MW00534800

SHAPING THE AMERICAN LANDSCAPE

Shaping the

Edited by Charles A. Birnbaum, FASLA, FAAR, and Stephanie S. Foell

A PROJECT OF THE CULTURAL LANDSCAPE FOUNDATION

Color galleries follow pages 176 and 320

Contents

University of Virginia Press
© 2009 by the Rector and Visitors of the University of Virginia
All rights reserved
Printed in the United States of America on acid-free paper

First published 2009

9 8 7 6 5 4 3 2 1

Library of Congress Cataloging-in-Publication Data
Shaping the American Landscape : new profiles from the pioneers
of American landscape design project / edited by Charles A.
Birnbaum and Stephanie S. Foell.
    p.   cm.
  Includes bibliographical references and index.
  ISBN 978-0-8139-2789-3 (cloth) : alk. paper)
   1. Landscape architects—United States—Biography. 2.
Horticulturalists—United States—Biography. 3. Planners—
United States—Biography. I. Birnbaum, Charles A.
II. Foell, Stephanie S. (Stephanie Sue), 1970–
  SB469.9.S53 2009
  712.092'273aB—dc22 2

                         2008031473

Title page illustration: Japanese garden by William Hertrich shortly
after completion in 1913, Huntington residence, San Marino,
California. (Reproduced by permission of the Huntington Library,
San Marino, California)

American Landscape

NEW PROFILES FROM THE PIONEERS OF AMERICAN LANDSCAPE DESIGN PROJECT

University of Virginia Press CHARLOTTESVILLE AND LONDON

Acknowledgments

THE PIONEERS OF AMERICAN LANDSCAPE DESIGN project could not be accomplished without the help of many generous individuals and institutions. Now, nearly two decades since the idea was first born, we are pleased and fortunate to have the continuing support of many university faculty, libraries, not-for-profit institutions, foundations, private collections, corporations, and federal and state agencies. It was also the collective efforts of diverse individuals, including landscape architects, historians, librarians, archivists, community activists, photographers, colleagues, and family members, who personally knew these pioneers or who developed a knowledge and a passion for their legacies.

Throughout the nine-year process of the Pioneers project, many have helped to shepherd manuscripts and to coordinate the Herculean volunteer efforts of over 117 contributing authors and more than thirty-five archives.

To begin with, many thanks go to my coeditor, Stephanie S. Foell, who volunteered her time and gave generously to this undertaking. Stephanie, who previously served as a contributor to earlier editions of *Pioneers,* brought editorial consistency, and when required, bracingly sharp editing. Stephanie also penned the essays in the present volume on architect Paul Philippe Cret and David Fairchild.

In addition to Stephanie, Nancy Slade has been involved in the development of this volume since nearly its conception. First as a volunteer, then as an employee of the National Park Service's Historic Landscape Initiative, and later as a project manager at The Cultural Landscape Foundation (TCLF), Nancy organized the massive illustration program and coordinated all of the authors' contributions. In the final months of the project she also received critical support from Andrea Hill who managed the database and color-corrected and enhanced a number of the visual images. Nancy also provided biographical essays for landscape architects John Simonds and Lester Collins.

During the period that this project resided at the National Park Service (NPS), special thanks go to H. Bryan Mitchell who managed the NPS's Heritage Preservation program. Under Bryan, the Pioneers project was afforded the essential critical support required. At TCLF, we are grateful for the support from the board of directors and the co-chairs that have served over the life of this project. Particular thanks go to former chairs, Sarah S. Boasberg, Behula Shah, and Noel D. Vernon, as well as the current co-chairs, Kurt Culbertson, Shaun Saer Duncan, and Douglas Reed.

Once again, the entire Pioneers team was fortunate to benefit from the expertise and assistance of Catha Grace Rambusch. Catha and I have collaborated on the Pioneers since the fall of 1989. During her tenure as the director of the CATALOG of Landscape Records in the United States at Wave Hill, and continuing following her retirement two years ago, Catha has provided indefatigable support to the entire team, offering editorial guidance, archival research, and acquisition support.

Special thanks must also go to our generous supporters and sponsors. First, thanks to the Hubbard Educational Trust and The Graham Foundation, who provided the critical philanthropic funds so that this

Pioneers publication could be richly illustrated. These two foundations, in particular, have been involved with the Pioneers' publications since 1995 when the Graham Foundation provided the first such grant to this ongoing endeavor.

In addition to philanthropic foundations, the richness of this volume is in large part because of the generosity from several key collections, private practitioners, and individuals. First, the Environmental Design Archives of the University of California at Berkeley, and The Smithsonian Institution, Archives of American Gardens, both provided extraordinary assistance, which is best illustrated by the great number of images that appear in this volume which have come from their collections.

Additionally, sponsorship for this publication was also provided by Edward B. Cella, Suzanne L. Turner, and Judith H. Robinson, and the firms of Pamela Burton & Company, EDAW, Inc., Hargreaves Associates, The Jaeger Company, Peter Lindsay Schaudt Landscape Architecture, Oehme van Sweden & Associates, and Quennell Rothschild and Partners.

On the editorial front, we are grateful to Susan Chamberlin, Robert E. Grese, Arleyn A. Levee, Patricia M. O'Donnell, Judith Tankard, Suzanne L. Turner, and Thaïsa Way, and to Melanie Macchio of TCLF, for their time and knowledge in conducting peer review. Their helpful direction and comments added immeasurably to the final product.

In addition to these supporters and friends, a project such as this is not possible without a tremendous effort by many others. Special thanks go to Joyce Connolly, Museum Specialist, at The Smithsonian Institution, Archives of American Gardens; Mary Daniels, Librarian, Special Collections at the Frances Loeb Library, Harvard University, Graduate School of Design; Waverly B. Lowell, Curator, at the Environmental Design Archives, University of California, Berkeley; and Art H. Miller, Archivist, Archives and Special Collections, Lake Forest College. In particular, these collections' managers and archivists assisted in making this publication both rich and diverse, each giving generously of their time and formidable knowledge.

Many library archives, research centers, colleges, universities, museums, municipalities, public agencies, and businesses generously supported this project and waived fees for the use of their images and materials. These include the American Academy in Rome; American Memory Collection, Library of Congress; Architectural Archive, Special Collection, Tulane University Libraries; Architectural Archives/Kroiz Gallery, University of Pennsylvania; Avery Architectural & Fine Arts Library, Columbia University Libraries; Barnard College Archives; Carl A. Kroch Library, Cornell University; City of Kent, Washington; City of Rolling Hills, California; The Cultural Landscape Foundation; Western History Collection, Jane Silverstein-Ries Papers, Denver Public Library; Fairchild Tropical Botanic Garden Archive; Fort Lauderdale Historical Society; French Lick Springs Resort Casino; Glorietta Conference Center; Hearst Communications Inc.; Hill-Stead Museum; Historic New England; Huntington Library, Art Collections and Botanical Gardens; Innisfree Foundation; Juliette Gordon Low Birthplace; Kenan Research Center, Cherokee Garden Library, Atlanta History Center; Kingwood Center; Manning Brothers Historic Photographic Collection; Milwaukee County Parks Department; Minneapolis Park and Recreation Board; Missouri Botanical Garden; Moorland-Spingarn Research Center, Howard University; Mount Vernon Hotel & Museum & Garden; Nassau County Department of Parks, Recreation and Museums, Long Island Studies Collection; National Baha'i Archives; U.S. National Park Service; Frederick Law Olmsted National Historic Site; New York State Library, Albany; North New Jersey Center of the Morristown & Morris Township Library; Eberly Family Special Collections Library, Penn State University Archives; Peridian Group; Principia College; Romer Collection, Miami Dade Public Library; Shellhorn Collection, Department of Special Collections, Charles E. Young Research Library, UCLA; Special Collections Library, University of Virginia; Special Collections, Charles E. Young Research Library, UCLA; Special Collections, The Morton Arboretum; Tennessee State Library and Archives; The Florida Memory Project, State Library and Archives of Florida; Tillinghast Association; Hargrett Rare Book & Manuscript Library, University of Georgia; Special Collections Division, University of Washington Libraries; and the Walter Schoel Engineering Company, Inc.

This publication has also been enriched by the contributions of visual materials from the private archives and collections of many landscape architecture firms, and as such we would like to acknowledge and thank those companies that provided access to such holdings, including: Carol R. Johnson Associates; Cornelia Hahn Oberlander; Environmental Planning and Design LLC; MPFP, LLC (formerly M. Paul Friedberg and Partners); Reed/Hilderbrand Associates, Inc.; Richard

Haag Associates, Inc.; Robert Marvin Howell Beach & Associates, Inc.; Royston Hanamoto Alley & Abey; Sasaki Associates, Inc.; Theodore Osmundson & Associates; the Office of Lawrence Halprin, Inc.; and Zion, Breen & Richardson Associates. Special appreciation also goes to Lawrence Halprin, who provided us with an original thumbnail drawing that precedes each individual pioneer essay. (This evocative icon is the postwar grandchild to the tree that was used in *Pioneers of American Landscape Design,* in 2000, adapted from Hubbard and Kimball's *An Introduction to the Study of Landscape Design,* in 1917.)

Rounding out the visual program, we would also like to thank the professional photographers who permitted use of their images free of charge, including Brian Goad, Geoffrey James, Lynn Johnson, Kevin Pasnik, Bob Labbance, and Allen Rokach.

In addition to the special collections, archives, practicing landscape architecture firms, and professional photographers, this publication was the fortunate recipient of visual materials from the private collections of those that penned individual pioneer essays, friends, and family members. In particular, thanks to the enthusiasm and personal commitments from Steven Baronti, Sydney Baumgartner, Russell Beatty, Stuart Bendelow, Susan Berg, Tina Bishop, Sarah S. Boasberg, Oliver Chamberlain, Susan Cohen, Collins Family, John Deimel, Lake Douglas, Grace Dunbar, Marc Dutton, Don Etter, Dr. Charles Fenzi, Eleanor Fisher, Lucina Furlong, Kathryn Gleason, Ken Guzowski, Archie Hanson, Milton Hicks, Mary Paolano Hoerner, Grayce Hollied, Sue Howland, Brian Katen, Joy Kestenbaum, Judy Kowalski, Donald Loggins, Kelly McCaughey Dent, Kevin R. Mendik, Baker H. Morrow, Geoffrey Movis, Shiro Nakane, Susan S. Nelson, Cornelia Hahn Oberlander, Laurie D. Olin, Theodore H. Osmundson, Ava Parks, Annemarie van Roessel, Peter Lindsay Schaudt, William Singer, Nancy Slade, Louise K. Smith, Frederick Steiner, David Streatfield, Maria M. Thompson, William H. Tishler, Marc Treib, Elisabeth Whitelaw, Kathy Wiedorn, and Anne Willson. Many of the individual essays have been visually enriched by their efforts.

Rounding out the visual documentation, we would also like to acknowledge the assistance of several individuals who worked with us to obtain particular images that were essential to this publication. Here, thanks go to Jane Amidon, Oliver Collins, Robert E. Grese, Gary Kesler, Lorraine Osmundson, and Alexandra Whyte.

The generosity of spirit that resulted in the 462 images contained herein is further amplified by the knowledge, enthusiasm, and dedication that is evidenced in the 151 pioneer essays that make up this collection penned by 120 contributors.

First, a special mention and thank you goes to those contributors who researched and wrote several pioneer essays including Virginia Lopez Begg, Carolyn Doepke Bennett, Susan Chamberlin, Pleasance K. Crawford, Rebecca Warren Davidson, Stephanie S. Foell, Barbara Geiger, Charles T. Gleaves, Joy Kestenbaum, Daniel Krall, Arleyn A. Levee, Joanna Lombard, Melanie Macchio, Linda Flint McClelland, Carrie Leah McDade, Kevin R. Mendick, Elizabeth K. Meyer, Arthur H. Miller, Baker H. Morrow, Therese O'Malley, Charlene K. Roise, Nancy Slade, David Streatfield, Noel D. Vernon, Thaïsa Way, and Cynthia Zaitzevsky

Rounding out the team of pioneer authors, we also are grateful to: Arnold R. Alanen, Lauren Muench Albano, Steven Baronti, Amanda Graham Barton, Sydney Baumgartner, Stuart Bendelow, Tina Bishop, John Bryan, Julie Cain, Margaret Carpenter, Ethan Carr, Suzanne Carter Meldman, Staci L. Catron, Oliver Chamberlain, Diane Brandley Clarke, Karen Cole, Kelly Comras, William G. Crawford Jr., Kurt Culbertson, Elizabeth Hope Cushing, Phoebe Cutler, Duane A. Dietz, Ced Dolder, Marc Dutton, Donald Elliott, Carolyn Etter, Don Etter, Barry Fitzpatrick, Lillie Petit Gallagher, Kathryn L. Gleason, Isabelle Gournay, Marlea Graham, Carol Grove, John Gruber, Ken Guzowski, Gary R. Hilderbrand, Mary Paolano Hoerner, Heidi Hohmann, Dorothée Imbert, Christine Jochem, Brian Katen, Gary Kesler, Julie Khuen, Judy Kowalski, Debbie Lang, Donna Tunkel Lilborn, Donald Loggins, Waverly B. Lowell, Catherine Maggio, Brice Maryman, Theresa Mattor, Kelly McCaughey Dent, Karen McLaren, Lauren G. Meier, Julie Moir Messervy, Susanne Smith Meyer, JC Miller, Donna M. Neary, Susan S. Nelson, Christine Edstrom O'Hara, Laurie D. Olin, Beth Page, Eliza Pennypacker, Doug Pulak, Susan M. Rademacher, Reuben M. Rainey, Chad Randl, Jennifer Hanna Reive, Marion L. Renneker, Donald Richardson, Gary O. Robinette, Seth Rodewald-Bates, Annemarie van Roessel, David A. Roth, R. Terry Schnadelbach, René D. Shoemaker, Melanie Simo, Frederick Steiner, Tim Tamburrino, Maria M. Thompson, William H. Tishler, Suzanne L. Turner, Mary Alice Van Sickle, Diana S. Waite, Peter Walker, Douglas A. Williams, Emily Herring Wilson, William McKenzie Woodward, Dorothy Wurman, and Emma Young.

To all of these contributing authors, we are extremely grateful to their multiyear commitment to working with us throughout the editing and permissions process, and for hanging in there while this project reached fruition.

None of this would have been possible without the dedicated staff at the University of Virginia Press. Thank you to our editor Boyd Zenner, who was our anchor throughout the publishing process; Mark Mones, our project editor, who kept us on track; Jonathan Aretakis, a freelance copy editor with extensive experience in reference projects who worked with us on the manuscript; Ellen Satrom, the managing editor, and Brandy Savarese, who shepherded us through the permission process required to publish images; and Martha Farlow and Chris

Harrison, who handled all of the 462 images submitted with the manuscript and transformed everything into the book you see today.

Finally, thank you to the visionary pioneers contained herein, who join the 160 revealing pioneer biographies included in the earlier volume. We are the fortunate beneficiaries of their astonishing and diverse landscape legacy that inspires each of us to be thoughtful stewards.

CHARLES A. BIRNBAUM, FASLA, FAAR
Founder and President,
The Cultural Landscape Foundation

Introduction

WELCOME TO THE LATEST ADDITION TO THE ever-expanding Pioneers of American Landscape Design project. From its modest genesis in a Manhattan coffeehouse conversation among Catha Grace Rambusch, Laura Byers, and myself in 1989, about how to document the lives and careers of those people who had shaped the American landscape, the Pioneers has slowly grown to encompass book projects of several types, a Web site with monthly dedicated features (e.g., pioneer profiles and online queries), and regional and national conferences. A word about how we got here might not be amiss.

It was clear from the beginning that we would need to enlist the help of a group of nationally recognized landscape scholars, archivists, practitioners, and librarians to help us further develop and clarify our initial vision. In 1992, provided with the invaluable administrative infrastructure of the National Park Service, we began to do so. In the early days, the Pioneers project also benefited very substantially from the assistance of the CATALOG of Landscape Records in the United States at Wave Hill, the Smithsonian Institution Libraries Office of Horticulture, Dumbarton Oaks Library and Studies in Landscape Architecture Program, and Frances Loeb Library Special Collections at the Harvard Graduate School of Design.

In 1993, the first written production of the Pioneers project—a paperback volume entitled *Pioneers of American Landscape Design*—was published by the National Park Service's Historic Landscape Initiative (NPS HLI). Edited by Lisa Crowder and myself—supported by the assistance of ten researchers—the book comprised a collection of sixty-two essays, each spotlighting a signifi-

cant figure in the history of American landscape design. The individuals singled out for biographical treatment in this initial collection were chosen from a master list of some 550 worthy pioneers, all of whom were listed in the book's appendix. Additionally, the volume contained an extensive annotated bibliography and one illustration for each profiled subject.

Obviously, in a project of such magnitude—with at least 550 figures already identified as deserving of biographical treatment—some basic editorial decisions had to be made for the sake of reasonably limiting the scope of the inaugural Pioneers volume. Such decisions would, it was understood, need to be revisited for later projects. The two winnowing editorial guidelines for the initial paperback collection were (1) that the figures treated were deceased and (2) that primary emphasis is placed on often overlooked lesser-known individuals who were not already the subject of books, monographs, and exhibitions. As a result, this first collection of pioneers—in marked contrast to many volumes whose principles of selection are chronological—did not include such towering figures as John Bartram, Frederick Law Olmsted Sr., Thomas Jefferson, Jens Jensen, or Beatrix Farrand.

As editorial work on this initial collection progressed, information on other major figures began to accrue dramatically, and as a result, a second softbound *Pioneers* volume was published by the National Park Service just two years later. Titled *Pioneers of American Landscape Design II,* the book was edited by Julie K. Fix and myself, and included an additional fifty-one essays, based on the same editorial guidelines as the initial volume. By this

San Francisco Golf and Country Club

The 14th Green

Typical of the design and contour which Tillinghast created in America. This great California course was planned by him and constructed under his supervision and definitely to his plan and specifications.

When building a course or reconstructing one, it might be well to confer with this architect.

A. W. TILLINGHAST, INC.

HARRINGTON PARK   NEW JERSEY

Telephone—Closter 1435

An advertisement for A. W. Tillinghast, one of seven golf course architects and designers profiled in this volume. (The Tillinghast Association)

time, the master list had grown from 550 to 635 important figures. In this collection, as in its predecessor, we noted that "the goal of this project is to document the lives and careers of those people who have shaped the American landscape. . . . This interim publication represents an attempt to make this resource available to researchers, practitioners, and home owners. However, it does not constitute a complete record of information received to date. Many important practitioners have been excluded due to space constraints . . . and the work continues." So more than a decade ago, we were already thinking expansively.

As important products of the National Park Service Historic Landscape Initiative (from 1992 to 1996), these first two published volumes were recognized by the American Society of Landscape Architects (ASLA) in 1996 with the President's Award of Excellence—the highest honor that can be bestowed upon a project by the ASLA.

The award unquestionably brought the Pioneers project to the attention of a greater community within the profession. Perhaps even more importantly, our own concept of the project broadened, and our goal shifted from simply educating people about the design legacies of these important figures to instilling respect and a sense of stewardship for their extant work. The product of this new, larger initiative, *Pioneers of American Landscape Design,* edited by Robin Karson and myself, was published in hardcover by the McGraw-Hill Companies in the spring of 2000. The cosponsors of the publication again included the National Park Service and the CATALOG of Landscape Records, in addition to the Library of American Landscape History and The Cultural Landscape Foundation.

To draw attention to the fact that the McGraw-Hill publication was more than an encyclopedic reference tool, and to help foster a stewardship ethic for this design legacy, the McGraw-Hill volume concluded with a listing of up to five publicly accessible sites for each pioneer. As has by now become necessary, the criteria for inclusion in the volume had been reconsidered. The collection now included individuals who had not appeared in previous Pioneer volumes because their work had been too frequently treated elsewhere—for example, the Olmsteds, Jens Jensen, Alfred Caldwell, and Thomas Jefferson, among others. The book, however, followed one of the original editorial guidelines and only included deceased practitioners, reflecting the small number of contemporary figures who died in the 1990s: Alfred Caldwell (d. 1998), J. B. Jackson (d. 1996), and James Rose (d. 1991). The book was widely praised, including admiring reviews in the *New York Times* and the *Washington Post.* In 2001, the ASLA gave the book a Merit Award in Research and Communications.

Like its predecessors in the Pioneers continuum, the collection you now hold in your hands also represents a recalibration, a broadening in scope. If the first paperback Pioneers volumes sought to establish a foundation for considering the idea of American landscape pioneers, many lesser known; and the McGraw-Hill volume dedicated itself to the idea of stewardship of built legacies, meanwhile showcasing some of the better-known figures earlier set aside; then the present work is notable for its argument that modernists, too, can be "pioneers," and for expanding the idea of landscape history ever further outward. The present volume is notable, too, in incorporating interrelated collateral disciplines not considered before. Thus you will find, for example, earthworks art-

M. Paul Friedberg's Riis Plaza, Manhattan. The Riis Houses were demolished in 1999, although part of the plaza remains. This iconic landscape is discussed in the entry on M. Paul Friedberg. (M. Paul Friedberg & Partners; courtesy of The Cultural Landscape Foundation)

Many of the pioneers discussed in the pages that follow were included in this 1950 survey of Harvard students by Lester Collins, among them Daniel Kiley, Ralph Gunn, Cornelia Oberlander, Hideo Sasaki, and Robert Zion. (Courtesy of Charles A. Birnbaum)

ists (Herbert Bayer), journalists (William H. Whyte Jr.), amateur botanists (Henry Shaw), community activist/ gardeners (Liz Christy), inventors (John Brooks), cemetery designers (Almerin Hotchkiss), librarians (Theodora Kimball Hubbard), seedsmen (James Vick), and a host of others.

You will find here a greater elasticity in time framework, both backward (to Sir Francis Nicholson, born in 1655) and, probably more controversially, forward, to include some individuals still living. This is probably the single greatest deviation from what were originally established as the Pioneers project's core principles, and it was not undertaken lightly. First, since publication of the McGraw-Hill collection we have sustained unprecedented losses in the profession: Garrett Eckbo, Daniel Kiley, Clermont H. Lee, Robert Marvin, Ian McHarg, Theodore Osmundson, Milton Meade Palmer, Jane Silverstein Ries, Robert Royston, Hideo Sasaki, Ruth Patricia Shellhorn, John O. Simonds, Richard Webel, William H. Whyte Jr., and Robert Zion. In fact, of these, Kiley, Lee, Osmundson, Ries, Royston, and Shellhorn were still living when their biographical profiles were initially submitted.

Second, other equally influential professionals who also practiced during this same period are now in their twilight years—with many of these figures often inextricably connected to those recently deceased postwar practitioners noted above. Thus, this suggested that the long and productive career canons of modernists such as Grady Clay Jr. (b. 1916), M. Paul Friedberg (b. 1931), Richard Haag (b. 1923), Lawrence Halprin (b. 1916), Carol R. Johnson (b. 1929), Cornelia Oberlander (b. 1924), and Robert Reich (b. 1913) could now also be evaluated and assessed.

It involves no great leap of the imagination to view a modernist as pioneering, as burgeoning interest in the postwar American landscape attests. The concept has been well established by Nikolaus Pevner's *Pioneers of Modern Design: From William Morris to Walter Gropius*. First published in 1949, this well-regarded reference book has been reprinted many times, with the most recent expanded edition published in 2005. The overall mission of the Pioneers project is to interpret and protect the extant legacy of visionary practitioners—and without a doubt these legacies must include those increasingly vulnerable built works from the recent past. This poses a particularly difficult dilemma, because a primary tool for protection, the National Register for Historic Places, requires that for a property less than fifty years old to be

Above: John Simonds (*far left*) and Ian McHarg (*center*) are both included in this volume. (Courtesy of Charles A. Birnbaum)

Left: An illustration from "The Cascade in Villa Torlonia, Frascati" by Edward Lawson, the first landscape architect to serve as a Fellow at the American Academy in Rome (from ASLA *Illustrations of Work of Members,* 1932). This volume considers the careers of Lawson, Thomas Drees Price, and Richard Webel, all of whom were fellows at the American Academy.

listed, sufficient scholarship must be available to attest to its value. In the event the designer is still living (and is not retired), a determination of significance is possible in the event that there are no new major commissions that would require a reevaluation of his or her extant built legacy.

Because of this lack of recognition, many modernist landscapes from the recent past have perished, often without any public discourse. To illustrate this unhappy reality, consider that in just the past few years we have witnessed the demolition of such revolutionary and iconic built works as Riis Plaza Park at Riis Houses, New York City (M. Paul Friedberg); Christopher Columbus Waterfront Park, Boston (Hideo Sasaki); Nations Bank Plaza (Dan Kiley), as well as threats to Freeway Park, Seattle (Lawrence Halprin), Gas Works Park, Seattle (Richard Haag), and Robson Square, Vancouver, B.C. (Cornelia Oberlander). These landscapes are not only

among the most significant works of the designers' careers, they were also enormously influential in the evolution of America's postwar landscape architectural legacy.

By recognizing that the stories and career canons of these individuals are not only worthy but *interconnected,* the design legacies of these pioneers may have a better chance of being designated locally and nationally and thus accorded the protection given National Register or National Historic Landmark properties. As was the practice with the McGraw-Hill volume, we have once again placed an asterisk—*—next to a pioneer's name to denote a separate biographical entry that appears in this same published collection. The present edition has enhanced this method of cross-referencing by applying **bold typeface** to the names of pioneers for whom there are biographies in the earlier McGraw-Hill volume.

From the outset of the Pioneers project, our goal has been to continue to generate biographical profiles of significant figures in the history of American landscape design. In 2001, taking advantage of new media opportunities, The Cultural Landscape Foundation (TCLF) created a dedicated Web site feature devoted solely to the Pioneers project. Using this ever-expanding site and monthly electronic newsletters, TCLF began hosting

ADAMS, CHARLES GIBBS
(1884–1953)
LANDSCAPE ARCHITECT

Charles Gibbs Adams was born on January 10, 1884, in Los Angeles, California, into a middle-class family. As a child he developed a strong fascination for natural landscapes and an understanding of the importance of water in semiarid landscapes, which resulted in a keen desire to become a landscape architect. He was unable to obtain a degree in landscape architecture in California because no colleges or universities offered coursework or degrees in the field. Therefore he studied architecture at the University of California, Berkeley. Following graduation, he went on an extended trip to Europe to study garden design in several countries.

Upon his return from Europe he opened an office as a landscape architect in South Pasadena, California, where he lived and practiced the rest of his life. His office in an adobe building built in 1841 by Manuel Garfias was very small. The size and dispersed nature of his practice coupled with his open and easygoing nature led to considerable laxity in billing practices, which irritated some of his clients.

The opening of his practice coincided with a phenomenal population expansion in the Los Angeles basin that made it the fastest-growing region in the country in the 1920s. His clientele included many actors associated with the movie industry as well as prominent figures in business and social circles. His practice encompassed a broad area from Pasadena, Hollywood, and West Los Angeles north to Montecito, Santa Barbara, and Paso Robles.

He achieved early prominence with his design for the Julian Eltinge garden overlooking Silver Lake in Los Angeles. This was an early attempt to develop a regionally appropriate design approach combining both traditional Hispanic walled enclosures and the use of native California plants. Unadorned painted retaining walls defined geometrically ordered spaces with simple tiled fountains that were planted with desert plants and native shrubs. The very steep slopes between the level platforms were planted with succulents and desert plants.

In numerous articles he wrote for popular journals and in public talks Adams advocated the use of California native plants, considerations of drought tolerance, and respect for historic precedent, especially the enclosed patio tradition associated with Spanish houses. However, his completed work confirms that he was not always successful in persuading his clients to adopt his ideas. While his finest work exemplifies these precepts his practice also included several designs that are virtually indistinguishable from the traditions of eclectic Southern California gardening that typified the 1920s and 1930s. These designs catered to a desire to create any landscape effect in this semiarid climatic region by using heavy nonseasonal irrigation where herbaceous borders adjoined extensive lawn areas. This portion of his work is really no different from the work of other contemporary landscape designers, especially the large number of nurserymen who provided design services during this period. Charles Greene's subtle design for the garden of the Cordelia Culbertson House, in Pasadena, was complemented by Adams with a very traditional garden of lawns and flower borders for Mr. and Mrs. Francis F. Prentiss, later owners.

Left: Prentiss garden, Pasadena, California. (Courtesy of the collection of David Streatfield)

Below: The Succulent Garden, Arabian Horse Ranch of W. K. Kellogg, Pomona, California. (Courtesy of the collection of David Streatfield)

Goodhue's formal layout of terraces and simple brick-paved walks.

Adams's most extensive desert garden design was The Succulent Garden on the Arabian Horse Ranch of W. K. Kellogg, the cereal magnate, in the Pomona Valley. Kellogg was keenly interested in the scientific study of plants that would grow in this very arid landscape. Adams was well equipped to assist him in this scientific venture, but he unfortunately ran afoul of Kellogg's rigorous accounting practices and was dismissed.

Adams also worked on a much larger scale on several remote mountain properties. He was hired by William Randolph Hearst to plant the extensive system of drives at San Simeon, his immense ranch in the coastal mountain range near Paso Robles. The trees and shrubs had to survive the aggressive grazing of Hearst's large and diverse collection of animals. Mature trees were planted but often moved after the initial planting to satisfy Hearst's imperious personality, but refined visual tastes. For director Cecil B. DeMille, Adams replanted a large, fire-damaged area of chaparral on his mountain estate Paradise, transplanting a large grove of mature pine trees and establishing an extensive wild-flower meadow.

On many of the large estates on which Adams worked, his contribution consisted of providing planting designs for elaborate formal garden designs already prepared by architects. Carleton Monroe Winslow's design for Arcady in Santa Barbara is a typical example. Adams created bold visual effects using color themes, such as yellow-orange and blue. His work at the Henry Dater estate at Santa Barbara reveals his skill in the semitropical mode of planting that had been established in the late nineteenth century and which was still favored by some clients. Adams's lush planting, which added to planting remaining from an experimental seed nursery, provided a striking contrast with the geometry of architect Bertram

Despite the seeming anomalies in his landscape design practice, Adams pioneered a number of new directions in garden design and garden writing in Southern California. He was among the earliest designers to advocate the use of the patio as an outdoor living space in the garden, reviving what was believed to have been Spanish and Mexican practice in the state. He was also an advocate for the use of California plants as well as desert and succulent plants, and the study of the history of Spanish gardens in California.

Adams displayed his broad knowledge and love of

California's Spanish history in numerous articles, lectures given to garden clubs, and in his service as vice president, president, and member of the Landmark Committee of the Historical Society of Southern California. In 1934 he collaborated with W. W. Robinson, the well-known Los Angeles historian, and Phil Townsend Hanna in producing the last *Annual Publications* of the society. While he was not a trained historian, he was virtually the first individual to write and speak about Spanish gardens in California who derived his information from a close study of original documents such as the diaries of travelers. This informed his attitudes toward historic restora-tion. He was a fierce critic of the early attempted resto-ration of Mission gardens in the 1920s, such as Father Sullivan's gardens at Mission San Juan Capistrano.

Charles Adams died on December 21, 1953.

Adams, Charles Gibbs. "Gardens of the Spanish Days of California." *Annual Publications, Historical Society of Southern California* 15 (1932), 347–55. Another insightful account of Spanish garden design.

"The Spanish Influence in California." In *Pioneer American Gardening,* comp. Elvenia Slosson. New York: Coward-McCann, 1951, 273–77. A general account of the influence of Spanish settlers in California derived from primary documentary sources.

David Streatfield

AFFLECK, THOMAS
(1812–1868)
HORTICULTURAL
JOURNALIST, NURSERYMAN

Born in Dumfries, Scotland, in 1812, Thomas Affleck was interested in the natural and physical sciences and large-ly self-taught in these areas. He immigrated to America in 1832, intent upon learning how Americans did busi-ness. His arrival coincided with the nation's physical, economic, and agricultural growth, but the 1830s also included periods of economic bust as well as boom; both farming and commerce were risky and unpredict-able. Nevertheless, as the nation expanded into frontier regions, regional markets grew for agricultural informa-tion, materials, and equipment, and technological ad-vancements made publication and distribution of new products affordable and accessible.

Ambitious and enterprising, he spent his first few years in various commercial ventures in New York, Penn-sylvania, Illinois, Ohio, and Kentucky. By 1837, he and his new family settled in Clinton, Indiana. Following a series of tragedies that included the deaths of his young wife and child, financial failure, and severe personal ill-ness, Affleck moved to Cincinnati in late 1838, expect-ing eventually to return to Scotland. However, by 1840, he had recovered and took a job as junior editor of the *Western Farmer,* an agricultural publication aimed at markets in the western and southern regions of the United States. Under Affleck's influence, the publication became the *Western Farmer and Gardener.* With his agree-able writing style, the publication changed from simply reprinting articles from other sources, as was then com-mon, to offering original writing that appealed to a wide

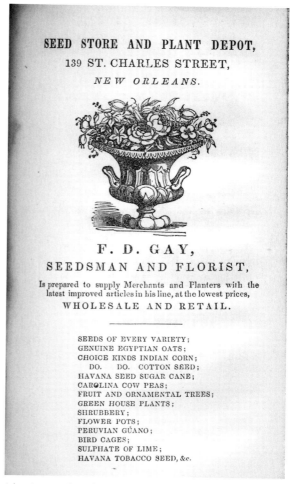

Advertisement for Affleck's Southern Nurseries, Washington, Mississippi. (Courtesy The Historic New Orleans Collection, Museum/Research Center)

[Village of log-huts.]

Illustration from the *Western Farmer and Gardener*, 1850, for which Affleck served as an editor. (Courtesy of the collection of Lake Douglas)

from European and American suppliers. Surviving commercial records show that Affleck corresponded extensively with clients throughout America and regularly conducted business with horticultural suppliers, publishers, merchants, lawyers, and others in New Orleans, which was one of America's largest and most important cities during the 1840s.

In 1846, Affleck began editing and writing for *Norman's Southern Agricultural Almanac,* published in New Orleans; in 1851 its name changed to *Affleck's Southern Rural Almanac and Plantation and Garden Calendar* when he assumed ownership and management responsibility. It offered practical advice on how, when, and what to plant; reported on local environmental conditions; and listed plant varieties available from his nursery. Though printed in quantity and distributed widely, few copies survive. Existing copies prove his role as a noteworthy American horticultural journalist and provide an important body of information about mid-nineteenth-century horticultural commerce in the Natchez–New Orleans region, an important center of agricultural wealth and activity in the antebellum South.

In spite of widespread renown, Affleck was never debt-free or financially secure. In 1855, he opened Central Nurseries in Washington County, Texas, and in 1857, he liquidated his Mississippi property and moved to Texas permanently. He turned his attention to livestock and plants, and by the time of his death, he had contributed greatly to Texas agricultural practices and livestock herds.

Affleck wrote throughout his career, and his highly regarded reports, articles, and commentaries appeared in a variety of contemporary journals, periodicals, and newspapers. While in Natchez, he contributed articles to the *Daily Courier* and was named agricultural editor of the New Orleans *Picayune* in 1851; later, Affleck's writings appeared in the Houston *Telegraph* and the Galveston *News.* Affleck's other works include *Bee Breeding in the West* (1841). His *Record and Account Books* (1847 to 1850s) for both cotton and sugar plantations were the first, best, and most extensively used accounting system for agricultural enterprise in the rural South. After the Civil War, Affleck embarked on an ambitious multivolume endeavor to write about plants for the South, but only one volume, *Hedging and Hedging Plants in the Southern States,* was published posthumously in 1869.

Affleck's early letters from the 1830s onward record vivid impressions of the American environment, and his later writings often discuss topics such as the ornamen-

audience, including women, whose sphere of influence included, according to the publication's senior editor, both the kitchen and the garden. Interested in livestock and improved agricultural methods, Affleck traveled to livestock and agricultural fairs in Ohio, Kentucky, and the Mississippi River Valley in 1841–1842, reporting on what he encountered.

Impressed by what he found and how he was received there, Affleck moved to Washington, Mississippi (near Natchez) in 1842, married the widow Anna Dunbar Smith, and began managing her plantations. Overcoming her debts, periodic crop failures, and financial reversals, he created the Southern Nurseries, one of the first commercial nurseries in the South, where he imported plants

tal value of plants, layout of the kitchen garden, suggestions for improving agricultural endeavors, and methods for increasing agricultural production and efficiency. Overviews of the contents of both *Western Farmer and Gardener* and *Southern Rural Almanac* during Affleck's editorial tenure suggest the awareness, if not outright endorsement, of the order, organization, and scientific approaches advocated by **Andrew Jackson Downing** and other prominent contemporaries.

The *Southern Rural Almanac* and the records of Affleck's commercial ventures provide important information about horticultural practices, techniques, and materials in antebellum Mississippi, Louisiana, and Texas. Affleck's importance to American landscape history is regional and lies in three areas: his tireless dissemination of horticultural information through publications and associations; his promotion of and advocacy for improved economic and commercial diversity, agricultural experimentation, new tools and techniques, and new varieties of plants and animals; and, finally, his commercial role in supplying horticultural materials throughout the southern Gulf region. Affleck passed away in 1868.

The Thomas Affleck Papers are housed at Special Collections, Hill Memorial Library, Louisiana State University, Baton Rouge.

Affleck, Thomas. *Affleck's Southern Rural Almanac and Plantation and Garden Calendar, 1851–1854.* New Orleans: Published at the office of the "Picayune"/New Orleans, 1851–1854. This volume is four years of *Affleck's Southern Rural Almanac* bound together in one volume.

Douglas, William Lake. "On Common Ground: Horticultural Commerce as a Unifying Factor among Diverse Communities in Nineteenth-century New Orleans." Ph.D. diss., University of New Orleans, 2001.

Hooper, E. J., Thomas Affleck, Charles Foster, and Charles W. Elliott, eds. *The Western Farmer and Gardener.* Cincinnati: J.A. and U.P. James, 1850. This volume, according to an introductory notice, is a compilation of the "largest and best part" of the five years of this periodical's publications, 1839–1845. Many of Affleck's shorter pieces are found here.

Williams, Robert Webb, Jr. "The Mississippi Career of Thomas Affleck." Ph.D. diss., Tulane University, 1954.

Lake Douglas

AUST, FRANZ
(1885–1963)
LANDSCAPE ARCHITECT, EDUCATOR

Franz Aust was born in 1885 in Defiance, Ohio. Shortly after receiving his master's degree in physics, Aust enrolled in the landscape architecture program at the University of Michigan where he became the first graduate from their five-year program. He then became an instructor at the University of Illinois, working with **Wilhelm Tyler Miller.**

In 1915, Aust received an appointment as associate professor of landscape design in the Department of Horticulture at the University of Wisconsin, becoming the first landscape architect hired at the campus. While at the University of Illinois, Aust met **Jens Jensen** and became a member of the Prairie Club—an organization of outdoor enthusiasts cofounded by Jensen. In 1913, Jensen organized another influential conservation group, the Friends of Our Native Landscape, based in Chicago. After moving to Madison, Aust quickly made powerful friends and in 1920 assembled a group of people in the senate parlors of the state capitol to organize a new Wisconsin chapter of the Friends of Our Native Landscape. Aust was designated the group's secretary—a position he held for

Franz Aust. (Photo courtesy of William H. Tishler)

Left: An example of a council ring, this one constructed by Aust at Glenwood Children's Park, Madison, Wisconsin. (Photo courtesy of William H. Tishler)

Below: One of Aust's plans for rock gardens, The Rock Garden, Red Brae Farm, Eagle, Wisconsin. (Photo courtesy of William H. Tishler)

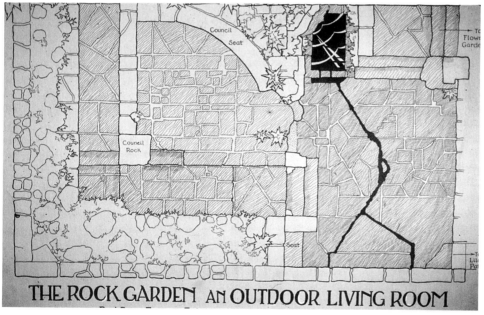

THE ROCK GARDEN AN OUTDOOR LIVING ROOM

more than a decade. In this capacity Aust became a driving force for the group organizing many of its meetings and spearheading its legislative activism with a vigorous public awareness campaign. He helped organize their meetings, which often were held at parks and endangered places. Aust also initiated the Wisconsin group's informative newsletter *Our Native Landscape.* Their first issue contained articles by Aust, Jensen, **Genevieve Gillette** (founder of the Michigan chapter), and other regional environmental luminaries. Working through the

Friends, Aust was also instrumental in organizing two regional and rural planning conferences, and lobbying for rural planning legislation, expanding the state park system, and billboard controls. With his guidance, and that of others, the group became a leading force for conservation action and landscape appreciation.

During his twenty-eight-year career at the University of Wisconsin, he became a pioneer in the challenging roles of teaching, research, and public service. In this capacity, his myriad of achievements included numerous speeches, articles, radio talks, and projects relating not just to landscape design, but also rural planning, horticulture, roadside development and soil conservation, outdoor advertising, and aesthetics. He also served as the campus landscape architect, designing several campus projects, which included a rock garden at the east wing of Agriculture Hall and a council ring, in collaboration with Jens Jensen, at the university arboretum.

As a professor and campus landscape architect, Aust possessed a broad understanding of the young profession, as well as a personal philosophy that embraced horticulture, aesthetics, urban and rural planning, conservation, and ecology. This coupled with the university's commitment to outreach programs, extended Aust's influence not only to his students and professional colleagues, but also to a large segment of the state's population. Throughout his career he wrote and spoke widely. Of special importance were the some thirty extension bulletins he authored or coauthored about topics that ranged from "Plantings for the Pioneer Home" to "What Name for the Farm." He also published in professional journals such as *Landscape Architecture,* and wrote many articles in popular magazines, particularly *Better Homes and Gardens.* During the Great Depression, Aust developed an innovative correspondence course that covered a broad range of topics relating to landscape architecture. This enabled many students without the financial resources to attend the university to learn about the profession.

Aust became a trusted friend of Frank Lloyd Wright. When Wright's reputation was marred by business and personal indiscretions that created extensive criticism, Aust supported his colleague. Many of Aust's students would later reflect on the enlightening field trips he led to Taliesin, Wright's home and studio, where they could interact and learn with Wright's apprentices. In 1923, Wright developed a proposal for a "Hillside School of the Allied Arts" at Taliesin, operated in conjunction with visiting instructors who were nationally significant artists and University of Wisconsin faculty. Instruction in landscape design was provided by Aust and Jens Jensen.

Meanwhile, Aust continued his innovative teaching that inspired scores of students. A popular public speaker he also brought an awareness of landscape architecture while speaking to many organizations and countless thousands of others with his periodic talks over Wisconsin Public Radio (said to be the oldest public radio station in the nation). Other significant aspects of Aust's prolific work in university extension included involvement with the American Civic Association and the Association of City Planners. A strong advocate for land-use planning in rural areas, he was a founder and secretary of the American Rural Planning Association. Research efforts included working with the Roadside Development committee of the National Research Council's Highway Research Board, shrub propagation, and, during World War II, developing better camouflage methods with experiments at the university arboretum.

Aust's interests lay not only with the theoretical aspect of his profession, but also with its practical application, and he was active as a private landscape designer and consultant. Some of his more important projects included developing a master instruction plan for the company town of Ojibway, Wisconsin; preparing county land-use plans; consulting for the greenbelt community of Greendale, Wisconsin; the university campus and arboretum; housing and neighborhood design projects; numerous parks; subdivisions; roadside rest areas; and gardens.

Aust retired from teaching in 1943 and spent the rest of his professional career in private practice. His son Alden, who went on to have a distinguished career as a planner for the City of Omaha, Nebraska, also attended the University of Wisconsin program, graduating in 1938. Franz Aust passed away in Madison in 1963.

Aust, Franz A., and Walter A. Duffy. *Rural-Regional Plan, Douglas County, Wisconsin: Preliminary Plan, part one.* Madison: University of Wisconsin Extension, 1932. An early report emphasizing a comprehensive and multidisciplinary approach to planning for a rural county in northern Wisconsin.

Aust, Franz A., and Robert S. Hanson. *The Values of Art in Advertising.* Menasha, Wisc.: George Banta Publishing Company, 1932. Sets forth the thesis that there are natural uniformities in art and beauty, which can be analyzed and evaluated and applied to pictorial composition in the practical world of advertising.

Drought, R. Alice. "Restoration Gardening." *American Landscape Architect,* February 1931, 32–35. Indicates how remnants of an early pioneer home setting were incorporated into a perennial and rock garden featuring Aust's skillfully designed stonework.

William H. Tishler

BALTIMORE, GARNET DOUGLASS
(1859–1946)
CIVIL ENGINEER, LANDSCAPE ENGINEER

Garnet Douglass Baltimore was born in Troy, New York, on April 15, 1859. His mother, Caroline A. Newcomb Baltimore, was the daughter of a physician. Garnet's father, Peter F. Baltimore, had studied Latin, Greek, and English literature under Henry Highland Garnet, the radical abolitionist who had taught in a school for African American children in Troy during the 1840s. Acclaimed as a "cultured gentleman and interesting conversationalist," Peter Baltimore owned a barbershop that became a popular gathering spot for local industrialists and politicians, as well as visitors to the city. Included in his wide circle of friends was abolitionist Frederick Douglass.

Having christened their second son in honor of two national African American leaders, Peter and Caroline Baltimore enrolled Garnet in the city's segregated public school and later at the elite Troy Academy. In June 1877, Baltimore joined the freshman class at Rensselaer Polytechnic Institute (RPI) in Troy, the country's first engineering school, and graduated in 1881 with a degree in civil engineering. Within a week, he had started work as an assistant engineer on the Albany and Greenbush bridge across the Hudson River. Over the next few years, he widened his professional experience by working for nearby railroads, a waterworks, a railroad-car company, and a project to improve navigation on the Hudson. In 1887, Baltimore was appointed an assistant engineer with the state canal system. He supervised work on the Shinnecock and Peconic Canal on Long Island and the construction of a lock built on quicksand on the Oswego Canal. Later, while in charge of the state's cement-testing department, Baltimore developed a test for strength that was still being used in the 1940s.

In 1891, shortly before his mother's death and not long before his marriage to Mary E. Lane, a schoolteacher and governess from Long Island, Baltimore resigned his state position and returned to Troy to become the assistant engineer with the city's Public Improvement Commission, which was charged with improving water service, sewers, and street paving. He worked under chief engineer Palmer C. Ricketts, who was soon to become head of RPI. Over the next decade, Baltimore consulted on parks and cemeteries in several upstate New York cities, including Glens Falls, Amsterdam, Johnstown, and Gloversville,

Garnet Douglass Baltimore. (Institute Archives and Special Collections, Rensselaer Polytechnic Institute, Troy, NY)

and in Brattleboro, Vermont. He is also credited with the designs of Graceland Cemetery in Albany and Forest Park Cemetery in Brunswick, just east of Troy.

At the turn of the century, Troy's small public parks were woefully inadequate for its growing population. In 1901, city leaders proposed that one substantial new park be created in a central location, on the hilltop grounds of two former estates. At a public hearing, Baltimore spoke in favor of the "bold promontory jutting out and extending over the city," standing "like a sentinel, guarding the valley of the Hudson, revealing a landscape of miles in extent and extraordinary beauty." Its spectacular vista, he predicted, would be "an incentive to youth, an inspiration to manhood and a solace to old age."

In February 1903, Baltimore was hired as the landscape engineer to create this new 80-acre facility, soon to

Right: Fountain and lawn in Prospect Park, Troy, New York, from *The Reporter,* 1908, photographer, Lloyd. (Collection of the Rensselaer County Historical Society, Troy, NY)

Below: Crowd at Sunday band concert in Prospect Park, Troy, New York, from *The Reporter,* 1908, photographer, Boice. (Collection of the Rensselaer County Historical Society, Troy, NY)

be named Prospect Park. His contract stipulated that he establish the grades, "make the necessary maps, designs and profiles for the embellishment and improvement" of the park and its approaches, and then superintend the work. That summer he set out on a ten-day study tour in the Northeast, intent on examining the "methods employed in the development and maintenance of the public pleasure grounds."

Baltimore filed a detailed report upon his return. While examining parks in the Bronx, he had had the good fortune to meet **Samuel Parsons Jr.**, the renowned landscape architect of the New York City Department of Parks. Parsons and Baltimore visited Prospect Park in Brooklyn and then spent the Fourth of July in Central Park, where, Baltimore recounted, he reveled in having "all its beauties . . . unfolded by one who had done much in giving it the distinction of being one the first parks of the world."

The two men went on to Riverside Park and Morningside Park, where, Baltimore reported, "the planting and arrangement of the trees and shrubbery gives a charming effect to what was otherwise an uninviting hillside." Over the next few days, with local park superintendents as his hosts, Baltimore enjoyed the magnificent views at New Haven's East Rock Park; the charms of Elizabeth Park in West Hartford, Connecticut; and the lakes, menagerie, casino, and band-concert facilities at Roger Williams Park in Providence, Rhode Island. In Boston, on the final day of his tour, Baltimore took in **Frederick Law Olmsted Sr.**'s "Emerald Necklace" parks.

"The primary object of the park," he advised in his report, was to be "a place where natural beauty can be en-

joyed free from the turmoil of the city." Baltimore took special note of playgrounds in parks, which typically consisted of "a square or tract of land set aside, with a running track, horizontal bars, swinging ladders, basketball, inclined ladders, etc., in fact, all the facilities of a gymnasium in the open air." He had been impressed with the hundreds of young people playing tennis on the lawn in Central Park, where the courts were "marked out on the turf by tapes," yielding an "animated picture" during play but afterwards becoming "an unbroken lawn, not marred nor disfigured by any so-called professional court." He also endorsed such features as band concerts, boating, croquet, baseball, merry-go-rounds, natural-history museums, and even the feeding of gray squirrels.

Over the next few years at Prospect Park, Baltimore successfully oversaw the construction of winding roads, curving paths, a lake with a concrete dam, a playground, well-concealed tennis courts, and two rustic lookouts. He worked with a local architect, H. P. Fielding, on designs for a music pavilion of Moorish design and the conversion of a mansion into a casino. Another residence on the site was made into a museum.

Baltimore undertook landscape and engineering work for St. Mary's Hospital in Troy and served as consulting engineer for Greenwood Cemetery in Rye, New York. Even late in life Baltimore continued his engineering work, sometimes engaged in "making surveys and maps for attorneys, of the scenes of accidents and crimes" and serving as an expert witness at trials.

"The calling and duty of the Landscape Engineer," he wrote, was "to devise ways of arranging land and its accompanying landscape so that whatever the particular purpose in view may be, the result shall be as thoroughly beautiful as possible." On his eighty-fourth birthday Baltimore was cited as a well-known civil engineer and landscape authority. He remained an active supporter of RPI and died on June 12, 1946, disappointed at having been too ill to attend his sixty-fifth class reunion. He was buried in Troy beside his wife in the family plot at Oakwood Cemetery, which had been designed by **James C. Sidney** in 1849 and where Baltimore himself had served as the landscape engineer for thirty years.

Obituary. *Troy Record,* June 13, 1946. A review of Baltimore's family history and his professional career.

"Park in the Chrysalis." *Troy Times,* August 22, 1905. Discussion of the design and construction of Prospect Park.

Report of the Municipal Improvements Commission. Troy, N.Y.: Bureau of Parks, 1903. Includes Baltimore's report of his tours in the Northeast.

Diana S. Waite

BASHFORD, KATHERINE EMILIE
(1885–1953)
LANDSCAPE ARCHITECT

Katherine Emilie Bashford was born August 19, 1885, in Prescott, Arizona, to Coles Allen Bashford and Henrietta Parker. In 1894, Coles Bashford brought his family to California. Katherine attended 17th Street School and then the exclusive and reputable Marlborough School for Girls from 1899 to 1905. Following her graduation, she took courses at the Polytechnic High School in Pasadena and the Otis Art Institute in Los Angeles.

She always wanted to be a landscape architect but received no formal training in the field. She reportedly traveled to Europe prior to 1920 and again in 1930. Those trips allowed her to study Italian, French, and English gardens in depth and, in conjunction with her extensive library of books and photographs, provided inspiration for her commissions, illustrated in her frequent use of formal bedding plans, courtyards, and sweeping lawns. During this period of time, large estates were being developed in Southern California and many owners wished to incorporate European themes into their gardens. Bashford's designs were grounded in the European tradition but they remained true to the California spirit in their use of plant material and appropriateness to setting.

She began her work apprenticing with **Florence Yoch** for two years and opened her own practice in 1923. A year later, the periodical *California Southland* began to feature her gardens. In 1924, a sketch for an intimate walled garden at the home of Mr. and Mrs. Cheesewright was included and described as "adapted skillfully to the existing conditions." It included promenades of flowers that softened the square edges of the garden, a lily pool, and two fountain sprays. The following year, her work at the Arthur Bourne house, designed by Wallace Neff, was featured. Bashford was praised by the architect for her ability to interpret in plants the pictures in his mind. Neff added that in a year, they would look like they had always been there. He believed that it was Bashford's eye for unexpected outdoor effects that distinguished her gardens of all sizes.

Along with being featured in *California Southland,* Bashford also contributed articles to the publication. In an article in the April 1924 edition, she encouraged the summer planting of annual seeds among perennials to add lightness and airiness to a garden.

The California estates designed by Bashford spanned from Santa Maria in the north to La Jolla in the south. They included gardens in Bel Air, Pasadena, Ojai, and

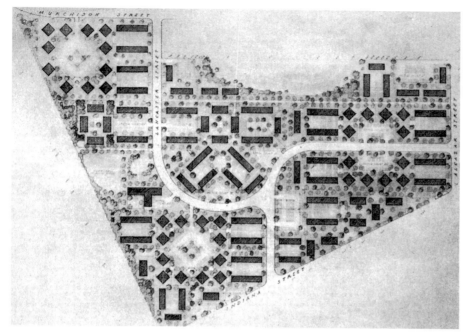

Left: USHA housing projects plan. (Illustration no. 118 from *Los Angeles in the Thirties,* by David Gebhard and Harriette von Breton, published by Hennessey + Ingalls, Santa Monica)

Below: Honeyman garden, San Marino, California. (Copyright 1996 by Allen A. Knoll, Publishers, from the book *California Gardens* by Winifred Starr Dobyns)

award for her work with Los Angeles architect Reginald Johnson on the William C. McDuffie estate.

In 1935, Bashford was chosen to be the landscape designer for the three demonstration homes in the House of Tomorrow exhibit at the National Housing Exposition in Los Angeles. It was in that year she also began a thirteen-year partnership with landscape architect Fred Barlow. He was first her office manager and assistant and later became a full partner.

As part of Franklin Delano Roosevelt's New Deal, Congress passed the Housing Act of 1937 to fund the building of decent and affordable housing for working families. Well-known architects and landscape architects were hired to design these low-rise communities based on the Garden City model. Bashford and Barlow completed four United States Housing Authority (USHA) housing projects in the Los Angeles area during the early 1940s. The Ramona Gardens Housing Project was a low-rent housing project of 610 dwelling units. Bashford and Barlow's landscape design reduced the typical number of public streets and increased walkways and play areas. Front yards planted with Bermuda grass were maintained

San Marino. *California Southland* reported that she also did landscape work in the desert. One of her best-known projects was the garden planned for Harry Bauer, president of the Automobile Club of Southern California. It was a hillside site in Pasadena, an area renowned for its natural gardens and expansive lawns. She also worked on the R. B. Honeyman and the John Barber estates in Pasadena and completed a landscape renovation for The Old Mill in San Marino. In 1933, the American Institute of Architects, Southern California Chapter, gave her an

by the owners, and were fronted with oriental plane trees on the parkways. The pair also completed work on the Harbor Hills Housing Project, which included 300 homes built on a terraced hillside with gardens in the rear, play areas with benches, tree-bordered walkways, and a spray pool. Their final two projects for the USHA were the Aliso Village War Housing Project, which included 802 units, and the 284-unit Rancho San Pedro Housing Project, both designed by architect Reginald Johnson.

Bashford again paired with Johnson for the development of another low-rise planned community designed to provide high-quality urban housing, Baldwin Hills Village, just southwest of downtown Los Angeles. Johnson led the project team, which along with Bashford and Barlow, included landscape architect Fred Edmondson, architect Robert Alexander, and consulting planner and architect Clarence Stein. Although it is difficult to discern what individual contribution Bashford made, the design included allées of olive and sycamore trees replicating early California scenes, lawns replaced by ivy ground cover, and decomposed granite used in small formal gardens and walkways. Baldwin Hills Village, now known as The Village Green, became a National Historic Landmark in 2001.

The American Society of Landscape Architects proposed Bashford for Fellowship in 1936. At that point she had been a member for six years. Her obituary printed in their publication, *Landscape Architecture,* recalled "the proposal was based on the outstanding quality and quantity of her work, her high ethical standards as a member of the profession, and her close collaboration with fine architects." Fellow landscape architect Ruth Patricia Shellhorn* remembered Bashford as being very skilled at designing perennial borders, and admirers often described her work as dignified and restful.

In 1943, Bashford retired from the landscape practice due to a heart condition. At the time of her death on June 3, 1953, she was living as an invalid with her sister, Caroline Louise Bashford York.

California Southland. A monthly periodical with descriptive articles about several of Bashford's gardens.

"Katherine Bashford: Biographical Minute." *Landscape Architecture* 44 (October 1953). Bashford obituary from her industry publication.

Scheid, Ann. *Historic Pasadena: An Illustrated History.* San Antonio: Historical Publishing Network, 1999. A section is devoted to Pasadena's rich garden history.

Carolyn Doepke Bennett

BAYER, HERBERT
(1900–1985)
ENVIRONMENTAL ARTIST, GRAPHIC DESIGNER

Herbert Bayer was born in the hamlet of Haag, Austria, on April 5, 1900. His father, a government revenue officer, and mother encouraged young Herbert's interest in nature and art, allowing him to roam into the hills and mountains near his childhood home in Linz with his sketchbook. Although Bayer had aspired to attend art school in Vienna, his father's early, unexpected death dashed those plans. Instead, Bayer took a position as an apprentice in the local architecture and decorative arts studio of Georg Schmidthammer, where Bayer gained valuable skills in graphic design, drafting, and production. Looking for a change, Bayer migrated in 1920 to Darmstadt, Germany, where he worked for the architect Emanual Margold. Between his duties creating package designs, Bayer heard stories of an emerging national

design school in Weimar. Bayer was accepted into the Bauhaus in October 1921.

The education Bayer received at the Bauhaus shaped the rest of his life. Under the influences of Walter Gropius, Laszlo Moholy-Nagy, and Wassily Kandinsky, Bayer gave himself over to the school's philosophy of functional design. Though Bayer maintained interests in painting and photography, he was encouraged by Gropius to focus in the areas in which he excelled: typography and graphic design. In 1923, Bayer took a break from his studies to travel in Italy. As in his boyhood, Bayer walked extensively, stopping to sketch or paint when the mood suited him. Complementing his academic focus on the functional arts, Italy nourished Bayer's respect and appreciation for nature and art. Upon returning to the Bauhaus in late

1924, Bayer continued to experiment with and explore a variety of techniques. After passing his examinations in February 1925, he was invited to the school's new home in Dessau to teach typography and graphic design.

Bayer's tenure as a master at the Bauhaus was as important to him as his education there had been. His Bauhaus position allowed him to accomplish two important goals. First, he was able to continue his experimentation with various media, resisting categorization into a single art form. Second, he was able to initiate his own professional design practice. Bayer was also instrumental in making the Bauhaus synonymous with an emerging, modern design aesthetic. Beginning in 1925, the Bauhaus adopted a fresh graphic design identity to use in all of its correspondence and publications. The Bauhaus graphics incorporated a newly created sans serif lowercase typeface called Universal that was designed by Herbert Bayer.

In 1928, Bayer along with Gropius, Moholy-Nagy, and architect Marcel Breuer left the Bauhaus for Berlin. Bayer established his own design firm. Berlin gave Bayer opportunities to increase his professional scope and acclaim. Working with such clients as *Vogue* magazine and the international advertising agency Dorland, Bayer incorporated his photography, which revealed the influence of surrealism and Dadaism on his work, into his graphic design commissions. Bayer was also asked—along with Gropius, Moholy-Nagy, and Breuer—to design an exhibition for the Societe des Artistes Decorateurs in Paris. Other design commissions to create exhibitions followed, including work for the Building Workers Union, Berthold Type Foundry, German Cork Industry, and various industrial and traveling exhibitions. This experience and his reputation as a modern exhibition designer would prove important for Bayer's successful move to America.

Fleeing the repression of Nazi Germany, Bayer moved to New York in 1938. He established an office below the Museum of Modern Art (MoMA), then housed in Rockefeller Center. Spurring Bayer's emigration was his nomination by a group of his former Bauhaus colleagues to assemble the first major Bauhaus exhibition in the United States, to be held at MoMA. Upon its opening, *Bauhaus 1919–1928* was hailed as a pioneering moment in American exhibition design. The acclaim of this success quickly led to two more exhibition design commissions: *Road to Victory,* directed by Edward Steichen at MoMA, and *Airways to Peace,* an exhibition on flying.

Herbert Bayer at Mill Creek Canyon Earthworks Park, Kent, Washington, 1982. (Photo by John Hoge; courtesy of the City of Kent, Washington)

Parallel to this exhibition design work, graphic design remained the mainstay of Bayer's practice, and while in New York he worked for a variety of high-profile clients. *Life* and *Fortune* magazines both used his services, as did book publishers and corporations, including General Electric and the Container Corporation of America.

During the holidays of 1945, Walter Paepcke, the head of the Container Corporation, invited Bayer as his guest to the old mining town of Aspen, Colorado. There Paepcke offered Bayer a position as the design consultant to both his company and the dilapidated town as it was being transformed into a world-class ski resort. The allure of the mountains combined with the scope of the project trumped Bayer's reservations about abandoning his successful practice in New York. Bayer moved to Aspen, where he remained until 1974.

Among several smaller projects in Aspen, Bayer's largest responsibility was the design of the Aspen Institute for Humanistic Studies. This project was Bayer's first opportunity to work within a site-specific context to create a

Mill Creek Canyon Earthworks Park, Kent, Washington, 1982. (Photo by John Hoge; courtesy of the City of Kent, Washington)

physical intervention that worked with its environment. Bayer's scheme harmonized the program elements of a conference center, hotel rooms, restaurants, and a health and exercise center with the surrounding natural topography. Bayer relished this environmental design challenge, and began to create several landscape pieces. In 1955, the first of Bayer's sculptural environments was built in Aspen. Marble Garden consisted of a series of up-ended marble slabs set onto a plinth to provide refuge from the open lawns of the Aspen Institute. Adjacent to this piece was Earth Mound (also called Grass Mound), dubbed by Jan van der Marck in his book *Herbert Bayer: From Type to Landscape* as "the first instance on record of landscape as sculpture." A 40-foot-diameter berm, Earth Mound formed a circular mound within the grassy plane, a place to sit and read within Aspen's expansive meadows. Although Bayer himself never acknowledged the relationship between his work and earthworks, he did not like the appellation nor did he like being labeled. His outdoor work in Aspen formed the precedent for the earthworks art movement that was to emerge a full decade later.

Though he continued his design work, developing marketing materials for Aspen and the Container Corporation, Bayer did not work with earth again until 1973, when he designed Aspen's Anderson Park, the largest of his environmental projects. Borrowing elements from both Marble Garden and Earth Mound, Bayer created in Anderson Park a series of paths that meandered over and around geometric berms, divots, and rings.

Bayer's work in the landscape expanded into outdoor sculpture as well, including Aspen's Kaleidoscreen (1955); Articulated Wall (1968), a commission for the Mexico City Olympics; and Double Ascension, built for Atlantic Richfield (ARCO, 1972). Bayer also remained active in graphic design, book layout, mural painting, publishing, exhibition design, and industrial beautification. His painting also flourished, with imagery influenced by surrealism, modernism, and color theory as well as his personal experiences.

Though these years were pleasant and productive for Bayer, the harsh extremes of Aspen's climate were taking a toll on his health. In 1975, Bayer moved with his wife, Joella, to Montecito, California. Removed from the place that he had shaped for thirty years, Bayer continued to work prolifically on a variety of projects. His work for ARCO occupied much of his time, particularly the Breakers project, which involved renovating and redesigning the interior and exterior spaces of an aging mansion overlooking the Pacific Ocean, transforming it into a plush executive headquarters for training. And as always, Bayer continued to paint. In California, his visual language became more introspective and regressive. Lifelong themes of mountains and geology, nature, and color came to the fore in his *Anthology* series of paintings.

Bayer's final environmental work, Mill Creek Canyon Earthworks Park in Kent, Washington, combined the sculptural vocabulary of his Aspen projects with ecological functionalism. The 2.5-acre site was designed to retain stormwater from the eponymous watercourse as it flowed down through a tight canyon. A series of berms, mounds, and excavated rings provided sculptural interest for viewers as they meandered through the composition. Mill Creek Canyon Earthworks Park is Bayer's most acclaimed work due largely to its successful resolution of two perceived competing interests: art and ecology.

However, the Bauhaus master likely saw both of these components as merely integrated parts of the larger field of design practiced in its myriad of expressions—an approach he had employed for his entire, remarkable professional career. Herbert Bayer passed away in Montecito, California, in 1985 at the age of eighty-five.

Baird, C. Timothy. "A Composed Ecology: After Twenty Plus Years, How is Herbert Bayer's Renowned Mill Creek Canyon Earthworks Holding Up?" *Landscape Architecture* 93, no. 2 (March 2003), 68–75. Post-occupancy design critique with special emphasis on the ecological sensitivities that the project displays.

Chanzit, Gwen F. *Herbert Bayer and Modernist Design in America.* Ann Arbor: University of Michigan Research Press, 1987. A lengthy text-based monograph that seeks to trace Bayer's design development and the manner in which the Bauhaus ideas filtered into his American works.

Cohen, Arthur A. *Herbert Bayer: The Complete Work.* Cambridge, Mass: MIT Press, 1984. The only encompassing monograph that spans the breadth and depth of Bayer's entire design portfolio with accompanying images.

Catherine Maggio and Brice Maryman

BAYLIS, DOUGLAS
(1915–1971)
LANDSCAPE ARCHITECT, AUTHOR

Douglas Baylis was born on January 7, 1915, in East Orange, New Jersey. At the age of sixteen and following the death of his father, Baylis moved to Long Beach, California, where he attended high school and worked with landscape designer George Carpenter. After completing a few years of study at a junior college and developing his general landscape construction and maintenance skills with Carpenter, Baylis moved to Berkeley to attend the University of California. There he studied under Hollyngsworth Leland Vaughan,* John W. Gregg,* and Harry Whitcomb Shepherd* and earned his undergraduate degree in landscape architecture from the University of California, Berkeley, graduating with high marks in 1941. That same year, he became the first recipient of the American Society of Landscape Architects student award.

Following graduation, Baylis worked in **Thomas Dolliver Church**'s San Francisco landscape design office from 1941 to 1942. Despite Baylis's short tenure in the office, Church mentored Baylis throughout the latter's career. After leaving Church's office, Baylis went to work for the San Francisco Housing Authority. Three years

Douglas Baylis, portrait by Fred Lyon, New York, ca. 1962. (Douglas and Maggie Baylis Collection [1999-4], Environmental Design Archives, University of California, Berkeley)

Left: A drawing of one of Baylis's nonresidential projects, Walter Doty Memorial Project, Palo Alto, California. (Douglas and Maggie Baylis Collection [1999-4], Environmental Design Archives, University of California, Berkeley)

Below: "Blueprint for Garden Living" by Douglas Baylis, undated clipping. One of Baylis's many illustrated articles, with its "how-to" approach. (Douglas and Maggie Baylis Collection [1999-4], Environmental Design Archives, University of California, Berkeley)

Opposite: William E. Egleston house and garden plan, Contra Costa County, California. An example of a residential landscape design. (Douglas and Maggie Baylis Collection [1999-4], Environmental Design Archives, University of California, Berkeley)

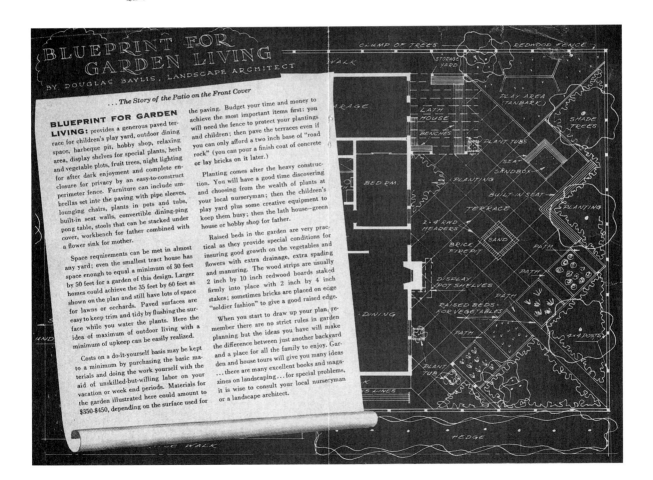

BLUEPRINT FOR GARDEN LIVING
BY DOUGLAS BAYLIS, LANDSCAPE ARCHITECT

... The Story of the Patio on the Front Cover

BLUEPRINT FOR GARDEN LIVING: provides a generous paved terrace for children's play yard, outdoor dining space, barbeque pit, hobby shop, relaxing area, display shelves for special plants, herb and vegetable plots, fruit trees, night lighting for after dark enjoyment and complete enclosure for privacy by an easy-to-construct perimeter fence. Furniture can include umbrellas set into the paving with pipe sleeves, lounging chairs, plants in pots and tubs, built-in seat walls, convertible dining-ping pong table, stools that can be stacked under cover, workbench for father combined with a flower sink for mother.

Space requirements can be met in almost any yard; even the smallest tract house has space enough to equal a minimum of 30 feet by 50 feet for a garden of this design. Larger homes could achieve the 35 feet by 60 feet as shown on the plan and still have lots of space for lawns or orchards. Paved surfaces are easy to keep trim and tidy by flushing the surface while you water the plants. Here the idea of maximum of outdoor living with a minimum of upkeep can be easily realized.

Costs on a do-it-yourself basis may be kept to a minimum by purchasing the basic materials and doing the work yourself with the aid of unskilled-but-willing labor on your vacation or week end periods. Materials for the garden illustrated here could amount to $350-$450, depending on the surface used for the paving. Budget your time and money to achieve the most important items first: you will need the fence to protect your plantings and children; then pave the terraces even if you can only afford a two inch base of "road rock" (you can pour a finish coat of concrete or lay bricks on it later.)

Planting comes after the heavy construction. You will have a good time discovering and choosing from the wealth of plants at your local nurseryman; then the children's play yard plus some creative equipment to keep them busy; then the lath house—greenhouse or hobby shop for father.

Raised beds in the garden are very practical as they provide special conditions for insuring good growth on the vegetables and flowers with extra drainage, extra spading and manuring. The wood strips are usually 2 inch by 10 inch redwood boards staked firmly into place with 2 inch by 4 inch stakes; sometimes bricks are placed on edge "soldier fashion" to give a good raised edge.

When you start to draw up your plan, remember there are no strict rules in garden planning but the ideas you have will make the difference between just another backyard and a place for all the family to enjoy. Garden and house tours will give you many ideas ... there are many excellent books and magazines on landscaping... for special problems, it is wise to consult your local nurseryman or a landscape architect.

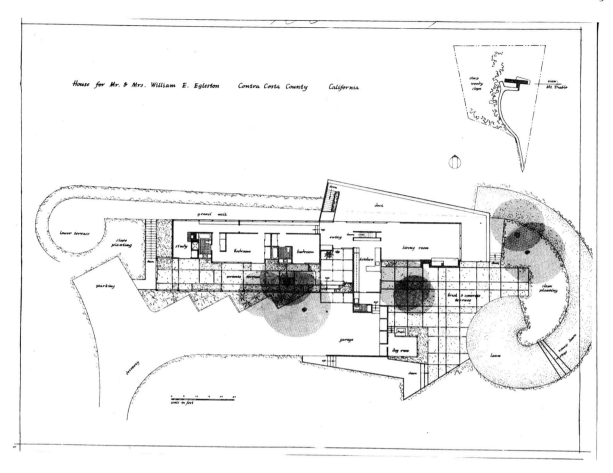

House for Mr. & Mrs. William E. Egleston   Contra Costa County   California

later, he opened his own office in San Francisco. In his private practice, Baylis promoted a modern and strongly regional design philosophy. He was especially interested in how people lived. Like his contemporaries, Garrett Eckbo,* Robert Royston,* and Lawrence Halprin,* Baylis embraced the natural landscape and climate of California and the lifestyle that such environmental aspects fostered.

Baylis articulated his design philosophy in his professional landscape projects and in a number of illustrated articles, which he wrote for both professional and popular journals such as *Landscape Architecture, Sunset, House Beautiful, Better Homes and Gardens, McCall's,* and *Family Circle.* Baylis's professional partner and wife, the talented graphic artist Margaret (Maggie) Hilbiber Baylis, whom he met in 1946, illustrated the couple's joint periodical contributions. Together, they are credited with pioneering a new "how-to" style of garden-article writing

that was eventually adopted by many popular magazines across the United States. In addition to specific site designs and journal articles, the Baylis team produced many drawings of landscape structures and garden furniture. Many of these details and sketches can be found in built projects, magazine articles, or as kits sold through magazines, such as their plywood play equipment designs. Both Douglas and Maggie Baylis were principal contributors to the 1948 Exhibition of Landscape Design, organized by the San Francisco Museum of Modern Art and the Association of Landscape Architects of the San Francisco region.

Douglas Baylis's earliest landscape work consisted primarily of residential garden designs, many of which were designed for clients and friends who had been his collaborators as architects, photographers, and other design professionals on larger public and commercial projects. One collaborator in particular, architect Gordon Drake, was a special colleague and friend of both Doug and Maggie. Doug worked with Drake on a house and garden in Carmel and on the "Unit House"—a house based on a three-foot module with five distinct zones for California indoor/outdoor living. After Drake's sudden death, Doug and Maggie Baylis contributed to the book *California Houses of Gordon Drake* (1956), a memorial to their dear friend and colleague.

Concurrent with his design practice, Doug Baylis was active in state and national professional organizations and design education. From 1948 to 1950, he served as the director for the California Association of Landscape Architects and he served as the vice president from 1953 to 1956. Supporting the licensing legislation that focused on the field of landscape architecture, Baylis helped realize the professional registration of landscape architects in the state of California, which became effective in 1953. During the 1950s, he was a visiting lecturer at the University of California, Berkeley, and he often contributed to the landscape department's publication, *Space*. Additionally, he served as the university's Supervising Landscape Architect for three years before Church assumed the position in 1959.

During his late career, Baylis's focus shifted from residential projects to larger, industrial ones. Applying the same interest in social function to these projects that he had demonstrated in his residential work, Baylis completed designs for San Francisco's Civic Center Plaza and Washington Square, as well as for the Monterey Freeway, San Bruno Mountain and Housing Preserve, Foothill Farms near Sacramento, and the IBM headquarters near San Jose. Commissioned to renovate Portsmouth Square in San Francisco, Baylis found himself embroiled in a highly charged political and civic debate from 1959–

1960. He also worked for the Redevelopment Agency and the Crocker Land Company, and remained active in professional organizations, especially the American Society of Landscape Architects, for which he served as a trustee from 1962 to 1965. In 1966, the organization honored him as Fellow. Baylis was also a dedicated member of the San Francisco Art Commission from 1948 to 1953.

Douglas Baylis passed away on November 28, 1971, at the age of fifty-six, in Stinson Beach, California. Maggie Baylis passed away on December 10, 1997, at the age of eighty-five in Sonoma, California.

The Douglas and Maggie Baylis Collection and office files are housed at the Environmental Design Archives, University of California, Berkeley. The collection spans the years 1938–1998 (bulk 1939–1943) and contains records relating to the Baylis firm's landscape design projects, publishing endeavors, and some personal items. Specifically, the holdings include personal papers, office files, project files, drawings, photographs, and writings.

Baylis, Douglas. "A Proposal for Product Development." *Landscape Architecture* 51 (Fall 1960), 2, 28–32. Includes a brief biographical note about Douglas Baylis.

Baylis, Douglas, and Joan Parry. *California Houses of Gordon Drake.* New York: Reinhold Publishing Corp., 1956. Architect Gordon Drake as a professional colleague and personal friend of Douglas and Maggie Baylis. This volume, which includes sketches, photographs, and commentary on Drake's short life and architecture career, was published as a tribute and memorial to Drake.

La Brecque, Suzan. *The American Published Articles and Books by the California School of Landscape Architects: Douglas Baylis, Thomas Dolliver Church, Garrett Eckbo, Lawrence Halprin, Theodore Osmundson, Robert N. Royston, John H. Staley,* ed. A. Williams. Pomona: California State Polytechnic University, Department of Landscape Architecture, 1992. Maggie's contribution to this oral history project includes many anecdotes on the relationship between her husband and Thomas Church.

Carrie Leah McDade

BENDELOW, TOM
(1868–1936)
GOLF COURSE DESIGNER

Born in Aberdeen, Scotland, on September 2, 1868, Tom Bendelow was one of nine children. At the age of five, his father taught him to play golf. As a young man, Bendelow was a proficient golfer and played many of the courses in Scotland and England. At that time, knowledge of the game and the ability to utilize the natural landscape were the essential qualifications needed to design golf courses. There was not a recognized profession of golf course

architect; instead greenskeepers or "club makers" designed the courses.

Bendelow trained as a typesetter for the Aberdeen newspaper. He then left Scotland, arriving in New York City on September 21, 1892. His first job was in the composing room of the New York *Herald* newspaper. Bendelow soon discovered the growing interest in America in the game of golf and in the need for places to play. He began by teaching others the game and then designing courses for friends, then for groups and communities. In 1895, Bendelow began an association with A. G. Spalding & Brothers, sporting goods manufacturers, to promote the development of golf courses in the New York and New Jersey area.

Bendelow's early foray into the realm of golf course design drew heavily upon his own experience on Scottish courses as well as the methods and writings of several British designers such as Old Tom Morris, Tom Dunn, Willie Dunn Jr., and Willie Park Jr.* Their methods of course layout—walking and staking the site—were the accepted and preferred practices of the time, allowing designers to get the full feel of the land, the wind, and the natural vegetation into which the course was to be laid.

Over the next several years Bendelow's reputation as a golf course designer grew rapidly in the metropolitan area. His personal contacts and working association with A. G. Spalding enabled him to redirect his profession from the newspaper business to golf course development. In 1898, the New York City Department of Parks hired Bendelow to redesign and expand the Van Cortlandt Park Golf Course in the Bronx, New York City. Van Cortlandt Park opened in 1895 and was the first public golf course in the United States. Bendelow supervised the construction work, the maintenance of the course, the operation of the facility, and the training of personnel. This combination of overseeing the design and the operation of a public golf course was unique for his day. It influenced his future manner of course design and consultations with local communities.

The overwhelming success at Van Cortlandt Park set examples that communities across the country sought to emulate. Recognizing the business potential, Spalding & Brothers hired Bendelow away from the New York City Department of Parks and assigned him to the firm's headquarters in Chicago as the firm's Golf Department Manager. As Spalding's representative, Bendelow traveled the United States and Canada laying out or remodeling golf courses for clubs and municipalities. He was a strong supporter of public golf courses and used every occasion to promote their development and use. He traveled to small towns that were

Tom Bendelow, 1899. (Courtesy of Stuart W. Bendelow)

French Lick Springs Resort, Springs Valley Golf Links Course, 12th green. French Lick, Indiana, 1920s. (Courtesy of Dave Harner, French Lick Springs Resort Casino)

lacking in public park facilities and convinced them to spend public monies on a landscape for golf, reassuring officials that the courses would not be financially burdensome to the local governments. He felt that the communities' enthusiasm for the game would grow and lead to improved recreational facilities.

Over the two-decade period that Bendelow was associated with Spalding & Company, he designed more than five hundred courses across the United States and Canada. He also established an association with the University of Illinois, where he conducted an annual series of lectures on golf course design and landscape maintenance. He was the first designer to encourage open discussions of course design and landscape usage. (This may have been the first instruction in golf course design by an academic institution in the United States.)

In 1920, Bendelow joined the staff of the American Park Builders, located in Chicago, as chief designer. It was during this time with the American Park Builders that he undertook some of his largest design efforts. Among his many designs were Lakewood Country Club in Colorado; Dubsdread Golf Course in Orlando, Florida; Evansville Municipal in Indiana; City Park Municipal in Baton Rouge, Louisiana; and the three courses at Medinah Country Club in Illinois, which may be some of his finest design work. He served as the firm's chief designer until the firm's demise in 1933.

Exactly how many golf courses Tom Bendelow was involved in designing, expanding, or remodeling is unknown. Many courses that he designed no longer exist, some of the clubs have moved to new locations, others have been altered by subsequent designs, or, in many cases, the records have simply been lost. An article by Myron Howard West* titled "Tom Bendelow: The Dean of American Golf Course Architects," which appeared in the February 1923 issue of *Golfers Magazine,* credits Bendelow with the design of over six hundred courses— and this was more than ten years before he ceased active design work. In a circa-1925 design pamphlet prepared for the American Park Builders, an estimate of over eight hundred courses is cited. He was possibly the most prolific golf course designer this country has seen or may ever see, deserving the designation given him as "the Johnny Appleseed of American Golf."

Bendelow passed away on March 24, 1936, at his home in River Forest, Illinois. Today, two of his golf courses— City Park Golf Course in Baton Rouge, Louisiana, and City Park Golf Course in Denver are listed in the National Register of Historic Places.

Bendelow, Thomas. *The Golfers' Magazine,* 1900 to 1919. Frequent contributions including: "The Finals" (August 1902, vol. 1, no. 4); "The Game of Golf" (January 1904, vol. 4, no. 3, pp. 108–9); "Long Grass on Golf Courses" (March 1911, vol. 18, no. 5, p. 222); "Sanding Putting Greens" (April 1911, vol. 18, no. 6, p. 278); "Rolling the Greens" (December 1912, vol. 22, no. 2, pp. 74–75); "Putting Greens" (March 1913, vol. 22, no. 5, pp. 216–18); "For the Consideration of the Green Committee," (March 1914, vol. 24, no. 5, pp. 29–30); "Tom Bendelow's Reply" (re: Harry Vardon's "What's Wrong With American Golf," June 1914) (August 1914, vol. 25, no. 4, pp. 42–44); and "Putting Greens" (February 1915, vol. 26, no. 4, pp. 59–61).

Bendelow, Thomas, ed. *Spalding's Athletic Library/Red Book Series.* New York: American Sports Publishing, 1909–1916. Published annually. Edited by Bendelow from 1909 to 1916, who also contributed such articles as "Hints to the Greens Committee," "Rolling of Greens," "Sanding of Putting Greens," "Hints on Laying Out a Golf Course," and "Golf in the Middle West."

Bendelow, Thomas. *Tom Bendelow's Caddie Manual.* Ashland Golf Department. Chicago: Thos. E. Wilson & Co., March 1917. Sixteen pages with illustrations.

Stuart Bendelow

BLOSSOM, HAROLD HILL
(1879–1935)
LANDSCAPE ARCHITECT

Known as Hal to his friends, Harold Hill Blossom was born in Brooklyn, New York, on October 6, 1879. After graduating from the Pratt Institute High School, he entered Amherst College with the class of 1901, but rheumatic fever delayed his graduation until 1902. This disease also left him with cardiac damage that would limit some of his future activities and eventually shorten his life.

After graduation, Blossom took courses at the Bussey Institute and worked on a fruit farm. He entered Harvard's Lawrence Scientific School in 1904 for the course in landscape architecture and engineering, becoming the first graduate of the Masters in Landscape Architecture program in 1907. Even before graduation, he had begun working on projects for the **Olmsted Brothers**, and according to his personal diary, had also spent leisure time sailing with **Frederick Law Olmsted Jr.**, or attending lectures with **Percival Gallagher**. His special status may have been due to his courtship of Minnie Motley Dawson, the sister of **James Frederick Dawson** of the Olmsted firm, whom he married in September 1908.

Blossom's early tasks at the Olmsted firm covered a range of projects working under various principals drafting plans and devising planting arrangements, such as that for South Mountain Reservation in Essex County, New Jersey, under Gallagher's supervision. Within the Olmsted office at that time, there was a strong emphasis on designs for major estates, particularly those on Long Island such as Nethermuir for Henry de Forest and Welwyn, for Harold Pratt, where his engineering and planting expertise made him a valuable on-site assistant. He accompanied **John Charles Olmsted** and Dawson to Seattle for the Alaska-Yukon-Pacific Exposition and other projects in this area, and went with Dawson to Cuba in 1910 for the planning of La Siguanea, a resort community on the Isle of Pines. In 1911, he became Olmsted Brothers' resident representative overseeing the problematic planning for the 1915 Panama-Pacific Exposition in Balboa Park, San Diego.

H. H. Blossom, ca. 1928. (Courtesy of the Blossom family)

As Dawson noted in recommending him to John Charles Olmsted, "[he] has enough knowledge of plants to cause him to take notice of new things in different places . . . He is intelligent and well-bred and gets on well with clients."

When the Olmsted firm resigned from this project in protest against the destruction of the park's natural scenery, Blossom returned east to continue estate work for the expanding Long Island clientele as well as for new Newport, Rhode Island, mansions. Additionally, he advised Stockbridge and Lenox, Massachusetts, on ways to preserve picturesque character and vistas in their town centers, and worked with John Charles Olmsted on such projects as Thompson Park in Watertown, New York. Among his notable residential designs during this period were his planting schemes for

"Wall looking to shelter from the North," in the Edwin S. Webster garden, Chestnut Hill, Massachusetts, June 1924. (Courtesy of the Blossom family)

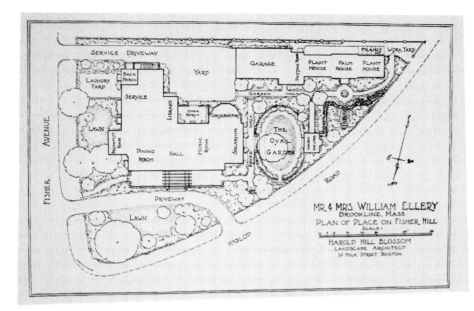

Left: Design for Ellery residence garden, Brookline, Massachusetts, from the *House Beautiful Gardening Manual*, 1926.

Below: Sketch of Harbour Court, John Nicholas Brown estate, Newport, Rhode Island, undated. (Courtesy of the National Park Service, Frederick Law Olmsted National Historic Site)

Oheka, the Otto Kahn estate in Cold Spring, New York, and Harbour Court in Newport, for John Nicholas Brown. The Browns remained as his clients even after he left the Olmsted firm, and his work on this estate garden won for him the 1923 gold Medal of Honor in Landscape Architecture from the Architectural League of New York for excellence in design using natural materials.

Blossom opened his own office on Milk Street in Boston in 1919, with a practice consisting primarily of residential design, both urban and suburban, along with some small subdivisions, mostly throughout Massachusetts. He became a Fellow of the American Society of Landscape Architects and in 1924 entered into an association with Guy Hunter Lee,* with whom he worked until 1927, occasionally sharing projects with Hallam Leonard Movius,* who had been Blossom's classmate at the Lawrence Scientific School. Eventually, Movius and Lee became partners. Additionally, Blossom taught landscape courses at both the Cambridge School and the Lowthorpe School. He was active in the Boston Society of Landscape Architects and in civic affairs in West Roxbury, where he lived, and an enthusiastic thespian in local productions. Whether for health reasons or because his wife Minnie had died unexpectedly in 1922, leaving him with four young chil-

dren, he did not travel far. He remarried in 1926 and had another daughter.

He understood the market value of publications to develop a practice and produced *The Landscape Beautiful* in 1923, which contained his own photographs of his work, which illustrated his richly textured assemblages of plantings, pavings, and architectural details. Over the next decade until months before his death, articles and photographs by or about Blossom and his work appeared in *The House Beautiful, The Garden Magazine, Country Life, Horticulture,* and other publications, including the American Society of Landscape Architects and the

Boston Society of Landscape Architects volumes illustrating works of members. Notably, within Massachusetts, his designs for Edwin S. Webster in Chestnut Hill; for William Ellery in Brookline; for the Hon. William Philips in North Beverly; and for John Saltonstall in Topsfield, reveal his sensitivity to site, his subtlety of scale, his horticultural deftness at plant combinations, and his consummate artistry in achieving what **Rose Ishbel Greely** called "studied luxuriance" and "a restful feeling of simplicity." Blossom saw his "garden magic," though well-schooled in European precedents, as an expression of "the language and thought of to-day" to fulfill a "beneficent purpose in the intricate web of modern human life."

In his 1936 obituary tribute to his longtime friend and colleague, **Edward Clark Whiting** wrote about Harold Hill Blossom, "'To garden finely' was his creed; and he gave nearly thirty years of untiring unswerving effort to its interpretation. He taught many to see a new breadth of meaning in that simple old-time phrase . . . his particular and outstanding contribution was in that subtle and intricate field of plant material: plant forms, plant qualities and habits, their groupings and associations, their happy and satisfying relationships to other forms whether natural or architectural . . . [and] his sensitive appreciation of beauty. . . ."

Note: It is very difficult to extract from the roster of Olmsted Brothers projects on which Blossom worked and in what capacity. Since many of his tasks lay in horticultural enhancement, these are the least likely elements to have survived the decades, and since many of the projects were, and still are, private, there is little opportunity for close inspection. Certainly, remnants of the Olmsted design are visible in the roads and paths in Balboa Park in San Diego, California, which Blossom influenced, as he did in Thompson Park in Watertown, New York, and South Mountain Reservation in Essex County, New Jersey.

Of the projects from the years of Blossom's independent practice, some of the private gardens remain, though in diminished horticultural condition, such as the grounds of the Saltonstall estate in Topsfield, Massachusetts. Harbour Court in Newport is now the New York Yacht Club, and while some property from Webster's Chestnut Hill estate remains as conservation land, the once-lush flower gardens were subdivided into separate lots. Pochet, a vacation subdivision on Cape Cod, designed by Blossom in 1926 for Orleans Associates, and where he owned a cottage, retains his well planned roads and most of its lot arrangements. However, intense development pressure has altered some of the original lot layout and the extensive beachfront was taken and made public by the town of Orleans.

Blossom, Harold Hill. *The Landscape Beautiful.* Boston: Derby Brown Co., 1923. Expressive photographs by Blossom, unidentified as to client, captioned to emphasize the paving and planting effects.

Blossom, Harold Hill. "The Transformation of a Field: The Flower Garden for Mr. Edwin S. Webster at Chestnut Hill, Massachusetts." *The House Beautiful* 57 (May 1925), 522–24, 572–74. Blossom's discussion of his melding of English, Italian, and colonial American styles into a distinctly "modern American garden" of horticultural richness, beauty, and variety, intermingling formal and informal elements in a suburban setting.

Steele, Fletcher. *The House Beautiful Gardening Manual.* Boston: The Atlantic Monthly, 1926. In this practical and aesthetic guide for gardeners, Steele uses Blossom photographs and descriptions of Blossom-designed gardens, particularly the Ellery estate in Brookline, to illustrate his various points.

Arleyn A. Levee

BOERNER, ALFRED L.
(1900–1955)
LANDSCAPE ARCHITECT

Alfred L. Boerner was born on November 1, 1900, in Cedarburg, Wisconsin. He was the eighth of ten children; nine boys (two who died in infancy) and one girl. He was the grandson of a Wisconsin pioneer who settled in Cedarburg in 1849 on a farm on Cedar Creek.

Boerner attended the University of Wisconsin for two years and then transferred to the University of Illinois, in Urbana, where he graduated in 1923 with a bachelor of science in landscape architecture. After leaving Urbana, he began his career in the office of **Albert Davis Taylor** in Cleveland, Ohio, where he gained a wide and diversified experience.

In 1926, he returned to Wisconsin where he was appointed to the position of Landscape Architect in the newly formed Milwaukee County Regional Planning Department. He served in this capacity until October 1952, when he became General Manager of the Milwaukee County Park Commission.

Boerner came to Milwaukee County at a time when the Park Commission had visionary ideas for a county-

Above: Alfred L. Boerner. (Milwaukee County Parks Department)

Below: "A Development Plan for Greenfield Park," Milwaukee, Wisconsin, County Park Commission, ca. 1931. (Milwaukee County Parks Department)

wide park system. Preliminary plans had been outlined for major parks connected by parkways that would follow natural streams creating pleasant drives while providing for storm water drainage and flood control. It was Boerner's sensitivity to the local landscape and his design philosophy that brought these dreams to reality.

Boerner's designs are representative of a time when the philosophy of park design was in transition from the landscape park providing peaceful respites to escape from arduous life in urban areas to places for active recreation. Boerner believed that "active recreation can be ingeniously woven into a sound park plan of artistic merit in a manner so unobtrusive that it will in no way hinder the effectiveness of the park as a landscape composition—a large recreational park must furnish the public many activities, as well as passive pleasures, in an environment of beauty."

Regarding the design of a small neighborhood park, he wrote, "If the property had been cleared of trees, graded to an absolutely flat plane, and fenced with a woven wire fence, it would probably have accommodated a few more children in competitive games." Instead, Boerner designed a park that "enhanced the natural assets of the property and was sensitive to the neighborhood character. Active play was incorporated in the plan, but not the type that would seriously affect the quiet of the neighborhood."

Larger parks were designed taking advantage of the existing topography and natural features of the site. In

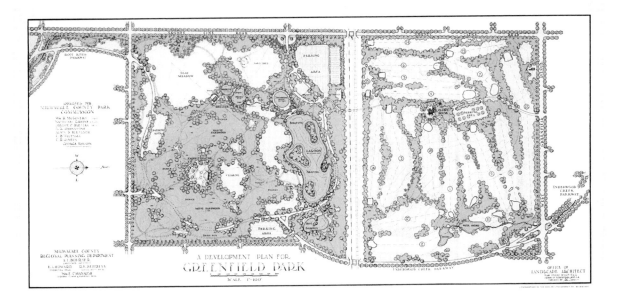

most parks water was used as a focal point. Lakes and waterfalls were incorporated into the landscape as well as "regrading the meander into many previously straightened stream channels" along parkways.

At the 600-acre Whitnall Park, native fieldstone was used to create the bridges, dams, walls, and buildings throughout the property. The gently rolling glacial terrain was developed into an arboretum park with the plant varieties that grow in the region assembled in ecological association. Native plant materials, especially hawthorns, were repeated throughout the scheme to maintain the appearance of a Wisconsin landscape. The north end of Whitnall Park was designed by Boerner as a botanical garden arranged on two formal axes ending in sweeping vistas of the surrounding parkland. The formal gardens contain a walled annual garden, perennial mall, shrub mall, rose garden, rock garden, and herb garden. The extensive collections contain plant material that thrives in the harsh Wisconsin landscape and were meant to serve as an educational model for the visitor and homeowner.

In Greenfield Park, the 320-acre property was bisected by a train track. The north portion of the park had been developed as an eighteen-hole golf course prior to Boerner's arrival. In the southern half of the park he created nature trails through a stand of native hardwoods with picnic areas developed on adjacent lawn areas. He sited a pavilion between a swimming pool and man-made lake. Both were fed by a deep well with water that was too cold for swimming. An ingenious plan evolved with water from the well appearing like a spring in the hillside. It then followed a course of rills and warming basins "designed to appear as kettle holes or pit lakes so common in this region" where a portion of the water eventually flowed into a wading pool for small children with the overflow bypassed into the lake. The bulk of the "warmed" water was taken underground to the swimming pool where it was chlorinated before being used.

Above: Warming basin waterfall, Greenfield Park, Milwaukee, Wisconsin, 1933. (Milwaukee County Parks Department)

Below: Arboretum at Whitnall Park, Wisconsin (later renamed the Alfred L. Boerner Botanical Gardens), 1947. (Milwaukee County Parks Department)

Prior to the Great Depression, Boerner and the Regional Planning Department produced a vast number of detailed park plans, which were gradually implemented. At the onset of the Depression, work came to a halt due to the lack of funding until the county implemented a relief project that would put unemployed men to work. This was later followed by many federal relief programs, allowing for many plans to be realized in a relatively short period of time. Boerner worked closely with workers and oversaw much of the fieldwork and construction undertaken in the parks by the Civilian Conservation Corps and Works Progress Administration programs assuring that work was completed according to plans.

Although the bulk of Boerner's work involved the design of parks, he also designed other county facilities such as the County Hospital Grounds and the Wustum campus of the Racine Art Museum. In 1942, he designed the display gardens for Jackson and Perkins nursery in Newark, New York, where his brother Eugene was a rose hybridizer.

Alfred Boerner became a member of the American Society of Landscape Architects in 1936 and a Fellow in 1952. He served on numerous committees, and was a trustee from 1946 to 1951. He served as president of the Chicago Chapter in 1941. He was a fellow of the American Institute of Park Executives, and was designated a Senior Fellow in 1930.

During his twenty-six years as County Landscape Architect and three years as the Parks' General Manager, Boerner's work included the planning of parks and parkways that were the nucleus of the current 15,000-acre park system and represent many of its finest achievements. On June 18, 1955, Alfred Boerner's career was cut short when he died of a heart attack. He was honored by the Park Commission after his death when one of his favorite projects, the Arboretum at Whitnall Park was renamed the Alfred L. Boerner Botanical Gardens.

The archives at the Milwaukee County Park files include numerous park plans drawn or approved by Boerner, as well as professional correspondence and reports.

Boerner, Alfred L. "The Influence of Nature on Park Design." Lecture by Boerner on file at the Milwaukee County Parks Department. November 26, 1940.

Boerner, Alfred L. "Saveland Park, A Small Park for a Residential Neighborhood," *Parks and Recreation* 15, no. 6 (February 1932), 323–26; "Greenfield Park, Unit of Milwaukee County Park System Designed to Satisfy Modern Needs," *Parks and Recreation* 17, no. 6 (February 1934), 185–91; and "New Trends in Park Design in Milwaukee County Parks," *Parks and Recreation* 22, no. 1 (September 1938), 3–6.

Cavanaugh, W. F., et al. *Milwaukee County Regional Planning Department First Annual Report*. Milwaukee, 1924. Original concept for parkway plan through Milwaukee County.

Laurie Muench Albano

BOGART, JOHN
(1836–1920)
CIVIL ENGINEER,
LANDSCAPE ARCHITECT

John Bogart was born in Albany, New York, to a successful merchant with business connections in Albany and New York City. Members of the Bogart family were prominent Albany citizens and city officials; Bogart's great-grandfather was the city surveyor. Bogart was educated at the Albany Academy. He was the first to win the top medals in mathematics and classics in the same year and, for a brief period, was an instructor at the academy. He earned a bachelor of arts (1853) from Rutgers College and subsequently was awarded an honorary master of arts (1856) and doctor of science (1912). An annual prize carrying Bogart's name is still awarded to an undergraduate mathematics major at Rutgers.

After graduating from college, Bogart worked for the New York Central Railroad, assisting with the construction of the direct line from Syracuse to Rochester. From 1856 to 1858, he was an assistant engineer on the reconstruction and enlargement of the Erie Canal for the State of New York. The work provided him with outdoor exercise that improved his delicate health. This early and practical experience in civil engineering secured his ap-

John Bogart, ca. 1895, from *Notable New Yorkers of 1896–1899: King's Handbook of New York City* (New York, NY: M. King, 1899). (Courtesy of Joy Kestenbaum)

pointment at twenty-two as an assistant engineer at New York City's Central Park, the first landscaped public park in the United States. The beginning of Bogart's longstanding association with **Frederick Law Olmsted Sr.** dates from this period.

Bogart interrupted his career to serve in the U.S. Army Corps of Engineers during the Civil War. In 1866, after the war, Bogart was an assistant engineer at Prospect Park in Brooklyn, New York, rejoining Olmsted and **Calvert Vaux**, who were the superintendents of the newly planned park. In 1870, Bogart became the chief engineer, but resigned the following year. He prepared the topographical surveys and working drawings, as well as carrying out the Olmsted and Vaux plan. His technical skills and experience were critical in planning and building the park's many features and in creating the intended artistic effects as well. Olmsted and Vaux acknowledged the special care Bogart used in the execution and elaboration of their designs during his five-year service.

While engaged at Prospect Park, in the summer of 1868, Bogart accompanied Olmsted to Buffalo and Chicago to examine several sites that the office was considering for future work. Bogart also undertook preliminary surveys for the suburb at Riverside, Illinois. He was closely associated with the initial planning of these important commissions. In Chicago he formed professional affiliations with architect and engineer William Le Baron Jenney and Louis Y. Schermerhorn, an engineer who had also worked at Prospect Park. They formed an architectural and engineering firm with Jenney as senior partner and designed the West Park system of Chicago as well as assisting in executing Olmsted, Vaux & Company's designs for Riverside. Bogart also formed a private partnership in New York City with his Prospect Park associate, Colonel John Yapp Culyer.* Together they undertook a number of projects, consulting with park commissions in several other American cities and adopting such titles as civil landscape engineers and landscape

Half of stereoscopic view of the drinking fountain shelter, Washington Park, Albany, New York. (Robert N. Dennis Collection of Stereoscopic Views, Miriam & Ira D. Wallach Division of Art, Prints & Photographs, The New York Public Library, Astor, Lenox and Tilden Foundations)

Branch Brook Park, Newark, New Jersey, 1902, E. F. Keller, photographer. (Courtesy of the National Park Service, Frederick Law Olmsted National Historic Site)

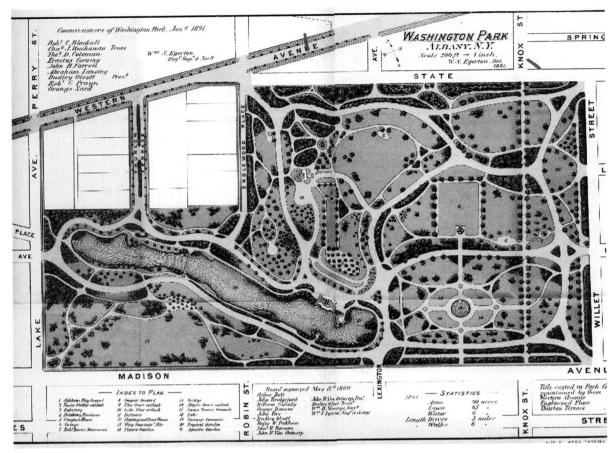

W. S. Ederton plan of Washington Park, Albany, New York, 1870-1872, by Bogart, Culyer & Company, from *The Public Parks of the City of Albany, N.Y.*, 1892.

architects. From 1870 to 1872, Bogart, Culyer & Company designed Washington Park, the major public pleasure ground in Albany. Undoubtedly, this assignment for his native city had special significance for Bogart. While engaged as landscape architects and consulting engineers, they developed the park's separate curvilinear carriage drives and pedestrian walkways, its underground drainage system, and a diverse variety of trees and shrubs were planted. Their original design also included an elongated and picturesque lake, its general location having been specified in a report that Olmsted, Vaux & Company had prepared for some Albany citizens earlier in 1868.

In the early 1870s, Bogart went to Nashville to improve the grounds of the Tennessee State Capitol, designed by the architect and engineer William Strickland before the Civil War. His plan for the steep site, respectful of an older scheme, included a series of graded sidewalks and staircases, and was carried out over a six-year period ending in 1877. The grounds, one of the earliest public parks in Nashville, were designated a National Historic Civil Engineering Landmark in 2003. In 1872, during the Reconstruction period, Bogart, Culyer & Company was also retained by the Commissioners of the New Orleans Park to improve the 100-acre site of City Park.

Following his departure from Prospect Park, Bogart continued his association with Olmsted, working with him on numerous public works. In 1872, he became chief engineer to the Department of Public Parks of the City of New York, charged with improvements to Central Park and smaller city parks. He also assisted with the early plans for Morningside and Riverside Parks, preparing the topographical map for the latter. Additionally, Bogart

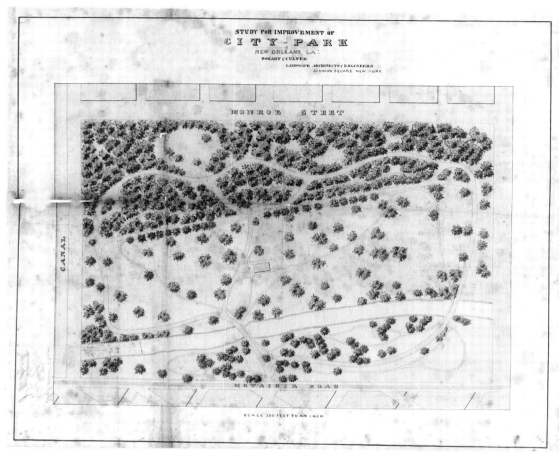

Study for the improvement of City Park, New Orleans, Louisiana, by Bogart, Culyer & Company. (Historical Archives of the Supreme Court of Louisiana, Earl K. Long Library, University of New Orleans)

executed Olmsted's designs for Baltimore's Washington Place (now Mount Vernon Place). In 1879, Bogart donated his services to Rutgers College, his alma mater, superintending improvements made on that campus.

Bogart was in charge of the engineering exhibit at the International Centennial Exhibition of 1876 in Philadelphia. A director of the Rapid Transit Underground Railroad Company and advisory engineer to the original Rapid Transit Commission, he was involved in planning New York's first subway system.

From 1886 to 1887, Bogart served as Deputy New York State Engineer, resigning to supervise the construction of the Washington Bridge over the Harlem River in New York City. Subsequently elected to two terms as State Engineer and Surveyor of New York, from 1888 to 1891, he oversaw the same department in which he had

worked more than thirty years earlier. He was responsible for the state's transportation network and infrastructure, including its canals, railroads, and highways, and served on the New York Water Power Commission and the New York Bridge and Tunnel Commission. While holding state office in 1890, Bogart was retained as consulting engineer by the Cataract Construction Company, a subsidiary of the Niagara Falls Power Company, which had been formed to utilize the waterpower of the falls. As one of the Board of Engineers, he traveled to Europe to study different methods of power generation and transmission. The trip resulted in the construction of the first major plant to generate and distribute alternating current electricity in the United States. Bogart became an expert in hydroelectric power, later consulting on the planning and construction of many other major power facilities in the United States and Canada, including those built on the St. Lawrence and Tennessee Rivers. The Cataract Construction Company developed a manufacturing center and a residential town for workers in Niagara Falls in anticipation of the area's imminent industrial development; Bogart planned the worker's village, Echota, collaborating with the architect Stanford White, the designer of the housing units. Bogart stated, "A district, not fit for comfortable residence, has been transformed into an ideal, healthful village. Ground upon which no vegetation would thrive has been changed to a region of velvet lawns and blooming gardens. Roads which were a discomfort from dust, or an annoyance from mud, have been made into well-paved, beautiful streets. An unattractive expanse of poor meadowland has become a model town."

In the 1890s, Bogart also resumed his earlier work planning public parks; two projects with which he was connected were ultimately completed by **John Charles Olmsted**. Twenty years after advising on City Park, he returned to New Orleans to consult on Audubon Park during the initial stages of its planning. In 1895, he was appointed landscape architect and engineer to the Essex County (New Jersey) Park Commission with **Nathan Franklin Barrett**. The following year they prepared a general design for a system of parks and parkways, the earliest county park system. They also created a plan for Branch Brook Park in Newark, New Jersey, the main park of the system, with construction progressing only in the southern division by the time their services were terminated in 1897. The **Olmsted Brothers** replaced Bogart and Barrett as landscape architects, but retained the latter's elabo-

rate features that had already been built in the park's southern section.

Bogart understood the important role that the engineer could play in the design and execution of landscape work, believing that a combined expertise in gardening, architecture, and engineering was required in order to be able to engage in landscape architecture. But Bogart remained first and foremost an engineer. He joined the American Society of Civil Engineers in 1869 and served as a director, treasurer, secretary, and librarian and, for many years, editor of the association's *Transactions.*

From 1913 until his death in 1920 Bogart practiced in partnership with the engineer Charles A. Pohl. Bogart died at his New York City residence and was buried in his family plot in the Albany Rural Cemetery.

Bogart, John. "Feats of Railway Engineering." *Scribner's Magazine* 4, no. 1 (July 1888), 3–34. Reprinted in Thomas Curtis Clarke et al. *The American Railway: Its Construction, Development, Management, and Appliances.* New York: C. Scribner's Sons, 1889. Discussion of the greatest engineering undertakings in the planning of railways, includes descriptions of major tunnels and bridges, with illustrations by artists and reproductions by engineers.

Bogart, John. "Industrial Village of Echota at Niagara." *Cassier's Magazine* 8, no. 3 (July 1895), 307–21. Reprinted in Bogart's *The Harnessing of Niagara.* New York: Cassier Magazine Co., 1895. Bogart's account of the planning and construction of the model town built by the Cataract Construction Company.

The Public Parks of the City of Albany, N.Y. Albany, N.Y.: Weed, Parsons & Co., 1892. Well-illustrated account of the history of the development of Albany's parks, prepared by William S. Egerton, Superintendent of Parks, who was the engineer in charge of constructing Washington Park, and containing the only known copy of the Washington Park plan by Bogart & Culyer.

Joy Kestenbaum

BRINLEY, JOHN ROWLETT
(1861–1946)
LANDSCAPE ARCHITECT

John Rowlett Brinley was born March 17, 1861, in Perth Amboy, New Jersey. Brinley attended Columbia University School of Mines, graduating in 1884 with a degree in civil engineering. Returning to Morristown after graduation, he worked for several years as the town's engineer. In 1885, he began receiving commissions for work as a landscape architect. In 1890, he married Elizabeth Hall Abeel, of Newark, New Jersey. They had five children. John Brinley was active in church and civic affairs; he was junior warden of Church of the Redeemer and served as

a trustee on the board of Morristown Memorial Hospital and the Morristown Library.

During the latter years of the nineteenth century, Morristown, New Jersey, was basking in the glow of the Gilded Age and there were many opportunities to design the estate homes and gardens of the millionaires who populated Morristown and the surrounding area. As Brinley built his reputation locally, he often took small jobs or preliminary work that better-known landscape architects might have declined. His notes suggest he may have even done some small jobs for little or no fee. This promotional tactic worked; in 1890, Brinley was engaged to complete the coveted job surveying Florham, the country estate of Hamilton and Florence Vanderbilt Twombly.

Surviving today as the campus of Fairleigh Dickinson University, Florham epitomized architectural splendor in Morris County, New Jersey, at that time. Working under the direction of **Frederick Law Olmsted Sr.**, Brinley was hired to survey the property and supervise the work of clearing away brush, draining a swamp, and planting trees that would be well established by the time the Twombly mansion was completed. Unfortunately, on May 24, 1890, fire swept through Brinley's office, destroying notes, maps, and surveys of Florham that had been returned to him the previous day for alterations.

With no fireproof safe and no insurance, the office fire was a setback for Brinley, but after establishing new offices, Brinley completed his work at Florham and went on to work on many other estates is the Morristown area. His landscapes often included elaborate formal gardens decorated with rocks, pools, arbors, pergolas, sweeping lawns, and circular driveways and walkways bordered by flowering trees.

In 1901, Brinley and John Swift Holbrook, also a graduate of Columbia University School of Mines, formed the partnership of Brinley and Holbrook, landscape engineers and architects, with offices in Morristown and New York City. However, in 1905, Holbrook followed his father into the Gorham Manufacturing Company when he was elected to the board of directors. When he became vice president of Gorham in 1906, Holbrook discontinued his connection with the firm. Although their partnership dissolved, Brinley chose to retain the firm name of Brinley and Holbrook throughout his career. It is not known if Holbrook served in any capacity after 1906, but it is clear from the records of the firm that Holbrook and Brinley re-

Stone Bridge at Blythewood, Kunhardt estate, Bernardsville, New Jersey. (From "Album of Landscape Architecture Photographs of John R. Brinley, 1903-1908," The Brinley and Holbrook Collection, North Jersey History Center, The Morristown & Morris Township Library, Morristown, NJ)

mained friends. In 1916, Brinley designed the landscaping for Holbrook's home in Providence, Rhode Island.

By 1906, the firm of Brinley and Holbrook had acquired good professional standing in the region and the business was thriving. Over the next forty years, Brinley designed landscape plans for dozens of estates, primarily in northern New Jersey, New York, and Connecticut.

Brinley often worked for larger, more notable offices, such as the Olmsted firm. He assisted Frederick Law Olmsted Sr. with preliminary designs for Blythewood, the Kunhardt residence in Bernardsville, New Jersey. This work brought him several more commissions, from

Left: Morristown Green, Morristown, New Jersey. (From "Album of Landscape Architecture Photographs of John R. Brinley, 1903-1908," The Brinley and Holbrook Collection, North Jersey History Center, The Morristown & Morris Township Library, Morristown, NJ)

Below: Estate walk and garden arbor at Blythewood, Kunhardt Estate, Bernardsville, New Jersey. (From "Album of Landscape Architecture Photographs of John R. Brinley, 1903-1908," The Brinley and Holbrook Collection, North Jersey History Center, The Morristown & Morris Township Library, Morristown, NJ)

for her into a Moorish-Italian palace. Grand sweeping carriage lanes carried family and guests past a vast array of landscapes including formal gardens with arbors, fountains, pergolas and pools, a 40-acre deer park, a golf courts, tennis and squash courts, and the shores of a private lake.

When working with larger, more prestigious firms, Brinley employed the style of the American romantic school of landscaping made popular by the Olmsted firm, using the natural features of the landscape and drawing the viewer's eye into the scenery. However, when working on his own, Brinley preferred to design traditional, formal gardens, embracing axial relationships, right angles, straight stonewalls, reflecting pools, and floral borders.

Brinley also created landscape designs for parks, schools, hospitals, prisons, asylums, churches, golf clubs, playgrounds, cemeteries, offices, and

1900 through 1919, to design the gardens and the extensive network of stone walls that surround the property.

Olmsted Sr. was also Brinley's entrée to work on Cedar Court, the Kahn estate in Morris Township, New Jersey. Otto Kahn, the financier and philanthropist credited with saving the Metropolitan Opera and the transcontinental railway system from bankruptcy, moved to Morristown when he married Addie Wolf in 1896. Kahn completely redesigned the 1,100-acre estate Addie's father built

government buildings throughout New Jersey. One of his most enduring legacies is the plan of walkways and gardens for the Morristown Green, a central square first laid out in the late 1600s. For many years, the Morristown Green was little more than a bare, open common, crossed by wagon roads, void of grass and shade trees. In 1908, Brinley laid out the green much as it appears today with paved, curving paths and associated planting embellishments.

In 1908, Brinley was elected a Fellow of the American Society of Landscape Architects. He became a member of the Executive Committee of the New York Chapter in 1920 and served on that committee for many years. He was also a member of the Board of Trustees from 1923 to 1927.

Commissions of the firm of Brinley and Holbrook covered a wide geographical area including Connecticut, Delaware, Maryland, Massachusetts, New Jersey, New York, North Carolina, Pennsylvania, Rhode Island, Vermont, Virginia, and Wisconsin. The majority of documented properties are in New Jersey and New York. Brinley did not leave any professional writings, but his grandson, A. Brinley Maury, deeded a collection of the firm's landscape drawings to the Local History Department of the Morristown and Morris Township Library in 1982.

The New York Botanical Garden (NYBG) association and professional work that Brinley carried on from 1895 to 1931 was a lengthy and highly important professional commission. Brinley is named in both the first survey of the NYBG acreage in 1895 and on the General Plan dated 1896. While **Calvert Vaux** is credited with the initial layout of the roads and walkways of the NYBG, Brinley appears to have stepped in upon Vaux's death as the landscape engineer and landscape architect. A particularly interesting component of the Brinley work for the New York Botanical Garden was a set of watercolors credited to John Brinley and Louis R. Bird dated to 1918. These images attractively portrayed proposed improvements planned for the NYBG that were seeking donors. A large number of Brinley linen and ink and pencil on trace drawings are located in the Metz Library at New York Botanical Garden.

Although he eventually closed his New York City office, Brinley maintained an office in Morristown until 1944. In an oral history interview, his daughter, Margaret Brinley, said her father climbed the three flights of stairs every day to his office in the Morris County Savings Bank Building at 21 South Street until he retired at the age of eighty-three. John Rowlett Brinley died January 31, 1946, at the age of eighty-five.

"Album of Landscape Architecture Photographs of John R. Brinley, 1903–1908." From the Brinley and Holbrook Collection. Morristown, New Jersey: The Morristown and Morris Township Library. A portfolio of photographs illustrating sixteen properties designed by Brinley between 1903 and 1908.

"The Brinley Family of Morristown, New Jersey." Collection of newspaper articles, oral histories, census records, maps, city directories and other miscellaneous material pertaining to the Brinley family of Morristown, New Jersey, 1870–1981.

John R. Brinley & John S. Holbrook, Landscape Architects, New York City, New York: Inventory of Landscape Drawing Collection in the Local History Department of the Morristown and Morris Township Library, Morristown, New Jersey. Revised 2004. Contains approximately 2,500 of the firm's landscape drawings, sketches, selected photographs, an inventory of plants, and indices that date from circa 1903 to circa 1930. The drawings include garden designs and planting plans.

Christine Jochem

BROOKS, JOHN A.
(1871–1958)
LANDSCAPE IRRIGATION INVENTOR, ENGINEER, MANUFACTURER

Born Abram Brooks on June 13, 1871, in the small town of Thornberry, Canada, this red-haired son of Mary and George Brooks was raised by his sister and brother-in-law after the death of his mother. He assumed the name John to honor his late brother of the same name. At the early age of twelve, John Brooks left his sister's home to embark upon his future.

Brooks studied plumbing, achieving the classification of master plumber, then opened his own plumbing company in Toledo, Ohio. It was here that a wealthy plumbing client challenged him to create a less labor-intensive way of watering the lawn than the traditional practice of hauling hoses about. In October 1915, Brooks installed his first underground pop-up sprinkling system at the home of Lillie I. Donat, clerk and acting treasurer of the Toledo Board of Education. One year later, he received both U.S. and Canadian patents for the product, which he named Lawn Sprinkling Means and called "rain's only rival." Although other inventors were also experimenting with underground irrigation, Brooks was the first to put his ideas together in a complete patented system.

In 1917, Brooks relocated to Detroit, Michigan, where both a favorable environmental and industrial climate continued to foster his ingenuity. The region, rich in

John A. Brooks in his office in Highland Park, a suburb of Detroit, ca. 1925. (From the Manning Brothers Historic Photographic Collection)

commissioned in 1926 to preserve an expansive area of meadows designed by the renowned Danish landscape architect **Jens Jensen**. The installation required over 1,100 sprinkler heads and was controlled by four massive three-inch Single Action Control Valves, another Brooks patent. Today, Fair Lane is maintained by the University of Michigan. Both the original landscape, as designed by Jensen, and the underground irrigation system, are undergoing a restoration and rehabilitation and are on public display.

While prominent citizens were employing Brooks's innovation, civic and governmental officials were also taking note in hopes of beautifying America's public places. Close to home, Brooks got his first big break in the public sector in 1921 when the City of Detroit commissioned him to install underground sprinklers in Roosevelt Park, the entrance to the Michigan Central Train Depot. At the time, mass travel by automobile had not superseded railway travel and the depot was considered one of the showplaces of the city. Detroit spent $700,000 over three years to develop the park, including land improvements and sprinkler installation. Over 900 sprinkler heads were used for consistent water saturation. Roosevelt Park became the ideal model that many leading cities hoped to emulate when beautifying their own regions.

Atlantic City, New Jersey, was not to be outdone. Brooks was broadening his operation through dealerships and franchises, and the Brooks dealer in Philadelphia completed the Brighton Park–Atlantic City installation in 1925. Meanwhile, officials in New York City also admired Roosevelt Park and in 1928 began installation in Central Park. Many companies bid on the job. John A. Brooks, Inc., supplied the winning bid, and subsequently the irrigation equipment for the installation through one of his successful franchises.

In 1937, Chicago also trusted the Brooks Company with the irrigation design of Grant Park, predating Brooks's most recognizable installation, the U.S. Capitol grounds in Washington, D.C. In 1939, Brooks's son, John Jr., was supervising most of the larger projects. He is be-

lakes and streams, provided a ready-made water supply for his irrigation systems, while Detroit's growing automotive factories were capable of mass-producing brass and copper irrigation parts. Brooks recognized that the booming auto industry provided something even more valuable: a class of newly affluent individuals with money to spend on large homes and attractive estates. With this niche in mind, he focused on inventing products for the luxury market, taking the lead in an emerging new field while his contemporaries continued to experiment with irrigation for agricultural purposes.

His focus paid off and soon prominent industrialists in and around Detroit, including Joseph Hudson, S. S. Kresge, and the Dodge and Fisher brothers all employed Brooks and his underground irrigation systems. Eventually Brooks's clients spanned the world and included the king of Siam, but perhaps the most notable entry in his ledger book was that of the legendary Henry Ford. Ford, who was always fascinated by mechanical invention, utilized underground irrigation at his automotive plants and at his beloved Fair Lane Estate. Though not Brooks's first major installation, Fair Lane is believed to be the second largest residential system that the John A. Brooks Company ever installed. It was

lieved to have overseen the work at the Capitol; however because of its prominence, there is little doubt that the senior Brooks made the final inspection himself.

As is the case so often, Brooks's accomplishments led to the success of many other individuals in the irrigation industry. After a twenty-five-year agreement expired, the Brooks of California franchise went on to become what is known today as Febco, a leading manufacturer of vacuum breakers. Max Snoody, secretary of the Brooks Company in 1936, later established Weather-Matic, a leading irrigation supplier that continues to operate. Austin Miller Sr. opened his own irrigation company called A. J. Miller in Detroit in 1922, after having served as superintendent for the Brooks Company. A. J. Miller Jr. later served as president of the Irrigation Association for many years.

Throughout his ambitious career, inventor John A. Brooks applied for twenty-seven patents in the United States and Canada. Eleven were fully U.S. patented. Three received patent status in Canada as well. Some inventions, like the Little Lu Lu, never gained patent rights, but earned recognition through Brooks's advertising instead. The Little Lu Lu was a mail-order product, a single pop-up sprinkler head designed to fit the small residential lawns of the 1940s. Advertised in magazines such as *Good Housekeeping,* it was purchased by homeowners across the country for approximately $55.

Brooks adapted his innovative ideas as the turf irrigation industry matured, improving individual parts

Above: A copy of Brooks's original patent no. 1,192,743—which he called "Lawn Sprinkling Means"—the first underground irrigation system patented in the United States. (Brooks Historical Papers, private collection)

Right: Rows of Brooks's pop-up sprinklers stand at attention at the Capitol building in Washington, D.C., ca. 1928. (Brooks Historical Papers, private collection)

and equipment as he saw fit. Yet he owed a lifetime of success to his original underground irrigation system, Lawn Sprinkling Means. Through innovation, he literally changed the way early twentieth-century landscape architects and designers envisioned the land, allowing them to plant vegetation, artistically and environmentally, in areas where survival would have been impossible previously.

John Brooks died on April 23, 1958, in St. Petersburg, Florida, from a blood clot in his brain. He was survived by his third wife Blanche, daughters Doris and Catherine, and son John. Another son, James preceded him in death.

Hawkins, Margaret E. *Rain's Only Rival: The Story of John A. Brooks.* Waterford, Mich.: Printed by Marc Dutton Irrigation, Inc., 1990. Overview of Brooks's life and career including a collection of patent illustrations, photographs, and business correspondences.

McLaren, Karen L. "John A. Brooks, Inc." *Crains Detroit Business, Detroit at 300: Then and Now* (Summer 2001). A commemorative edition documenting the important people, businesses, and events that shaped Detroit's rich three-hundred-year history.

Morgan, Robert M. *Water and the Land: A History of American Irrigation.* Cathedral City, Calif.: Adams Publishing Corp., 1993. An illustrated overview of the irrigation industry, including its origins and scientific methods.

Marc Dutton and Karen McLaren

BULLARD, HELEN ELISE
(1896–1987)
LANDSCAPE ARCHITECT

Born in rural Schulyerville, New York, in 1896, Helen Elise Bullard was the daughter of Dr. Thomas and Elizabeth Huggins Bullard. She was descended from an early New England family who were key players in both the American Revolution and the French and Indian War. In 1918, she graduated from Cornell University with a B.S. degree in landscape architecture and following a brief employment with the American Locomotive Company, she became director of the Small Home Grounds Department at the Wagner Park Nursery Company in Sidney, Ohio, where she worked under the pseudonym Janet Brown.

In 1921, Bullard was engaged by **Warren Henry Manning** to work in his Boston office as chief plantsman and planting designer. Here she originated and executed many plans for city and regional developments, educational and industrial institutions, parks, and private estates. Included among her projects were those for North Carolina State College, International Harvester Company at Fort Wayne, and parks and private estates on Lookout Mountain. In 1927, Bullard became assistant to landscape architect Annette Hoyt Flanders* in New York City where she was responsible for layout and construction projects for several private estates, many on Long Island. During this time she had some fifty men under her supervision and was responsible for the general direction of work under contract.

With the onset of the Great Depression and subsequent decline in private practice, Bullard joined the

Helen Bullard, from *The Cornellian*, 1919. (Courtesy of the Rare and Manuscript Collections, Carl A. Kroch Library, Cornell University)

New York Civil Service. Her early work in this capacity included the gardens and plantings for Creedmoor and King's Park State Hospitals. At this time, Bullard became acquainted with Robert Moses, then head of the Long Island Parks Commission and went to work for him under the supervision of **Gilmore David Clarke**, another Cornellian. The parks in Montauk, Hither Hills, Sunken Meadow, and Jones Beach reflect, at least in part, the beauty and skill of her design. During this period she also created the planting designs for the new parkways on Long Island including the Grand Central, Montauk, Wantagh, Southern State, and Jones Beach Causeway. For a period, she was the official hostess at Jones Beach State Park and supervised female employees. Additionally she organized and oversaw the spring and summer flower bedding programs for the Long Island state parks.

In 1935, Bullard was named Assistant Landscape Supervising Engineer for the New York City Department of Parks. Her most notable works include planting contributions at the Hayden Planetarium, Randall's Island, and Jefferson, Highbridge, and Sunset Parks as well as Alley Pond, Clove Brook, La Tourette, Central and Prospect Parks in Manhattan, Queens, Brooklyn, and the Bronx. She was largely responsible for the creation of the Colonial Revival garden at the Morris-Jumel Mansion in Manhattan and also executed the design and construction of New York City's first nature trail. During this period, Bullard designed and supervised flower-bedding programs for all five boroughs and was in charge of the city flower shows. In 1938, Helen Bullard became Junior Landscape Architect for the New York State Department of Public Works. In this role she was intimately involved with planting design and construction for more than fifty institutions statewide.

Working under Gilmore Clarke, Bullard became involved with the 1939 New York World's Fair where she served as one of several landscape designers. When asked about her work on a "modern landscape" for the Fair, Helen Elise Bullard noted that, "Landscape design has for the most part to date utilized straight beds and pattern gardens . . . (while) modern principles for this field are still undeveloped." However, she continued, "with modern buildings we cannot depend on the classic forms. We have no precedents to follow, but in general the planting will be designed in directional lines to give the feeling of motion."

A job offer from the New York State Department of Public Works, however, lured her away from completing her work at the World's Fair site. Employment with the state provided the opportunity to design and travel to various sites as well as to indulge her love of New York history. In her later years, she returned to her home to care for her aging parents and enjoy the beauty of upstate New York. During a long life marked by professional achievements, Helen Bullard combined a remarkable dedication to her community and friends, a quiet generosity, a stubborn pride in her state and nation, and a keen sense of the natural beauty around her.

Helen Bullard died in 1987.

Note: Helen Bullard is frequently confused with Elizabeth Bullard, who worked with Frederick Law Olmsted Sr. between 1862 and 1863 and then later with John Charles Olmsted on his firm's work at Smith College in Northampton, Massachusetts. Another Elizabeth Bullard (though by marriage), living in the Hartford area, was also a landscape architect. It is possible that these Bullards are distantly related, but any connection is unknown.

The Helen E. Bullard Collection, in the Department of Manuscripts and Archives, Kroch Library, Cornell University, Ithaca, N.Y, includes some of Bullard's drawings and personal effects.

"Bullard, Helen Elise 1896–1987, United States Landscape Architect." In *Chicago Botanic Garden Encyclopedia of Gardens: History and Design,* ed. Candice A. Shoemaker. Vol. 1. Chicago and London: Fitzroy Dearborn Publishers, 2001, 208–9.
"Leading Women in the Big Performance of Building a World's Fair on Flushing Meadows." *New York Sun,* October 19, 1937.
"Women Take Lead in Landscape Art." *New York Times,* March 13, 1938.

Daniel Krall

BUTTON, FRANK MORSE
(1866–1938)
ENGINEER, LANDSCAPE ARCHITECT

Frank Morse Button was born on August 14, 1866, in Brandon, Vermont, the oldest of three boys. Button graduated from Brandon High School in 1883 and from the University of Vermont as a civil engineer in 1887. The origins of Button's design intent can be traced to his early education as an engineer.

Employed as civil engineer in the quartermaster department in the U.S. Army from 1889 to 1895, Button spent six months as assistant engineer at the World's Columbian Exposition during 1891, where he was privy to the planning and construction issues. As engineer and construction superintendent for **Ossian Cole Simonds**, Button later coordinated work with the Olmsted office and perhaps acted as a liaison in matters of construction as suggested in a note dated March 12, 1904, from Button to **John Charles Olmsted**.

During the period that Button worked for the Army Corps of Engineers, he completed drawings for Fort Sheridan in Highland Park, Illinois, working with Simonds's office. The drawings show the fort's formal sections of planting are offset by naturalistic areas in a manner similar to the plans of the Columbian Exposition. In 1903, Button formalized his partnership with O. C. Simonds.

Simonds worked on the design of the extension of Lincoln Park, in Chicago, completed in the 1920s. The design integrates the roadway and buildings and includes several miles along Lake Michigan shore from the northern boundary of the original park at Fullerton Avenue to Hollywood Avenue, where the building and roadway features are executed in the Art Deco style.

In November 17, 1921, Button wrote an article titled "Suburb Beautiful," an advertorial that ran in a number of newspapers. Within this piece and in two newspaper interviews, he describes his philosophy of plants, which included the preservation of native materials as well as "bringing together plant materials that have a link." This philosophy can be seen in his subsequent work in Coral Gables, Florida, George Merrick's idealistic town just south of Miami. In the article, Button also referred to some of his projects, which included the Forester Arden, a private park; Higinbotham, in Joliet, Illinois; the grounds of Governor Frank O. Lowden's home, in

Frank Morse Button, from a portrait by Bob Lamm.
(Courtesy of Arva Parks)

Oregon, Illinois; the estates of George A. McKinlock and Edward L. Ryerson in Lake Forest, Illinois; and a master planting list of Coral Gables.

The design for Buena Vista, the Charles Deering estate in Florida, is attributed to Simonds, with Button having supervised the implementation of the Simonds plan. This vast estate was the subject of study and collaboration between the owner and John Kunkel Small of the New York Botanical Garden. Buena Vista also hosted a plant introduction station overseen by David Fairchild* for the U.S. Department of Agriculture.

Charles Sterns, who owned property in Coral Gables, introduced Frank Button to George Merrick. After

Button's wife died in 1918, he and his daughter Florence moved to Florida. Various snippets of news articles credit Button with the design of the Charles Deering Estate at Cutler and the Biltmore in Havana. Mrs. Merrick in her later years advised Arva Moore Parks that Button was one of three people, the other two her husband George Merrick and his cousin, Denman Fink, who were primarily responsible for the vision of Coral Gables. Little remains to archivally document Button's work but the City of Coral Gables stands as evidence that the wisdom of its planning and design have established a legacy for generations to come.

On April 18, 1921, Button typed a proposal to Merrick outlining his fees to develop plans for the new town of Coral Gables, at a charge of $1 per acre, for the 2,000-acre project. Button proposed a preliminary study with subsequent plans of blocks and parkways or parks and other details as became necessary. Button expected to perform this work over a two-month period. George Merrick also considered engaging William Lyman Phillips,* who was working with the Olmsted office in Lake Wales but ultimately selected Button.

While few of the detail plans exist today, the maps and overall site plans that Button and engineer Whitney C. Bliss laid out reveal a design based on an infrastructure of an inherited grid of fruit trees from the days of the Merrick family's citrus plantation, as well as the native pineland. Button describes his task as a matter of infilling plant materials that would work as accents against the existing framework.

Button included shady and cool spaces to provide respite from the tropical sun. He designed courtyard gardens and arcades that extended even to the city's business district. And like the architects Phineas Paist and Denman Fink, Button found aesthetic purpose in revealing the oolitic limestone that is the foundation of the city and using the limestone as a decorative element in the architecture and fountains of the plazas that mark the intersection of the most scenic roadways and entrances.

The concept of the city as a vast garden complete with

Looking toward the bay from the Deering Estate in Cutler, Florida, 1921. (JK Small Collection, SM1508, Florida Memory Project, Florida State Archive)

botanical parkways and winding canals is still evident in Coral Gables today and can be attributed to the master planning as well as the planting plans of Button. His construction experience kept him directly involved in field supervision and he was often described on the site selecting limestone or dynamiting the holes that needed to be opened in the limestone in order to allow for the planting of trees.

Unfortunately, Button's close participation in field-work lead to his untimely death on August 4, 1938, when, according to his obituary in the *Miami Herald,* Button was killed when he slipped and fell into the path of a truck that was moving in reverse while he was supervising the installation of the now immense *Ficus benjamina* trees in the median of Bird Road in Coral Gables. Button's body was sent to Graceland Cemetery in Chicago, where he is buried in a section that was set aside for its designer O. C. Simonds.

Button became a member of the American Society of Landscape Architects in 1902 and was elected to Fellowship in 1910.

"Beautiful Landscaping Makes Gables an Eden." *Miami Riviera* 1, no. 44 (1926). Illustrated newspaper account of Button's design.
"Landscaping in Southern Florida." *Southern Architect and Building News,* February 1930, 41–43, 71. Laying out home grounds to make them both useful and ornamental.

Debbie Lang

BYE, ARTHUR EDWIN, JR.
(1919–2001)
LANDSCAPE ARCHITECT

Arthur Edwin Bye Jr., known as Ed, was born in Arnhem, Holland, on August 25, 1919. He was a shy Quaker boy, the youngest of four children, who loved nature and absorbed his parents' interest in art. Although it is unclear exactly when Bye's family settled in the United States, they eventually made Pennsylvania their home. Bye's father was a professor of art history at Swarthmore College; his mother, Maria Heldring, studied art and nurtured artistic awareness in her children. In addition to this enriching atmosphere, Bye's boyhood landscape experiences were formative. He lived on an 800-acre estate in pastoral Bucks County, Pennsylvania, and spent summers on his aunts' estate near Oosterbeek, Holland. He enjoyed exploring the fields and forests of both landscapes, an avocation he continued while a student at the George School in Newtown, Pennsylvania. Recognizing Bye's interests, a teacher suggested that Ed study forestry in college.

Bye matriculated at the Pennsylvania State College, planning to study forestry, but because he lacked necessary prerequisites, he instead entered the landscape architecture program. In this field, his interests in art and nature coalesced. The textbook *An Introduction to the Study of Landscape Design* (1917) by **Henry Vincent Hubbard** and Theodora Kimball (Hubbard)* influenced him, but (as Bye later declared) only the chapters that focused on the designer's necessary understanding of natural systems to create compositions that capitalize on nature's aesthetic unity impacted him. Frank Lloyd Wright's work, which Bye discovered in an art history class, also influenced Bye, who read extensively on Wright's organic architecture and visited many of Wright's works in Pennsylvania and Illinois.

Graduating in 1942, Bye, like many contemporaries, found work in governmental agencies, first with the National Park Service and then the National Forest Service in 1944. In 1946, he moved to the private sector, and in 1951 opened his own office in Greenwich, Connecticut, which he maintained for the rest of his life, although he moved the location first to Cos Cob and then to Ridgefield, both also in Connecticut. (Bye partnered with Irving C. Herrmann for a period in the 1950s and 1960s.) Within his first year of private practice, Bye

A. E. Bye Jr., ca. 1955. (A. E. Bye Collection, Penn State University Archives, Pennsylvania State University Libraries)

obtained a formative commission to design the landscape for Wright's Reisley House in Pleasantville, New York. Emulating Wright's approach at Fallingwater, in Pennsylvania, Bye limited his plant palette to native plants thriving on site. This was the beginning of a personal style that married Bye's sensitivity toward nature with his artist's eye.

Bye's distinctive approach focused on intensifying a site's natural features through subtle design manipulations. Inspired by natural conditions on a site, Bye chose key existing characteristics to enhance through deft subtraction or addition of plants, rocks, or landforms. The resulting landscape presented its natural features with greater intensity and unity than the original site. Bye took pleasure when viewers could not tell that the site was designed. This deferential aesthetic was grounded in Bye's

Bye's sensitivity to the natural conditions of the site is seen at the grounds of the Montgomery Residence, New Hope, Pennsylvania, 1970. (Department of Landscape Architecture, Penn State University)

emphasis upon human experience of nature's systems, from its cycles to its compositional beauty.

While his designs appear simple or even simplistic, Bye's descriptions of his efforts reveal his artistic hand and eye. For the Heap Residence in Greenwich, Connecticut, he explained, "Only those plants that have similar textures to the surrounding woods were used. This gives coherence and unity to the landscape scene." Of a spare composition of limestone outcropping and juniper at the Herring Property in Ridgefield, Connecticut, Bye enjoyed employing the compositional power of "opposing forces," as he called them, stating, "Ounces against tons; white against dark grey-green; animate opposing inanimate, the temporary opposing the permanent." His consistent design goal was to achieve a sense of timelessness, both through making natural processes integral to the design (allowing dead trees to decay, for example) and by employing an aesthetic that would never seem outdated. Bye's thoughtful-but-subtle work is not identifiable as part of any single historical design style but hints of abstraction, minimalism, and ecological con-

cern. These characteristics, coupled with his deferential response to existing conditions of a site, mark Bye's work as a product of the twentieth century.

While his office undertook some public and business projects, Bye's greatest influence was in the area of residential design. He preferred the creative freedom of working with a homeowner rather than with bureaucracies. He counted as clients many wealthy Americans, including Leonard Lauder, John R. Gaines, and George Soros, who appreciated the subtle elegance of his designs and gave him considerable freedom.

Regardless of the commission, Bye consistently focused on nature's processes and beauty. In 1965, ahead of his time, Bye recognized a bog on the Stein property in New England as a landscape amenity, and subtly enhanced its features. Another important project in 1965 was the Soros residence in Southampton, Long Island. The solution of a drainage problem led Bye to create undulating grassy mounds, punctuated by existing bayberries, elegantly revealing ephemeral natural processes of snowmelt and shadow play. Sculpted

Right: Grounds of George Soros residence, Southampton, New York, 1965 (Peter Johnson, staff landscape architect). (A. E. Bye Collection, Penn State University Archives, Pennsylvania State University Libraries)

Below: The ha-ha wall at Gainesway Farm, Lexington, Kentucky, 1975. Bye famously sketched the wall's shape in seconds, then labored on site for two months to ensure the naturalistic appearance of the surrounding landform. (A. E. Bye Collection, Penn State University Archives, Pennsylvania State University Libraries)

landforms became a recurring element in Bye's work, especially in his period of collaboration with Janis Hall (who had studied sculpture with Isamu Noguchi), which lasted from 1984 to 2001. Shadows playing across the mounds animated the landscape of the Massachusetts Seaside Landscape (1986), the Pittman residence (1988), the Meltzer residence (1988), and the Wilson residence (1992), among others. A famous long-term project, the Gaines residence and Gainesway Farm in Lexington, Kentucky (1974–1986), included a ha-ha wall that Bye swiftly conceptualized on an envelope, then labored on site for two months sculpting a natural-looking surrounding landform. This was, in fact, Bye's design approach. He took great pride in arriving at a design concept "in two or three seconds," then, rather than developing the design through drawing, he went straight to the site. There he physically sculpted the land and placed the plants in situ to derive his desired visual effects. Plan drawings, if created at all, were often rendered after the fact to document the design as implemented.

The extent and significance of Bye's private designs could have been lost to the public and profession, but Bye made them accessible through his book *Art into Landscape, Landscape into Art* (1983, 1988). It is a book of few words but many eloquent photographs, which display another of Bye's lifelong interests, landscape photography. Bye used this medium both to record potential sources of design inspiration and to document his projects. Through photography, he also captured landscape "moods," an ongoing infatuation traceable back to Hubbard and Kimball. In 1999, Bye published *Moods in the Landscape,* a marriage of his photography with brief statements on the emotive qualities he found in landscapes around the world.

Bye's enduring influence also occurred through teaching. For much of his professional life he was an adjunct professor at Cooper Union, where he formed a strong relationship with architect John Hedjuk. Though never built, Hedjuk's Second Wall House (1974) was designed for Bye for a site near Ridgefield, Connecticut. In addition to Cooper Union, Bye taught at Columbia and the University of Pennsylvania, and lectured at many universities nationwide.

A. E. Bye became a Fellow of the American Society of Landscape Architects in 1993. He died on November 25, 2001. His *New York Times* obituary remarked on his "naturalism so artful that students said he knew how to make snow fall where he wanted."

Bye, A. E. *Art into Landscape, Landscape into Art.* Mesa, Ariz.: PDA Publishers Corporation, 1983. This book stands as the most complete record of Bye's work, presented as he wished it to be seen through his own photographs, brief text descriptions, and an occasional plan. The book also includes his philosophical statement and a list of references on a variety of Bye's design projects. A second edition (1988) adds two projects from the period of his partnership with Janis Hall, as well as some color photographs.

Howett, Catherine, ed. *Abstracting the Landscape: The Artistry of Landscape Architect A. E. Bye.* University Park: Department of Landscape Architecture, The Pennsylvania State University, 1990. Exhibition catalog for a traveling interpretive exhibition, presenting five essays on facets of his work: one on Bye's photography; one each on his link to the English Landscape School, to Modernism, and to the Ecological Aesthetic; and one essay citing sources of inspiration.

Rainey, Reuben. "The Landscape Artistry of A. E. Bye." *Princeton Journal: Thematic Studies in Architecture: Landscapes 2,* (1985), 114–23. This article presents an excellent analysis of Bye's design approach, identifying four consistent themes: respect for regional landscape character; design composition through abstraction of natural conditions; understanding of the relationship between building and site; and use of mood in the landscape.

Eliza Pennypacker

CALVERT, FRANCIS
(1830–1909)
LANDSCAPE GARDENER

Francis Calvert was born in Scotland in 1830 and came to Chicago in 1851. After marrying Jane Wallace in 1857, Calvert, who was known as Frank, designed many of the estate landscapes in Lake Forest, Illinois, a suburb of Chicago on the North Shore of Lake Michigan. Calvert's Lake Forest designs occurred within the 1857 town plan of Almerin Hotchkiss.* Calvert set the character for such development in a community destined to play a significant role in the history of American landscape design in the years following the 1893 World's Columbian Exposition. Working in the period between Hotchkiss and a host of later well-known designers, Calvert implemented the streetscapes envisioned by Hotchkiss and undertook the plantings that provided the structure for later developments.

Calvert is one of many British gardeners who immigrated to America to work on estates, villas, and cottages; his work was influenced by the ideas promulgated by **Andrew Jackson Downing**. Scottish gardeners especially were at a premium in more northerly climes because of their ex-

perience with the narrower planning palette required by shorter growing seasons. The system of Victorian-era gardener training included a journeyman's range of experiences on great estates and glasshouse work in the years following 1845. How much of this rich cultural heritage and varied practical experience came to Lake Forest with Calvert is not known, but he soon set up a nursery with glasshouses in Lake Forest.

Calvert appears to be responsible for a number of Lake Forest estates established before the onset of the Civil War. Properties belonging to Quinlan Holt, Harvey L. Thompson, and C. F. Quinlan were among the first houses in Lake Forest. The Quinlan property was surrounded by sophisticated gardens and landscape. Mrs. Quinlan wrote about some of Calvert's work, including the hillside wooded park; the parterre west of the terrace on which the house was sited; arbor; orchard; and curving drive. The parterre included a range of flowering plants and shrubs as well as scotch roses. Landscapes by Calvert appear in early photos of the D. R. Holt and H. L.

Right: An example of Francis Calvert's estate work is the planting of the Elisha Barber–Edwin S. Skinner residence, Lake Forest, Illinois, 1899. (Lake Forest College Library Special Collections)

Below: An early example of Calvert's work is the centered entry drive, though in an informal landscape at Lake Forest Academy, 1865. (Lake Forest College Library Special Collections)

Thompson villas; the former was beautiful and the latter picturesque according to the Downing manner. The Thompson property included a ravine that was developed in the gardenesque style with architectonic wooden bridges, fences, terraces, statuary, and paths.

The completion of the transcontinental railroad in 1869 and the 1871 Chicago fire spurred the boom in economic fortunes during the years following the Civil War and Calvert appeared to capitalize on these historic events by marketing his skills to wealthy clients. Calvert laid out the landscape for John Farwell, a wholesale, dry-goods merchant circa 1869. Calvert surrounded a glasshouse with ponds and flower beds on the property.

The extent of Calvert's design career in the years following 1877 is unknown. He retired to California, where he developed a nursery in the early 1890s. The property contained two hothouses, a barn, and two dwellings. Calvert's son, Francis Jr., succeeded him as a nurseryman and florist on the site. Calvert died in 1909.

Arpee, Edward, and Susan Dart. *Lake Forest, Illinois: History and Reminiscences, 1861–1961.* Enlarged ed. with *Supplement* by Susan Dart. Lake Forest, Ill.: Lake Forest-Lake Bluff-Historical Society, 1991. Includes a written description of the Quinlan garden, apparently from a first-hand account.

Coventry, Kim, Daniel Meyer, and Arthur H. Miller. *Classic Country Estates of Lake Forest, Architecture and Landscape Architecture, 1856–1940.* New York: W. W. Norton, 2003. Discusses and illustrates early Lake Forest gardens, attributed to Calvert.

Lake Forest Foundation for Historic Preservation. *Lake Forest: A Preservation Guide to National Register Properties.* 2nd ed. Lake Forest, Ill.: 1994. Includes a photo of the first Quinlan estate house and immediate grounds.

Arthur H. Miller

CAPARN, HAROLD AP RHYS
(1864–1945)
LANDSCAPE ARCHITECT

Harold A. Caparn was born at Newark on Trent, Nottinghamshire, England. A number of his family members shared his interest in horticulture, landscape design, and the arts.

His grandfather, William Horner Caparn, owned a successful nursery and seed firm. His uncle, W. H. Caparn Jr., was an organist, composer, and conductor, and it was in his home that Harold learned about music at an early age. Harold's father, Thomas John Caparn, was an artist, businessman, and horticulturalist; he owned the largest nursery in the English Midlands. His father no doubt provided encouragement in drawing and horticulture to the young Harold, as he had earlier to his nephew William John Caparne, who became a figure of note in both art and horticulture.

Harold Caparn received his education at the Magnus Grammar School in Newark, then continued his studies at the University of London. Following a stint as a teacher at Canterbury Cathedral School, he studied art and architecture at the prestigious École des Beaux-Arts, and later in Buray's Atelier, both in Paris.

Thomas J. Caparn, Harold's father, left England in 1884 and settled in Short Hills, New Jersey. There he built a partnership designing gardens with his younger son, Arthur Tom Caparn, a nurseryman. By 1899, the father had opened a landscape architecture office in Newark, New Jersey. With much in common, Harold later often visited his father and brother in Short Hills.

After coming to America, Harold Caparn worked for about six years in the 1890s for J. Wilkinson Elliott, a landscape gardener from Pittsburgh, Pennsylvania. He then moved to New York in 1899 as an independent practitioner, opening an office there in 1902, just three years after the profession of landscape architecture was founded.

From about 1899, he and **Warren Henry Manning** each provided advice to the New York Zoological Park in the Bronx. Over the next several years Caparn designed parts of the landscape and Great Steps of the Bronx Zoo. The general foreman of maintenance said many years later about the design, "Much of the massive planting that today is so natural . . . actually was planted about 1905."

Caparn married Clara Howard (Jones) Royall, a suc-

Harold A. Caparn, ca. 1940, photograph from Associated News. (Caparn collection, courtesy of Oliver Chamberlain)

cessful voice teacher in New York City. They had two daughters, Anne Howard, a writer, and Rhys, a sculptor of note. In 1909, Caparn bought 5 acres in the village of Briarcliff Manor, about 30 miles up the Hudson River from their home in Manhattan. He proceeded to landscape the property and built an Arts and Crafts–style dwelling, complete with a large music studio for his wife, as a country retreat.

During the summer of 1911, Columbia University offered for the first time, on an experimental basis, a course in landscape architecture taught by Caparn with six students enrolled. The university decided to continue coursework, leading to a degree, so in summer 1912 through spring semester 1913, Caparn taught together with **Charles Wellford Leavitt Jr.** and **Ferruccio Vitale**, each presenting separate topics. He thus helped to establish a degree curriculum at Columbia in landscape architecture.

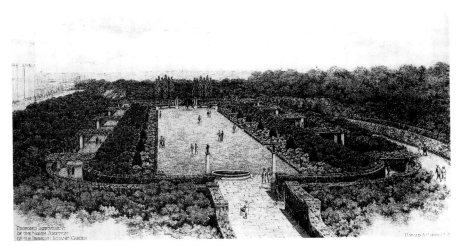

Left: "Proposed Improvement of the North Addition of the Brooklyn Botanic Garden," undated; entrance to the garden approaching from Eastern Parkway, with the Brooklyn Museum of Art at left. (Caparn collection, courtesy of Oliver Chamberlain)

Below: "Entrance Court" of the Griggs Estate, at Ardsley on the Hudson, New York, undated photograph by R. V. Smurby. (Caparn collection, courtesy of Oliver Chamberlain)

On January 1, 1912, the Brooklyn Botanic Garden appointed Caparn its consulting landscape architect. His work there for over thirty-two years was his greatest achievement. He designed the overall plan after site layout and preparation by the **Olmsted Brothers**. He then designed, among others, the Cranford Rose Garden, the Magnolia Plaza, the Osborne Garden (known then as the North Addition), the Herb Garden, the Horticultural Section, and especially the Systematic Section, now called the Plant Family Collection, presenting plants in botanic order of their evolution on earth. Beside his own work, during 1913 and again in 1919, his cousin William John Caparne of Guernsey, who had painted with and taken irises of his own propagation to Claude Monet at Giverny, sent him bulbs, plants, and seeds for the garden. Harold and his daughter Rhys jointly designed an armillary sphere that was erected in 1933 and stands at the center of the Magnolia Plaza. In 1980, Rhys gave her 1968, bronze sculpture, *Moonrise,* in memory of her father.

The parks Caparn designed include Grant Park and Columbus Park in Yonkers, New York; Lincoln Park and Milford Park in Newark, New Jersey; and John Jay Park on the upper east side of Manhattan. He also designed other park-like areas, including the grounds of the National Soldiers Home in Johnson City, Tennessee; the Woodland Garden in the Parade of Gardens at the 1939 New York World's Fair; Lake View Cemetery near Ithaca, New York; the campus of Brooklyn College from 1937 to 1945; country club grounds in Montclair, New Jersey; and the grounds of an office building of the House of Representatives in Washington, D.C.

Among outstanding private estates, he designed those of Mrs. Ben Ali Haggin, wife of the theatrical designer, at Onteora Park in the Catskills, now restored and known as Wildetur; Maitland F. Griggs, Esq., art collector and donor, at Ardsley on the Hudson; J. C. Willever, officer of Western Union, in Millburn, New Jersey, of which the East Gate with waterfall still exists on Glen Avenue; and the Honorable Joseph E. Willard, Ambassador to Spain, in Fairfax, Virginia.

He was elected a Fellow of the American Society of Landscape Architects in 1905. He faithfully served on committees and in various offices of the ASLA Board of Trustees, being elected president of the society in 1912,

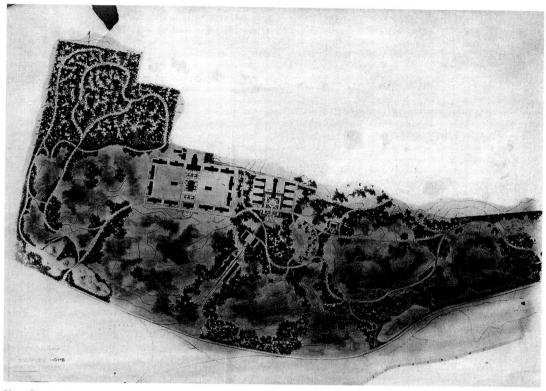

Plan of National Soldiers Home grounds, Johnson City, Tennessee, ca. 1902. (Caparn collection, courtesy of Oliver Chamberlain)

and of the New York Chapter in 1920. In the necrology for the ASLA by **Charles Downing Lay**, he said of Caparn, "In all his associations as in his writings and many activities, he was distinguished by his probity."

During his fifty-year career, Caparn made lasting contributions to landscape architecture in three principal areas: designing and writing about parks, designing and writing about botanic gardens, and teaching, including a course on landscape architecture, in presentations at professional meetings, and in more than eighty articles in various journals. He also wrote early letters to newspapers and public officials to influence thinking on environmental issues such as soil erosion and air pollution, and supported Jackson Hole National Monument in the debate in Congress over whether to abolish it, since "such scenery is a national, not an individual or local possession."

His varied interests included photography, painting in watercolors, and especially music. He attended many musical performances and wrote knowledgeable letters to well-known conductors and newspaper critics. He died at New York General Hospital at the age of eighty, after a brief illness.

Caparn, Harold A. "The Founding of the American Society of Landscape Architects." *American Landscape Architect* 4 (January 1931), 20–23. Gives background and documentation of the gathering of eleven individuals in 1899, mostly from Boston and New York, into the professional Society. Describes individuals he knew.

Caparn, Harold A. "The Planning of a Botanic Garden." *Landscape Architecture* 22 (July 1932), 261–69, illus. Rationale for and detailed diagram of the Brooklyn Botanic Garden systematic section as grown, in 1928; cf. same journal, July 1915, for the original plan, diagram; systematic botanic garden of smaller design, at Lebanon Valley College, *American Landscape Architect* 3 (December 1930), 12–16, 38–39, diagram.

Caparn, Harold A. Articles on parks: *Transactions of the American Society of Landscape Architects* (1899 to 1909), *Landscape Architecture* (1911 to 1930), *National Municipal Review* (1921), *Parks and Recreation* (1921 to 1933). Articles describing parks, solutions to park problems, and encroachment on parks, especially Central Park in New York City, Niagara Falls, and Yellowstone National Park, among other topics.

Oliver Chamberlain

CHRISTY, ELIZABETH (LIZ)
(1945–1985)
GARDENER, ACTIVIST

Elizabeth Christy, known as Liz, was born on April 16, 1945, in New York City. Her mother, Patricia Law Christy, was a distant relative of **Frederick Law Olmsted Sr.** Liz Christy had a diverse educational background that included attending Columbia University, New York University, and the New School. She took painting and drawing classes at the New York Studio School; city planning classes at the New York University Graduate School of Public Administration; and classes in botany, agronomy, and landscaping at the New York Botanical Garden.

In 1973, Christy, who was then living as an artist on the Lower East Side of Manhattan, and a group of friends and neighbors were interested in beautifying their community with plantings.

Elizabeth "Liz" Christy relaxing in the Lower East Side community garden, New York, New York, ca. 1978. (Photograph by Donald Loggins)

They encouraged residents to install flower boxes and plant trees in their neighborhood. They also developed instructions for constructing seed bombs, a mixture of seeds, fertilizer, and peat moss in either balloons or discarded Christmas ornaments, which could be tossed into abandoned or vacant lots to improve them with plants. One day, Christy noticed a rubble-filled vacant lot on the corner of the Bowery and Houston Street. She gathered the group, which called themselves the Green Guerillas, to haul away the debris, spread topsoil, plant seeds, and construct fences, thereby creating New York City's first community garden.

In April 1974, New York City's Office of Housing Preservation and Development agreed to rent the lot, known as the Bowery Houston Community Farm and Garden, to the Green Guerillas for $1 per month. Local residents installed sixty raised beds and planted them with vegetables, adding trees and herbaceous borders. The following year the garden won the Mollie Parnis Dress Up Your Neighborhood Award. The resulting publicity raised awareness of the trend of neighborhood gardening and residents in other parts of the city sought out information to establish their own gardens, a trend which has changed the appearance of communities throughout the five boroughs. Christy became the driving force in the creation of the modern community garden movement by developing urban green spaces in the poorest sections of the city. The Green Guerillas developed workshops and planted experimental plots to learn how to best grow a range of plants in the sometimes hostile urban environment. Gardeners, along with local nurseries, garden centers, and professional horticulturalists, donated plants, shrubs, and trees to help establish new gardens in other parts of the city. The Green Guerillas continue to assist more than 200 groups each year by giving away plants, providing gardening support, and protecting community gardens from development pressures.

From 1974 to 1981, Christy hosted a radio program called "Grow Your Own" on WBAI-FM in New York City. This program covered such topics as urban forestry, landscaping, community gardens, community environmental issues, and urban design and planning. In 1975, she was appointed as the first director of the Open Space Greening Program, which was part of the New York City government's Council on the Environment. She held this position until her death in 1985. The Open Space

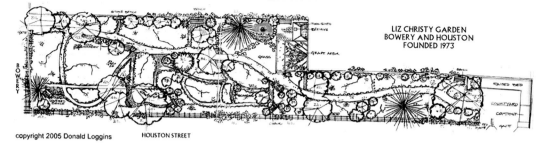

LIZ CHRISTY GARDEN
BOWERY AND HOUSTON
FOUNDED 1973

copyright 2005 Donald Loggins   HOUSTON STREET

Liz Christy Garden, on the corner of the Bowery and Houston Street, as designed in 1973. (Courtesy of Donald Loggins)

Greening Program was responsible for designing and developing green spaces in the poorest areas of New York City. Working with local community leaders Christy directed the creation of over twenty new community green spaces and play lots. She considered the desires of local residents, stating that "people who live on the block, in the neighborhood, have the best feelings for and understanding of what can or will work. . . . Without feeling for the pulse of the neighborhood, taking all people into consideration, a project is doomed to eventual apathy."

In the ten years that she directed the Open Space Greening Program, she changed the face of the city. In addition to the sites she designed, she provided technical assistance, resources, and training to support the approximately seven hundred community gardens in New York City. Visitors to New York City saw her spirit and vision for the development of urban community gardens, and she helped people create similar programs in Boston, Philadelphia, San Francisco, and Seattle, sometimes consulting directly with groups in these cities. During this period, she developed a twelve-hour pruning and tree maintenance course for the New York City Parks Department to certify Citizen Street Tree Pruners. She also instituted a program to educate the public on their neighborhood trees, teaching citizens about different species and installing identifying plaques on city trees.

Liz Christy lectured widely on the topic of community gardening and urban green spaces. She was the recipient of numerous awards that recognized her commitment to improving the urban landscape. Among these are the Municipal Art Society Award for Urban Improvements (1976), Parks Council Award for Community Service (1977), U.S. Environmental Protection Agency Region II Award (1979), and the American Forestry Association Urban Forestry Award (1982).

In 1985, Liz Christy passed away from cancer. The following year, the garden she established was renamed in her honor and is now officially known as Liz Christy's Bowery-Houston Garden, although it is most commonly referred to as the Liz Christy Garden. Today, individual gardeners maintain their own plots and share general maintenance on common areas. In 1990, the Cooper Square Committee pledged to preserve the garden in its entirety as part of its neighborhood renovation plans. In 2002, the City of New York and the New York State Attorney General called for the preservation of the garden, recognizing its importance to the Lower East Side neighborhood. Most recently, in 2006, a local developer agreed to curtail plans to excavate a portion of the garden for construction work on adjacent parcels that would have removed a towering dawn redwood and smaller blue Atlas cedar. Although minor impacts will occur, the trees will be preserved, due in large part to the advocacy efforts of local gardeners and the Green Guerillas, and the developer has agreed to provide funds to enhance the garden.

Christy's legacy is evident throughout New York City, but is perhaps most apparent in the garden that bears her name. The garden has progressed and now houses a pond with fish and turtles, beehive, wildflower habitat, grape arbor, grove of weeping birch trees, fruit trees, a dawn redwood, berries, vegetable gardens, and hundreds of flowering perennials.

Christy, Liz. "The Greening of Cities." In *Urban Open Spaces*. Rev. ed. New York: Rizzoli, 1981. Article on methods to bring more green spaces to urban areas.

www.Greenguerillas.org. A Web site for the Green Guerillas. The site has historical data on Liz Christy and the Green Guerillas.

www.LizChristyGarden.org. A Web site for the Liz Christy Garden with historical documents, photographs, and sound files related to Liz Christy. Also included is a history of Open Green Space in New York City written by Liz Christy.

Donald Loggins

CLARKE, HELEN HAWKINS

(1892–1974)

LANDSCAPE ARCHITECT,
HORTICULTURIST

Helen Hawkins was born on May 19, 1892, in Americus, Georgia, the eldest of four children. In the late 1890s her parents, William and Helen Hawkins, moved their family to Atlanta, where her father opened an insurance company in 1899. After graduating from high school, young Helen became a favorite in the Atlanta social world, marrying insurance agent Arthur Clarke on November 4, 1914.

As was commonplace for middle- and upper-class women in the 1920s and 1930s, Clarke juggled her domestic responsibilities with civic duties and educational interests. She was an active member of the Junior League

Above: Helen Hawkins Clarke, ca. 1940. (Cherokee Garden Library, Kenan Research Center at the Atlanta History Center)

Left: Clarke home, West Andrews Drive, Atlanta, Georgia, 1933, with a garden designed by Helen Hawkins Clarke. (Cherokee Garden Library, Kenan Research Center at the Atlanta History Center)

of Atlanta, established in 1914 to promote volunteerism for educational and charitable causes. In a 1937 article in the Atlanta Junior League's publication, *The Cotton Blossom,* Clarke voiced her concerns about the difficulties of combining family life with professional work, humbly claiming that she was not doing either task as well as she should.

As one of the founding members of the Cherokee Garden Club of Atlanta, Clarke was part of a national phenomenon that was sweeping early twentieth-century America—the garden club movement. Established in 1923, Peachtree Garden Club was the first garden club in Atlanta. By 1926, Peachtree Garden Club had produced their first book entitled *The Garden Schedule.* With guidance from the Peachtree Garden Club, Clarke and thirty-one other women formed Atlanta's second garden club, the Cherokee Garden Club, in 1928. By June of the same year, the two Atlanta clubs, along with nine other clubs in Georgia, established the Garden Club of Georgia. Over the next decade, the Garden Club of Georgia grew rapidly, recording over four thousand members in 1936.

As part of Georgia's bicentennial celebration in 1933, the Peachtree Garden Club of Atlanta compiled and published *The Garden History of Georgia, 1733–1933,* an influential volume in southern garden history. Both publications by the Peachtree Garden Club of Atlanta helped fuel the garden frenzy that occurred in Georgia in the 1920s and 1930s.

As a member of the Cherokee Garden Club of Atlanta, Clarke was involved with community service projects, including the development of a garden at Egleston Hospital for Children, as well as flower shows and horticultural courses. Clarke quickly became a prizewinning flower arranger and respected flower-show judge in Georgia.

In 1929, Helen and Arthur Clarke purchased a home on West Andrews Drive in the Northside neighborhood of Atlanta. In the 1930s and 1940s, Clarke designed and executed an extensive garden at her home, combining her love of horticulture with her keen eye for design. An article in the *Atlanta Journal* on June 26, 1938, described the Clarke garden as a place in which "the beauty of the native forest trees . . . makes an effective background for the masses of flowers, columbines, foxgloves, hollyhocks, bee balm and rudbeckia. A trellis, overgrown with honeysuckle and rose vines shelters a swing."

Garden clubs provided some women, like Clarke, the vehicle to work as professionals in the field of landscape architecture. After raising her daughter, also named Helen, Clarke increased her knowledge of design by attending landscape architecture classes at the University of Georgia taught by Hubert Bond Owens.* Clarke also took several courses at the Georgia Institute of Technology and spent two summers studying landscape architecture at Harvard University. She entered college at the University of Georgia in 1935, the same year her daughter enrolled as a freshman.

In conjunction with her university studies, Clarke continued gaining horticultural knowledge through her participation in the Cherokee Garden Club and the Garden

Unidentified garden sketch by Helen Hawkins Clarke. (Cherokee Garden Library, Kenan Research Center at the Atlanta History Center)

Club of Georgia. Clarke served as the horticultural chairman for the Garden Club of Georgia in 1936 and 1937. During her chairmanship, she wrote numerous articles for the club's publication, *Garden Gateways,* and became recognized as a horticultural authority throughout the state.

Clarke's writings show her extensive knowledge of horticulture and garden design. Lengthy discussions regarding varieties of plants, shrubs, and trees suitable to the Georgia Piedmont region, references to garden history and plant introductions, and practical gardening advice reflected Clarke's expertise in field.

In a 1937 article in *The Cotton Blossom,* Clarke explained that her decision to study landscape architecture stemmed from years of diligent home study of horticulture and an abiding love of flowers. On her design philosophy, she remarked, "Every garden must have form and symmetry. The term 'formal garden' has acquired a connotation of severity and coldness which should never be the case. A garden must always have harmony of line and color and at the same time natural beauty and spontaneous charm. One should always want to relax, talk and sip tea in a garden."

Like most other women landscape designers in the first half of the twentieth century, Clarke worked in the arena of residential garden design. One of the first women in Atlanta to practice in the field of landscape architecture, Clarke worked with the firm of Newberry and Johnson in the late 1930s. She also formed a landscape architecture partnership with Perry Hunt Wheeler* prior to World War II. In a 1944 letter, Wheeler asked Clarke if she would consider establishing another partnership with him—combining a landscape architecture practice with a nursery business in Atlanta—but the plans never came to fruition. After World War II, Wheeler set up a private landscape architecture practice in Middleburg, Virginia. He became known for his work on private gardens in Georgetown and for designing the White House Rose Garden during the Kennedy administration.

Clarke contracted polio in the 1940s, and consequently only practiced as a landscape designer for a decade. She continued to assist close friends and family members with their garden designs in the 1950s and 1960s. Helen Clarke died on July 26, 1974, in Atlanta, Georgia, at the age of eighty-two.

The Helen Hawkins Clarke Collection, MSS 976, at Cherokee Garden Library, Center for the Study of Southern Garden History, Kenan Research Center, Atlanta History Center, Ga., contains landscape sketches drawn by Clarke, correspondence from Perry Hunt Wheeler* to Clarke, photographs of Clarke at work and of her garden, articles regarding her work, articles written by Clarke, and her drawing instruments.

Ansley, Florence Bryan. "Helen Hawkins Clarke." *The Cotton Blossom,* Newsletter of the Atlanta Junior Urban League, November 1937, 6. A biographical article about Clarke, including a discussion of her education and work, involvement with garden clubs, and quotations from a Clarke lecture to the Junior League of Atlanta.

Clarke, Helen. "Beauty in the Autumn Garden." *Garden Gateways,* October 1936, 1. The first in a series of articles written by Clarke while serving as horticultural chairman for the Garden Club of Georgia, showing her extensive knowledge in horticulture; subsequent articles appeared September 1936 (p. 1), November 1936 (p. 2), December 1936 (p. 2), May 1937 (p. 5).

Staci L. Catron

CLAY, GRADY, JR.
(1916–   )
AUTHOR, JOURNALIST

Grady Clay was born in Atlanta, Georgia, in 1916. He spent much of his early life at the family's Ashland Farm, in Walnut Grove, Georgia. Clay's father, Grady Clay Sr., an ophthalmologist on the faculty at Emory University, followed scientific farming techniques on the 1,600-acre holding. Young Grady Clay graduated from Emory University with a B.A. in journalism in 1938. After a short stint publishing a newspaper on St. Simon's Island, Georgia, he enrolled and completed a master's degree in journalism at Columbia University in 1939. Following graduation, Clay got a job reporting the police beat for the *Louisville Times* in Louisville, Kentucky.

Clay served as a second lieutenant during World War II and was stationed in Italy, France, and Alaska. He was assigned to work on *Yank,* the weekly Army magazine for soldiers. During his time in the service, he read *Geography and Human Destiny* by Roderick Peattie, which altered the course of his professional life. The discipline of geography became the filter through which Clay began evaluating places. He took a job at the *Courier-Journal,* in Louisville following the war, and in 1948, Clay applied for and was awarded a Neiman Fellowship to the Harvard Graduate School of Design where he studied urban geography. His adviser was William L. C. Wheaton, and G. Holmes Perkins and Joseph Hudnut were on the faculty. Clay formed lasting friendships with classmates Ian L. McHarg,* David Wallace, and Jackie Tyrwhitt.

Upon Clay's return to the *Courier-Journal* following the year at Harvard, he assumed the position of the first editor of the new real estate section. He reported on national trends in real estate, urban renewal, suburban development, land-use issues, and the development of the interstate highway system. Clay gained national recognition for his writing on important land issues across post–World War II America. He created the position of Urban Affairs Editor at the *Courier-Journal,* the first in the United States.

In 1959, Clay left the *Courier-Journal* and became editor of *Landscape Architecture* (then a quarterly). He moved the magazine's office from Boston to Louisville, Kentucky, in 1961. Clay reported on the trend, now known as suburban sprawl, and linked it to the expansion of federal road projects and bridge construction. The discussion of suburban sprawl had been brought to the forefront during the late 1940s by William Hollingsworth Whyte Jr.* in articles he wrote as editor of *Fortune* and in the book *The Exploding Metropolis.* Clay contributed an essay to that book and advanced the discussion in the 1960s when he called for a "Girth Control" movement. Clay's writings and public speaking on the matter gained him a national forum for the issues of urban planning and community design. What some saw as signs of American progress and bounty, Clay rightly identified as threatening the future of American cities.

Clay sought to broaden the appeal for landscape architecture and community planning. He concluded that updating the magazine (published since 1910) was the way to achieve that goal. Clay set out to change its focus and its feature articles. This plan would result in a publication of truly national proportions and interest that would highlight professional practice. Clay directed the new editorial stance to focus on community planning and natural ecology within the context of landscape design.

Under Clay's leadership, *Landscape Architecture* was the first publication to feature the work of his former classmate, Ian McHarg. Clay promoted ecology as a component of landscape architecture. This new direction was a turning point for the magazine. It resulted in subscriptions and income for the magazine quadrupling between 1959 and 1964. Clay's work at the magazine showed his ability for identifying and locating the new talent in landscape architecture and including these designs in the magazine. Clay recalls that he had to convince many of the proponents of the evolving ecological trend in landscape architecture that the magazine was a proper forum for their work and ideas. He developed the magazine to provide a professional voice for landscape architects, and expanded the content to include international issues and projects. Under his direction, *Landscape Architecture* published the work of Robert Smithson and Michael Heizer, turning the lens onto "Earth Art" and

Grady Clay and Maya Lin atop the Vietnam Veterans Memorial prior to opening ceremony, 1982. (© *The Courier-Journal*)

profoundly influencing the next generation of landscape architects. During Clay's tenure, the magazine often featured special thematic issues, including topics such as historic preservation and residential garden design.

Clay's work led to his creation and development of the cross-section technique. It is a way to read development of a landscape over time and to predict the emerging development patterns. In his seminal book *Close-Up: How to Read the American City,* published in 1973, Clay for the first time in urban planning established a template, with spatial geography at its center, for understanding the development of cities and suburbs. He focused attention on a hidden resource in American cities—the alley—with his Louisville study published in 1978. His fascination with the language used to describe place and his skill at wordsmithing resulted in the publication of *Real Places* in 1984. He identified and named, in encyclopedic treatment, the words and phrases that societies create to describe vernacular places.

Clay was elected president of the American Society of Planning Officials, serving from 1973 to 1974. Clay held several other national posts including service on the Potomac Planning Task Force, as an advisor to Secretary of the Interior Stewart Udall, and as a member of the Housing and Urban Development Advisory Committee on Urban Development during President Lyndon Johnson's administration.

In 1981, Clay was chairman of the selection committee for the Vietnam Veterans National Memorial. The committee reviewed more than 1,400 entries during a five-day period before selecting the winning submission of an undergraduate student, Maya Lin, which Clay characterized as minimalist. Clay was awarded the 1999 Olmsted Medal, presented to a non-architect by the American Society of Landscape Architects, for his "outstanding contributions to the environment through action and treatment."

A popular lecturer, Clay took his ideas to a new audience when he began broadcasting a regular feature titled "Crossing the American Grain" on Louisville public radio from 1995 to 2006.

Grady, Clay, Jr. *Alleys: A Hidden Resource.* Louisville: Grady Clay and Company, 1978. Explores the origins, uses, natural character, and occurrences of these hidden thoroughfares in Louisville, Kentucky. By using case studies, Clay examines the changing functions of alleys and argues their usefulness in modern city design.

Grady, Clay, Jr. *Close-Up: How to Read the American City.* Chicago: University of Chicago Press, 1973. Close-up refutes the idea that cities are confusing and randomly arranged. Clay discusses several organizing principles and illustrates them with numerous diagrams and photos using examples across the country.

Grady, Clay, Jr. *Real Places: An Unconventional Guide to America's Generic Landscape.* Chicago: University of Chicago Press, 1984. This illustrated guidebook to our ever changing cultural landscape is in three parts—The Center: The Life and Death of Centrality; The Front: The Struggle for Control; and Out There: Life in the Great Beyond-the-Bypass. These sites are unlisted on maps but they are ubiquitous. From "The Good Address," "Downtown," and "Drug Scene" to "Back Forty," "Boondocks," and "The Last Chance," Clay vividly describes these generic places.

Donna M. Neary and Susan M. Rademacher

COLLINS, LESTER ALBERTSON
(1914–1993)
LANDSCAPE ARCHITECT

Lester A. Collins was born in Moorestown, New Jersey, on April 19, 1914. He was one of five children born to Lester and Ann Collins. His Quaker family had lived and farmed in western New Jersey since 1678.

Collins's grandfather was John Collins, a farmer, nurseryman, and founder of the New Jersey Horticultural Society. He was also an entrepreneur and adventurer who bought beach front property in Miami, Florida, which he and his family farmed and developed. In 1913, to facilitate the shipping of his farm products and to develop the beachfront land, the family financed the Collins Canal, and later the Collins Bridge across Biscayne Bay, connecting the city of Miami to Miami Beach. Collins Avenue in Miami Beach is named for John Collins.

Lester A. Collins, grew up in Moorestown, New Jersey. He was educated at Choate and Harvard University. He graduated from Harvard in 1938 with a degree in English. Before returning to Harvard for a master of landscape architecture degree in 1940, he traveled for a year to the Far East with fellow student John Ormsbee Simonds,* visiting China, Japan, India, and Tibet. These travels would profoundly affect both men and would influence Collins's thinking, future study, and design esthetic.

Collins was a student of landscape architecture at Harvard from 1940 to 1942 during the years that Walter Gropius, as dean of the School of Architecture, was advancing the ideas of modernism. In 1939, at Gropius's invitation, Christopher Tunnard joined the Harvard facility. Tunnard, also educated in European modernism, continued the program's promulgation of these ideas. He exposed the students to the study of the occult balance, a means of studying relationships in a composition. Collins continued to study space configured with occult balance throughout his career.

From 1942 to 1945, Collins served as a captain in the American Field Service, serving with the British Eighth Army in North Africa. It was there that he met Petronella Le Roux, a nurse in the South African army. They would later marry and have three children.

After the war, he returned to Harvard, and was an instructor in the Department of Landscape Architecture from 1945 to 1950. In 1947, he was instrumental in developing a new program called the Field Laboratory at the Case Estates in Weston, Massachusetts. The Field Laboratory afforded students the opportunity to gain practical knowledge by providing a site and materials where they could build their studio designs, and learn from their choices.

Collins served as the dean of the Department of Landscape Architecture at Harvard from 1950 to 1953. In

Above: Innisfree Garden, Millbrook, New York. (Courtesy of the Innisfree Foundation)

Left: Lester Collins, 1975. (Courtesy of the Collins family)

1951, he edited, with Thomas Gillespie, the book *Landscape Architecture.* It commemorated Harvard's fifty-year history teaching landscape architecture. Included in this book were projects and papers by students and practicing graduates of the program including Lawrence Halprin,* Daniel Urban Kiley,* Hideo Sasaki,* Garrett Eckbo,* **Fletcher Steele**, Robert Lewis Zion,* Ralph Ellis Gunn,* Sidney N. Shurcliff, and others.

A year in Japan in 1954 as a Fulbright scholar and other travels to South Africa and China contributed to Collins's appreciation for the gardens and design aesthetic of other cultures. While in Japan, he became interested in an ancient Japanese garden book, *Sensai Hisho,* translated as the *Secret Garden Book.* During this time he worked with Japanese scholar Fuku Ikawa on an English translation. The principles of this ancient text were a remarkable source of practical garden instructions for designing and constructing gardens.

Returning from Japan, Collins and his family moved to Washington, D.C., where he was a lecturer at Harvard's Dumbarton Oaks Landscape Studies program, from 1954 to 1955. In Washington, he developed a successful design practice working with leading architectural firms on residential and public planning projects. Among his most notable projects in Washington are the 1977 redesign of

the Hirshhorn Museum's Sculpture Garden; the design of the Smithsonian Institution's Enid A. Haupt Garden in 1987; the landscape design at The Podium of the John F. Kennedy Center for the Performing Arts; and the gardens for the Embassy of Ghana in Washington, D.C., in the 1970s. He advised many Washington schools and universities on their campus designs, including The Beauvoir School on the National Cathedral campus; Georgetown University; American University; and George Washington University. He designed twenty-nine small parks along Pennsylvania Avenue, SE, for the National Park Service. He also served as a consultant to architects Faulkner, Fryer & Vanderpool on many projects, including the 1972 master plan for the National Zoo in Washington. Other designs outside of Washington include the landscape for the Comsat Laboratory campus (Clarksburg, Maryland, 1969) and a design for the residence at the U.S. Embassy in Cairo, Egypt. He also consulted on many municipal projects including the plaza and garden design of Market Square in Alexandria, Virginia, and the rehabilitation of three city squares for the Historic Savannah Foundation in Savannah, Georgia.

Collins also worked for many other public and private clients from Maine to Florida. Prominent architects around the country admired him for his able and original

Hirshhorn Museum Sculpture Garden, Smithsonian Institution, Washington, D.C., 1981.
(Hirshhorn Museum and Sculpture Garden, Smithsonian Institution; Lee Stalsworth,
photographer)

solutions. Mark Simon, FAIA, partner in Centerbrook Architects and Planners, LLC, in Centerbrook, Connecticut, said, "He was fun to work with. At the heart of all that, [he] was a brilliant designer who made difficult situations simple, but who could make simple solutions interesting." Collins was a minimalist who used common sense. He found fresh solutions to problems by understanding the requirements of the site; he had the ability to distill the design requirements to their essence and give the client a design that was a unique complement to the architecture and was appropriate and suitable for the client's needs.

From 1955 to 1970, he was the Washington partner in the firm Collins, Simonds and Simonds, landscape architects and planners, with offices in Pittsburgh, Pennsylvania, and Washington, D.C. Friends and traveling companions from their Harvard years, Lester Collins, John Simonds, and Philip Simonds of Pittsburgh, Pennsylvania, worked on projects in both Washington and Pittsburgh and across the country. Their firm was instrumental in shaping new town development in southern Florida in the 1960s and 1970s. In 1970, the firm became Environmental Planning and Design (EPD) to whom Lester Collins continued to consult.

In 1962, Lester Collins worked for the Graham family in Dade County, Florida, developing the master plan for the new town of Miami Lakes. Collins based his ideas on those of garden city planners Ebenezer Howard, Clarence Stein, and **Henry Wright**. It was the first Florida development that was conceived as a complete community. Unlike conventional Florida developments, Miami Lakes' plan conserved and enhanced the natural resources of the site. It featured an organic street design, extensive park-like open spaces and greenways, and a network of artificial lakes. It included public amenities, such as golf courses, which it combined with diverse housing sizes and styles and a viable commercial district. Today, this community of more than 22,000 is still considered one of the most successful new town developments of its era. Over the years, Collins continued to work with the Graham family on new phases of Miami Lakes. Its success led to many other Florida development projects for EPD, including the communities of Indian Trace, Saga Bay, and Pelican Bay.

Collins's knowledge of Asian garden philosophy gave him the opportunity to work successfully on another venerable project, the Innisfree Garden in Millbrook, New York. This garden estate was the home and passion of Marion and Walter Beck. Collins began consulting to the Becks while he was at Harvard in the 1950s. Walter Beck, an artist who turned his talent from painting to garden design, built his garden at Innisfree based on the garden ideas of Wang Wei, a Chinese gardener, artist, and poet from the eighth century. The Becks transformed their landscape into a series of self-contained arranged views, or cup gardens. Collins was involved with the Innisfree Garden for forty years. In 1960, he became president of the Innisfree Foundation and helped guide Innisfree from a private garden to a public one, and in doing so would more than double the garden's size. At Innisfree, Collins had the opportunity to use his years of work and study to refine the garden so that it expressed the subtle relationships between garden elements. He did so by carving out spaces, creating lawns and berms, and enhancing the flow from garden to garden, creating a series of linked spaces, which led the visitor to carefully planned views. The garden would be an expression of his and the Becks' dreams. A master of the unconventional and the unexpected, he unified the parts of the garden to enhance the experience of the whole.

In 1964, Lester Collins was honored by his profession and made a Fellow of the American Society of Landscape Architects. In 1981, Lester and Petronella Collins moved from Washington, D.C., to Key West, Florida. The Collinses divided their time between Key West and Millbrook, New York. Lester Collins died in 1993 at the age of seventy-nine.

Collins, Lester. *Innisfree, An American Garden,* ed. Barbara Probst Morrow. New York: Sagapress, Inc./Harry N. Abrams Inc., 1994. Richly illustrated monograph of Collins's masterwork.

Collins, Lester, and Thomas Gillespie, eds. *Landscape Architecture.* Cambridge, Mass.: Harvard University, 1951. Collection of student projects celebrating the program's first fifty years including such graduates as Hideo Sasaki, Ralph Gunn, and Robert Zion.

Collins, Lester A. "Ise, Ancient and Flourishing Center of Shinto Religion." *Landscape Architecture* 45, no. 2 (January 1955), 93–94.

Nancy Slade

COTTRELL, LOIS PAGE
(1896–1997)
LANDSCAPE AND GARDEN DESIGNER

Lois Lee Page was born in 1896. She attended The Masters School in Dobbs Ferry, New York (class of 1913). She married Donald C. Cottrell, whose family firm, C. B. Cottrell & Sons, was the foremost manufacturer of printing presses in the United States during the late nineteenth and early twentieth centuries. She began working with her sister, Helen Page Wodell, around 1924, and they practiced as Wodell and Cottrell, Landscape and Garden Consultants, beginning in 1931.

Lois Cottrell is credited with popularizing herb gardens in the Great Lakes area, one of which she designed for Edith Farwell, later a well-known writer on the subject. Cottrell herself characterized her style as a blend of formal and natural, with one or the other predominating depending on the view, the terrain, and the architecture of the house. She believed in the importance of extensive interviews with her clients, in order to design the sort of garden that would suit their way of living. Although not a self-described advocate of the Prairie style, she did prefer using native plant materials whenever possible.

In 1933, Lois Cottrell moved to Lake Forest, Illinois, where her husband had relocated with his firm. There she designed portions of the estates of W. A. P. Pullman and Donald Welles, among others, as well as the Lake Forest Village Square (1933–1936). Subsequently, Cottrell and her husband moved to Milwaukee, Wisconsin, where she designed gardens for A. J. Kieckhaefer, Mrs. Ludington Patton, and others. She also continued to work with her sister and their firm in New Jersey. This long-distance practice was handled by correspondence and during Cottrell's frequent visits with her sister.

In 1950, Lois Cottrell retired and moved to Stonington, Connecticut. She died in Milwaukee, Wisconsin, in 1997, shortly before her 101st birthday.

See also the individual entry on Helen Page Wodell and the joint entry on Wodell and Cottrell. Reference list follows the Wodell and Cottrell entry.

Rebecca Warren Davidson

CRET, PAUL PHILIPPE
(1876–1945)
ARCHITECT, PLANNER

Paul Philippe Cret was born in Lyons, France, on October 24, 1876, to Paul Adolphe Cret and Anna Caroline Durand, a working-class couple. When his father passed away in 1881, young Cret and his mother moved into the household of his mother's sister. Cret's uncle was the brother of Joannès Bernard, an architect in Lyons for whom Cret would later work while studying at the École des Beaux-Arts.

Cret received a private education focused on academia rather than trade skills. Despite his natural academic abilities, Cret's desire to study architecture was so great that he left school in 1893 before graduating to attend the École des Beaux-Arts in Lyons. Cret distinguished himself at the École and after four years, he won the prestigious Prix de Paris, which allowed him to study at the École in Paris. There he entered the atelier Pascal, whose teacher, Jean-Louis Pascal, was renowned for encouraging students to approach each project as distinct and unique. Cret, who later would become a respected teacher himself, adopted this approach with his students as well as with his own work.

Cret was one of the more talented students at the École in Paris during his tenure, earning his *diplome* in June 1903. However, he opted not to stay in France to compete for the Prix de Rome, but instead accepted a teaching position at the School of Architecture at the University of Pennsylvania in Philadelphia. The position of Professor of Design afforded Cret the opportunity to promulgate his ideas while simultaneously engaging in the practice of architecture. In 1904, he briefly returned to France, where he married Marguerite Lahalle, whom friends affectionately referred to as Madame Cret upon the couple's return to Philadelphia.

A kind yet demanding teacher, Cret remained at the University of Pennsylvania until 1937. He trained numerous foreign students, most notably from China and Russia, in Beaux-Arts ideology and Western construction methods.

Cret's first major commission resulted from his winning entry for a competition for a design for the Pan American Union (now the Organization of American States). In 1907, Cret and Albert Kelsey developed a plan for an eclectic building that merged Beaux-Arts features

Paul Philippe Cret, 1928. (The Architectural Archives, University of Pennsylvania)

with Latin-American characteristics, including a substantial courtyard garden and open patio. Essentially a geometric plan, the classically inspired patio features a central fountain and lush foliage. Taking cues from Latin-American building materials, Cret adorned the space with natural wood, stucco, and colorful tiles.

Beaux-Arts training prepared Cret for much more than building design. In 1907, in association with the firm of Trumbauer & Zantzinger, Cret developed a plan for the Benjamin Franklin Parkway in Philadelphia. Cret's scheme was not executed, but a plan by Jacques-Henri-Auguste Gréber* was implemented in 1917. However, Cret's skillful, elaborate renderings for lamp posts were retained and executed. Although Cret initially complained that Gréber borrowed heavily from his 1907 plan,

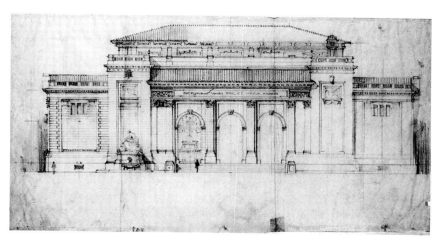

Left: Pan American Union drawing, circa 1908. (The Architectural Archives, University of Pennsylvania)

Below: Schematic drawing of fountain at Pan American Union, ca. 1908. (The Architectural Archives, University of Pennsylvania)

he did not appear to harbor a grudge and later worked with Gréber on several prominent projects.

Cret redesigned Rittenhouse Square in Philadelphia in 1913, and it retains much of his original plan. Main walkways radiate from the corners of the square and converge in a central oval. The plaza contains a large planted bed and reflecting pool surrounded by a balustrade and a circular walkway.

In 1914, at the onset of World War I in Europe, Cret interrupted his burgeoning practice, which was simply called Paul Philippe Cret, and enlisted in the French army, serving as an interpreter until the armistice. Although he attempted to complete designs from the trenches, he finally relinquished, admitting he found it difficult to work under such conditions. When he returned to the United States in 1919, he was partially deaf from exposure to exploding shells. For his service, the French military made Cret an officer in the Legion of Honor and awarded him the Croix de Guerre.

Despite the interruption in his career, Cret soon received a commission to design a new museum for the Detroit Institute of Arts in 1919. Cret included a court and garden in the new museum, placing sculpture among plants. The garden contained raised planting beds and water features surrounded by ornate walls decorated with recessed niches, moldings, and mascarónes. However, only five years after the museum opened, renowned artist Diego Rivera painted bold frescoes on the surrounding walls, destroying Cret's intentions for the space.

Cret found that his developing style of modern classicism adapted well to bridges, and he enjoyed collaborating with structural engineers. In 1922, he designed

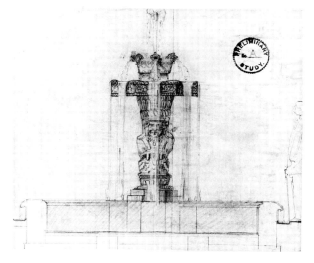

the Delaware River Bridge (now the Benjamin Franklin Bridge) in Philadelphia. Cret continued to design numerous bridges, most notably in Philadelphia and Washington, D.C. After his wartime experiences, Cret's diversity as a designer took another form. He served as the Consulting Architect for the American Battle Monuments Commission from 1925 until his death. He developed plans for war-related monuments and memorials throughout the United States and Europe, consequently influencing the image of the United States abroad by executing solemn yet triumphant Beaux-Arts structures.

Cret's interest in planning never waned, and he was involved with numerous institutions throughout his career, forming long-term relationships with his clients. He developed campus plans and buildings—both built and

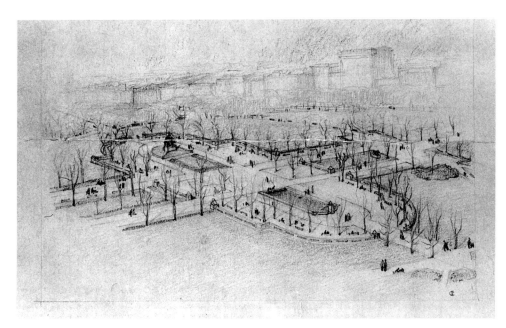

Pencil drawing of Rittenhouse Square, Philadelphia, 1913. (The Architectural Archives, University of Pennsylvania)

unbuilt—for the University of Pennsylvania, U.S. Naval Academy, and Brown University. In 1930, he was retained by the University of Texas in Austin to serve as consulting architect for a development plan and continued to design landscape plans and buildings for the campus until his death. His approach to planning was holistic; he developed ideas for roadways, pedestrian walkways, landscape features and furnishings, and placed administrative, residential, and service buildings in logical arrangements. His planning work was not limited to educational institutions; in the late 1920s, he developed designs for the Philadelphia Zoological Gardens in Fairmount Park. During the Great Depression, Cret designed the Tygart River Reservoir and Dam in West Virginia in 1934 for the U.S. Army Corps of Engineers.

Applying his campus planning experience to a hospital site, Cret laid out the U.S. Naval Medical Center (now the National Naval Medical Center) in Bethesda, Maryland, designing buildings, circulation patterns, and landscape features in 1938–39. He consulted with the firm of Clarke & Rapuano (**Gilmore David Clarke** and **Michael Rapuano**) on landscape issues, but was responsible for the overall site plan and individual component landscapes. Despite the classicism of his architecture for the site, his landscape abandons Beaux-Arts principles in favor of a picturesque setting with a pond, pergola, and stone retaining walls and bridges.

Residential commissions comprise a minute portion of Cret's vast body of work. Photographs show that his houses—most of which were in Pennsylvania—usually included some type of Beaux-Arts garden situated close to the building. Drawings show designs for fountains, birdbaths, benches, tiles, paving materials, and lampposts, attesting to Cret's attention to detail.

Cret continued to design sophisticated buildings that simplified classical traditions, evoking historically derived architecture yet responding to modernism. His two architectural masterpieces are the Folger Shakespeare Library and the Federal Reserve Board Building, both in Washington, D.C. The Federal Reserve Board Building contains two open courtyards that essentially function as intimate outdoor rooms, one of Cret's favorite type of space.

Cret published many papers and delivered speeches, writing and speaking impeccable English. Later in his life, a bout with cancer robbed him of his voice. However, he remained active, continuing to design and write. Although Cret is best remembered for his civic architecture, his planning, landscape architecture, and monument and memorial work deserve in-depth study, as do his teaching, participation in architectural competitions, and lengthy record of public service.

Cret was affiliated with numerous organizations during his prolific career. He was a member of the Society of Beaux-Arts Architects, National Academy of Design, T-Square Club, National Institutes of Arts and Letters, American Philosophical Society, and American Institute of Architects, which awarded him the prestigious Gold Medal in 1938. He received honorary degrees from the University of Pennsylvania, Brown University, and Harvard University. Cret served on the Commission of Fine Arts from 1940 until his death on September 8, 1945. After his death, his surviving partners renamed the firm Harbeson, Hough, Livingston, and Larson. It continues today as H2L2.

The Paul P. Cret Collection, located at the Athenaeum of Philadelphia, Penn., is the most complete and diverse collection of Cret drawings.

Grossman, Elizabeth. *The Civic Architecture of Paul Cret.* Cambridge, England: Cambridge University Press, 1996. An excellent analysis of several of Cret's most notable public buildings.
White, Theo. *Paul Philippe Cret: Architect and Teacher.* Philadelphia: The Art Alliance Press, 1973. A warm recollection of Cret and his work by a former pupil. Also provides a collection of some of Cret's writings as well as historic photographs.

Stephanie S. Foell

CULYER, COLONEL JOHN YAPP
(1839–1924)
CIVIL ENGINEER, PARK SUPERINTENDENT, LANDSCAPE ARCHITECT, ARCHITECT, EDUCATOR

John Yapp Culyer was born in 1839 and raised in New York City. In the 1850s, he studied at New York University's newly established School of Engineering and Architecture, followed by one year in the office of an unidentified New York architect. This early training led to his employment on the original corps of engineers responsible for constructing New York's Central Park under the supervision of **Frederick Law Olmsted Sr.** While engaged on this major public works project, Culyer served as clerk to the Engineering Department under the superintending engineer, William H. Grant. Several years later, he identified his positions at Central Park as rodman and assistant engineer.

John Culyer on top of a tree-moving machine, date unknown. (Collection of The New-York Historical Society)

With the outbreak of the Civil War, Culyer followed Olmsted to Washington, D.C., to assist in the administration of the United States Sanitary Commission. He developed an organizational chart, which graphically rendered the Commission's chain of command and division of labor. After joining the Army Corps of Engineers under General John G. Barnard, he was engaged in the building of fortifications in Virginia, south of the Potomac River. While in Washington, Culyer attended the fateful performance at Ford's Theatre the night that President Lincoln was assassinated.

After the war, Culyer briefly resumed an appointment at Central Park, but soon resigned to become an assistant engineer at Prospect Park in Brooklyn, New York. Collaborating with a talented team of specialists assembled by Olmsted and **Calvert Vaux** to construct their newly designed park, Culyer was initially charged with the organizing, disciplining, and keeping track of the work force. In 1871, he became chief engineer, and, in 1874, succeeded Olmsted and Vaux as the park's superintendent. Culyer held these two positions until his resignation four-

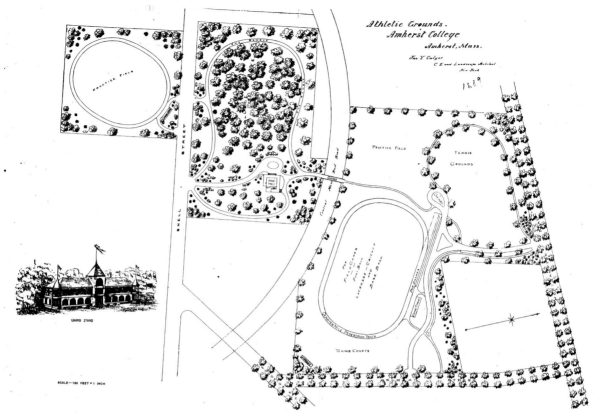

Plan of athletic grounds, Amherst College, Amherst, Massachusetts, 1889. (Amherst College Archives and Special Collections, by permission of the Trustees of Amherst College)

teen years later. Under his direction, Prospect Park was substantially completed and Brooklyn's smaller parks, including Washington (Fort Greene Park), were laid out. Culyer designed two types of trucks for the transplanting of large trees that were said to have improved upon those used in Paris. He also devised ways of improving road construction. Olmsted and Vaux had designed Prospect Park to be the centerpiece of a citywide system of parks and connecting boulevards. Culyer planned and supervised the original construction (and later, the repair and maintenance) of Brooklyn's two pioneering parkways: Eastern Parkway (1870–1874) and Ocean Parkway (1874–1876). When completed, the latter, a six-mile drive from the park's southern entrance to Coney Island, was described as "the most magnificent drive in the world." At its terminus on Coney Island, he also planned the Concourse (1876), a boulevard that extended for about half a mile near the Atlantic Ocean. For twenty-five years, he maintained an avid interest in protecting the

Concourse lands from private development, supporting an original plan to make it a seaside park and, later, in 1897, proposing a boardwalk for the site. From 1890 to 1893, while consulting engineer to the Brooklyn Board of Park Commissioners, and, twenty years after the laying out of Eastern Parkway, Culyer designed its two-mile extension linking Prospect Park to Highland Park. He also planned new smaller parks. Culyer's long tenure working for the Brooklyn Park Commission provided an important consistency of management and vision, in support of Olmsted and Vaux's designs for Brooklyn's park system. Culyer was also closely associated with James S. T. Stranahan, the first and longtime president of the Park Commission. In 1896, he himself was considered as a viable candidate for commissioner, although he was not appointed.

Culyer also worked as an architect, landscape architect, and engineer independent of his work for the Brooklyn park system. Initially, he practiced in partner-

Eastside Park overlooking the Passaic River, Paterson, New Jersey, ca. 1905. (Courtesy of Joy Kestenbaum)

ship with John Bogart,* his associate at Prospect Park, securing work from park commissions in several American cities including Albany and New Orleans. Their extensive experience in all aspects of landscape work led to numerous appointments. Culyer also designed the High Victorian Gothic Flatbush Town Hall (1875), a designated New York City Landmark. During this period, he prepared plans for a gate lodge at Brooklyn's Cemetery of the Evergreen (which was partially designed by Vaux and **Samuel Parsons Jr.**) along with improvements to its main entrance, modeled on that of Prospect Park. In 1876, Culyer also served as an advisor to the commissioners planning the New York State Soldiers' Home in Bath, New York, a facility for disabled volunteers of the Civil War, advising on the location of the buildings and laying out the grounds.

Following his forced resignation in 1886 by the newly appointed Brooklyn Park Commission, Culyer was actively engaged in private practice. Maintaining an office in Lower Manhattan, he was considered an expert in site planning and landscape development, and frequently called upon to plan and supervise the laying out of a variety of public and private properties. In 1887, Culyer prepared designs for Laurel Grove Cemetery, located just south of Paterson, New Jersey, for a group of prominent citizens. He also served as a consultant to Paterson's Board of Aldermen, and then its Park Commissioners, helping to plan a new park system. His recommendation of a site rising from the Passaic River on the easterly side of the city led to the purchase of that property for Eastside Park. Later, in 1889, after a limited competition, Culyer's plan was awarded first prize and he was selected

to supervise the park's construction, although limited funds prevented its full development according to the original design. His plans included a circulation system with curvilinear drives and walks; lawns for tennis and croquet; and several park structures. The park's main feature was a terrace in the center of the park, reached by masonry stairways. In 2004, the Eastside Park Historic District was listed on the State and National Register of Historic Places.

In 1889 to 1890, Culyer was retained by the trustees of the Grand Lodge of the State of New York to survey the grounds of the proposed Masonic Home (now Masonic Care Community of New York) in Utica. He devised and laid out a circulation system for the 160-acre site, which overlooked the picturesque Mohawk River Valley.

For Charles Pratt, the prominent Brooklyn resident and philanthropist, he planned improvements to the Pratt property in Glen Cove, Long Island, and developed a system of drives. Commissioned by Charles's son Frederic B. Pratt, with whom he shared an interest in educational matters, Culyer also designed and laid out new athletic grounds for Amherst College (1889–1891), Frederic Pratt's alma mater. Planned with a drainage and sewerage system, the 13-acre site featured ornamental plantings, drives, and walks, and was connected by an iron bridge to an adjacent grove and ball field. Culyer's design included a grandstand structure, which seated 500 and contained up-to-date hygienic facilities. Upon its completion, the Pratt Field was considered one of the finest recreational grounds at an American college. Concurrently, Culyer prepared designs for an athletic field for Columbia College in New York City. Later, in the mid-1890s, he planned, graded, and laid out a summer resort at Point O'Woods on Fire Island with groves, drives, and buildings for the Long Island Chautauqua Assembly Association. After the association's bankruptcy a few years later, Point O'Woods continued as a private beach community.

Culyer remained an ardent spokesman for the planting of street trees in urban and suburban areas. He recognized their increased aesthetic quality, contribution to land value, sanitary importance, provision of comfort in warm weather, and use as shelters by birds. While abroad in 1874, he studied the culture and growth of trees in the major cities of Europe. Culyer advocated a systematic approach to tree planting, care, and maintenance in connection with street improvement, urging that this work be done under the charge of parks departments. In 1897, he was elected secretary to the Tree Planting Association of New York. Later, he served as its advisory landscape architect, providing advice regarding varieties of suitable street trees and the conditions under which they were to be most favorably planted and maintained.

A dedicated public servant, Culyer was a prominent figure in Brooklyn's civic affairs. For over twenty-five years, beginning in 1872, he was an influential member of the Brooklyn Board of Education and an active promoter of art education and drawing in the public schools. In 1899, he spoke on the practice of landscape architecture to the art education section of the Brooklyn Institute of Arts and Sciences (now known as the Brooklyn Museum of Art). Culyer promoted the educational requirements of this emerging profession and the varied opportunities it offered to those so inclined, including women. He noted that, "the drawing and designing faculty of the art student, some knowledge of mathematics, acquaintance with botany, horticulture and forestry, knowledge of methods of road construction, and above all, ability to grapple with practical problems, are among the numerous faculties and acquirements demanded of the landscape architect."

For many years, Culyer and his family resided on Prospect Hill, just east of the Prospect Park Plaza. He was also a longtime resident of Mount Kisco, New York, in Westchester County, where he and his family summered and, for many years he offered his expert services as tree warden to the village. Known as Colonel Culyer, he served in the New York State National Guard, attaining the rank of lieutenant colonel and engineer. He was a member of the American Society of Civil Engineers and was also associated with the planning of railroads and rapid transit in Brooklyn. Culyer died at his home in Mount Kisco in 1924 and was buried in his family plot in Brooklyn's Greenwood Cemetery.

"Brooklyn Institute News; Art Students in Landscape Architecture." *Brooklyn Eagle,* April 21, 1899, 13. Discusses Culyer's address, "Openings for Art Students in Landscape Architecture."

"Death of Col. John Y. Culyer." *Mount Kisco Recorder,* March 21, 1924. Obituary from newspaper published where Culyer resided for over fifty-five years.

Johnson, Rossiter, ed. "Culyer, John Yapp." *The Twentieth Century Biographical Dictionary of Notable Americans,* vol. 3. Boston: Boston Biographical Society, 1904. Major biographical account, written during Culyer's lifetime.

"To Beautify the City; the Importance of Tree Culture in Urban Ornamentation." *Brooklyn Eagle,* January 29, 1882, 2. Article quoting Culyer and his views on the importance of street tree planting.

Joy Kestenbaum

CURTIS, JOSEPH HENRY
(1841–1928)
LANDSCAPE GARDENER, LANDSCAPE ENGINEER

Joseph Henry Curtis was born in 1841. He attended Brown University from 1859 to 1861, then served in Company F, 44th Regiment of the Massachusetts Volunteers from 1862 to 1863 during the Civil War. After the war was over, he briefly enrolled in the Massachusetts Institute of Technology from 1867 to 1868. In 1880, Curtis purchased a portion of the steeply sloping eastern shore of Northeast Harbor, Maine, and with William C. Doane, an Episcopal Bishop from Albany, New York, and Charles W. Eliot, the president of Harvard University, became one of the founders of the Northeast Harbor summer colony. George E. Moffette, a Boston architect, designed a rustic-style cottage for Curtis, who named it Thuya Lodge after the indigenous white cedar in the area. In 1886, Curtis married Amelie Eugenie Lewandowski, a native of Paris, France, and they had one son, Henry J. Curtis. For the remainder of his life, Curtis summered in Northeast Harbor and wintered in Massachusetts, in or near Boston.

No collection of Curtis's papers or records is known, but evidence indicates that he referred to himself as a landscape gardener and as a landscape engineer. Despite his association with Massachusetts, Curtis's known works were all in Maine. One of his first designs was for a cemetery in Bucksport in 1872. His remaining work appears to be primarily garden plans for private residences, including Mrs. Bowler's Cottage in Bar Harbor in 1884; Hulls Cove Point in Mount Desert in 1888; Heights of Buena Vista in Hancock in 1888; High Head in Mount Desert in 1888; Spruce Point Road in Boothbay, in 1888; The Breeze (Mrs. A. P. Peabody Cottage) in Bar Harbor in 1896; and a garden for Joseph Bowen at Hulls Cove in Mount Desert (date unknown).

Curtis published several pamphlets between 1910 and 1925. Topics included tobacco and the oldest tree in Boston Common. One essay purported to consist of a conversation between an apple tree and Curtis. However, the writing demonstrates that he read widely in history and botany. The sixty-three-page essay is a witty, closely reasoned argument against the prohibition of alcohol. He traces the intertwined roots of his own family, the origins of attitudes toward alcohol, and various species of apple trees back to Tudor England. He argues that "man and his best vegetable friend the Apple progressed side by side in the early settlement of New England" and that hard cider was a principle "source of nutriment" in the American colonies. He rejoices in fermentation as a natural process and denounces the temperance movement as a wrong-headed rejection of one aspect of creation. He concludes by noting that the native fruits of Northeast Harbor—including apples, cherries, huckleberries, blueberries, strawberries, raspberries, blackberries, and cranberries—fill the air with the "the perfume of potential alcohol" and he joins the plants and the bees in a murmuring "chorus of approval" celebrating the fruitful relationship between man and nature.

Asticou Terrace steps, Mount Desert Island, Maine. (Photo courtesy of Nancy Slade)

After establishing his residence at Thuya Lodge, Curtis began working on his own Thuya Gardens, a project that commenced in 1880 and continued until his death in 1928. His concept for Thuya Gardens is wholly in keeping with the rustic style of his home. The lookouts, steps, and retaining walls are all composed of rough, local granite; constructed elements are kept to a minimum and follow the contours of the land. His plans incorporated the paths adjacent to his summer home, adding plantings to enhance the existing landscape. The use of native conifers—juniper, cedar, and spruce—to define the setting and frame the vistas make the garden seem natural.

In 1905, he created a trust to maintain the 5-acre site as a public park; by 1928, he had added 15 acres to the park, and in that year he appointed Charles K. Savage, a local resident and proprietor of the nearby Asticou Inn, as sole trustee. Today the gardens reflect Savage's realization of Curtis's vision, and although it is impossible to assign some specific elements to either of them, the lower pathways and lookouts are attributed to Curtis.

Curtis passed away in 1928. Today, visitors to Asticou Terrace on Mount Desert Island, in Maine, will find a carved granite memorial that recognizes Joseph H. Curtis's design and stewardship contributions: "The Asticou Terraces are his gift for the quiet recreation of the people of this town and their summer guests."

Curtis, Joseph Henry. *As long as there is a Single Apple Tree left, New England never can be made Bone Dry, is the message received by Joseph Henry Curtis from a friend, a Wise Old Apple.* Published by the author, 1917.

Curtis, Joseph Henry. *Life of Campestris Ulm, The Oldest Inhabitant of Boston Common.* Boston: W.B. Clark, 1910.

Description of the Great Fight Waged by the Grim Puritans of Massachusetts Bay to Suppress Tobacco. Published by H.C. Baker, 1925.

Savage, Charles K. *Asticou Terraces Trust, Report of the Trustee,* 1937–1965. Typescript in the collection of the Northeast Harbor Library, Northeast Harbor, Maine. Provides insight into Curtis's contributions and Savage's ongoing realization of Curtis's vision.

John Bryan

DAHL, HILBERT EINAR
(1893–1967)
LANDSCAPE ARCHITECT,
ENGINEER, PLANNER

Hilbert Einar Dahl was born in Chicago in 1893 to parents of Norwegian descent. The family relocated to the Pittsburgh area shortly after his birth. He received his bachelor of science in landscape gardening from Pennsylvania State College in 1917, and then served in the United States Army from 1918 to 1919 as a sergeant in the 319th Regiment Infantry. He continued his studies at Penn State in 1920, writing a thesis with direction from the Department of Horticulture on possibilities for "The Regional Plan of State College and Vicinity." As a result, Dahl earned a master of science degree. He stayed on, working as an assistant professor of landscape architecture from 1923 to 1927. Briefly Dahl served as landscape architect for the State of Pennsylvania, and then opened a private practice as a landscape architect, registered professional engineer, and site planner.

A member of the new Baha'i faith since 1905, Dahl visited Chicago in 1926 to see the site that had been selected for the first Baha'i temple in the country, and to get married. At this time, the unusual structure was still on architect Louis Bourgeois's drawing board. No landscape improvements had been made to the 6-acre plot in the residential, lakefront community of Wilmette, Illinois. Dahl was deeply concerned that there was no overall site plan. He offered to start a design for the lawn and garden areas around the caretaker's home, the only structure built at that time; however, the trustees were not yet ready to proceed. Dahl returned to Pennsylvania, living and working in the town of Erie, until he moved to Chicago in 1936.

Carl Berg and Hilbert Einar Dahl at the construction of Baha'i Temple gardens, Wilmette, Illinois, 1952. (National Baha'i Archives, United States)

While there, he became a judge for the Chicago Flower Show, held annually at Navy Pier, an interest that he would keep for the rest of his life.

Within a few years, the Dahls moved to Charleston, West Virginia, where he established another private practice, according to his letterhead, designing parks, recreational projects, subdivisions, housing, and private estates. He also worked as the associate chief of the West Virginia State Parks. By 1951, Dahl and his wife had moved to the Louisville, Kentucky, area, and there Dahl partnered for some years with engineer and designer Carl Berg. They belonged to many professional organizations, including the American Society of Landscape Architects, American Institute of Planners, American Institute of Park Executives, and American Society of Planning Officials, as well as being registered Professional Engineers. Berg and Dahl expanded their business in 1956 by opening the Cloverleaf Garden

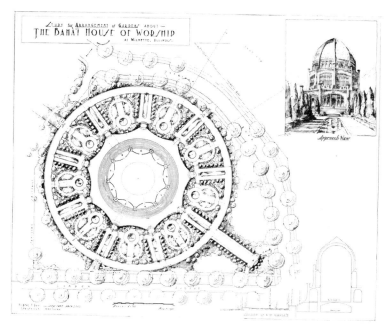

"Study for the Arrangement of Gardens at The Baha'i House of Worship, at Wilmette, Illinois," 1951. (National Baha'i Archives, United States)

Center offering "The Best of Everything for the Garden," while continuing their professional practice. Dahl also served as the associate director of the Kentucky State Parks, working with both parks and state-run tuberculosis sanatoria.

In the meantime, construction had moved along on the ornate, 190-foot high Baha'i Temple in Wilmette. Finally, in 1938, the trustees asked Dahl for a garden plan. To complement the nine-sided building, and incorporate such Baha'i sacred symbols as the circle and sacred numbers (nine and nineteen) into a cohesive and workable plan, Dahl devised a simple and elegant solution. Nine nearly circular individual gardens, separated by nine approaches, would surround the building in a ring. Each garden contained a 19-foot wide circular pool with a fountain, part of Dahl's intention to create an Oriental atmosphere reminiscent of Persian gardens. This reference complemented the Middle Eastern roots of the faith and the exotic edifice they were to encompass. In his original concept, Dahl planned long reflecting pools in each of the approaches as well, and concrete seating ringing each of the interior gardens. (Due to financial constraints, the rough Chicago climate, and

a simplified aesthetic on the part of the trustees, these were never installed.) However, all available funds were needed to complete the building at this time, and no substantial work was done in the gardens.

Nevertheless, an ongoing concern for Dahl was the immense amount of fill that the trustees had decided to put around the basement of the temple. The trustees had decided to elevate the building above the rest of the neighborhood by raising the grade about ten feet immediately surrounding the building. The visual impression was that the temple was sitting on higher ground. Without even minimal site planning, they began to purchase fill of questionable quality from lakeshore and railroad grade-change excavations in the area. Dahl conscientiously asked that they stop until a plan could be developed, but they rejected this advice and continued to fill.

Finally, in January 1951, with the temple completed inside and out, and the surrounding grade level raised, all attention turned to the gardens, which now needed to be installed for the May 1953 dedication. The trustees reexamined Dahl's 1938 plan, "deemed it basically sound," and asked him to elaborate on the design. They also asked several other area landscape architects to submit plans, including F. A. Cushing Smith, Swain Nelson, C. D. Wagstaff, and Ralph Rodney Root.* By early June, when they finally chose Dahl's plan, there was just a little over a year for construction, plant selection, and installation.

Overseeing the work himself, Dahl was able to complete the grading, walks, terraces, and garden bed layout before the dedication ceremony. The major planting was accomplished, including the columnar juniper allées along the approach walks. Their similarity to the cypresses of Persia contributed to a more Middle Eastern than Midwestern effect. The new gardens were featured in an article by Dahl called "Baha'i Temple Gardens: The Landscape Setting of a Unique Architectural Monument" in the July 1953 issue of *Landscape Architecture.*

During the next several years, Dahl, with the help of head gardener Wyatt Cooper, managed to implement the rest of his planting plan, amend the soil to adjust the uneven quality of the fill, and change plant species as needed. By the early 1960s, they had achieved the gardens Dahl had envisioned. Dahl and Cooper also won awards for a model of the temple and gardens they exhibited at the Chicago Flower and Garden Show. After retiring to Royal Oak, Michigan, Dahl continued to consult on management of the temple grounds, until his death in 1967.

Dahl, Hilbert Einar. "Baha'i Temple Gardens: The Landscape Setting of a Unique Architectural Monument." *Landscape Architecture* 43 (July 1953), 145–49. Insight into the concept and design of the Baha'i Temple garden.

Geiger, Barbara. *The Creation of the Gardens and Terrace at the Baha'i House of Worship in Wilmette, Illinois.* Baha'i National Spiritual Assembly of North America, 2002. This comprehensive historic narrative recounts the Baha'i Temple's formative first five decades. The article utilizes the extensive holdings of the Temple Archives in Wilmette, Illinois, including correspondence between Dahl and the Temple Trustees.

Whitmore, Bruce. *The Dawning Place.* Wilmette, Ill.: Baha'i Publishing Trust, 1984. A history of the entire site, which includes information about the gardens.

Barbara Geiger

DE FOREST, ELIZABETH KELLAM
(1898–1984)
LANDSCAPE ARCHITECT, WRITER

Elizabeth Kellam was born in San Francisco, California, in 1898. She was the daughter of Frederick B. and Edith Bishop Kellam, knowledgeable and enthusiastic gardeners who had an extensive botanical library. The young Kellam attended Miss Hamlin's School in San Francisco and studied at Vassar College, where her literary career began as editor of *Miscellany News.* In 1919, she graduated cum laude with bachelor's degrees in English and psychology. Returning to San Francisco, she matriculated at Stanford University where she earned her master's degree in psychology in 1920.

In 1916, Elizabeth went to Santa Barbara for the first time to visit a San Francisco friend. Santa Barbara was a small, summer community, and Elizabeth met landscape architect **Lockwood de Forest III**. They married in 1925, the same year as the devastating Santa Barbara earthquake. After the earthquake, the de Forests joined with other prominent architects, philanthropists, artists, and planning visionaries, forming the Community Arts Association. Together with such locals as George Washington Smith, **Francis Townsend Underhill**, Lutah Maria Riggs, Pearl Chase, Reginald Johnson, James Osborne Craig, Bernard Hoffman, Carlton Winslow, and Wright Ludington, the de Forests rebuilt Santa Barbara in the Spanish Colonial Revival style.

In that same year, the de Forests were approached by the Community Arts Association to start a monthly garden publication to educate Santa Barbarans on appropriate plantings and horticulture for the new architecture and the mild climate of Santa Barbara. The response was the modest periodical *The Santa Barbara Gardener,* co-produced by the energetic and knowledgeable couple. It was a literary work of genius; it combined Elizabeth's elegant prose; Lockwood's landscape design philosophy; Elizabeth's exhaustive knowledge of plants and their culture; and Lockwood's discussion of style, color, composition, and proportion, with spirited responses and commentary from prominent horticulturists and designers. There were regular contributions from such luminaries as E. O. Orpet, **Kate Olivia Sessions**, Lucy Foster Sexton, W.

J. Pettingill, **Lester Rowntree, Florence Yoch,** and **Lucille Council,** Hugh Evans, Francis E. Lester, Sydney B. Mitchell, Theodore Payne, and Victor Reiter Jr. Elizabeth de Forest's strengths in planting design were featured particularly in her articles on gray foliages, bulbs of South Africa, and perennial beds. There were also regular columns from San Francisco, Pasadena, and Los Angeles. Eventually included were poignant commentaries on the invasion in Europe, victory gardens, and appeals to send seeds to the Finnish Relief Fund in 1940. In 1942, Lockwood joined the United States Air Corps to work with the Camouflage Division disguising California defense factories with special paint finishes and landscaping. Elizabeth, not wanting to carry on alone, ceased publication of *The Santa Barbara Gardener.*

Elizabeth and Lockwood de Forest in the front seat of a 1930 "Buffalo" car. (Courtesy of the collection of Syndey Baumgarter)

During its short publication, *The Santa Barbara Gardener* became a pioneering garden publication that was extremely influential in the community. The publication touted the importance of regionally unique landscaping, and in doing so, encouraged new planting trends throughout Southern California.

Lockwood returned from service after World War II and was engaged to assist his friend Wright Ludington with the transformation of the entrance to the Santa Barbara Museum of Art. It was in the midst of this commission, in 1949, that pneumonia suddenly claimed Lockwood's life. Elizabeth rose to the challenge and, while raising their two sons alone, finished the commission with Ludington and architect Lutah Riggs as a memorial to her husband. Lockwood had many other major commissions underway at the time of his death, including a residence and garden for Dr. Ernest Watson, which Elizabeth finished with her signature palette of gray plants and the native California plants so beloved by Lockwood. The resulting garden melded seamlessly into the oak woodland of Montecito.

She continued on with his commissions and received her own California Landscape Architect's license in 1952, the first year of licensing in the state. Among her own commissions were two residences for Wright Ludington. Hesperides, the Ludington residence on a mountaintop in Montecito, was designed by Lutah Riggs. Together Riggs and de Forest built a Classical/Moderne house and garden for Ludington's collection of Roman and Greek artifacts and paintings. The gardens spilled down the hillside with lavender and rosemary fields. California native mountain lilac beneath olive groves, accents of Italian cypress, acanthus, lily ponds, a classical Roman outdoor bath, and a plein air theater were all a simple frame for the view of the mountains above and the sea far below. Another Ludington residence, October Hill, was also built as a gallery for art and antiquities on a similar hill, lower in elevation, again with a gray/black/green plant palette, and an even more modernistic rendition of classic Roman architecture by Riggs.

De Forest collaborated with **Thomas Dolliver Church** on many of his projects in Santa Barbara by advising on appropriate plantings for the Montecito climate, much as she had assisted Lockwood in his landscape work. Other projects included the Dorothy Crofton-Atkins and the John Mitchell Jr., gardens. For thirty-four years, starting in 1950, she served on the Santa Barbara Botanic Garden Board, following the tradition of her father's chairmanship and Lockwood's service and design work. Hers was a hands-on service to the garden, as she frequently walked the grounds and advised on design as chairman of the Grounds Committee. Her favorite regional historical garden project was that of the La Purisina Mission restoration, with twelve years of service on the Advisory

Left: Alice Keck Park, Santa Barbara, California, 2002 view. (Photo by Charles A. Birnbaum)

Below: One of de Forest's residential garden designs is seen at "October Hill," Santa Barbara, California, ca. 2000 view. (Photo by Charles A. Birnbaum)

Committee. She helped found the Santa Barbara Senior Center, providing housing for elderly, low-income Santa Barbarans. She designed its gardens and served for thirty-two years as their Garden Committee Chairman.

As the California vice regent for the Mount Vernon Ladies Association from 1957 to 1984, de Forest reorganized the accounting system and served as chairman of the Grounds Committee. In 1983, she designed the Lamont Garden at the new Ann Pamela Cunningham Building on the Mount Vernon grounds. Her literary talent shone in the 1982 publication of her authoritative book *The Garden and Grounds at Mount Vernon.*

She advised on the launching of *Pacific Horticulture Magazine.* She provided articles including a piece, "A Parcel of Rosemaries," outlining the many species in Santa Barbara, including the Lockwood de Forest variety. She was an articulate speaker, notably on historic Santa Barbara gardens and estates, illustrated by the many slide lectures that she delivered on the region.

Beginning in 1975, de Forest served as the supervising landscape architect for a new city park in Santa Barbara in cooperation with the Santa Barbara Botanic Garden and Mrs. Alice Keck Park, the donor of this horticultural garden to the city. The resulting park continues to be a mid-city refuge full of unusual plant specimens, year-round flower color, and a small lake.

The de Forests' design philosophies were in complete agreement: "The garden should take advantage of the climate, with outdoor rooms, affording privacy, while borrowing the view." Furthermore, selectively chosen materials appropriate for the site, attention to proportion, and usability for those inhabiting the garden were essential priorities. While de Forest recognized the need for an overarching functional idea in a landscape plan, she saw contrast as the energy of design and believed the form must express order, balance, and rhythm. Most of all, though, de Forest believed that the relation of the garden scheme to its surroundings, with a progression of the form and materials of the garden leading to a view of the greater natural landscape was of utmost importance.

Elizabeth de Forest died in Santa Barbara in 1984. Following her death, the Santa Barbara Art Museum's public memorial for Lockwood de Forest was extended to include Elizabeth.

de Forest, Elizabeth Kellam. "The Gardens and Grounds at Mount Vernon: How George Washington Planned and Planted Them." February 1982. Original transcript drafts by Sydney Baumgartner. The Mount Vernon Ladies Association of the Union, Mount Vernon, Virginia.

de Forest, Elizabeth. "A Parcel of Rosemaries." *Pacific Horticulture* 37, no. 4 (1976), 40–42. Origin of the "Lockwood de Forest" variety of rosemary in the de Forest Garden.

de Forest, Lockwood, and Elizabeth Kellam. *The Santa Barbara Gardener.* 1925–1942. Published under the auspices of the Planting Committee of the Community Arts Association. Volumes 1 through 17. A monthly magazine with garden design and cultural advice written by the de Forests with contributions from California designers and horticulturists.

Sydney Baumgartner

DETMER, JULIAN FRANCIS
(1865–1958)
NURSERYMAN, HORTICULTURIST

Julian Francis Detmer was born in Cleveland, Ohio, on December 4, 1865, to Henry and Josephine Detmer. Both parents were merchant tailors who founded a small but successful business. As a child, Julian Detmer was interested in only two things—acting and gardening. After a failed attempt at acting, Detmer entered the family business and trained as a tailor. Soon after, his remarkable business savvy took over as he formed a number of woolen distribution companies including the Detmer Woolen Company, one of the largest in the world at the time. As a result, Detmer attained great wealth. By 1900, he moved his headquarters to New York City and settled in a country estate in Tarrytown, New York. Detmer's incredible success allowed him to launch his second career into his lifelong passion of landscape design.

Without any formal training, Detmer set upon a task that seemed preposterous: to design and then landscape more than 180 acres of land into two separate arboretums. However, true to his confident form, Detmer created two enchanting arboretums; Edgemont was a part of the estate in which he lived and, the Evergreens was just 2 miles east of Edgemont. Detmer traveled the world in search of specimens that not only fit the different schemes of the arboreta, but were also unique to North America. Accordingly, he is credited with introducing a number of species of evergreens and flowering shrubs to this country.

Julian Francis Detmer (*on right, in rocking chair*). (Courtesy of the collection of Steven Baronti)

5. LAWN WALK.

Above: Lawn Walk at Edgemont Nursery, Tarrytown, New York, postcard image, ca. 1937. (Courtesy of the collection of Steven Baronti)

Right: Fountain Pool at Evergreens Nursery, Tarrytown, New York, postcard image, ca. 1937. (Courtesy of the collection of Steven Baronti)

The arboreta, also known as Detmer Nurseries, contained intricately laid out pathways that led visitors through an array of stunning shrubs, trees, and perennials. The Azalea Ring, Hemlock Hill, and Lover's Walk were three of the vistas set up to lead visitors through a tapestry of plantings. The Detmer Nurseries gained legendary status among the locals, who were encouraged to visit. As an indication of the site's beauty, one visitor stated, "I hope to go to heaven some time but I don't expect to find it any more beautiful than here." Visitors from as far away as California would flock to the nurseries on the weekends. It was commonplace to see a long line of cars lined up waiting for the gates to be opened. Students of art and landscape design would come to study Detmer's design. There was no entrance fee; Detmer simply wanted people to bask in the beauty of his gardens.

Although the nursery business thrived, Detmer's focus remained on the design of the arboreta. The Detmer style (at least as far as the arboreta were concerned) was neither eclectic nor formal; rather, it could be called a stream of consciousness approach to design. However, planning was a part of their development. For example, a vista consisting of azaleas, laurels, and andromeda was carefully connected to a field of perennials, which in turn was bordered by a veritable forest of pines and firs.

The Detmer Nurseries also served as proving ground for the propagation of thousands of varieties of evergreens. Detmer experimented with the

FOUNTAIN POOL.

hybridization of perennials and was recognized for his design of a rock garden at the International Flower Show at the Grand Central Palace in 1920. He also received awards for his designs and assortment of evergreen propagations.

Julian Francis Detmer died on November 26, 1958, but his legacy as a visionary remains. One of his life aims was to "have a cheerful countenance and always wear a smile," something he achieved with the design and construction of Detmer Nurseries. Detmer's landscape designs were small in number, yet their influence is still felt today. His arboreta culminated fifty years of a dedicated love of landscaping. Detmer forged the way for those who lack formal training, but whose talents may nonetheless contribute greatly to the world of landscape design.

After Detmer's death, the Detmer Nurseries designed and installed the gate exhibit for the 1964 World's Fair and designed and installed the landscaping for the Tarrytown Hilton and other office developments in the area. One of its great magnolia trees now proudly stands in front of the Baltimore Museum of Art. Sadly, the arboreta were sold to corporations that were unconcerned with the history of Detmer and his work. They were gutted and ravaged by office and condominium developers. The design and blueprints of the Detmer Nurseries still exist and are the property of Detmer's grandson, Eugene Julian Detmer.

Good, Paul. "Sleepy Hollow Estate, Wonderland of Nature," *New York World Telegram and Sun,* October 3, 1953. Article on Detmer's arboreta with interview.

Griffin, Ernest Freeland. "Julian Francis Detmer." *Who's Who in America: Westchester County and Its People, A Record.* New York: Lewis Historical Publishing Company, Inc., 1946. Historical analysis of Julian Francis Detmer.

"Julian F. Detmer Marks The Fiftieth Anniversary Of His Estate, Nursery." *Tarrytown Daily News,* June 24, 1950. Article detailing origins of Detmer's interest in landscaping with interview.

Steven Baronti

DILLON, JULIA LESTER
(1871–1959)
LANDSCAPE ARCHITECT, GARDEN WRITER

Julia Lester was born on March 9, 1871, in Warren County, Georgia. Her family had deep southern roots; both parents were Georgians. The family garden made a deep impression on young Julia, she later recalled, remembering the roses that survived an 1875 tornado. In 1882, the Lesters moved to an ancestral family home in Augusta, Georgia, where her garden interests flourished as she grew up. Deciding on education as a profession, Julia Lester attended Nashville's Peabody College, now part of Vanderbilt University, graduating in 1890. She taught school in Augusta for several years and married William Bennett Dillon in 1892. Tragedy struck when he died little more than one year later. In addition to this bereavement, Julia Lester Dillon had suffered a profound hearing loss, probably from diphtheria.

Dillon resumed her teaching career in 1896 but by 1907 was seeking a new direction. Although her hearing loss was progressively worsening, she went north to study landscape design. Newspaper articles report that she studied in "the landscape branch" at Columbia University and art history at Harvard. The first degree in

Julia Lester Dillon, from *House and Garden,* November 1926.

Memorial Park, Sumter, South Carolina, ca. 1917, from Dillon's book, *The Blossom Circle of the Year in Southern Gardens,* 1922.

landscape architecture in the United States was granted in 1901. With academic programs in their formative years, many landscape architects still learned their profession by working with existing practitioners and through reading and travel. Displaying both ingenuity and determination, Dillon may have done the same, utilizing professional connections in the Boston area.

Julia Lester Dillon was committed to learning how to read lips. Boston might have attracted her because the Muller-Walle School of Lip Reading, founded in 1902, provided advanced training techniques for the deaf. In addition, the Boston area offered women several opportunities for the study of landscape design, including programs at the Bussey Institute and the Massachusetts Institute of Technology. Most pertinently, Julia Lester Dillon herself indicated that her studies included a Harvard connection.

Julia Lester Dillon was widely known in her home city through her involvement with numerous municipal activities. **James Sturgis Pray**, head of Harvard's program in landscape architecture, who was instrumental in the foundation of the Cambridge School in 1915, had strong ties to Augusta, completing public and private commissions during the years Dillon contemplated a career change. Several principals of the Boston firm of Pray, Hubbard & White (**Henry Vincent Hubbard** and **Stanley Hart White**) showed a strong commitment to the education of women as well as men in the profession of landscape architecture. In 1911, the year Julia Lester Dillon entered practice, Pray, Hubbard & White designed the Francis Hardy garden in Augusta, Georgia. Dillon and Pray likely met at this time. Dillon was almost certainly

associated with that project, featuring it in numerous illustrations in her book, *The Blossom Circle of the Year in Southern Gardens,* as well as on the cover.

Beginning her practice in Augusta, Julia Lester Dillon worked on residential commissions but, in marked contrast to other women practitioners, entered the public sector by designing the grounds of post offices and custom houses for the U.S. Department of the Treasury. From 1914 to 1917, she planned and executed such projects in North Carolina, South Carolina, Georgia, and Florida. Dillon also designed parks and school landscapes throughout the South. In 1916, she designed the landscape at the post office in Sumter, South Carolina, where she made many friends.

At the close of World War I in November 1918, Julia Lester Dillon was among the landscape architects who engaged in the design of memorials to the dead. She urged the "planting of memorial trees and hero groves" in her home state. In early 1920, Sumter officials, remembering her work in that city, asked her to design a park, to be called Memorial Park, out of what she described as a wilderness, which included a house, outbuildings, a burned garage, an abandoned auto, cotton stalks, cockleburs, and rubbish. The site also featured wonderful old trees and rolling ground. Dillon set to work immediately, paid on a day-to-day basis by the City Council. Three months later, pleased with her work, the council offered her a full-time position as city landscape architect, the only such appointment in South Carolina at that time. Dillon accepted, determined to see her design fully implemented and maintained.

Julia Lester Dillon remained the city's landscape architect until 1948. In addition to Memorial Park, she designed other parks, as well as church, school, library, and hospital properties. She planted hundreds of trees and shrubs along the city's streets and maintained these plantings for decades. As time permitted, she also engaged in private residential work. Affected by illness, her voice was difficult to understand; an African American man, regrettably known only by his first name, Bob, assisted her in her work.

Dillon's training as an educator was not forgotten. In

1931, she wrote a locally published pamphlet, *Landscape Design, Twenty Lessons,* using *Landscape Gardening* by **Frank Albert Waugh** as a text. She encouraged the knowledge and appreciation of landscape design through her work with civic organizations and by founding the Sumter Garden Club. This association was important at a time when garden clubs played a critical role in stimulating the growth of the profession of landscape architecture.

Through her writing about gardens and landscape design, Julia Lester Dillon reached beyond Sumter to a regional and national audience. Focusing on gardening in the South, early in her career she wrote a column with practical information for *House and Garden,* as well as several important articles about notable southern gardens. During these same years in the 1910s and early 1920s, she also wrote for *The Florists' Exchange,* a how-to garden magazine. Dillon also wrote assiduously for newspapers in South Carolina and Georgia.

The 1922 publication of her book, *The Blossom Circle of the Year in Southern Gardens,* cemented Julia Lester Dillon's reputation as an authority on southern gardens. *House and Garden* noted the fact in 1926, proclaiming her "prominent place" in the garden world. The attractive green volume was addressed to the many amateur gardeners who had written to her from all over the South, requesting advice relevant to their region. Dillon sought to answer these questions, not only on the "practical and helpful side," but "something higher, which is the esthetic side of landscape work." She spoke to women in particular who, she asserted, "are now thoroughly awakened to their responsibility and opportunity." She noted how southern women were planting school grounds, courthouse squares, parks, railroad stations, and the highways rapidly being built in the new automobile age. While Dillon's book is oriented more toward horticulture than design, its numerous illustrations of effective residential gardens, coupled with textual references, advanced knowledge of landscape design for southern residences.

Julia Lester Dillon also reached a wide audience through *The Flower Grower* magazine, a popular national gardening publication. She wrote a column about gardening in the South from June 1936 through June 1954. Again, while horticultural in focus, the column offered suggestions for better landscape design in southern gardens. Her audience included many in other parts of the country, who traveled in growing numbers to winter residences in the South.

Increasing disability, including blindness, eventually ended Dillon's long career. She died in 1959.

Dillon, Julia Lester. *The Blossom Circle of the Year in Southern Gardens.* New York: A. T. De La Mare, 1922. The practitioner's only book, it includes twenty-one chapters and is heavily illustrated. It is a seasonal approach to gardening in the South.

Dillon, Julia Lester. "A New Home in an Old Suburb." *House and Garden,* December 1914, 358–60, 391–92. Dillon's description of "Coniston," a Country Place–era estate in Augusta, Georgia, in whose landscape design she likely assisted.

Erdeljac, Diane. "Blossom Circle, The Life of Julia Lester Dillon." *Magnolia* 16, no. 3 (Spring 2001). An introduction to Dillon, including many oral-history reminiscences from her niece.

Virginia Lopez Begg

DORMON, CAROLINE CORONEOS
(1888–1971)
WRITER, HORTICULTURIST, CONSERVATIONIST, TEACHER

Born in 1888 at Briarwood, her family's summer home in the piney woods of north Louisiana, Caroline Dormon claimed for herself the "gift of wild things," her ability to experience "a thousand things that no one else sees." Her landscape designs were efforts to offer this gift to others, through preservation, education, and the cultivation of hundreds of species indigenous or adapted to the southern climate. Self-taught as a landscaper and a horticulturist, Dormon took part in a number of projects that changed the look of and the response to landscape in the South, particularly in Louisiana. "The native trees and flowers of a state constitute a natural heritage," she wrote, "one which should be protected and shared in common."

Dormon, who was affectionately known as Carrie, attributed her love of the outdoors to her parents. Her father, James, was an attorney and amateur naturalist; her mother, Carolyn, was a writer whose novel, *Under the Magnolias,* celebrated a legacy of agrarian values. After earning a bachelor of arts from Judson College in Marion,

Caroline Dormon in her "wildwood."
(Dormon Collection, Cammie G. Henry
Research Center, Watson Library,
Northwestern State University of Louisiana)

Welfare, Dormon designed native plantings on the grounds of hospitals in Pineville and Monroe from 1938 to 1941. Less successful was her effort in the early 1940s as consultant to the state's Highway Department. Collecting photographs of naturalistic roadsides, she encouraged the planting of pines, oaks, magnolias, hollies, redbuds, and crabapples. Too often nurserymen with non-native plants to sell prevailed.

Advocating native landscaping in lectures and publications, Dormon also influenced home gardening in the South. In the 1920s, Dormon caught the enthusiasm for native irises, collecting widely and experimenting with their cultivation in the bog garden at Briarwood. Working within the network of "irisiacs," which included John K. Small of the New York Botanical Garden and Mary Swords Debaillon in New Orleans, she popularized their use in her "Louisiana Iris Notebooks," introduced several important cultivars, and helped to establish the Louisiana Iris Society. From 1930 to 1950, she and her sister-in-law, Ruth Dormon, operated Felicity Wild Gardens, a mail-order business offering "native plants and shrubs & rare Louisiana irises."

Alabama, in 1907, Dormon returned to Louisiana to teach. By 1917, she and her sister, Virginia, had settled permanently at Briarwood in a log home. Here Dormon found the central theme of her life's work: "This unspoiled beauty must be preserved for future generations to enjoy."

For three decades, Dormon held appointments that allowed her to shape Louisiana landscape in broad, if sometimes indirect ways. In two terms with the Department of Conservation, Division of Forestry (1921–1923 and 1927–1931), she created the state's first program of conservation education and published *Forest Trees of Louisiana*. The first woman to work in the state's forestry division, she visited parish schools with a slide presentation and a mission for schools to teach forestry and plant trees. As Chairman of Forestry for the Louisiana Federation of Women's Clubs, she helped to initiate the campaign to save what historic maps called the Kisatchie Wold, some 600,000 acres of "kingly longleaf pines" growing "to perfection in an idyllic setting" over seven parishes. In 1930, after nearly a decade of her tireless advocacy, the tract was designated the Kisatchie National Forest.

After leaving forestry work, she continued lecturing on conservation issues and campaigning for a state arboretum and park system. She was also instrumental in the designation of El Camino Real, the extension of the Natchez Trace through central Louisiana and into Texas. As a landscape consultant to the state's Board of Public

In her mid-fifties, Dormon settled into a habit of home at Briarwood, dividing her time among gardening, writing, and illustrating. She contributed regularly to *Home Gardening for the South,* which focused on the "great garden movement in the South," from 1940 to 1952. In its first issue, she argues in her article, "Louisiana, Our Garden," that the unsurpassed beauty of the state's flora had been planted by nature's "lavish hand" and must be protected from humans, "the most destructive animals known." The titles of her botanical books—all of which she illustrated with her own line drawings, photographs, and watercolors—reveal a similar passion: *Wild Flowers of Louisiana* (1934), *Flowers Native to the Deep South* (1958), and *Natives Preferred* (1965). Dedicated to amateur gardeners for whom the "finding of a new flower is a real adventure," these handbooks favor an invisible hand in design. A plantswoman first, Dormon typically was fond of the beauty of a wild spot, framing it by laying a path of pine straw, making a clearing to give the view the needed margin, or adding an understory of wildflowers. "Wild" and "native" and "preserve" were the key words in her design vocabulary. Her design tendency was from naturalistic toward natural, in the tradition of the landscape architect whom, as she often noted in her correspondence, she most admired, **Jens Jensen**. Dormon also corresponded extensively with Elizabeth Lawrence.* Together, they promoted southern gardening practices for residents of the region.

With **Ellen Biddle Shipman**, in the 1930s and 1940s, she consulted on the gardens at Longue Vue in New Orleans for Edgar and Edith Stern. (Edith, a native plant enthusiast, had underwritten the publication of *Wildflowers of Louisiana*.) While the master design was decidedly Shipman's, Dormon consulted frequently with Edith Stern, usually through the mail, proposing native plantings and identifying local nurseries with dependable stock. The Dormons' nursery, Felicity Wild Gardens, supplied Louisiana irises and violas; Nik Nak Garden in Raleigh, North Carolina, supplied three species of crabapple, to ensure continuous bloom at the Bamboo Road entrance. Through her network of garden correspondents, Dormon hand-shaped and developed Shipman's plans. Her work at Hodges Gardens near Many, Louisiana, was similar. To forest-magnate-turned-conservationist A. J. Hodges, she wrote, "Let me hasten to disabuse your mind of the idea that I have 'gardens'! I have 120 acres of wildwood . . . I do have many rare and beautiful things—but often you have to look through the briars to see them!" She was hired by Hodges as "Consultant on Natural Areas" to create natural gardens to frame the formal rose garden and beds of annuals.

In her life's work at Briarwood, the natural landscape was at the center, not the periphery. In her sixty years of tending, she created an iris bog, the bay garden, a writer's cabin overlooking a human-made pond similar in dimensions to that of Thoreau's Walden, a wildflower plot near the log cabin, and miles of rambles through the pine woods. "You can see native Louisiana trees and flowers 'as is,' with no landscaping. I have a few other attractive shrubs native to other parts of the South, but specialize in Louisiana flora," she wrote.

In 1960, Dormon was awarded the Eloise Paine Luquer Medal for achievement in botany from the Garden Club of America and she received an honorary doctorate of science from Louisiana State University in 1965. In 1966, Briarwood was named a "sanctuary for the flora of the South" by the American Horticultural Society. Today Briarwood is under the protection of the Foundation of the Caroline Dormon Nature Preserve, in accordance with her wishes in her last days in 1971.

The Caroline Dormon Collection, at the Cammie G. Henry Research Center, Watson Memorial Library, Northwestern State University of Louisiana, Natchitoches, (318-357-4585. www.nsula.edu/watson_library/CGHRC.HTM), includes archival records, correspondence, illustrations, and photographs of and by Dormon.

Bonta, Marcia Myers. "Carrie Dormon, Queen of the Forest Kingdom." *Women in the Field: America's Pioneering Women Naturalists*. College Station: Texas A&M University Press, 1991, 250–61. A valuable overview of Dormon's life and work within the context of women's work in various disciplines.

Cole, Karen. "A Chapter in Southern Garden Writing: The Correspondence of Elizabeth Lawrence and Caroline Dormon." *Journal of the New England Garden History Society* 9 (Fall 2001), 45–54. A study of Dormon's collaboration with Elizabeth Lawrence in their work to bring southern gardening practice from the estate to the backyard garden.

Johnson, Fran Holman. *"The Gift of the Wild Things": The Life of Caroline Dormon*. Lafayette, La.: The Center for Louisiana Studies, 1990. A book-length biography of Dormon, drawing upon her writings, memoirs, and correspondence.

Karen Cole

DOUGLASS, DAVID BATES
(1790–1849)
ENGINEER, CEMETERY DESIGNER

David Bates Douglass was born on March 21, 1790, in Pompton, New Jersey. In 1810, Douglass entered Yale University as a sophomore intending to become a civil engineer, and graduated with a bachelor's degree in 1813. Immediately after graduating, he was commissioned by the army as second lieutenant in the Engineering Corps and promoted to captain in 1814 for his distinguished and gallant performance in the field. Douglass's remarkable service during the War of 1812 led the army to offer him a teaching position at West Point in 1815; he became chairman of the mathematics department in 1820 and professor of civil engineering in 1823. Douglass taught at West Point until 1831, when he left to pursue his engineering work full time.

Like many educated men of his generation, Douglass was well versed in several disciplines and his career reflects a broad range of skills and interests. At age thirty, he was assigned to survey the northwestern regions of the Michigan Territory for the 1820 Lewis Cass Expedition. In 1825, Douglass accepted a position from DeWitt Clinton, supervising the construction of a section of the Erie Canal, ultimately becoming a national expert on canal construction and assisting with projects in New York, Pennsylvania, and New Jersey. Douglass became chief engineer on the Morris & Essex Canal in New Jersey. In 1831, he moved to Brooklyn and in 1832, was appointed a professor of mathematics at the University of the City of New York, where he later became a lecturer in civil engineering and architecture. While there, he designed the university's new building in Washington Square.

In 1833, Douglass surveyed the railroad route from Brooklyn to Jamaica, New York. Subsequently from 1833 to 1836, he was appointed engineer of the Croton Aqueduct, which supplied drinking water to Manhattan for many years. Douglass made the requisite survey examinations and created all the plans and details of this great work. Douglass's tenure in Brooklyn and New York City led to his greatest design achievement, the layout of Green-Wood Cemetery, one of the earliest and largest rural cemeteries. Green-Wood was important for its progressive role in defining the aesthetic character of rural cemeteries, while also contributing to the perceived

David Bates Douglass. (Greenslade Special Collections and Archives, Kenyon College, Gambier, Ohio; used by permission)

value of large picturesque landscapes as places of relaxation and renewal for an urban population.

Douglass first became aware of the physical qualities of the hills of Brooklyn in 1833 while surveying railroad lines and land for the Croton Water Works. This was just two years after the first celebrated rural cemetery in America, Mount Auburn Cemetery designed by **Jacob Bigelow** and **Henry A. S. Dearborn**, was founded in Cambridge, Massachusetts.

Douglass believed that whenever plans for a rural cemetery would "be acted upon, with a proper estimate of its magnitude and importance, the hills back of Brooklyn would furnish, not only the best locality in the vicinity, but probably one of the finest in the world." Henry Evelyn Pierrepont and others negotiated the purchase of 175 acres from Brooklyn farmers in a rural portion of the city for the new cemetery, which was officially incorporated on April 18, 1838. An act of the New York State Legislature created the cemetery as a joint stock company for the purpose of establishing a public burial ground in the City of Brooklyn, with an appropriate name reiterating "that it should always remain a scene of rural quiet, and beauty, and leafiness, and verdure."

Accustomed to the complexities of large civil engineering projects, David Bates Douglass's design for Green-Wood achieved a unique and beautiful picturesque design of unprecedented scale and topographic variation. Before construction began in 1839, Douglass wrote how "a considerable portion of the ground is now covered with a fine old forest of native growth. . . . this will of course be preserved and cultivated, and in due time those parts which have been cleared off for purposes of agriculture, will also be covered with appropriate plantations of shrubbery and trees, till the whole shall have acquired a character of sylvan still life in harmony with the quietness and repose of the grave."

Douglass designed the roads, paths, and plots as a series of curvilinear forms that followed the dramatic topography of the site, so that the picturesque scenery unfolds as one travels through the grounds. The founding trustees determined that the grounds would be subdivided into family or individual lots, contained within the winding drives and paths. Douglass described this concept as "the design of the interior arrangement of the Cemetery precinct is to intersect every part of it with convenient winding avenues and walks, and in connection with them, to lay out the Cemetery lots of the proper size for family burying places."

Nehemiah Cleaveland, who wrote most of the early descriptions of Green-Wood, described the design approach as taking great "advantage of the [site's] natural inequalities." Douglass brought to Green-Wood a nationally recognized understanding of site engineering and surveying and a keen interest in the natural environment. By emphasizing the topographic change instead of regrading the site, the character of Green-Wood dramatically emphasizes its picturesque qualities. Douglass's plans and the trustee's rules for managing the cemetery ensured that the overall topographic design for the entire landscape would take precedence over the desires of individual lot owners.

Green-Wood Cemetery, Brooklyn, New York. A map of "The Tour," a route for visitors that passed main attractions in the cemetery, from *Green-Wood Illustrated*, 1847.

In his 1849 essay, "Public Cemeteries and Public Gardens," that appeared in the *Horticulturalist,* **Andrew Jackson Downing** described Green-Wood as "the largest and unquestionably the finest [rural cemetery] . . . grand, dignified, and park-like. It is laid out in a broad and simple style, commands noble ocean views, and is admirably kept." Douglass himself sought to improve the site's rural qualities to make it a suitable park for tourists and area residents to visit, and he described the intentions of the cemetery corporation as having an explicitly civic, almost public role of openness and service to the community.

Green-Wood was one of Douglass's most significant and personal projects in his career as a surveyor, site designer, and engineer. He remained as president of Green-Wood Cemetery through its initial construction, departing to become president of Kenyon College from

1840 to 1844, where he also served as a professor of intellectual and moral philosophy, logic, and rhetoric. While at Kenyon College, Douglass is credited with the first improvement of the college grounds, which included the design and construction of paths and gates. After leaving Kenyon College, he returned to engineering and consulting work and, using Green-Wood as his model, laid out the Albany Rural Cemetery in New York, from 1845 to 1846, and the Protestant Cemetery in Quebec, Canada, in 1848. After moving that year to Geneva (now Hobart) College, in Geneva, New York, to teach mathematics and natural philosophy, he fell and suffered a stroke that led to his death on October 21, 1849. Douglass is interred at Green-Wood Cemetery in Brooklyn, New York.

The best source of information about Douglass's life and work is the William L. Clements Library at the University of Michigan in Ann Arbor, where the David Bates Douglass Papers are housed; additional family papers are contained in the Douglass-Hale Papers at Hobart (formerly Geneva) College in Geneva, N.Y.

Cleaveland, Nehemiah. *Green-Wood Illustrated. In highly finished line engraving, from drawings taken on the spot. By James Smillie. With descriptive notices, by Nehemiah Cleaveland.* New York: R. Martin, 1847. Smillie's cemetery series was widely distributed through the United States, and documented the earliest rural cemeteries with compelling etchings that illustrated picturesque landscape style.

Douglass, David Bates. *Exposition of the Plan and Objects of the Green-Wood Cemetery an Incorporated Trust Chartered by the Legislature of the State of New York.* New York: Narine & Company, 1839. This pamphlet contains a detailed description of the cemetery and Douglass's design intent.

Richman, Jeffrey. *Brooklyn's Green-Wood Cemetery, New York's Buried Treasure.* Lunenberg, Vt.: The Stinehour Press, 1998. Contains the history of Green-Wood Cemetery, focused on a description of noteworthy burials with excellent color photographs.

Lauren G. Meier

EARLE, ALICE MORSE
(1851–1911)
AUTHOR

Alice Morse Earle was born Mary Alice Morse on April 27, 1851, in Worcester, Massachusetts. Her parents, Edwin and Abby Clary Morse, provided an upper-middle-class upbringing for her, her sister, and half-brother. Importantly, they were enthusiastic gardeners and active in the Worcester County Horticultural Society, one of the oldest in the nation. The family also visited important private gardens of the day, including the Hunnewell estate in Wellesley, Massachusetts. In addition, Earle received far more education than most Americans of her day, when few of her peers graduated from high school. After completing studies at Worcester Classical and English High School, she also did advanced work at Boston's Gannett Institute and Brooklyn's Pratt Institute. In 1874, she married Henry Earle, who hailed from Providence, Rhode Island, and the couple moved to Brooklyn, New York. They had four children.

It is not clear when or why Alice Morse Earle began her research and writing about preindustrial America. She indicated that she had been working for many years before the publication of her first book, *The Sabbath in Puritan New England,* in 1891. This unlikely topic became an instant bestseller. Among her many titles, *Home Life in Colonial Days* (1898) and *Child Life in Colonial Days*

Alice Morse Earle. (Courtesy of the American Antiquarian Society)

(1899) are perhaps her most popular works and have rarely, if ever, been out of print.

Alice Morse Earle based her writing on detailed research in primary sources. Her two chief archival sources were the Long Island (now Brooklyn) Historical Society and the American Antiquarian Society in Worcester, Massachusetts. However, she also explored the cities and villages of the original thirteen colonies including areas of New England and New York. She read court records, diaries, letters, old newspapers, and other such material. Furthermore, she investigated material culture, searching old attics, storerooms, and farm buildings, for example. She also interviewed elderly citizens everywhere she went. Her thorough research gave credence to her writing, although she wrote in an anecdotal style without scholarly documentation.

Gardens were of intense interest to Earle. In fact, *Old Time Gardens* (1901) may be her most ambitious work. She had previously addressed the topic of gardens when she wrote several articles about plants and gardens for important magazines at a time when interest in these subjects was just growing in this country. In addition, Earle penned a number of important reviews of American and British garden books. These reveal her indepth knowledge of gardens and landscape design. Self-confident and assured, Earle never hesitated to express her frank opinions. The respect given to these opinions is underscored by their appearance in the most influential publications of the day. She was the author of more than fifteen books and numerous magazine articles about the life and material culture of preindustrial America. Most of her work was produced in an intense literary effort from 1891 through 1903.

Her most important contribution to American gardens was her 1901 book, *Old Time Gardens*. The volume features almost five hundred pages, augmented by over two hundred photographs, describing the plants, gardens, and landscapes of an earlier America, as well as of her own time. *Old Time Gardens* must be considered separately both as Earle's garden masterwork and for its influence on Colonial Revival gardens then and now. The book appeared at a critical time during the evolution of the American landscape. A new century had dawned and, with it, the Victorian era—with all of its fustiness, landscape features of bedding out, tropical foliage extravaganzas, and gingerbread hardscape—was scorned. Earle encouraged a new type of garden design for the new century, as did her contemporaries, Gertrude Jekyll and **Helena Rutherfurd Ely**. Earle's work encouraged her

Colonial Revival quincunx design garden, Haverford, Pennsylvania, as featured in Earle's *Old Time Gardens*, 1901.

readers to look to the American past in designing and planting gardens for the new century. She was among the earliest writers of the era to promote formal design, enclosure, privacy, historic garden furnishings and ornaments, perennials, and iconic plants such as boxwood.

Based on Earle's thorough research and familiarity with gardens and garden literature, *Old Time Gardens* features twenty-two loosely connected chapters emphasizing design, plants, and architectural features. Uniting her themes was her core belief that material culture only has meaning in terms of its human associations. Earle's chapters are filled with the anecdotes and lore that made her books popular in her day and have kept them useful and readable today. Her underlying purpose was serious. America's old gardens had much to teach a new generation. *Old Time Gardens* is an alluring yet insistent plea for her audience to embrace a specific garden design, expressed in specific plants and architectural features.

Dooryard garden, Deerfield, Massachusetts, as featured in Earle's *Old Time Gardens,* 1901.

descriptions of numerous gardens admired by Earle. Many were old gardens but it is perhaps surprising to discover her admiration for the lavish new Italian gardens of the day, which she believed were descendants of old estate gardens. She singled out several for extensive coverage.

Ornamental plants are another of Alice Morse Earle's most important topics. Among the earliest to advocate "old-fashioned" hardy plants, she also favored other plants redolent of the past. These included lilacs, boxwood, apple trees, and herbs. Each received its own chapter. Earle linked plants with stories of the people who grew them, an emotional resonance that has captivated readers for a century. She also, however, enthused about new plant introductions from Asia and elsewhere, noting that many seemed like long-lost family.

Alice Morse Earle looked back at old plants and gardens in part to shape those of the new century. *Old Time Gardens* quickly became one of the most popular garden books of its era, remaining in print for three decades until the expense of printing its photographs put it out of print. With the long success of her book, Earle is considered to be one of the most influential garden writers of her time. Many referred to her work with affection and admiration. As interest in the Colonial Revival has increased in recent decades, Earle's work is exerting increased influence once again. Her portrait of preindustrial America, including its gardens, remains of great value to both gardeners and landscape historians today.

Alice Morse Earle died in 1911. In addition to her advocacy of the Colonial Revival style for gardens, she was a pioneer in women's writing in the field of landscape architecture.

Earle strongly advocated enclosure, privacy, and formal design. She devoted a chapter to hedges, walls, and fences, for instance. Privacy was a critical concept and the very soul of a garden, she believed. She used the gardens of the Puritans as examples for a new generation. She insisted that formal design is deeply embedded in American history and gave examples from New York and elsewhere. The architectural features and ornament of such gardens received frequent mention. Pergolas, seats, gates, summerhouses, and sundials were found in old gardens, modest and grand. Such features made gardens spaces to live in, rather than Victorian spectacles for public view. The book's text and photographs offered

Begg, Virginia Lopez. "Alice Morse Earle, Old Time Gardens in a Brave New Century." *Journal of the New England Garden History Society* 8 (Fall 2000), 13–21. An overview of the author's life and career as they relate to landscape history.

Earle, Alice Morse. *Old Time Gardens.* New York: Macmillan, 1901. New edition with introduction by Virginia Lopez Begg. Hanover, N.H.: University Press of New England, 2005. This is Earle's influential garden masterwork, as described in this biographical entry.

Earle, Alice Morse. *Sun-Dials and Roses of Yesterday.* New York: Macmillan, 1902. Earle discusses the title subjects, and offers interesting commentary on a variety of garden and landscape topics.

Virginia Lopez Begg

ECKBO, GARRETT
(1910–2000)
LANDSCAPE ARCHITECT, AUTHOR, TEACHER

Although born in Cooperstown, New York, to Theodora Munn and Axel Eckbo on November 28, 1910, Garrett Eckbo identified with California. In 1912, following his parents' divorce, he moved with his mother to Alameda, east of San Francisco, where he grew up with very limited social opportunities. Prospects improved in 1929 with a six-month visit to a wealthy and enterprising paternal uncle in Oslo, Norway, spurring young Eckbo's ambition to pursue a higher education. After a year at Marin Junior College, Eckbo entered the Division of Landscape Design and Floriculture at the University of California at Berkeley, in the fall of 1932. He later credited Professor Hollyngsworth Leland Vaughan,* a former student of **Thomas Dolliver Church** at Ohio State University, as being influential in his professional development. Vaughan and the Great Depression years impressed Berkeley landscape students with the need for pragmatic and reductive design, even

Garrett Eckbo in Southern California, ca. 1946. (Garrett Eckbo Collection [1990-1] Environmental Design Archives, University of California, Berkeley)

though their projects rarely strayed from adaptations of historical styles, as witnessed in Eckbo's 1934 design entitled "Estate in the Manner of Louis XIV." Upon graduating in June 1935, Eckbo moved south. Employed by Armstrong Nurseries in Ontario, California, for a year, he produced approximately one hundred garden plans and acquired a wide knowledge of Southern California plants. A scholarship to Harvard University's Graduate School of Design allowed him to move beyond the service industry. In the fall of 1936, Eckbo drove east to enroll in the Department of Landscape Architecture. Soon disillusioned with the school's traditional curriculum, Eckbo questioned the legacy of **Frederick Law Olmsted Sr.** and the program's reliance on *An Introduction to the Study of Landscape Design* by **Henry Vincent Hubbard** and Theodora Kimball (Hubbard),* a textbook which he condemned as formulaic and overly aesthetic. While the landscape department conformed to a Beaux-Arts tradition and the formal/informal dialectic, the architecture department at Harvard was undergoing a complete transformation under the leadership of Walter Gropius, who had joined the faculty in 1937. Eckbo began to de-

fine his own modernist theory by establishing connections among landscape design, architecture, and art. He collaborated with architecture students on projects such as a recreation center and park in underprivileged South Boston. He announced his beliefs that "what is good for the rich is good for the poor," and that design required a multidisciplinary approach. He further explored the relationships between private gardens and public space, and urban and suburban design, in both his master's thesis project, "Contempoville—a superblock with a central common"—and "Small Gardens in the City." The publication of the latter in the architectural periodical *Pencil Points* in September 1937 brought him notoriety at home and abroad.

Eckbo quickly understood the necessity of advancing his ideas in writing. He joined forces with fellow students and modernism champions Daniel Urban Kiley* and **James C. Rose** to produce the three-part seminal text "Landscape Design in the Urban Environment," "Landscape Design in the Rural Environment," and "Landscape Design in the Primeval Environment," which appeared in *Architectural Record* in May and August 1939

Above: Park plan for community building, Farm Security Administration, Weslaco Unit, Texas, 1939. (Garrett Eckbo Collection [1990-1] Environmental Design Archives, University of California, Berkeley)

Below: ALCOA Forecast Garden, Wonderland Park, Los Angeles, California, 1959. (Photo by Garrett Eckbo, courtesy of Marc Treib)

and February 1940, respectively. These articles argued for collaborative, cohesive design and planning, from city garden to natural preserve, stressing the interdependency of such environments.

On September 19, 1937, he married Arline Williams, the sister of his future business partner. Having received a Master in Landscape Architecture degree in 1938, Eckbo took a series of project-based jobs, each lasting six weeks. He worked on the Federal Building for the 1939 Golden Gate International Exposition at the office of Kastner and Berla in Washington, D.C. While in Washington, Eckbo designed prototypical open spaces for housing projects at the request of Frederick Gutheim of the United States Housing Authority. In addition, he conceived several unbuilt landscape schemes for Norman Bel Geddes's General Motors pavilion at the 1939 World's Fair in New York.

Having returned to California, Eckbo worked for the San Francisco office of the New Deal's Farm Security Administration from 1939 to 1942, where he designed environments for migrant-worker camps across the valleys of California, Washington, and Texas. Collaborating with architects Vernon DeMars and Burton Cairns and landscape architect Francis Violich, Eckbo would further his spatial explorations and provide shelter at the human scale within the expansive agricultural landscape. At Tulare and Ceres, in the San Joaquin Valley, his grand and richly varied planting schemes offered shade, wind protection, and a sense of place for a transient population. With the same group of designers, Eckbo founded Telesis, an organization that focused on the impact of development in the Bay Area. From 1942 to 1945, he participated in the World War II effort by contributing landscape designs for defense housing in the San Francisco region.

In the postwar era, Eckbo founded a firm with Robert Royston* and Edward Williams. Eckbo Royston and Williams soon expanded their scope of work from residential gardens to suburban parks (the 1949 Standard

Oil Rod and Gun Club in Richmond and 1957 Mitchell Park in Palo Alto) and planned communities (Ladera on the San Francisco Peninsula). From 1946, Eckbo headed the firm in the Los Angeles area with the assistance of Francis Dean. The early years were marked by a multitude of garden designs for the wealthy and the more modest, and by collaborations with modernist architects on several developments. His unbuilt 1946 to 1949 design for Community Homes in Reseda remains exemplary in its sophisticated use of vegetation as a tool for structuring neighborhoods. Other designs included the semi-urban Park Planned Homes from 1946 to 1947, and Mar Vista Housing in 1948, both with Gregory Ain; and the dramatically canyon-sited Crestwood Hills in 1948 and Wonderland Park in 1950.

In 1950, Eckbo coalesced his ideas in *Landscape for Living,* defining the modern discipline of landscape architecture for his professional peers and a broader readership. A quintessential twentieth-century text in a field that has shied away from theory, *Landscape for Living* stands apart with **Christopher Tunnard**'s *Gardens in the Modern Landscape* (1938, 1948) and Ian L. McHarg's* *Design with Nature* (1969) as remarkable attempts to define the field in relation to planning and the environment. Eckbo illustrated its theory, defined as "a generalization of social experience," with his own projects and those of the firm. He reiterated the call for an organized and planned landscape, from garden to nature, a designed landscape that would stress the relations between human and land without apologizing for the human presence.

Eckbo continued to balance design and writing in his mature years. He taught in the School of Architecture at the University of Southern California from 1948 to 1956. His widely publicized 1956 to 1959 Forecast Garden, commissioned by the Aluminum Company of America, tested aluminum as a spatial and decorative force in landscape design. The year 1956 also saw the publication of *The Art of Home Landscaping,* a garden and site planning manual aimed at a popular audience. Eckbo's innovative design for the pedestrian blocks of the Fulton Street Mall in Fresno, developed with Victor Gruen in the early 1960s, proposed an urban alternative to shopping centers. In 1962, Eckbo began a twenty-year design and planning process for the University of New Mexico at Albuquerque. He published *Urban Landscape Design* in 1964 and *The Landscape We See* in 1969.

His firm continued to evolve as well. In 1958, Eckbo Royston and Williams divided into Royston Hanamoto and Mayes, and Eckbo Dean and Williams. In 1964, Donald Austin became a partner and the firm was recast as Eckbo Dean Austin Williams, later known as EDAW. Ultimately, the laboratory for progressive landscape design with a focus on the relationship between individual and community grew into a multinational planning corporation. Eckbo returned to the San Francisco Bay Area in 1963 to head the Department of Landscape Architecture at Berkeley until 1969. He received the Medal of Honor from the American Society of Landscape Architects in 1975; he retired as professor emeritus in 1978, and left EDAW a year later.

In an attempt to start anew, Eckbo formed Eckbo Kay Associates with Kenneth Kay in 1979 with whom he collaborated until 1983. During the final years of practice, Garrett Eckbo and Associates addressed the scales of planning and garden design, having come full circle. His involvement in writing and debating the state and future of landscape architecture never abated. Eckbo still believed in landscape design as an agent of societal change, publishing *People in the Landscape* two years before his death on May 14, 2000, in Oakland, California.

The Garrett Eckbo Collection, in the Environmental Design Archives, University of California, Berkeley, spans the years 1933 to 1990 and includes Eckbo's papers, writings, projects, photographs, and scrapbooks; see www.ced.berkeley.edu/cedarchives/profiles/eckbo.htm.

Eckbo, Garrett. *Landscape for Living.* New York: Architectural Record with F. W. Dodge Corporation, 1950. His first and most pointed book, it instantly became a polemic for modern landscape architecture and its relationship to the environment and other design disciplines. Illustrated with projects by Eckbo and Eckbo Royston and Williams.

Eckbo, Garrett. *Urban Landscape Design.* New York: McGraw Hill, 1964. Like *Landscape for Living,* this volume is situated at the intersection of theory and practice and addresses a variety of scales from the patio to the region. Eckbo included projects by designers other than himself, with the intention to illustrate that the "landscape revolution" of the mid-1930s had spread well beyond California.

Treib, Marc, and Dorothée Imbert. *Garrett Eckbo: Modern Landscapes for Living.* Berkeley: University of California Press, 1997. This publication accompanied an exhibition of the same name held at the University Art Museum in Berkeley. The two essays focus on Eckbo's development as a landscape architect and on his view of landscape as conductor for social pattern, with a brief survey of projects between 1935 and 1955.

Dorothée Imbert

EGAN, WILLIAM CONSTANTINE
(1841–1930)
HORTICULTURIST, AUTHOR, ROSARIAN

William Constantine Egan was born on April 1, 1841, in New York City. His father, Dr. William Bradshaw Egan, brought the six-month-old infant to Chicago via the Erie Canal four years after the fledgling town was incorporated. The senior Egan had pioneered Chicago's development as a real estate investor. He was the first City Physician, and also a noteworthy storyteller and orator who gave the Fourth of July speech at the groundbreaking for the Illinois-Michigan Canal in 1836.

The senior Egan was particularly interested in horticulture, planting hundreds of trees, shrubs, and flowers on a 600-acre tract in Hyde Park he named Egandale. He hoped to evoke the memory of the Irish landscape from which he emigrated, but did not live to complete the project. Local lore suggests that Egan, a classically trained Latin scholar, urged Chicago's adoption of the motto *urbs in horto*—City in a Garden—for its corporate seal.

William Constantine Egan at Egandale, Highland Park, Illinois, 1917. (Photo courtesy of Susan Tippey Berg)

William Constantine Egan inherited his father's love of the Midwestern landscape. From 1882 to 1897, he was a trustee of the Chicago Academy of Sciences, whose institutional charge was to survey the area's natural history, creating a Smithsonian-like model for the Midwest. An amateur paleontologist, Egan combed the Bridgeport quarries, contributing over ten thousand invertebrate fossils that comprise the core of the academy's collections. Egan also nourished an interest in botany and excitement about findings of plant explorers and their introductions. Despite these avocations, Egan pursued a career in the business world, retiring from H. H. Schufeldt and Co. at age fifty because of concerns about his health. After retirement, Egan devoted himself entirely to the stewardship of a 5-acre tract he selected for his country place on a ravine-bluff site in Highland Park, Illinois, overlooking Lake Michigan. He named the place Egandale, and lived and worked there from 1888 until his death in 1930.

When Chicago was selected as the site for the World's Columbian Exposition of 1893, Egan and his colleagues aimed to raise the profile of horticulture in the Midwest, and members filled William Le Baron Jenney's 69,000-square-foot Horticultural Hall with exemplary displays. Egan was a founding trustee of what became the Chicago Horticultural Society, parent organization and manager of today's thriving Chicago Botanic Garden. He also served as secretary on the executive board of the World's Columbian Exposition, where a formal architectural layout contrasted with the naturalistic landscape designed by Henry Sargent Codman and **Frederick Law Olmsted Sr.** Egan developed a friendship with Codman's uncle, **Charles Sprague Sargent** of the Harvard Arnold Arboretum. Egan and Sargent maintained a lively correspondence, sharing the latest horticultural discoveries of their day. Sargent nominated Egan as a corresponding honorary member of the Massachusetts Horticultural Society in 1918, and Sargent visited Egandale circa 1922.

A number of plant introductions bear Egan's name: the W. C. Egan Japanese iris and phlox, *Egandale canna;* a hawthorn, *Crataegus egani;* the large-flowered rambler rose *William C. Egan;* and the *Mrs. William C. Egan.*

Egandale, Highland Park, Illinois, 1912. (Image, captured from original glass autochrom, courtesy of Susan Tippey Berg)

Roses were a particular interest for Egan. Egan was vice president of the American Rose Society. He was referred to as "the eminent horticulturist of northern Illinois" by Conard and Jones Co., in the twelfth edition of the volume *How to Grow Roses,* which was published in 1916. Egan's passion for roses was memorialized in an extant rose garden designed by **Jens Jensen**'s protégé and son-in-law, Marshall Liston Johnson.* The garden was dedicated in 1942 and adjoins Highland Park's City Hall. The garden pays tribute to Egan's contribution as Highland Park's "first Rosarian who proved that the 'Queen of Flowers' could be successfully grown in this climate." Egan's fondness for roses was remembered by colleagues long after his death. In the early 1960s, thirty years after his death, landscape architect Gertrude Deimel Kuh* would recall Egan's love of roses.

In the September 1895 issue of *Landscape Gardening,* describing "how I made my garden," Egan wrote that one secret of "good landscape work" is to create "agreeable surprises." He was referring to a sunken bridge he built in the ravine. He named the wooden footbridge and hand-hewn bench Wychwood, homage to his avid horti-

culturist friend Charles Hutchinson's country place in Lake Geneva, Wisconsin. Hutchinson reciprocated with a similar spot on his property which he in turn named Egandale.

Liberty Hyde Bailey, editor of *Country Life In America,* selected a team of experts for an article on maintaining good lawns in various parts of the country for an article published in 1902. His chosen experts were **Samuel Parsons Jr.**, who wrote from his New York landscape gardening perspective; **Warren Henry Manning**, who described the treatment of established lawns in Boston; and W. C. Egan, who wrote of his experience with the hard compact soil of his Chicago suburb.

Egan wrote extensively of his observations about lawns, the value of native herbs in the garden, and every detail of his experience developing Egandale—both successes and failures. Manning, publisher and director of *Billerica,* chose him as a regular Midwest contributor to North Shore, Illinois, editions of the magazine. In April 1915, the magazine noted that Egan was widely recognized as Dean of Amateur Horticulturists.

In September 1912, *Country Life In America* published a

horticultural edition. Dr. Wilhelm Miller wrote an article entitled "How the Middle West Can Come Into Its Own," which stated that "the best-known small garden, in the Middle West is Egandale. There is no five-acre place in the East that can vie with it for pictorial quality and finish. The great principle illustrated by Egandale is that the universal element in gardening lies in design, while the local color resides in material."

In June 1922, one year after the Garden Club of Illinois hosted Egan's eightieth birthday celebration, forty-two members of the Oak Park, Illinois, Garden Club visited Egandale. The community newspaper, *Oak Leaves,* reported that Egan "treated his guests as experienced botanists and garden planners. . . . His scientific manner in regard to plant life contrasts agreeably with affable philosophical witticisms regarding life in general."

In March 1903, *Country Life* published Egan's "Why and How I Made My Country Home." His last paragraph stated, "My physician's prescription should be incorporated in the *material medica* of all nations. It was extremely pleasant to take, and not only restored my shattered health, but was the means of awakening in me a love for the greatest of all delights—one's own garden."

Egan passed away in 1930. Today, Egan's Craftsman-style home and his garden are no longer extant. A street named for his home remains, as do Sargent's gifts, a towering ginkgo and an entry katsuratree.

Egan, W. C. "How I Made My Garden: Six Years Ago It Was Wild Woodland." *Gardening* 3, no. 73 (September 1, 1895).

Meldman, Suzanne Carter. *The City and the Garden: The Chicago Horticultural Society at Ninety.* Glencoe, Ill.: Chicago Historical Society, 1981.

Miller, Wilhelm. *How To Make a Flower Garden.* New York: Doubleday, Page & Co., 1903. Egan articles pp. 92, 97, 205, 311, 323. Reprinted 1905, 1910, 1914.

Suzanne Carter Meldman

ELIOT, CHARLES W., II
(1899–1993)
LANDSCAPE ARCHITECT, PLANNER, CONSERVATIONIST, EDUCATOR

Charles W. Eliot II was born in Cambridge, Massachusetts, on November 5, 1899. He was the grandson and namesake of the president of Harvard College, Charles William Eliot, and the nephew of **Charles Eliot**, the renowned landscape architect. The elder Eliot was famous for modernizing and enhancing the Harvard curriculum, for overseeing the institution's transition from a college to a modern university. In 1986, Charles William Eliot II recollected, "On the day of my birth my grandfather strode through the door of the house, right into this very front hall, and announced in a firm voice 'This boy will be a landscape architect.'" The premature loss of Charles Eliot, the brilliant landscape practitioner, in 1897 at thirty-seven years old was a tragedy for the nascent profession, but a devastating blow to the elder Charles William Eliot, hence the importance to him for his namesake and the nephew of his departed son to follow in the profession.

Young Eliot was raised and educated in Cambridge, Massachusetts, graduating from Harvard College in 1920, interrupted by a 1918 to 1919 stint in the American Red Cross Ambulance Service on the Italian Front during

Charles W. Eliot II, 1955. (Courtesy of the Frances Loeb Library, Harvard Graduate School of Design)

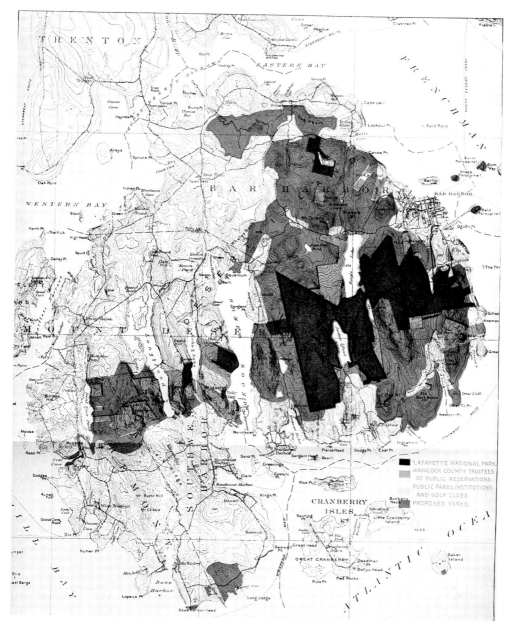

Map of Mount
Desert Island, Bar
Harbor, Maine, 1928.
(Courtesy of the
Frances Loeb Library,
Harvard Graduate
School of Design)

World War I. In 1923, he received a master's degree from the Department of Landscape Architecture at Harvard, then spent the following year holding their Sheldon Traveling Fellowship in Planning, touring Europe, studying urban planning, landscape design, and what he termed "historic preservation procedures" in Belgium and Holland.

Upon returning to the United States, he quickly set up an independent practice in Boston, where he specialized in city planning as well as working on private estates. He also served as the Assistant Editor of the American City Planning Institute's monthly magazine, *City Planning.* Later, he was a Contributing Editor for *Planning and Civic Comment* (1935–1943), on the Editorial Board of the *Journal of the American Institute of Planners* (1955–1958) and on the Publication Board of *Landscape Architecture* (1956–1959).

From 1926 to 1933 he served as a city planner for Washington, D.C., serving as director of the National Capital Park and Planning Commission. Here he helped implement the Mall development recommended by the 1901 McMillan Commission. His areas of influence came to include the creation of a wider park system for Washington and nearby Virginia and Maryland, in particular the 28 miles along the Potomac River from Great Falls, Maryland, to Mount Vernon, Virginia. He helped defeat efforts to establish a proposed electricity-producing dam that would have destroyed the river scenery above Washington. He also shepherded the 1930 Shipstead-Luce Act into law. The act was the first to encourage protection of the visual fabric of urban environments—specifically the areas surrounding Washington's public buildings and parks, including the north side of Pennsylvania Avenue, which was threatened with haphazard development.

In 1933, at the depth of the Great Depression, Franklin D. Roosevelt appointed him director of the National Resources Planning Board (NRPB); thus began what Eliot characterized as "the most important part of my career." This work over the next decade cemented his early commitment to better public housing, improved urban recreational facilities, increased numbers of public parks, and large-scale, nationwide planning—advocacies he never relinquished. The NRPB was established within the Public Works Administration, and Eliot structured the agency to deal with natural resources and planning issues nationwide. Eliot gathered experts and immediately established water, land, science, and technology committees. The NRPB laid the groundwork for the coordination of local, state, and regional planning. Eliot was proud to have a national network for policies, plans, and structures within which to best harness and utilize "human, natural, manmade and institutional resources of this country" in order to protect national natural assets and plan for future necessary development.

When Congress dissolved the NRPB in 1943, Eliot moved to California where he spent one year as director of the Haynes Foundation, lecturing at the University of California. He also maintained a private planning practice, preparing master plans and advising on zoning issues for numerous towns surrounding the Los Angeles area. He served for two years as Director of Resources Programs for the newly established Ford Foundation where he organized a program called Resources for the Future.

In 1954, he returned to Cambridge, joining the faculty of the Harvard Graduate School of Design where he held the Charles Eliot Professorship of Landscape Architecture for four years. Then he became a professor of city and regional planning until 1966, choosing to teach half-time so that he might continue his private practice as a planning consultant for the towns surrounding Boston. He thought it imperative for teachers to have experience with current practice as well as theory. During this time he helped found the Cambridge Historical Commission and served as its president from 1970 to 1978.

Eliot maintained a longtime professional and personal involvement with planning at Mount Desert Island in Maine (a place beloved by his Uncle Charles) beginning with his 1928 *The Future of Mount Desert Island* and later, with the development of Acadia National Park. Eliot was affiliated early on with the Trustees of Reservations, a private land conservation group founded in Massachusetts by his uncle in 1891. Among other contributions, he conceived and began the process of establishing a green belt of parkland called the Bay Circuit Beltway approximately 25 miles out and encircling the Boston area.

In an editorial published after his death in March of 1993, the *Boston Globe* characterized him as "the most persistent of planners . . . a lifelong preservationist" and "a proponent of sensible planning as the antidote for mindless growth." They praised his founding of the Bay Circuit and urged its completion as "a splendid tribute to his memory." As it continues to move toward completion, it still seems a fitting memorial to a landscape architect who devoted his life to public service and the preservation of our natural resources.

Eliot was a member of the American Institute of Planning. He was a Fellow of the American Society of Landscape Architects and, in 1982, Eliot was rewarded for his public service as well as his extensive contribution to the fields of landscape architecture, city planning, housing advocacy, conservationism, and education with the ASLA Medal, the organization's highest honor.

The Frances Loeb Library, Special Collections at Harvard includes Eliot's original gift of papers pertaining to the National Resources Planning Board and its predecessor agencies, as well as a substantial collection of reports made to the board. In 1987, Eliot added to the archive those materials documenting—in formats ranging from manuscript (his 1927 plan) to a 1986 videotape—his long-time professional and personal involvement in planning at Mount Desert Island and the development of Acadia National Park. Subsequently, materials related to his planning projects and postwar activities were also presented to the library. In addition to Harvard, the Cambridge Historical Society holds a collection of Eliot material pertaining to his work as an officer of the Cambridge Historical Society from 1970 to 1978.

"The Career of Charles Eliot, 2nd, FASLA-AIP." Video recording: an interview with Sidney N. Shurcliff, Hubbard Trust, 1980. Cambridge, Mass.: Visual Resource Center, Loeb Library, Graduate School of Design, Harvard University.

Eliot, Charles W., II. *The Future of Mount Desert Island.* Bar Harbor, Me.: Privately printed, 1928. The planning of this site was of deep personal and professional interest to Eliot.

Krueckeberg, Donald A. "From the backyard garden to the whole USA: a conversation with Charles W. Eliot, 2nd." In *The American Planner: Biographies and Recollections,* ed. Donald A. Krueckeberg. New York: Methuen, 1983, 350–365. Among the first discussions of Eliot's career and his place in landscape history.

Elizabeth Hope Cushing

ENGELHARDT, HEINRICH ADOLPH
(1830–1897)
LANDSCAPE GARDENER, AUTHOR, CEMETERY DESIGNER, SUPERINTENDENT

According to church records in Mühlhausen, Germany, Heinrich Adolph Engelhardt was born Johann Heinrich Engelhardt on December 1, 1830, the third child and only son of Christoph Adolph Engelhardt and Christiane Tamm. At age nineteen, after completing studies in civil engineering at University College in Berlin, he spent the mandatory two years in military service there, followed by a voluntary year in Schleswig-Holstein. Immigrating to America in 1851, he became a landscape gardener in Baltimore, Maryland. Then, according to accounts published in Ontario around 1880, he assisted in the laying out of Central Park in New York City, New York; Hollywood Cemetery in Richmond, Virginia; and Oakwood Cemetery in Raleigh, North Carolina.

In 1870 H. A. Engelhardt—as he was known by this time—went to Canada and settled in Ontario. (According to the province's 1871 census, the population was nearly 10 percent with German origins.) His arrival was timely. After Confederation in 1867, the resulting provinces began planning new institutions, many requiring imposing buildings complemented by extensive grounds. Ontario had no other qualified landscape gardeners, so Engelhardt caught the attention of officials in the province's Department of Public Works. Beginning in 1871 and continuing into 1873, this department employed him for at least three projects. He designed and supervised construction of the grounds of the Institution for the Deaf and Dumb at Belleville and the Institution for the

Advertisement for Englehardt's *The Beauties of Nature Combined with Art,* 1872.

Mount Pleasant Cemetery, Toronto, Ontario, May 2007. (Photograph by Geoffrey James, courtesy of Geoffrey James, Mount Pleasant Group of Cemeteries and Mount Pleasant Cemetery)

Blind at Brantford, and he proposed landscape improvements for an aging Parliament Building at Toronto.

Engelhardt soon had other clients. He laid out municipal parks in Brantford and Port Hope in 1871; designed the non-denominational Belleville Cemetery in 1872–1873; and advised on new cemeteries in the towns of Picton and Port Hope in 1873.

Each undertaking helped further his reputation as a skilled landscape gardener. So, too, did occasional mentions of his skill and taste, in editorials and letters in local newspapers. His own letters to the editor of the Belleville *Intelligencer,* in favor of a non-denominational cemetery and an agricultural college where "science and the dignity of labor [could] go hand in hand," promoted his egalitarian ideals.

Engelhardt's *The Beauties of Nature Combined with Art,* published in 1872 by James Lovell of Montreal and distributed through book and seed stores and the Toronto Nurseries, was his most far-reaching emissary. Henry S. Codman's bibliography on landscape architecture (*Garden and Forest,* 1890) included the 174-page work. Rare copies survive today, and Canadian scholars consider it the country's first treatise on landscape gardening. Stating that he wished "to advance the art of rural improvement to a higher perfection," Engelhardt wrote about site selection, drainage, soil preparation, landscape types, design elements, and plant selection. He declared the work "in its main points . . . original" and included many examples bespeaking a Prussian background, a broad education, and a knowledge of resorts

and "watering places" in the United States and Canada. He added that he had written the book at the request of friends in both countries. (One of these friends may have served as editor. The phonetic spelling and idiosyncratic syntax that characterize Engelhardt's surviving letters do not occur in his book.) He signed the introduction as "Prof. of Agriculture and Landscape Gardener, Belleville, Ontario," although no evidence of an academic affiliation has been found.

Engelhardt's best-known work is Mount Pleasant Cemetery in Toronto, an undertaking that occupied him from 1874 through 1888. Upon learning that the Toronto General Burying Grounds Trust had purchased a 200-acre site outside the city limits late in 1873, Engelhardt applied to lay out the grounds of what was to become the nonsectarian trust's third cemetery. His rough sketches impressed the trustees, who then hired him to prepare an overall site plan plus a detailed design for its westernmost 53 acres, and to superintend construction of that first portion.

The new cemetery fronted on Yonge Street (Toronto's principal north/south thoroughfare) and lay just beyond the terminus of a streetcar line, so the press and the populace watched its development with great interest. Engelhardt gradually created an intricate system of curvilinear paths and roadways (the latter, as in the United States, named for trees); replaced thistles with ornamentals; transformed a creek into a series of small lakes connected by cascades and rustic bridges; and introduced two white swans sent from Germany. When the cemetery opened on November 4, 1876, with Engelhardt as its newly appointed superintendent, journalists praised his enhancement of the natural scenery. Torontonians adopted Mount Pleasant as a favorite place for weekend outings as well as burials. Newspapers continued to report Engelhardt's improvements there, one declaring in 1882 that "when the plans of the company are brought to a termination Mount Pleasant will be one of the handsomest burying grounds in America."

Engelhardt and the trustees apparently agreed that Mount Pleasant's rules should foster the landscape-lawn concept by prohibiting "fences, walls, and hedges in or around lots." They differed, however, about monuments. Although the superintendent feared these would give the cemetery "the appearance of a marble yard," the trustees decided to allow lot owners unrestricted expression of taste and means.

Differences of opinion notwithstanding, the trustees credited Engelhardt in 1887 with "designing, engineering, laying out, and superintending [the work] well and in good taste." In July 1888, however, they cited his offensive behavior and diminishing usefulness as grounds for terminating his employment. Engelhardt then moved from a house near the cemetery to a room downtown where he lived, a bachelor in declining health, until his death of consumption, at age sixty-six, on November 8, 1897. Finding neither a will nor any close survivors, the trustees buried him in Mount Pleasant Cemetery in a grave that remained unmarked until 1991. Obituaries in Toronto newspapers praised Engelhardt's accomplishments, while a German-language publication declared, "He has shown the English citizens of Toronto what a German can accomplish." Engelhardt's estate, totaling nearly $10,000 (reputed to be partly from a private income from Germany) passed to cousins in Mühlhausen.

No single repository of Engelhardt papers has been found. The Mount Pleasant Group of Cemeteries, Toronto, has a few of his drawings; and the Archives of Ontario has one watercolor-and-ink drawing and several handwritten letters to the Inspector of Asylums, Prisons, and Public Charities.

Crawford, Pleasance. "H. A. Engelhardt (1830–1897): Landscape Designer." *German-Canadian Yearbook* 8 (1984), 163–81. This fully documented paper includes an appendix on Engelhardt's entries in a parks-design competition sponsored by the City of Toronto in 1876.

Crawford, Pleasance. "Letters on Landscape." *APT Bulletin* 19, no. 2 (1987), 61–63. These exchanges between Engelhardt and his Ontario-government contact provide insights into the travails of a pioneering landscape designer.

"H. A. Engelhardt." In *History of Toronto and the County of York,* vol. 2. Toronto: C. Blackett Robinson, 1885. Aside from what appears in newspapers, this is the only biographical information about Engelhardt published during his lifetime and contains some details not found elsewhere.

Pleasance K. Crawford

FAIRCHILD, DAVID
(1869–1954)
HORICULTURALIST,
PLANT EXPLORER

David Grandison Fairchild was born in 1869 in Michigan, where his father, George, taught at the Michigan State College of Agriculture. Fairchild remembered his childhood days exploring nature and evenings reading *Robinson Crusoe*. He was destined to be a horticulturalist, stating that "I do not believe that I consciously chose its direction, but rather wandered down its attractive way." Fairchild cited the publications of **Liberty Hyde Bailey**, a Michigan State graduate, with influencing intelligent gardening and spurring his own interest in horticulture.

When he was ten, his father accepted a position as president of the Kansas State College of Agriculture. The younger Fairchild matriculated there, studying horticulture, botany, and the emerging field of plant pathology and graduating in 1888. Byron Halsted, Fairchild's uncle who was a renowned botanist and horticulturalist, then invited Fairchild to study with him in Iowa. However, Halsted soon accepted a position teaching at Rutgers College, and Fairchild followed him there to engage in postgraduate studies. Before becoming entrenched in his studies, Beverly T. Galloway invited Fairchild to work for him in the U.S. Department of Agriculture's Plant Pathology Section. Fairchild accepted, making his way to Washington, D.C., in 1889.

There Fairchild immersed himself in the new science of plant pathology and his research was groundbreaking. In 1893, Galloway dispatched Fairchild to the Chicago World's Fair to staff an exhibit on plant pathology at the

David Fairchild (*right*) with a botany colleague, from *The World Was My Garden*, 1938.

Agricultural Building. Following his return, Fairchild secured a fellowship to the Naples Zoological Station. On his way to Naples, Fairchild met Barbour Lathrop, who had traveled extensively in Java, and upon hearing of Fairchild's desire to visit the country, encouraged him to seek a job collecting plant specimens for the Smithsonian Institution as a means to travel there, an idea that Fairchild dismissed because he wanted to study living tropical plants. Fairchild later became reacquainted with Lathrop, who offered him $1000 to travel to Java as an investment in science. To prepare for his journey, Fairchild embarked on a course of study in Germany, Switzerland, Corsica, and France. Arriving in Java in 1896, Fairchild was filled with wonder at the flora that surrounded him. Particularly enthralled with exotic fruits, he sent seeds to his associates in Washington to determine their viability for growth in the United States. After rendezvousing with his benefactor Lathrop, the two men embarked on a lengthy journey through the South Pacific.

Returning to America after a four-year absence,

Fairchild espoused the idea that plant introduction was an activity in which the federal government should be involved. After drafting a clause for a Congressional appropriation bill that would provide $20,000 to establish the Section of Foreign Seed and Plant Introduction within the Department of Agriculture, Fairchild approached key officials for support. He received funding, hoping to discover appropriate plants that could flourish in unsettled areas of the United States and allow for westward and southern expansion. As Fairchild prepared for his new role, his thoughts turned frequently to the tropical plants of Java with which he had become enthralled. Because Florida was the only place in the United States where these plants could thrive, he visited there and was captivated by the climate and the flora.

Fairchild settled into his new position, but Lathrop had doubts about Fairchild's ability to build the new section without having seen South America, India, or South Africa and without having professional contacts in these places, so he offered to finance a worldwide journey for Fairchild and accompany him on the voyage. The two men embarked on a five-year trip, with Fairchild bearing the title of Agricultural Explorer of the Section of Foreign Seed and Plant Introduction with the mission of collecting plants. Before setting sail, Fairchild met Dr. Francesco Franceschi,* whose work he admired greatly and who he credited with the foresight to realize the potential of the Santa Barbara region. Fairchild made him a collaborator with his federal office, arranging to have suitable plants sent to Franceschi.

Fairchild and Lathrop traveled to the Caribbean, South America, and Europe, where they sampled exotic fruits and vegetables to determine if these delicacies would appeal to American citizens if they could be cultivated in the United States. Fairchild collected specimens of cultivated plants that he observed locals growing, but he also scoured fields and forests for new specimens. He championed mangos, alfalfa, dates, horseradish, nectarines, and bamboo. Although he acknowledged that he was primarily interested in practical plants, he also took samples from what he called dooryard plants, which were purely ornamental.

The men stopped in Egypt, where Fairchild observed irrigation practices, noting similarities between the Nile Valley and the agricultural potential of both the Rio Grande and Colorado River valleys. In December 1899, the pair returned to Java to explore some of the lesser known islands in the region. In 1900, they went to Sweden, Finland, and Bavaria, followed by travels to Persia, North

Africa, and South Africa, where Fairchild collected eucalypts, sending the seeds to John McLaren* who planted them in Golden Gate Park. Years later, Fairchild visited McLaren there to see the plants in bloom.

Fairchild traveled to regional and state agricultural experiment stations across the United States to observe the viability of his samples. Some specimens that Fairchild sent back were incorporated into early Florida gardens. His work dramatically affected agriculture and related economic aspects of farming, as well as eating habits and settlement patterns within the nation.

In 1903, Fairchild returned to his office in Washington at the U.S. Department of Agriculture's Bureau of Plant Industry in the Office of Seed and Plant Introduction. The same year, on a trip west, Fairchild stopped to meet **Ossian Cole Simonds**, whose philosophy that native plants should compose the major part of a landscape greatly influenced the remainder of Fairchild's career.

As a public education effort, Fairchild spoke at a National Geographic Society meeting and through contacts made there, he met Marian Bell, a daughter of Alexander Graham Bell, the president of the society. Fairchild married Marian in 1905. The couple settled in their estate, In the Woods, in the suburbs of Washington, D.C., where they employed a Japanese gardener who planted blossoming cherry trees that Fairchild particularly admired. Children Alexander Graham Bell, Barbara Lathrop, and Nancy Bell soon completed the Fairchild family. Fairchild continued to travel, both internationally and nationally, including a visit to Ralph Ellis Gunn's* garden designed for Edward McIhenny on Avery Island, Louisiana.

Fairchild believed in the viability of southern Florida as a habitable area and was encouraged when the grapefruit that he championed yielded profits for local farmers. In 1913, Charles Deering met with Fairchild to discuss O. C. Simonds's work on his Buena Vista estate in Florida and various native plants that existed on his property.

Assisted by students, Fairchild planted the first Japanese flowering cherry trees around the Tidal Basin in Washington, D.C., hopeful that citizens and tourists would enjoy their beauty. Because of publicity surrounding Fairchild's efforts, the Mayor of Tokyo sent 2,000 trees to the United States in 1912, with **George Elberton Burnap** offering an appealing landscape design that established the nation's capital as a major tourist destination during the spring when the trees blossom.

When Washington winters took their toll on Fairchild's health, he relocated to Coconut Grove, Florida, building his masterpiece gardens at his house, christened The Kampong after similar family compounds in Java, between 1927 and 1930. There he planted his beloved tropical trees and plants gathered during his travels. The overall effect was that of a natural tropical paradise. In 1929, Fairchild became the first president of the Tropical Everglades Park Association.

Fairchild retired to The Kampong in 1935. In 1938, Robert Montgomery opened the Fairchild Tropical Botanical Gardens, named to honor his plant-explorer friend who helped him realize his dream of establishing an outdoor, year-round garden. Designed by William Lyman Phillips,* the garden contains many specimens collected and planted by Fairchild. In 1940, Fairchild embarked on a collecting expedition to the Indonesian archipelago for the garden that bears his name.

Fairchild wrote articles and took photographs for *National Geographic.* He authored several books that are valuable not only for their detailed information about his life and work but also for their abundant expedition photographs.

Fairchild passed away in 1954. In 1984, The Kampong was listed in the National Register of Historic Places and became part of the National Tropical Botanical Gardens.

Fairchild, David. *Exploring for Plants.* New York: The Macmillan Company, 1930. Accounts of Fairchild's travels as a plant explorer, including numerous photographs of his adventures.

Fairchild, David. *The World Grows Round My Door; The Story of The Kampong, a Home on The Edge of the Tropics.* New York: C. Scribner's Sons, 1947. Discussion of Fairchild's Florida home and the methods used to acquire the plants there.

Fairchild, David. *The World Was My Garden: Travels of a Plant Explorer.* New York: C. Scribner's Sons, 1938. Fairchild's recollections of his life, travels, and work, and exceptional photographs.

Stephanie S. Foell

FLANDERS, ANNETTE HOYT
(1887–1946)
LANDSCAPE ARCHITECT

Annette Hoyt Flanders was born in Milwaukee, Wisconsin, on September 6, 1887. She grew up in a well-established family spending summers at a fashionable resort on the shores of Lac LaBelle in Oconomowoc, Wisconsin. Her parents shared their appreciation of the arts, education, gardens, and gardening with her, taking her abroad to travel and providing tutors for her education.

While in her early twenties, she enrolled at Smith College, probably in their botany program, and graduated in 1914 with a bachelor of arts degree. She married Roger Yale Flanders in 1913. They were divorced in 1920; however, she retained the title of Mrs. Annette H. Flanders throughout her professional life. In the fall of 1918, she received her bachelor of science in landscape architecture from the University of Illinois. From 1918 to 1919, she worked for the American Red Cross in France. While in Paris, she enrolled in courses in design, architecture, and the history of architecture at the Sorbonne. Upon her return to Milwaukee she took courses in civil engineering at Marquette University.

From 1920 to 1922, Flanders was an associate in the firm of Vitale, Brinckerhoff and Geiffert (**Ferruccio Vitale**), in New York City. She was in charge of design work and supervising the planting for a variety of projects. The firm specialized in estate work and Flanders worked on two important projects, both of which were published under her name: the Myron C. Taylor gardens on Long Island and the garden of F. E. Dury, the Oasis, in the heart of Cleveland, Ohio. In 1922, she opened her own office with Helen Swift Jones,* Associate Landscape Architect, in New York City soon moving to a prestigious Park Avenue address. In 1923, she was elected to membership in the American Society of Landscape Architects. She traveled widely in Europe and also devoted time to studying the vegetation of the tropics in the West Indies. In the early 1930s, Flanders unofficially added a Master of Landscape Architecture to her title, a degree she appears to have bestowed upon herself in recognition of her own extensive studies and practice.

Annette Hoyt Flanders, ca. 1935. (Sophia Smith Collection, Smith College, Northampton, MA)

Estate of Charles E. F. McCann, Esq., Oyster Bay, Long Island, New York, from ASLA *Illustrations of Work of Members*, 1932.

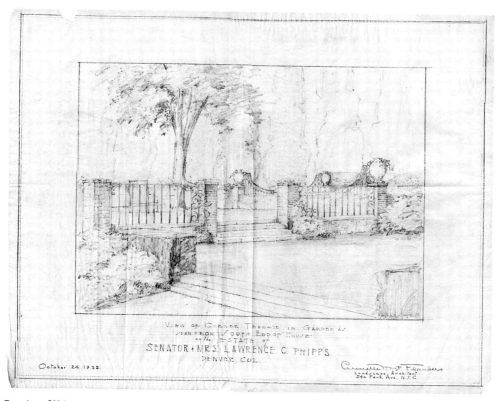

VIEW OF CORNER TERRACE IN GARDEN AS SEEN FROM SOUTH END OF HOUSE on the ESTATE of SENATOR + MRS LAWRENCE C. PHIPPS DENVER COL.

October 24, 1935.

Annette Hoyt Flanders
Landscape Architect
590 Park Ave, N.Y.C.

Drawing of Phipps estate, Denver, Colorado, 1935. (Annette Hoyt Flanders Collection, Lawrence C. Phipps Memorial Conference Center Archives, copyright University of Denver, Denver, Colorado)

In 1930 *House & Garden*'s Hall of Fame recognized Annette Hoyt Flanders for "her broad grasp of horticulture, landscape design, architecture and practical engineering, and her ability to apply them to the creation of lovely gardens. And for that essential which no training gives—native genius."

Flanders produced at least eighty-five projects including private estates, real estate subdivisions, recreational developments, and exhibition gardens. She worked throughout the United States from the Canadian border to North Carolina and Texas, to Colorado and New Mexico as well as a project in Hawaii and another in the south of France. She was the designer for many of the large estates in the Midwest including those for the Pabst (with **Warren Henry Manning**), Phipps, and Simonds families. She also designed model gardens in Chicago and New York City and was commissioned for the initial design of Adams Park in Wheaton, Illinois, in the 1940s.

Flanders's landscape designs reflected her education and training as well as the fashions of the time. Royal Cortissoz, a *New York Times* art critic, described her work "as the epitome of the present temper of the art in this country." Her estate designs blended a traditional formal style with a naturalistic approach that was increasingly viewed as "American." She worked closely with the existing landscape, stating that the "soundest, most beautiful design possible is always the one which, in the simplest way, takes advantage of every natural beauty which the land offers." She often included native trees, at times moving large ones to sites. She also used existing trees to frame and focus her designs. However, she did not hesitate to alter the landscape to create more dynamic spaces and experiences. Flanders emphasized changes in elevation by creating sunken gardens and raised terraces, each framed and linked by beautifully crafted walls and steps. Her designs featured strong sight lines and well-balanced plans created by an interweaving of the plant materials and the architecture.

Phipps estate, Denver, Colorado; Hyskell photograph. (Annette Hoyt Flanders Collection, Lawrence C. Phipps Memorial Conference Center Archives, copyright University of Denver, Denver, Colorado)

Flanders knew her materials well and was exacting on the craftsmanship necessary to produce the results she desired. For her award-winning design for Mrs. McCann on Long Island, Flanders created an elaborate treillage that was "as handsome as a piece of lace." The garden was awarded the Architectural League of New York's Medal of Honor in Landscape Architecture in 1933.

Plant materials were critical to what **Richardson Wright** described in 1932 in *House & Garden* as the "distinction and rare beauty" of a Flanders garden. Her design (ca. 1920s) for the gardens at Morven for Mrs. and Mr. Stone in Charlottesville, Virginia, was in the Colonial Revival style with boxwood-lined beds for flowers, extensive hedges of boxwood, and delicate white fencing with a romantic rose-covered arbor at the entrance. The plants spilled over a strict geometry and the colors, fragrances, and textures were choreographed for each season.

While Flanders created beautiful gardens for private estates, she was also commissioned to design model gardens open to the public. She designed a modern classic garden for Chicago's Century of Progress Exposition in 1934. The fair, a celebration of a century of scientific and technological advances alongside the growth of the city of Chicago, was open from the spring of 1933 to the fall of 1934. The architecture represented applications of the most advanced concepts in design and construction, featuring a rainbow of colors while the landscape, designed by Vitale and Geiffert, was generally in the more traditional style of the Beaux-Arts. Flanders was commissioned by *Good Housekeeping* magazine to design a model garden in the second year of the fair, placed just west of the South Lagoon. The exhibit was described in the magazine by the editor Helen Koues as a "Classic modern garden, a formal garden, in green and white, [with] a pavilion containing a Classic Modern living room and two loggias." By classic modern, the sponsors meant classic treated in a modern way. General Electric provided extensive lighting including in the pools under the water-lilies and along the allée of white birch trees. William Wheeler contributed the white marble sculpture, *Maya,* which stood on axis with the pavilion in front of a green arborvitae hedge. Demonstrating a modern approach to garden design, it was judged to be the finest of the landscape exhibits.

A second model garden by Flanders was "America's Little House" in New York City in 1934. The house was designed by Roger H. Bullard, and the interior included a kitchen designed by the renowned Lillian Gilbreth for the New York Herald-Tribune Institute. The model home and garden were to promote family life and the qualities of convenience and economy in order to increase the apparent viability of single-family home ownership. The garden featured a simple Colonial Revival design using lawn, flowering shrubs, boxwood, and apple trees. Citizens of New York City were delighted to realize thirty-six apples growing on the trees the following fall. Flanders used these model gardens to teach the public the value of well-designed gardens and landscapes.

Flanders hired women to work as designers in her office, including Helen Swift Jones* and Helen Elise Bullard,* as well as women graduates of the Lowthorpe and Cambridge schools. Her collection of source materials and images were available to her employees as well as being used for her "landscape school." It was not a formal school but rather a series of courses offered by Flanders in landscape design, drafting, construction, grading, soil preparation, planting, and maintenance. She would make arrangements with a local sponsor such as a museum, civic organization, or garden club to offer the series for a reasonable fee to the public. Attendees included young landscape architects (both men and women) alongside amateur gardeners and designers. These courses served to educate young designers as well as clients and to promote the profession.

As with many practitioners, Flanders advocated for the profession of landscape architecture by lecturing for botanical societies, schools, and garden clubs. She wrote extensively on the principles of design for magazines including *House and Garden, Country Life in America, House Beautiful,* and the *Bulletin of the Garden Club of America.* She was *Good Housekeeping*'s Consultant Garden Editor in 1933–1934 and published a four-part series on her design philosophy for small suburban gardens in 1934.

Flanders retained the New York office until 1942, simultaneously maintaining a second office at the family's summer home, The Shelter, in Wisconsin. This arrangement allowed her to establish herself within the elite families of both the East Coast and Midwest. She was actively engaged with members of the ASLA and was elected as a Fellow in 1942 in recognition of her extensive work throughout the nation, the quality of her designs, and her dedication to the advancement of the profession. Flanders left New York in 1943 to open an office in Milwaukee that she ran until her death.

Annette Hoyt Flanders died of cancer on June 7, 1946, at the age of fifty-eight. A collection of her papers has been placed in the Smith College Archives in Northampton, Massachusetts.

Filzen, Patricia. "Annette Hoyt Flanders: From Beaux Arts to Modernism." In *Midwestern Landscape Architecture,* ed. William H. Tishler, 231–42. Urbana: University of Illinois Press in cooperation with Library of American Landscape History Amherst Mass., 2000. A brief biography of Flanders and her most important works.

Filzen, Patricia Louise. "Garden Designs for the Western Great Lakes Region: Annette Hoyt Flanders and Early Twentieth Century Women Landscape Architects." Master's thesis, University of Wisconsin, 1988. The most comprehensive biography of Flanders and contemporary women landscape architects in the Midwest between 1915 and 1945.

Flanders, Annette Hoyt. *An Exhibition of Landscape Architecture.* New York: Privately published, 1932. Flanders published this herself with a foreword by Richardson Wright. It is a collection of images of her garden designs with captions for additional images that were a part of a larger exhibition.

Thaïsa Way

FRANCESCHI, DR. FRANCESCO (EMANUELE ORAZIO FENZI)
(1843–1924)
HORTICULTURIST, BOTANIST, AUTHOR, NURSERY OWNER, LANDSCAPE GARDENER, HYBRIDIZER

Emanuele Orazio Fenzi was born in Florence, Italy, in 1843. His paternal family was in banking and railroad development, and his mother was from the Gherardesca family. After the death of his parents, young Fenzi was raised by his grandfather at Palazzo Fenzi in Florence. He attended the University of Pisa, where in 1864 he obtained a doctor of law degree in preparation for entering the family businesses. His passion, however, was horticulture. He made the family's Villa Sant'Andrea south of Florence into a botanical showcase. He also became a significant Italian horticulturist, contributing to publications such as *The Gardeners' Chronicle* in London. He served as president of the Royal Tuscan Society of Horticulture. He also introduced plants, including bamboo, to Italy.

An economic crisis consumed the family fortune. Fenzi retained the title of Doctor and changed his name to Francesco Franceschi. In 1891, he moved with his wife, Cristina, and three of their six children to Los Angeles, California. He opened a shop as a nurseryman and horticultural book dealer. Always curious and full of energy, he surveyed and collected plants on Guadalupe Island, off of the Mexican coast, in the winter of 1892–1893. Franceschi published an article on the trip in the scientific journal *Zoe,* and began contributing to *Garden and Forest.*

In 1893, landscape architect Charles Frederick Eaton convinced Franceschi to move to Santa Barbara. Together, they established the Southern California Acclimatizing Association (SCAA) at Eaton's Montecito estate. They hybridized and introduced plants, grew California native plants, raised cut flowers for florists, and laid out orchards and gardens. The SCAA was the first nursery to scientifically evaluate new plants for California's unique

Dr. Francesco Franceschi (also known as E. O. Fenzi) by his lath house at Montarioso, Santa Barbara, California, 1912. (Photo used by permission of Dr. Charles Fenzi, courtesy of the Warren E. Fenzi collection)

climatic conditions. In 1895, Franceschi published *Santa Barbara Exotic Flora* (an essential reference for reconstructing California's version of the Victorian garden), ended his partnership with Eaton, and moved the SCAA to downtown Santa Barbara.

Using seeds obtained from his contacts all over the world and assisted by his talented daughter, Ernestina, Franceschi introduced and propagated little-known plants and wrote about them throughout his career. His 1897 SCAA *General Catalogue and Garden Guide* is one of California's important early references. In 1903, Franceschi's wife purchased 40 acres of land on a remote ridge overlooking Santa Barbara and the Pacific Ocean. Franceschi built a house on the property and moved his SCAA stock to the site from downtown. He laid out a botanic garden based on his analysis of microclimates, soil, topography, and water requirements. Hoping to create an educational resource as well as a nursery, he designed the site so plants were "picturesquely arranged

but grouped in scientific order." In 1904, his nursery supplied 360 palm trees (mainly Canary Island date palms) to line the principal drives in a nearby new suburb called Hope Ranch. The Franceschis called their property Montarioso and in 1905 built their house in the Arts and Crafts style.

From 1907 to 1909, Franceschi legally incorporated the SCAA. At this time, he established a partnership with horticulturist and landscape architect Peter Riedel, who moved the SCAA in the direction of design-build garden contracting. Franceschi's main role was as a landscape gardener specializing in plant propagation. He supplied Dr. A. B. Doremus, Santa Barbara's first park superintendent, with trees, including the famous stone pines that were raised from seed and planted on Anapamu Street. When the partnership ended, Riedel kept the SCAA business and Franceschi founded the Montarioso Nursery with his daughter, Ernestina F. Franceschi, as proprietor.

Franceschi was always interested in finding the right fit between plant and place. Long before it was popular, he increased awareness of the value of drought-tolerant landscaping and promoted California's native flora. By 1912 his plant collection at Montarioso was among the most exotic growing in the open anywhere in the United States. It included 100 varieties of palms and many other species unknown elsewhere in the United States.

Franceschi's influence on the California landscape is most deeply felt in Santa Barbara, where his introductions of succulents and flowering trees, such as *Erythrina, Bauhinia, Chorisia,* and *Tipuana,* enhance the city's reputation as a Riviera-like paradise. In addition to these tangible reminders of his presence, he was a significant horticultural authority. He contributed to compilations such as **Liberty Hyde Bailey**'s *Cyclopedia of American Horticulture,* and collaborated with David Fairchild* for the U.S. Department of Agriculture's Office of Foreign Seed and Plant Introduction. Franceschi conducted plant surveys, hybridized the Montecito rose, and introduced zucchini squash to the United States.

Franceschi was a relative latecomer to the thriving California horticultural scene, yet he introduced more plants than anyone else to Southern California, including more than 800 to the Santa Barbara region. Of these, at least 200 were completely new introductions to the state of California. Widely admired for his work and intellectual ability, Franceschi was the first to describe *Brahea elegans;* today, it is called the Franceschi palm in his honor. For his plant introductions, he was awarded the third Meyer Memorial Medal by the Council of the American Genetic Association in 1922.

Despite his achievements, Franceschi never experienced financial success in the United States. At the age of seventy, after twenty years in Santa Barbara, he returned to Italy in 1913 at the request of the Italian government. There, he resumed using the name Fenzi, published a definitive book devoted to growing rare fruits (*Frutti Tropicali e Semitropicali*), and moved to what was then the Italian colony of Libya in North Africa. Assisted by Ernestina, Franceschi had a tremendous impact on that landscape. He died in Tripoli in 1924, and was often referred to as Dr. Franceschi Fenzi in the years after his death. In California, a portion of Montarioso became Franceschi Park in 1931, and in 1934, Dr. Franceschi Fenzi Boulevard in Tripoli was named in his honor.

Beittel, Will. *Dr. F. Franceschi: Pioneer Plantsman*. Santa Barbara, Calif.: Santa Barbara County Horticultural Society, 1984. This extensive examination of Franceschi's life and work is more thorough than Victoria Padilla included in her 1961 landmark book, *Southern California Gardens*.

Chamberlin, Susan. "The Life of Dr. Francesco Franceschi and His Park [in two parts]." *Pacific Horticulture* 63 (July 2002), 4–12; (October 2002), 13–20. Surveys Franceschi's career, his plant introductions and life in Libya, and the evolution of Franceschi Park in Santa Barbara; includes bibliography.

Franceschi, Dr. F. *Santa Barbara Exotic Flora: A Handbook of Plants from Foreign Countries Grown in Santa Barbara, California ...* Santa Barbara, Calif.: Privately published by the author, 1895. One of numerous Franceschi publications, this important contribution to our understanding of Victorian gardens describes native and introduced plant material and Santa Barbara gardens prior to 1895.

Susan Chamberlin

FRIEDBERG, M. PAUL
(1931–   )
LANDSCAPE ARCHITECT, EDUCATOR

M. Paul Friedberg was born in 1931 in New York City. He spent much of his youth in rural Pennsylvania and Middletown, New York. When his father became a weekend landscape contractor and established a nursery business, the teenage Friedberg actively assisted. After finishing high school, he studied ornamental horticulture in the agriculture school at Cornell University. College proved a formative experience for Friedberg. He took classes in the liberal arts department and met worldly colleagues and faculty, who introduced him to classical music, history, and art. Despite this academic focus he pursued a career in horticulture after graduation. He moved to New York City and instead found work in architecture and landscape architecture offices. His assignments were mundane, and his limited drafting abilities were quickly revealed, but during this time Friedberg gained valuable experience and a familiarity with prevailing urban park planning processes. Most importantly, he began to develop an interest in design.

In 1958, after two years outfitting city parks with stock features in standard configurations, he established his own practice, M. Paul Friedberg and Associates. It was fortuitous timing. Landscape architecture was just emerging as a distinct, professionalized field. A small group of pioneers including Lawrence Halprin,* Robert

M. Paul Friedberg. (M. Paul Friedberg & Partners)

Left: Plan detail of Jacob Riis Plaza, New York, New York. (Photo by Charles A. Birnbaum)

Below: Plan of Jacob Riis Plaza, New York, New York. (Photo by Charles A. Birnbaum)

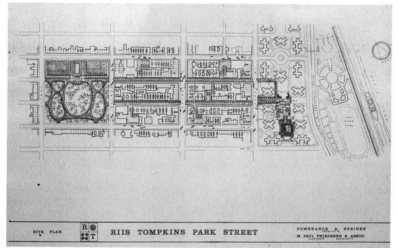

RIIS TOMPKINS PARK STREET

lic needs and was increasingly frustrated by the waste, thoughtless inertia, and condescension that seemed to characterize the process of public landscape design.

In 1963, Friedberg's firm was hired to remodel the outdoor areas surrounding Carver Houses, a public housing project in New York City. They removed chain link fences, asphalt, and the standard playground pieces and introduced a spray pool and sandbox and a few other modest changes. It was a tentative step beyond typical playground form. Two subsequent public housing playground projects showed how varying gradients and topography contributed to exciting play places, and provided insights into appropriate ways of integrating modular manufactured playground pieces into more dynamic environments.

Thanks to a private grant, Friedberg was free to combine these new approaches with his first "total play environment" at Jacob Riis Houses in Manhattan's Lower East Side. Opened in 1965, it featured a series of experiences—a tree house, mounds, a tunnel—made primarily of granite block and separated by changes in the landscape. Paths, slides, and swings linked the various features within a unified landscape, the boundaries of which were delineated not by fences, but by changes in materials and other tactile and visual cues.

Riis Plaza was a watershed event. It was widely publicized (even appearing in *Life* magazine) and made the thirty-four-year-old Friedberg an instant expert. Riis Plaza and his other playground designs were distinct from other play spaces because they were not composed of isolated play features that could only be used in one

Lewis Zion,* Garrett Eckbo,* and Daniel Urban Kiley* were opening landscape design to modern ideas and exploring new forms of public spaces. It was clear that urban open spaces needed help. Cast aside by postwar suburbanization, the urban environment was increasingly considered threatening, dehumanizing, and in hopeless decline. Public parks and playgrounds were regarded as escapes from the malevolent city, but their designs were often unresponsive to the users' needs.

Bound by convention and bureaucracy, Friedberg's early work was unexceptional. Yet he was increasingly aware of the disconnect between public spaces and pub-

Jacob Riis Plaza, New York, New York.
(M. Paul Friedberg & Partners)

way, by one child, from one age group, at a time. His playgrounds and their linked experiences, shifting grades and points of prominence and seclusion, provided opportunities for discovery, experimentation, exploration, creativity, and cooperation. Friedberg's empirical approach—studying his past work to identify successful and failed elements, and observing how landscapes are used—gave voice to the user and enabled him to design play places that met the needs of those users.

With these projects Friedberg's reputation as a preeminent designer of urban play areas was firmly established. He furthered this expertise with publications. His 1970 book *Play and Interplay* criticized the existing play area design process that provided isolated facilities without acknowledging or understanding the intended users "true needs, habits, nature, and desires" and without appreciation for the larger urban environment. It called for a "new recreation" in which the design of multifaceted play areas was integrated with education, housing, commerce, and transportation planning. In 1975, Friedberg published *Handcrafted Playgrounds: Designs You Can Build Yourself.* The book illustrated how amateur builders could construct customized play facilities with simple materials. By linking together assemblies of stacked timbers, nets, poles, tire swings, and drums designers can produce stimulating play areas that were adaptable to different age groups, lot sizes, and budgets.

Friedberg also became a leading designer of new public spaces including diminutive vest-pocket parks, municipal and corporate plazas, and main street malls. The 1972 A.C. Nielsen headquarters near Chicago, though a suburban setting, included early versions of features that became central to his public space design vocabulary. The primary landscape element was a retaining pond with a plan characterized by right angles. Small islands, one connected to the shore by bridges, complicated the pond's shape and accommodated additional plantings. Ringed by paths and benches, the pond was set into the site and emphasized with sloping terraces above. Changes in grade screened the parking lot and introduced variety to the otherwise flat site.

Subsequent designs in the 1970s and 1980s, like Peavey Plaza in downtown Minneapolis and the Fulton County Government Plaza in Atlanta, Georgia, showed Friedberg adapting and reworking these elements. Paths and bridges interspersed among pools, ponds, and water courses immersed visitors in the landscape. To encourage year round use, the 1979 Pershing Park in Washington, D.C., and Calgary's 1987 Olympic Plaza both featured pools that were converted to ice rinks in the winter. This flexibility was carried over from earlier playground work as well as Friedberg's continued observations of what made public spaces successful. Also in common with his designs for play areas was the interconnection of park features as a means to encourage discovery and initiate an active engagement with the environment.

Friedberg has proven adept at making the most of the city's vertical nature. His 1982 Park Place is set above a parking garage. In 1989 he retrofitted a rooftop plaza for New York's Fordham University, converting the space to a lush campus green. The design featured a large lawn area, amphitheater, flower and sculpture gardens, and a connected entrance and seating area for the school's dining facility. Friedberg's playground at Yerba Buena Gardens, atop a San Francisco convention center, remained true to his established approach to play area design. It is a three-dimensional linked environment where play features, from sandboxes to a maze, are joined with slides, stairs, paths, catwalks, and tunnels.

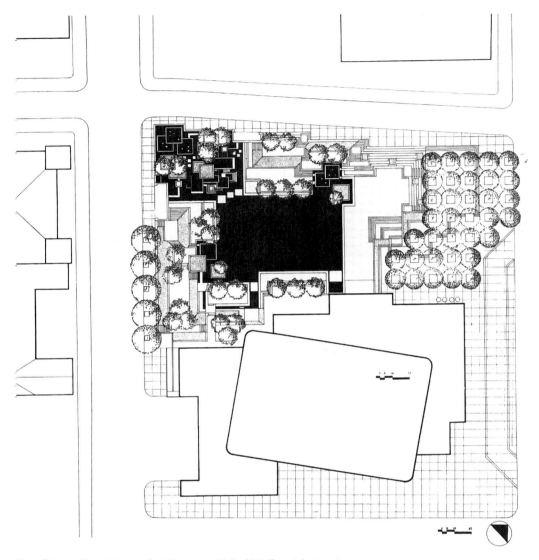

Plan of Peavey Plaza, Minneapolis, Minnesota. (M. Paul Friedberg & Partners)

A sundial, learning garden, and a mural inscribed with measurements, emphasize experiential education as a component of play. The result: a continuous flow of play, exploration, and revelation.

Friedberg's recent work illustrates his varied talents and convictions. Battery Park on Manhattan's southern tip represents his continued interest in fostering public-private partnerships. Holon Park in Holon, Israel, mixes contemporary recreational activities (entertainment and shopping) with public urban spaces. The

Hascoe Residence in Greenwich, Connecticut, and the Promenade Classique in Alexandria, Virginia, were collaborations with other artists. La Jolla Commons in San Diego, California, and Andromeda Houses in Jaffa, Israel, show Friedberg's philosophy of linked experiences and multi-use spaces applied to private housing developments that blend with the surrounding public environment.

Friedberg has served on the faculty at Harvard University, Columbia University, Pratt Institute, and other

Battery Park City, World Financial Center 1, New York, New York. (M. Paul Friedberg & Partners)

universities. Recognizing the need to educate a new generation of professionals, he founded the Urban Landscape Architecture Program at the City College of New York in 1970. He was the director of the department, the first of its kind in the country, for the next twenty years.

Numerous awards confirm Friedberg's contribution to the field of landscape architecture and the design of urban public spaces. In 1979 he was made a Fellow of the American Society of Landscape Architects. The following year, the American Institute of Architects recognized Friedberg's efforts to integrate the design work of various disciplines and presented him with the AIA Medal for an allied professional. Ball State University conferred a doctorate of laws on him in 1983, and in 1984 France awarded him the Chevalier de L'Ordre des Arts et de Lettres. In 2004 he received the American Society of Landscape Architect's Design Medal, the organization's highest honor. Additionally Friedberg's individual designs have received eighty-five national and international awards.

Today, Friedberg remains active at his firm M. Paul Friedberg and Partners. His career has been one that questioned established convention. His designs replaced fences and signs with spaces that were open to the broader urban environment and open to a multiplicity of uses. Friedberg's varied landscapes accommodated the differing recreational desires of children, adolescents, adults, and the elderly, providing independent spaces that still allowed encounters, exchange, and observation. They countered the city's image as a lonely and unnatural place. His designs were not set apart as refuges from the city but enmeshed within it. They engaged the whirl of urban life and were unapologetically vital and active. In all, Friedberg's work shares a common conviction: that designed landscapes can enhance life by revealing beauty in the environment and in human contact.

Bennett, Paul. *M. Paul Friedberg: Social Force, Projects 1988–2000. LandForum* 8. Berkeley, Calif.: Spacemaker Press, Palace Press International, 1999. Chronological survey of late work. Includes an introductory essay that places this work in context by Bennett and an editorial by Peter Walker. Concludes with current projects. Richly illustrated.

Friedberg, M. Paul. *Process 82. M. Paul Friedberg: Landscape Design.* Tokyo: Process Architecture Publishing Company, Ltd., 1989. Includes probing essays by Jonathan Barnett and William Hollingsworth Whyte Jr.* that places Friedberg's work in context. Chronological survey of critical projects beginning with Riis Park Plaza in 1965 through the 1980s.

Friedberg, M. Paul, and Ellen Perry Berkeley. *Play and Interplay: A Manifesto for New Design in Urban Recreational Environment.* New York: The Macmillan Company, 1970. Practical design solutions for all age groups from children to the elderly. Many Friedberg design projects are richly illustrated with extensive black and white photography.

Chad Randl

FURLONG, ETHELBERT ELY
(1894–1993)
LANDSCAPE ARCHITECT

Ethelbert Furlong was born in Dover, New Jersey, in 1894, and was raised in Newark. After his father's death, he left school for work. His long career in landscape architecture began inauspiciously when he applied for a "nursery job," believing it would be with children. It was instead a landscape nursery needing a day laborer. Although barely in his teens, he was hired and started digging and driving the wagons. Eventually, he was planning and supervising installation and attending night classes at Pratt Institute in Brooklyn. In 1917, he was hired by Mann & MacNeille as a draftsman and later by Brinley and Holbrook (John Rowlett Brinley*), both landscape architecture firms in New York City. Furlong married and had two sons. In 1921, he opened his own landscape architecture office at 15 Washington Street, in Newark. Later, he moved his family to Montclair and his office to Glen Ridge, neighboring New Jersey towns.

In 1932, when presenting his portfolio to the American Society of Landscape Architects, Furlong wrote he had "come to landscape architecture as a craftsman not an academic" and for his commissions he "personally assumed full responsibility of design, construction, planting and business management." He joined the Society and The Architectural League of New York.

Before World War II, many of Furlong's commissions were for large properties in New Jersey, and some in New York and Connecticut. Most were English, French, or Mediterranean in style; a few of the others he labeled "Rocks and Water," foreshadowing his later Japanese gardens. In an early 1930s sales brochure, Furlong listed his design projects: thirty-two private residences, six apartments, one cigar factory, one sewage pumping installation, two cemeteries, one bank, one country club, and one construction company.

The Ladies' Home Journal commissioned Furlong to design the "Garden of Flexible Forms" for its House of Tomorrow at the North American Home Exposition at Madison Square Garden, New York City, in 1937. The same year Charles Nichols's Pleasantdale Farm, a Furlong design, was included in The Architectural League of New York's exhibit and his article about it appeared in *Landscape Architecture*. Photos and information about that design and four others of his were

Ethelbert Furlong. (Courtesy of the Furlong family)

included in the 1947 exhibit, The Contemporary House and Its Neighborhood, at the Trenton State Museum in New Jersey.

Furlong volunteered for service in the U.S. Navy Seabees in 1943. He trained at Pace Institute and shipped out to England where, as a member of the 81st Construction Battalion, he supervised the building of military housing. After D-Day, he camouflaged military equipment on the Normandy beaches until he was ordered to Paris to design tennis courts for officers. He ended his tour of duty in the Pacific as a chief petty officer designing landing strips.

Returning to his practice, many of Furlong's commissions now reflected his longtime knowledge of and in-

Above: Pace-Setter House garden (Garden of 100 Stones), Orange, New Jersey. (Gottscho-Schleisner, photographers; Library of Congress, Prints and Photographs Division, Gottscho-Schleisner Collection)

Right: Furlong's residential work is seen at the Sunken Garden of Mrs. Jay R. Monroe, South Orange, New Jersey, from ASLA *Illustrations of Works of Members,* 1934.

terest in the Orient, especially Japanese gardens. These gardens brought him the most acclaim. The postwar building boom gave him many opportunities to design in this style including *House Beautiful*'s "The 12 Month-a-Year Garden" for its Pace-Setter House. Landscape architect **Thomas Dolliver Church** served as consultant. This contemporary house and garden in Orange, New Jersey, was open to the public and featured prominently in the magazine's November 1949 issue. Photos of this garden appeared numerous times in the magazine over the next several years with glowing references to Furlong's mastery of both design and texture with plant and hardscape material that gave interest year-round.

Furlong's article about the Pace-Setter House garden, renamed the Garden of 100 Stones, which appeared in *Landscape Architecture,* elicited a letter from **Fletcher Steele**, who stated, "It is a charming surprise to come on the photographs of your Garden of a 100 Steps (*sic*) in *Landscape Architecture.* The design shows stalwart poetry with a true understanding of the best of Japan made comfortable for an American. Truly I admire it more than any garden in this country that I remember. The foliage texture appeals more than in Japan, which you evidently like better than I. They have a cruel way of trimming shrubs. Yours are let alone and look free. The more I look at it,

the more I think you have improved on the Japs. It is fine. Congratulations."

According to Furlong's diary, he met the architects Philip Johnson and Edward Durrell Stone at The Architectural League of New York Awards Dinner on June 1, 1950, where Furlong received honorable mention for his Garden of 100 Stones. Two weeks later he noted in his diary that he and Johnson had met regarding the Museum of Modern Art garden. Subsequently, Johnson visited New Jersey to view some of Furlong's commissions including the Garden of 100 Stones, and Furlong gave him a plan. On July 15, 1950, Furlong wrote in his diary that he sent a print of the Museum plan to Johnson. This plan, labeled A Kare-sansui Garden (Natural Style), could have been the inspiration for the sansui garden of the Museum of Modern Art's Japanese Exhibition House, which opened in 1954. Philip Johnson and Tansai Sano were listed as designers of the garden, and Ethelbert Furlong as consultant. In this capacity, he selected, purchased, and supervised the installation of the plant material.

In 1950, *The Ladies' Home Journal* once again called upon Furlong, this time to design the properties of fifteen or more of its demonstration Portfolio Houses in Pennsylvania, New York, and New Jersey. These were mostly small houses on small lots. His designs were attractive, innovative, and inexpensive ways for the homeowners to individualize and utilize their limited outdoor areas. For those who couldn't visit these properties, photos, plans, and approximate costs were detailed in the magazine from 1951 until the early 1960s.

Ethelbert Furlong was honored in 1965 at a White House ceremony where Lady Bird Johnson presented him with the American Association of Nurserymen's Industrial Landscaping Award for the Japanese garden at Capital Car Company Distributors in Lanham, Maryland.

In addition to his two articles in *Landscape Architecture,* references and photos of his work also appeared in the magazine over the years as they did in the *New York Times,* the *Brooklyn Botanic Garden Record, House and Garden, House Beautiful* and *The Ladies' Home Journal* plus many other garden magazines and books. In the 1940s, several Furlong prewar gardens were featured in *Casas y Jardines,* an Argentinean publication. He served as a design judge at the International Flower Shows held at the Grand Central Palace and later at the New York Coliseum.

In the late 1960s, Furlong began to simplify his life. He reduced his workload and office staff so he could take longer overseas trips. This also afforded him more time for painting and reading. He retired in 1984 and died nine years later in 1993. He was fondly remembered by many clients, and by one as "a true gentleman who always arrived in a Lincoln, wearing saddle shoes."

Among Furlong's professional papers in the Ethelbert E. Furlong Collection at the Joint Free Public Library of Morristown and Morris Township, N.J., are over six hundred plans of his commissions including private residences, apartments, libraries, schools, factories, churches, and country clubs. Slides of thirty-two of Furlong's commissions are in the Archives of American Gardens, Smithsonian Institution, Washington, D.C.

Ascher, Amalie. "Breezewood: A Japanese Garden." *The Green Scene. Pennsylvania Horticulture Society's Magazine,* September/October 1981, 13. Discusses the wonders of Breezewood.

Furlong, Ethelbert E. "The French Provincial: The Atmosphere of an Old-World Garden." *Landscape Architecture* 27, no. 4 (July 1937), 179–85. Discusses the design principals of a French Provincial style garden.

Furlong, Ethelbert E. "Garden of 100 Stones: Contemporary American Conception in the Japanese Style." *Landscape Architecture* (October 1952), 5–11. Discusses the ideas behind the design of a Japanese garden that Furlong designed for the "House Beautiful" Pace-Setter House in 1949.

Diane Brandley Clarke

FURNESS, FAIRMAN
(1889–1971)
HORTICULTURIST

Fairman Rogers Furness was born in 1889, the grandnephew of noted architect Frank Furness. He grew up in Philadelphia, traveled Europe with his parents, attended St. Paul's and Harvard College, and served as the Third Secretary at the United States Embassy in St. Petersburg, Russia, from September 1912 through March 1915. He resigned the diplomatic post to return to Delaware County, Pennsylvania, where he bought land along Ridley Creek that was once part of a cotton mill known as Upper Bank. He called the place Upper Bank Farm. It was not far from Wallingford where his parents had a suburban house on an 80-acre estate belonging to his grandfather, Shakespearean scholar Horace Howard Furness. In 1894, the elder Furness wrote to a friend about the joys of gardening: "I take endless delight in flowers whose language is distinct to my deaf ears; and my only recreation in winter is in my green house, where I potter among the flowers, making cuttings, trying experiments, hybridising [*sic*], and having a real good time," never dreaming his grandson would transform a similar love of gardening into a life's work.

The Wallingford property, known as Lindenshade, featured an allée from the railroad station to the house, water garden, maze, rose garden, orchard, a collection of magnolias, and a Japanese garden with a teahouse. Formal plantings were integrated with naturalistic ones, and these, in turn, led to fields and woodland. In the summer of 1870 Horace Furness won a prize for his champion corn and six years later guests exclaimed over his night-blooming cereus (*Hylocereus undatus*). As a boy and young man, Fairman Furness spent considerable time at Lindenshade where he especially enjoyed the portion of the property that had once been the Wallingford Nursery. Skills learned at Lindenshade served as the foundation of his horticultural knowledge and the base upon which he built a career in which he was self-taught.

By July 1915, the nucleus of Upper Bank Farm belonged to Furness and he oversaw construction of an entry drive and bridge over Ridley Creek and a barn. He renovated an old stone farmhouse and repaired various outbuildings including a chicken house and tool shed. When he moved to the property in 1917, the lower field was planted in corn and a formal flower garden was laid out near the house. The site required extensive grading to create areas for the cultivation of ornamental plants and the eventual transformation of farm into nursery, but the planting plan retained the association between the two with location designations such as an orchard field where he grew hybrid azaleas.

In 1921, Furness was elected a member of the Pennsylvania Horticultural Society as a nurseryman and seven years later began a term on the Executive Council that was renewed continuously through 1954. As he was establishing himself in the twenties and thirties, changes were afoot at several great nearby gardens. Longwood opened in 1921, Winterthur expanded under H. F. du Pont who inherited the property in 1927, and Mount Cuba was being established by the Copelands, whose house was completed in 1937. Fairman Furness had a hand in all these gardens, designing a rock garden for Mrs. Copeland, moving large specimen plants at Longwood, and supplying H. F. du Pont with trees and shrubs like *Magnolia sieboldii, Catalpa speciosa,* and *Cercis canadensis.*

In addition, his involvement at Gibraltar and St. Anom estates for H. Rodney Sharp and Lammot du Pont can also be attested to as they appear on Furness's client list. Besides Wilmington and Odessa, Delaware, clients, Furness had an association with landscape architect **Fletcher Steele**, who he met through another client, Grahame Wood. Steele became a Wood family friend and advised two generations on landscape matters. Furness met Naumkeag's owner, Mabel Choate, through Wood and went to Naumkeag in Stockbridge, Massachusetts, for house parties. He often brought plants. In June 1958, six months before Mabel's death, he wrote that "after lunch we all sat in the little garden while a painter put samples of color on the new gondola posts and Mabel and Fletcher approved or corrected."

Furness supplied plants for several Steele-designed

Fairman Furness, watercolor self-portrait, 1946. (Private Collection)

gardens in and around Philadelphia, where Upper Bank was the nursery of choice for many horticulturalists. As testified by a 1932 price list, the earliest surviving catalog of Upper Bank Nurseries, the commercial grower offered an impressive list of perennials, rock plants, shrubs, vines, and ground covers. Its catalog also carried the notice that in addition to plants listed, the nursery would sell more common shrubs and evergreens at nominal prices to make space available for rare and unusual plants. Ten years later, the results of Furness's collaboration with Mary G. Henry, a noted field botanist, were offered in a catalog of rare native shrubs available to the public for the first time. *Rhododendron chapmanii,* identified by Dr. Rehder, a rhododendron specialist, is described as the "hardy form of one of the rarest and most beautiful of all native rhododendron . . . never before found outside of Florida." Furness and Henry also contributed rare, nonnative plants to the trade and several appear in the catalog. An example is *Magnolia cylindrica,* "a very beautiful small tree from dry slopes in the Himalayas."

In demand as a lecturer, Furness traveled to garden clubs and horticultural societies where he illustrated his talks with hand-colored lantern slides (all lost), botanical illustrations, or quick sketches with colored pencils done while speaking to the group. When the Garden

Club of America held its annual meeting in Philadelphia in 1938, Furness served on the visiting gardens committee and perhaps this was the impetus behind his creation of the Spanish Steps, a display area at the nursery begun in 1939.

After World War II, Furness no longer sold perennials but he continued to hybridize daylilies, keeping meticulous records of his crosses and participating in trials sponsored by the U.S. Department of Agriculture. A quote from *The Merchant of Venice,* "How poor are they that have not patience," is on the first page of his hybridizing notebook, a reference that would have pleased his scholarly grandfather, who published a variorum edition of the play in 1888. Furness also crossed azaleas and rhododendrons, grafted lilacs, experimented with hollies, and expanded his collection of bamboo while continuing the fundamental business of the nursery. Upper Bank was also a destination for members of the holly, magnolia, and other plant societies and local arboreta interested in viewing mature specimens of unusual varieties or cultivars. When Furness bought Upper Bank in 1915 he described it as the Promised Land. He lived and worked there over fifty years, dying at Upper Bank on September 30, 1971.

Darke, Rick. "The Garden Artistry of Upper Bank." *The Green Scene* 23 (March/April 1995), 3–7. Illustrated with photographs by Rick Darke, this article showcases the creative vision and design talent of Fairman Furness and other family members.
Furness, Fairman. "Journals and Notebooks, 1939–43, 1944–47, 1957–60, 1961–64." Private Collection, Media, Pa. These handwritten and typewritten papers record the development of the nursery and mention clients, although they do not, generally, describe the nature of the work.
Upper Bank Nurseries. "Catalogs. 1932–1965" (incomplete series). Very few catalogs survive and no one repository has a complete run. Most are available at the McLean Library of the Pennsylvania Horticultural Society, several are at Winterthur Library, and eight are among the Furness papers in a private collection at Media, Pa.

Maria M. Thompson

GRÉBER, JACQUES-HENRI-AUGUSTE
(1882–1962)
LANDSCAPE ARCHITECT, URBAN PLANNER, AUTHOR

Jacques-Henri-Auguste Gréber was born in 1882 in Paris, to a family of artists of Austrian origin. In 1901, he gained admission to the architecture section of the Paris École des Beaux-Arts, receiving his diplôme (M.Arch.) in 1908.

Gréber's focus of activity in the 1910s was formal gardens in the spirit of André Le Nôtre's seventeenth-century creations. Achille Duchêne, who worked in the United States and whose pencil rendering techniques Gréber emulated, assumed a leadership position in promoting this landscape revival. Based on the serious study of historical precedents, the best examples of the revival combined authenticity in detail with a truly creative breadth of vision. Like Le Nôtre, Duchêne and Gréber used symmetry and optical devices to compose sweeping vistas where horizontal surfaces, such as intricate *parterres de broderie,* grassy *tapis vert*, stepped terraces, and foun-

Casa de Serralves, Porto, Portugal, 1995 view. (Photo by Charles A. Birnbaum)

tains played against vertical elements of bosquet, treillage, balustrades, or allegorical statuary. The fact that neo-rococo groups by his father, the sculptor Henri-Léon

A perspective drawing of the formal Gardens at Harbour Hill, Roslyn, New York, from Gréber's *L'Architecture aux Etats-Unis*, Paris, 1920.

Gréber, were sought after to adorn French-style gardens explains in part Gréber's initial career path.

A cosmopolitan phenomenon, the Le Nôtre revival had its counterpart in architectural design and interior decoration. Wealthy Americans were particularly attracted to this aristocratic "package." One of Gréber's earliest clients was Pecci Blunt, for whom he re-created the garden of the Hôtel Cassini, using treillage to terminate its axis and conceal a tennis court. During Gréber's first visit to the United States, in 1910, he formalized the existing landscape design by Boston architect and École graduate Guy Lowell. Gréber respected the lateral vista at Harbor Hill, the Roslyn, Long Island, estate of Clarence Mackay. Stanford White patterned Harbor Hill after François Mansart's château at Maisons, so Gréber's design complemented the property.

Most of Gréber's American gardens were for homes designed by the Philadelphia office of Horace Trumbauer, whose adaptations of European classical models were often heavy-handed, but not devoid of panache. In 1913, Gréber was called to transform the stodgily designed grounds of Lynnewood Hall, the neo-Georgian estate of Peter A. B. Widener in Elkins Park near Philadelphia; its garden ornaments included sculptures by Gréber's father. Gréber's most splendid American garden was Whitemarsh Hall, the 300-acre estate of Edward T.

Stotesbury in Chestnut Hill, Pennsylvania. It combined French and English formal traditions, brilliantly adapting elements traditionally intended for flat land to the undulating terrain. However the garden is no longer extant. Gréber's surviving gardens are located at private residences. For example, Miramar, the property of Alexander Hamilton Rice, who married the widow of George Widener, was designed by Trumbauer and is located in Newport, Rhode Island. In Jericho, Long Island, Gréber designed a more modest but very sophisticated creation for Hautbois, the Walter E. Maynard residence that Ogden Codman had designed in the spirit of a Louis XV hunting lodge.

In 1917, with Stotesbury's support, Gréber was hired as consultant to the Fairmount Park Commission in Philadelphia and made the transition from landscape to urban design. David Brownlee credits him for transforming what is known today as the Benjamin Franklin Parkway "from an urban boulevard to a green wedge of park reaching toward the congested center of the city." Gréber also refined "some of the awkwardness of the earlier plan" and developed the idea of erecting replicas of the Place de la Concorde twin buildings on Logan Circle. Gréber's plan for the landscape surrounding the Philadelphia Museum of Art hangs in the museum today.

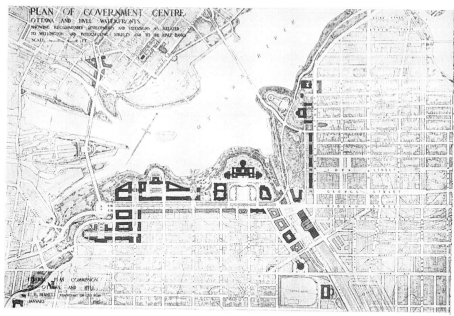

Left: Plan for the Canadian National Capital (Ottowa), 1950. (Courtesy of Charles A. Birnbaum)

Below: Philadelphia's Benjamin Franklin Parkway as seen from the Capitol, from Gréber's *L'Architecture aux Etats-Unis,* Paris, 1920.

After 1920, Gréber was primarily active outside of the United States. A pragmatist with regards to stylistic and functional issues, he imparted a synthetic and broad vision to his various endeavors. His architectural output—schools, houses, and apartment buildings—was modest. Garden commissions were occasional but significant. In addition to the Parc Kellerman (1937–1950) in Paris, Gréber fashioned the grounds of the Villa Trianon in Versailles (for Elsie de Wolfe), the Casa de Serralves in Porto, Portugal; and designed and restored the grounds of the Villa Reale di Marlia in Tuscany, Italy. Named Inspecteur Général de l'Urbanisme in 1942, he coordinated the reconstruction of Rouen, Abbeville, and Calais. His 1939 and 1950 plans for Ottawa played a major role in fashioning the present landscape and infrastructure of the Canadian capital by combining Ottawa and Hull into one city. It also included proposals for a park system, (known as the Greenbelt), satellite towns, formal boulevards and plazas, and an efficient transportation system.

However, Gréber never severed his ties with the United States. In 1920, his book *L'Architecture aux Etats-Unis* (where he publicized his own designs) gave American achievements in the field of civic art, estate design, and low cost housing their first extensive examination in France. In the early 1920s, Gréber's proposal to fashion the zone separating Paris and its suburbs into a recreational greenbelt, and his garden city in Vitry-sur-Seine, were influenced by American precedents. In the 1920s,

Gréber acted as consultant to the Regional Planning Federation of the Philadelphia Tri-State District. In 1929 in Philadelphia, he designed the grounds for the Rodin Museum designed by architect Paul Philippe Cret.* He developed the plan for the grounds of the American military cemetery in Suresnes (near Paris). Gréber also designed the grounds of the U.S. pavilion at the 1931 Exposition Coloniale (a replica of Mount Vernon). His position as architect in chief of the 1937 International Exposition in Paris led him to act as consultant for the 1939 New York World's Fair. As a professor at the Institut d'Urbanisme, Gréber shared his American expertise with a new and influential generation of French architects and planners. Gréber died in Paris in 1962.

There is no dedicated Gréber archive. Architectural Archives of the University of Pennsylvania and the Philadelphia Museum of Art keep a few of his drawings.

Brownlee, David B. *Building the City Beautiful. The Benjamin Franklin Parkway and the Philadelphia Museum of Art.* Exhibition catalog. Philadelphia: Philadelphia Museum of Art, 1989, 30–37.

Gréber, Jacques. *Jardines Modernes: Exposition Internationale de 1937.* Printed in France. Photographic portfolio of garden designs for the modern exposition of gardens curated by Gréber who had the title of Architecte en chef de l'Exposition. Also includes a brief introduction by Gréber.

Griswold, Mac, and Eleanor Weller. "Green Grandeur: American Estate Gardening in the French style 1890–1940." *Antiques* 140 (September 1991), 386–401.

Isabelle Gournay

GREGG, JOHN W.
(1880–1969)
LANDSCAPE ARCHITECT, LANDSCAPE EDUCATOR

Born in Weare, New Hampshire, on January 8, 1880, John William Gregg spent much of his childhood on a farm. His fascination with chemistry and botany led him to attend Massachusetts Agricultural College, now University of Massachusetts, Amherst, where professor of horticulture **Frank Albert Waugh** introduced him to the emerging field of landscape architecture. With course work in horticulture, civil engineering, and landscape design, Gregg received a bachelor of science degree from the college in 1904. Through an intercollegiate program he received a liberal arts degree from Boston University at the same time. As an educator and designer, Gregg promoted landscape design as a fine art and an essential compo-

nent of community development and everyday life. Late in life, his mentor Waugh would name him "Dean of the Teachers of Landscape Architecture in the United States," recognizing his broad influence.

Gregg's first jobs were primarily horticultural. Working first at the Louisiana Purchase Exposition in St. Louis in 1904, he experienced the City Beautiful grandeur of the fairgrounds designed by the **Olmsted Brothers** and **George Edward Kessler**. After working briefly in Texas, Gregg secured a position at Arbor Lodge, the estate of Arbor Day founder J. Sterling Morton in Nebraska City, Nebraska. From 1905 to 1907, he managed an active farm, the forest plantations established by Morton decades earlier, and

John Gregg, portrait sketch by Peter Van Valkenburgh, 1931. (College of Environmental Design Collection, Environmental Design Archives, University of California, Berkeley)

the formal gardens that **Warren Henry Manning** designed for Morton's son and heir, Joy Morton. Gregg married Mary Jennings on January 27, 1906; together they would raise three children.

Gregg began his teaching career in 1907 at the Baron de Hirsch Agricultural School in Woodbine, New Jersey, where he taught horticulture to young Jewish men preparing for careers in agriculture. From 1910 to 1913, as an assistant professor at Pennsylvania State College, now Pennsylvania State University, Gregg organized and headed the Department of Landscape Gardening and Floriculture under Dean Thomas F. Hunt, who soon after went west to head the College of Agriculture at the University of California at Berkeley. In 1913, Gregg accepted Hunt's invitation to join the faculty at Berkeley, where he served as professor and founding chair of the Division of Landscape Gardening and Floriculture until retiring in 1947 as a professor emeritus. A land-grant institution endowed by the Morrill Act of 1862, the College of Agriculture was nationally famous for its study of California plants and endeavored to train students in practical applications of science and agricultural enter-

prises. The East Bay region had an ideal growing climate and became a thriving center of large commercial nurseries, many devoted to propagating popular floral varieties and garden plants. In addition to horticultural preparation, Gregg's division provided training in the landscape design of schools, public buildings, residences, estates, parks, and playgrounds.

Gregg understood the democratic values and socioeconomic gains inherent in agricultural research and public education. Through the university's extension service, supported by the Smith-Lever Act of 1914, Gregg and his colleagues engaged in community outreach, encouraging town planning, countryside improvements, and landscape conservation throughout California. His 1919 design for Durham, a planned agricultural settlement in California's Great Valley, incorporated many landscape improvements and even included a planting plan for the new community building.

Immersed in a rapidly changing environment, Gregg and his students drew inspiration from the region's Mediterranean-like climate, widely diverse native flora, Hispanic roots, and pioneer heritage. Gregg embraced California's natural beauty and economic prosperity as an ideal environment in which to gain recognition for his profession and prepare his students for useful careers. He also encouraged his students to study in Europe or undertake graduate studies at East Coast schools, particularly Harvard University. His teaching led students to have an inventive and forward-looking perspective. Two of his students, **Thomas Dolliver Church** and Garrett Eckbo,* would transform the California landscape after World War II, and, with practitioners Daniel Urban Kiley* and **James C. Rose**, define an internationally recognized modernist landscape style. In addition, Gregg equipped several generations of landscape architects to tackle the problems of national park design and construction; most prominent was **Thomas Chalmers Vint**, who modeled a landscape division for the National Park Service after a professional design office in the 1920s. During the New Deal era, Vint hired many Berkeley-trained landscape architects to plan Public Works Administration projects and direct the work of the Civilian Conservation Corps in both national and state parks.

As Landscape Architect for the University of California, Gregg consulted on campus projects, including the President's House. From 1915 to 1930, he collaborated with University Architect John Galen Howard on new design and construction. For Gregg and his students, the Berkeley campus was a ready-made laboratory for apply-

Community Center Plan, Durham, California, 1919. (College of Environmental Design Collection, Environmental Design Archives, University of California, Berkeley)

ing the theoretical principles of design to practical contemporary problems. His students later recalled, "Gregg guided both the planting of the Berkeley campus, and the protecting of its native growth, tree by tree and shrub by shrub." Soon his consulting role extended to the entire California university system, and in the late 1920s he collaborated with architect George W. Kelham on the design of the new 400-acre campus at Los Angeles, which included an 80-acre subdivision of faculty residences.

Throughout his career, Gregg maintained an active private practice. Only a small portion of his work, which ranged from New Jersey to California, is currently known. In the 1920s *Landscape Architecture* highlighted his Berkeley designs for John Hinkel Park, the J. B. Havre Estate, his own Villa Greggoria, and the Roy O. Long Estate, a hillside estate featuring a garden vista

and Spanish tile pool. Using plantings archetypically Californian in quality, Gregg's work reflected simple and understated formal compositions, an excellent treatment of details, and a penchant for Spanish Colonial–inspired features such as intimate patio gardens. He also designed the Berkeley homes of Dean Charles Gilman Hyde and Richard J. McCarthy, and with, architect Albert Farr, a Menlo Park residence. In the mid-1930s he served as a consultant to the U.S. Bureau of Reclamation on the All-American Canal Project in California's Imperial Valley. Gregg was an active member of the Pacific Chapter of the American Society of Landscape Architects beginning in 1921, serving on its board for many years. Not only did this put Gregg in touch with West Coast practitioners, it also supplied new ideas to his teaching as well as his practice.

Gregg's writings in *Architect and Engineer, American City,* and *Landscape Architecture* covered a variety of topics from landscape education to campground planning, often drawing attention to the expanding role of landscape architects in shaping the built environment. In "Universities Broaden Scope of Training in Landscape Design," which appeared in *Architect and Engineer* in November 1937, Gregg described the profession's valuable service in designing large-scale public works, National Park Service and Forest Service work, and city and subdivision planning. His writings in *Landscape Architecture* on West Coast designers, such as **Stephen Child** and **Ralph Dalton Cornell**, communicated the profession's progress in California. Gregg also drew national attention to the artistic achievements, talent, and innovations of West Coast designers.

In June 1949, Gregg received an honorary doctorate of landscape architecture from the University of Massachusetts, his alma mater. Self-deprecating and kindly in character, with a dry sense of humor, Gregg's efforts were critical in establishing the profession of landscape architecture in California. Upon Gregg's retirement in 1947, landscape architect and former classmate **Albert Davis Taylor** wrote: "No man has done more than he to develop Landscape Architecture in the Far West to its present stature as an established profession." Gregg passed away in 1969.

Eckbo, Garrett, Robert B. Litton Jr., H. L. Vaughan, and Francis Violich. "John William Gregg, Landscape Architecture: Berkeley at 1970 University of California: in Memoriam." dynaweb. oac.cdlib.org:8088/dynaweb/uchist/public/inmemoriam/inmemoriam1970/995. Compiled by four graduates of the Department of Landscape Architecture at University of California, Berkeley, this tribute enumerates Gregg's many professional accomplishments and focuses on his pioneering role in defining the professional field of landscape architecture.

Gregg, John William. "A Half-Century of Landscape Architecture." Oral history conducted by Suzanne B. Riess, Regional Cultural History Project, University of California, Berkeley, 1965. Capturing his personal energy and character, this exemplary oral history documents Gregg's reflections on his life and career as well as the advancement of landscape architecture in the West.

Laurie, Michael, and David C. Streatfield. *75 Years of Landscape Architecture at Berkeley: An Informal History, Part I: The First 50 Years.* Berkeley: Department of Landscape Architecture, University of California, 1988. Includes Gregg's founding of the Department of Landscape Architecture in 1914 and the more than three decades when he served as professor, department head, and adviser to the California University System on campus planning and design.

Linda Flint McClelland and Noel D. Vernon

GUNN, RALPH ELLIS
(1908–1976)
LANDSCAPE ARCHITECT, ENGINEER

Ralph Ellis Gunn was born in Florida on September 16, 1908. One of the first generation of Texas landscape architects, Gunn received an undergraduate degree in engineering and entered Harvard's Graduate School of Design in 1930 where he received a master's degree in landscape architecture in 1934. Soon after graduation, Gunn returned to Florida. In 1936, Gunn designed the original 55-acre section for the Key West Botanical Garden located on Stock Island. The project was founded and developed by the Federal Emergency Relief Administration as a tourist destination during the Great Depression. Gunn's design included the design and construction of an amphitheater, aviary, greenhouses, tropical gardens, and the installation of over 7,000 plants.

In 1938, he began working for E. A. McIlhenny of Jungle Gardens Nursery in Avery Island, Louisiana. Gunn's official title was chief engineer, and he was the nursery's representative on the newly completed Louisiana State University (LSU) campus in Baton Rouge, designed by the firm of Theodore Link, where he supervised the construction and planting of a formal garden, an elaborate terraced garden with a long reflecting pool that served as the backdrop for the campus's Greek Theater. Though the pool was filled in decades later, the enclosed garden space with its linear plantings of cypress trees survives. Later in 1938, he also supervised the procurement and installation of plant material for a replanting project at Louisiana's Old State Capitol and the New State Office Building, part of the state government complex north of the LSU campus in downtown Baton Rouge.

During his stay in Baton Rouge, Gunn met his future wife, Esme Patterson, the daughter of a Texas oilman. They married in 1940 but had no children. In 1943, Gunn started a branch of Jungle Gardens Nursery in Houston

Ralph Gunn during restoration of the grounds of Rosedown Plantation, St. Francisville, Louisiana, 1957. (Texas A&M University Library)

continued to refine his work at Rienzi for many years, accommodating various additions to the property.

By 1956, Gunn was a well-established landscape architect in Houston and was engaged by the Underwood family to restore the grounds of Rosedown Plantation in St. Francisville, Louisiana, an extensive project that lasted several years. The garden here, one of the oldest in Louisiana, featured parterres, Italian marble sculpture, camellias, and other plantings dating from the 1840s, documented with the extensive records of the plantation mistress from the garden's beginnings until her death in the 1890s.

Up until the time the Underwoods purchased the property, the house was occupied by surviving elderly children of the original owners—hence, both house and garden possessed a high degree of historic integrity. Gunn's first move, before clearing or removing any materials, was to document the gardens and plantings as he found them, following the basic protocol of landscape preservation protocol two decades before it had been codified. Then Gunn worked systematically to restore the landscape to its antebellum condition, while adapting plantings to the changes in canopy. Gunn's restoration stood Rosedown's gardens in good stead, as the property was sold by the Underwoods' heirs in the 1990s to an out-of-state owner who was not a preservationist, and then in turn Rosedown was sold to the State of Louisiana a decade later. Though some of the original garden ornaments were removed prior to the state's acquisition, much of Gunn's restoration remains.

Rosedown represented the pinnacle of Gunn's career. In 1959, he opened Ralph Ellis Gunn and Associates, continuing his successful residential practice in Houston, where he designed as many as two hundred residential landscapes found in the exclusive River Oaks neighborhood. In addition to Rosedown, Gunn worked on a number of historic properties that were open to the public including the Liendo Plantation, one of Texas's oldest cotton plantations in Hempsted; and, Centennial House, one of the finest examples of masonry classic revival

for McIlhenny. By 1945, the branch nursery employed nine men, and Gunn worked as both landscape architect and plantsman.

In 1946, Gunn received what was probably his first large commission, designing the grounds for the Shamrock Hotel, built between 1946 and 1949 by oilman Glenn H. McCarthy for a reported cost of $21 million. The eighteen-story hotel, on a 15-acre tract, featured extensive gardens, a terrace, and swimming pool that at 165 feet by 142 feet, was one of the largest in the world. The Shamrock was also immortalized in 1956, as the Conquistador, in the film version of Edna Ferber's popular novel, *Giant,* directed by George Stevens. The hotel elevated Gunn's professional status but was never financially viable and was demolished in 1987.

Throughout this time, Gunn maintained his connection with McIlhenny's Jungle Gardens Nursery in Avery Island through its branch in Houston. Upon McIlhenny's sudden death in 1949, Gunn acquired full ownership of the Houston operation and records at the McIlhenny Archives indicate that at least until 1954, the nursery was still operational.

In 1952, Gunn was approached by Mr. and Mrs. Harris Masterson III to design the grounds of their home Rienzi. Now part of the Museum of Fine Arts in Houston, housing the Mastersons' collection of European decorative arts, Rienzi's landscape was restored in the early 1990s. It was here at Rienzi that Gunn, influenced by travels throughout Europe, developed his characteristic classical style, which suited his clients' taste perfectly. Gunn

Above: Menil House, Houston, Texas. (Photo by Charles A. Birnbaum)

Below: Entrance to Rosedown Plantation, St. Francisville, Louisiana. (Texas A&M University Library)

architecture in existence south of Austin in Corpus Christi. For this latter 1963 commission, Gunn was part of a consulting team that included Houston colleague David Warren, curator of Bayou Bend, and New Orleans historical architect Samuel Wilson. Gunn also worked on projects in Mississippi, Indiana, and Florida. In 1956, Gunn was awarded the Arp Award by the Texas Nursery and Landscape Association, an award bestowed on an individual who made significant and lasting contributions to the nursery industry.

As one of the first practicing landscape architects in Texas, Ralph Gunn refined the traditional Beaux-Arts approach that he would have learned at Harvard. His prolific residential practice left a lasting mark, primarily on southeast Texas and Louisiana. His work encompassed both horticulture and design for new installations and historical renovations. Gunn died in Houston, Texas, in March 1976.

The Technical Reference Center, Texas A&M University, holds a partial archive of the work of Ralph Ellis Gunn. The collection includes over 950 of Gunn's slides, which illustrate many of his projects.

Collins, Lester, and Thomas Gillespie, eds. *Landscape Architecture.* Cambridge, Mass.: Graduate School of Design Harvard University, 1951, 57. A selection of material from a exhibition of student, faculty, and alumni celebrating the fiftieth anniversary of the Harvard program. Includes Gunn's model of the Shamrock Hotel, Houston, Tex.

Jon Emerson and Associates. "A Plan for the Preservation, Management, and Interpretation of the Landscape of Rienzi." Baton Rouge, La., 2000. An unpublished management plan for Rienzi, with historical documentation of Gunn's work. Copies located at Rienzi and with Jon Emerson and Associates, Baton Rouge, La.

"Rosedown, That Beauty of the Old South Not Forgotten." *Architectural Digest* 23, no. 1 (Summer 1966), 4–17. Photography by Max Eckert. Details the work by architect George Leake and landscape architect Ralph Gunn.

Seth Rodewald-Bates

HAAG, RICHARD
(1923–)
LANDSCAPE ARCHITECT, EDUCATOR

Richard Haag was born October 23, 1923, in Louisville, Kentucky, the oldest of six children. His father, who owned and operated a nursery, introduced him to fundamental aspects of landscape and ecology. As a child, Richard astonished a national meeting of horticulturalists by identifying a series of rare and unusual plants. When he was eighteen, he volunteered for military service and shipped out to the Pacific in May 1942.

At the end of the World War II, he returned from Asia and enrolled in the landscape architecture program at the University of Illinois, Champagne-Urbana. There he met **Stanley Hart White**, an inspirational teacher who introduced students to ecological issues on local field trips. White, who had worked in the **Olmsted Brothers** office, emphasized fundamental physical landscape experiences and formal considerations. During this time, Haag became friendly with Hideo Sasaki* who graduated in 1948. In 1949, Haag took two important and influential trips. The first was to the East Coast with White, where the two visited towns, parks, arboreta, museums, and rural landscapes, including many by the Olmsteds. They proceeded to Maine, staying with White's brother, the critic and writer E. B. White, and visited with Buckminster Fuller. The second trip was with Sasaki. They drove across the country from Illinois to the West Coast in a surplus army jeep. Observing and discussing vernacular landscapes and towns, they formed a lasting friendship and a deep impression of the virtues, dilemmas, and landscape needs of modern Americans.

Haag transferred to the University of California, Berkeley, where he received a bachelor of landscape architecture degree in 1950. During the summers of 1949 and 1950, Haag worked for Sasaki. During the summer of 1951, he worked for Daniel Urban Kiley* in Vermont, another formative experience. Haag then went to Harvard where he received a master of landscape architecture degree in 1952. Soon thereafter, he relocated to San Francisco. Shortly after his arrival there, he won a Fulbright scholarship and spent the next two years, from 1954 to 1955, studying in Kyoto.

Haag studied the gardens and design of Japan enthusiastically. The influence of this period, both visually and philosophically, can be seen in his subsequent design

Richard Haag, ca. 1980. (Photo courtesy of Laurie Olin)

work. While Haag has never asserted an affiliation with any religious group, the principles and spiritual tenets of Zen Buddhism and Taoism deeply inform his work.

Returning to the United States, Haag worked for Lawrence Halprin* from 1956 to 1957 in San Francisco. In 1957, he left Halprin's office to establish his own practice in the Bay Area, producing several award-winning projects. The Dux Corporation project in Burlingame shows the clear influence of his experience with Dan Kiley with tightly planted rectilinear grids of paper birch trees framing the site, walks, courts, and buildings.

Haag's time in San Francisco ended in 1958, when **Thomas Dolliver Church** recommended Haag to the University of Washington, where the College of Architecture

View of Gas Works Park, Seattle, Washington. (Photo courtesy of Laurie Olin)

and Urban Planning intended to create a landscape architecture department and wished to hire a promising person to set it up and teach within the program. In the autumn of 1958, Haag joined their faculty in Seattle. Moving his family to the Northwest, he also opened a small office near the university. Until the new department was established, he taught site planning and studio design to architectural students. The department officially opened in 1964 and has grown into a nationally recognized program.

From 1958 to the present, Haag has maintained a small professional office that is an intense and lively studio enterprise. Preparing numerous landscape master plans and district plans, Haag proposed designs with tree-lined pedestrian ways, squares, and quadrangles. Faced with limited budgets, he employed ordinary materials and simple furnishings, insuring pragmatic but effective horticulture as well as long-term strategies for structuring the landscape and spaces of these campuses. With his quiet manner, Haag convinced architects and clients to invest their small budgets into long-term landscape solutions that often appeared simple and sparse in their early stages. Years later, strong masses and ranks of trees characterize these sites, giving them a handsome quality.

Despite his wisdom and accomplishment, Haag's somewhat quiet, elusive, uncompromising character and deep convictions made some clients uneasy. Nevertheless, from 1958 to 2000, Haag participated in over 500 built projects, the majority of which are located in the Pacific Northwest. The two most prominent

are Gas Works Park (1971–1988) on Lake Union in Seattle and the Bloedel Reserve (1979–1984) on Bainbridge Island in Puget Sound.

The significance of Gas Works Park lies in its prescient concept and uncompromising realization. Although officials and citizens wanted a former plant that converted coal to gas to be removed and replaced with a bucolic park, Haag convinced them to keep a considerable amount of the industrial apparatus. He embraced industrial ruins rather than attempting to erase or beautify them, accepting them as a valid portion of history worthy of retention. He also embarked upon what was possibly the first soil remediation experiment for a public space in the country. His methods of remediating the soil using plants and natural biological processes, original and highly controversial at the time, became accepted standards.

The Bloedel Reserve is located in a forest near Agate Point on the former estate of timber baron Prentice Bloedel. Haag created a series of landscape events, rooms, and places, which were stunning. Beautiful and calm, simple in concept, yet rich in material and spiritual properties, they form an artistic landscape masterpiece. This was a formerly ravaged landscape, having been clear-cut in logging operations at the beginning of the century. Working within the second growth woodland Haag created a sequence of spaces, each with its own character. The highlight is the Reflection Garden where 12-foot-high clipped yew hedges form a perfect rectangular clearing among the Douglas firs. A long shallow basin filled with groundwater reflects the surrounding trees and sky. Serene and beautiful, Haag plunges visitors into a physical and spiritual experience of concentration and release that is remarkable, accomplished, and unique.

Strikingly different is Steinbrueck Park located immediately north of the Pike Place Market in Seattle. Working in collaboration with Victor Steinbrueck, the principal designer of Seattle's Space Needle who was instrumental in saving the market, Haag developed a small but socially important park atop a garage. While it serves as an overlook for Puget Sound and a neighborhood park, it is also a remarkably abstract and introspective design stripped down to basic typological components and emblematic elements.

Haag's design vocabulary is a self-imposed limited one. The most fundamental aspect of his work has consistently been a concern for landform and sculpting of the land. His predilection is for prime forms, clarity of shape, and simple and direct plan organization, as well as a modernist abstract imagery. He frequently employs circles, squares, truncated cones and pyramids, and a generous use of vertical relief, stairs, and ramps. He combines simple and direct plan organization with an encyclopedic knowledge of plants and horticulture. His choice of plants and their juxtaposition is often rich, bold, and strong, yet accomplished with the use of only a few species and groups at a time. In some projects, he juxtaposes native flora with contrasting Asian or other ornamental species. Emphasizing the natural and physical dynamics at work in the world and on his sites, Haag realizes that his works are cultural productions, made by and for society. One favorite motif, for instance, is that of the council ring, a circular seating area adapted from the work of **Jens Jensen**. Unlike Jensen's council rings, which were invariably made of freestanding circular fieldstone walls, Haag's are imbedded in the earth and the concentric rings of circular seats made of inexpensive concrete.

Haag's frustrations with the commercial nursery industry led him to grow some of his own plants. Purchasing land on the Stillaguamish River north of Seattle in the 1980s, he began his own nursery.

As a teacher and as a designer, Haag places a great emphasis upon spirit, feeling, direct contact with sites, and informed intuition. Although a strong supporter of Ian L. McHarg* and deeply committed to the facts, theories, and study of ecology, he has reiterated that his approach to design is more akin to the methods of Zen monks than it is to any quasi-scientific one. Haag has also expressed great interest in psychological needs and behavior found in human experience of landscape.

Throughout his career, Haag has continued to teach. He stepped down as chairman after ten years, with the landscape architecture department fully fledged and a fresh group of professors hired, but continued to teach, even after retirement as professor emeritus, influencing several generations of students. Within his office, his role as a mentor is as notable as his success as a designer.

Haag is a Fellow of the American Society of Landscape Architects (ASLA), an Honorary Member of the American Institute of Architects, and a Resident of the American Academy in Rome. He is the only person ever to have received two Presidential Awards for Design Excellence from the ASLA, one for Gas Works Park, the other for the Bloedel Reserve. In 2003, he received the ASLA's medal for lifetime achievements and contribution to the profession. He was honored by the Harvard Graduate School of Design with a symposium and exhibition in 1996 followed by the publication of the book *Richard Haag: Bloedel Reserve and Gas Works Park*. Haag continues to teach and lecture internationally and practice and participate in design award and competition juries.

Kreisman, Lawrence. *The Bloedel Reserve, Gardens in the Forest*. Bainbridge Island, Washington: The Arbor Fund, Bloedel Reserve, 1988. An account of the estate before, during, and after Haag's involvement, with extensive photography by Mary Randlett, drawings.

Rozdilsky, John, "Profile: Richard Haag." *Cascadia Forum* 1, no. 1 (October 1993), 43–48. An affectionate portrait with reminiscences by Haag, Rozdilsky was an Associate Curator of the Burke Museum, University of Washington, Seattle, at the time.

Saunders, William, ed. *Richard Haag: Bloedel Reserve and Gas Works Park*. New York: Princeton Architectural Press, 1998. Includes essays by Patrick Condon ("The Zen of Garden Design"), Elizabeth K. Meyer ("Seized by Sublime Sentiments, between Terra Firma and Terra Incognita"), and Gary R. Hilderbrand ("A Teacher's Teacher"), and two portfolios of excellent black-and-white photographs with plan drawings. Bibliography and project list, 1964 to 1996.

Laurie D. Olin

HALL, ALFRED V.
(ca. 1880–ca. 1961)
LANDSCAPE ARCHITECT, TOWN PLANNER

Information about Alfred V. Hall's early life is elusive. In October 1906, however, he became employee number 516 in **Warren Henry Manning**'s office in Cambridge, Massachusetts. Listed as an employee from Toronto, Hall received an initial monthly salary of $40, twice that of the lowest-paid employees. Hall rapidly rose through the ranks, increasing to $75 per month in less than a year.

In May 1912, Hall left Manning's office for Toronto, where he immediately began work with the year-old firm of H. B. and L. A. Dunington-Grubb, Landscape Architects. In January 1914, Hall and his younger fellow employee, William E. Harries,* formed their own partnership, Harries & Hall, which Arthur M. Kruse* joined later. While Harries and Kruse eventually returned to the United States, Hall maintained the firm's presence in Toronto until 1961.

In April 1919, the Ontario Bureau of Municipal Affairs selected Harries & Hall as consultants on town planning. Hall, representing the firm, traveled around Ontario for the next several years advising municipalities on site plans for new housing. In 1921, when the province and the Spruce Falls Lumber Company created the model town of Kapuskasing in northern Ontario, Hall was the principal town planner. In 1926, he helped produce a housing scheme for the Paymaster Mine in South Porcupine, Ontario.

In 1919, at its first general meeting, the Town Planning Institute of Canada (today's Canadian Institute of Planners) elected Hall an associate member. The following year, he gave a talk entitled "The Garden's Relationship to Nurserymen and Landscape Work" at a conference on establishing a botanical garden at University of Toronto. He became vice president of Harries, Hall & Kruse in about 1925, and president and manager in about 1935. Over the years, he lived in several attractive Toronto neighborhoods. He had a wife, née Ely, from New York state. His name disappeared from Toronto city directories after 1961 but no mention of his death has yet been found.

See also the individual entries on Harries, William Edward, and Kruse, Arthur M., and the joint entry on Harries, Hall & Kruse. References follow the Harries, Hall & Kruse entry.

Pleasance K. Crawford

HALPRIN, LAWRENCE
(1916–   )
LANDSCAPE ARCHITECT, THEORIST

Born on July 1, 1916, Lawrence Halprin was raised in Brooklyn, New York. After graduation from high school, he lived for several years in Israel on a kibbutz. In 1935, he began his studies in plant sciences at Cornell University where he also played varsity baseball with hopes of playing professionally. After graduation, Halprin pursued advanced studies at the University of Wisconsin receiving an M.S. in horticulture in 1941. During this time, Halprin married Anna Schuman, a dance student whose work played a significant role in Halprin's ideas about landscape movement as well as his developing new graphic techniques to represent landscape experience. Halprin has recounted that, while living in Wisconsin, he visited Taliesin East, Frank Lloyd Wright's home-studio, and decided to study architecture focusing on landscape. He entered the B.L.A. program at Harvard's Graduate School of Design in 1942, studying with landscape architect **Christopher Tunnard** whose book *Gardens in the Modern Landscape* (1938) Halprin credited with confirming his interest in landscape design. During his studies at Harvard, Halprin was also inspired by professors Walter Gropius and Marcel Breuer, and was "vitally influenced" by the writings of László Moholy-Nagy, a Hungarian artist and Bauhaus educator who immigrated to the United

Left: Lawrence Halprin leads a blindfolded awareness walk as part of a 1979 RSVP Workshop in Japan. (The Office of Lawrence Halprin, Inc.)

Below: Auditorium Forecourt fountain (Ira Keller Fountain), Portland, Oregon, 1998 view. (Courtesy of The Cultural Landscape Foundation)

soon hiring Jean Walton, Donald Carter, Satoru Nishita, and Richard Vignolo who would remain with him for several decades while the practice grew to over sixty staff.

During the 1950s, Halprin's practice comprised typical project types of the postwar period—residential gardens, small housing projects with prominent Bay Area architects, such as William Wurster, and eventually several campus master plans as well as suburban shopping centers. By the early 1960s, he was taking on new types of projects on formerly marginal urban sites and innovating with the very process of design, not only with forms and spaces. His site plan for Sea Ranch (1962–1967), a 5,000-acre second home community on the Pacific Coast north of San Francisco, can be seen as a response to the coastal landscape structure and environmental phenomena of wind and water erosion. It is also a significant critique of, and alternative to, standard suburban site planning standards. By the mid-1960s, after several trips to Europe, Lawrence Halprin and Associates were known more for their urban than suburban landscape projects, as they designed and built Ghirardelli Square (1962–1968) and Embarcedero Plaza (1962–1972), both in San Francisco; Nicollet Mall, Minneapolis (1962–1967); four of Portland, Oregon's public spaces—Lovejoy Plaza, Pettigrove Park, Auditorium Forecourt, and the Transit Mall (1965–1978); and Freeway Park, Seattle (1970–1974). These projects, where he reasserted the landscape architect's role in regenerating the American city, made vital social and pedestrian spaces out of formerly marginal sites such as historic industrial complexes or the spaces

States in 1937. This particular influence is readily discerned in Halprin's articles and books about process, space-time, and motion from the early 1960s throughout the late 1990s.

Halprin's career as a landscape architect was delayed by two years as he, like many of his peers, enlisted in the U.S. Navy during World War II and served in the Pacific theater. In spring 1945, he returned to the United States and joined **Thomas Dolliver Church**'s firm in San Francisco, where he worked for four years. There, he collaborated with architect George Rockrise on the renowned Dewey Donnell garden in Sonoma, California. In 1949, Halprin opened his own firm in San Francisco,

Left: Freeway Park, opened 1976, Seattle, Washington; 2006 view. (Courtesy of The Cultural Landscape Foundation)

Below: View of the Franklin Delano Roosevelt Memorial, Washington, D.C. (The Office of Lawrence Halprin, Inc.)

essence of the art of landscape design." The sheer volume of work in the office, coupled with Halprin's responsibilities on several national commissions, such as White House Council on Natural Beauty and the Advisory Council on Historic Preservation, afforded young designers in his office, such as Charles Moore and Angela Danadjieva, the chance to make major contributions to the design language that has come to characterize Halprin's urban spaces. This vocabulary, a fractured urban ground terraced to choreograph the movement of bodies and water, was rendered in poured-in-place concrete that simultaneously evoked monumental geological forms and dynamic ecological processes.

By the mid-1970s, Halprin's office was considerably smaller, having weathered several recessions and infamous staff revolts. Still, at an age when many consider retirement, Halprin's talent and enthusiasm were undiminished. He continued to receive major commissions for another three decades. These included the Charlottesville Mall in Virginia;

over or under freeways. In doing so, they reimagined a public realm for American cities that had been cleared by federal urban renewal programs and abandoned for new suburban developments.

These projects are memorable for their striking forms and sequences that evoke multiple associations and recall varied references. As Halprin wrote in 1995, "My own way has been to design the *outward forms* of nature but emphasize the results of the processes of nature. . . . This act of transmuting the experience of the natural landscape into human-made experience is, for me, the

the Franklin Delano Roosevelt Memorial in Washington, D.C.; Levi Strauss Plaza in San Francisco, California; Bunker Hill Steps and Library Garden in Los Angeles, California; the 52-acre approach to Yosemite Falls in Yosemite National Park, California; the Haas Promenade in Jerusalem; and Lucas Studio campus at The Presidio and Stern Grove, both in San Francisco, California.

For a generation that often divided landscape practice into landscape art versus ecological design, Halprin's works and his writings demonstrate how to link creative artistic impulses with the ecological sciences. He excels at connecting phenomenological experience with environmental awareness and ethics. For his ability to create memorable landscape forms, spaces, and experiences, Halprin was awarded numerous honors such as the AIA Medal for Allied Professions (1964), Fellow of the American Society of Landscape Architects (1969), ASLA Gold Medal (1978), ASLA Design Medal (2003), American Academy of Arts and Sciences (1978), the University of Virginia Thomas Jefferson Medal in Architecture (1979), and the National Medal of the Arts (2002), the nation's highest honor for an artist.

Halprin's legacy may reside as much in how he restructured the process of design as in what he built. Recognizing that landscape design requires, in Moholy-Nagy's terms, "vision in motion," Halprin translated notational systems for dance and music scores into a new landscape drawing convention. Called "motation," this diagram documented and imagined movement through space over time in the landscape. Concerned about the hierarchical relationship between designers and the public and informed by artistic events and happenings conducted by Anna Schuman Halprin and others, he worked with facilitators such as Jim Burns to insert community participation workshops into the design process. This contribution is manifest in his design works and his numerous articles, reports, and books and is documented in his extensive office files and drawings housed in the University of Pennsylvania Architectural Archives.

The Architecture Archive of the University of Pennsylvania has the entire body of Halprin's drawings, project files, and correspondence. The archives are located on the Philadelphia campus in the Fisher Fine Arts Library. For additional information and a finding aid go to: www .design.penn.edu/archives/archives/index.html

Halprin, Lawrence. *Lawrence Halprin: Changing Places.* San Francisco: San Francisco Museum of Art, 1986. Catalog for a retrospective (Frank Gehry–designed) exhibition that coincided with Halprin's eightieth birthday, it includes numerous drawings, models, and photographs of Halprin's built works. The catalog includes essays by Halprin, Jim Burns, Charles Moore, Teddy Kollek, and Robert Maguire.

Halprin, Lawrence. *Process Architecture,* no. 4. Tokyo: Process Architecture Publishing, 1978. First volume in a process series dedicated to a landscape architect. Includes Halprin's most significant early projects.

Halprin, Lawrence. *RSVP Cycles: Creative Processes in the Human Environment.* New York: Braziller, 1969. A design manifesto, the book is graphically striking and theoretically innovative in its coverage of temporality, movement, and flow in landscape architecture. Includes an excerpt from his 1965 *Progressive Architecture* article "Motation" and demonstrates how scores were used in workshops as well as to study sites such as Nicollet Mall and Sea Ranch.

Elizabeth K. Meyer

HANSON, A. E.
(1893–1986)
LANDSCAPE ARCHITECT, PLANNER, DEVELOPER, AUTHOR

Archibald E. "Archie" Hanson was born on December 20, 1893, in Chino, California, at that time a small town east of Los Angeles. Hanson's father had emigrated from Canada in 1885 to become a land developer who planted and sold small orange groves to Midwesterners. Hanson's mother was from Ohio.

Hanson, a middle child, finished just two years of high school and then began to acquire the experiences that would form the basis of his future career. He worked in British Columbia for a company that developed apple orchards and small towns. Returning to Los Angeles in 1914, he learned to appreciate native plants while working for Theodore Payne, the British-born specialist in California flora. A 1915 visit to the Panama-California Exposition in San Diego convinced Hanson to become a landscape architect. Hanson was just starting out on his own, following a brief apprenticeship with Paul J. Howard, when he was sent to France to join American forces in World War I. While on leave, he visited notable French gardens. He returned to Los Angeles when he was discharged in 1919.

After approximately two years as a design-build landscape contractor, Hanson began to actively seek larger commissions. In addition to a Beverly Hills landscape architecture office, he had a landscape construction business in the industrial section of Hollywood. Like most landscape architects of this era, he designed estates as natural-looking parks with axial and walled formal gardens either near the building or tucked into the grounds as discrete units.

A. E. Hanson, 1927. (Architecture & Design Collection, University Art Museum, University of California, Santa Barbara)

Hanson always acknowledged that the key to his success was his staff of gifted craftsmen and his talented designers, including Lee Rombotis and landscape architect Geraldine Knight Scott.* Typical of the practice at large offices, they expanded, added detail, and rendered the designs that Hanson sketched during site visits. Although he had no formal education, Hanson was savvy about spatial relationships, light/shadow qualities, and plant material. His pragmatic, "can-do" attitude endeared him to clients.

Harold Lloyd, the silent-film star, hired Hanson in 1925 to design his 16-acre Beverly Hills estate, Greenacres, because he was the only landscape architect interviewed who was confident he could fit a golf course on the property. Hanson planned the site and suggested the architect. Based on European models, much of the garden was formal. Hanson included a miniature village for Lloyd's daughter. The outlying areas were naturalistic with an informal barbecue house, three lakes, and a 100-foot waterfall that fell into a streambed by the golf course.

Hanson toured Europe in 1927 during a lull in the Lloyd job. This trip influenced his subsequent projects, which exhibited more sophisticated design tenets than his early work. Two notable 1929 designs, both in collaboration with architect George Washington Smith, are La Toscana and the Archibald Young garden. La Toscana, the Kirk Johnson estate that is now called Sotto il Monte, is in Montecito, California, and is regarded as a successful Italian-inspired garden. The Young estate, since subdivided, was admired for its abstraction of Spanish design principles.

The stock market crash of 1929 had an immediate impact on Hanson's business as many clients were forced to abandon their projects. Two notable Depression-era commissions were the landscape for the Doheny Memorial Library at the University of Southern California from 1931 to 1932; and the Mrs. Daniel Murphy garden in Los Angeles in 1932. Palos Verdes, Frank A. Vanderlip's "Millionaire's Colony," planned by the Western office of the **Olmsted Brothers** (**James Frederick Dawson** project lead, with **George Gibbs Jr.** and Hammond Sandler) and Charles H. Cheney, was starting to suffer the Depression's effects when Vanderlip contacted Hanson in 1930 to design a small garden for the gatehouse of his estate. Vanderlip subsequently hired Hanson in 1932 to be General Manager of the Palos Verdes Corporation and sell the corporation's thousands of remaining acres. Hanson coined the term Palos Verdes Peninsula and with the help of Cheney, extended Palos Verdes Drive north to create a scenic highway that encircled the entire peninsula.

Hanson made significant contributions to the gardens of the American Country Place era while working with wealthy clients. As society changed, he then became the designer and developer of themed, planned communities for the rising middle class. Freed from the historicism of his earlier gardens, Hanson helped create the modern California built environment with its emphasis on an informal, outdoor lifestyle revolving around the suburban ranch house.

In 1934, Hanson asked Cheney to help him develop the newly accessible, northern 600 acres of grassland into a village called Rolling Hills. In contrast to opulent Palos Verdes, with its Mediterranean villas and golf course, Rolling Hills would be an equestrian-oriented, family community of modest, ranch-style houses. White, split-rail fences lined the roads, which were informally planted with California pepper trees and mature olive trees obtained from an old orchard. There were stables and riding trails. Hanson trucked in sand to enhance a

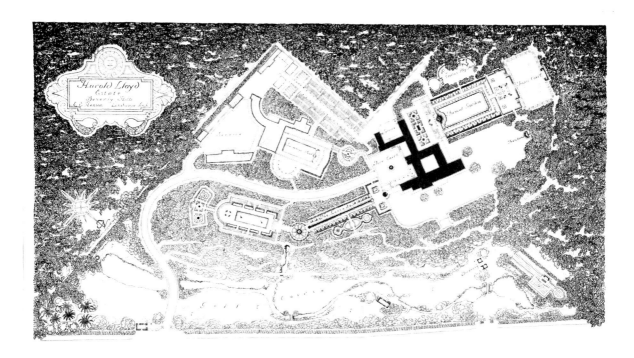

Presentation plan, Greenacres, Harold Lloyd estate, Beverly Hills, California, 1925-1929. (Architecture & Design Collection, University Art Museum, University of California, Santa Barbara)

beach he named Abalone Cove. Throughout the project area, gatehouses, beach clubhouse, and community buildings were in the approved, ranch-house style with tall Canary Island date palms to signify their presence. New homeowners were required to match the fencing and build architect-designed ranch houses. Lutah Maria Riggs was a consulting architect. Following a trip to Virginia, Hanson invited architect Paul R. Williams to design speculative, Colonial Revival–style homes along Williamsburg Lane. He never mentioned it, but by employing Riggs and Williams, Hanson selected a female architect and an African American architect at a time when few opportunities existed for minorities.

In 1948, Hanson founded, developed, and was the majority owner of Hidden Hills, a planned community in the San Fernando Valley, which was incorporated in 1961. He also developed other projects, including a mobile-home park at Lake Casitas. To document his career, he wrote two books about his work.

A. E. Hanson possessed a firm grasp of plant material and a keen sense of humor. Entirely self-educated, he absorbed and was able to articulate fundamental prin-

ciples of architecture and landscape. He passed away in 1986.

Hanson's papers are archived in the Architecture and Design Collection, University Art Museum, University of California, Santa Barbara; the Palos Verdes Library District holds an oral history and miscellaneous materials.

Bricker, David. "Ranch Houses Are Not All the Same." *Preserving the Recent Past 2,* eds. Deborah Slaton and William G. Foulks. Washington, D.C.: Historic Preservation Education Foundation, National Park Service, and Association for Preservation Technology International, 2000. Places Rolling Hills in the evolution of ranch house developments and architecture; excellent notes.

Hanson, A. E. *An Arcadian Landscape: The California Gardens of A. E. Hanson, 1920–1932.* Introduction by David Gebhard. Los Angeles: Hennessey & Ingalls, Inc., 1985. This is the definitive study of his early work and the era in general by Hanson and architectural historian David Gebhard. Hanson also wrote *Rolling Hills: The Early Years* in 1978.

Streatfield, David C. "The Evolution of the California Landscape 4: Suburbia at the Zenith." *Landscape Architecture* 67 (September 1977), 417–24. The author's insight into this period and his interviews with Hanson and Geraldine Knight Scott nicely supplement *An Arcadian Landscape.*

Susan Chamberlin

HARRIES, WILLIAM EDWARD
(1886–1972)

LANDSCAPE ARCHITECT, ENGINEER, GOLF COURSE ARCHITECT, SUPERINTENDENT

William E. Harries was born on March 13, 1886, in Buffalo, New York, attended public schools there, and graduated from Buffalo's Masten Park High School. After receiving a bachelor of science degree in agriculture from Cornell's College of Landscape Architecture circa 1908, he continued landscape architectural studies in Berlin. He then completed nursery and landscape work in France's Loire District before joining Thomas H. Mawson's construction force in England. Returning to the United States in 1910, he worked briefly in Arthur F. Brinckerhoff's New York office, but left to become superintendent of the New York State Reservation at Niagara Falls, where his duties included supervising the reforestation of Goat Island.

He resigned in 1912 and in May, like Alfred V. Hall,* entered the Toronto office of Howard B. and Lorrie A. Dunington-Grubb (the former also a Cornell alumnus and Mawson protégé). From 1913 to January 1914, when Harries and Hall left, the firm was called Dunington-Grubb & Harries.

In 1916, Harries married a Cincinnatian and returned to Buffalo, where he established with Hall the office of Harries & Hall for projects south of the border. He was appointed Buffalo's Superintendent of Parks in 1919 and designed numerous public open spaces before resigning in early 1922 to return full-time to private practice. He formed Harries & Reeves, whose projects included site plans for several federal housing projects in Buffalo and many golf courses.

About 1960, Harries sold Harries & Reeves to Tryon and Schwartz & Associates Inc., of East Aurora, New York, but continued working with Russell Tryon until 1969. By then Harries, himself an avid golfer, had helped lay out at least a dozen courses in the Buffalo area alone. His 1920s entrance design for the Cherry Hill Club near Fort Erie, Ontario (not far from his summer home at Windmill Point), is still intact.

About 1952, Harries moved to Clearwater, Florida. There, with Arthur M. Kruse,* he helped organize the planning board on which he served from 1955 until shortly before his death on May 23, 1972.

See also the individual entries on Hall, Alfred V., and Kruse, Arthur M., and the joint entry on Harries, Hall & Kruse. References follow the Harries, Hall & Kruse entry.

Pleasance K. Crawford

HARRIES, HALL & KRUSE

Estate of Levon Babayan, Esq., York Mills, Toronto, Canada, from ASLA *Illustrations of Work of Members,* 1931.

William Edward Harries and Alfred V. Hall formed W. E. Harries & A. V. Hall, Landscape Architects & Engineers, on January 1, 1914, and added Arthur M. Kruse as associate in 1919. The firm became Harries, Hall & Kruse, Landscape Architects & Town Planners, in 1925, and added Ltd. about 1928. Its office in downtown Toronto, with Hall as vice president and then president and manager, appeared in city directories through 1961. To date, information about the firm's activities after the 1920s has proven as elusive as that about Hall himself.

The early years are fairly well documented. Articles about Harries & Hall's landscapes for a new Toronto hos-

Plan of Kapuskasing, Ontario, 1922; from the *Ontario Bureau of Municipal Affairs Housing Report for 1921, Including Town Planning for the Town of Kapuskasing,* 1922. (Archives of Ontario)

pital and several branch libraries appeared in 1915 and 1917, respectively. An impressive list of work on both sides of the border, sent in January 1919 to the director of the Ontario Bureau of Municipal Affairs, survives at the Archives of Ontario. Although some of the projects listed were actually carried out under previous employers, most involve clients of the new partnership.

Photos and descriptions of thirteen Harries & Hall projects, most with Kruse as associate, plus the latter's article entitled "Landscape Architecture," were pub-

lished in 1921 in *Construction.* Summaries of their work as town planners for the Bureau of Municipal Affairs appeared in the bureau's annual reports for 1919, 1920, and 1921. Toronto city council minutes record their applications for plans of subdivision and other dealings with that municipality during the 1920s.

Three public landscapes in Ontario suggest the range of the firm's early work: the grounds of the 1919 Parker house (now owned by the City of Mississauga); the downtown core of Kapuskasing, laid out in 1921; and the 1928

Amsterdam Square Park and Fountain, designated by Toronto City Council in 2003 as being of architectural and historic value.

Crawford, Pleasance. "The Forgotten Landscape Architectural Firm of Harries, Hall and Kruse of Toronto and Buffalo." Available online at www.apa.umontreal.ca/gadrat/formcont/seminar98/conferences/ Crawford/Crawford.htm. This paper presents the author's findings as of 1998. A similar but more fully documented version appears in *Environments* 26 (1999), 29–35.

Hall, A. V. "Considerations in the Laying Out of the Town of Kapuskasing." *The Canadian Engineer* 43 (August 15, 1922), 260–62. First published in the *Journal of the Town Planning Institute of Canada,* this is Hall's description of the process and the resulting plans, eleven of which appear in Ontario Bureau of Municipal Affairs, *Report re Housing for 1921, Including Town Planning for the Town of Kapuskasing* (Toronto: King's Printer, 1922).

Harries, W. E. "Planning of Hospital Grounds." *The American Architect* 107 (April 7, 1915), 217–20. The only example of Harries's writing found to date, this article discusses Harries & Hall's Toronto General Hospital project and the importance of an intimate connection between building and grounds.

Kruse, Arthur M. "Landscape Architecture" and "Professional Practice in Landscape Architecture." *Construction* 14 (August 1921), 224–36. In a periodical read mainly by Canadian architects, Kruse illustrates and explains the complementary role played by landscape architects.

See also the individual entries on Hall, Alfred V.; Harries, William Edward; and Kruse, Arthur M.

Pleasance K. Crawford

HAVEY, RUTH MILDRED
(1899–1980)
LANDSCAPE ARCHITECT

Ruth Mildred Havey was born February 4, 1899, in Roslindale, Massachusetts. One of seven children, Havey attended the Girls' Latin School in Boston from 1911 to 1916. After receiving a bachelor of arts from Smith College in 1920, she entered the Cambridge School of Domestic Architecture and Landscape Architecture (known as the Cambridge School) directed by Henry Atherton Frost. While at the Cambridge School Havey was a student of Charles Killam. Her application noted her intended area of specialization as the "house and garden." Havey received her certificate from the Cambridge School in 1923. In 1932, the Cambridge School became an affiliated graduate school of Smith College, and previous graduates of the Cambridge School who were certified by the school faculty became eligible to be granted master's degrees from Smith College. After being duly certified by the faculty, Havey was granted a master of architecture degree from Smith College in June 1934. She was a member of the Association of Women in Architecture and became a member of the American Society of Landscape Architects in 1941.

Little information has survived regarding Havey's first decade of practice. Upon receiving her certificate from the Cambridge School, she was employed by the Home Builders Service Bureau of the House Beautiful Publishing Company. In May 1925, she began practicing architecture and landscape architecture in West Roxbury, a suburb of Boston. It is not known if she was

Ruth Havey ca. 1923. (Dumbarton Oaks Archives, Washington, DC)

The Pebble Garden at Dumbarton Oaks,
Georgetown, Washington, D.C.
(Photo courtesy of Sarah S. Boasberg)

in independent practice or employed by an established firm. The only clues to her work during this period are the updates she sent to the Smith College Alumni Association, which indicate that she practiced in both New York and New England. Sometime during this period she may have first been associated with the office of **Beatrix Jones Farrand** in New York. By 1929, it appears she was working in the New York office of Farrand, as she listed the office as her "temporary address" in correspondence with the Smith College Alumni Association. The exact nature of her association with the office is unclear. In 1930, she reported her address as Jamaica Plain, Massachusetts. By 1935, Havey seems to have settled permanently in New York City, and by 1936 she had established her own independent landscape architecture practice there. She kept her practice in New York for the remainder of her career.

The landscape architecture legacy of Ruth Havey rests almost entirely on her association with the office of Beatrix Farrand and her work spanning nearly forty years on a single project, the gardens at Dumbarton Oaks in Washington, D.C. The design of this signature landscape began in 1921, as a collaborative effort between Beatrix Farrand and the garden's patron, Mildred Bliss. This collaboration grew to include a series of garden advisers and landscape architecture consultants including Ruth Havey, Robert Patterson, **Alden Hopkins, Ralph E. Griswold,** the French designer and sculptor Armand Albert Rateau, and the staff of Harvard University, which took ownership of the house and gardens in 1940.

Although Ruth Havey likely began working on the design of Dumbarton Oaks shortly after her arrival at Farrand's office in 1929, the first mention of her in the garden's extensive correspondence files is in 1933. Havey was developing the design of the Aquarias Fountain. It is significant that the first mention of Havey in the Dumbarton Oaks files reveals her role in detailed design work at the garden. Havey's skill at detailed design would be highly valued by Farrand and Bliss for the next three decades.

Havey was shy and unassuming in her professional life, often characterized as a "designer" or a "drafter associated with" Farrand's office. In 1942, Farrand described Havey as "my assistant." Certainly, her contribution to the design evolution of the garden has never been fully appreciated. Documents in the Dumbarton Oaks archives indicate that she was consistently charged with the design of detailed elements throughout the garden. Designs for steps, paving, walls, finials, copings, consoles, gates, tablets, benches, metalwork, lanterns, and inscriptions were developed by Havey for review by Farrand and Bliss. But Havey was also involved in larger design projects. In 1942, Farrand noted Bliss's request that she and Havey study "possibilities for the ultimate designs" for the North Vista. Later that year, Havey assumed a more equal role with Farrand, who proposed a six-month "trial marriage . . . to see how we are going to work together, especially at Dumbarton Oaks . . . our four hands and two heads melded into one." The arrangement concluded Farrand, "promises well." This arrangement appears to have lasted at least into 1944, when Havey's insights were sought out by Farrand on the redesign of the Ellipse. By 1946, however, Farrand's correspondence to garden director John Thatcher indicated that her successor at Dumbarton Oaks should be someone more independent who could bring an "original point of view" to the garden. In 1946, Robert Patterson was chosen as Farrand's successor, and for the next two years Ruth Havey is absent from the garden.

Yet this would not mark the end of Havey's influence at Dumbarton Oaks. In fact, the next fifteen years would be the most significant period of her involvement with the garden. Havey returned in 1949, at the request of Bliss, to assist with the detailed design of the North Vista walls and other pre-1940 design elements that had remained unexecuted. During this period, Havey completed the working drawings for the final North Vista redesign and, working closely with Bliss, redesigned the Arbor and Box Terraces. She also designed the R Street gates, the landscape for the new Garden Library and the Pebble Garden that replaced the tennis court, and continued to provide detail design studies for elements throughout the garden. Although many of these detailed studies were not realized, Havey's work continued the long history of experimentation and collaboration among the designers, Bliss, and the garden staff that characterized the garden's evolution. Havey's designs reflected Bliss's evolving ideas about the design of the garden. Over time, these ideas began to focus on more elaborate details and ornamentation. This interest culminated in Havey's intricate design of the Pebble Garden. Ruth Havey's continued presence provided an important element of continuity as the garden evolved and unfinished work from the pre-1940s era was undertaken. Her work reflected not only new ideas but continued to incorporate design elements from earlier work at the garden, including the detailed designs developed by Albert Armand Rateau.

Little is known about Ruth Havey's other work while at the Farrand office or her commissions while in independent practice. Her office records were no longer in her possession at the time of her death, and their whereabouts remain unknown. Most of her commissions are assumed to have been in New Jersey, New York, and New England, but only a few projects in addition to Dumbarton Oaks have been identified to date. Through her connection to Mildred Bliss, Havey was commissioned to design a fountain for the Meridian House in Washington, D.C., and the Lawrence Coolidge cemetery plot in the Hamilton Cemetery, Hamilton, Massachusetts. She also designed a playhouse for the garden of Mr. and Mrs. Sidney Gamble in Fieldston, New York.

Ever in the shadow of Beatrix Farrand, Ruth Havey's last visit to Dumbarton Oaks was in 1980, when she attended a colloquium on the work of Farrand. Later that same year, on October 18, she died at the age of eighty-one at her home in New York City.

The holdings of the Dumbarton Oaks Research Library, the Dumbarton Oaks Archives, Washington, D.C., contain correspondence and project files, architectural plans, and drawings related to Ruth Havey's work at Dumbarton Oaks, including correspondence regarding Havey's work on the Meridian House fountain and the Lawrence Coolidge cemetery plot, records of Havey's education at the Cambridge School, Smith College Alumni Bulletin excerpts, Havey's article in *House Beautiful*, and correspondence with Havey's relatives.

Havey, Ruth. "The Garden as an Outdoor Living Room." *Farm and Garden* 12, no. 4 (November 1924), 20–21. Describes the design of an outdoor living-room for a narrow property. Includes a planting plan.
Tamulevich, Susan, and Ping Amranand. *Dumbarton Oaks: Garden into Art*. New York: The Monacelli Press, 2001. Richly illustrated by photographer Amranand, this work notes Havey's contributions throughout the garden and includes a 1920s photograph of Havey.

Brian Katen

HEGEMANN, WERNER
(1881–1936)
PLANNER, THEORIST, CRITIC, AND AUTHOR

Born in Mannheim, Germany, in 1881, Werner Hegemann attended universities in Berlin, Munich, and Paris from 1901 to 1904, and then moved to the United States to attend the University of Pennsylvania, where he studied with Simon N. Patten, a leader in America's Progressive movement and the eventual founder of the Wharton School of Economics. After a year in America, Hegemann returned to Germany, where he earned a doctorate in economics from the University of Munich in 1908. Immediately thereafter, Hegemann once again departed for America, this time working for a brief period as a housing inspector in Philadelphia's poorer neighborhoods.

Moving to Boston in 1909, Hegemann played a major role in preparing the exhibition for "Boston 1915," a comprehensive planning proposal that called for the inclusion of almost forty Boston area communities into a single metropolitan district. It was also during this period that Hegemann became acquainted with several influential American planners and writers, including **John Nolen**, **Frederick Law Olmsted Jr.**, **Charles Mulford Robinson**, and Benjamin C. Marsh.

DR. WERNER HEGEMANN

Above: Washington Highlands, Wauwatosa, Wisconsin, 2004 view of median absorbing grade differential. (Photo by Charles A. Birnbaum)

Left: Sketch of Werner Hegemann, from the *Cleveland Plain Dealer*, May 17, 1913.

In 1910, the indefatigable Hegemann was back in Germany, this time directing a planning exhibition for Greater Berlin, which included a two-volume catalog with a significant number of American planning examples. One year later, Hegemann's interests in Boston's park system and Chicago's public parks were expressed in an exhibition and accompanying publication, *Amerikanische Parkanlagen,* which traveled throughout Germany.

Ever willing to pursue opportunities in America, Hegemann eagerly accepted a 1913 invitation from the People's Institute, a Progressive group established to promote educational discourse, in New York to participate in a coast-to-coast lecture tour of some thirty cities. Hegemann's familiarity with planning activities on both sides of the Atlantic, and his obvious passion for American democratic ideals, proved very popular with audiences. Ending his lecture tour in California, Hegemann then spent a few months preparing plans for the cities of Berkeley and Oakland that were published in 1915.

Intending to travel back to Germany by way of Japan, China, and Australia in 1914, the outbreak of war in August of that year forced Hegemann to remain in America, this time for seven years. By 1915, Hegemann had established himself as an urban planning consultant in Milwaukee, Wisconsin, a city with a significant German population. Even though he had to register as an enemy alien after the United States entered World War I in 1917, Hegemann was able to travel throughout the country and pursue a number of consulting opportunities.

In early 1916, Hegemann published *City Planning for Milwaukee,* a report that was sponsored by the Wisconsin Chapter of the American Institute of Architects and several of the city's civic organizations. During that same year, Hegemann also worked on a plan for the model industrial village of Kohler, Wisconsin. Joining Hegemann at Kohler was **Elbert Peets**, a recent graduate of Harvard University's landscape architecture program who provided design and graphics expertise. Hegemann recommended that the 3,000-acre Kohler site, with its "rolling land, fine trees, a most surprisingly winding stream, high ravine, with perfectly formed views," be planned as a garden city. Disagreements between company president Walter J. Kohler and Hegemann and Peets, however, led to the termination of their contract in late 1916. Only portions of Kohler's future development followed the Hegemann-Peets plan, but the two men were much more successful in laying out the elite subdivision of

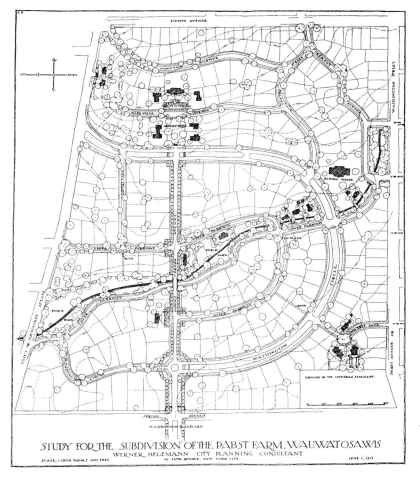

STUDY FOR THE SUBDIVISION OF THE PABST FARM, WAUWATOSA WIS.
WERNER HEGEMANN CITY PLANNING CONSULTANT
SCALE, 1 INCH EQUALS 100 FEET
70 FIFTH AVENUE, NEW YORK CITY
JUNE 1, 1916

Plan of Washington Highlands, Wauwatosa, Wisconsin, from *City Planning for Milwaukee: What It Means and Why It Must be Secured* (Milwaukee: Wisconsin Chapter of the American Institute of Architects, 1916).

Hegemann and Peets planned other subdivisions in Wisconsin, including Hi-Mount, Grand Circle, Maplewood Place, Pabst Acres, Jackson Park, and Jefferson Heights, but it was their 1919 proposal for Wyomissing Park, a garden suburb of Reading, Pennsylvania, that most favorably compares with Washington Highlands. Here, Hegemann called for a blending of architecture and landscape design that resulted in the construction of traditional housing forms throughout the 500-acre community, and the retention of the most scenic and hilly areas as parks and open space.

The Hegemann and Peets collaboration culminated in 1922 with the publication of their magnum opus, *An American Vitruvius*. The volume, subsequently reprinted in 1972 and 1988, continues to serve as one of the seminal urban design and planning manifestos of the twentieth

Washington Highlands in Wauwatosa, a community situated along Milwaukee's western border. Their proposal for the 133-acre subdivision, built on part of a farm owned by the Gustaf Pabst family, was prepared between 1916 and 1919 and was the first large subdivision in Milwaukee County. The plan was notable for the consideration it gave to topographic features and vegetation, and to the successful relationship it established between the gridded streets of Milwaukee and Wauwatosa and the curvilinear circulation system of Washington Highlands. Hegemann and Peets laid out Washington Highlands' topographically determined circulation system complimented with parks, plazas, and a waterway, and such decorative and functional objects as bridges and entryways. Its sensitive preservation of natural features made the community unusual for the region in its time.

century. Containing some 1,200 images that represent a broad range of historical periods and European and American locations, the volume is arranged similarly to the planning exhibitions that Hegemann so successfully organized during his early career.

Hegemann returned to Germany with his American wife and their family in 1921. Finding employment as the editor of two German-language planning journals, Hegemann wrote voluminously about a range of topics; however, by the late 1920s, he was devoting himself to the fight against Fascism. In 1933, after one of Hegemann's books was burned in Berlin because of its criticism of Adolf Hitler, the Hegemann family fled to New York City. Over the next four years Hegemann worked on what would become a three-volume survey of housing, and also taught at The New School for Social Research and

Columbia University. Deeply dismayed over the fate of his colleagues who remained in Germany, Hegemann's concerns may have contributed to his relatively early death at the age of fifty-five in 1936.

Collins, Christiane Crasemann. "A Visionary Discipline: Werner Hegemann and the Quest for the Pragmatic Ideal." In *Modernist Visions and the Contemporary American City.* New York: Rizzoli, 1989, 74–85. A publication that features Hegemann's role in the European-American dialogue, which provided a foundation for the modern discipline of city planning.

Collins, Christiane Crasemann. *Werner Hegemann and the Search for Universal Urbanism.* New York: W. W. Norton, 2005. The definitive assessment of Werner Hegemann's life and career, by his biographer.

Hegemann, Werner, and Elbert Peets. *The American Vitruvius: An Architect's Handbook of Civic Art.* New York: Architectural Book Publishing, 1922. One of the seminal urban design primers of the twentieth century; the 1988 reprint includes a thorough overview, by Christiane Crasemann Collins, of the Hegemann and Peets partnership.

Arnold R. Alanen

HERTRICH, WILLIAM
(1878–1966)
HORTICULTURIST

William Hertrich was born on January 23, 1878, in Baden, Germany, which lies close to the Swiss border. Inspired by the natural beauty of this region, he decided to pursue a career in horticulture and left school at the age of fourteen to gain practical experience in fruit and vine cultivation. When he was sixteen, he began working as an apprentice for Joseph Smetana in Voralberg, Austria, and remained with this firm for four years. In 1900, after completing his mandatory two years of military service he immigrated to the United States. For two years, he worked for the firm of John Reck and Son, in Bridgeport, Connecticut. He then took courses in agriculture, horticulture, landscape gardening, and estate management. He subsequently moved to California to be near an uncle who lived in Orange County. Hertrich worked for two employers before being hired in 1904 by Henry Edwards Huntington, the real estate and transportation magnate. Hertrich became the foreman on the 600-acre Ranch San Marino, located east of Pasadena. Huntington had purchased the property the previous year.

By this time, Hertrich had become an experienced and skilled horticulturist. He was responsible for realizing Huntington's ideas about transforming the ranch into a grand estate. Despite Hertrich's subsequent claims for

William Hertrich. (Reproduced by permission of The Huntington Library, San Marino, California)

complete responsibility for the design of the estate's gardens, Huntington was very much in charge, although he trusted Hertrich completely. In fact, Hertrich was largely responsible for the vision of transforming the magnificent private estate into a major botanical garden of national and international significance.

Huntington appreciated natural landscapes and Hertrich developed the numerous gardens as a series of

Left: Bronze statue of *Bacchante* by Frank McMonies, Huntington residence, San Marino, California, ca. 1920. (Reproduced by permission of The Huntington Library, San Marino, California)

Below: Japanese garden shortly after completion in 1913, Huntington residence, San Marino, California. (Reproduced by permission of The Huntington Library, San Marino, California)

specialized plant collections in naturalistic spaces, avoiding any formality except in the immediate vicinity of the mansion. Hertrich's careful preservation of the existing Englemann design as well as the extant Coast Live Oaks was a critical component of his design strategy. Since the Huntingtons only lived at San Marino in the winter months, Hertrich was required to provide flower color throughout the winter and into the early spring. To meet Huntington's desire for an established appearance, Hertrich pioneered the transplanting of large tree specimens, moving them in wooden boxes using horse-drawn trucks and flat-bed cars belonging to Huntington's Pacific Electric Railroad Company. This frequently necessitated complicated arrangements with cities to close streets and temporarily remove overhead wires. However, the most audaciously ambitious project involved moving two, large palm trees from the garden of Collis Huntington, Huntington's uncle, in San Francisco, a distance of more than 400 miles.

In 1905, Hertrich established the Palm Garden. This was essentially an experimental garden designed to test the suitability of various species of Huntington's favorite tree for use throughout the Los Angeles Basin on numerous real estate ventures for the Huntington Land and Improvement Company. Successful species were grown in the ranch nursery and then used as street trees. Hertrich was also responsible for creating the Desert Garden, one of the largest collections of desert plants outside a natural desert.

The development of the Desert Garden was a specialized form of plant collecting that evolved without a definitive master plan. Hertrich persuaded his skeptical employer that the scientific study and collection of desert plants was a worthy endeavor. For this, Hertrich traveled throughout the deserts of the southwest collecting specimens and obtained specimens from other plant collectors. In 1910, he initiated the Cycad collection with plants he brought back from Mexico. Three years later, he obtained a shipment of plants from Japan, and also purchased the important Louis Bradbury cycad collection in Duarte, California.

In 1911, Hertrich began the development of the Japanese garden in a western canyon beyond the rose garden. He purchased the plants and structures of a failed Pasadena commercial tea garden, created by George Turner Marsh. Hertrich designed the garden and hired Japanese craftsmen to build the moon bridge over the lake, and a tile-roofed pavilion to house a bronze bell. The garden was not designed as an authentic representation of a classical Japanese garden but was a popular evocation of the idea of a Japanese garden.

In 1912, Hertrich began the development from seed of the extensive collection of camellias that grew beneath the canopy of a large, existing grove of oak trees flanking both sides of the North Vista, the major formal feature of the garden conceived by architect Myron Hunt, who designed the mansion.

By the mid-1910s, the Huntington estate had become the location of one of the finest collections of plants on the West Coast. It typified the popular conception of an estate garden as a series of specialized collections. The gardens were as splendid as Huntington's remarkable collection of paintings, sculpture, and manuscripts. The presence of this important collection of plants coupled with Hertrich's preeminence as a horticulturist ensured the public recognition and appreciation of the garden. In 1919, a trust was established to create the Huntington Art Gallery and Botanic Garden. After Huntington's death in 1927, the art gallery and gardens were opened to the public. Hertrich became the first curator, a position he retained until 1948 when he was forced to retire because of poor health.

In addition to his work on the Huntington estate, Hertrich was an adviser on street-tree planting on Huntington's numerous real-estate ventures in the region. Hertrich also designed the grounds of the Hotel Huntington, an elegant hotel in Pasadena. He also designed its golf course and oversaw the rehabilitation of the Old Mill, an adobe building built by the Franciscan Fathers of Mission San Gabriel, into a clubhouse.

Hertrich played a significant role in the small, surrounding, exclusively residential city of San Marino. He served on its city council for twenty-three years, and worked tirelessly to improve and promote the city's appearance. He obtained street trees from the Ranch San Marino's nurseries and designed Lacey Park, the city's park, which is its principal open space.

After his retirement in 1948, he returned to the Huntington Art Gallery and Botanic Garden as Curator Emeritus and devoted himself principally to writing about the collections. However, he continued to monitor developments in the garden until he died. Hertrich's significant contributions to horticulture were recognized by two major horticultural institutions. In 1950, the Massachusetts Horticultural Society awarded him the George Robert White Medal of Honor, and in 1955 he received the Medal of Honor from the Garden Club of America. Very frail, he died at the age of eighty-eight on May 18, 1966, in San Marino.

Hertrich, William. *Camellias in the Huntington Gardens: Observations on their Culture and Behavior and Descriptions of Cultivars.* San Marino, Calif.: The Huntington Library, 1955. An important scientific monograph on the large collection of camellias at the Huntington Gardens.

Hertrich, William. *The Huntington Botanical Gardens, 1905–1949, Personal Recollections of William Hertrich, Curator Emeritus.* San Marino, Calif.: The Huntington Library, 1949. A highly personal account of the development of the Huntington estate and its subsequent development as a botanic garden until his retirement in 1948.

Hertrich, William. *Palms and Cycads. Their Cultivation As Observed Chiefly in the Huntington Botanical Gardens.* San Marino, Calif.: Henry E. Huntington Library and Art Gallery, 1951. A scientific monograph on the cycad collection at the Huntington Gardens.

David Streatfield

HOLLIED, CLARENCE EDMUND "BUD"
(1896–1954)
LANDSCAPE ARCHITECT, HORTICULTURIST

Clarence Edmund Hollied, better known as Bud, was born into a family of horticulturists in Horton, Kansas, in 1896. Five generations of his family had been in the practice of plant cultivation, beginning in Germany and continuing after the family emigrated to the United States. Hollied started his career in the commercial greenhouse business in Iowa before entering military service as a member of the famous Rainbow Division in World War I. Following the war, Hollied moved to New Mexico at age thirty-three to recover from chlorine gas exposure. His twenty-five-year career there began at a commercial greenhouse. He later managed the design and construction of Roosevelt Park in Albuquerque for Mayor Clyde Tingley in 1934 at the height of the New Deal era.

From 1934 to 1936, Hollied also served as landscape engineer for the state and as New Mexico State Parks commissioner. This era saw the design and construction of many of the state's modern parks, including Cahoon Park in Roswell; Hillcrest Park in Clovis; and the Butte Gardens near Hot Springs (today known as Truth or Consequences).

Roosevelt Park, the crown jewel of Albuquerque's park system, is one of New Mexico's best examples of a New Deal park design. The park was listed on the National Register of Historic Places in 1996. Hollied sketched the park design on cardboard in late 1933 or early 1934, according to his late wife, Grayce. The 6-acre city park, built in 1934–1935 for $122,338 in Federal Emergency Relief Administration funds, was originally heavily planted with imported ornamental trees and shrubs to create a passive park atmosphere. Hollied asked a friend in Iowa to send truckloads of arborvitae, Pfitzer juniper, and blue spruce for the new park, which also counted honeysuckle, lilacs, forsythias, rose bushes, umbrella catalpas, and Siberian elms among its plantings. This "Frontier Pastoral" landscape, a Western version of the English Landscape School style, is generally naturalistic, with groves of trees and undulating, sweeping lawns. The site, originally a sandy arroyo serving as a city dump, became the focal point of an active Albuquerque neighborhood. With its stately Siberian elms, one of Mayor (later Governor) Clyde Tingley's favorites, and rolling green

Bud Hollied in Roosevelt Park, Albuquerque, New Mexico, 1937. (Photo courtesy of Grayce Hollied)

hills, the park retains its original pastoral feel, despite several renovations over the years. The park also contains some excellent Works Project Administration stonework in retaining walls and picnic area abutments.

Nearing the end of his life and in declining health, Hollied moved to Santa Fe, where he was commissioned by Allison Herron to heal the construction scars in the landscape of the newly constructed Glorieta Baptist Assembly retreat in the foothills of the Sangre de Cristo Mountains. Hollied began a master plan for the 10-acre landscape terraces of Glorieta Gardens, located some 20 miles east of the state capital. Concerned about his ability to finish the gardens before he died, Hollied asked his Albuquerque friend Cecil Pragnell* to take over for him should he be unable to complete the task. It was a prescient move. In May 1954, Hollied died suddenly of a heart attack at the age of fifty-eight while on a fishing trip to Pilar on the Rio Grande. With Cecil Pragnell, Harvey Cornell at Carlsbad, Elephant Butte, and Santa Fe; and, the work of **Sidney J. Hare and S. Herbert Hare** at the Villa Philmonte in Cimarron, Hollied laid the foundation for modern landscape architecture in the far Southwest.

Beibel, Charles D. *Making the Most of It: Public Works in Albuquerque during the Great Depression, 1929–1942.* An Albuquerque Museum History Monograph. Albuquerque, N.Mex.: The Albuquerque Museum, 1986. A detailed discussion of Depression-era public works projects, including the funding and construction of Roosevelt Park.

Comfort, Mary Apolline. "Place of Glory's Summer Ranch." *Sun Trails* 7, no. 6 (July 1954), 15–18. Report on the opening of the Glorieta Baptist Assembly conference center in Glorieta, New Mexico, including a description of Hollied's garden designs.

Morrow, Baker A. "Rio Grande Landscape Architecture." In *A Dictionary of Landscape Architecture.* Alburquerque: University of New Mexico Press, 1987, 280–81. Cites Cecil Pragnell and Bud Hollied as influential figures in early twentieth-century Southwestern regional style.

Roosevelt Park, Albuquerque, New Mexico, 2005. (Photo by Judy Kowalski, courtesy of Morrow Reardon Wilkinson Miller Ltd.)

Judy Kowalski and Baker H. Morrow

HOLZBOG, WALTER CHARLES
(1900–2002)
LANDSCAPE ARCHITECT

Walter Charles Holzbog was born in Milwaukee, Wisconsin, in 1900. At the age of six, the Holzbog family moved from the Midwest to Louisville, Kentucky, then to Indiana and finally Tennessee. The Holzbogs maintained family ties to Wisconsin, and during his formative childhood years, young Walter was able to observe the differences among the cultural and natural environments of the places that he lived and visited. He worked with his grandmother on the landscape of her cottage on Cedar Lake in Wisconsin, where he built trails and steps on the hilly slope on her property. These early experiences contributed to a lifelong interest in travel and historic architecture, and would influence his belief in designing on a human scale in a way that related to the natural environment.

Beginning in 1918, Holzbog began studies at the University of Wisconsin at Madison in the School of Agriculture. That same year, he also joined the Army ROTC, just one month before the armistice. Holzbog earned a bachelor of science degree in agriculture and horticulture. Using the fundamentals of his undergraduate studies, Holzbog initiated postgraduate work at the University of Illinois at Urbana-Champagne with a focus on botany and horticulture.

In 1926, Holzbog returned to Wisconsin and became involved in farming and nursery work. His position with the nursery quickly evolved from laborer to salesman and design consultant. After the stock market crash of 1929, Holzbog was forced to start his own nursery business with a focus on landscape design. Though he was not formally trained in landscape architecture, he advocated that good survey and design could save the client money and provide better results for their garden and landscape designs.

During the Great Depression years, the nation's economic situation limited Holzbog's vision that landscape architecture was a combination of art and utility. He competed with untrained laborers and struggling nurseries for scarce landscape commissions. Consequently, his work during this time did not allow him to fully express his design ability.

Holzbog received several inquiries and job offers during this time, including invitations to work for landscape architect **Jens Jensen** and architect Frank Lloyd Wright. Both offers would have required relocating his young family, which included his wife Dorothy and two sons, away from other relatives during the height of the Depression. Instead, Holzbog began work with the Civilian Conservation Corp in 1935. Working as a landscape architect at Pattison State Park, located 12 miles south of Lake Superior, Holzbog was responsible for master planning activities resulting in the design and construction of trails and other facilities within the park. Holzbog did later serve as a landscape consultant to Wright, although the projects that he worked on are unknown at this time. Unfortunately, their relationship was limited because of Wright's problems with overdue payments to his consultants.

As the economy strengthened, Holzbog continued his landscape design-build practice, embracing his desire to design romantic gardens. An early influence in Holzbog's design aesthetic was the 1933 Century of Progress Fair in Chicago. There he toured the Belgian Village, a re-created medieval town of meandering streets that stood in stark contrast to the orderly towns of the Midwest. The village displayed a variety of building masses and elevations that were united by the use of indigenous materials. Holzbog learned that good design involved vegetation in harmony with bricks, stone, wood, ground forms, and water. This understanding, united with his childhood experiences, galvanized his belief of fusing nature with human creations.

His interest in the early American architecture of New England and the southern states, particularly his travels to the formal gardens of Williamsburg, also influenced his work. Holzbog's college roommate and lifelong friend, Lester J. Cappon, also a native of Milwaukee, was an archivist for Colonial Williamsburg in Virginia and director of the Institute of Early American History and Culture in Williamsburg. Many of Holzbog's designs include red-brick gardens in the Colonial Revival style, an obvious inspiration from his visits to Williamsburg and his lively correspondence with Cappon. Jens Jensen's

Walter Charles Holzbog. (Courtesy of the family of Walter Holzbog)

Prairie School of design also influenced Holzbog's work in both design and plant materials. As a result, Holzbog incorporated native plants into his garden designs. This impact is also evident when reviewing Holzbog's design plans, which reveal skillful applications of Jensen's principles.

His body of work includes projects that vary in scale and scope, ranging from single-family residences to urban and rural parks in the Milwaukee County area. He designed domestic, commercial, and civic projects. He completed landscape designs for several churches, including Community United Methodist Church in Elm Grove, Wisconsin. However, the majority of projects were completed for single-family residences. Working primarily in southeastern Wisconsin, Holzbog designed landscape plans for hundreds of residential projects. His work is characterized by the frequent use of masonry retaining walls, terraces, and cost-effective design solutions. Holzbog often approached potential clients that lived in his community as a neighbor rather than a landscape architect. He would discuss other projects he had completed and walk the site with the homeowners, describing ideas and developing sketches. If their houses were not yet built, Holzbog showed them how skillfully siting their homes could allow them to retain desirable mature trees. He promoted early coordination between landscape design and site preparation. He stated, "With landscape design at the start you are buying a combination of art, conservation, preservation, function and experience, and taking full advantage of what the site has to offer before you barge in on the ecocycle which took years to create and which, once destroyed, cannot be replaced."

In the 1960s, Holzbog built a house designed by his son Thomas, an architect, landscape architect, and planner, at Amy Belle Lake in Wisconsin. Another son, Charles, a landscape architect, assisted with site selection and landscaping.

Holzbog also served on several architectural review boards and the Wauwatosa Planning Commission for fourteen years prior to his semiretirement in the mid-1970s. His practice continued beyond retirement with the help of his son Charles.

During his latter years of semiretirement, Holzbog continued to express his ideas in naturalism, conservation, and ecology through art works and several self-published volumes of poetry. In 2001, Holzbog was inducted into the Hall of Fame of the Wisconsin Green Industry Federation, formerly the Wisconsin Landscape Federation. Holzbog resided at Friendship Village retirement center for the last twenty-five years of his life, where he wrote about his family's history, penned poetry, and created watercolor paintings. He also wrote a self-published autobiography with numerous details of his professional philosophy and career, crediting his

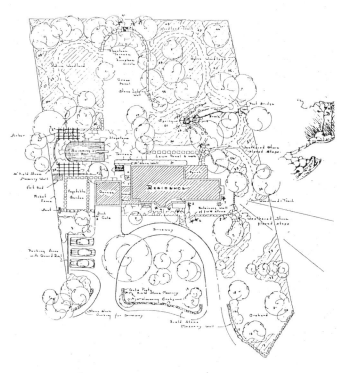

An example of Holzbog's work is seen in the landscape and development plan for French residence, Elmgrove, Wisconsin. (Courtesy of the family of Walter Holzbog)

friend Grady Clay Jr.* for teaching landscape architects how to write about their work. Holzbog passed away on September 17, 2002, at the age of 102.

Behm, Don. "Holzbog designed gardens; consulted with Wright." Milwaukee *Journal Sentinel,* September 23, 2002. Holzbog's obituary describing his life's work and personal interests.

Holzbog, Walter. *My Life as a Landscape Architect in the Midwest.* Milwaukee, Wisc.: Self-published, 1994. An insightful autobiography by Holzbog that describes his influences, personal and professional experiences, design philosophy, and includes a collection of his ecological poetry, landscape plans, and photographs.

Tim Tamburrino

HOTCHKISS, ALMERIN
(1816–1903)
LANDSCAPE GARDENER, CEMETERY SUPERINTENDENT

Almerin Hotchkiss was born in 1816. He began his career at Brooklyn's Green-Wood Cemetery, one of the earliest rural cemeteries in the country. Survey work began at the cemetery in 1833, just two years after the incorporation of the nation's first rural cemetery, Mount Auburn Cemetery, in Cambridge, Massachusetts. Green-Wood was incorporated on April 18, 1838, with construction of the design by David Bates Douglass* beginning just one year later. As the newly appointed superintendent, Hotchkiss played a pivotal role in this work, including the expansion of the original 178-acre Green-Wood Cemetery by more than 200 acres. Consistent with Douglass's original design intent and sympathetic with the site's unique topographic variation, Hotchkiss's addition is characterized by undulating, sweeping curves. For this design Hotchkiss worked with Zebedee Cook on the expansion, which occurred in the 1840s.

In June 1849, a massive cholera epidemic broke out in St. Louis, Missouri, killing 10 percent of the city's population, which averaged approximately one hundred funerals each day. To address this crisis, cemetery board member James Yeatman traveled east to Brooklyn where he visited Hotchkiss and the Green-Wood Cemetery. Following this visit, Hotchkiss was selected for the Bellefontaine Cemetery commission and within the next few months moved west.

Above: Brooklyn's Green-Wood Cemetery, from Nehemiah Cleaveland's *Green-Wood Illustrated* (New York: R. Martin, 1847).

Below: Bellefontaine Cemetery, St. Louis, Missouri. (Photo by Charles A. Birnbaum)

The 138-acre cemetery was the first large-scale rural cemetery to be designed west of the Mississippi River. The picturesque site overlooking the river would prove perfect to replace the older in-town cemeteries that stood in the path of expansion.

As with his Brooklyn work, Hotchkiss integrated gradually curving roadways into the terrain, while offering scenic prospects and preserving existing vegetation. The renowned tree collections that survive today are attributed to the vigilance of Hotchkiss. While Hotchkiss remained the superintendent at Bellefontaine, he also completed designs for properties in Illinois, across the Mississippi River from St. Louis. His tenure at Bellefontaine spanned more than forty-six years, during which

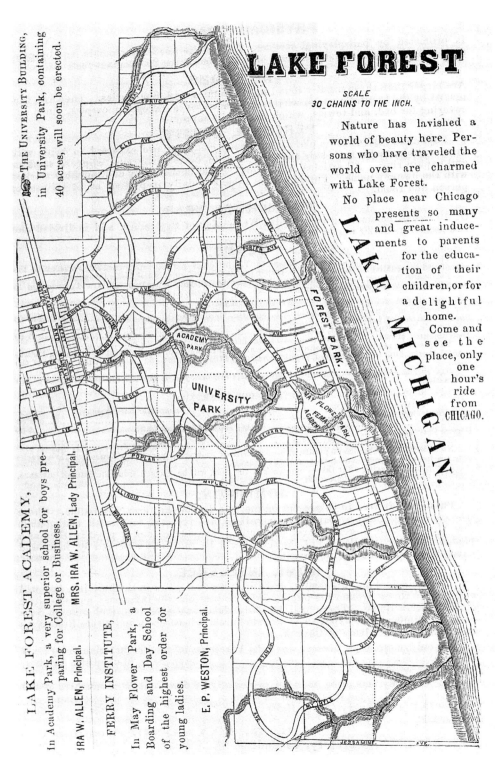

LAKE FOREST

SCALE
30 CHAINS TO THE INCH.

Nature has lavished a world of beauty here. Persons who have traveled the world over are charmed with Lake Forest.

No place near Chicago presents so many and great inducements to parents for the education of their children, or for a delightful home.

Come and see the place, only one hour's ride from CHICAGO.

THE UNIVERSITY BUILDING, in University Park, containing 40 acres, will soon be erected.

LAKE FOREST ACADEMY, a very superior school for boys preparing for College or Business.

IRA W. ALLEN, Principal.   MRS. IRA W. ALLEN, Lady Principal.

FERRY INSTITUTE, In May Flower Park, a Boarding and Day School of the highest order for young ladies.

E. P. WESTON, Principal.

Lake Forest town plat, 1857, from the *Lake Forest Academy and Ferry Institute Catalog*, 1869. (Lake Forest College Library Special Collections)

time the cemetery grew from its original 138 acres to 332 acres, including 14 miles of picturesque roads.

Hotchkiss also laid out Chippiannock Cemetery in Rock Island, Illinois. Platted in 1855, "Chippiannock" is a Native American term meaning "place of the dead." The original 62 acres purchased by the founders of the cemetery, as with Brooklyn's Green-Wood, was selected for its steeply sloping topography that afforded picturesque views. Here again Hotchkiss integrated undulating drives and pedestrian circulation routes in harmony with the subtle grade changes. However, these drives intersected with triangular traffic islands that were espoused through **Andrew Jackson Downing**'s writings characteristic of the English landscape school.

In 1856, Hotchkiss visited Illinois to consult on the plan to create a university and suburb called Lake Forest, just 27 miles outside of Chicago. Hotchkiss registered his plat for Lake Forest in July 1857. His design was in response to another cholera outbreak and was an attempt to make a refuge for urban dwellers to escape the city. Lake Forest was incorporated in 1861 under a charter granted by the Illinois State Legislature and was primarily founded to support the establishment of church-related educational institutions. It was among the earliest large-scale, commercial residential developments in the Chicago region—predating Olmsted & Vaux's design (**Frederick Law Olmsted Sr.** and **Calvert Vaux**) for Riverside (1869) and **Nathan Franklin Barrett**'s design for Pullman, Illinois (1870s), by more than a decade. Lake Forest was established just five years after the first such planned community in America, Llewellyn Park, in West Orange, New Jersey, was founded in 1852. While other designed suburbs predate Lake Forest, no other is of a scale comparable to Lake Forest's 1,200 acres, including a substantial town center.

The landscape setting for Lake Forest included both natural and man-made features, including Lake Michigan, lakeside bluffs, an existing rail line, and ravines. As with his earlier cemetery work, Hotchkiss took full advantage of the scenic and topographic features the site offered, and his general plan could be described as a city in a park. As with the earlier A. J. Davis, **Howard Daniels**, and Eugene Baumann design for Llewellyn Park, Lake Forest was laid out in an organic manner so that the topography, hydrology, and vegetative features guided the street plan, rather than a formal grid. To reinforce and protect this idea, residential and commercial areas were strictly defined, and Hotchkiss designated an area of Lake Forest for a cemetery. The site, which was high on a bluff overlooking the lake, was laid out by architect William Le Baron Jenney in 1882 and refined by landscape architect **Ossian Cole Simonds** in 1901. Simonds and Jenney had previously collaborated on Chicago's great rural cemetery, Graceland Cemetery.

The Lake Forest Association was unable to pay Hotchkiss's fee following the Panic of 1857. However, he was granted one of the lots in lieu of cash. It is possible that this experience curbed Hotchkiss's enthusiasm for pursuing outside projects because it appears that he worked exclusively at Bellefontaine after this time. Hotchkiss remained superintendent there for the rest of his career and was succeeded by his son Frank, for the following twenty. Hotchkiss passed away in 1903.

Bellefontaine Cemetery, 1863. St. Louis: Bellefontaine Cemetery Company, 1863. Includes a fold-out map of the cemetery (25 by 30 inches), a narrative history, and discussion of individual plots.

Coventry, Kim, Daniel Meyer, and Arthur H. Miller. *Classic Country Estates of Lake Forest: Architecture and Landscape Design 1856–1940.* New York: W. W. Norton and Co., 2003. An overview of the community, including its houses, landscapes and country clubs built during the Gilded Age. Richly illustrated, including renderings, plans, drawings, and photographs, many not previously published.

Miller, Arthur H., and Shirley M. Paddock. *Lake Forest: Estates, People, and Culture.* Chicago: Arcadia Publishing, 2000. Reprint, 2003. Richly illustrated with over two hundred images. Historical survey from the Civil War era to the Great Estate period includes Hotchkiss's role in planning the community.

Arthur H. Miller

HOWLAND, BENJAMIN CREGAN, JR.
(1923–1983)

LANDSCAPE ARCHITECT, EDUCATOR

Benjamin Cregan Howland Jr. was born on January 28, 1923, in Saratoga Springs, New York, and grew up in Tonawanda, a small town outside of Buffalo. In 1940, he joined the Civilian Conservation Corps, where he managed forests in Almond, New York. The following year, Howland enlisted in the U.S. Marines, an institution that was formative in shaping his personal and professional character, including his sense of duty, discipline, and love of country. During World War II, he served in the South Pacific with Edson's Raiders, the First Marine Raider Battalion, the most decorated Marine regiment in history. This experience honed skills that were central to Howland's success as a landscape architect, including his keen ability to read the lay of the land in the field and by using maps. After returning to the United States, he applied these skills to his studies at New York State College of Forestry where, in 1950, he earned a bachelor of science degree in landscape architecture. After graduation, following the example of his department chair, George J. Albrecht, a former National Park Service (NPS) employee with whom he corresponded frequently after graduation, Howland opted for employment with the NPS.

Howland worked in three NPS regions during his career: the National Capital Region and Eastern Service Center in Washington, D.C.; the Western office in San Francisco; and the Eastern office in Philadelphia. His impact on the planning and design of federal lands in and around Washington, D.C., cannot be understated. His projects ranged from significant historic sites, such as the White House, where he served as the restoration landscape construction supervisor in 1952, to complex engineered landscapes such as the Baltimore-Washington Parkway grading, site work, and bridge design from 1952 to 1955. He was particularly proud of his lead role in the major park planning initiative for the Anacostia River, a project that he guided for almost a decade. It was the first effort in the area since the McMillan Commission report.

Howland contributed to the design of the Old Stone House garden in Georgetown; the Iwo Jima Memorial grounds; the Washington Monument site improvement that translated Robert Mills's unrealized plans for a

Benjamin Howland in the field in the 1970s. (Courtesy of Sue Howland)

peristyle base into a ring of fifty American flags; the preliminary alignment of the George Washington Memorial Parkway north and west of Spout Run; the Master Plan for the National Capital Parks System; the initial task force for the Potomac River Basin; and the proposed alignment of the interstate highway adjacent to the monumental core. He was also proud of his leadership in the master planning efforts at three national seashores: Point Reyes, California; Cape Cod, Massachusetts; and Assateague, Virginia. Many of his contributions in the field were behind the scenes but highly influential, setting the conceptual plans and programs for subsequent consulting landscape architects such as **Gilmore David Clarke**, Horace Peaslee, Ian L. McHarg,* and Lawrence Halprin.*

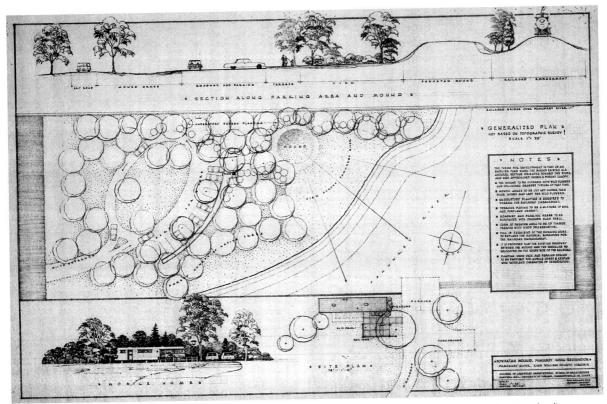

Site plan of proposed visitor center, Pamunkey Indian Reservation, King William County, Virginia, 1977. (Courtesy of Sue Howland)

The NPS afforded Howland extraordinary opportunities to design new visitors' centers within renowned established parks as well as occasions to develop master plans for newer types of parks, such as national seashores and urban recreational areas. Much of this work was realized under Director Conrad Wirth's *Mission 66,* a ten-year, $670 million park construction, renovation, and expansion program leading up to the NPS's fiftieth anniversary in 1966.

For Howland, national parks were places where people simultaneously experienced and protected the land, which he believed was the greatest source of natural and cultural history. Howland believed that the national parks belonged to the people. His social commitment was especially evident during his last major project, the Anacostia River waterfront, a long-neglected area in Washington's park planning efforts. Howland moved his design team from the regional office headquarters to a maintenance building closer to the African American neighborhoods that would be served by his project. There, he believed

he could better "serve as the pencil" for his clients during the planning process. This approach was not standard in landscape architecture practice and was one of Howland's many contributions to National Park Service master planning.

Howland was recognized for his superior professional accomplishments during this period with a Department of Interior Meritorious Service Award (1966) and a Citation for Distinguished Service (1971). Those awards noted that "Howland's creativity, sincerity and untiring ambition led him to be recognized as one of the foremost landscape architects in the National Park Service" and commended him for his unusual qualities of initiative, drive, and dedication as well as his technical excellence, sincerity of purpose, and unselfish contribution. In addition to the projects previously noted, others cited as proof of Howland's significant contributions included Big Bend National Park Development Plans, the San Francisco Bay Area Recreation Study, the Death Valley National Recreation Area, Lake Meade National

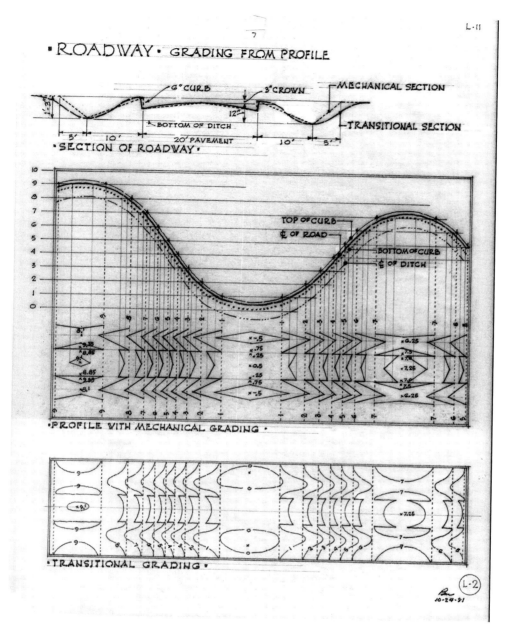

L-11

Road grading profile from Howland's Road Design class at the University of Virginia, 1981. (Courtesy of Sue Howland)

Recreation area, and Catoctin Mountain Park Jobs Corps Camp.

By the time of his retirement, Howland was supervising the architecture, engineering, landscape architecture, ecological services, and historic architecture programs in the National Capital Region. His concern for both historic landscapes and the wilderness and his ex-

pertise in planning, design details, and construction was unprecedented.

Howland's vast experience and excellent reputation made him a welcome addition to the newly established landscape architecture program at the University of Virginia (UVA). Harry W. Porter Jr., chair of the department, was also a Syracuse alumnus. He had known

Howland for twenty years, since interning in the NPS San Francisco office. The two of them became the intellectual and ethical foundation of the program. For two years, from 1975 to 1977, Howland taught at UVA through a temporary assignment under an innovative program, the Intergovernmental Personnel Act, Mobility Assignment Agreement. In 1978, Howland accepted a full-time tenured professorship. He taught construction courses including the legendary "Park Roads and Parkways" course, and master planning studios often addressing public landscapes such as Assateague Island, Pamunkey Indian Reservation, and Brandy Station Battlefield. Howland's course "Historic Sites" that researched and documented cultural landscapes, such as the Barboursville estate and Jefferson's Rivanna River mill and canal, was a popular course for students interested in landscape preservation. In that course, Howland advocated expanding the NPS Historic American Building Survey (HABS) with a new program, the Historic American Landscape Survey (HALS), twenty years before that program was finally initiated. As in his NPS tenure, when he was known for putting in long, unpaid hours rendering beautiful landscape tableaus for master planning document cover sheets, Howland inspired those who worked with him through example. He was often in the UVA design studios late at night—accompanied by a big thermos of coffee, a pipe, and an encouraging word.

For his superior accomplishments as a park planner and designer, Howland received a Meritorious Service Award and a Citation for Distinguished Service. He was made a Fellow of the American Society of Landscape Architects in 1981. Howland died on June 24, 1983. His legacy continues at UVA through annual programs endowed by his wife of thirty-five years, Sue Wilder Howland (m. 14 February 1945), their children Creg, Pamela, Sue Ann, Marlis, and Jane, and UVA alumni, such as a traveling fellowship, a lecture, and a student design competition. On Founder's Day in 1984 an ash tree was planted on the UVA Lawn in his memory.

Archival material related to Howland's teaching and design work can be found in several locations: The Department Alumni Archives, Faculty of Landscape Architecture, School of Environmental Sciences and Forestry, State University of New York, Syracuse, contains faculty correspondence from 1950–1960s, as well as seventeen drawings by Howland. In addition, the Department of Landscape Architecture Records, University of Virginia Alderman Library Archives, contains Howland's correspondence and related course files from 1975 to 1982. The NPS Regional Office Project Files (Group 79.6) at the National Archives contain broad listings for specific Regional Offices, as well as specific listings for the Cape Cod National Seashore and Anacostia Park; future scholars researching Howland's professional accomplishments will find these records invaluable.

"A Great Park Man Retires." *The National Park Courier* 22, no. 8 (August 1975), 3. This article covers Howland's retirement from the National Park Service and lists his many professional accomplishments.

Howland, Benjamin C. "Park Roads and Parkways." 1982. Unpublished lecture notes from Howland's course at the University of Virginia that he was working into a book manuscript. The topics range from the history of parkways to the detailed design of horizontal and vertical alignments for roadways. The University of Virginia library has a copy of the manuscript.

Parker, Don. "Howland Elected ASLA Fellow." *ASLAVA Virginia Landscape Architect Newsletter* (Fall 1981), 1, 5. This short article documents the Virginia chapter's reasons for nominating Howland as a Fellow.

Elizabeth K. Meyer

HUBBARD, LOUISE STONE
(1887–1932)
LANDSCAPE DESIGNER

Born in 1887, Louise Stone was the daughter of prominent Chicago attorney Horace Greeley Stone. She married Charles Walcott Hubbard, a Chicago real estate and trust company executive, on November 17, 1906. They were the parents of twin sons, Charles Jr., and Horace Stone. The family lived in east Winnetka, north of Chicago on Lake Michigan, where their garden was well-known for its spring display. Louise Stone Hubbard was a member of the original Garden Club of Illinois, organized in 1912 by women from Winnetka and Lake Forest. In 1913, her club became the westernmost founding member of the Garden Club of America; by 1922, this original group split off into the Winnetka and Lake Forest Garden Clubs.

Widowed in 1924, Hubbard turned her avocation of gardening into a profession. She soon began designing gardens and landscapes along Chicago's North Shore for

Welles garden, Winnetka, Illinois.
(Smithsonian Institution, Archives of
American Gardens, Garden Club of America
Collection)

some of the most high-profile clients of the day. It was an era when suburban Chicago professional garden design was a field dominated by men and East Coast women practitioners such as **Rose Standish Nichols** and **Ellen Biddle Shipman**. However, Hubbard carved important niches as both a cosmopolitan, locally based, expert creator of gardens and as an ensemble player with other nationally recognized landscape architects.

Hubbard's design skills were particularly suited to the American Country House movement, with its large estates and elaborate gardens and landscapes. Within just a few years, Hubbard contributed to some of the best known estates of the period. Hubbard designed a tennis court, lily pond, rock garden, and rose garden for Rosecrana, the estate of James Simpson, in Glencoe, just north of Winnetka. The designs prepared for Simpson, who was the president of Marshall Field & Company, were typical of classic suburban estate gardens of the era. At Rosecrana, Hubbard was part of a greater group of designers that included **Jens Jensen**, who designed a park-like landscape, and Root & Hollister (Ralph Rodney Root*), who designed a reflecting pool and plant borders. Hubbard's rock garden design was a notable feature of the estate.

Hubbard also completed designs for the estate of Edward K. Welles on the edge of Lake Forest's Onwentsia Club golf course. The Welles property was designed in the late 1920s. Hubbard reputedly spent several years in the Orient at one point in her life. Consequently, she was considered to be an expert on Chinese gardens. Her designs at both the Simpson and Welles properties may reflect Chinese design philosophies. She juxtaposed the soft, feminine *yin* of water with the hard, rough, and unmoving, or masculine, *yang* of stone. Her designs may have also reflected an awareness of *feng shui,* the ancient Chinese art of placing houses and gardens within a landscape. However, these Chinese influences are seamlessly interwoven into the fabric of these artful suburban estate gardens of the time.

Perhaps Hubbard's largest project in the mid-1920s was Old Mill Farm, the 400-acre estate of Chicago advertising genius Albert Lasker. The eminent classical architect David Adler was the designer of the estate and Louise Hubbard collaborated with him about the gardens around the house, including the rose garden and main gardens to the east. A trio of other Lake Forest commissions demonstrates the range of garden design challenges met by Louise Hubbard. Working as part of an ensemble that included Rose Standish Nichols, Hubbard was charged with planting the main south garden of Two Gables, the estate of Laurance Armour. This high-profile garden was pictured in the 1940 monograph of the architect Harry T. Lindeberg. At Laurence Scudders's mid-1920s Colonial Revival home, designed by New York architects Electus D. Litchfield & Rogers, in Connecticut, she planned the suburban-scaled landscape. The new estate incorporated part of an 1875 estate. She designed a large, open meadow south of the house, a native, rough-hewn, dry-laid limestone wall, and a rectangular refined pool bordered with Bedford limestone that is served by a winding flagstone path from the terrace. Hubbard's design still survives today.

At the Homestead, Hubbard worked on the D. R. Holt garden, attributed by the family to **Frederick Law Olmsted Sr**. She was in the midst of careful restoration when she died in 1932. According to her obituary, her death came suddenly during a talk she was delivering in Cleveland on the subject of Asian gardens.

A file on Hubbard (Louise Stone), landscape designer, is housed at the Lake Forest College Library Special Collections. The file includes material on Hubbard's biography, Holt and Scudder commissions, and other ephemera.

Coventry, Kim, Daniel Meyer, and Arthur H. Miller. *Classic Country Estates of Lake Forest: Architecture and Landscape Design, 1856–1940*. New York: W. W. Norton, 2003. Illustrates the Lasker estate and provides a brief biographical sketch on Hubbard.

Griswold, Mac, and Eleanor Weller. *The Golden Age of American Gardens: Proud Owners, Private Estates, 1890–1940*. New York: Harry N. Abrams, 1991. Archives of American Gardens listings include the Simpson and Welles gardens.

Salny, Stephen M. *The Country Houses of David Adler*. New York: W. W. Norton, 2001. Discusses the Lasker estate and Hubbard's role.

Arthur H. Miller

IREYS, ALICE RECKNAGEL
(1911–2000)
LANDSCAPE ARCHITECT, HORTICULTURIST, AUTHOR, TEACHER

Alice Recknagel was born and lived all of her life in Brooklyn, New York. In her youth, she volunteered at the recently established Brooklyn Botanic Garden, and from this experience determined to work with plants for the rest of her life. She studied at the Cambridge (Massachusetts) School of Architecture and Landscape Architecture, a college for women closely associated with Harvard, graduating in 1935. She worked for **Marjorie Sewell Cautley** for a year, and then for Charles N. Lowrie, one of the founders of the American Society of Landscape Architects. When Lowrie died suddenly in 1939, she took over his practice, completing the planting plan of the now-notorious Red Hook housing project in Brooklyn. The trees from the original design still stand today. However, only a few of Lowrie's clients stayed with her. She worked from his office on Park Avenue in New York City until 1943, in association with Cynthia Wiley, primarily producing landscape plans for public housing projects in New York City. In 1943, she married Henry Tillinghast Ireys III, and subsequently had three children. After her marriage, she opened an office in her home and worked from there until her death in 2000.

Ireys was associated with Clara Coffey from 1945 to 1947, and together they worked on landscape plans for public projects. Ireys later became an accomplished designer of hundreds of home and estate gardens for private clients, usually working with one or two assistants. Many of the estate gardens were built on the cleared, flat ground of Long Island potato fields, where coun-

Alice Ireys. (Photo by Allen Rokach)

Garden, Abigail Adams Smith Museum (now the Mount Vernon Hotel Museum and Garden), New York, New York, 2005. (Courtesy of the Mount Vernon Hotel Museum and Garden, New York, NY)

try houses proliferated. The city gardens, in contrast, were often very small yards associated with Brooklyn brownstone row houses. A less significant portion of Ireys's design work consisted of gardens for small public institutions such as churches, libraries, hospitals, and the like. In the 1950s, she began teaching in the Landscape Design Schools of the Federated Garden Clubs of America, which she continued to do until the early 1980s. At the same time, she began lecturing and teaching at the Brooklyn Botanic Garden and garden club meetings. All of her teaching and lecturing was on the subject of home landscape design. Her design, teaching, and lecturing for the Brooklyn Botanic Garden continued for the rest of her life.

From 1952 to 1955 she designed what may be her most well-known work, the Garden of Fragrance for the Blind, at the Brooklyn Botanic Garden. It was the first public garden in the country designed for the sight-impaired and is extant. It is an oval space, approximately 60 by 100 feet, with a central lawn and wide path at the edge. The garden is surrounded by waist-high stone walls enclosing beds of strongly fragrant plants that are placed to be easy to touch and smell. Plants are identified by labels in Braille. A small fountain provides both a pleasing sound for those with acute hearing, and also a place to rinse strong aromas off of the fingers.

Between 1955 to 1965, Ireys designed the Clark Botanic Garden in Albertson, Long Island, New York, a 10-acre site affiliated with the Brooklyn Botanic Garden, as well as several other projects for the Brooklyn Botanic Garden. In 1974, she designed a historically themed garden renovation for the Abigail Adams Smith Museum (now the Mount Vernon Hotel Museum and Garden) in Manhattan. Today, it remains a heavily visited garden on an outcrop of Manhattan schist.

In 1967, Ireys published her first book, *How to Plan and Plant Your Own Property.* It became very popular as a gardener's guide and was republished multiple times. This was followed in 1978 by the very well received *Small Gardens for City and Country.* Both of these books are directed to homeowners. The books present the basic principles of residential landscape design, using Ireys's many designs to illustrate her points. In them, she taught people how to scale-down the grandness of the estates of the rich to make gracious outdoor living possible on modest properties. In particular, she emphasized a properly welcoming and visible approach to the house, well-situated and proportioned areas for outdoor living, proper siting and selection of trees, and the use of a water feature in every garden. Her clients' gardens, which she used as examples, were notable for their multilayered and horticulturally sophisticated planting designs. In 1978, she was made a Fellow of the American Society of Landscape Architects, primarily in recognition of her writing, teaching, and horticultural work.

In the mid-1980s, Ireys began an association with the W. Atlee Burpee Seed Company, designing small flower gardens utilizing Burpee seeds. These garden plans were packaged with an artist's illustration and the necessary seeds. They were sold through both the Burpee mail-order catalog and the company's retail seed distribution system. Hundreds of thousands of these packaged designs were sold. In 1991, Burpee published those designs, and many new ones, in *Garden Designs,* and also published a second book, *Designs for American Gardens,* which returned to Ireys's past writing and teaching style. It showed fourteen of her residential designs, each in a detailed chapter discussing the plan, features, and planting material. In that same year, the American Horticultural Society awarded her the Liberty Hyde Bailey Award, its highest honor. She won the 1992 Quill and Trowel Award from the Garden Writers Association of America.

In 1994, the Brooklyn Botanic Garden awarded her the Distinguished Service Medal, and in 2000, they published a videotaped documentary of her work. At the time of her death in 2000, she was scheduled to receive the Brooklyn Botanic Garden's Better Earth Award, which recognizes people who are engaged in important environmental work in the community.

Alice Ireys's papers are held at Smith College. For a finding aid to the collection go to: www.smith.edu/libraries/libs/ssc/collectij.html.

Brooklyn Botanic Garden. *The Living Landscapes of Alice Recknagel Ireys.* New York: Brooklyn Botanic Garden, 2000. Videocassette. Made in the year of her death, at eighty-nine, this shows the designer talking about her career, her designs, and her association with the Brooklyn Botanic Garden. Filmed at many of her existing gardens, and showing many archival pictures, this is the most complete overview available of Ireys's work.

Ireys, Alice Recknagel. *Designs for American Gardens.* New York: Prentice Hall, 1991. A reworking and updating of a 1967 book, this shows the material on home garden design that Ireys taught and lectured about for sixty years.

Ireys, Alice Recknagel. *Small Gardens For City and Country: A Guide to Designing and Planting Your Green Spaces.* Englewood Cliffs, N.J.: Prentice-Hall, 1978. Ireys's most popular lectures and courses were about designing for small spaces. Here, she illustrates her material with images from her own designs.

Donna Tunkel Lilborn

JOHNSON, CAROL R.
(1929–)
LANDSCAPE ARCHITECT, EDUCATOR

Carol Johnson was born in Elizabeth, New Jersey, on September 6, 1929. She was the second child born to her parents. Her father was a lawyer, and her mother, a school principal. From them she inherited a love of the outdoors. She was shaped by the landscape experiences of her childhood spent in Killington, and Sherborn Valley, Vermont, as well as on the Gay Head Cliffs on Martha's Vineyard in Massachusetts. During this time she climbed trees, hiked, and camped out. Her earliest memories of living in a consciously designed landscape were of her time as a student at Wellesley College, and in particular, her introduction to **Frederick Law Olmsted Jr.**'s campus concept of building on the hills and leaving the valley open. She graduated in 1951 with a bachelor of arts in English. Following Wellesley, she worked in a commercial nursery in Bedford, Massachusetts. While there, she met John Frey, Pat Manhart, and Eric Desty, students who were studying landscape architecture at Harvard.

Carol R. Johnson on the campus of Agnes Scott College, Decatur, Georgia, 2001. (Photo by Sue Clites, courtesy of Agnes Scott College)

John Marshall Park, Washington, D.C., 1984. (Photo courtesy of Carol R. Johnson Associates, Inc.)

With their encouragement, she decided to pursue a career in landscape architecture, a field she knew little about.

While at Harvard's Graduate School of Design, Johnson attributed her personal growth to professors Serge Chermeyoff, Hideo Sasaki,* **Norman Thomas Newton**, and Walt Chambers. Later she would recall that they all gave her their time and attention. From these mentors, she gained confidence, and an understanding of design. In particular, her studies under Sigfried Gideon, the author of *Space, Time, and Architecture*, would be a great influence on her attitudes toward urban design. Also during this time, Johnson became familiar with collaborative design processes and environmentally sensitive landscape design—two concepts that formed the foundation of her design approach and ethic. She earned her degree from Harvard in 1957.

Between 1955 and 1958, Johnson acquired her earliest professional experience, initially with the Bucks County Park Board in Doylestown, Pennsylvania; and subsequently with engineering and planning firms in the greater Boston area. In September 1958, she was one of the first landscape architects to be hired by The Architects Collaborative (TAC), the renowned architectural practice founded by Walter Gropius in Cambridge, Massachusetts. Despite the prestige of her position, and with the encouragement of colleagues, she left TAC after only one year to start her own practice, taking advantage of projects offered to her through her Wellesley and Harvard contacts.

When she founded her firm in 1959, there were few women landscape architects working on urban design and planning issues. There were also few male landscape architects who would choose to work for a talented woman landscape architect when they had opportunities to work for talented men. As a result, her earliest employees included artists and sculptors who, under her tutelage, learned the art and craft of landscape architecture. At first, the project work in the office emphasized suburban private gardens, which allowed Johnson to learn quickly about building landscape details. Very soon, Johnson had opportunities that were unusual for a woman, such as her first foreign project, the landscape associated with the U.S. Pavilion at Montreal's Expo '67, where she collaborated with Buckminister Fuller and Cambridge Seven Associates.

Other early Johnson commissions included two pioneering visual impact assessment projects: in 1975, for the Chevron Oil Refinery in Perth Amboy, New Jersey, Johnson collaborated with a team of environmentalists on a phased program of visual improvements, including a new color palette for the refinery; and, in the Finger Lakes region of Upstate New York, in 1981, she directed the site reclamation for the Bell Station on Lake Cayuga. This disturbed area had been abandoned following site preparation for a proposed power plant. Johnson transformed the site into a natural lakeside meadow. As is evident with these early corporate projects, Johnson based her practice upon the traditional values of dedicated public service, an unrelenting insistence upon quality in design and construction, and educating future practitioners about the social value of good design. Johnson's first project where she worked closely with an affected community was in 1972 at the North Common in Lowell,

John Fitzgerald Kennedy Memorial Park, Cambridge, Massachusetts, 2001 view. (Photo courtesy of Carol R. Johnson Associates, Inc.)

Work in the office during the 1980s and 1990s included many of Johnson's most important built works. Among them are the Old Harbor Park, where she created a waterfront linear park between South Boston and the Kennedy Library in 1990; the John F. Kennedy Memorial Park, which unites the Charles River Reservation with nearby Harvard Square in Cambridge, Massachusetts, completed in 1987; and the Lechmere Canal Park in East Cambridge, the first phase of which was completed in 1983. In addition, her extensive commissions and consulting work on campus landscape master plans and site improvements at colleges and universities from Maine to Florida expanded. In all of these projects, Johnson's signature design style of establishing harmony with the setting and surroundings; respecting the site's natural and cultural history; offering respite to users; and providing elements of delight and surprise is present.

Massachusetts, part of Lyndon Johnson's Model Cities Program. In other community-based planning projects, such as the Mystic River Reservation in Medford and Somerville, Massachusetts, Johnson was able to meld her interest in history (in this case **Charles Eliot**'s approach to scenic and natural resource values) with state-of-the-art environmental sciences. For the once-polluted Mystic Reservation, Johnson worked with consultants who developed new soil mixes and drainage techniques to solve problems posed by toxic soils.

With her reputation established, opportunities for Johnson in the 1970s and 1980s increased. In addition to serving on many planning committees, during President Jimmy Carter's administration, she served on the Treasury Department's Commission on Small Business, and in the 1980s on the Department's Committee on Development Options. Also during this time she began to travel abroad extensively in Europe, Asia, the Middle East, and Africa. While visiting colleagues in Nairobi, she camped out in the desert and visited Kenyan wildlife parks. In Iran, Johnson directed the firm's first overseas work for a new community, Farahzad. This commission provided her an opportunity to visit the great Persian gardens and civic spaces.

She taught in the Planning Department at Harvard's Graduate School of Design from 1966 to 1973, and in 1984, Johnson taught and lectured at several architecture schools in Taiwan. This opportunity also provided the impetus for Carol R. Johnson Associates (CRJA) to undertake projects for the first time in the Far East.

Marshall Park in Washington, D.C., was completed in 1983. This original conceptual design was integrated into the overall streetscape design for Pennsylvania Avenue itself and the access to the district court on one side and the Canadian Chancellery on the other. Johnson's new design provides a stronger memorial to John Marshall, recalling his long tenure in the Supreme Court and its impact on the federal government as we know it today.

Johnson became a Fellow of the American Society of Landscape Architects in 1982, and in 1998 she was the first American woman to receive the ASLA Gold Medal. She is also a member of the Boston Society of Landscape Architects, an honorary member of the Boston Society of Architects, a trustee for the Hubbard Educational Trust and Chairman of the Board of Designators for the George B. Henderson Foundation. For ten years, she was a City of Boston Civic Design Commissioner. She holds honorary degrees from Wentworth Institute of Technology and Gettysburg College.

Beyond the positive impact of her work on the public, Johnson's contribution can be measured by the influence that she has had on new generations of landscape architects. She is recognized as a role model, especially for young women entering the profession.

Johnson, Carol R. "Monuments: Their Environment, Theme and Construction." *1990 IFLA Yearbook,* 123–32. Proceedings of the International Federation of Landscape Architects Central Region Symposium, Leningrad and Moscow, USSR. Includes essay on the effect of monuments on the environment, their thematic messages, and their detailed design, citing John F. Kennedy Memorial Park as a case study.

Johnson, Carol R. "The Unconsidered Northern Landscape." *Simultaneous Landscapes, Journal of the Alaska Design Forum,* no. 2 (Summer 1994), 14–18. Essay on opportunities for public enjoyment and celebration provided by the winter landscape.

Johnson, Carol R. "Urban Open Space and Transit Development." *Landscape Architecture* 6, no. 2 (February 1993), 22–24. Commentary on opportunities for urban open space and pedestrianization to interface with new or rehabilitated transit stations, using CRJA projects as case studies.

Mary Alice Van Sickle

JOHNSON, MARSHALL LISTON
(1892–1967)
LANDSCAPE ARCHITECT

Marshall Johnson was born in Minneapolis, Minnesota, in 1892. After receiving education in Oak Park, Illinois, and Kansas City, Missouri, he entered the landscape architecture program at Cornell University in 1911, studying under its founder **Bryant Fleming** and **Liberty Hyde Bailey**. Upon graduation in 1915, Johnson immediately applied for work with **Jens Jensen**, just as the Prairie-style master was embarking on his collaboration with architect Howard Van Doren Shaw on a major project in Lake Bluff, Illinois, at industrialist William V. Kelley's estate, Stonebridge. The project (now the Harrison House Conference Center) remains one of the best surviving North Shore Jensen projects. It includes many of Jensen's defining vocabulary elements. Jensen welcomed Johnson's energy and quick grasp of the requirements of the Kelley project, and they worked together, traveling daily from Chicago by train, for nearly a year.

From 1917 to 1919, Johnson distinguished himself in combat service during World War I and was awarded the *Croix de Guerre* in 1918. After returning from the war, Johnson was associated with Jensen in his office and after 1919 as his son-in-law. Johnson managed the office at The Clearing, on Ellison Bay, in Door County, Wisconsin, and was responsible for many handsome drawings of Jensen's projects. Johnson designed the archetypical shoreline council ring at The Clearing, constructing it in 1925.

In 1935, at the age of seventy-four, Jensen relocated to Ellison Bay to start the noted folk school at his long-time retreat, The Clearing, and Johnson succeeded him in his

Marshall Johnson (*right*), with Mrs. Howard Peabody and August Kock, 1942. (Lake Forest College Library Special Collections)

Left: Roads of the World—Belgium, from The Century of Progress Exposition, Chicago, 1934. (Courtesy of Robert E. Grese)

Below: Aerial view of Greenfield Village, Dearborn, Michigan. (Courtesy of Robert E. Grese)

signed personal projects for Edsel Ford and numerous company offices and plants in the Midwest. He also completed plans for Greenfield Village and Dearborn Inn, in Dearborn, Michigan; and exposition pavilions for the company for the World's Fair's in Chicago (The Century of Progress) in 1933 to 1934, and New York City in 1939. In the 1950s, Johnson collaborated with historian Leonard K. Eaton in the preservation of Jensen's drawings at the University of Michigan.

In addition to his work with Jensen, Johnson was developing his own notable practice in the 1920s. He designed a plan for Howard B. Peabody's Lake Forest estate, and provided alterations in 1951. In 1940 and 1941, Johnson designed the layouts for the flower shows of the Lake Forest Garden Club. One member, Mrs. Laurance Armour, commissioned Johnson to modify the flower garden (planned earlier by **Rose Standish Nichols**) of her estate, Two Gables, in 1947. Jensen had designed the park at the estate for its original owner, Orville Babcock, in 1910–1911. Celebrated examples of his City Beautiful–era work in Illinois include his 1935 plan for the Highland Park town center and the 1948 Lake Forest College campus feasibility study. Also in Illinois, his residential commissions from this period include the Harold Florsheim estate, in Highland Park, and W. Paul McBride estate, in Lake Forest.

Chicago North Shore practice. Examination of Johnson's surviving records, drawings, and renderings indicate he provided continuity and stewardship on many of Jensen's notable projects. Johnson often conducted additional work, especially in the late 1930s and 1940s, on parks such as Rosewood in Highland Park, where he lived in Jensen's original studio, and at Columbus Park in Chicago's Austin community. Johnson continued Jensen's relationship with the Ford family. He de-

Johnson's half century on the North Shore saw him adapting artfully to changing economic conditions and aesthetic tastes. As the estate era waned, Johnson adapted successfully to smaller-scale projects, commercial clients, and the influences of modernism. Amid bleak

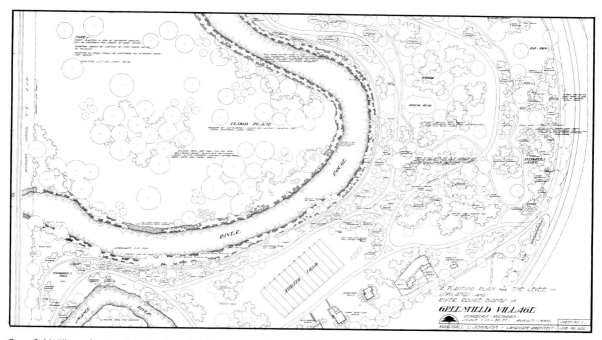

Greenfield Village planting plan, Dearborn, Michigan, 1940. (Courtesy of The Sterling Morton Library, The Morton Arboretum, Lisle, IL)

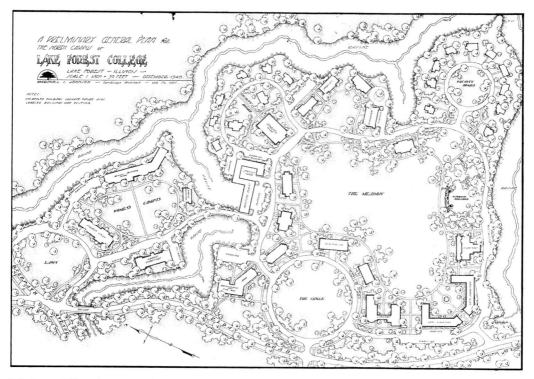

Lake Forest College plan, 1948. (Lake Forest College Library Special Collections)

post–World War II housing in Highland Park, Illinois, Johnson created a successful model landscape for the new forms of housing. The design featured a few well-placed spruce trees in proportion for the low ranch house, a horizontal split rail fence, and a clump of birch trees. In 1951, Johnson developed a subdivision plan for the 200-acre formal Lake Forest Villa Turicum, designed by **Charles A. Platt** for Edith Rockefeller McCormick in 1909–1912. Johnson managed to preserve most of Platt's key Italian villa garden elements on the proposed lakefront lots. Today, these famous features survive or have been restored.

Johnson's career seemed effortlessly to span the transition from the City Beautiful plans in the 1930s and 1940s to modernism in the 1950s. By 1958, Johnson was collaborating with Miesian architect I. W. Colburn on the bluff-sited William L. McLennan place on Lake Forest's high-profile Lake Road. The project earned a double-page spread in a July 1962 *Life* feature on new architectural styles.

Johnson was prolific with over 2,500 commissions, most of them on Chicago's North Shore. Three decades after Jensen's departure, he competed with other capable local and national landscape architects, among them Annette Hoyt Flanders,* Gertrude Deimel Kuh,* Franz Lipp,* Helen Milman, and C. D. Wagstaff, for commissions. Fortunately, sophisticated clients, often educated in the many garden clubs that sprang up during the period, appreciated Johnson's ability to adhere to classic and Prairie principles while adapting to new styles and conditions.

Few individuals or firms have contributed so substantially to an area for so long as did the Jensen-Johnson affiliation, led by the former for three decades, and then continued by the latter for three more. Much of the public and private character of the region still reflects this long stewardship. Johnson passed away in 1967, ending his long period of influence.

The Marshall L. Johnson collection, at the Sterling Morton Library, Morton Arboretum, Lisle, IL, contains Johnson's drawings, his renderings, several Jensen projects (e.g., the Shakespeare Garden at Northwestern University, Evanston), and his job book. A copy of the job book is also at Lake Forest College Library Special Collections.

Coventry, Kim, Daniel Meyer, and Arthur H. Miller. *Classic Country Estates of Lake Forest: Architecture and Landscape Design, 1856–1940.* New York: W. W. Norton, 2003. Includes illustrations of the William V. Kelley and W. Paul McBride estate landscapes.

Fitch, James, and F. F. Rockwell. *Treasury of American Gardens.* New York: Harper & Brothers, 1956. Features Johnson's Peabody estate, one of only two Illinois gardens discussed and illustrated.

Grese, Robert E. *Jens Jensen, Maker of Natural Parks and Gardens.* Baltimore: Johns Hopkins University Press, 1992. Includes a brief biographical sketch of Johnson.

Arthur H. Miller

JONES, HELEN SWIFT
(1887–1982)
LANDSCAPE ARCHITECT, WRITER, EDUCATOR

Helen Swift Jones was born on July 13, 1887, in Brooklyn, New York, to Helen Jeanette Swift and Wallace Thaxter Jones. In 1910, she received her bachelor of arts from Smith College and, in 1912, she taught her first botany course at Adelphi College in New York. Jones continued to work in the botany department until 1917, when she took a hiatus from her career to join the war effort. During the war, Jones worked as an inspector in a gas mask factory and then later as a clerk in the delinquency draft board office.

Jones returned to school in 1921 and began taking courses in plant materials at Harvard Summer School and for three years at the Cambridge School of Architecture and Landscape Architecture. Within a year, Jones took the first of what became lifelong trips abroad to study gardens. Her first trip was limited to Western Europe, but she eventually expanded her travels to include Japan and India. In 1924, Jones moved to New York City and spent a year working for Annette Hoyt Flanders.* Jones opened her own practice in 1925, working first from her home and then from her office on Park Avenue.

By 1930, her practice was flourishing. Jones was retained to design and execute the mall and Levermore Memorial Elms on Adelphi's Garden City, New York, campus. The plantings included a double row of elm trees connecting two main campus buildings. During this time, Jones also began the first of her projects for hospitals, including the site plan and planting of the

40-acre campus of the Mary Avery Convalescent Hospital in Hartford, Connecticut; a large, interior courtyard for the Stamford Hospital in Connecticut; and an urban garden for the Prospect Heights Hospital in Brooklyn, New York.

In 1932, Jones was hired by the New York City Department of Parks to supervise playground design under **Gilmore David Clarke**. Jones also served as secretary and treasurer for the New York Chapter of the American Society of Landscape Architects from 1932 to 1936 and, by 1934, Jones became the first female landscape architect to join the Architectural League of New York. In January 1936, she married naval architect Winthrop Merton Rice and moved to Stamford, Connecticut. She continued to work from her office in New York City and, the following year, she earned a masters in landscape architecture from Smith College.

Throughout her career, Jones wrote and lectured on the subject of landscape architecture. She spoke at local garden clubs and participated in nationally broadcast talks, including a series of garden talks from the 1939 World's Fair in Flushing Meadows, in Queens, New York, entitled "Gardens of the World: Their Influence on Our Gardens." Her articles on landscape design were published in several magazines, including *House and Garden, House Beautiful,* and *Arts Magazine.* Jones also wrote a series of pamphlets on gardening and garden design for publisher William H. Wise. Throughout her writing, Jones expressed her belief that a garden should not be an extravagance. Instead, it is an integral part of any home or surrounding. Jones believed that the garden offered a place for children to play and learn, a place for adults to relax and entertain, and, of course, it was a place of practicality where one could grow fruits and vegetables. Jones argued that this usefulness, along with restraint in planning, was what separated the modern garden from its traditional predecessor.

Jones's philosophies are most evident in the commis-

An integrated garden room design is seen at the Frank Barbour garden, Canojoharie, New York, 1931. (Smithsonian Institution, Archives of American Gardens, Garden Club of America Collection)

sion she completed for Bellevue Hospital in New York City. In 1938, she began work on a series of roof gardens for the hospital's children's wing. The project included three adjoining rooftop gardens: one for play, one for gardening, and one for rest. When she later wrote about the design, Jones expressed that making a garden useful as well as inviting kept it a welcome diversion rather than an overwhelming chore.

In 1940, Jones was elected vice president of the Architectural League of New York. The following year, she again put her career on hold in order to join the war effort. Jones trained as a Red Cross Nurse's Aide and served the organization until 1945. By the end of World War II, Jones had moved her practice to Stamford, Connecticut, where she continued to work until her retirement.

Her relatively prolific career included over half a dozen estate designs, a dozen private gardens, and landscape designs for four hospitals. Her commissions stretched from New Jersey to Canada and her clients included philanthropists Vincent Astor and Nora Mellon, entrepreneur Bartlett Arkell, and architect Raphael Hume.

Jones retired from her formal practice in 1970 and spent the remainder of her life traveling and gardening at her new home in Hightstown, New Jersey. Along with being a member of the Architectural League of New York and a Fellow of the American Society of Landscape

Architects, Jones was an active member of the Garden Club of America. She died in 1982.

Jones, Helen Swift. "Plan First, Then Plant." *Modern Hospital* 54, no. 4 (April 1940), 45–48. In this article, Helen Jones Swift explains the benefits of a garden in a convalescent environment as well as the importance of planning in keeping maintenance expenditures to a minimum.

Jones, Helen Swift, and E. L. D Seymour. *Landscaping the Small Home.* New York: William H. Wise and Co., Inc., 1950. This is one of a series of informational pamphlets in which Helen Swift Jones discusses the importance of planning and maintenance in the modern garden.

Peterson, Anne. "Women Take the Lead in Landscape Art." *New York Times,* March 13, 1938. This article provides basic information on Helen Swift Jones and her contemporaries' presence in the field of landscape architecture.

Melanie Macchio

KELLAWAY, HERBERT J.
(1867–1947)
LANDSCAPE ARCHITECT, PLANNER

Herbert J. Kellaway was born in Kent, England, but moved with his family at an early age to Needham, Massachusetts, where he graduated from high school. With no possibility to formally study the emerging profession of landscape architecture, Kellaway began his early career in 1892 as a draftsman in the Boston offices of Olmsted, Olmsted, and Eliot. There he worked with **Frederick Law Olmsted Sr.** (until his retirement in 1892), **John Charles Olmsted**, **Frederick Olmsted Jr.**, and **Charles Eliot**. During this time, Olmsted's plan for a continuous green corridor from the Boston Common to Jamaica Pond, commonly referred to as the "Emerald Necklace," was nearly completed. In addition, a newly formed Metropolitan Park Commission was implementing Eliot's vision for a system of metropolitan parks, parkways, and preserved open spaces in greater Boston. Kellaway also worked on campus plans for Smith, Amherst, and Middlebury colleges during his tenure at the Olmsted firm. After leaving the firm in 1906 to open his own office, Kellaway continued to promote preservation and connection of open spaces, ideals that were no doubt enriched in his formative professional years at the Olmsted firm.

Kellaway's career continued to overlap with projects initially designed by the Olmsted firm. In his hometown of Newton, Massachusetts, in 1908, he made changes to

Newton Centre Playground, a park originally designed by Olmsted Sr., in 1891. Reflecting the public's growing awareness in the value of sports and outdoor exercise, Kellaway changed the original open, park-like layout to include basketball courts, a croquet lawn, and archery grounds. The picturesque meandering brook was rerouted underground to create more play areas.

Also in 1908, Kellaway was asked by the city of Brookline, Massachusetts, to submit a plan to connect the northern and southern groups of Metropolitan Park Commission parks. His plan called for a tree-lined parkway that would link two of the commission's newly created green spaces: Charles River Reservation (near Watertown Square) and the West Roxbury Parkway. Kellaway wrote that he believed the beauty of this parkway would be in the diversity of its landscape, incorporating woods, swampland, glacial outcroppings, and streams. Although the plan was approved by the adjoining municipalities, Hammond Pond Parkway was the only part of the plan that was built.

In 1913, Winchester, a residential suburb north of Boston, hired Kellaway to develop a plan to improve the waterways in the town. Although Winchester had many scenic natural features, its waterways in the town center were polluted with industrial waste, sewage, and

Above: Webster rose garden (with 2,700 roses), Falmouth, Massachusetts, photo by Herbert Kellaway, from *Landscape Architecture,* October 1932. (Courtesy of the Frances Loeb Library, Harvard Graduate School of Design)

Left: Herbert J. Kellaway, photo by Frezell Studio, from *Landscape Architecture,* January 1948. (Courtesy of the Frances Loeb Library, Harvard Graduate School of Design)

rubbish from nearby tanneries, lumberyards, and tenements. Kellaway's plan called for removal of unsightly mill buildings, rebuilding of bridges, and removal of a large dam at the Mill Pond in the center of town. In its place, he designed a large, semicircular, stepped dam. Central to the plan was the use of water to connect spaces throughout the town. Kellaway wrote that water, "if it can be secured in a natural manner," can be "fully as beautiful as the formal" in creating an informal style civic center. This approach would reappear fourteen years later in 1928, when Winchester once again called upon Kellaway to develop a plan to improve the Aberjona River that flowed through the town. Similar to his earlier plans of connected parks, this plan called for a continuous corridor of green, with tree-lined parkways, ponds, and parks stretching from one end of town to the other. The effect was an emerald necklace for the scenic small town. New bridges, ponds, and parks were implemented. During the Depression many were built with help from government-sponsored work programs. Today, almost all of Winchester's numerous parks, ponds, and scenic roadways are the result of the design and preservation efforts of both Charles Eliot and Herbert Kellaway. Kellaway's semicircular, stepped dam continues to serve as a scenic focal point of the town.

Kellaway's town planning expertise was utilized during World War I. He was part of a nationwide group of city planners charged with rapidly planning and overseeing construction of enormous military complexes, or cantonments, for the U.S. Army. This group of city planners was carefully selected and recommended by Frederick Law Olmsted Jr., then chairman of the National Conference on City Planning. Under Kellaway's direction, the Fort Devens complex in Ayer, Massachusetts, was built in four months and housed 45,000 soldiers. Using the experience and nationwide recognition for developing timely, low-cost housing for the military, Kellaway also designed low-cost housing projects for war workers of the Fore River Shipbuilding Works in Quincy, Massachusetts, and the Salvation Army Fresh Air Camps in Sharon, Massachusetts. Other projects included the grounds of the Newton-Wellesley Hospital and the Andover-Newton Theological Seminary, both in Newton, Massachusetts, and the Mission Hill Project in Roxbury. Projects outside of the Boston area including Mountain View in Springfield, Vermont, and villages in Plainfield, Connecticut, and Winnsboro, South Carolina.

Herbert Kellaway's work was not exclusively large-scale town or campus planning. In 1907, the year after he left the Olmsted firm, he published *How to Lay Out Suburban*

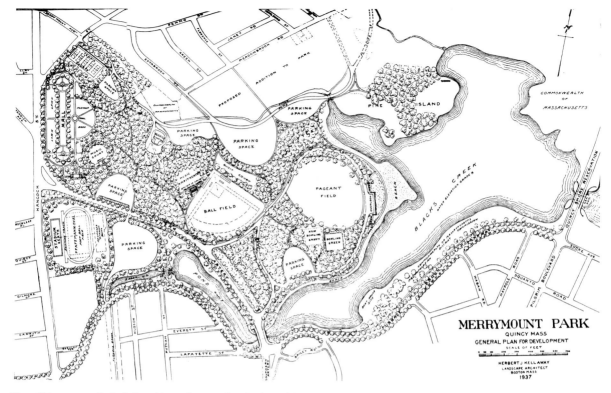

Plan of Merrymount Park, Quincy, Massachusetts, from *Parks and Recreation,* March–April 1938. (Courtesy of the Frances Loeb Library, Harvard Graduate School of Design)

Home Grounds. Similar to **Andrew Jackson Downing**'s pattern books of the mid-1800s, his book was directed to the homeowners of suburban properties. Like Downing, he encouraged homeowners to analyze the natural features of the site before locating the house and laying out the gardens. His residential designs for larger properties were more formal, with symmetrical garden beds, and axes and cross-axes tying elements of the garden together. Many of his residential plans included extensive rose gardens, which he designed with the help of rosarian **Harriett Risley Foote**. The two most noteworthy rose gardens were for Mrs. Henry Ford in Dearborn, Michigan, and for Mrs. Edwin Webster in Falmouth, Massachusetts.

In 1937, Kellaway redesigned the aging 90-acre Merrymount Park in Quincy, Massachusetts. The narrow paths that had accommodated pedestrians and horse and buggy traffic were no longer safe for automobile use. Kellaway divided the park into three parts. The Mall, closest to town, was the most formal section with a tree-lined

avenue for strolling, flower gardens, and a bandstand. Roads were moved to the periphery of the park. The second area contained ball fields and a horseshoe pit. In the third area, he took advantage of the broad views, rerouting the road to include overlooks along the edges of Quincy Bay. Kellaway also designed smaller parks in other Massachusetts towns, including Doyle Field in Leominster, Hitchcock Memorial Field in Amherst, and Hastings Park in Lexington.

Kellaway had great affection for his profession. He was one of eight landscape architects listed as initial incorporators of the American Society of Landscape Architects in Massachusetts. In 1912, he was elected a Fellow of the same organization where he later served as a Trustee and member of its Examining Board. He frequently wrote articles about his work, believing that greater public attention should be focused on land planning. In one such publication entitled "Landscape Architecture A Fine Art," he mused that unlike a building or statue that can be signed the authorship of landscapes is often lost. "Yet

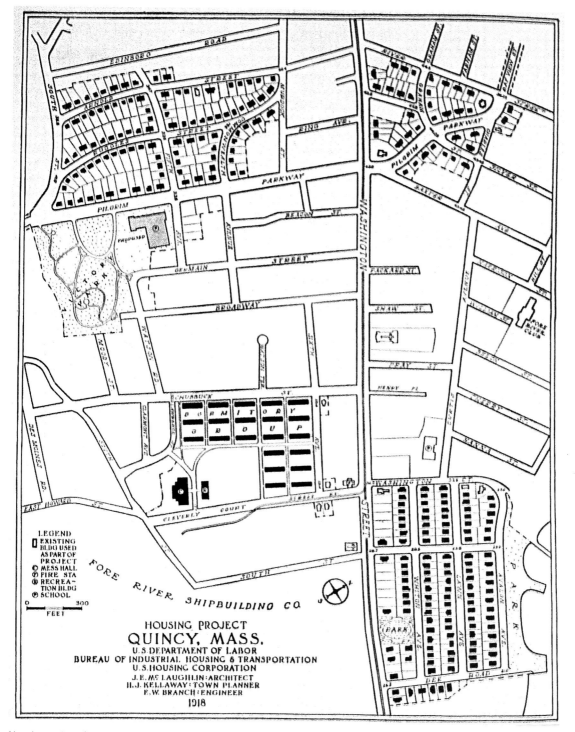

Housing project plan, Quincy, Massachusetts, 1918, from *Report of the U.S. Housing Corporation Houses, Site-Planning Utilities*, 1919.

Kellaway's estate work is seen at the Auchincloss estate, Newport, Rhode Island. (Courtesy of the Frances Loeb Library, Harvard Graduate School of Design)

in some instances, after the designer has left this sphere, his genius is found out and memorialized," he wrote. Herbert Kellaway died in Bath, Maine, on September 6, 1947, only three years after closing the doors of his Boston practice. His plans for preserving open space for public use and connecting those spaces through green corridors can still be seen in parks, ponds, and parkways throughout greater Boston.

Kellaway, Herbert J. *How to Lay Out Suburban Home Grounds.* New York: Wiley and Sons, 1907. A book directed to the homeowner, with detailed instructions on site analysis, garden layout, grading, and planting plans; includes before and after photographs and plans of suburban homes.

Kellaway, Herbert J. "Planning Cities: A List of Cities Which Have Shown an Interest in City Planning . . ." *Proceedings of the Fourteenth National Conference on City Planning, Springfield, Mass. June 5–7, 1922.* National Conference on City Planning (Springfield, Mass., 1922), 200–210.

Khuen, Julie. "Herbert J. Kellaway: Linking Water, Parks and Parkways in the Olmsted Tradition." *The Architects of Winchester, Massachusetts,* no. 2, ed. Maureen Meister. Winchester, Mass.: Winchester Historical Society, 1995. Copies filed at the Society for the Preservation of New England Antiquities (SPNEA) archives, Boston, Massachusetts; Fine Arts Dept., Boston Public Library, Boston, Massachusetts; Loeb Library Special Collections, Harvard University, Cambridge, Massachusetts. A definitive study of Kellaway's professional work with detailed plans of his Winchester projects; extensive document citations with footnotes that will refer the reader to further primary source material.

Julie Khuen

KESSLER, WILLIAM HARRY
(1880–1966)
PLANTSMAN, LANDSCAPE ARCHITECT, PLANNER

William H. Kessler was born in Ashland, Nebraska, in 1880. Despite sharing the same last name, he is not related to landscape architect **George Edward Kessler**. During his childhood, the Kessler family moved often. Consequently, he attended public schools in Los Angeles, California, Quincy, Illinois, and Atlanta, Georgia, before graduating from high school in Gainesville, Florida. Kessler expanded his education through field experience, and studied civil engineering through various correspondence schools. From 1898 to 1912, Kessler worked as secretary and landscape designer for Fruitland Nurseries in Augusta, Georgia, where he gained extensive horticultural knowledge.

Kessler traveled to Birmingham, Alabama, on behalf of Fruitland Nurseries, between 1905 and 1907, to supervise the planting and landscape development of Robert Jemison Jr.'s residence in Mountain Terrace. Jemison, a developer with vision, endeavored to "build and beautify" the city of Birmingham and its neighborhoods. Kessler also oversaw the planting installation at the town of Corey (later named Fairfield), Alabama, from 1909 to 1911. Landscape architect George H. Miller designed Corey, which was Jemison's model industrial town. While working on these projects, Kessler became familiar with prominent designers in the field of landscape architecture. Miller had worked in **Warren Henry Manning**'s office before opening his own office in Boston, and **Samuel Parsons Jr.** initially planned Mountain Terrace and Glen Iris Park.

In 1912, Kessler moved to booming Birmingham permanently. During his first few years in Alabama, Kessler appears to have worked for Jemison and other prominent clients on their personal estates and commercial ventures. An undated, curriculum vitae shows that although he lacked academic training, Kessler held the title of Designing Landscape Architect Engineer for Fleet Corporation in Jacksonville, Florida, and was Designing Landscape Engineer for the U.S. Army Corps of Engineers in Muscle Shoals, Alabama, from 1918 to 1919. Beginning in 1919, Kessler was Landscape Engineer of Plant Properties and Employee Housing for Alabama Power Company. He held this position until 1947.

In 1921, Kessler registered as a landscape architect with

William Harry Kessler at Chickasaw steam plant, Gorgas, Alabama, July 22, 1944. (Courtesy of Louise G. Smith)

the Alabama Department of Agriculture and Industries, which administered examination for other professional licenses in the nursery trade. Because he was concerned about the integrity of the profession, Kessler sponsored an effort to create a more suitable regulatory law for licensure. However, Alabama licensure law did not pass until 1972, six years after his death.

Kessler served as a consultant for Redmont Park, a neighborhood on Red Mountain in Birmingham developed by the Jemison Company, between 1911 and 1935. Redmont Park was planned during the Country Place era of American landscape design. George H. Miller drew the first master plan, but Jemison hired Kessler for consultation during subsequent phases of development. Kessler

Drawing of Cahaba Road entranceway to Mountain Brook Estates, Birmingham, Alabama, 1926. (Courtesy of Walter Schoel Engineering Company, Inc.)

located individual estates on the ridge-top knolls with views of the city below. It was costly and therefore unusual for a land company to build neighborhoods such as Redmont Park on such difficult terrain, with street lighting, curbs and gutters, sidewalks, asphalt paving, sewage connections and other improvements. Many Redmont Park residents hired Kessler to provide individual landscape plans for their property. He planned terraces for the steep hillsides, and designed detailed perennial borders, rose gardens, tea houses, swimming pools, lily ponds, arbors, light fixtures, retaining walls, sundials, and entrance gates to complement the architecture and topography.

Kessler continued to work for Jemison on notable real estate development projects, establishing a lifetime collaboration and friendship. One major project was Mountain Brook Estates, a suburb of Birmingham, for which Kessler was the landscape architect from 1926 to 1929. Warren Manning of Boston, Massachusetts, served as landscape consultant for the project. Jemison and the designers of Mountain Brook Estates took great care to retain the natural beauty of the land, designing naturalistic winding roads to fit the topography. Advertisements

for property in this development described a retreat from city life and a return to country living where children "can romp in protected freedom and grow up with a knowledge and love of nature." Kessler also designed the interior and exterior of The Old Mill, a picturesque building overlooking a streamside park. Constructed near the site of a former mill, this rustic building added to the romantic character of the development and served as a community clubhouse and tea room. Tree-lined, curvilinear parkways, wooded areas, stone walls and bridges, a shopping village, horse stables (no longer extant), and miles of bridle trails contribute to the success of the development.

Kessler also worked with a local civil engineer to lay out the roads and estates in the Glenwood and Redmont Park neighborhoods. Throughout his career, Kessler's office was small, employing only one or two designers at a time. During the Great Depression, Kessler closed his office and found work with the government. Beginning in 1933, Kessler traveled throughout the state as supervising landscape architect for the Civil Works Administration's projects. He resigned from this post in 1934 to become chief of engineering and architecture of

Drawing of the Old Mill, Mountain Brook Estates, Birmingham, Alabama, 1926. (Courtesy of Walter Schoel Engineering Company, Inc.)

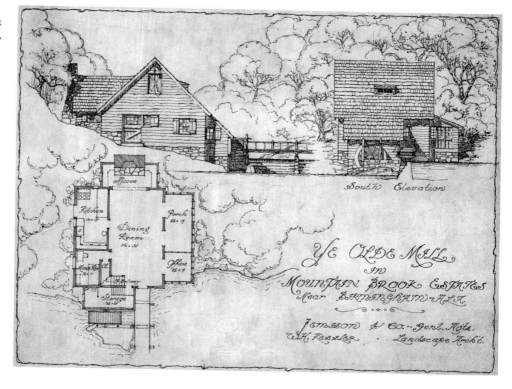

the Fourth Regional Resettlement Administration head-quartered in Montgomery, Alabama. From 1935 to 1942, Kessler was landscape engineer and landscape architect for the U.S. Housing Administration and Defense Administration Projects Birmingham, Sylacauga, Talladega, Childersburg, and Montgomery, Alabama. From 1936 to 1942 Kessler served as the site planning engineer and landscape architect for the Central City Project, a $3 million government housing project in Alabama. Projects of the 1930s and early 1940s include the Lange Residence Garden, Grove Park, and Valley View, all in Alabama.

Other Birmingham work includes Cherokee Road, Central Park neighborhood, the Club, Mountain Brook Village, Woodrow Wilson Park (now Linn Park), the Country Club of Birmingham, and Mountain Brook Club (with golf course architect Donald Ross). Kessler worked on various projects such as educational institutions, churches, hospitals, residential subdivisions, shopping centers, industrial-plant grounds, housing communities for electric power plants, parks, playgrounds, cemeteries, country clubs, and grounds for public buildings. This work varied in scale and scope and included proj-

ects that were federal, state, and private commissions in Alabama, Georgia, Mississippi, and Tennessee.

Although Kessler had a broad range of design experiences, residential design and estate planning dominated his career. He had many satisfied clients who appreciated his artistic sensibility. Plans for the Swann estate, near Birmingham, show that Kessler designed houses and furniture in addition to detailing the sign and laying out the entrance road and grounds. Kessler was respected for his horticultural knowledge and was an expert on native plants of Alabama. Some early plant lists include native oak leaf hydrangea, indicating that Kessler promoted its use in Birmingham landscapes. Hallmarks of his design included naturalistic woodland plantings, formal gardens, and curvilinear, tree-lined roads and entrance drives. Kessler was also known for his site-sensitive placement of houses—ranging from narrow lots to large estates—that accommodate the challenging hills and ridges of Birmingham.

Serving on the Mountain Brook Planning Commission and designing a set for a local theater production were among Kessler's many volunteer pursuits. In a tribute composed in 1962, Robert Jemison Jr., wrote, "Mr.

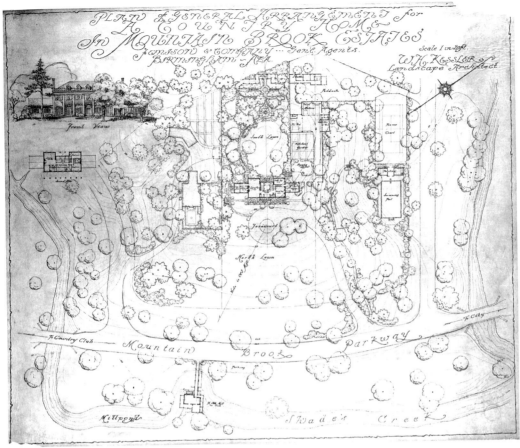

An example of Kessler's work in Mountain Brook Estates is the plan of the Tutwiler estate, Birmingham, Alabama. (Courtesy of Walter Schoel Engineering Company, Inc.)

Kessler deserves much of the credit for the beautiful developments in and around Birmingham. A great deal of this work he has done with very little, and often, practically no compensation, but, because of his love for the beautiful, and loyalty for Birmingham, he has always been most unselfish, and generous with his time and talents." Kessler was elected an honorary member of the Alabama Chapter of the American Institute of Architects in 1942 for his achievements in landscape architecture and planning. He died in 1966, and was remembered fondly for his loyalty to friends, service to the community, civic spirit, and artistic talent.

Unfortunately, much documentation of Kessler's work was lost. The remaining business records, letters, drawings, and photographs are cataloged and stored in the Kessler Collection and the Robert Jemison Jr. Collection in the Archives of the Birmingham Public Library. William H. Kessler did not publish his design philosophy and has no living descendants. What has been written about him was culled from his files, Jemison's archived files, and anecdotes told by those who knew him.

Adams, Cathy. *Worthy of Remembrance.* Birmingham, Ala.: Redmont Park Historic District Foundation, 2002. A history of the Redmont Park neighborhood and its developers, architects, residents, and gardens.

Morris, Philip A., and Marjorie Longenecker White, eds. *Designs on Birmingham.* Birmingham, Ala.: Birmingham Historical Society, 1989. A landscape history of Birmingham and its suburbs from early planners and developers to contemporary landscape architecture projects.

Marion L. Renneker

KILEY, DANIEL URBAN
(1912–2004)
LANDSCAPE ARCHITECT

Daniel Urban Kiley was born in Roxbury Highlands in Boston, Massachusetts, in 1912. He grew up and attended public schools, graduating from high school in 1930. Kiley credits the beginning of his interest in the outdoors and nature to a series of vacation visits to his grandmother's farm in New Hampshire and to a job caddying at the Charles River Country Club in Boston.

In 1932, Kiley began a four-year apprenticeship with **Warren Henry Manning,** who had offices in Harvard Square in Cambridge, Massachusetts. There he learned the rudiments of office practice and procedures, drafting, and was exposed to Manning's great interest in planting design. Because he was outgoing and quick-witted, Kiley was often assigned to supervise construction and select plant materials from nurseries, often transplanting plant materials from various site locations. He loved these outdoor assignments and the experience became an important element of his long practice. Over the years, Kiley, who was noted for his vigorous and creative plant selections and for adventurous plant choices, often searched out available plants even before beginning his design. His interest in extending the planting possibilities in use and location is at the heart of his design innovation. Planting was the first important element that would affect his professional work.

In 1936, Kiley entered the landscape architecture program at Harvard University. Harvard at that time was undergoing a revolutionary curriculum change in the architecture department with the arrival of Walter Gropius from the Bauhaus in Germany. The landscape architecture department, however, was less driven by an interest in modernism than by the study of estate gardens, the Beaux-Arts traditions, and faculty

Above: Dan Kiley. (Photo by Todd Eberle; collection of Charles A. Birnbaum)

Below: South garden at the Art Institute of Chicago, Illinois, 2004. (Photo by Charles A. Birnbaum)

Above: The Miller garden, Columbus, Indiana, 2006. (Photo by Charles A. Birnbaum)

Below: Lincoln Center Plaza, New York, New York. (Photo by Aaron Kiley, courtesy of Dan Kiley)

advocacies of naturalism versus formalism. Kiley and his classmates Garrett Eckbo* and **James C. Rose**, while accepting the earlier ideas of **Frederick Law Olmsted Sr.**, **Frederick Law Olmsted Jr.**, and **John Charles Olmsted**, were extremely interested in the emerging European social, spatial, and artistic interests. The three classmates were involved in a series of confrontations, both in design and theory, in which they attempted to adapt, without the aid of Gropius, the new architectural thinking to landscape design. Though not by nature a writer, Kiley led in the design innovations, leaving the polemics to Rose and Eckbo. Their joint efforts can be read in three articles published in *Architectural Record* in 1939 and 1940. This interest in the new modernism became the second major element in Kiley's work.

Kiley left Harvard in 1938 without graduating. He worked briefly for the National Park Service in Concord, New Hampshire, and then in Washington, D.C., at the U.S. Public Housing Authority under **Elbert Peets**. There he met the young architect Louis Kahn, whom he worked with on several Defense War Housing projects. In 1940, Kiley left the Housing Authority and opened the Office of Dan Kiley in both Washington, D.C., and Middleburg, Virginia. His first commission was a "modernistic" (Kiley's term) garden for the Collier family in Falls Church, Virginia.

In 1942, he married Anne Lathrop Sturges, with whom he would have eight children. He opened his own office in Franconia, New Hampshire, and was licensed to practice architecture in New Hampshire in 1943 with a recommendation from Kahn.

From 1943 to 1945, Kiley served in the U.S. Army. Due to his design background, he was assigned to the presentations branch of the Corp of Engineers in the Office of Strategic Services, where he became director of the design staff. At the end of the war in Europe, Kiley designed the courtroom for the war crimes trials at Nuremberg. While in Europe, he first visited the German countryside and the great French gardens of Le Notre and others. The European landscape and these gigantic formal works left a strong impression on the young Kiley and were perhaps the third informing element in his career.

Kiley absorbed the work of the Olmsted firm and the early ecological planning of Manning, but after his return to the United

Nations Bank Plaza, Tampa, Florida, ca. 1985. (Courtesy of Peter Lindsay Schaudt)

States, his professional contacts, particularly with American modern architects, such as Eero Saarinen, I. M. Pei, Louis Kahn, and Gordon Bunshaft of Skidmore Owings & Merrill (SOM), provided not only professional opportunities but shaped his modern design direction as well.

As the post–World War II American built environment exploded in the 1950s, Kiley found himself one of the few practitioners of modern landscape architecture, particularly on the East Coast and in the Midwest. After a brief trip to the West Coast to visit his friend Eckbo and see the work of **Thomas Dolliver Church** and the developing group of California modernists, Kiley chose to continue his practice first in New Hampshire and later in Vermont. He chose these locations in part because of his love of skiing and hiking. He and his wife Anne supplemented his design income as ski instructors during his early years of practice.

A series of important projects came into Kiley's office through his association with Saarinen and the other modern architects. In 1947, he was on the winning team with Eero Saarinen for the Jefferson National Expansion Memorial Competition, known as the St. Louis Arch, although the landscape was not built precisely to Kiley's plans. In 1955, again with Saarinen and his junior partner Kevin Roche, he designed the garden for J. Irwin Miller's family in Columbus, Indiana, perhaps the most important garden of its era in the United States. In Columbus, he also designed the landscape for the Irwin Union Bank and Trust (1954) and North Christian Church (1964). Kiley's contributions at these three properties were part of the first multiple property National Historic Landmark to recognize postwar landscape architecture in America. In 1963, he designed the gigantic approach gardens for Saarinen's Dulles Airport in Chantilly, Virginia.

In 1968, Kiley with Walter Netch of SOM designed the gardens for the new U.S. Air Force Academy in Colorado Springs, Colorado, followed in 1969 with the remarkable rooftop gardens at the Oakland (California) Museum with Kevin Roche, Saarinen's surviving partner.

Working with Myron Goldsmith of SOM, and later with Paul Kennon of CRS, Kiley produced a series of urban plans for Columbus, Indiana, followed by dozens of specific public and private projects within and just outside the small city.

Like other postwar landscape architects, Kiley has many important works that were not properly built or

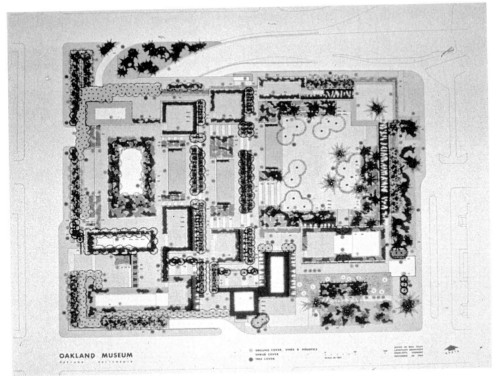

Oakland Museum plan, Oakland, California, 1969. (Courtesy of Jane Amidon)

maintained. Nevertheless, a number of Kiley's projects remain today. These include his modern masterpiece, the Miller Garden; the Dallas Museum of Art Sculpture Garden with Edward Larabee Barnes (1983); and Fountain Place in Dallas, Texas, designed with Harry Cobb of Pei Cobb Freed (1985). In 1988, Kiley designed both the complex Nations Bank Plaza in Tampa, Florida, with Harry Wolf, and the elegant Henry Moore Sculpture Garden at the Nelson Atkins Museum of Art in Kansas City, Missouri.

Unlike many of his contemporaries, Kiley never wrote nor taught. On the advice of Warren Manning, he never joined the American Society of Landscape Artists. Kiley's forte may have been in mentoring; he apprenticed many distinguished designers and teachers, including Richard Haag* and Peter Hornbeck, in his office.

Kiley's work displays both the monumental clarity of the French Baroque gardens and the influence of the classical constructivist and spatial elements in the early postwar works of the new generation of American architects. His gardens use hedges and walls in a manner influenced by the work of modernist architect Ludwig Mies van der Rohe, and his grids of trees perhaps owe more to the columnar grid of contemporary architecture than to early designers such as Le Notre. Kiley passed away at his home in Charlotte, Vermont, in February 2004.

Kiley, Dan, and Jane Amidon. *Dan Kiley: The Complete Works of America's Master Landscape Architect.* New York and London: Bullfinch Press Book/Little Brown and Company, 1999. Despite Kiley's international renown, this is the first published survey of his work. Richly illustrated with plans and chronology.

Process: Architecture 108. Dan Kiley: Landscape Design II in Step with Nature. Tokyo, Japan: Morotani Bunji, 1993. Introduction by architect Harry C. Wolf, essays by Kiley, Jaquelin Robertson, Yoji Sasaki. Portfolio of projects includes urban plazas, parks, corporate campuses, museums, universities, libraries, public gardens and private residences. Chronology.

Saunders, William S., ed. *Daniel Urban Kiley: The Early Gardens.* New York: Princeton Architectural Press with Harvard University, Graduate School of Design, 1999. Preface by James Marston Fitch. Essays on housing and garden projects, ca. 1940s to 1950s, by Anita Berrizbeitia, Joe Disponzio, Daniel Donovan, Mark A. Knopfer, Gary R. Hilderbrand.

Peter Walker

KIMBALL HUBBARD, THEODORA
(1887–1935)
AUTHOR, LIBRARIAN

Theodora Kimball Hubbard, a librarian by training, played an important role in the development of the intellectual foundations of landscape architecture and city planning. She was born Theodora Kimball on February 26, 1887, in West Newton, Massachusetts. She and her younger brother, the noted architectural historian Sidney Fiske Kimball, were raised in a middle-class family. Her father, Edwin Fiske Kimball, was a public school teacher, eventually becoming a headmaster at the Gilbert Stuart School in Dorchester, where the family moved sometime after 1888. Academic achievement appears to have been a family expectation. Kimball Hubbard graduated from the Girls' Latin School in Boston in the spring of 1904 and matriculated at Simmons College that September. In college, where she was known as Ted, she was described as a "glowing, dark-eyed girl," whose eager intelligence inspired the devotion of her classmates. She graduated in 1908.

Her professional career began with a short stint as an editorial writer for *The New England Historical and Genealogical Register,* where she compiled a subject index and conducted historic research and bibliographic work. In 1910, she became an assistant in the Art Department of the Boston Public Library. Shortly thereafter, in 1911, she became the librarian at the School of Landscape Architecture at Harvard University, a position she may have learned about from her brother, who was by then a student in Harvard's School of Architecture. In the position, she found her niche as a "special librarian," one who combines subject knowledge with library science methods, and she retained the position for thirteen years, until 1924, when she married **Henry Vincent Hubbard**.

Kimball Hubbard's years at Harvard set the productive tone for the rest of her professional career. In addition to building the library collection at the School of Landscape Architecture, she served the school's early researchers and students, seeking out bibliographic references and sources for their papers and projects. She fashioned the library into "a clearing house for information," fielding research queries from around the globe. A talented bibliographer, she also began the work of cataloging books for the new professions of landscape

Theodora Kimball Hubbard, 1928. (Philadelphia Museum of Art Archives: Fiske Kimball Papers)

architecture and city planning. In 1913, she collaborated with **James Sturgis Pray** in producing *City Planning: A Comprehensive Analysis of the Subject.* The book was the first thorough examination of the young field's numerous subject areas, and became the standard for classifying information in the field. The authors hoped that the classification scheme would organize the rapidly growing profession, provide "a more general rational conception of this vital field," and be "useful in pointing out special fields of desirable research." *City Planning* was followed by a similar catalog entitled *Landscape Architecture: A Comprehensive Classification Scheme,* which she co-authored with Henry Vincent Hubbard in 1920. Together, the two books provided a research base and intellectual foundation for the emerging fields of city planning and landscape architecture.

In 1912, Kimball Hubbard began writing articles for *Landscape Architecture* on topics ranging from how to organize a professional office to garden vegetation. By 1917, she had become a contributing editor, responsible for the book review department and for conducting an annual review of city planning progress. Also in 1917, she received a master's degree in library science from Simmons College, with a minor—and thesis—in English landscape gardening. Perhaps she used this thesis research in the writing, with Henry Vincent Hubbard, of the first landscape architecture textbook, *An Introduction to the Study of Landscape Design,* first published in 1917. The book was republished several times and remained in print through the 1960s. She also wrote short articles for popular magazines such as *House Beautiful* and *The Garden.*

In 1918 and 1919, as part of the war effort, she was called to Washington, D.C., to head the library of the U.S. Bureau of Industrial Housing and Transportation. In 1918, she became an associate member of American Society of Landscape Architects, along with **Charles A. Platt** and **J. Horace McFarland**. In 1919, she became a member of the American City Planning Institute, where she was the only woman member and the honorary librarian. By the 1920s, she was teaching (in what we might today consider an adjunct role) at both the Cambridge School for women and in the Landscape Architecture Department at Harvard, where she taught English, with a strong emphasis on professional communication. She also began writing more extensively. In 1920, **Frederick Law Olmsted Jr.** engaged her to edit his father's papers for publication. *Volume I* was published in 1920, and Kimball Hubbard wrote eleven of its thirteen chapters, which comprise an early history of the park movement. *Volume II* was published in 1928.

For Kimball Hubbard, the 1920s were characterized by an intensifying interest in city planning. In 1923, she published, with Katherine McNamara, the *Manual of Information on City Planning and Zoning,* a combination how-to manual and reference resource for city managers. Between 1921 and 1931 she served as an expert on two federal planning committees: the Advisory Committee on Zoning and the Committee on Research of the President's Conference on Home Building and Home Ownership. In 1924, after leaving Harvard, she and Hubbard co-founded *City Planning Quarterly,* where she continued publishing her annual city planning re-

views. These yearly analyses eventually culminated in the book *Our Cities To-Day and To-Morrow,* a field study of the results of city planning in 120 cities across the country. In 1929, she became the "Editor of Research" of the Harvard City Planning Studies at the newly established School of City Planning, overseeing the publication of numerous planning studies. The series began publication the following year with *Airports: Their Design, Location, Administration and Legal Basis* by Henry V. Hubbard; and continued through the 1930s. Other topics in the series included *Urban Land Uses* by **Harland Bartholomew** published in 1932; and *Parkways and Land Values* by **John Nolen** and Henry V. Hubbard published in 1937.

In the early 1930s, Kimball Hubbard's health began to decline and she worked her last few years from her home and bed in Milton, Massachusetts. She died in 1935 at the age of forty-eight. The loss of her "keen mind and a dynamic personality," as well as her "benevolence, self-effacement and thoughtfulness for others"—traits typically associated with librarians—were perhaps not surprisingly mourned by her colleagues in a 1936 eulogy in *Landscape Architecture.* They noted her larger legacy— an exemplary set of books, articles, and classification systems—produced to both broaden and deepen the professional knowledge and literatures of her two adopted fields. In the words of her eulogists, the fields of landscape architecture and city planning were "both the richer and the better ordered for her contribution."

Hubbard, Henry Vincent, and Theodora Kimball. *Landscape Architecture: A Comprehensive Classification Scheme For Books, Plans, Photographs, Notes And Other Collected Material, with Combined Alphabetic Topic Index and List of Subject Headings.* Cambridge, Mass.: Harvard University Press, 1920. Based on Kimball Hubbard's earlier classification scheme for *City Planning* with James Sturgis Pray, this work organized the professional literature of landscape architecture in the NAB classification scheme, based on the Library of Congress NA classification scheme for architecture.

Hubbard, Theodora Kimball. *Manual of Information on City Planning and Zoning, including References on Regional, Rural, and National Planning.* Cambridge, Mass.: Harvard University Press, 1923. This book was intended to encourage civic managers to employ city planning principles in their work, by providing professional advice and resources.

Hubbard, Theodora Kimball, and Henry Vincent Hubbard. *Our Cities To-day and To-morrow: A Survey of planning and zoning Progress in the United States.* Cambridge, Mass.: Harvard University Press, 1929. Kimball Hubbard's last and major publication, which is essentially a comparative analysis of city planning progress in 120 American cities.

Heidi Hohmann

PLATE 1: Katherine Emilie Bashford. An example of Bashford's design work is seen at the rose garden of the President's House, University of Southern California, San Marino, California. Photo by Elise Mudd Marvin, daughter of Dr. Seeley G. Mudd. (Smithsonian Institution, Archives of American Gardens, Garden Club of America Collection)

PLATE 2 (*left*): Arthur Edwin Bye Jr. Clingendael, England, as featured in Bye's book, *Moods in the Landscape*, 1999. (A. E. Bye Collection, Penn State University Archives, Pennsylvania State University Libraries)

PLATE 3 (*below*): Harold ap Rhys Caparn. Osborne Garden, Brooklyn Botanic Garden, Brooklyn, New York. (Caparn collection, courtesy of Oliver Chamberlain)

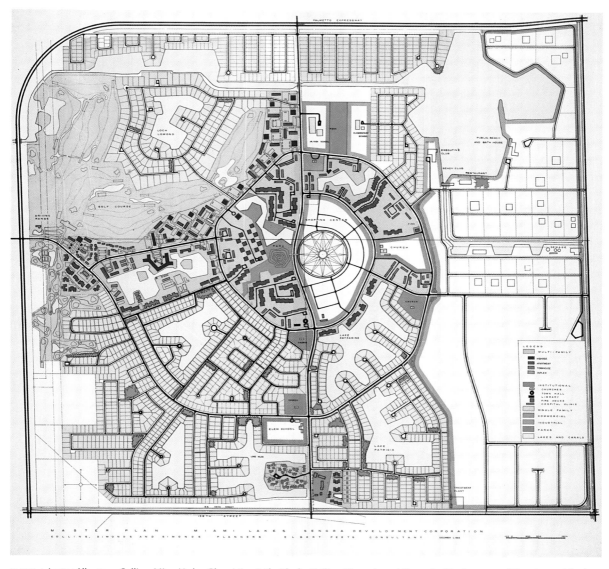

PLATE 4: Lester Albertson Collins. Miami Lakes Plan, Miami, Florida, by Collins, Simonds and Simonds. (Environmental Planning and Design, LLC)

PLATE 5 (*above*): Elizabeth Kellam de Forest. The garden at the residence of Elizabeth and Lockwood de Forest. (Photo by Charles A. Birnbaum)

PLATE 6 (*right*): Julia Lester Dillon. Cover of Dillon's book, *The Blossom Circle of the Year in Southern Gardens,* 1922.

PLATE 7 (*opposite, top*): David Bates Douglass. Sylvan Water, Green-Wood Cemetery, Brooklyn, New York. (The Green-Wood Cemetery & Jeffrey I. Richman)

PLATE 8 (*opposite, bottom*): Garrett Eckbo. An example of Eckbo's modernist work is seen at Union Bank Plaza, Los Angeles, California. (Photo by Marc Treib)

The Blossom Circle Of the Year In Southern Gardens

JULIA LESTER DILLON

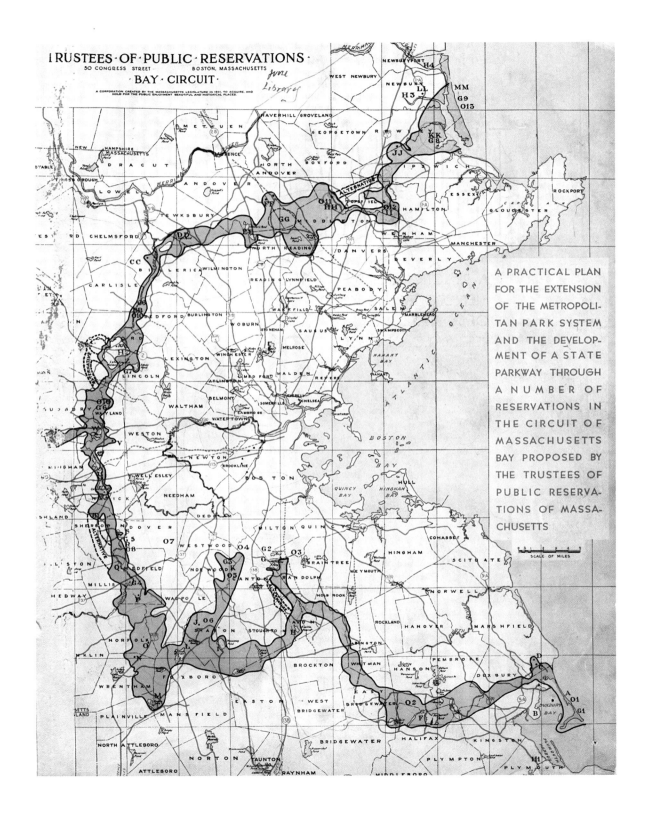

TRUSTEES·OF·PUBLIC·RESERVATIONS·
50 CONGRESS STREET   BOSTON, MASSACHUSETTS
·BAY·CIRCUIT·

A CORPORATION CREATED BY THE MASSACHUSETTS LEGISLATURE IN 1891, TO ACQUIRE, AND
HOLD FOR THE PUBLIC ENJOYMENT BEAUTIFUL AND HISTORICAL PLACES.

A PRACTICAL PLAN
FOR THE EXTENSION
OF THE METROPOLI-
TAN PARK SYSTEM
AND THE DEVELOP-
MENT OF A STATE
PARKWAY THROUGH
A NUMBER OF
RESERVATIONS IN
THE CIRCUIT OF
MASSACHUSETTS
BAY PROPOSED BY
THE TRUSTEES OF
PUBLIC RESERVA-
TIONS OF MASSA-
CHUSETTS

SCALE OF MILES

PLATE 9 (*opposite*): Charles W. Eliot II. Plan of Bay Circuit Beltway expansion, Boston, Massachusetts, 1937. (Frances Loeb Library, Harvard Graduate School of Design)

PLATE 10 (*left*): Annette Hoyt Flanders. Morven garden, Charlottesville, Virginia, ca. 1930. (Smithsonian Institution, Archives of American Gardens, Garden Club of America Collection)

PLATE 11 (*below*): M. Paul Friedberg. Pershing Park, Washington, D.C. (National Park Service files)

PLATE 12 (*opposite, top*): Ethelbert Ely Furlong. Furlong's design work is seen at Seven Oaks Park, Orange, New Jersey, in a photo by Diane Clark. (Smithsonian Institution, Archives of American Gardens, Garden Club of America Collection)

PLATE 13 (*opposite, bottom left*): Fairman Furness. *Spanish Steps in Snow*, watercolor, 1944. (Private Collection)

PLATE 14 (*opposite, bottom right*): Jacques-Henri-Auguste Gréber. Villa Reale di Marlia, Tuscany, Italy. (Photo by Charles A. Birnbaum)

PLATE 15 (*left*): Ralph Ellis Gunn. Grounds of Rosedown Plantation, St. Francisville, Louisiana. (Photo by Charles A. Birnbaum)

PLATE 16 (*below*): John W. Gregg. The drawing of the garage-pergola plan for Prince A. Hawkins residence, Reno, Nevada, 1919, is an example of Gregg's hand. (College of Environmental Design Collection, Environmental Design Archives, University of California, Berkeley)

PLATE 17 (*left*): Richard Haag. Bloedel Reserve, Bainbridge Island, Puget Sound, Washington. (Photo by Charles A. Birnbaum)

PLATE 18 (*below*): Richard Haag. Gas Works Park, Seattle, Washington. (Courtesy of Richard Haag)

PLATE 19 (*opposite, top*): Lawrence Halprin. Condo 1, The Sea Ranch, Gualala, California. (The Office of Lawrence Halprin, Inc.)

PLATE 20 (*opposite, bottom left*): Lawrence Halprin. Sketch of approach to Yosemite Falls, Yosemite National Park, California. (The Office of Lawrence Halprin, Inc.)

PLATE 21 (*opposite, bottom right*): A. E. Hanson. Sotto il Monte, Montecito, California. (Photo by Charles A. Birnbaum)

PLATE 22 (*left*): A. E. Hanson. La Toscana, the Kirk Johnson estate (now called Sotto il Monte), Montecito, California, ca. 1925. (Smithsonian Institution Archives of American Gardens, Garden Club of America Collection)

PLATE 23 (*below*): Ruth Mildred Havey. Box Terrace, Dumbarton Oaks, Washington, D.C. (Photo courtesy of Brian Katen)

PLATE 24 (*opposite, top*): Werner Hegemann. Business Center, Wyomissing Park, Pennsylvania, adapted from Hegemann and Peets, *Wyomissing Park: The Modern Garden Suburb of Reading, Pennsylvania, A Stepping Stone Towards Greater Reading*, 1919.

PLATE 25 (*opposite, bottom*): Clarence Edmund "Bud" Hollied. Glorieta Baptist Assembly gardens, Glorieta, New Mexico. (Baker A. Morrow, courtesy of Morrow Reardon Wilkinson Miller Ltd.)

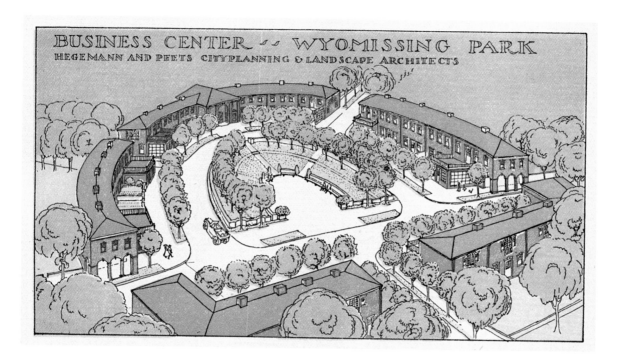

BUSINESS CENTER - WYOMISSING PARK
HEGEMANN AND PEETS CITYPLANNING & LANDSCAPE ARCHITECTS

PLATE 26 (*left*): Louise Stone Hubbard. Rosecrana garden, Glencoe, Illinois. (Smithsonian Institution, Archives of American Gardens, Garden Club of America Collection)

PLATE 27 (*below*): Carol R. Johnson. Mystic River Reservation, Medford and Somerville, Massachusetts. (Photo courtesy of Carol R. Johnson Associates, Inc.)

PLATE 28 (*opposite, top*): Daniel Urban Kiley. Jefferson National Expansion Memorial Park (St. Louis Arch), St. Louis, Missouri. (Photo by Charles A. Birnbaum)

PLATE 29 (*opposite, bottom*): Daniel Urban Kiley. The Miller garden, Columbus, Indiana. (Photo by Charles A. Birnbaum)

PLATE 30 (*left*): Clermont "Monty" Huger Lee. Troup Square, Savannah, Georgia. (Photo courtesy of Ced Dolder)

PLATE 31 (*below*): Franz Lipp. Fountain garden at Cantigny Park, Wheaton, Illinois. (Photo courtesy of Annemarie van Roessel)

KOCH, KATE RIES (CATHERINE E.)
(1885–1974)
LANDSCAPE ARCHITECT, EDUCATOR

Kate Ries Koch attended public schools in Buffalo, New York, the city where she was born on November 28, 1885. Following her graduation with a bachelor of science degree from Michigan State College in 1909, she taught science for five years at Western State Teachers College in Kalamazoo, Michigan. Entering Cornell University in 1915, Koch graduated the following year with a master of arts degree. She then relocated to Poughkeepsie, New York, where she taught landscape gardening at Vassar College for two years. Returning to Cornell for a master's degree in Landscape Design she studied with fellow students Edward Godfrey Lawson,* Ralph E. Griswold, and Norman Thomas Newton; and under E. Gorton Davis, head of the department, Bryant Fleming, visiting lecturer, and Ralph Curtis, who taught plants and planting design. At the same time she also served as a graduate teaching assistant. In 1919, she joined the Botany Department at Smith College where she was a member of the faculty until her retirement as associate professor in 1952.

At Smith College, Kate Koch quickly realized the limitations of teaching landscape gardening in the botany department. Changing the course name to landscape architecture, she divided her work into two parts, offering a course in plant materials plus additional courses in design. Approaching the Art Department, she received agreement for the inclusion of the course in landscape architecture in their schedule. This arrangement with the two departments continued until Koch developed the interdepartmental major in landscape architecture, from which evolved her specialty, city planning. A July 1929 announcement in *Landscape Architecture* noted the development as follows: "An entirely new departure for women's colleges has been added to the Smith College curriculum—namely, an Interdepartmental Major in Landscape Architecture. The major is planned for students who wish to make the subject a profession, and is under the direction of Miss Catherine Koch, Associate Professor in Landscape Architecture. One of its most progressive features is the inclusion of a course in Civic Art, which is intended to make the student cognizant of higher responsibility in her home community."

During her years at Smith, Koch served as consultant to the president of the college on planning and was the

Catherine Koch, 1907, image cropped from the original. (Michigan State University Archives and Historical Collections)

designer of the Capen House gardens as well as the crab-tree plantings around the Alumnae House gardens. Koch was also the first faculty head of Sunnyside House, a student self-help organization, and served in that capacity for eighteen years. She served on the Northampton Planning Board from the time it was established in 1946 until 1966, serving as chairperson from 1953 until her retirement. Under her guidance the board developed a city master plan, zoning maps, and subdivision controls. Koch had been appointed to the city's initial planning board in 1924 and served for three years at which time she was appointed to the City Improvement Committee on which she served until 1943. Koch also designed several private gardens in Northampton and was instrumental in the design and development of the Sheldon Playground in the city.

Kate Koch was awarded a scholarship from the Albright Art Gallery in Buffalo, and a Scandinavian Fellowship with which she attended the University of London. In 1930, she attended the International Town Planning Congress in Berlin. She also traveled extensively in Europe studying architectural gardens and city planning, especially in northern European cities. Her studies and travels included Canada and Mexico.

Koch was a member of the League of Women Voters, the Northampton Board of Engineers, the Massachusetts Planning Board, the Northampton Historical Society, and a founding member of the American Horticultural Council. Upon her retirement from Smith, Koch was praised for her "passionate devotion to the conception of landscape architecture as an art; a conception which has been communicated to students who are affecting civic thought in many parts of the country. Your high craftsmanship, careful consideration of detail, always controlled by a broad view of the whole; your ingenuity in combining scientific knowledge with artistic perception, have given a visual stimulus and satisfaction to young people of assorted backgrounds and potentialities for the future." Kate Ries Koch died on February 9, 1974, in Williamsville, New York.

There is a small collection for Kate Ries Koch in the College Archives at Smith College, in Northampton, Massachusetts.

Koch, Catherine E. "Landscape Architecture at Smith College." *Bulletin of the National Council of State Garden Clubs, Inc.* 10, no. 4 (January 1940). Description of the landscape architecture curriculum with photos of some student projects.

Koch, Catherine E. "Landscape Architecture Takes Its Place as a Fine Art." *Journal of the American Association of University Women* 31, no. 2 (January 1938), 94–96.

Koch, Catherine E. "Some Wild Marsh Plants." *Landscape Architecture Quarterly,* July 1916. A description of her research on wetland plants undertaken while a graduate student at Cornell.

Daniel Krall

KRUSE, ARTHUR M.
(1889–1980)
LANDSCAPE ARCHITECT, TOWN PLANNER

Arthur M. Kruse was born in Moravia, New York, on April 2, 1889. After graduating in landscape architecture from Cornell circa 1910, he worked in Detroit for T. Glenn Phillips, with whom he formed a partnership in 1915. Kruse was in Washington, D.C., from 1917 to 1918 with the Town Planning Division of the U.S. Housing Corporation. Arriving in Toronto in 1919, he became Harries & Hall's associate (William Edward Harries* and Alfred V. Hall*) on both residential and town-planning projects. Kruse joined the American Society of Landscape Architects in 1914 and was elected a Fellow in 1924. He became a partner in Harries, Hall & Kruse* about 1925.

Kruse's Toronto-area residential landscapes appeared in the *Studio Garden Annual* for 1935 and in *Canadian Homes and Gardens* throughout the 1930s. He joined the Canadian Society of Landscape Architects and Town Planners (today's CSLA) soon after its founding in 1934. He was designer and superintendent of installation for the National Flower and Garden Show held in Toronto in the spring of 1938.

Returning to the United States in 1941, he became a liaison officer with the Air Traffic Control Board and a consultant to the Prisoner of War Operations Division and the Office of Provost Marshal. After the war, serving with the Army Corps of Engineers, he planned several military camps. In 1947, he initiated the planning of the National Memorial Cemetery of the Pacific in Punchbowl Crater above Honolulu, Hawaii.

Kruse retired from the U.S. Army as a colonel in 1952, moved to Clearwater, Florida, in 1954, and immediately became involved in community service. He headed the Beautification Committee, the Clearwater Beach Association, the Memorial Civic Center Association, and the Florida Planning and Zoning Association, and he chaired the Clearwater Planning Board for eighteen years. He donated his designs for several Clearwater parks and a garden (named in his honor in 1967) at the Memorial Civic Center. In recognition of his outstanding contributions, the city awarded him medals, titles, and citations. Kruse died in Clearwater on May 19, 1980.

See also the individual entries on Hall, Alfred V., and Harries, William Edward, and the joint entry on Harries, Hall & Kruse. References follow the Harries, Hall & Kruse entry.

Pleasance K. Crawford

KUH, GERTRUDE DEIMEL
(1893–1977)
LANDSCAPE ARCHITECT

Gertrude Kuh was born Gertrude Virginia Eisendrath on September 11, 1893, in Racine, Wisconsin. Her parents, Benjamin and Francis Haas Eisendrath, moved their six children, including young Gertrude, to Chicago in 1899. Starting in 1912, Kuh spent a year at Sweet Briar College in Virginia before transferring to the Lowthorpe School of Landscape Architecture, Landscape Gardening, and Horticulture for Women in Groton, Massachusetts, in 1917. While at Lowthorpe, Kuh studied all facets of landscape architecture, including design, construction, propagation, and planting. She also began her professional work as an intern in the office of **Ellen Biddle Shipman**. Kuh received her degree in 1917 and was subsequently hired into the office of Francis Robinson in Des Moines, Iowa.

In 1921, Kuh returned to Chicago and started her own practice. Kuh's first designs were private garden commissions in Pennsylvania, where she had family connections. While she continued to work from an office in her home, her clientele expanded quickly and she soon began designing gardens, landscape plans, and site plans for projects located in Chicago and along the city's North Shore, including Winnetka, Highland Park, Glencoe, and Lake Forest.

In September of 1925, Kuh married Chicago mortgage broker Jerome Deimel. The couple had one son, John, before Jerome Deimel passed away in November 1927. Kuh continued her landscape work while raising her son and, in 1931, she took a yearlong sojourn to Europe. Kuh was based in Germany during the trip and traveled to France, Holland, Italy, and Spain. Though she traveled with her family and young son, Kuh likely took the opportunity to study Western European garden and landscape traditions.

Kuh became a member of the North Shore Garden Club early in her career and served as its president during the 1930s. She was awarded consecutive blue ribbons by the club from 1937 to 1939 for her entries in the Navy Pier Flower Show. Her success and active participation with the club led to many of her commissions. During this period, she further solidified her standing by executing several gardens for shoe manufacturer Irving Florsheim's estate in Libertyville, Illinois.

Gertrude Kuh, ca. 1965. (Courtesy of John E. Deimel)

Along with landscape plans for existing homes, Kuh's work included collaborations on new constructions with architects including Edward Dart, Jim Keiser, Herman Lackner, and Sam Marks. Along with **Jens Jensen**, Kuh became the exclusive landscape architect of choice for several North Shore architects including Ernest A. Grunsfeld Jr. and later his son Ernest Grunsfeld III. Both father and son also commissioned Kuh for work on several of their own homes. By 1940, Kuh was so well established that she was often hired before the project architect with the understanding that she would assist in making the selection.

A plan for one of Gertrude Kuh's North Shore residential clients, the Friedman residence property plan, Glencoe, Illinois, 1953. (Gertrude Kuh Papers, Ryerson and Burnham Archives, The Art Institute of Chicago. Digital file © The Art Institute of Chicago)

In June 1942, Gertrude Kuh married her second husband, clothing manufacturer George Kuh. The marriage lasted only a short while, though, as Kuh's husband passed away later that summer.

By 1950, Kuh developed a professional association with landscape architect Mary Long Rogers. After Rogers relocated from Illinois to Santa Barbara, California, Kuh made extended trips to the beachside town in order to continue the collaboration. The pair continued their working relationship for over twenty-five years, ultimately completing over 200 designs together. Kuh also worked with designers Betty McAdams, Beth Howerton, and Edith Antognoli during her career. Her longest as-

sociations, though, were with her principal stonemason "Twin" Morelli and nurseryman and landscape contractor Robert Louden, both of whom she utilized throughout her career.

A key facet of Kuh's work was her ability and desire to integrate borrowed landscape features into her designs. In many of her designs, she integrated adjacent woods or existing ravines with minimal plant additions in order not to detract from the existing landscape. During the mid-1960s, she produced designs for two houses that exemplified this talent most clearly. The Logan House was a new construction that sat on a multi-acre site at the edge of a ravine in Highland Park. Kuh took special

One of Kuh's many residential commissions is the Searle residence grounds, Chicago, Illinois, ca. 1971 view. (Gertrude Kuh Papers, Ryerson and Burnham Archives, The Art Institute of Chicago. Digital file © The Art Institute of Chicago)

care to integrate the existing landscape in order to create a transition between the steep ravine and the immediate surroundings of the house. Kuh applied a similar design method to the site selected for the Epstein House in Northfield. The site included a drainage ditch that Kuh rerouted and integrated as a water feature traversed by a bridge that led to the modern glass and steel house.

Though the overwhelming majority of Kuh's work was residential, she also completed commissions for several hospital and religious institutions. In 1947, she executed a design for the Jewish Center in Muskegon, Michigan. In 1950 and 1951, respectively, she produced plans for the Home for Aged Jews and the Jewish Orthodox Home for the Aged, both located in Chicago. In 1963, she completed work on the grounds of the Children's Memorial Hospital in Chicago, and, ten years later, she designed the landscape for the North Shore Senior Center in Winnetka, Illinois.

During her fifty-year career, Kuh executed over four hundred designs throughout Chicago's North Shore as well as within the city itself. Kuh relied heavily on her instinct and was willing to make drastic changes in the field. Her designs reflected her attention to detail and high regard for quality craftsmanship in the carefully planned pathways and subtly integrated stonework. She seldom included flowers, choosing instead to utilize greens and browns to create fluctuating textures and she often repeated the same species while diversifying their layout for each individual site.

Kuh became a member of the American Society of Landscape Architects in 1956 and continued to produce designs until she was eighty years old. Gertrude Kuh died in 1977.

The Gertrude Kuh Collection is housed at the Ryerson and Burnham Archives, the Art Institute of Chicago. The collection includes images and papers documenting Kuh's career from 1942 to 1976, with the bulk dating from 1967 to 1972. Though Kuh culled the majority of her plans and papers from the first part of her career, the remaining drawings are housed in the permanent collection of the Department of Architecture at the Art Institute of Chicago.

Fitzsimmons, Mary Elizabeth. "Outdoor Architecture for the Midwest: The Modern Residential Landscapes of Gertrude Eisendrath Kuh, 1937–1977." Master's thesis, University of Minnesota, Minneapolis, 1994. In this unpublished manuscript, Fitzsimmons takes an in depth look at the residential work of Gertrude Kuh.

Oral History of Ernest Alton Grunsfeld, III. Interview by Annemarie van Roessel. Chicago Architects Oral History Project, Department of Architecture, Art Institute of Chicago, 2004. During this interview, Grunsfeld discusses the work that Kuh produced in collaboration with him and his father, Ernest A. Grunsfeld Jr.

Melanie Macchio

LAMSON, MARY DEPUTY
(1897–1969)
LANDSCAPE ARCHITECT, WRITER

Mary Lois Deputy was born in southern Indiana into a family that greatly appreciated gardens and plants. She studied for two years at the State Normal School in Mankato, Minnesota, and then transferred to Indiana University in Bloomington, where she received a bachelor of arts and a master of arts in 1919, both in English. At Bloomington, she also studied fine arts, free-hand drawing, trigonometry, surveying, and botany. She entered the Cambridge School of Domestic Architecture and Landscape Architecture in 1920, completing the three-year program in only two years. Shortly after finishing the Cambridge course, she returned to Minnesota, where she was director of physical education at Bemidji State Teachers College, where her father was president. She began her practice of landscape architecture at this time. To date, no projects have been identified with Mary Deputy in Bemidji, a logging town in northern Minnesota.

Mary Deputy moved to New York City in 1924, where she worked for **Ruth Bramley Dean** until Dean's death in 1932. With others, she carried on the firm's work as Ruth Dean Associates, for another two years. In 1926, she married Frank Vernon Lamson, an engineer. Seven years later, they bought a farm called Briar Patch in Milan, near Rhinebeck, along the Hudson River in New York. The following year, in 1934, she opened her own office in New York City. In 1935, with four other graduates of the Cambridge School, which by then had merged with Smith College, she was awarded a masters in landscape architecture from Smith. By 1952, she and Lamson had divorced, and, around 1954, she married William Cattell.

Mary Deputy Lamson published numerous short, practical articles in monthly periodicals such as *House and Garden* and *House Beautiful.* In these articles, she rarely illustrated her own work. She was never a member of the American Society of Landscape Architects and so did not publish in *Landscape Architecture* or the series *ASLA: Work of Members,* issued by the New York Chapter in the early 1930s. However, she published two books: *Gardening with Shrubs and Small Flowering Trees* in 1946 and *Garden Housekeeping* in 1951. These were practical "how-to" books with an intended audience of average

homeowners who would not have had garden help. As with her articles, her own work was not featured.

This authorial modesty, along with an absence of her archives, makes it difficult to get a sense of the full scope of Lamson's work. After the first six months of her independent practice, Lamson wrote Henry Atherton Frost, the director of the Cambridge School, that she was "comfortably busy" with a number of small jobs. In 1942, she told him that her firm did private work exclusively, primarily in the New York City area. In 1946, she had three assistants in her office. Obviously, she had many more projects in the course of her career than are currently known, but the names of most of them may be irretrievably lost.

Fortunately, the dust jackets of her books give additional, albeit general, information. According to this information, Lamson designed city backyards and penthouses, small suburban gardens, large estates, farms, and college campuses. The farms would have included Lamson's own Briar Patch property, but no other farms and no college campuses designed by her are currently known. Geographically, her work extended from Maine to Florida, and from Long Island and New York City, to Kansas City, Missouri. Also, a few high-profile clients are mentioned on the dust jackets, including Philip Barry, presumably the playwright, who had homes in Hobe Sound, Florida, and in East Hampton on Long Island. Specific documentation regarding Lamson's involvement is lacking. Another client was Mrs. Dwight Morrow, mother of writer Anne Morrow Lindbergh. Most likely, Lamson was involved at Next Day Hill, the Morrow property in Englewood, New Jersey, where the Lindberghs were married in 1919.

Lamson designed four residential properties on Long Island. She completed the garden for the George Roberts residence in East Hampton that Ruth Dean began in 1930. This led to another commission to design a city garden for the Roberts's New York City townhouse.

In the 1930s, Lamson laid out the grounds of Pretty Penny, the home of Helen Hayes and her husband Charles MacArthur in Nyack, New York, on the west side of the Hudson River. Lamson's project was published in *House and Garden* in August 1937, and in Margaret

Right: An example of Mary Deputy Lamson's residential work is seen at the Warren Kinney garden, New Vernon, New Jersey, ca. 1965. (Smithsonian Institution, Archives of American Gardens, Maida Babson Adams American Garden Collection)

Below: Lamson's formal design leads to a garden room at Elmwood, Pawling, New York, photo by Marjorie Greville. (Smithsonian Institution, Archives of American Gardens, Garden Club of America Collection)

Olthof Goldsmith's 1941 book, *Designs for Outdoor Living.*

At Pretty Penny, Lamson transformed a scenic but steep and narrow site into terraced spaces for gardens and outdoor recreation, each terrace running the entire width of the lot. Lamson kept some of the existing trees in situ and moved others, such as a large pine, which was moved from beside the house and transplanted to one of the upper terraces. On the level immediately below the house terrace was a pergola. Below the pergola, there was a rose garden, its central beds filled with tulips in the spring. At one end of this terrace was an old pear tree over which wisteria climbed. A lower terrace housed a tennis court with a backstop especially designed by Lamson, who cleverly disguised the court by concealing it from view by a sharp drop in grade. Near the bottom of the site, planted with dogwoods, was an elegant swimming pool. At one of the ends of this terrace was a bath house inspired by a Dutchess County schoolhouse. Beyond were sweeping views east of the Hudson River, framed by elms and other trees.

In 1954, the landscape architect, now personally and professionally known as Mary Deputy Cattell, designed the grounds of Mrs. H. Donald Baker's residence on North Street in Greenwich, Connecticut. She planned driveway and turn-around plantings and appears to have again made use of existing, mature trees. A double-stemmed gray birch appears to have survived ice storms by listing markedly to one side. There seems to have been no garden as such at this property.

Mary Deputy Cattell died in Red Hook, New York, on December 19, 1969, leaving no close relatives.

Lamson, Mary Deputy. *Garden Housekeeping*. New York: Oxford University Press, 1951. Practical garden tips for the average homeowner with illustrations by Jess Robinson. Contents include: Housekeeping Outdoors; Fall Housecleaning; Getting Ready for Winter; Staking and Labeling; Pruning; Feeding Plants; Outdoor Enemies; Watering; Terraces, Drives, Walks; Routines of Special Gardens; Tools; Garden Housekeeping Calendar.

Lamson, Mary Deputy. *Gardening with Shrubs and Small Flowering Trees*. New York: M. Barrows and Company, Inc., 1946. Multiple printings through 1952. A popular book with practical how-to information for the average homeowner.

Zaitzevsky, Cynthia. *Long Island Landscapes and the Women Who Designed Them*. New York: W. W. Norton & Company, 2004. Includes a short biographical profile of Lamson and references several projects.

Cynthia Zaitzevsky

LAWRENCE, ELIZABETH
(1904–1985)
GARDEN DESIGNER, AUTHOR

Elizabeth Lawrence was born in Marietta, Georgia, on May 27, 1904, in her paternal grandparents' house. Her father, Samuel Lawrence, a Marietta native, was a civil engineer, who built railroads in the South. Her mother, Elizabeth Bradenbaugh Lawrence, was born in Baltimore and grew up in the house of her maternal grandparents in Parkersburg, West Virginia. After their marriage, Samuel and Elizabeth Lawrence moved to Hamlet, a small North Carolina railroad town, and then to Garysburg, North Carolina, where Mr. Lawrence operated a sand and gravel business. Mrs. Lawrence was active in village life and gave a great deal of attention to bringing up young Elizabeth, and her sister, Ann, younger by two years. In Garysburg, young Elizabeth enjoyed solitary walks to find wildflowers growing on creek banks and planted her first garden, which set her on a path that she was to follow for the rest of her life. In 1912, the family moved to the state capital of Raleigh in order to enroll Elizabeth and Ann at St. Mary's School, an Episcopal preparatory school for girls. The Lawrence home was close to St. Mary's, in a neighborhood of large, old, clapboard houses, about a mile from downtown Raleigh and Christ Episcopal Church, where the Lawrences became active members. Christ Church also sponsored a small mission church in a downtown working-class neighborhood, where Elizabeth later taught Sunday school. Family, home, church, and garden became the cornerstones of her life.

After receiving a good education in science, Latin, French, and classical literature, Lawrence graduated from St. Mary's in 1922 and enrolled at Barnard College in New York City. In the small, familial setting of St. Mary's, Lawrence had felt at home, which was always her most cherished feeling; in classes there, she had loved to argue, and she was recognized as a good writer. At Barnard College, Lawrence was initially unsure of herself and afraid of the city, but she summoned up her determination to stay. While making up courses at the Columbia University extension division, she met Ellen Bracelen (Flood), a woman her age who was living with her widowed father in a penthouse on Park Avenue. They became lifelong friends, and Bracelen introduced Lawrence to the cultural life of New York—concerts, museums, shops, and botanical gardens. After Lawrence graduated from Barnard in 1926, she spent a winter with her grandmother in Parkersburg, and then she went on a European tour.

In 1928, when she returned to Raleigh, Lawrence made the decision to live at home for the rest of her life. At this time, she chose gardening as her profession. In 1932, she was the first woman to graduate with a landscape architecture degree from present-day North Carolina State University. She became active in the state garden club movement and was a popular lecturer and garden designer. She had a business with another female gardener, Isabel Busbee, who was also a neighbor. They designed small, residential gardens, city streets, and parks. Sometime in the early 1930s, Lawrence became friends with another neighbor, Ann Preston Bridgers, whose early success as co-author with George Abbott of a Broadway play, *Coquette*, had steered her toward a professional writing career. Ann's sister, Emily, was also a writer, and together they became Lawrence's mentors, encouraging her to publish garden articles in popular magazines that included *House & Garden* and *American Home,* and *Southern Home and Garden.* After an apprenticeship where she wrote garden articles, Lawrence published her first book, *A Southern Garden: A Handbook for the Middle South,* with the University of North Carolina Press, in 1942. It acquired an audience of appreciative readers, not only in the South. Readers wrote to her, and she wrote back, beginning a lifetime of correspondences that linked her to many gardeners throughout the county. Lawrence's own garden in Raleigh, where she lived for thirty-six years and which she shared with her mother, was the talk of the town, and she wrote about the hundreds of native and exotic plants that she grew there. She thought of her garden as a laboratory in which to experiment with many different kinds of plants and a place to enjoy almost every day of the year. She also wrote about the gardens of friends and about her favorite gardening books, which included ones by Mrs. Loudon (Jane Webb), Gertrude Jekyll, Elizabeth von Arnim, E. A. Bowles, and **Louise Beebe Wilder.** In 1943, Lawrence received the Herbert Medal from the American Amaryllis Society, and the society's journal, *Herbertia,* was dedicated to her. In a rare autobiographical statement, written for *Herbertia,* she stated that when her mother read her the Parable of the Sower from the Bible and she planted her first garden when she was only a child, she understood "the relation between poetry and the soil." Her many allusions to literature were perhaps her signature contribution to garden writing.

In 1948, Lawrence and her widowed mother (her father died in 1936) moved to Charlotte, North Carolina, to live next door to her sister Ann, and her family. Ann was married to Warren Way, and had two young children, Warren Jr. and Elizabeth. Lawrence designed a small modern bungalow for herself and her mother and started on a new garden. As she had done from the beginning of her gardening life, she kept careful records of her failures and successes in her own garden. In 1957, she published *The Little Bulbs: A Tale of Two Gardens,* based on her own garden and that of Carl Krippendorf, who grew thousands of bulbs in a vast woodland estate near Cincinnati, Ohio. That year Lawrence also began writing a Sunday garden column for the *Charlotte Observer,* which brought readers through her garden gate. She urged everyone—readers, visitors, correspondents—to try to grow many different kinds of plants and to follow their own tastes. As a landscape designer, she gave free advice about plants

Elizabeth Lawrence in her Charlotte, North Carolina, garden. (*Charlotte Observer*)

to countless numbers of gardeners, and she accepted a small number of North Carolina clients for garden designs. Among them were the Nolle Medical Clinic in Charlotte, the Country Doctors' Museum in Bailey, Linda Lamm's residential garden in Wilson, and Historic Hope Plantation near Windsor.

In 1961, Lawrence published *Gardens in Winter,* and she continued working on two unpublished manuscripts, one about rock gardens, and another based on her long correspondence with women who advertised their plants in southern agricultural market bulletins. By the late 1960s, she had thousands of correspondents and a following of faithful readers. Among her admirers, Eudora Welty praised her style as that of a "lyricist." Katharine S. White, writing in *The New Yorker,* said that she had "learned more about horticulture, plants, and garden history and literature from Elizabeth Lawrence than from any other one person." Beverly Seaton, writing a biographical profile for the *Guide to America's Women Writers,* called Lawrence "one of America's foremost authorities on southern gardening."

After her mother's death in 1964, Lawrence lived alone, still gardening, working on her unfinished manuscripts, and entertaining friends and family. She was especially devoted to her nephew and niece. After they each married, she entertained their young children in her garden. After her sister's death in 1980, however, and because of her own deteriorating health, she found it difficult to cope with the upkeep of her house and garden. In 1983, she sold her property and moved to Maryland to live near her niece, Elizabeth Way Rogers. After almost a year of decline, Lawrence died on June 11, 1985. She is buried in the churchyard of St. James Episcopal Church in Lothian, Maryland.

Lawrence, Elizabeth. *The Little Bulbs: A Tale of Two Gardeners.* Durham, N.C., Duke University Press, 1986. First published in 1957 by Criterion Books, Lawrence's prose was enlivened by the appearance of "Mr. Krippendorf," a friend of hers who grew hundreds of thousands of bulbs in his woodland estate near Cincinnati, Ohio.

Lawrence, Elizabeth. *A Southern Garden: A Handbook for the Middle South.* Chapel Hill: University of North Carolina Press, 1942. Lawrence's first book, reissued in four editions from UNC Press, is today considered a classic.

Wilson, Emily Herring, ed. *Two Gardeners/Katharine S. White and Elizabeth Lawrence: A Friendship in Letters.* Boston: Beacon Press, 2002. A collection of some one hundred letters written between Lawrence and White, an editor at *The New Yorker.*

Emily Herring Wilson

LAWSON, EDWARD GODFREY
(1884–1968)
LANDSCAPE ARCHITECT

Born on October 29, 1884, in Buffalo, New York, Edward Godfrey Lawson was the adopted son of working-class parents, John F. and Sophia Hall Lawson. He attended classes in Rural Art, Outdoor Art, and Landscape Art—the forerunners in courses of landscape architecture—taught at Cornell University. After graduating with a bachelor's degree in 1912, he worked in the Buffalo firm of Townsend and Fleming and taught in the Cornell undergraduate program while obtaining his master of landscape architecture in 1914. Lawson was one of two first graduates in Cornell's new program. Upon graduation Lawson entered and won the first national competition in 1915 for the Rome Prize in Landscape Architecture at the American Academy in Rome. In winning the coveted fellowship to study at the academy's Rome facilities for three years, Lawson set off a bitter rivalry between Harvard University's Lawrence Scientific School of Landscape Architecture and the Cornell program of landscape architecture, which was based in the fine arts. Harvard professor **James Sturgis Pray** led a five-year personal vendetta against Lawson, first attempting to stop his departing for Rome, then to deny his attending the academy, disapproving at first Lawson's study program, and finally blocking Lawson's fellowship renewal in 1920. In Lawson's defense were two of the founders of the Rome Prize in Landscape Architecture: **Bryant Fleming** and **Ferruccio Vitale**. The third Rome Prize founder, **Frederick Law Olmsted Jr.**, recused himself from the fray. However, the conflict highlighted opposing views of the practice of landscape architecture and its young professional society: scientific versus artistic; public versus private (both in commission and practice); pictorialism versus formalism; all playing out within the American Society of Landscape Architects' two centers of activity in New York City and Boston.

Lawson arrived in Rome in October 1915 at the onset of World War I. Italy was at war, Rome was on military alert, and the academy was closed. Lawson had to take residency with an Italian family and conduct his studies independently. As a conscious objector, he served in the Red Cross during the war. It was during this period that Lawson developed the skills and techniques to measure the Italian villa landscapes, beginning with the readily accessible Villa Borghese in Rome. Lawson compiled notebooks with drawings of fountains, terrace balustrades, gates, and other architectural garden elements as well as a plan of its gardens and parklands. His measured drawings of the Villa Piranesi Gates were the first such measured drawings by a landscape architect at the academy.

During this period Lawson met Geoffrey Scott, the author of *Humanism in Architecture,* one of the most influ-

Right: Edward Lawson in his studio at the American Academy in Rome, ca. 1916. (American Academy in Rome Photographic Archive)

Below: Measured drawing of Bosco Parrasio, Rome, from Lawson's article, "Bosco Parrasio, Rome," in *Landscape Architecture,* April 1929.

ential books on Renaissance architecture. Lawson was introduced to the collection of modernist landscape designers practicing in Florence— Diego Suarez,* Cecil Pinsent, Geoffrey Scott, and Petro Porcinai. He came to know the owners of many outstanding Florentine villa patrons including Bernard Berenson, Giovanna Ghyka, and Arthur Acton, who were actively engaged in the re-Tuscanization of the classical Italian garden on their own properties. Enraptured by the beauty and asymmetry of Princess Ghyka's Villa Gamberaia, at Settignano, outside of Florence, Lawson began measuring its plan, especially documenting its planting composition. This planting plan, the first such recorded research in this specialty was a first for the academy and for the garden. (This detailed planting plan would later prove critical for the garden's restoration after World War II when it was later described as a charred ruin.)

It was also during this period that Lawson translated to English Maria Pasolini Ponti's book *The Italian Garden.* Ponti wrote her work as a landscape sequel to Scott's book setting out the basis of Renaissance garden design using the gardens at the Gamberaia as among her examples. This translation, never published, found its way into the library collections of leading American landscape architects through Lawson's limited distribution of his translation.

When the war ended and the academy was reopened, Fellows were given a new start date for their interrupted fellowship. However, Harvard professor Pray in another acrimonious flurry of correspondence argued that Lawson had already been in Rome for three years, and challenging the talent and quality of Lawson's work produced, claimed Lawson was not deserving of further time under the academy's sponsorship. The Rome Prize founders, Fleming, Vitale, and Olmsted, differing from Pray in their assessment personally funded Lawson for another two years so that he could complete his studies.

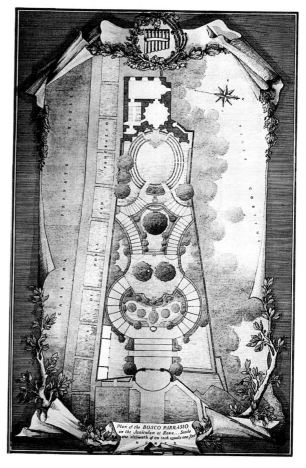

Above: Grounds of Swan House, Atlanta, Georgia, 1998 view. (Photo by Charles A. Birnbaum)

Left: Lawson measuring cascade at Villa Corsini, for one of his many drawings recording the architecture and landscape architecture of Rome. (American Academy in Rome Photographic Archive)

At the end of his academy stay, Lawson bestowed his oeuvre to the academy to influence future Fellows in their research. He left a photographic record of one of his numerous sketchbooks entitled *Italian Villas: Plans and Details,* an original bound manuscript containing thirty-two leaves of plates, chiefly photographs of Lawson's measured drawings at the academy and his collection of over 780 photographs of Italian villas, which started the Landscape Collection at the academy, a resource that he expected succeeding Fellows to augment. He also left prints of his two problem competitions, executed by teams of Fellows comprising an architect, painter, and sculptor, a practice meant to encourage future collaborations.

Lawson published several articles in *Landscape Architecture* magazine, then a quarterly, on his most important garden research. He wrote on the Bosco Parrasio in Rome, a review of the unique Plato-derived model for an artistic and philosophical academy of the Renaissance. Bosco Parrasio was home to the Arcadian Academy, an elective academy comparable to the one Lorenzo de Medici established at the Villa Medici in Fiesole. Its baroque terraced garden and staircase acted both as its entry and an amphitheater for meetings of the Arcadian

Fellows. Another article was on the baroque water works and fountains of Frascati's Villa Torlonia. In yet another research breakthrough, his article on the villa comprises a practicum of garden hydraulic engineering absent from any known studies of Renaissance gardens. Unfortunately, the Villa Torlonia was badly damaged during World War II and much of it exists today as a ruin.

During this time, Lawson encountered additional personal problems; he formed a homosexual relationship with the architectural fellow **Philip Trammell Shutze**. Shutze accompanied Lawson on almost all Lawson's Florence trips and Lawson collaborated exclusively with Shutze on his several architectural commissions. This personal relationship was critically commented on by other fellows, and by academy director Phillip Gorham Stevens, and probably was added fuel to Pray's dislike for Lawson.

Upon leaving the academy in 1921, Lawson moved to Paris and accepted an opportunity to work on American cemeteries in Europe for the U.S. Graves Registration Service. His planning and designs were primarily for five sites: the main European memorial to America's war dead, the American Cemetery, located in Surense, an eastern suburb of Paris, and four smaller sites dispersed in the Allied countries: Belleau Woods, near Chateau Thierry, just north of Paris, and Argonne Rovare sois Montfalcon cemetery to the southwest in France; in Belgium, the American Cemetery at Flanders Field; and the American Cemetery at Surrey, a suburb to the west of London in England.

In the fall of 1922, Lawson returned to America as assistant professor of landscape architecture at Cornell University, where **Gilmore David Clarke** was dean. He joined a distinguished group of Cornell alumni; nine of the first ten Rome prizewinners were from Cornell. Lawson began teaching two courses, Design Studio and Planting Design. He became one of the program's most distinguished professors. Ed, or Eddie, as he was called on campus, taught until 1942 when he retired. During this period, he made frequent returns to Rome and continued his research in the field and at the academy's renowned library. He brought with him to Cornell a wealth of research in historic Italian villa gardens, and developed course material in Beaux-Arts landscape design as well as the emerging modernist idiom. Together, the Lawson archives at the university's main library and the visual resource library of the College of Architecture, Cornell University, contain almost the entirety of Lawson's work. Among the archives are five unpublished volumes on an acclaimed Italian villa

Estate of J. Lakin Baldridge, Ithaca, New York, from ASLA *Illustrations of Work of Members*, 1932.

(utilizing the research findings of later academy Fellows, and Cornell alumni, **Norman Thomas Newton, Ralph E. Griswold**, and **Michael Rapuano**); copies and lantern slide originals of the photographic villa collection he established at the academy; and, several originals of his masterful, color-rendered Beaux-Arts measured drawings.

During the height of the American Depression, 1933–1934, Lawson took leave from Cornell and began a short-lived private practice in Rochester, New York. It is during this time that Lawson executed the majority of his built landscape architectural works. Among them were: residence for Frank E. Plankenhorn, Williamsport,

Pennsylvania; Libanus M. Todd residence, Rochester, New York; the atelier and residence of the American muralist Ezra Winter and his wife, Pat, a horticulturist, in Falls Village, Connecticut; the Swan House in Atlanta for Mr. and Mrs. Edward H. Inman, a collaboration with Philip Trammell Shutze; and an extensive Ithaca residence for the architect J. Lakin Baldridge. Baldridge was a young Cornell assistant professor of architecture. During this period, Lawson designed his one public commission, the master planting and landscape plan for the Main Street campus, Greater University of Buffalo, a campus of new buildings around quadrangle spaces.

After his retirement form Cornell in 1943, Lawson moved to Lakeville, Connecticut, taking up the growing of herbs at Pat Winter's commercial enterprise, House of Herbs, in nearby Falls Village, Connecticut. From that time until his death in 1968, Lawson led a hermetic life with no known outside interests or friends. When Lawson died, having no survivors, nor any extended family, Mary T. Williams, the Executive Secretary of the American Academy, and someone with whom Lawson had regularly corresponded, organized what amounted to an academy-sponsored funeral. She arranged for her brother-in-law, a Protestant minister, to perform services at the sole church in Lakeville and sent the academy's director, Richard Kimball, to represent the academy. Kimball gave a glowing account of Lawson's achievements in scholarly research of Italian garden design. Another attendee was landscape architect Michael Rapuano, president of the Society of Fellows. Lawson was buried in Salisbury Cemetery, Lakeville, Connecticut.

Material on Lawson can be found at the Edward G. Lawson Archives, Carl A. Kroch Library, and the Visual Resources Facility, College of Architecture, Art and Planning, Cornell University, Ithaca, N.Y. In addition, the Photographic Collection, *Archives,* at the American Academy in Rome, Italy, has copies of his photographs and measured drawings.

Lawson, Edward G. "Bosco Parrasio, Rome." *Landscape Architecture* 19, no. 3 (April 1929), 170–74. The amphitheater and entry garden to the Arcadian Academy in Rome, measured by Lawson during his Rome Prize Fellowship.
Lawson, Edward G. "The Cascade in Villa Torlonia, Frascati." *Landscape Architecture* 11, no. 4 (July 1921), 186–88. The baroque gardens, a fragment of the original villa's extensive gardens, which he measured during his Rome Prize Fellowship, includes a unique description of a typical hydrologic system of baroque fountain engineering.

R. Terry Schnadelbach

LEE, CLERMONT "MONTY" HUGER
(1914–2006)
LANDSCAPE ARCHITECT

Clermont "Monty" Huger Lee was born in Savannah, Georgia, in 1914. Her father was a physician and her mother was an avid gardener, who was active in the local garden club. After schooling in Savannah and Charleston, South Carolina, she attended Barnard College in New York City where she became captivated with the sciences. She then transferred to Smith College, in Northampton, Massachusetts, eventually deciding to major in landscape architecture. After completing her undergraduate degree, she attended the Smith College Graduate School of Architecture and Landscape Architecture (formerly the Cambridge School), near Harvard University in Cambridge, Massachusetts, obtaining a master of landscape architecture degree in 1939. Although at this time, Harvard faculty promulgated Modern Bauhaus architecture, Lee always preferred the traditional, less severe landscape styles.

During the Great Depression, Lee returned to Savannah looking for employment. She realized that government work would likely be the most fruitful possibility because government contracts specified degreed personnel. The U.S. Housing Authority (later the Federal Housing Authority) employed architects that could select their own landscape architects. She become an assistant to Talmadge "Bummy" Baumgardner, a landscape architect associated with the Sea Island Company, during the war years after his male assistant was drafted into military service. While working there, she planned landscape designs and supervised planting operations for many federal housing projects in Savannah and Brunswick. Because of wartime labor shortages, she noted on one occasion during World War II that she had a work crew consisting of fifty African American women and one male tractor driver.

Her interest in historic gardens began in the 1940s, when, at the request of a family friend, she drew plans for a small garden at Hofwyl-Broadfield Plantation, in Brunswick, Georgia, based on circa 1910 photographs. In 1944, she made measured drawings of ten Victorian-era gardens in Savannah for Laura Bell and the Georgia Historical Society. She later researched antebellum plants to develop a planting plan for the formal garden of the Andrew Low home newly purchased by the Georgia Chapter of the Colonial Dames of America. She researched antebellum plantings and used the Garden Club of Georgia's 1933 book, *Garden History of Georgia, 1733–1933,* as references to install the most authentic garden possible. In 1949, Lee left the Sea Island Company to establish her own practice, thereby becoming the first female professional landscape architect in private practice in Savannah.

In the early 1950s, Lee began her long and continuing involvement with historic landscapes. Despite the simplified Colonial Revival viewpoint of historic gardening that was in favor at the time, Lee did extensive research to provide an accurate reproduction of a 150-year-old landscape for the Owens-Thomas House on Oglethorpe Square in Savannah. Later her appropriate design and planting plans for historic buildings in the city included the Juliette Gordon Low Birthplace, Andrew Low House, and Green-Meldrim House. Elsewhere in Georgia, Lee consulted on landscapes for the Chief Vann residence near Chatsworth and the New Echota Cherokee Capital near Calhoun for the Georgia Historical Commission.

Clermont "Monty" Huger Lee in Juliette Gordon Low Birthplace garden, ca. 1955. (Courtesy Juliette Gordon Low Birthplace)

From 1951 to 1972, Lee worked with Mills B. Lane Jr., former president of the Citizens & Southern Bank, and his wife to develop landscapes for their business of purchasing and renovating historic homes in the northeast section of Savannah. She also worked with the Lanes to develop plans for the renovation of five Savannah squares that were integral to the colonial plan by James Edward Oglethorpe:* Green, Madison, Troup, Warren, and Washington. Her designs to preserve the sanctity of the squares brought her into conflict with the city, which wanted drive-through lanes for emergency crews and buses crossing the middle of all squares. To address the problem of the turning radius required by the buses, the city adopted Lee's suggestion that the curves of entry into the squares be rounded. In addition, efforts were made to eliminate unattractive structures in the squares such as utility poles and concrete walks. Lee's strong, simple designs used variations in materials and ground forms to give each square a unique character.

In addition to becoming one of the few women in landscape architecture in Georgia, Clermont Lee also worked for recognition of her profession. The American Society of Landscape Architects (ASLA) began in 1899 with only one woman, New York's **Beatrix Jones Farrand**, among its founding members. Clermont Lee joined the ASLA

in 1950, and later worked in conjunction with Hubert Bond Owens,* head of the Department of Landscape Architecture at the University of Georgia, to establish the Georgia State Board of Landscape Architects. Clermont Lee was the fourth landscape architect and first female landscape architect to be registered in the state. (Interestingly, the next 125 registrants were male civil engineers, perhaps alarmed that certified landscape architects might take their commissions.) Lee served on the state board for three years.

Clermont Lee remained active in preparing both historic and current landscape and planting plans throughout the remaining years of her life. She also organized independent research and kept a detailed log on blooming times and characteristics of regional herbaceous plants, planning to author a book on the subject. In addition, she pursued personal interests in genealogy, writing and editing several books on her personal family line and those of others in Savannah. In 2002 she wrote *The Joseph Alston Huger Family: Their Line of Descent from Daniel and Margaret Pedriau Huger of France and South Carolina.*

She was also active in historic associations and commissions, including preparation of the landscape guidelines for the Savannah Victorian District. As noted in her local obituary, she served on the boards of Historic

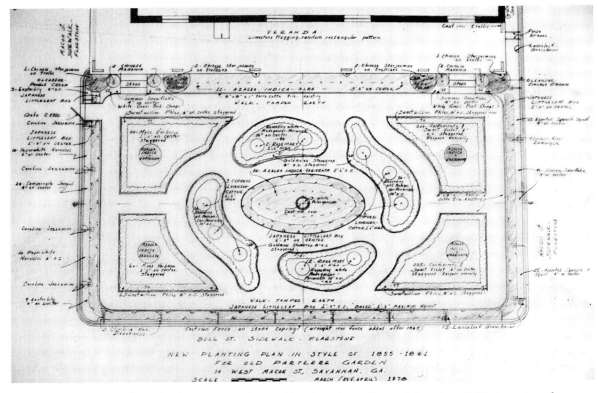

An example of Lee's garden plans is her design of the garden at 14 West Macon Street, Savannah, Georgia, 1978. (Photo courtesy of Jim Cothran)

Savannah Foundation, Inc., the Savannah Public Library, Savannah Science Museum, The Georgia Conservancy, and the Savannah Academy of Lifelong Learning. She held memberships in the Bartram Trail Conference, the Bluffton Historical Preservation Society, Inc., the Georgia Historical Society, the Pendleton Historic Foundation, Inc., the Georgia Botanical Society, and the Savannah chapter of the League of Women Voters. Clermont Lee died in Savannah on June 14, 2006.

The Clermont Lee Collection, MS 1480, at the Library of Georgia Historical Society, Savannah, contains approximately 300 original landscape plans of Savannah area gardens, as well as plans for several Savannah public squares, restored by Lee; drawings date from 1940–1970s.

Beehive Foundation, 208 W. Harris Street, Savannah, Georgia 31401. Mills Lane Family Restoration Projects Collection. Application by permission. Records of projects from the long working association of Clermont Lee and Lane, including both private homes and public squares. Photos, construction details, some plant lists, sketches, and plans.

An earlier version of this entry appears in the *New Georgia Encyclopedia* (www.georgiaencyclopedia.org), and is reprinted here by permission of the Georgia Humanities Council and the University of Georgia Press.

Ced Dolder

LEE, GUY HUNTER
(1894–1953)
LANDSCAPE ARCHITECT, AUTHOR

Guy Hunter Lee, a scion of one of the oldest and most prominent Massachusetts families, was born on January 27, 1894, and grew up in Chestnut Hill, Massachusetts. This area of formerly agricultural land was developed in the mid-nineteenth century into a residential enclave for Boston's civic and financial leaders, with an extraordinary grouping of mansions by notable architects surrounded by well-designed, horticulturally significant grounds by equally meritorious landscape architects. He was influenced by this setting and by his education at the Berkshire School in rural Sheffield, Massachusetts, and at Harvard University where he was a member of the class of 1916, and received a bachelor of arts in 1917. Lee's educational concentration on fine arts refined his interest in the land. He received a master's degree from Harvard's Graduate School of Landscape Architecture in 1921, after having spent 1917 through 1919 in the military, assigned to the infantry in the Argonne. He returned to France in 1920 to work with the Harvard Reconstruction Unit, which probably influenced the topic for his master's thesis, "The Preservation of the Individuality of Cities." He published an account of his French experience in January 1921 in *Landscape Architecture*, noting that the planning for new towns in devastated rural areas instilled him "with the profound belief that anything that can be done to aid France in reconstruction helps the world to regain its equilibrium."

After graduation, Lee became an associate and later partner of Harold Hill Blossom* until 1927. Then he entered into partnership with Hallam Leonard Movius,* with a practice in both New York and Boston that specialized in residential designs for a socially prominent clientele. Since several of the earlier Blossom-Lee designs had been published in various journals of the period, Lee continued this practice. From 1929 through 1931, he embarked on a series of articles for *The Sportsman* describing the estates of notable American sportsmen from the Northeast to South Carolina. His purpose was to explore these great private enclaves, focusing on their facilities for "sports of any sort or specialized agricultural features of interest to sportsmen." His articles reviewed the architectural arrangements and the layout on the land for

Guy Hunter Lee, from "Your Neighborhood L.A.," *House Beautiful*, April 1933.

horse-training, dog-breeding, hunting, fishing, and the like, while numerous photographs illustrated the designed beauty of these vast and luxurious retreats, many of which had been planned by the eminent practitioners of the day.

In addition, Lee maintained an abiding interest in Japanese garden design, which likely developed when he spent nearly a year in 1916–1917 traveling through China and Japan to explore their fine arts. He lectured widely on this topic. He observed in his 1929 review of *The Gardens of Japan* by Jiro Harada for *Landscape Architecture,* that although this pictorial book was educationally noteworthy, it only glanced at the intricacy, variety, and artistry of this refined landscape heritage. Therefore, in 1935, Lee published his own volume, *Japanese Gardens: Their*

Left: An example of Lee's work, creating informal garden rooms at the Forbes residence, Wellesley, Massachusetts, from "Easily Cared for Garden," *House Beautiful,* January 1931.

Below: Lee, in conjunction with H. H. Blossom, creates a design which meld walls, rocky outcrops, and plantings at the Forbes residence garden, Wellesley, Massachusetts, from "Easily Cared for Garden," *House Beautiful,* January 1931.

History, Sources of Inspiration and Value to Western Gardening Art. In this small volume, he examined the varied historical, political, and spiritual allegiances that gave rise to early artisans of the Japanese garden. The influence of picturesque volcanic topography and unique types of vegetation upon design values fascinated him. He admired the restrained architecture and its integral relationship to a garden regardless of the scale, noting that Japanese designs were "meant to suggest natural scenery . . . but never to reproduce it, . . . [to] set the mind of the beholders working along certain contemplative channels . . . to refresh and restore the soul." He ruminated about the lessons of Japanese gardens for the American landscape, particularly for the country park or estate, which were intended for respite in both cultures. Americans, whose taste emphasized quantity and size, had much to learn from the Japanese mastery of "using appropriate material in the proper place . . . drawing together all of these elements into a unified and satisfactory artistic composition. . . . The Japanese can teach us ways 'undreamed of in our philosophy' to understand, to appreciate and to utilize the aspects, moods, and methods of nature in the design of our own gardens."

In his own design work, Lee reflected much of this training and the rich texturing of plant materials that he had learned under Blossom's tutelage. His plans give evidence of balanced compositions of boulder, border, and lawn flowing along varied terrain to form attractive spaces for repose around suburban homes. In addition to his residential clientele, in the early 1930s, Lee, together with Movius, did some master planning for his alma mater, the Berkshire School, in Sheffield, Massachusetts, where young Hallam Movius Jr. had also been a student. Lee also prepared multiple design variations for the Small House Project for *Better Homes and Gardens in America* in 1933, but as he wrote in his Harvard College 25th Anniversary Report (1941), he found work during the Depression years, "not so hot," eventually working on public housing plans in Washington, D.C. With the outbreak of World War II, Lee returned to the army, this time with military intelligence. Because of his fluency in French, he was stationed in Paris and then Belgium, organizing prisoners of war to replace American labor forces near the front. He expressed his shock at the abject poverty, demoralization, and disorganization he found in France in the postwar period. He retired from active practice upon his return, spending his summers fishing at Lake Champlain, and his winters in South Carolina, where he died in 1953.

Lee, Guy H. "Estates of American Sportsmen . . . [with various subtitles]." *The Sportsman,* July–December 1929, February–December 1930, January–May 1931; vols. 6, 7, 8, 9. An interesting collection of articles about selected grand estates of prominent leaders in "society" in a magazine directed toward the tastes of the rich and famous.

Lee, Guy H. "The Harvard Reconstruction Unit in France." *Landscape Architecture* 11 (January 1921), 70–75. Planning for the post–World War I reconstruction of French rural communities as seen through the eyes of an optimistic young man.

Lee, Guy H. *Japanese Gardens.* Boston: Private printing, ca. 1935. A charming small volume, with delicate line drawings by Alden Ripley, Lee's paean to Japanese culture, taste, and garden design.

Arleyn A. Levee

LIPP, FRANZ
(1897–1996)
LANDSCAPE ARCHITECT

Born in 1897 and raised in Leipzig, Germany, Franz Lipp graduated from technical high school with a specialty in civil engineering at the age of sixteen. He spent the next several years as a crew member on merchant ships sailing around the world and was detained in a civilian internment camp in Plymouth, New South Wales, Australia, with his fellow shipmates during World War I. While interned, Lipp learned basic horticulture and civil engineering from his fellow Germans. At the end of the war, Lipp returned to Germany to study horticulture under Karl Foerster at the Gartenbauschule in Potsdam, graduating in 1921 with a degree in landscape architecture. Foerster and Camillo Schneider then arranged for Lipp to conduct postgraduate work in dendrology with E. H. Wilson and Alfred Rehder at Harvard University's Arnold Arboretum, where Lipp cataloged plant specimens collected by Wilson in East Asia before World War I.

Interested in the work of distinguished Midwestern landscape architect **Jens Jensen**, Lipp moved to Chicago in 1923 to work as a construction supervisor for Jensen. After a brief return to Germany in 1925, Lipp worked for several landscape architects in New York and Chicago before establishing an independent landscape architecture practice in Chicago in 1929. Accepting projects

Franz Lipp at Yellowstone Park, ca. 1945. (Photograph by Lester Brideham. Gift of Jim & Margaret Young. Franz Lipp Papers, Ryerson and Burnham Archives, The Art Institute of Chicago. Digital file © The Art Institute of Chicago)

Stornoway, the McLennan Residence in Ligonier, Pennsylvania, designed by Lipp in 1964. (Photo by Joseph W. Molitor; Joseph W. Molitor Photographs and Papers, Avery Architectural and Fine Arts Library, Columbia University)

throughout Illinois and Wisconsin, Lipp also relied on associations with architects such as Holabird & Root for work landscaping several public housing projects during the difficult years of the Great Depression. For the largest of these projects, the Trumbull Park Homes complex in Chicago, Lipp chose to plant large deciduous trees, low hedges, and climbing vines to soften the fairly austere buildings and to define areas between housing units. In addition to his commissions from public and private clients, Lipp was also involved in the annual Spring Flower and Garden Show in Chicago, frequently winning awards for his strikingly modern floral and garden designs during the early 1930s.

With the outbreak of World War II and the marked decline in landscape commissions, Lipp joined the noted Chicago architectural photography company Hedrich-Blessing, learning the technical and aesthetic language of photography. In 1942, Lipp began a monumental photographic survey of landscapes in Idaho, Wyoming, and Yellowstone National Park, a selection of which became the basis of an exhibition at the Art Institute of Chicago in 1951.

After the war, Lipp reopened his landscape practice

with landscape engineer Carl Pathe, choosing an office in downtown Chicago near the Tavern Club and the Cliff Dwellers Club, where Lipp and many of Chicago's prominent artists and architects frequently gathered. Always keeping a small office, Lipp hired Marvin "Bud" Wehler as a field supervisor in 1959, naming him partner in 1970, although Lipp remained chief designer until his retirement in 1978. In the later years of his practice, Lipp moved his office from Chicago to Winfield, Illinois.

Lipp's reputation was principally made through his landscapes for commercial buildings, shopping centers, hospitals, schools, and churches throughout the Midwest. He maintained long-standing relationships with many of Chicago's major architectural offices, including Holabird & Root; Perkins & Will; Schmidt, Garden & Erikson; Paul Schweikher and Winston Elting; and Loebl, Schlossman & Bennett, working on sites across the United States. Among his more than 325 identified projects, Lipp's most important designs include the 1350 Lake Shore Drive Apartments in Chicago; the Allstate Insurance Company building in Northbrook, Illinois; Badger Meter Plant in Brown Deer, Wisconsin; the Bertha Evans Residence in Palm Beach, Florida;

Houston during the last five years. Another five will undoubtedly make secure the well-earned title, 'Garden City of the Southwest.'"

Perhaps the best documented of London's designs to date is the East Garden of Bayou Bend, Ima Hogg's residence; however, the authorship of the implemented garden still remains unclear. Ellen Shipman is credited with a sketch for the East Garden, one that is similar to the present design. However, most sources credit London with the design. In 1932, London made two sketches of a pool design for the East Garden, but neither was used for the implemented design. The East Garden would be the only garden London was actively involved with at Bayou Bend, yet it is the garden most commonly associated with London by many Houston residents.

One of Ruth London's courtyard designs is seen at the Evans residence, location unknown, pre-1939. (Collection of Kelly Dent)

London's designs are characterized by simplicity and reflect the changing attitudes of her clients toward their outdoor spaces. Houston homes in the 1930s followed the national movement in using eclectic architecture, and the gardens designed around the homes were expected to follow the same stylistic model. Gardens were used as outdoor living areas, essential for domestic life in Houston's subtropical climate. London's designs included well-proportioned elements in relation to each other and to the architecture, most often acting as extensions of living spaces or outdoor rooms. London began designing gardens in the 1930s, employing the Beaux-Arts principles of design, including the use of the axis of the house, symmetry, incorporation of clipped hedges, restrained plant palette, fountains, reflecting pools, and statuary. Her designs reflect a propensity toward clearly defined spaces and sparse ornamentation. London's gardens reveal a tendency for abstraction and a reliance on simple geometric shapes for spatial definition.

She tended to use a restrained plant list, often relying on textural contrasts, masses of plants, clipped evergreen hedges, and espaliered plants for visual interest. Clients often retained her services after the installation of her designs, enabling her to follow the maintenance of her landscapes and to carefully monitor the growth and development of the designs. By the 1950s, London had taken several ideas from modernism, including the lack of a focal point and combinations of curvilinear and rectilinear forms. **Thomas Dolliver Church** designed a residential garden in Houston, which appeared in *Architectural Record* in 1956. Being located in Houston, perhaps this garden was a source of inspiration that spurred on London's transition to using modern design forms and materials. By 1954, London was recommending native plants in plantings to clients, indicating an openness to emerging horticultural ideas.

Ruth London established herself in Houston and owned a small independent practice in the city for over thirty years. Her designs reflect national garden styles adapted to the Gulf South over three decades. She entered Houston when the city was emerging as a major cultural center. She helped define the gardens of the city, putting them on par with the finest in the nation. The picture of her left by fragmentary historical records shows she was a strong-willed individual with high standards and an excellent understanding of design principles. London remained and worked in Houston for the rest of her life, dying on February 4, 1966, at the Methodist Hospital.

Garden Club of Houston. "Annual Garden Pilgrimage." *Houston Scrapbooks* 25 (1938 and 1939). Houston Metropolitan Research Center. These pamphlets attribute several gardens to Ruth London and also list several garden designers who were active in Houston in the late 1930s.

Nevins, Deborah. "The Triumph of Flora: Women and the American Landscape, 1890–1935." *The Magazine Antiques* 127 (April 1985), 904–22. This is a good introduction to the contribution of women in landscape architecture and sets the scene for London's contributions.

White, Robert F. "Memorial Minute: Ruth London, ASLA." *ASLA Bulletin*, no 144 (1 July 1966), 4–5. One of the few known printed mentions of Ruth London, this obituary documents some of her late-career designs.

Kelly McCaughey Dent

MACDONALD, CHARLES BLAIR
(1855–1939)
GOLF COURSE DESIGNER

Charles Blair Macdonald was born in Niagara Falls, Canada, to a Scottish father and Canadian mother. Shortly thereafter, the family moved to Chicago. In 1872, he went to Scotland to attend the University of St. Andrews. His grandfather William Macdonald, a member of the Royal and Ancient Golf Club, introduced him to golf. The day after his arrival, the younger Macdonald was brought to the club and introduced to Old Tom Morris, one of the game's greatest players, clubmakers, and greenkeepers, who along with his son, Young Tom Morris, won numerous championships. By his second year, Macdonald had become proficient enough to be invited to play matches with both Old and Young Tom, along with many other skilled players of that time.

Macdonald returned to Chicago in 1874. In 1884, he married Frances Porter of Chicago, and they had two daughters, Janet and Frances. He referred to these years as his "Dark Ages," which lasted until 1892, when he began designing golf courses. During those years, there were no golf courses in the Chicago area, so he only played during trips abroad. His first layout, in 1892, was a seven-hole course in Lake Forest, Illinois, on the grounds of Fairlawn, the summer estate of Senator Charles B. Farwell. Macdonald then organized the Chicago Golf Club and laid out its original nine holes in Belmont, Illinois. That layout was expanded to eighteen holes the following year, and in 1895 he laid out a new eighteen-hole course when the club moved to Wheaton, Illinois.

Macdonald is credited with sixteen original golf

C. B. Macdonald, from *Scotland's Gift: Golf*, 1928.

course designs; unfortunately only nine courses retain integrity today, while many have vanished altogether. He never accepted a fee for his services in golf course design. For him, it was an enduring passion, and fortunately, his family was rather well off, which afforded him the ability to work without payment. During Macdonald's years in Illinois he was a member of the prestigious Chicago Board of Trade. In 1900, he moved his family to New York to become a partner in the stockbrokerage firm of C. D. Barney & Co.

Macdonald believed most existing American courses were designed with little imagination. In 1897, while still in Chicago, he wrote in *Country Life* that "ideal first-class golf links has yet to be selected and the course laid out in America." The 1899 patent for a rubber-cored ball changed the game as golfers then knew it. The new Haskell ball flew farther (rendering many courses obsolete), was easier to hit, and placed less stress on the hickory shaft clubs. Macdonald was determined to build "a classical golf course in America, one which would eventually compare favorably with the championship links abroad and serve as an incentive to the elevation of the game in America."

When Macdonald developed an idea, he worked to achieve its fruition. In 1902, he traveled abroad to gather information on design and spent the better part of the next four years studying foreign courses, mostly in the United Kingdom. He returned to the United States in 1906 with surveyors' maps of the more famous courses, plus twenty or thirty of his own sketches of courses with distinctive features. Some called his idea of essentially copying the great holes humorous, while others thought it visionary. Macdonald's definitive statement on the matter was, "The flowers of transplanted plants in time shed a perfume comparable to their indigenous home."

By 1904, Macdonald drew up an agreement proposing to advance the game of golf in America by constructing a

Above: An existing MacDonald design, Crater, hole 12, St. Louis Country Club, St. Louis, Missouri (MacDonald and Raynor). (Photo by Kevin R. Mendik)

Below: Yale University Golf Course, holes 3 and 4, New Haven, Connecticut. (Photo by Kevin R. Mendik)

course where each of the holes would be modeled on the most famous ones from overseas, with each hole being "representative and classic in itself." He identified a 450-acre unsurveyed tract of land adjacent to the Shinnecock Hills Golf Club in eastern Long Island. The land was filled with bogs and swamps and covered in entangling bushes such as blackberry and bayberry. He and his future son-in-law, H. J. Whigham, spent a few days riding the land and noted that the contours and sandy soils provided ideal natural conditions for a links course. He signed up seventy subscribers at $1,000 each, including among others Devereaux Emmet, Henry Frick, Robert Lincoln, J. C. Parrish, and William Vanderbilt.

By the spring of 1907, Macdonald obtained the title to 205 acres and the course known today as the National Golf Links of America began to take shape. The bogs were drained, the bushes cleared, and over 10,000 loads of good soil and manure were laid on the land. Macdonald then partnered with a local surveyor by the name of Seth Raynor, who oversaw construction on much of Macdonald's future work and became an accomplished course designer himself. Some land was remolded to accommodate the blueprinted, but naturalistic, Scottish links holes; other holes were altered, and entirely new types of holes were simply created. The first play on the rough course occurred in 1910 and writing in *Metropolitan Magazine,* Horace Hutchinson stated that "several of the best . . . holes [in the United Kingdom] are here seen reproduced with a faithfulness which is a testimony to the scientific care, the labor and the money which have been lavished upon it." He noted that roughly five holes were accurate representations of those in the United Kingdom, but the greater number and "possibly the best in character, have been planned out of the designer's brain with such suggestions as his experience, gathered in Europe, and the natural trend of the ground he had to deal with, supplied to it." Hutchinson went on to state that when the course officially opened the following year, it would be by far the best in the United States.

Hutchinson's prediction was accurate. Clubs all over the country, especially at nearby Shinnecock, were clamoring for Macdonald's design services. He eventually redesigned Shinnecock in 1916, but only two of those holes, including the infamous Redan, exist today.

Raynor, who did not play golf, had an extraordinary eye for topography and was able to adapt the types of holes laid out at National Golf Links of America to other locations, even recreating its topography elsewhere. The Macdonald-Raynor courses were equally suitable for the duffer and the champion as they offered alternative routes of play on most holes. Probably the best surviving example of a Macdonald-Raynor course hewn out of rock and forest is the Yale Golf Course, which cost almost $400,000 to build in the mid-1920s, an extraordinary sum for those days. Macdonald, Raynor, and their colleague Charles Banks also designed numerous courses during the 1920s that were part of island subdivision

resorts. Several of those were done in close collaboration with the **Olmsted Brothers** and include the Gibson Island Golf Course, Annapolis Roads in Maryland, and the Fishers Island Club in Long Island Sound. Of those, Fishers Island retains its design integrity, and is attributed to Seth Raynor. Only nine holes were built at what is now the Annapolis Golf Club, and that layout is attributed to Banks. All that survives at today's Gibson Island Club is a nine-hole course, with some Macdonald and Raynor features.

Macdonald's primary residence, which he called Ballyshear, was constructed on 117 acres overlooking fifteen holes at National Golf Links of America. The house is extant. He retained Annette Hoyt Flanders* to design a formal plan for its grounds. Her work there illustrates several varied styles, including a half-mile drive surrounded by trees and lawn in the English style, as well as rustic and informal terrace furnishings, brick pathways, and local plant materials such as blue hydrangea and beach roses.

In Macdonald's 1928 book, *Scotland's Gift: Golf,* he reminisced about his design philosophy and experiences. He wrote, "There can be no really first-class golf course without good material to work with. The best material is a sandy loam in gentle undulations, breaking into hillocks in a few places. Securing such land is really more than half the battle. Having such material at hand to work upon, the completion of an ideal course becomes a matter of experience, gardening and mathematics." He also believed strongly that "glaring artificiality of any kind detracts from the fascination of the game." Macdonald passed away on April 23, 1939, in Southampton, New York, and was buried alongside Seth Raynor in the Southampton Cemetery.

Bahto, George. *The Evangelist of Golf: The Story of Charles Blair Macdonald.* Chelsea, Mich.: Clock Tower Press, LLC, 2002. A detailed analysis of Macdonald's best known courses, along with substantial information relating to time frames for Macdonald, Raynor, and Banks designs.

Macdonald, Charles B. *Scotland's Gift: Golf.* New York and London: Charles Scribner's Sons, 1928. Macdonald's classic work in which he describes his early experiences with golf and his design philosophy.

Whigham, H. J. "The Evangelist of Golf." *Country Life Magazine,* September 1939. A biographical essay on the life and times of Macdonald written shortly after his death in 1939.

Kevin R. Mendik

MARVIN, ROBERT E.
(1920–2001)
LANDSCAPE ARCHITECT

Robert Marvin was raised in Colleton County in the rural South Carolina coastal plain. Influenced by his native landscape, the work of Innocenti and Webel (**Umberto Innocenti** and Richard K. Webel*) on Bonnie Doone plantation where his family resided, and a family nursery, he chose to study horticulture and received a degree in 1942 from Clemson University. After college, he served as a U.S. Army captain in the Pacific until 1945. Upon his return to civilian life, he pursued advanced studies in landscape architecture from 1945 to 1947 at the University of Georgia.

Marvin started his firm in the small town of Walterboro, South Carolina, in 1947. His early practice included garden designs for area plantations. These were among the few commissions available in an otherwise economically depressed region where the practice of landscape architecture was relatively unknown. During this time, he became concerned about the treatment of the landscape during construction and established a landscape construction company that he ran until 1980. Marvin foresaw the future development potential of the region and the threat to the fragile natural and cultural landscape. Consequently, his ethics and design philosophy were formulated early in his career.

In the early 1950s, Marvin and his wife, Anna Lou, penned the mission statement for his firm, Robert E. Marvin & Associates: "The dominant reason for the existence of Robert E. Marvin and Associates shall be to create and design an environment in which each individual within it can grow to be a full human being as God intended him to be." He pioneered and guided development in the region through his positive environmental practices and belief in people. Over his career of fifty-four years, he mentored many landscape architects, who he armed with strong principles and design expertise.

Marvin promoted a team approach to design as the best way to plan the environment. By the mid-1960s, he promoted the concept that cooperation between disciplines was paramount from project inception. If this did not occur, the environment would not meet the needs of

Robert Marvin. (Robert Marvin Howell Beach & Associates, Inc.)

the society it served. Marvin believed landscape architects have the qualities to lead the design team through knowledge of site, skills to coordinate other disciplines, and an understanding of the integration of man and nature.

The projects Marvin designed throughout his career were diverse, and included residential landscapes, planned communities, public parks, and corporate headquarters. He was a versatile and a strongly principled designer who insisted his firm be in control of everything outside of the building and often conceived the design intent of the building.

In 1958, Marvin & Associates designed Glen Cairn Gardens in Rock Hill, South Carolina. It is a fine example of a small park design and one of the first projects that won him regional acclaim, including a 1963 Plant America Award. The 6-acre property had been owned by David and Hazel Bigger who planted azaleas and other southern heritage plants. Marvin preserved and enhanced the site adding flowering specimen trees, canopy trees, lily ponds, and bulb masses. There is a new plan to renovate site features and add additional property to the park.

The Jones Bridge Headquarters of the Simmons Company, completed in the 1970s, was Marvin's favorite

Above: Finlay Park, Columbia, South Carolina, 1991. (Robert Marvin Howell Beach & Associates, Inc.)

Below: Southern Progress Headquarters, Birmingham, Alabama 1993. (Robert Marvin Howell Beach & Associates, Inc.)

over the ground of the oak hickory forest, allowing natural storm water patterns to flow. The project won an American Society of Landscape Architects Honor Award in 1978. The design was so successful, in fact, that it was used as a model in the 1994 publication *Storm Water Infiltration* by Bruce Ferguson.

From the 1960s to the 1980s, Marvin performed a multitude of site work on Hilton Head Island, South Carolina. He worked primarily for developer Charles Fraser, master planner for Harbor Town and Sea Pines Plantation with Sasaki Associates (Hideo Sasaki*). Fraser's then-unique concept was to leave as much of the natural environment intact as possible. He was convinced that it could be profitable to do so. He found Marvin to be the perfect designer for sensitive environments requiring subtle detailing. Marvin won awards from the American Institute of Architects and the American Association of Nurserymen for his work on the island.

The National Landscape Award–winning Henry C. Chambers Waterfront Park in Beaufort, South Carolina, completed by 1981, was a more urban design than many of Marvin's other projects. The waterfront promenade comprised a series of spaces with gathering areas, plantings, and enclosures, all with simple detailing allowing the vista to be the jewel of the design. The modernist design with various rooms, angular walkways, seat walls, and elegant elevation changes has been significantly altered by a renovation in progress.

design project. Located outside of Atlanta, this corporate headquarters was nestled on the fragile banks of the Chattahoochee River. Marvin skillfully graded the roads and parking with minimum site disruption and preserved existing trees. The steel-truss building designed by Thompson, Hancock Witte, and Associates, Inc. floats

Marvin was the prime consultant for the 1984 Sibley Center at Callaway Gardens in Pine Mountain, Georgia. This passive solar structure housing an open-air greenhouse and garden pavilion was conceived through Marvin's absolute certainty that architecture is secondary to the land. Craig Gaulden Davis's architectural work was subordinate to Marvin's vision of an earth-formed, formal design sited to benefit from environmental exposures. This project received a National Landscape Award from the American Association of Nurserymen in 1986.

Planning for the Southern Progress Headquarters began in 1987 with Marvin working directly for the owner. Teaming with Jova/Daniels/Busby Architects, he designed a campus plan sensitive to the topography and vegetation of the site with buildings spanning ravines, thus melding the site and architecture. The project received an American Society of Landscape Architects Design Merit Award in 1994. An addition was completed in 1995, and Marvin's firm continued working on the campus after his death.

In Columbia, South Carolina's capitol, two well-known projects illustrate the work of Robert Marvin. The 18-acre Finlay Park is an excellent example of Marvin's principles. The challenging natural features of the site were manipulated to create a pedestrian-friendly environment that has been heralded for its designer's vision. Over the years Marvin worked on the Governor's Mansion, renovating formal gardens and the park-like setting. The Governor's Mansion was honored with a 1990 Grand Award from the American Association of Nurserymen.

Marvin was the recipient of over forty national and fourteen regional awards and honors throughout his lengthy career, including the 1967 Slater Wright Award from the Southern Nurseryman Association; the 1988 University of Georgia Distinguished Alumni Award; and the South Carolina Arts Commission's Elizabeth O'Neill Verner Award. He was inducted into the South Carolina Hall of Fame and received the South Carolina Order of the Palmetto, two of South Carolina's most meritorious awards. Marvin was elected a Fellow of the American Society of Landscape Architects in 1990. In 2001, Marvin received the ASLA Medal for Lifetime Career Excellence from the American Society of Landscape Architects. The ASLA Medal is the highest honor a society member can receive.

Henry C. Chambers Waterfront Park, Beaufort, South Carolina, 1996 view. (Photo by Charles A. Birnbaum)

In 1997, Marvin changed the firm name and structure to Robert Marvin/Howell Beach & Associates PA to ensure that the firm's mission would continue and allow Marvin to spend more time on creative concept development. His contributions to the profession include impacting regional design practices through his design expertise and sensitive development as well as his mentoring and leadership among landscape architects. A well-known Marvin statement that best illustrates his philosophy is, "we need to knock the walls down and let nature in again. The environmental movement proves that man needs to get out of his box that technology has created. He needs to wrap his arms around nature." Marvin passed away in June of 2001.

Freeman, Allen. "Finely Wrought Garden Pavilion John A. Sibley Horticultural Center, Pine Mountain, Georgia." *Architecture,* December 1984, 36–41. Synthesis of landscape and architecture produces work of art.

Marvin, Robert E., and James Paddock. "A Corporate Headquarters Achieves Minimum Landscape Impact." *Landscape Architecture,* January 1979, 70. Harmonious blending of building and site on the Chattahoochee River.

Thompson, J. William. "Southern Savior." *Landscape Architecture,* June 1997, 74–79, 93–95, 97. An overview of Marvin's philosophy and work.

Amanda Graham Barton

McHARG, IAN L.
(1920–2001)
LANDSCAPE ARCHITECT, EDUCATOR, AUTHOR

Ian L. McHarg was born in Clydebank, a shipbuilding town northwest of Glasgow, Scotland, on November 20, 1920. During his youth, he explored the rugged coastal terrain of western Scotland. Hiking and American jazz were his teenage passions. McHarg took a deep interest in religion and worked for the Associated Scottish Newspapers as a copy boy and editor's boy.

In 1936, McHarg discovered landscape architecture. He withdrew from high school to become a pupil-apprentice to Donald A. Wintersgill, a landscape architect with the Glasgow firm Austin and McAslan, Ltd. He also enrolled in the Glasgow College of Art and the West of Scotland Agriculture College.

He enlisted in the British Army in May 1938, and was mobilized into the regular army on September 2, 1939, at the onset of World War II. McHarg distinguished himself during the war, rising through the ranks from private to major. As a commando in the Second Parachute Squadron, McHarg participated in campaigns in North Africa, Italy, France, and Greece. In Italy, he led the reconstruction of the Acquedotto Pugliese during 1943. This aqueduct helped provide water supplies to Allied troops as well as Italian citizens. In 1945, McHarg won the competition to design the British military cemetery in Athens.

After the war, McHarg decided to enter the Master of Landscape Architecture program at Harvard University. This presented a challenge since he had neither a high school diploma nor an undergraduate degree. Still, Harvard admitted him. Early in his Harvard days, McHarg met a Dutch Radcliffe College student. Pauline Crena de Iongh was from a prominent Dutch family. She and McHarg married in 1947 and had two sons, Alistair and Malcolm. In his four years at Harvard, McHarg earned both a bachelor of landscape architecture degree in 1949 and a subsequent master of landscape architecture degree in 1950. The atmosphere at Harvard encouraged cross-disciplinary collaboration, due in large part to the model of the modernist German Bauhaus model that influenced instructors in the architecture department. McHarg took advantage of opportunities offered in architecture and city and regional planning, collaborating with three architecture students on a plan for downtown

Ian McHarg (*foreground*) at University of Pennsylvania jury with colleagues Robert Hanna and Nicholas Muhlenberg, 1979. (The Architectural Archives, University of Pennsylvania, photo by Becky Young)

Providence, Rhode Island. In 1951, McHarg earned a master of city planning degree from Harvard, receiving the distinction after he returned to Scotland.

In Scotland, McHarg discovered he had tuberculosis. He almost died at the Southfield Colony for Consumptives in Edinburgh. Fortunately, he went for treatment to Hotel Belvedere in Leysin, Switzerland, where he regained his health. The contrast between the dank conditions in the Scottish hospital and the clean Swiss sanatorium instilled an interest about the rela-

Lake at The Woodlands, near Houston, Texas; ecological plan by Wallace McHarg Roberts & Todd for the Mitchell Energy and Development Company, 1970–1974. (Photo courtesy of Frederick Steiner)

tionship between health and the built environment that would have a lasting influence on McHarg's approach to design and planning.

From 1951 to 1954, McHarg worked as a planning officer for the Department of Health for Scotland. During this time, he offered lecture courses in landscape architecture at Edinburgh College of Art and Glasgow College of Art. In 1954, his former Harvard professor and then dean of the University of Pennsylvania Graduate School of Fine Arts, G. Holmes Perkins, invited McHarg to Philadelphia. He was appointed assistant professor of landscape architecture and city planning with the charge to create a Department of Landscape Architecture at the University of Pennsylvania. An undergraduate program in landscape architecture had existed at Penn since 1924. McHarg established the Master of Landscape Architecture degree and the department. In 1959, he introduced the "Man and Environment" course. Destined to become one of the most popular courses at Penn, McHarg invited prominent designers, theologians, and scientists to the class to discuss the relationship between people and their environments.

This course led to the CBS television series *The House We Live In,* which McHarg produced and hosted from 1960 to 1961. Guests included Margaret Mead, Paul Tillich, Eric Fromm, Julian Huxley, Loren Eiseley, Lewis Mumford, Arnold Toynbee, Luna Leopold, and others.

The ideas generated in his classes and on the television series about people and their environments influenced McHarg's teaching and burgeoning practice.

With planner-architect David Wallace, he founded Wallace-McHarg Associates in 1962. Their first two projects were the Plan for the Valleys and the Baltimore Inner Harbor Plan, both in Maryland. McHarg led the innovative Plan for the Valleys, which addressed a bucolic Maryland landscape threatened with suburban sprawl and the construction of an interstate. The plan pioneered concepts like the transfer of development rights, the protection of environmentally sensitive areas, and conservation-based clustered village settlements. In 1965, Wallace and McHarg expanded their practice, adding landscape architect William Roberts and architect Thomas Todd.

At Penn, McHarg began to explore and to expand ideas about using ecology as a basis for design and planning. His exploration was reinforced by grants from the Rockefeller and Ford foundations that permitted him to engage in exploratory studies. His growing practice with Wallace McHarg Roberts & Todd (WMRT) allowed him to apply these theories and to reflect on their utility. For example, his work on siting highway routes in the late 1960s laid the groundwork for national environment impact assessment policy and procedures. Meanwhile, McHarg became a more prominent public personality.

President Lyndon Johnson appointed him to the White House Task Force on Conservation and Natural Beauty in 1966 and Secretary of Interior Stewart Udall invited him to serve on the American Institute of Architects Potomac Planning Task Force from 1965 to 1967.

At the urging of Russell Train, then president of the Conservation Foundation and noted ecologist Raymond Dasman, McHarg started to pull together his theories for an ecological approach in 1966. He tested several ideas in various articles and public speeches. McHarg hosted a PBS documentary titled *Multiply and Subdue the Earth,* which was filmed in 1968 and broadcast the following year. In 1969, the fruits of his exploration, the now classic, *Design with Nature,* was published.

The book appeared at a time of great environmental awakening. Few environmental books were available then and even fewer addressed design and planning. With the Earth Week celebrations of April 1970 across the nation, book sales of *Design with Nature* skyrocketed and McHarg was in high demand for speaking engagements. Student applications increased as a Master of Regional Planning degree was created at Penn and the department was renamed the Department of Landscape Architecture and Regional Planning in 1965.

The "Environmental Decade" of the 1970s was productive for McHarg as both a scholar and practitioner. However, the decade was personally sad as McHarg lost his wife Pauline to cancer in 1974. Among the important projects that McHarg was involved with as part of WMRT were community plans for The Woodlands near Houston, Texas (1970–1974); the Amelia Island resort community in Florida (1971); and the new Nigerian capital Abuja (1978–1979). Other projects included the design of the Pardisan environmental park in Tehran, Iran (1973–1975) and the plan for the Toronto Central Waterfront (1976). He also completed regional ecological studies and plans for Minnesota's Twin Cities (1969); Denver (1971–1972 and 1978); Wilmington and Dover, Vermont (1972); Lake Austin in Texas (1976–1977); Toledo (1977); Detroit (1978); and northwestern Colorado (1978). Important transportation studies included Wilmington, Delaware (1973); Easton, Pennsylvania (1973); and Washington,

D.C. (1977). These projects broke new ground in the areas of new community design and regional planning. For example, The Woodlands is widely regarded as the most successful new town in the United States planned at that time. During the early 1970s (and again in the 1990s), McHarg worked with the U.S. Environmental Protection Agency on a comprehensive plan for environmental quality that envisioned a nationwide, computer-based, ecological mapping system.

In 1977, McHarg married Carol Smyser and they would have two sons, Ian and Andrew. McHarg resigned from WMRT in 1979, which continues today as Wallace Roberts & Todd, LLC. He continued to teach at Penn, long after stepping down as department chair and retiring in 1986. In addition, he was a visiting professor and guest speaker at universities throughout the world. From the 1980s on, he devoted much of his considerable energies to advocating national and global systems for mapping environmental and social information through computing technologies.

He remained active through his seventies as a lecturer and writer, publishing two more books: *A Quest for Life* (1996) and *To Heal the Earth* (with Frederick Steiner, 1998). McHarg received the National Medal of Art in 1990 and the Japan Prize in 2000. He received honorary doctoral degrees from Amherst College (1970), Lewis and Clark College (1970), Bates College (1978), and Heriot-Watt University in Edinburgh (1998). Ian McHarg died in Chester County, Pennsylvania, on March 5, 2001.

McHarg, Ian L. *Design with Nature.* Garden City, N.Y.: Natural History Press/Doubleday, 1969 (2nd ed., New York: John Wiley & Sons, 1994). An approach to design and planning grounded in an understanding of ecological systems and human values. Widely influential, the book was a National Book Award finalist, and has been translated into French, Italian, Japanese, and Spanish.

McHarg, Ian L. *A Quest for Life: An Autobiography.* New York: John Wiley & Sons, 1996. McHarg recounts his life from his boyhood in Scotland through his career in Philadelphia. The story is peppered with amusing anecdotes about human nature.

McHarg, Ian L., and Frederick R. Steiner, eds. *To Heal the Earth: The Collected Writings of Ian L. McHarg.* Washington, D.C.: Island Press, 1998. McHarg's major writings are collected on ecological design and planning theory and practice.

Frederick Steiner

McLAREN, JOHN
(1846–1943)
HORTICULTURIST

John McLaren was born on December 20, 1846, to Donald and Catherine McLaren on a farm near Stirling, Scotland. After serving an apprenticeship as a dairyman, he became a gardener at Bannockburn House. He continued to learn horticulture at a succession of country estates and at the Royal Botanic Garden in Edinburgh, and finally at the Earl Of Wemyss's estate in East Lothian. Here he planted sea bent grass to bind dunes on the edge of the Firth of Forth. McLaren immigrated to the United States in 1872, by which time he was a very accomplished horticulturist. His experience in sand dune reclamation earned him a position as Head Gardener on George Howard's estate, El Cerrito, in Hillsborough, on the San Francisco peninsula. This was the earliest estate developed south of San Francisco. During his tenure on this estate McLaren was involved in extensive tree planting. The most visible of these efforts were beautification projects such as the planting with eucalyptus trees of El Camino Real, originally the principal north-south road on the peninsula, and Coyote Point. He also frequently provided design services to the owners of nearby properties.

In 1886, McLaren was invited, together with **Frederick Law Olmsted Sr.**, by the San Francisco Park Commissioners to examine Superintendent of Parks **William Hammond Hall**'s tree plantations at Golden Gate Park. This design was a remarkable exercise in advanced plant succession, but was in a parlous condition of neglect owing to years of inadequate funding. McLaren and Olmsted vindicated Hall's planting design and proposed forest management techniques. Hall had become the state engineer and he was unable to continue in his position. However, he agreed to train McLaren for three years as his successor.

In 1889, McLaren became superintendent of parks for the San Francisco system, a position he held for fifty-three years until his death in 1943. He immediately implemented an aggressive program of tree planting and new projects. Under his direction, the parks assumed a more gardenesque character with large plantations of rhododendrons (grown from seed) and other broad-leafed, evergreen plants. McLaren built on the foundation of Hall's design by applying the principles of imitation and experimentation. He hiked frequently in the

Portrait of John McLaren, Parks Commission, San Francisco. (Courtesy of the collection of David Streatfield)

Sierra Mountains with his friend John Muir and his designs in the park attempted to evoke the wooded slopes, wildflower meadows, waterfalls, and fern canyons that he had seen in the mountains. He corresponded with botanists and horticulturists in India, Japan, China, Australia, Tasmania, New Zealand, England, and France, seeking plants that would grow well in San Francisco. The products of these extensive searches were grown in the parks' nursery and were used throughout the city's park system. It has been estimated that McLaren was responsible for introducing more than 600 plant species into northern California.

In addition to completing Golden Gate Park, McLaren designed large estate gardens with his son Donald, who owned a nursery in San Mateo. His design approach was stated very clearly in *Gardening in California Landscape and Flower,* which was published in 1904, and reissued in three subsequent editions. This book rapidly became

Left: Huntington Falls, in Golden Gate Park, San Francisco, California (1910), was inspired by McLaren's hikes in the Sierra Mountains. (Courtesy of the collection of David Streatfield)

Below: Rotunda and colonnade of the Palace of Fine Arts, Panama Pacific International Exposition, San Francisco, California, 1910. (Courtesy of the collection of David Streatfield)

one of the most influential books on the use of plants in California. McLaren advocated natural gardens. "As our greatest painters do, go into the natural forests of our hills and hillsides, or the meadows and haughs of our valleys, and select, from the innumerable beautiful scenes, the one whose beauty most appeals to them and which seems to best fit the general outline of the site.... Let the measurement of this part of Nature's garden be carefully taken."

McLaren studied the works of William Gilpin and John Claudius Loudon very carefully and advocated planting groups with three or four varieties of a single genus. Form and habit were the most important ordering properties. Groups could be created with trees with similar shapes, such as round-headed and pyramidal, but the groups were not to be mixed. Evergreen and deciduous trees could be mixed provided they had the same shape. Where different groups met, they were to be blended

together.

In 1912, McLaren was appointed landscape engineer for the Panama Pacific International Exposition, which was to be held in 1915 on a very exposed site close to the Golden Gate Straits. He was responsible for running a huge nursery of trees, which were moved fully grown, and other stock. His designs for the various garden courts responded to Jules Guerin's color scheme, which was inspired by native wildflowers and the soft browns and gold colors of the Bay-area landscape. The various interior courts were planted to complement the diversity of architecture. In the Court of Flowers, he used Lophantha trees trimmed to a height of four feet. In The Garden of Hyacinths, Italian cypresses and balled acacias provided structure for the geometric seasonal plantings. Much of the exposition site was enclosed by a huge hedge wall, 50 feet high and 10 feet wide, which was actually a wood frame, covered with vines, suggesting an old wall covered with ancient plants.

McLaren worked closely with Bernard Maybeck at the Palace of Fine Arts to use plants that reinforced the mood of romance and melancholy that Maybeck sought. Maybeck used McLaren as a horticultural consultant on a number of his residential projects, although there is little documentation on these collaborations. An important exception is the Fagan house, Woodside (1920); the drawings are annotated by McLaren with plant names.

McLaren was a highly respected authority on plants and landscape design throughout California and elsewhere on the West Coast. In 1907 he was invited to design Graceada Park in the Central Valley city of Modesto. In 1914 he redesigned Lithia Park in Ashland, in southern Oregon.

When McLaren reached the age of mandatory retirement in 1917, the city passed a resolution allowing him to keep the position until his death and also doubled his salary. His work as a horticulturist was recognized by the Massachusetts Horticultural Society in 1923 when it awarded him the George Robert White Medal. In 1930, the Royal Horticultural Society made him an Associate of Honour, and in 1931 the University of California gave him a doctor of laws degree. By 1936, he was a local leg-

Cover of *Gardening in California* by John McLaren (San Francisco: A. M. Robertson, 1909).

end and June 7 of that year was declared McLaren Day. He died on January 12, 1943, at Park Lodge in Golden Gate Park.

Burke, Hugh M., ed. *Fortieth Annual Report of the Board of Park Commissioners of San Francisco For the Year Ended June 30th, 1910.* San Francisco: Dickinson & Scott, 1910. One of the most complete early histories of Golden Gate Park.

McLaren, John. *Gardening in California Landscape and Flower.* San Francisco, Calif.: A. M. Robertson, 1904. This book went through three editions and was widely regarded as the seminal text on gardening in California, especially the northern part of the state.

David Streatfield

MISCHE, EMANUEL TILLMAN
(1870–1934)
HORTICULTURIST, LANDSCAPE ARCHITECT

Emanuel Tillman Mische was born in Syracuse, New York, on January 29, 1870. Following his primary education, he went to work at the Missouri Botanic Garden at St. Louis. In 1894, he studied at the Bussey Institute at Harvard University. Mische secured a coveted scholarship to study at the Royal Botanic Gardens at Kew, England, in 1896 as a result of his association with Ernest O. "Chinese" Wilson, a Kew graduate, and Alfred Rehder, who traveled to and corresponded with numerous European botanical institutions. Kew personnel were so impressed with Mische that he was allowed to stay an additional six months. Mische's experience at Kew helped to develop his writing and speaking abilities and perfected his gardening and horticultural skills.

Upon returning from Kew, Mische married Nellie Mae Carpenter (1873–1963) and moved to Brookline, Massachusetts, to work in the **Olmsted Brothers** office. He arrived in 1898, the first year of the partnership between the brothers John Charles and Frederick Jr., and was trained in all aspects of the firm. He was involved in the Essex County Park commission in New Jersey, assisted with the George W. Vanderbilt estate in Asheville, North Carolina, and selected plants for arrangement in the firm's final planting plans. **John Charles Olmsted**'s influence allowed Mische to learn the diplomatic skills necessary to sell a project to a client, and also exposed Mische to the early theories of city planning. The Olmsted Brothers considered him the best-versed horticulturist in the country. In fact, in his daily letter to his wife, Sophia, John Charles Olmsted expressed his wish that Mische had joined him on his first trip to the Pacific Northwest to assist with plant identification.

Mische was influenced by the English manner of life, and the Vandyke he wore all of his life was due to that influence. He was six feet tall, pleasant-faced and bald, with mild, steady, blue eyes.

In 1906, John Charles Olmsted recommended Mische for the position of first park superintendent for Madison, Wisconsin. Mische was involved in all aspects of the mature park movement in Madison. He hired the first playground director after outfitting the parks with apparatus. Mische designed and laid out the 11-mile Boulevard Drive, Henry Vila Park, and Tenney Park. He

Emanuel T. Mische, ca. 1928. (Courtesy of the collection of Ken Guzowski)

was a member of the local horticultural society and gave valuable service to the Cemetery Commission for the improvement of Forest Hill Cemetery. Mische resigned as park superintendent in 1908. It took two men to replace him, **John Nolen** as landscape architect and William G. MacLean as park foreman.

Mische was hired as Portland, Oregon's, park superintendent on February 26, 1908. The attractive wage of $2,500 a year lured him away from Madison. Mische preceded his family by train, and Nellie Mae followed with their four children: Dorothy, Lawrence, Olive, and Clifford. Mische immediately took on responsibility for the city's street trees and all aspects of the young park system, including management of the park police, recreation department, general maintenance, engineering, horticultural division, and purchasing. All foremen and employees were under his supervision.

Before the services of the Olmsted Brothers were terminated by the Portland Park Commission on March 16, 1910, the firm completed their 1903 Park Plan for Portland. Mische took responsibility for all design work, planting plans, and maintenance for city-owned parks. These included Sellwood, Columbia, Kenilworth, Peninsula, Laurelhurst, City, Macleay, and Mt. Tabor parks, and Terwilliger Boulevard and neighborhood parks.

During Mische's Portland park years, he worked with an extremely limited budget. Under a sweeping new regime the Park Board was eliminated in 1913, and Mische was assigned the position of Landscape Architect for the City of Portland. Following a dispute with City Commissioner William L. Brewster, Mische tendered his resignation on September 9, 1914. He continued for an additional year as consulting landscape architect.

Mische submitted a plan for the design of the capitol site at Canberra, Australia, in 1912, and wrote a review of the competition in *Park and Cemetery* magazine. **Walter Burley Griffin** won this competition. As early as 1911, Mische took on the cause of the national park preservation movement in the West. He was active in the development of Oregon's only national park at Crater Lake.

From 1917 to 1919, Mische was the investigator for the Town Planning Department of the United States Housing Corporation on projects in Bremerton, Washington, and Mare Island, California. Mische wrote on the species Quisqualis and Toxylon in the first edition of **Liberty Hyde Bailey**'s *Standard Cyclopedia of Horticulture* (1916). He was a prolific writer and served as the editor of the landscape and art departments for the magazine *Parks and Recreation* from 1921 to 1923. Mische wrote the memorial and tribute for John Charles Olmsted in the April 1920 issue of the magazine. Mische was the president of the Portland City Club in 1922 and 1923 and wrote articles on topical issues related to city planning.

Mische continued with a successful private practice. In 1923, he was hired to assist Herman Brookman with the planting selections for the Lloyd Frank estate, and Julius Meier's estate, Manukah, on the Columbia River. Mische worked with Peter Kerr to finalize plant selections for the Olmsted Brothers' design at Kerr's house and garden at Elk Rock. Mische was enticed to develop parks in Los Angeles, California, and his decision to relocate resulted in a divorce from his wife. Mische's contributions to *Parks and Cemetery* magazine during his California period discussed park acquisitions in Los Angeles.

Mische was also involved in the movement to save California's redwood trees and helped to establish California's state park policies. He was committed to forest preservation, undoubtedly from his exposure to the remarkable forests in the Pacific Northwest. He wished

Bandstand at Peninsula Park, Portland, Oregon. (Photo by M. Dickel; Oregon Historical Society, OrHi89554)

to preserve native vegetation and animal life in their virgin conditions so that future generations could see a bit of the forest as it was when Lewis and Clark first explored the region. As an early environmental planner Mische labored to preserve the native flora of the West. His work contributes to the natural resource legacy that exists in the West today.

Mische became a member of the American Society of Landscape Architects in 1905, and was elected a Fellow of the Society in 1920. During his Portland years he was active in the Pacific Coast Chapter of the American Society of Landscape Architects, serving as president during 1929 and 1930.

On October 29, 1931, Mische and his son Clifford, who studied landscape architecture at Harvard, came to New York City to assist the Olmsted Brothers with the construction of Fort Tryon Park. Mische coordinated the arrival and placement of nursery stock that came from all over the East Coast. He was taken to St. Elizabeth's Hospital on April 20, 1934, with a severe case of pneumonia and pleurisy. He died in the early morning of April 23, 1934, and his body was transported to Syracuse for burial in the family plot.

Guzowski, Kenneth J. "Portland's Olmsted Vision (1897–1915): A Study of the Public Landscapes Designed by Emanuel T. Mische in Portland, Oregon." Master's thesis, University of Oregon, June 1990. This thesis documents the public landscape work of Emil Mische in Portland, Oregon, following the recommendations of John Olmsted's 1903 Park Report.

Mische, Emanuel Tillman. "In Memoriam." *Parks and Recreation,* April 1920, 52–54. A tribute to John Charles Olmsted following his death.

Mische, Emil. "Boston's Metropolitan Park System [Five Part Series]." *Park and Cemetery,* March–August 1905. A series of essays that summarize the ambitious park plans by the Olmsted firm for Boston, Massachusetts.

Ken Guzowski

MOTT, SEWARD HAMILTON
(1888–1965)
COMMUNITY PLANNER, LAND-USE ENGINEER, ADMINISTRATOR

Seward Mott was born in New York State in 1888 and was raised there. He attended high school in Rochester and briefly took classes at the University of Rochester, where he acquired strong skills in the mechanical arts. Around 1910, he went to Flint, Michigan, to work for Weston-Mott, an axle manufacturer affiliated with the General Motors Corporation. Mott married Erma Alice Willson of Flint in 1912. In 1914, he joined the practice of William Chase Pitkin Jr.,* also of Rochester, who married Mott's sister and at the time was designing a housing subdivision in Flint for General Motors employees. Mott, the able civil engineer who described himself as a "land use engineer," complemented Pitkin's training in landscape architecture and strong horticultural knowledge, enabling the firm to take on large-scale projects that blended Olmsted-inspired principles with advances in Garden City planning. The firm's work was particularly influenced by **Charles Mulford Robinson**, also from Rochester, whose writings—*Modern Civic Art* (1903) and *The Width and Arrangement of Streets* (1911)—sparked nationwide interest in the City Beautiful movement and provided the basic principles of subdivision design, the layout of streets, and neighborhood development. Pitkin & Mott* quickly gained a strong reputation for the design of fine estate grounds and residential subdivisions that attracted commissions across the Midwest and as far south as Florida. The combined talents enabled the firm to take on ambitious projects that required close attention to natural topography and streams, and to create idyllic, pastoral, and naturalistic environment.

Residential commissions waned during the Great Depression, and in 1932 Mott left the partnership, turning his attention to the new opportunities in public service. In 1934, he went to work for the Federal Housing Administration, where he headed the new agency's small-house and land-planning programs, which were intended to lower housing costs and stimulate the home building industry. In this capacity, he set standards for the attractive design of neighborhoods of small modest homes and worked with builders who were seeking federal loans. Mott brought to this field knowledge of planning and zoning deed restrictions, as well as a long practice of curvilinear subdivision design and commitment to sound neighborhood planning. Mott helped bring sound planning conventions as well as good design into the mainstream of American middle-class life. His methods of laying out curving tree-lined streets to follow the contours of the land and restrict traffic through the use of courts, circles, crescents, and cul-de-sacs would influence the landscape design of American suburbs for decades to come.

In 1944, Mott became the executive director of the Urban Land Institute, an independent research organization. There, with Max Wehrly and Harold Lautner, he edited the first edition of the *Community Builders Handbook,* a manual of professional practice, which immediately became an authoritative guide for community planning when first published in 1947 and would continue in print and be revised for several decades. Under Mott's leadership, the institute encouraged high standards for urban revitalization and suburban development in the postwar period and established councils to study the planning and design of residential areas, shopping centers, and industrial centers.

Mott returned to private practice in 1951, first as Seward H. Mott Associates and after 1955 as Mott & Hayden Associates. He gained a strong reputation for the planning of shopping centers, rental housing, and residential suburbs in the 1950s. His private commissions included Cameron Village in Raleigh, North Carolina; Seven Corners Regional Shopping Center in Fairfax County, Virginia; Village Market, in La Grange Park, Illi-

nois; and Utica Square, in Tulsa, Oklahoma. He gained considerable praise for the resort and marina complex at Mahoe Bay in the British West Indies, and won several awards from the National Association of Home Builders for his design of residential communities, including Clairemont near San Diego, California; Cotswold in Charlotte, North Carolina; Fairless Hills, Pennsylvania; and Kearney, Arizona. Mott passed away in 1965.

See also the individual entry on William Chase Pitkin Jr. and the joint entry on Pitkin & Mott. References follow the Pitkin & Mott entry.

Linda Flint McClelland and Charles T. Gleaves

MOVIUS, HALLAM LEONARD
(1880–1942)
LANDSCAPE ARCHITECT

Hallam L. Movius was born on September 22, 1880, in Buffalo, New York. Movius grew up on Delaware Avenue, surrounded by the lifestyle privileges of being a member of the Rumsey family, long prominent in that city's history. He was educated at the Nichols School, the Hill School in Pottstown, Pennsylvania, and Harvard College, graduating in 1902. Returning from a postgraduate European tour, he obtained some early work experience in the office of S. Burnett of New York, acting as landscape agent on several estates, and in **Arthur Asahel Shurcliff**'s office, before entering Harvard's Lawrence Scientific School as a student in landscape architecture. After graduation in 1907, he set up an office on State Street in Boston, later forming a partnership with Arthur G. Rotch, with another office on Park Avenue in New York City. Their practice primarily consisted of residential design for an elite clientele. In 1917, Movius was assigned to a field artillery unit that served in France. Upon his return he entered and won the competition for a campus plan for the University of Buffalo in 1919 with a design praised as showing "a breadth and simplicity of treatment together with a comprehensive grasp of the problem." Ground was broken a year later for the first McKim, Mead & White building placed according to that plan. As the university's needs changed, Ralph Adams Cram was engaged in 1930 to revise the campus plan.

Hallam L. Movius, ca. 1935. (Courtesy of Geoffrey Movius)

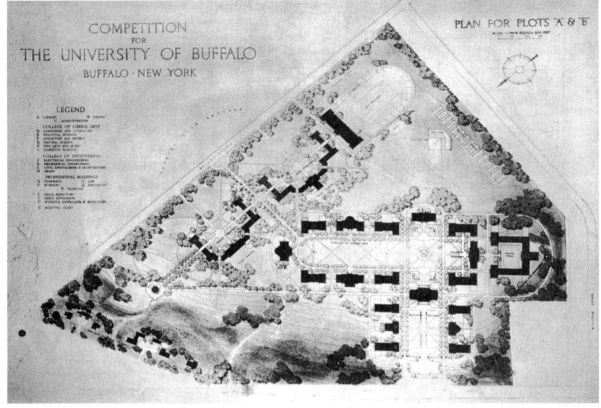

University of Buffalo campus competition plan, 1919. (Courtesy of Geoffrey Movius)

Movius continued to operate his practice out of offices in both Boston and New York until the mid-1920s, although his plans remaining in the Special Collections of the Frances Loeb Library at Harvard indicate a clientele mainly in the New England area. Additionally, Movius maintained the Red Lodge Farm in Millis, Massachusetts, where he engaged in apple and dairy farming and breeding hunting dogs, the "Boggestow Beagles." He had three children, one of whom, his son and namesake, Hallam L. Movius Jr., became a prominent professor of anthropology at Harvard, responsible for significant Stone Age discoveries.

In 1927, he entered into a partnership with Guy Hunter Lee.* Lee had previously worked with Harold Hill Blossom.* From the extant plans, it appears that these three landscape architects had a loose association, cooperating on several developments, both individual properties and small subdivisions, over the next decade. Movius often worked with architect Charles S. Keefe,

preparing the landscape layouts for substantial residential projects to achieve "a well-ordered design . . . [in] all its parts." His client roster included several prominent Bostonians whose country home grounds he designed. Included in this list was Christian Herter, his neighbor in Millis, who was appointed by Charles Hurley, then governor of Massachusetts, to work on public housing needs. Through that connection, Movius was engaged in 1940 as landscape architect for the Boston Housing Board, responsible for the site planning for Orchard Park. The challenge was to create harmonious designs for housing, providing for the necessities of drying yards, playgrounds, and common space in "dignified, livable but inexpensive projects" In this same time period, Movius was involved in the development of a master plan for the Bowdoin College campus in Brunswick, Maine, to plan for future growth. (This plan has not yet been located.) These were his last two projects. He died in Edgartown, Massachusetts, in 1942, praised in his obituary by Fletcher

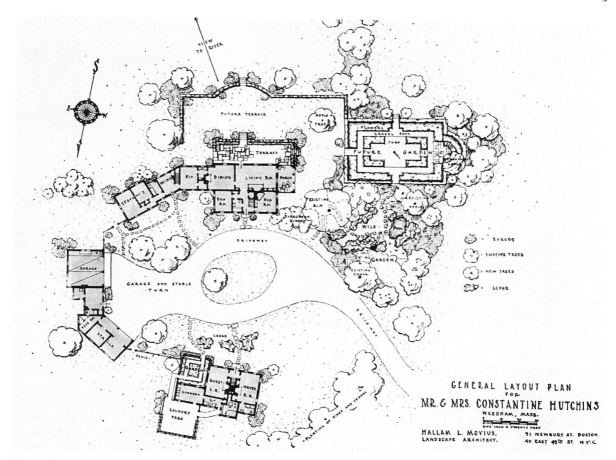

"General Layout Plan for Mr. & Mrs. Constantine Hutchins, Needham, Massachusetts," by Movius and his frequent collaborator, architect Charles S. Keefe, from "Building: Planting: Furnishing: A Collaborative Problem," *House Beautiful,* September 1931.

Steele and architect Charles Keefe for his creative skills and "sympathetic understanding" of design problems.

Heath, Richard. "Architecture as Public Policy: The History of Bromley-Heath Public Housing Development." Unpublished manuscript, 1999. Available at www.jphs.org/locales/2005/10/15/bromley-heath-public-housing-development-history.html. Interesting examination of the history of workingmen's or low-cost housing in Jamaica Plain, Massachusetts, looking at the development of public policies, philanthropy, and architectural design over the decades.

Lee, Guy H. "Building: Planting: Furnishing: A Collaborative Problem." *The House Beautiful* 70 (September 1931), 199–102, 260. Exploration of the collaborative process between architects and landscape architects; in this example, fitting a Cape Cod style complex designed by Charles Keefe into a hilly site above the Charles River with a Lee and Movius plan to preserve the scenic vistas.

Arleyn A. Levee

NAKANE, KINSAKU
(1917–1994)
LANDSCAPE ARCHITECT

Kinsaku Nakane was born in 1917 in Iwata-shi, Shizuoka Prefecture, Japan, and earned his bachelor of landscape architecture degree from the Tokyo University of Agriculture. He started his firm, Nakane and Associates Garden Research and Landscape Consultant Company, on September 1, 1966, and proceeded to research and restore many of the most important temple gardens in Kyoto, including Daisen-in Temple Garden and Jonangu Shrine Garden. He also designed and built many new Japanese-style gardens, both in Japan, including the famous Adachi Museum Garden in Shimane Prefecture (1972) and the Obori Park in Fukuoka City (1984), and around the world, including Seiwa-en Japanese Garden in Jurong New Town, Singapore (1971), the Japanese Garden at the Jimmy Carter Library and Conference Center (1986), and the Garden of the Heart of Heaven, at the Museum of Fine Arts, Boston (1988).

Nakane spearheaded the restoration of the famous Daisen-in subtemple garden. One of the most celebrated gardens in Japan, it was constructed in 1509 on the grounds of the Zen temple, Daitokuji, and was completed with the main hall in 1513. The narrow *karesansui* (dry landscape) garden surrounds the main hall on all four sides. Thought to depict a metaphorical journey through life, the garden is centered on a river that begins at the mythical Mount Horai in the northeast corner. The streambed narrows to suggest the rapids of youth and broadens to denote maturity and adulthood. In 1959, Nakane's research uncovered several missing elements that were then restored to the garden: a bell-shaped window-wall and the famous "treasure boat"—a stone in the shape of a Chinese sailing vessel that had belonged to Ashikaga Yoshimasa.

One of the most famous Nakane-designed gardens is Rakusui-en at Jonangu, the ancient Shinto guardian shrine for Kyoto that dates from 794. This two-hectare landscape has several sub-gardens, inspired by the hundred or more plants mentioned in the famous book *Genji Monogatari* (Tales of the Genji). They represent the different major periods of time in Japanese garden history: Heian, Muromachi, Momoyama, and modern. In November, an elegant poetry game is played by men and women dressed in the clothing of Heian aristocrats along the shores of the azalea stream.

The gardens that surround the Adachi Museum in Shimane Prefecture make use of the technique called *shakkei* or "borrowing the landscape." Here, Nakane used distant mountain views to form the background of his composition; the forest makes up the middle ground; and the carefully shaped mounds, highly pruned pines, and trimmed shrubs create a foreground that echoes the background landscape. Stones were collected by the owner of the museum, Zenko Adachi, from the mountains of Okayama. Windows from within the museum further frame the borrowed landscapes without.

One of Nakane's most famous creations outside of Japan is Tenshin-en, the Garden of the Heart of Heaven at the Museum of Fine Arts in Boston, which opened in 1988. This one-quarter-acre garden, located on the north side of the museum's West Wing, is named for Okakura Kakuzo, also known as Okahura Tenshin, former curator of the Museum's Department of Asiatic Art and author of *The Book of Tea*. Funded by the Nippon Television Network Corporation, the garden was built by a team of Japanese and American craftsmen. The landscape is entered through a *bukemon* medieval-style gate built by specially trained carpenters (*miya daiku*) who traveled to Boston from Kyoto, Japan, to build it. A *tsuijibei*-style traditional garden wall encloses the whole. Under Nakane's direction, 178 boulders were placed in the *karesansui* (dry landscape) garden, where scenes of nature are suggested by stones and raked gravel, forming waterfalls, mountains, islands, and the sea. *Kare* means "dry," *san* means "mountain," and *sui* means "water"—a style that harkens back to Zen temple gardens of fifteenth-century Japan. Each stone and plant was chosen from local materials. Since its opening, Tenshin-en has become a contemplative sanctuary in the city of Boston.

Nakane, who taught at the Osaka University of the Arts, always told his students that a true Japanese garden derives from the landscape around it. Toward that end, the project team that built the garden flew over New England in a small plane, exploring the region's rocky coastlines, deep forests, soft hillsides, and craggy mountains. For the next six days, Nakane, accompanied by his son and chief assistant at the time, Shiro Nakane, set the elements that made up the structure of the garden. He directed the placement of the stones, with the aid of a one-hundred-foot hydraulic crane and eight tractor-trailer truckloads of boulders, some weighing as much as eight tons. He created the traditional elements of a Japanese garden with a touch of New England: a *takiguchi* (waterfall), a *tsurujima* (Crane Island), and a *kamejima* (Tortoise Island). Three arched granite bridges link the Tortoise and the Crane islands to Tenshin-en's "mainland." Stone lanterns (*ishidoro*) from the museum's collection grace the garden, along with an ever-flowing water basin (*chozubachi*). Using the technique known as *shakkei,* Nakane captures the background landscape of Fredrick Law Olmsted Sr.'s Back Bay Fens, making it an integral part of the garden space.

Kinsaku Nakane at the Adachi Museum Garden, Shimane Prefecture, Japan. (Courtesy of Shiro Nakane)

As Nakane wrote, "One of the most important points of *karesansui* garden building is the treatment of stones. The designer must have an extremely keen sense of artistry in arranging the rocks and stones. Dozens, or even hundreds, of stones must be positioned in harmony as if they are all connected by a single invisible thread. Single stones or groups of stones must be set at exactly the spots that imply the movement of flowing water, its rush, and lethargy. Even one single rock placed out of synchronization may greatly affect the result."

In September 1986, Nakane completed a Japanese-style garden for the 35-acre Carter Center in Atlanta, Georgia, the home of the Jimmy Carter Library and Museum. The small stroll garden with a pond and two waterfalls (said to represent President Carter and his wife, Rosalynn) is known simply as the "Japanese Garden." The miniature landscape inspired by tall mountains and deep valleys is open to the public.

Nakane's influence in America is strongly felt through the impact of his writings and the works of his students and professional protégés—Nakane authored five books, including *Kyoto Gardens* published by Hoikusha and *NIWA: Meitei no Kansho to Sakutei* (Japanese Gardens: Their Enjoyment and Construction). He generously sponsored many Japanese and international students as interns in his office, many of whom have gone on to become influential in their fields, including author and landscape designer David Slawson, author of *Secret Teachings in the Art of Japanese Gardens,* and landscape architect Shinichiro Abe, principal of Zen Associates of Concord, Massachusetts, and designer of many important Japanese-style gardens in the United States, including the Peace Bell Garden at the United Nations Headquarters.

Nakane passed away in 1994. His son, Shiro Nakane, now heads Nakane and Associates, and continues his father's work by creating Japanese-style gardens around the world.

Messervy, Julie Moir. *Tenshin-En, The Garden of the Heart of Heaven.* Boston: Museum of Fine Arts, 1993. Discussion of Nakane's design intent by his former student for this 1988 commission.

Nakane, Kinsaku. *Kyoto Gardens.* Translated by Money L. Hickmans and Kaichi Minobe. 22nd ed. Osaka: Hoikusha, 1987.

Julie Moir Messervy

NICHOLSON, SIR FRANCIS
(1655–1728)

GOVERNOR, TOWN PLANNER

Born in 1655, Francis Nicholson graduated from Magdalene College in Cambridge, England, in 1677 before going into military duty, where he served in both France and Tangier. He first came to the New World in the 1680s as an infantry commander and stayed through a term as lieutenant governor of Virginia. In that period, he played a key role in the founding of the College of William and Mary, the only college ever granted a royal charter in English America and the second oldest institution of higher learning in the American colonies. As lieutenant governor, he began his planning career as he pushed for the town planning act of 1690, which stipulated that the capital of Virginia move from Jamestown to Middle Plantation, renamed Williamsburg.

Nicholson was made governor of Maryland in 1693, the second royal governor of Maryland since its change from a proprietary colony to royal province in 1691. Among his first acts as governor was the legislation that allowed him to found two new towns, Oxford and Anne Arundel. He then secured the removal of courts and Assembly from St. Mary's City to Anne Arundel, renamed Annapolis. The removal from the early colonial capital was argued in terms of the inaccessibility of the old town.

The plan for Annapolis has been described by scholars as the first baroque city plan in the New World, diverging radically from the usual grid plan of most colonial towns exemplified by the plans of Philadelphia and New Haven. The site had the commercial advantage of being on the Severn River, but also offered a variety of elevations for dramatic settings and compelling prospects. The plan of Annapolis includes two great circles, two squares, and several radiating diagonal streets. Public Circle measuring over 500 feet in diameter was the highest site and intended for the statehouse. Church Circle (now State Circle) was 300 feet in diameter. Bloomsbury Square, 350 feet on each side, inspired by the residential square of the same name in London, was never developed. The smallest square contained the public market.

Nicholson's education, social class, and military training would have brought him into contact with military and civil architecture, town planning, and landscape design. Scholars have speculated that Nicholson would have known well the baroque projects of London and Paris and presumably had direct contact with Christopher Wren and John Evelyn in the period in which both were involved with the redesign of London following the Great Fire of 1666. The plan for Annapolis is discussed as Wren-like in its system of radiating and diagonal streets leading to open spaces for monumental buildings. Planning history pioneer John Reps argued that Nicholson's design resembles Evelyn's plan for London in its irregular pinwheel of streets entering the circular or square open areas. Reps claimed Nicholson borrowed ideas from Evelyn's *The Compleat Gardener* (1693) in which garden designs employed pure geometric spaces and emphasized terminal perspectives.

Late in 1698, Nicholson returned to Virginia as governor and promoted himself as "the founder of a new City." On June 7, 1699, "An Acte Directing the Building of the Capitoll and the City of Williamsburgh" became law. It directed that ". . . two hundred and twenty acres . . . be . . . sett apart for ground on which the said City shall be built and erected according to the formal and manner laid downe in the said draught or plott." A series of buildings acts he oversaw are among the earliest detailed architectural and city planning regulations enacted in America. They had the dual concerns of the character of individual buildings as well as their surroundings. They specified lots for warehouses, half-acre house lots, setbacks of six feet for houses on the main streets, dwelling measurements of at least 20 by 30 feet, and heights of at least 10 feet at the roof's edge. Property owners had to build substantial houses within twenty-four months or forfeit their property; fencing was mandatory within six months. As the streets were laid out, they were named by the governor for the royal family and, unabashedly, for himself: Francis Street and Nicholson Street.

The plan was conceived to join the preexisting College of William and Mary and Bruton Church with a central avenue. The "Duke of Gloceter" Street, 99 feet wide, ran due east and continued almost a mile in length from the college to the new capitol, the design for which Nicholson is often credited. This boulevard linked the two grandest buildings in the British colonies. Although primarily a

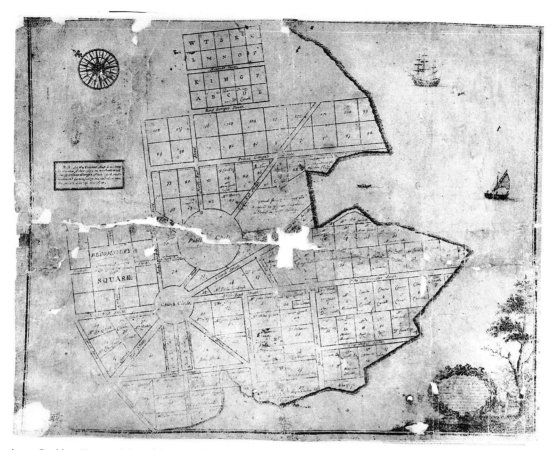

James Stoddert, "A ground platt of the citty and port of Anapolis," 1718. (Courtesy Maryland State Archives, Special Collections [Maryland State Archives Map Collection])

grid plan after the traditional orthogonal model, a grand view along the main axes culminating in public buildings gave the plan monumentality not found in other colonial towns. A broad cross axis, running in front of the Bruton Church, was twice as wide as Duke of Gloucester Street and led to the site of the governor's house. Although it is difficult to recognize them in the plan today, the grid was once embellished with diagonal avenues that formed royal initials *W* and *M*.

By 1705, the proud and difficult Nicholson was recalled from Williamsburg by Queen Anne after arousing the dislike of many. He went on from Virginia to be governor of Nova Scotia and South Carolina. In 1720, Nicholson was knighted by George I and died in London in 1728.

Hugh Jones, chronicler of Virginia in 1724, reported that in Williamsburg, "the first design of the town's form is changed on a much better [one]." Robert Beverly, author of *The History of Virginia* (1722) explained that the streets were realigned "From fanciful Ws and Ms to much more conveniences." Still, the basic design of Williamsburg remained intact.

John Stilgoe, in his *Common Landscape of America,* wrote that Francis Nicholson's designs objectified the governor's obsession with pure forms as circles and straight streets and the outdated attempts to stress form over use. Indeed, Reps called his plan for Annapolis a "caricature of baroque design." Yet, Nicholson was one of the first professional colonial administrators, held the highest government positions in six colonies, and was a tireless promoter of higher education and science,

Desandrouins Map of Williamsburg, ca. 1781–1782. (Louis Alexandre Berthier Papers, Manuscripts Division, Department of Rare Books and Special Collections, Princeton University Library)

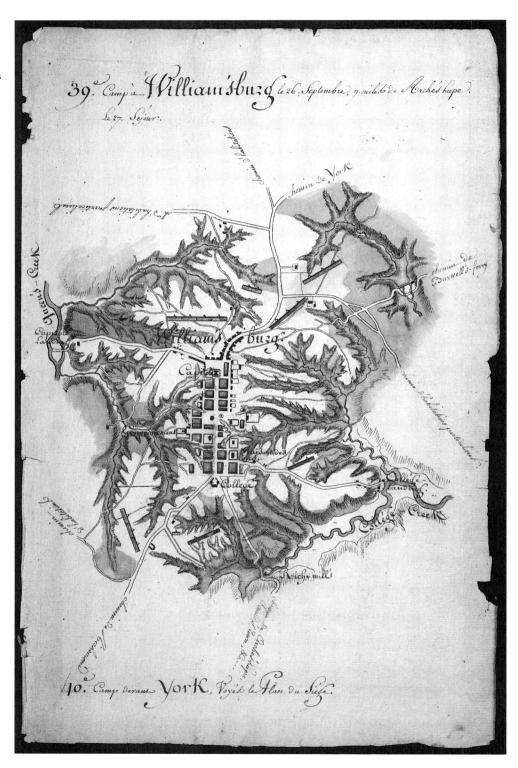

The Bodleian Plate, ca. 1738. Given by Richard Rawlinson in 1755 to the Bodelian Library, Oxford, and to the Colonial Williamsburg Foundation in 1930, it shows the public buildings of Williamsburg: the College of William and Mary, the Capitol, and the Palace. (The Colonial Williamsburg Foundation)

specifically botanical exploration. What is most significant about his career is that Nicholson raised the standard of public architecture and town planning to its highest level in the colonial period. James Kornwolf claims that he can be associated with eighty-two building projects in the course of his career in the colonies. No surviving portrait has been identified of Francis Nicholson.

Kopper, Philip. *Colonial Williamsburg*. New York: Abrams in association with Colonial Williamsburg Foundation, 1985. This work relies heavily on an earlier architectural history by Marcus Whiffen from 1949, *The Public Buildings of Williamsburg, Colonial Capital of Virginia*.

Martin, Peter. *The Pleasure Gardens of Virginia, From Jamestown to Jefferson*. Princeton, N.J.: Princeton University Press, 1991. This book represents Nicholson's plans in terms of landscape design. Martin claims that Nicholson was "aware of the exchangeability of town and garden in their architectural heritage."

Reps, John. *The Making of Urban America: A History of City Planning in the United States*. Princeton, N.J.: Princeton University Press, 1965. In his many publications, Reps has given the most complete account of how Nicholson laid out the two towns. He expounds on the impact of Wren and Evelyn on Nicholson and how he worked with the skills of a landscape designer.

Therese O'Malley

OBERLANDER, CORNELIA HAHN
(1924–)
LANDSCAPE ARCHITECT

Cornelia Hahn Oberlander was born at Muelheim-Ruhr, Germany, in 1924. Her engineer father died while she was still a child. However, predicting Germany's future course, he already had decided to move his family to the United States; her mother, a trained horticulturist, brought Cornelia and her sisters to New York. Later Cornelia's mother moved the family to an idyllic 200-acre truck farm in New Hampshire. Oberlander has said that she knew at the age of eleven that she would design parks and green spaces.

Oberlander attended Smith College in the early 1940s, attracted to its interdepartmental program in Architecture and Landscape Architecture. At Smith, she was strongly influenced by faculty member Kate Ries Koch,* a Cornell landscape architecture alumnus, who taught

Cornelia Oberlander, 2007. (Photo by Susan Cohen)

at Smith from 1919 to 1952. From Koch, Oberlander learned that landscape architecture was not just about gardens. A student paper she wrote on Pierre L'Enfant's plan for Washington, D.C., further demonstrated for her the scope of her profession and introduced her to issues of historic landscape preservation.

After gaining her diploma from Smith, Oberlander attended the Harvard Graduate School of Design, graduating in 1947. By the time Oberlander arrived, Walter Gropius and Marcel Breuer were well established in the Architecture Department. Christopher Tunnard was teaching Modern Landscape Architecture. The program encouraged collaboration across disciplines, which later would become an Oberlander trademark.

After graduating from Harvard, Oberlander worked briefly for landscape architect James C. Rose. From 1949 until 1951 she was at the Regional Plan Association in New York City, working primarily on plans for small metropolitan-area communities. By 1951, Oberlander moved to Philadelphia to serve as Community Planner for the Citizens' Council on City Planning, an organization dedicated to involving local citizens in the planning process. Here she designed landscapes for community gardens; in one case, members of the community implemented a local park she designed. Such work brought her to the attention of the noted architect Oskar Stonorov, who enlisted her for his Schuylkill Falls public housing project (1952 to 1955), with Daniel Urban Kiley* as senior landscape architect. Kiley then asked her to come and work with him at his office in Charlotte, Vermont. Here she learned how to write specifications and the technical side of landscape installation. She also worked with Kiley and architect Louis Kahn on Philadelphia's Millcreek Housing Project. During these years, she established and confirmed her central ethic of the social responsibility of the landscape architect; over time, she would extend this ethic to include site ecology. She did not rely on a "style" of design, but rather followed a process that allowed each project to be a unique solution, from conception to installation. She learned how, as a designer, to exert control over projects through developing careful details and specifications as well as actively engaging in the design implementation and installation process.

In 1953, Oberlander moved to Vancouver, Canada, with

her husband and classmate, architect and city planner H. Peter Oberlander, who had been asked to found a School of Community and Regional Planning at the University of British Columbia. For Cornelia, this was a new landscape to understand and interpret, with its unique native flora and fauna. One of Oberlander's powerful early Canadian works was the landscape for the University of British Columbia faculty club (1956 to 1958) designed in collaboration with architect Frederick Lassarre. She also continued to collaborate on projects in the United States, including a 4-acre playground at 18th and Bigler streets in Philadelphia, the Philadelphia International Airport landscape, and Cherokee Housing in Germantown, Pennsylvania, again with Oskar Stonorov. She continued to design playgrounds; her most influential, the Children's Creative Center at Expo '67 in Montreal, served 30,000 children. She eventually designed some seventy playgrounds in Canada and worked toward the establishment of a national Task Force on Play.

Oberlander's first very large project was Robson Square in Vancouver, a provincial government center and courthouse complex (1974 to 1979), with architect Arthur Erickson; Erickson, Raoul Robillard and Oberlander collaborated as the landscape architecture team to create the extensive roof garden. Another major challenge for Oberlander was the integration of the building and site of the University of British Columbia's Museum of Anthropology (1975 to 1977), with Arthur Erickson. Oberlander collaborated with Erickson in designing this landscape as an outdoor museum, specifying the native vegetation used by Canada's First Nations based on ethnobotanical studies.

For the National Gallery of Canada in Ottawa, designed by Parkin/Safdie Architects, Oberlander based her vision for the site on the painting *Terre Sauvage* by A. Y. Jackson, a member of the Group of Seven. She used it as a con-

Above: The Retention pond at Discovery Parks, Burnaby, British Columbia, completed 1982, creates a parklike setting and exhibits Oberlander's commitment to stormwater management and ecological design. (Photo by Cornelia H. Oberlander)

Below: Cornelia Oberlander's first residential project in Vancouver, a low-maintenance heather planting on a slope bordering gravel courtyard, Friedman garden, Vancouver, British Columbia, completed 1953. (Photo by Cornelia H. Oberlander)

ceptual starting point from which to interpret Canada's northern "taiga" landscape for this 1984 to 1989 commission. The resulting designed landscape showed Oberlander's ability to create an elemental, primordial design, merging the landscape's primal strength with her own minimalist design. From 1989 to 1994, she developed the landscape design for Safdie's Ottawa City Hall, and from 1992 to 1995, she worked with Moshe

The University of British Columbia's Museum of Anthropology, Vancouver, British Columbia. (Photo by Charles A. Birnbaum)

Safdie and Associates/Downs Archambault and Partners in the design of an inaccessible (for viewing only) roof garden for Library Square in Vancouver.

Working with Rolland/Towers, Oberlander served as landscape architect for the 1995 to 1997 master plan of her alma mater, Smith College, in Northampton, Massachusetts, a plan based upon work done by **Frederick Law Olmsted Sr.** in 1892. Some of her other recent designs include the landscape setting for the New York Times Building in New York City, with H. M. White Site Architects and Architect Renzo Piano; the landscape for the Canadian Embassy in Berlin, with Kuwabara Payne McKenna Blumberg Architects; and the landscape with a green roof of the Waterfall Building in Vancouver, with Erickson and Nick Milkovich Architects. In 2001, she also completed the Jim Everett Memorial Park on University of British Columbia Endowment Lands, with a wetland that permits the site not to require connection to the city storm sewer system. The American Institute of Architects cited the C. K. Choi Building–Institute for Asian Research by Matsuzaki Architects with Oberlander at the University of British Columbia as one of North America's best examples of environmentally responsible design.

Cornelia Hahn Oberlander is considered by many to be the "Dean of Canadian Landscape Architects" and has done much to bring world-class landscape design to western Canada. For her life's work and contributions to the profession of landscape architecture, Oberlander as been awarded fellowship in the both the Canadian and the American Societies of Landscape Architects, as well as honorary doctoral degrees from the University of British Columbia (1991), Ryerson Polytechnic University (1999), Simon Fraser University (2002), and Smith College (2003). Oberlander served as president of the Canadian Society of Landscape Architects from 1986 to 1987. In addition to her many published articles Oberlander recently coauthored with Elisabeth Whitelaw and Eva Matsuzaki an *Introductory Manual for Greening Roofs for Public Works and Government Services Canada.*

Leccese, Michael. "Canadian Modern." *Landscape Architecture* 79, no. 10 (December 1989), 64–69.

Moorehead, Steven, and Gordon Grice, eds. "Cornelia Hahn Oberlander." *Landscape Architecture.* Gloucester, Mass.: Rockport Publishers, Inc., 1997, 164–169.

Preston, Brian. "An Affinity for Natural Beauty." *Imperial Oil Review* 78, no. 413 (Summer 1994), 18–21.

Noel D. Vernon

OGLETHORPE, JAMES EDWARD
(1696–1785)

CITY PLANNER, FOUNDER OF THE STATE OF GEORGIA, PHILANTHROPIST

James Edward Oglethorpe was born in December 1696 in London. In 1714 he entered Corpus Christi College in Oxford, the same year he enlisted in the army of Prince Eugene of Savoy. On the recommendation of John Churchill, 1st Duke of Marlborough, he secured the position of aide-de-camp to the prince. From 1716 to 1717, he served with distinction in the campaign against the Turks. He returned to England in 1722.

In the late 1720s, as a member of the English House of Commons, Oglethorpe and a group of prison reformers conceived the plan to develop a colony on the right bank of the Savannah River. The colony would provide a shield for the southern frontier of the British colonies against incursions of Spaniards, attacks of Indians, and depredations of fugitive slaves. The resulting city of Savannah was an agricultural experiment, a piece of practical philanthropy, and a military expedition.

Oglethorpe secured the cooperation of wealthy and influential patrons with the promise of relieving the burden of debtor's prisons and workhouses through colonization. On June 9, 1732, a charter was made for "The Trustees for establishing a Colony of Georgia in America." Georgia was the last of the thirteen colonies to be founded in America. Oglethorpe proposed the new colony with goals beyond the defense against the Spanish in Florida to protect the Carolinas: England's poor and victims of religious persecution would find refuge and the colony would be a buyer's market for raw materials and a seller's market for manufactured goods. Although the poorest of the colonies, it had an elaborate promotional campaign that was so successful that during recruitment the debtors and disenfranchised were usurped by small businessmen. Recent scholarship suggests that James Oglethorpe was the author of many of the important promotional tracts and maps for the Savannah experiment.

City planning historian John Reps wrote that the design for Savannah was truly a regional plan. While it owed much to the agricultural village patterns of New England, it brought these patterns into geometric order. Each colonist was deeded one house lot, one garden lot of 5 acres, and one farm of 50 acres. The grid plan of the city of Savannah, still intact today, was based on a repeating module made up of a public square surrounded by

Portrait of James Edward Oglethorpe, 1744. (Courtesy of Edwin Jackson, Carl Vinson Institute of Government, University of Georgia)

four trust lots and four "tythings" of ten house lots each. Major axial streets divided the town in four quarters or wards, each with a single module. This model was repeated over the first twelve years so that by the mid-eighteenth century there were twenty-four squares. Savannah's public squares were an integral part of the town's circulation system and served as the site of markets, military drills, and playgrounds. The typical houses were freestanding against the streets with ample gardens to the side and to the rear. The plan has been described as equalitarian because it established no central point of authority and its neighborhood unit was indefinitely repeatable without ultimate borders.

Savannah was an integrated society not only by virtue of its pattern of open squares and system of land tenure but by the organization of public services. It had a public mill, a public granary and storehouse, and a public nursery from which settlers could procure plants for

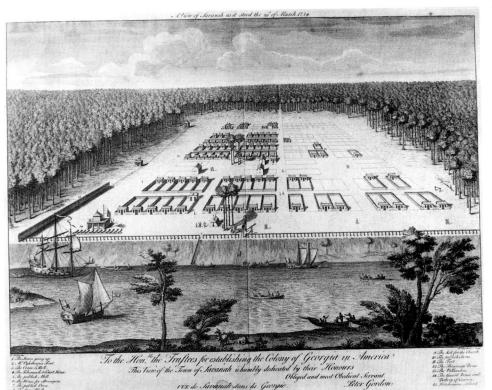

View of Savannah, Georgia; engraving by P. Foudrinier after a drawing by Peter Gordon, 1734. (University of Georgia Libraries, Hargrett Rare Book and Manuscript Library)

their gardens and where the colony's experimental horticulture was directed. One side of the corporate seal of Georgia depicted two figures carrying spades, suggesting agriculture as the chief employment of the new colony. On the reverse of the seal, silk worms in various stages of labor suggest silk production as the most profitable employment. The Trustees Garden was established at the colony's founding on 10 acres located to the east of town. Robert Miller, a trustee gardener and botanist, was employed to collect various seeds from many countries to be sent to Georgia where they were to be grown for experimental purposes. Documents in 1740 reported that the garden had "a nursery of oranges, olives, white mulberries, figs, peaches, and many herbs; besides which there is cabbage, peas, and other European pulse and plants, which all thrive." Oglethorpe insisted that the "arts of Indian agriculture" be taught to the Georgia colonists. The concept was supported by Sir Hans Sloane, the Duke of Richmond, the Earl of Derby, and Lord Petre, who were among the richest and most active botanical collectors in England.

Sephardic Jews and German Protestants were among the first colonists in Georgia, attesting to a notable level of toleration. However, toleration had its limits in Savannah; Roman Catholics and attorneys were prohibited. Oglethorpe believed that three critical laws were essential to the creation of a model society: Indians had to be treated fairly, particularly in regards to trade; there was a prohibition against entry of free blacks or Negro slaves into Georgia; and rum and any other kind of "spirits or strong waters by whatsoever name" were forbidden both in Savannah and Indian country.

Few American new town plans have received the scholarly attention of Savannah. Its author drew upon great learning and experience as a military man and ardent imperialist. Suggested sources for Oglethorpe's model range from Roman castramentation to seventeenth- and eighteenth-century treatises (including Scamozzi, Castell, and Cataneo) to contemporary English urban planning (particularly fortified towns in Northern Ireland). Recent scholarship has argued persuasively that Freemasonry was integral to the Georgia colony

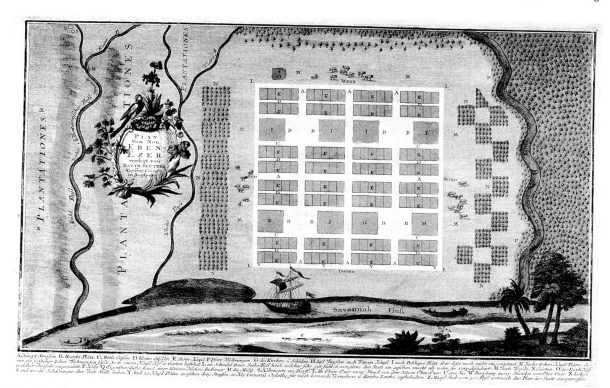

Plan of New Ebenezer, Georgia, 1740. (Courtesy of John W. Reps)

experiment, based on the predominance of Freemasons among the trustees, including Oglethorpe, as well as the ritual and policies recorded in the founding documents. Oglethorpe's military career travels in Sicily may have influenced his plan for Savannah, which resembles town plans in that country. However, Oglethorpe and his aids fashioned a new community out of older models that constituted real innovations in urban design. In addition to allowing for urban expansion, the basic module of ward, public square, and local streets provided a humanly scaled, convenient, and socially cooperative pattern ideal for frontier settlement.

James Oglethorpe is given credit for several other town plans in Georgia, including New Ebenezer and Darien, communities planned or influenced by the Savannah model of common land and sites reserved for public use. Two other new towns planned by Oglethorpe, Frederica and Augusta, were defense outposts and not based on the Savannah pattern of wards with open squares. Oglethorpe returned to England in July 1743. Renowned as a heroic colonizer, he continued his career in Parliament and the life of a gentleman among the literary and artistic luminaries of the day. He passed away at Cranham Hall, in Essex in 1785.

Kornwolf, D. James, with Georgiana W. Kornwolf. *Architecture and Town Planning in Colonial North America.* Baltimore: Johns Hopkins University Press, 2002. This massive, three-volume comprehensive survey of architecture, landscape design, and town planning is the result of decades of study and collection and is a major source of maps, drawings, and photographs as well as bibliography.

Reinberger, Mark. "Oglethorpe's Plan of Savannah: Urban Design, Speculative Freemasonry and the Enlightened Charity." *The Georgia Historical Quarterly* 81, no. 4 (Winter 1997), 839–62.

Reps, John. *The Making of Urban America: A History of City Planning in the United States.* Princeton, N.J.: Princeton University Press, 1965. John Reps has written more than anyone on the plan of Savannah.

Therese O'Malley

OSMUNDSON, THEODORE
(1921–2009)
LANDSCAPE ARCHITECT, PHOTOGRAPHER

Theodore Osmundson, known as Ted, was born in Portsmouth, Virginia, in 1921, and graduated from Iowa State University with a bachelor of science degree in landscape architecture in 1943. In that same year he married his wife Lorraine Wiese, with whom he has raised three sons, one of whom, Gordon, is a landscape architect. Osmundson began his professional career in San Francisco working for brief stints with **Thomas Dolliver Church** and Garrett Eckbo,* as well as a landscape superintendent in a Bay area nursery. By 1946 he opened his own office. At a time when there were very few landscape architects in the San Francisco Bay area, his first commission was the $200 design for a garden for a doctor in Berkeley. During nearly sixty years of professional practice, he was responsible for designs of numerous residential landscapes, parks, playgrounds, college campuses, recreation areas, historic properties, and rooftop landscape developments (now referred to as landscape on structure). Osmundson is best known for his design, with David Arbegast, of the Kaiser Center Roof Garden in Oakland, California. During these early years, he designed a great many private gardens throughout the Bay area. He used his emerging skills as a photographer, documenting his own work, and sent photographs to many popular magazines, including *Sunset, House Beautiful,* and *House and Garden.* The photographs were published with full credit to him as both designer and photographer. Throughout the rest of his career, he built up an impressive body of work of landscape photography. Wherever he traveled, he seldom was without one or more cameras from his extensive collection.

His writings included articles on school site design, flood control, integration of art into the landscape, electrical transmission line alignment, and rooftop landscape development. His book *Roof Gardens, History, Design and Construction* (1999) is the definitive reference on this subject and is widely used throughout the world.

In addition to these accomplishments, Osmundson was a supreme builder of institutions and organizations related to his chosen profession. Early in his career, he realized that the individual professional, working alone, had very little impact, while a group, working together, could accomplish a great deal in a very short period of time. Osmundson joined the California Association of

"Ted" Osmundson and John Simonds on a trip to the Grand Canyon, 1994. (Courtesy of Lorraine Osmundson)

Landscape Architects in 1950 and quickly became its president. This organization spearheaded the movement toward the passage of the first state licensing law for landscape architects in the United States in 1953. He became the trustee of the American Society of Landscape Architects (ASLA) representing the Northern California Chapter. During this time he served on visiting teams for the accrediting of landscape architecture programs under the auspices of the ASLA Committee on Education. In 1963, he was elected a Fellow in the ASLA and at the same time became a vice president of the society. In 1967, he was elected the national president. On July 4, 1966, he was one of the six founders of the ASLA Foundation (now the Landscape Architecture Foundation) at Independence Hall in Philadelphia, Pennsylvania.

Osmundson made his greatest contribution to the profession in his capacity as president of the ASLA and the ASLA Foundation. His 1968 work program called for engaging a professional association management firm to assist in the reorganization and management of the ASLA; the development of a "Handbook of Professional Practice" and a "Handbook of Landscape Architectural Construction"; the organization of a Landscape Architecture Bookstore; a program of minority recruitment; the development of guidelines for barrier-free site design; a study of the improved school site design; the initiation of an index to graduate work in landscape architecture; and study of the profession. All of these projects were accomplished during his term as president and were expanded as he became the president of the ASLA Foundation. In that position, he initiated a publications program, organized a leadership meeting at the Roland Conference Center, and sought and obtained grants from the Educational Facilities Laboratory, the National Endowment for the Arts, the Ford Foundation, the National Park Service, and the Department of Housing and Urban Development. At the end of his term with the Foundation, the income generated from the sale of publications, grants, and contracts exceeded the income of the society itself from membership dues and the annual meeting. In 1968, during his presidency of the ASLA, his leadership success enabled the hiring of the first staff to the newly emerging Council of Landscape Architectural Registration Boards (CLARB) until that organization could generate the necessary capital to support its own independent operations.

In 1991, Osmundson was elected to the presidency of the International Federation of Landscape Architects (IFLA), where his expansive management style came in conflict with the more conservative approach of some of the other national organizations. As a result of his observations, he recommended that the ASLA withdraw from the international organization until they improved and

Above: Kaiser Center, Oakland, California. (Photo by Ted Osmundson)

Below: Kaiser Center roof garden under construction, Oakland, California. (Photo by Ted Osmundson)

streamlined their organizational structure and management practices. The ASLA complied with his suggestions and when the problems were corrected he recommended that the ASLA support the international organization once again.

When Osmundson was awarded the ASLA Medal in 1983 for his extraordinary contributions to the profession, the award read: "Few landscape architects, if any, have made a greater contribution to their profession than has Theodore Osmundson. As talented designer, as world-wide spokesman for the profession, as renowned lecturer and accomplished author, his dedicated concern for excellence brings honor and recognition to our profession."

Theodore Osmundson maintained his practice for sixty years while contributing to the profession through his volunteer efforts on behalf of all of the major organizations related to landscape architecture. His impact affected everyone who has practiced landscape architecture in the last half century, and this influence will likely continue for many years to come. Osmundson resided with his wife Lorraine in Kensington, California, where he died on April 9, 2009. Their son Gordon is a landscape architect practicing in the Bay Area.

Osmundson, Theodore. Articles in *Landscape Architecture:* "How A Profession Began," January 1965; "The Changing Technique of Roof Garden Design," March 1979; and "Sculpture Garden/Garden Sculpture," January 1983.

Osmundson, Theodore. *Roof Gardens, History, Design and Construction.* Evanston, Ill.: W. W. Norton & Co., 1999. The definitive textbook on the subject. Richly illustrated.

Osmundson, Theodore. "What Accreditation Has Meant to Landscape Architecture." *Hortscience,* January 1968. An important early article on the topic.

Gary O. Robinette

OWENS, HUBERT BOND
(1905–1989)
LANDSCAPE ARCHITECT, EDUCATOR

Hubert Owens was born in 1905 in Canon, Georgia, in the foothills of the Blue Ridge Mountains in northeast Georgia. Both his father and mother came from planter families. The Owens family farm operation consisted of large tracts of cotton land, acreage in corn and wheat, pasturage for dairy and beef cattle, timberland, and fruit orchards. The family also operated gins, a fertilizer warehouse, and a cottonseed mill.

After graduating from Canon High School, Owens spent a year preparing for college in Beaumont, Texas, with an older sister and her husband. The new and different natural environment, the dynamism of the southeast Texas oil economy, and the scholarly environment provided by his brother-in-law's family had a marked influence on Owens. As he witnessed lots for new houses being developed under the supervision of a New York landscape architect, he became interested in pursuing the profession of landscape architecture.

Owens attended the University of Georgia from 1922 until his graduation in 1926 with a bachelor of science degree in agriculture, majoring in horticulture and landscape gardening. He took a teaching position in northwest Georgia at Berry Junior College and the Boys High

Hubert Owens with foreman, Athens, Georgia. (Courtesy of Owens Library, School of Environmental Design, University of Georgia)

School in Mount Berry in the fall of 1926. His pursuit of a landscape architecture degree led him to travel to numerous colleges to continue his studies and to follow his vision for a landscape architecture program at the University of Georgia. By May 1928, funds had been appropriated by the Georgia State Legislature for the establishment of a landscape architecture program at the University of Georgia and Owens was offered a position as adjunct professor. For the first nine years of the program, Owens was the program's only professor. During this time, he spent five summers studying landscape architecture with Professor E. Gorton Davis at Cornell University and with Professor **Bremer Whidden Pond** at Harvard. He drew on resources within the University of Georgia, particularly with Dr. T. H McHatton in the Horticulture Division, and H. W. Harvey at the University of Georgia Extension Service. Also during this time, Owens completed a master's degree in education at the University of Georgia in 1933.

Serpentine garden, Founders Memorial Garden, University of Georgia, Athens, Georgia. (Courtesy of Owens Library, School of Environmental Design, University of Georgia)

Owens instituted the practice of student field trips to inspect and study estates, highway projects, Civilian Conservation Corps public works, college campuses, and towns throughout the southeast. At the University of Georgia, Owens also instituted the "terminal project" as a graduation requirement for both the undergraduate and graduate degrees. This was an actual assignment in landscape architecture working with a client outside the school. The student was required to create a design; make freehand sketches, construction drawings, and a scale model; and produce a typed and bound written report. The terminal project concept not only provided valuable experience to the student but also channeled talent and resources into the community at large. The terminal project has since been adopted at other schools across the country.

Over a forty-five-year tenure, Owens built a nationally recognized landscape architecture program at the University of Georgia, which became one of the largest departments in the United States. In the late 1960s, the program became a separate school within the university due to Owens's vision and perseverance. In 1969, he was named the first dean of the School of Environmental Design. Owens retired as dean emeritus in 1973.

Owens served as president of the International Federation of Landscape Architects (IFLA) from 1974 to 1976. He was a Fellow of the American Society of Landscape Architects (ASLA), and served as the society's president from 1965 to 1967. Owens was active in research on the education of landscape architects in both organiza-

tions. In the late 1960s, as the IFLA's chairman of the Committee on Education, he managed a worldwide survey of landscape architecture schools. As a result of the survey, the committee was able to develop a set of minimum requirements for landscape architecture education. Owens insisted, however, that local needs and conditions be respected and taken into consideration in the recommendations.

Owens enthusiastically supported garden clubs in Georgia and across the United States. He believed that any social benefit that landscape architecture's contribution of technical and horticultural knowledge might bring to the clubs would be multiplied many times over through the member's work in conservation, beautification, and historic preservation. In the late 1930s, Owens began work with the Garden Club of Georgia to establish a plant collection and memorial on the University of Georgia campus. This project incorporated a two-story, brick former residence and a brick kitchen and smokehouse on a 2.5-acre garden site. The garden became known as the Founders Memorial Garden in honor of the twelve original members of the Ladies' Garden Club of Athens, which was established in 1891 as the first garden club in America.

Owens worked with garden clubs on highway beautification projects and on establishing national standards for judging club flower shows. From 1952 to 1957, he served on the National Council of Garden Clubs' executive board. Owens worked to pair members of the ASLA across the country with local garden clubs in order to share resources. He also promoted the establishment of garden-club scholarship funds at the state and national level for the study of landscape architecture.

Continuing an active private practice for more than forty years, Owens's strongest influence and design vocabulary was in the Colonial Revival style. He designed numerous private gardens for clients throughout Georgia. He worked on such prominent and diverse projects as the Oak Ridge National Laboratory Grounds in Oak Ridge, Tennessee; the Berry College campuses near Rome, Georgia; and Callaway Gardens in Pine Mountain, Georgia. He was president of the Georgia Urban Design Council in the late 1960s. He received an award from the Georgia Trust for Historic Preservation and from the Athens-Clarke Heritage Foundation for his work in preservation.

Owens's memoir, *Personal History of Landscape Architecture in the Last Sixty Years 1922–1982,* was published by the University of Georgia Alumni Society in 1983. The book covers his personal quest to become a teacher of landscape architecture; his involvement in the organizations of ASLA, IFLA, and the National Council of University Instructors of Landscape Architecture; his years at the University of Georgia and the formation of the School of Environmental Design and his service to garden clubs; and the building of the Founders Memorial Garden. Owens relates the difficulties he encountered in the early 1920s in his search for an education in landscape architecture. As faculty member and administrator he spent his professional career not only educating students but also improving teaching techniques and educational methods. Sir Geoffrey Jellicoe states in the prologue to Owens's autobiography that Owens "was dedicated to the cause of landscape architecture rather than landscape architects."

In 1963, Owens contributed an essay on landscape architecture professional training to the *Encyclopedia Britannica.* He lectured on landscape architecture all over the world. He had a fundamental personal commitment to the profession of landscape architecture. The landscape architect, he once wrote, "works for beauty and order in the face of thoughtless bulldozers . . . the ravages of time and weather, and a modern tempo of living which often leaves little time or patience for the conservation of natural resources or the preservation of human dignity."

In a speech to the International Federation of Landscape Architects in Istanbul in September 1976, Owens reviewed landscape architecture's changing role over the course of the mid-twentieth century. He noted that at the universities where landscape architecture training was offered, their staff had risen to the challenge of adapting their curricula to meet a whole new range of profession-transforming public needs in landscape architecture, public planning, and historic preservation. Though speaking of university staff at institutions across the world, he might have been commenting on and summing up his own life and career when he said: "Through constant, dedicated hard work, they comprehended and analyzed . . . and built curricula to train landscape architects to meet the challenges of contemporary life." Owens passed away on March 13, 1989, in Athens, Georgia.

The Hubert Bond Owens Collection and the Dean Hubert Owens Private Practice Landscaping Projects, 1939–1967 Collection, University of Georgia Libraries, University of Georgia, Athens, include Owens's records as a designer, professor, and dean, with project drawings, client files, and photographs.

Owens, Hubert Bond. *Personal History of Landscape Architecture in the Last Sixty Years 1922–1982.* Athens: University of Georgia Alumni Society, 1983. Owens's personal reminiscences of the years spent building the program at the University of Georgia, and espousing the benefits of landscape architecture.

René D. Shoemaker

PALMER, MILTON MEADE
(1916–2001)

LANDSCAPE ARCHITECT, EDUCATOR

M. Meade Palmer, Meade to all who knew him, was born May 13, 1916, in Washington, D.C. He was raised in Arlington, Virginia, and graduated from Washington-Lee High School. His father was a Washington landscape contractor who inspired a keen interest in plants and landscape. Meade recalled, "I can't remember when I didn't want to be a landscape architect." He attended Cornell University and received a bachelor's degree in landscape architecture in 1939.

Palmer's academic training at Cornell was shaped by the Beaux-Arts tradition and influences from the modernist movement of the 1930s. He observed that design education at Cornell encouraged a close relationship and exchange of ideas between students of architecture and landscape architecture, an experience that prepared him for many collaborative associations with architects in later years.

He began his professional career as an employee with the Arlington County, Virginia, Planning Department. From 1941 to 1942 he was an intern in the office of **Charles Freeman Gillette**, noted landscape architect in Richmond, Virginia, and protégé of **Warren Henry Manning**. Palmer enlisted in the United States Naval Reserve during World War II, serving in the South Pacific. After the war he stayed for a two-year period to work on housing reconstruction as a site-planning engineer. In 1963, he retired from the U.S. Navy as a lieutenant commander.

Palmer opened a landscape architecture practice in Warrenton, Virginia, in 1948, maintaining a small professional office at 57 Culpeper Street for over fifty years. Described as a general practitioner of landscape architecture, he designed parks, historic sites, schools, residences, country estates, parkways, urban plazas, and town plans. Meade's work emphasized the importance of site context and was inspired by an intuitive, practical, and harmonious reading of the landscape. Palmer

Meade Palmer at pedestrian bridge, Lyndon B. Johnson Memorial Grove, Washington, D.C., 1976. (Papers of Meade Palmer, MSS 12210, Special Collections, University of Virginia Library)

expressed his belief that "we should treat nature with the greatest of care and try to do what we do so that it blends with nature . . . that when we get through, a person can not tell whether we have been there or not."

He commonly used traditional building forms and materials such as stone, wood, and brick, interpreted with a contemporary eye for simplicity, abstract line, and form. The site plan for Bull Run Regional Park in Virginia was conceived to preserve the existing natural piedmont landscape while introducing park facilities and roads as unobtrusively as possible. Picnic shelters in the park illustrate creative design interpretation using simple line and form to recall the region's history and imagery of Civil War camp tents. Palmer observed that "as far as landscape architecture is concerned, less is more, because we're dealing with a very dynamic process, a growing process."

Recognized for his prodigious knowledge and affection for plants, Palmer had a particular interest in the

Right: Aerial view, Lyndon B. Johnson Memorial Grove, Washington, D.C., 1976. (Papers of Meade Palmer, MSS 12210, Special Collections, University of Virginia Library)

Below: Carter's Grove Country Road, Tutter's Neck Creek Bridge over tidal marsh, Colonial Williamsburg, Virginia, 1979. (Papers of Meade Palmer, MSS 12210, Special Collections, University of Virginia Library)

native plants of a region. He often specified native species for use in his work. He championed the unique role of plants in design, stating "the designing of plants in the out-of-doors is one of the finest of the fine arts and I can think of none that compares with it in complexity. We, landscape architects, are the only ones that are trained to do planting design and I think we ought to glory in it."

A regionalist by nature, Palmer knew the Virginia landscape intimately and found inspiration in the region's particular beauty, varied topography, and history. Virginia, Maryland, and Washington, D.C., became the canvas for many of his built projects. Experiences in the South Pacific during and after World War II and travels through Southeast Asia and China in later years broadened his appreciation of regional landscape.

Selected projects spanning many years of practice include: Lyndon B. Johnson Memorial Grove on the Potomac, Washington, D.C.; Carter's Grove Country Road, Colonial Williamsburg, Virginia; Bull Run Regional Park, Fairfax, Virginia; Mount Rogers State Park, Grayson County, Virginia; The Garth at Washington National Cathedral, Washington, D.C.; Lake Anne Village Center at Reston, Virginia; Historic Green Springs Land-use Study, Louisa County, Virginia; James Madison University, Harrisonburg, Virginia; Woodlawn Plantation, Mount Vernon, Virginia; State Office Building and Governor's House, Annapolis, Maryland; St. Albans School and National Cathedral School, Washington, D.C.; Mason Neck State Park, Fairfax, Virginia; J. D. Rockefeller Residence, Washington, D.C.; Organization for American States Headquarters, Washington, D.C.; Point of Honor Historic Site, Lynchburg, Virginia; Adams Morgan Community Park West, Washington, D.C.; Marriott Corporation Headquarters, Montgomery County, Maryland; Virginia Museum of Fine Arts, Richmond, Virginia; Tomb of the Unknowns at Arlington Cemetery, Arlington, Virginia; Capitol Street Development and Darden Garden, Virginia State Capitol, Richmond, Virginia; Restoration at Dumbarton Oaks, Washington, D.C.; President's Garden, University of Virginia, Charlottesville, Virginia.

Palmer was commissioned in Washington, D.C., to design the Lyndon B. Johnson Memorial Grove in 1972. This "living memorial," completed in 1976, is a distinct example of a nonarchitectural celebration of a U.S. president in the nation's capital. A grove of 800 white pines was planted throughout the 17-acre Lady Bird Johnson Park. A spiraling walkway flanked by pines culminates in a large flagstone terrace with a 19-foot granite megalith quarried in Texas as the central focus.

From the terrace, a view opens across the Potomac River to a panorama of Washington, D.C. The memo-

"General Development Plan for Bull Run Park," Manassas, Virginia, 1967. (Papers of Meade Palmer, MSS 12210, Special Collections, University of Virginia Library)

rial received the National Landscape Award from the American Association of Nurserymen and the Grand Award from the American Landscape Contractors Association.

The design for Carter's Grove Country Road was conceived as a 7-mile parkway and journey back into early American history. Completed in 1979, the one-way, 12-foot-wide, non-engineered roadway between Colonial Williamsburg, Virginia, and the eighteenth-century Carter's Grove Plantation on the James River meanders through an unspoiled landscape of forest, field, and tidal marsh. Noted architect and colleague Jaquelin Robertson commented, "those who know that road understand the subtlety of its design and can see there landscape art at its most refined level." The project was given a National Award for Design Excellence from the U.S. Department of Transportation and the National Endowment for the Arts.

With colleagues Joseph Bosserman and Harry Porter, Palmer was a founding member of the Department of Landscape Architecture at the University of Virginia. For more than thirty years, he taught courses on plant identification and planting design to students at the university.

A fellow teacher described "the often repeated scene of a first-year class struggling to keep pace with the white-haired, yet spry and wiry gentleman in a bow tie, scrambling up hill and dale through tangled woods in search of a plant specimen." He was well known for an annual spring class fieldtrip to Washington, D.C., where the National Arboretum became his outdoor classroom. In 1986, Palmer was the honored speaker at the Fifth Annual Symposium on Landscape Architecture at the University of Virginia entitled "The Work of Meade Palmer—Sixty Years of Landscape Architecture."

An active member of the American Society of Landscape Architects, Palmer was made a Fellow in 1958. He served the ASLA in many official capacities including chairman of the Council of Fellows and first vice president of the society.

Awards and honors include the Allied Professions Award (1988) from the Virginia Society of the American Institute of Architects, the American Society of Landscape Architects Medal (1991), the society's highest award, and an Honorable Mention in the design competition for the Vietnam War Veterans Memorial. In 2003, in his honor, the Virginia Chapter of the American

Society of Landscape Architects created the M. Meade Palmer Medal to be awarded to a selected individual for outstanding contributions to landscape architecture.

Palmer served the community in numerous advisory roles including chair of the Fauquier County, Virginia, Planning Commission and County Zoning Administrator, as well as contributing as an active member to state and national organizations. Recognized for his light-hearted sense of humor and gracious manner, he was affectionately regarded among colleagues, clients, and students and established an enduring legacy of excellence in design and teaching. Refusing retirement,

Palmer continued in active practice in Warrenton until he died on July 16, 2001, at the age of eighty-five.

Meade Palmer's archives are housed in Alderman Library at the University of Virginia, Charlottesville.

Leach, Sara Amy. "Landscape Artist, Meade Palmer Sculpts Gardens of Perennial Appeal." *New Dominion,* Spring 1987, 82–85. Interview with Meade Palmer, general overview of life and work.
Levy, Claudia. *The Washington Post,* July 19, 2001. Obituary.
"The Work of Meade Palmer—Sixty Years of Landscape Architecture." *Proceedings of the Fifth Annual Symposium on Landscape Architecture,* University of Virginia, April 19, 1986. Edited by Nancy Takahashi. Charlottesville, Va.: University of Virginia School of Architecture, 1990.

Susan S. Nelson

PAOLANO, JOHN L.
(1902–1993)
LANDSCAPE ARCHITECT

John L. Paolano was born in Abruzzo, Italy, on June 24, 1902. Although he was raised in America, landscapes and classical architecture that he saw on childhood trips to Italy inspired him and influenced his work, providing the basis of his love of plants and landscapes. One of his early memories was a valley near Rome filled with fruit trees in bloom and surrounded by snow-capped mountains. After graduating from high school in Barberton, near Akron, Ohio, Paolano worked his way through Ohio State University studying landscape architecture during the period when **Albert Davis Taylor** was a professor there.

Upon his graduation in 1927, Paolano won a scholarship to the Foundation for Architecture and Landscape Architecture in Lake Forest, Illinois, founded by **Ferruccio Vitale** (among others) who promptly hired Paolano for his New York office, Vitale and Geiffert (**Alfred Geiffert Jr.**). Paolano worked on many projects such as the Clarence Dillon, Esq., estate in New Jersey (including a detailed design of the elliptical swimming pool), and the John Vietor (where he completed the "Guide Planting Plan

John L. Paolano at the rose garden at Fellows Riverside Gardens, Youngstown, Ohio, September 1965. (Courtesy of Mary Paolano Hoerner)

for the Flower Garden") and A. V. Davis estates on Long Island, New York. His trained eye and extensive knowledge of plants served him well. Spotting a great old wisteria on the side of a shed on the way to work one day, he moved it to a glaringly new wall at an estate, immediately imparting age. While the exact location of this anecdote is unknown, it may have been at the Chalmers Wood, Esq., estate on Long Island where he completed the design for the entrance court and walls.

By 1933, Vitale had passed away, and the Depression was underway. Paolano was hired by the National Park Service in Washington, D.C., as Associate Landscape Architect in the National Capital Parks Program. He worked on a range of projects, among them the master plan for the National Capital Parks in the District; the completion of Meridian Hill Park; Lafayette Park near the White House, where he removed, transplanted, and added elm, oak, and Magnolia grandiflora trees near the Jackson Monument; the planting plan for the Mt. Vernon Memorial Parkway, and Rock Creek Park, where he completed the planting plan for Pierce Mill.

In 1938, Paolano returned to the Barberton area, and began his private practice. A plan he designed in 1949 transformed a swampy lake in the middle of the city of Barberton into the setting for the Lake Anna Cherry Blossom Festival, still attended by over 25,000 citizens annually. From 1940 to 1957, he worked for the Akron Metropolitan Housing Authority as Technical Assistant supervising site development work on public housing projects. In 1957, he became the first Planning Director for Barberton, tackling new zoning and subdivision issues. As reported in the *Barberton Herald,* he advocated preservation and acquisition of parkland and construction of "tot lots" (playgrounds for small children). He and his wife, Jeannette

Above: Rose alleé leading to the Lake Glacier overlook, Fellows Riverside Gardens. (Courtesy of Mary Paolano Hoerner)

Below: Lake Anna Park, Barberton, Ohio. (Courtesy of Mary Paolano Hoerner)

McCafferty Paolano, collected and cultivated approximately 1,000 varieties of daffodils at their Elmbrook Farm, displaying the cultivars at garden shows. Paolano was active in the community, and often gave lectures to groups as diverse as the Kiwanis and the Junior League. As reported in *The Alliance Review,* he described gardening as an outlet for creative desires, and "matching wits

with the elements." He advocated that landscape architecture should be recognized as a practice, and not just as a title.

In 1958, the Akron *Beacon Journal* reported that the Stan Hywet Hall Foundation, at what had been the home of F. A. and Gertrude Seiberling in Akron, Ohio, had hired Paolano as its first executive director. In 1959, Paolano left the position, though he remained on the board of directors, and went to work as Akron City Planner II. He became Chief City Planner in the Planning Department in 1960 at a time when the city of Akron was undergoing urban development. Old city parks were being redesigned and new ones added. Coworkers recalled his exceptional knowledge of plant materials, most notably his willingness to experiment with plants. Paolano mentored others in the profession, and served as consultant to individuals and organizations because he "believed landscapes create quality of life and possibilities in people's lives, and make them happy."

Paolano went on to serve as Akron's Landscape Architect in the Planning Department. He undertook an ambitious program of rezoning the entire city, building new parks and planting boulevards, expanded staff positions, and established the tradition of selecting a landscape architect as the city's design administrator, which continues to this day.

Paolano retired in 1969 to work full-time in his growing solo private practice. Some of his commissions included the grounds for the Rosemont Country Club; the Municipal Center in Barberton; the Canal Fulton Library; and many of the Akron area's fine residences, businesses, and parks. An article in the *Beacon Journal* described Bina Carter's French-Provincial style house and garden built in 1962. Its rock walls, terraces, and the wide flagstone approach to the front entrance were noted. Among the unusual plants used were golden chain trees, one planted on either side of the front entrance against the pale brick house.

In 1962, Paolano began work on Fellows Riverside Gardens, at Mill Creek MetroParks in Youngstown, Ohio. Elizabeth Fellows had willed her hilltop property with spectacular views to the Youngstown Township Park District so all could enjoy it. Olmsted Associates was asked to do a plan, and proposed formal gardens

throughout. Paolano was invited to visit the property. He wrote to the park superintendent, "The Panoramic View to the North of part of the Industrial Area of the City is of great value by way of contrast and adds humanness to the development. . . . I believe that formality should have a very minor role in this planning program. This is determined, in my mind by the interesting rolling topography of the site, and also by the surrounding natural existing landscape, specifically on the Park Side of the area." As a result, Paolano was commissioned to design the Fellows Riverside Garden. He used his substantial knowledge of plant materials to create a landscape that has been sustainable to maturity. In 1998, *The National Geographic Guide to America's Public Gardens* recognized Fellows Riverside Gardens as an outstanding garden, and one of the 300 best to visit.

In 1990, Paolano's contribution was recognized with an award from the Ohio Chapter of the American Society of Landscape Architects. He died in 1993 at age ninety-one. In his final years, macular degeneration took Paolano's eyesight, but nothing took his humanistic vision of landscape architecture.

Paolano's plans for the National Park Service are housed at the National Archives II, College Park, Maryland. Plans for the city of Akron are archived at the Engineering Department, Akron, Ohio.

Jenkins, Mary Zuazua. *National Geographic Guide to America's Public Gardens: 300 of the Best Gardens to Visit in the U.S. and Canada.* Washington, D.C.: The National Geographic Society, 1998. A compendium of public North American gardens, provides information about Fellows Riverside Gardens including its history, plantings, and features.

Melnick, John C., M.D. *The Green Cathedral: History of Mill Creek Park, Youngstown, Ohio.* Youngstown, Ohio: Youngstown Lithographing, 1976. This local history includes text and photographs on Fellows Riverside Gardens.

Potter, Carol, and Rick Shale. *Historic Mill Creek Park, Ohio. Images of America Series.* Chicago: Arcadia Publishing, 2005. Includes a chapter of Fellows Riverside Gardens including a history of its design and installation. Includes photos.

Mary Paolano Hoerner

PARK, WILLIE, JR.

(1864–1925)

GOLF COURSE ARCHITECT

Willie Park Jr. was born in Musselburgh, Scotland, in February 1864. He grew up in an area with strong ties to golf—both playing and equipment making. A number of Park's family members were distinguished golfers. His

father, Willie Sr., was one of the best-known golfers of his time and won the first British Open in 1860 and won it again in 1863, 1866, and 1875. Park's uncle Mungo won the Open in 1874. Willie's younger siblings, Mungo, Jean,

Willie Park Jr., from *American Golfer*, 1917.

is a match for anyone." In 1895, Park played Willie Dunn in one of the first professional golf events in America—a series of three games with a total prize of $600. This was also the year of the first U.S. Open, held in Newport, Rhode Island. Although Park continued playing throughout his life, including with Princess Victoria in December 1902, his game peaked in the late 1890s.

In 1884, Park had returned to assist his ailing father in the family business. Later, the enterprising Park used his prominence within the golf community to successfully expand the business. During the first half of the 1890s, the company expanded to Edinburgh, London, Glasgow, and Manchester, and established a branch office in New York City in 1895, during his first visit to the United States.

Park joined his father in laying out golf courses in the 1880s. His first formal commission was at Innerleithen in southeast Scotland in the autumn of 1886. From there, his course design career quickly grew and took up the majority of his time.

Park pioneered the parkland course. Unlike other designers of the day, who were laying out holes on convenient, mostly seaside terrain, Park molded seemingly unsuitable land into scenic courses that appeared to have always existed. His designs typically had open holes, with the area in front of the green free of hazards. He incorporated trees into courses, a design departure from earlier approaches. His designs moved golf from traditional coastal locations, where nature had laid out the courses along river estuaries, to diverse inland sites. Although he emphasized using the existing landscape to its best advantage, he was among the first architects to reshape the natural contours of a site to create greens, tees, and hazards. Through practical experience based on widely differing sites, he became an expert not only on layout but also course maintenance.

In February 1895, Park traveled to North America to design a course for the St. Andrews Golf Club in Yonkers, New York. During his five-month stay, he instructed a number of socialites including members of the Astor and Vanderbilt families. He reportedly planned a course for the Vanderbilts at Shelbourne Farms, the 3,800-acre farm laid out by Frederick Law Olmsted Sr. near Burlington, Vermont. Park returned to the United States again briefly in the summer of 1896.

Two courses associated with residential development plans greatly increased Park's reputation and secured his place in the history of golf course architecture. In 1899, he began work on Sunningdale in Berkshire, some 20

Jack, and Margaret, were all accomplished players. His elder brother Frank, also an esteemed player, instructed him as a boy. The family had a business designing and manufacturing clubs and balls in Musselburgh—one of the primary centers of golf at the time. From the age of six he was spending time in his father's shop creating clubs and by twelve was experimenting with ball production. He would eventually patent a number of his designs.

Little is known of Park's first wife, who died in 1894 after the birth of their daughter, Rebecca. Park remarried in October 1895. His wife, Margaret Inglis, gave birth to four daughters and a son by 1904. The family made its home at Springfield in Inveresk, although Willie was frequently away traveling for work—often for extended periods. Willie and Margaret's eldest daughter, Meta, died in 1903 (the same year as Willie Park Sr.) and their only son, Willie, died in 1906. The three younger daughters all lived into adulthood. Doris, the eldest of the three, was a successful golfer from the 1920s through 1940s.

Park first entered the British Open in 1880 at age sixteen. He won the Open in 1887 and 1889, and was runner up in 1898. He was known for his putting abilities, and is credited with the phrase "the man who can putt

miles west of London. The course is considered among the first created on heathland (dry sandy soil covered with rough heather), which required extensive alteration to make it suitable for golfing. It was also part of a pioneering real estate venture, which included adjacent plots for large, exclusive residences—today's ubiquitous golf course community. The contract to design, construct, and equip the course for a fixed sum is also one of the earliest examples of a "turnkey project." Opened in 1901 complete with a man-made pond, eighteen-hole Sunningdale was a success from the start and today is considered Park's masterpiece.

Huntercombe, in Oxfordshire, opened the same year and is another of Park's superb inland courses. Park's brother Mungo, who had been in the United States for three years, returned to Britain in 1900 to help with Huntercombe. Although the course was hailed as a great design success, its financing was a failure, with insufficient funds to build a clubhouse. Unlike at Sunningdale, residential lots remained unsold for many years, being more remote at 40 miles west of London and some distance from the nearest train station. The comfortable Park family, which had supplied much of the initial capital, suffered considerable strain as a result. Park then focused more on the retail side of his business before once again devoting himself almost exclusively to course design.

From 1886 until the outbreak of World War I in 1914, the industrious Park worked on over 100 courses in Europe. With the pursuit of golfing interrupted by the war, he returned to the United States in 1916 for a seven-year period, returning three times to Scotland during this time. During his tenure in North America, he designed, redesigned, and oversaw construction of nearly seventy courses, mostly in the Northeast and Midwest, as well as across Canada.

Two of Park's notable courses in North America are Olympia Fields-North, outside of Chicago, Illinois, and Maidstone Club on Long Island, New York. Olympia Fields Country Club was founded in 1915 and Park worked on the championship fourth course from 1919 to 1922. He had previously designed nine holes at Maidstone Club that were completed in 1899, and in 1922 redesigned eleven holes that were finished in 1925.

Throughout his active professional life, Park also found time to write. In April 1896, he published his own illustrated instruction book, *The Game of Golf,* the first complete book on golf written by a professional player. In it, he proclaimed that "laying out of a golf course is by no means a simple task." His second book, *The Art of Putting,* was published in 1920. He also wrote three sizable articles, "The Beginning of My Golf" for *Golf Illustrated* in 1905, and "The Construction of a Golf Links" and "My Experiences in America" for *The Golf Monthly* in 1911 and 1920, respectively.

His brother Mungo brought Park back to his native Musselburgh following what appeared to be a nervous breakdown sometime in late 1923. He was hospitalized in Edinburgh and died in May 1925.

Adams, John. *The Parks of Musselburgh: Golfers, Architects, Clubmakers.* Worcestershire, U.K.: Grant Books, 1991. History of the Scottish Park family beginning with Willie Sr. in the 1850s and continuing for over a century, with a particular focus on the career of Willie Jr.

Cornish, Geoffrey S., and Ronald E. Whitten. *The Architects of Golf.* Rev. ed. New York: HarperCollins, 1993. The history and evolution of golf course design, and a catalog of over 12,000 courses and their architects.

Klein, Bradley S. "Willie Park, Jr.: Golf Course Architect." golfonline.com.

Doug Pulak

PARKER, CARL RUST
(1882–1966)
LANDSCAPE ARCHITECT

Carl Rust Parker was born in Andover, Massachusetts, in 1882. An only child, he attended local public schools and graduated from Phillips Andover Academy in 1901. The academy's Scientific Department provided Parker's only training in landscape architecture, as he did not seek a college education. Instead, he began working for the **Olmsted Brothers** in Brookline, Massachusetts, in 1901, the same year that **Henry Vincent Hubbard** was hired. Parker remained until 1910, serving as a draftsman, planting designer, and supervisor of construction and planting. Other contemporaries at the Olmsted firm included **James Frederick Dawson** and **Percival Gallagher.**

While working for the Olmsteds, Parker married Jessie Merrill of Yarmouth, Maine, in 1906. Their only child, Marjorie, was born in 1908. In 1910, Parker "voluntarily retired" from the Olmsteds to start his own firm in Portland, Maine. When Parker left the Olmsteds, a few residential clients followed him in private practice, which resulted in slightly strained relations between Parker and the Olmsted firm. This minor tiff apparently went no further; eight years later Parker returned to work for the Olmsted Brothers.

In 1911, Parker was listed as "the only practitioner of his profession in the state" in a Maine newspaper article. An advertisement in the 1911–1912 *Maine Register* lists his services as "Designer of Parks, Playgrounds, Private Grounds, Gardens and Land Developments. Special attention given to Continued Care of Summer Residents' Property. Construction and Planting Plans furnished and work supervised."

Parker had a relatively short but prolific career in Maine that lasted until 1917. During that time he worked on several residential projects with John Calvin Stevens, one of Maine's most talented and respected architects. One of the most significant of these collaborations was for John S. Hyde of shipbuilding fame. His brick mansion in the Colonial Revival style was the largest house constructed in Maine in 1913. Located in Bath, the property featured an Italian-style sunken garden, carriage drives throughout the 160-acre site, and a naturalistic pond with a stone footbridge. Another project with Stevens was for the summer residence of Murray Shipley, Esq., on a narrow Maine coast peninsula. The plan featured a saltwater swimming pool, formal entrance and service drives, tennis court, and an "old-fashioned flower garden" aligned on axis with the Colonial Revival house.

A sampling of his nonresidential projects in the greater Portland region between 1911 and 1917 includes the Village Green in Yarmouth, Boulevard Park Subdivision in Portland, and the grounds of the Curtis Memorial Library in Brunswick. Parker also traveled to rural communities, designing the grounds of the Mount Kineo House resort on Moosehead Lake, the grounds of the Goodwill Hinckley Home & School for Boys & Girls in

Above: Carl Rust Parker, ca. 1910. (Maine Historic Preservation Commission)

Below: Stone entrance gates and drive of the Goodwill Hinckley Home and School for Boys and Girls, Hinckley, Maine, designed Carl Rust Parker, 1929. (Photo by Deanne Herman)

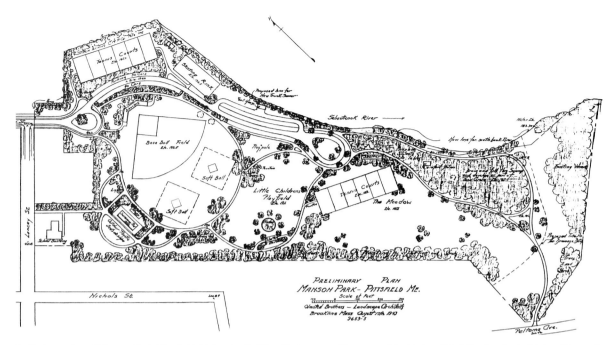

Preliminary plan of Manson Park, Pittsfield, Maine, by Carl Rust Parker, 1943. (Courtesy of the National Park Service, Frederick Law Olmsted National Historic Site)

Fairfield, and a cemetery for the town of Gilead in Maine's western mountains.

While self-employed, Parker worked primarily in Maine, with the exception of his work for the Boca Grande Land Company on Gasparilla Island, Florida. In 1910, the land company began to develop a year-round resort in an area that was famous for sports fishing. After Parker's site visit in 1911, a newspaper article noted that he "is now at work upon plans for laying out streets and the grounds for an immense hotel which will be constructed immediately." The Gasparilla Inn was finished in time for the 1912–1913 season.

Parker's writings and his service on public committees reflect his interest in community planning and civic duty. In 1912 he delivered a paper entitled "Possibilities for Civic Improvement in Maine" to the Board of Trade, of which he was a member. Parker divided civic improvements into three classes: those to be made by the individual, the community, and the state. In Maine, he promoted simple, pragmatic improvements as opposed to the "impractical and extravagant ideas" offered at the time in other locations. In 1913, Parker joined John Calvin Stevens and other community leaders in advocating

for the creation of a planning department in Portland. The following year, he addressed the Yarmouth Village Improvement Society, urging the formation of a town civic center and social hall, among other improvements. In 1916, he served on the City Planning Committee of the Portland Chamber of Commerce, which sponsored an illustrated lecture on city planning by landscape architect **Arthur Asahel Shurcliff**.

Parker's downtown office was listed in the *Portland Directory* and the *Maine Register* consistently between 1911 and 1919. He apparently had connections to Springfield, Massachusetts, as well; the *Maine Register* and records in the Connecticut Valley Historical Museum verify that he had offices in both Portland and Springfield from 1916 to 1917. To date, no information is known about his Springfield association.

During World War I, Parker worked in Washington, D.C. He served six months as the principal civilian assistant for the Camp Planning Section, Construction Division of the War Department, and eighteen months as Assistant Manager and Manager, Town Planning Division, U.S. Housing Corporation, U.S. Department of Labor.

Postcard view of
George Washington
Masonic Memorial
grounds plan,
Alexandria, Virginia.
(Alexandria Library,
Special Collections,
Alexandria, VA)

GROUNDS PLAN
GEORGE WASHINGTON MASONIC NATIONAL MEMORIAL
ALEXANDRIA, VA.

In 1919, after the war, Parker returned to the Olmsted Brothers, working for them in Maine on residential projects, Colby College, and the University of Maine, among others. Some of his major projects for the firm in the 1920s were in Augusta, including Capitol Park & Driving Grounds, the grounds of the Maine State House, and the grounds of the Governor's Mansion. Due to state budget problems, Parker's formal design for the mansion's entrance was not completed at the time; the design was finally installed in 1988–1990 after the creation of a private, nonprofit restoration fund.

While working for the Olmsteds, Parker worked on private estates, industrial plants, land subdivisions, town and city planning problems, parks and recreation areas, and cemeteries. One of his major projects was at the George Washington Masonic Memorial in Alexandria, Virginia. In correspondence from 1931, Parker discussed bumps and low spots on the new road and stressed that he "was anxious to get this road one hundred percent perfect." In his characteristically practical manner, he suggested the type of machinery and method to best achieve his desired results.

In the 1940s and 1950s, Parker worked extensively at Kohler Village in Wisconsin, where he served as the key representative of Olmsted Brothers. Parker was involved in rethinking plans for expansion of the village residential area, relandscaping the American Club, and landscaping the cemetery and some of the churches built during the period. However, due to World War II and a major Kohler strike in the 1950s, the residential projects did not get started until the 1960s, when the Olmsted firm was no longer involved.

Other projects attributed to Parker include those in New Jersey for the Bell Telephone Laboratories and for parks in Essex and Union counties. He also worked on the grounds of the National Cash Register Company in Dayton, Ohio, as well as at the University of Mississippi in Oxford.

In 1950, Parker became a partner of the Olmsted Brothers where his contemporaries were Artemis P. Richardson and Charles Scott Riley. Parker remained with the Olmsteds until his retirement in 1961 at age seventy-nine. He was involved with the American Society of Landscape Architects throughout his career, becoming a member in 1908 and a Fellow in 1915. He was one of the authors of *Transactions of the ASLA, 1909–21*. He submitted "A Note from the Business Manager" to the 1930 issue of *Landscape Architecture*. In it, he summarized the first twenty years of the magazine and offered his thoughts for the future, expecting the magazine to "grow in wisdom and strength" with help from younger members of the profession.

Carl Rust Parker suffered a stroke on Thanksgiving Day in 1966 and died five days later. He was eighty-four years old and had practiced landscape architecture for sixty years.

There is no single archive for the work of Carl Rust Parker. In Maine, drawings and articles are located at the Curtis Memorial Library in Brunswick; the John Calvin Stevens Collection at the Maine Historical Society in Portland; L. C. Bates Museum in Fairfield; Maine Historic Preservation Commission in Augusta; Maine Maritime Museum in Bath; Maine Olmsted Alliance for Parks & Landscapes in Portland; and Yarmouth Historical Society. Other documents are located at the Kohler Company Archives in Wisconsin and the George Washington Masonic Memorial in Alexandria, Virginia. Projects related to his tenure with the Olmsted Brothers are located at the Frederick Law Olmsted National Historic Site, Brookline, Massachusetts, and the Library of Congress, Manuscript Division in Washington, D.C.

"Mass Meeting Adopts Resolve in Favor of Planning Commission." *Portland [Maine] Sunday Telegram,* March 9, 1913. The bulk of the article is Parker's paper presented to the Portland City Council advocating for a "City plan commission and the services of a City plan expert."

"Possibilities For Civic Improvements in Maine." *Portland [Maine] Evening Express,* March 15, 1912. A lengthy article derived from Parker's presentation at the Maine State Board of Trade meeting. Parker's motive was to create a statewide interest in civic improvement.

"Village Green an Added Attraction to Yarmouth." 1910 article from unknown newspaper. Scrapbook located at Yarmouth (Maine) Historical Society, Collection 118, Vol. 16. Describes the process of creating Yarmouth's first town park, illustrated with Parker's plan.

Theresa Mattor

PATTEE, ELIZABETH GREENLEAF
(1893–1991)
LANDSCAPE ARCHITECT, EDUCATOR

Elizabeth Greenleaf Pattee was born in Quincy, Massachusetts, on June 7, 1893. Born at a time when few women received any form of formal education, Pattee enrolled at the Massachusetts Institute of Technology (MIT) in 1912, graduating in 1916 with a degree in architecture.

Following graduation, Pattee began teaching and served as assistant principal at the Lowthorpe School of Landscape Architecture, Gardening and Horticulture for Women in Groton, Massachusetts. Founded in 1901 by Mrs. Gilchrist Low, this was the first school of landscape architecture to be established in America for women. Not only did Pattee teach courses in architecture, she studied landscape architecture there, graduating in 1918. Her education in both architecture and landscape architecture was the foundation for her career as an educator and designer.

During her tenure at the Lowthorpe School, she worked with various design offices in the Boston area. She was employed by Stone & Webster, Harold Hill Blossom,* and Howe and Manning, established by Lois Lilley Howe and Eleanor Manning and the first women-owned architectural firm founded in Boston and the second in the country. Pattee opened her own office of architecture and landscape architecture in 1922 in Boston with Constance Peters, a 1920 Lowthorpe graduate. This partnership produced a landscape master plan, designed in 1929, for Dr. and Mrs. George Kimball of Concord, New Hampshire. This residence, now known as the Kimball-Jenkins Estate, is currently maintained as a charitable trust and is used as an educational historic site and community art school. A formal perennial garden, designed for the property's lower lawn, exists today due to the historic preservation efforts undertaken in the 1990s.

Pattee published numerous articles early in her career that reflected her interest and expertise in residential landscape architecture. An article entitled "Planting the Herbaceous Border," published in October 1919 in *House Beautiful,* gave a brief and concise lesson on the important elements of a perennial border. A sample planting plan is illustrated with the article. Later, an article called "Little Lessons in Landscape Design (No.1)," published in the March 15, 1939, issue of *Horticulture,*

Elizabeth Greenleaf Pattee, ca. 1950. (Rhode Island School of Design Archives)

compared design treatments of stairs in different landscape settings.

Pattee continued teaching at Lowthorpe through the prosperous years of the 1920s, a period of unparalleled participation by women in the field of landscape architecture, and the lean years when it struggled with enrollment and financial troubles during the Great Depression and the onset of World War II. In 1945, the Lowthorpe School announced a merger with the Rhode Island School of Design (RISD) in Providence, Rhode Island. The RISD landscape architecture program became part of the Division of Planning and was referred to as the Lowthorpe Department of Landscape Architecture. Four

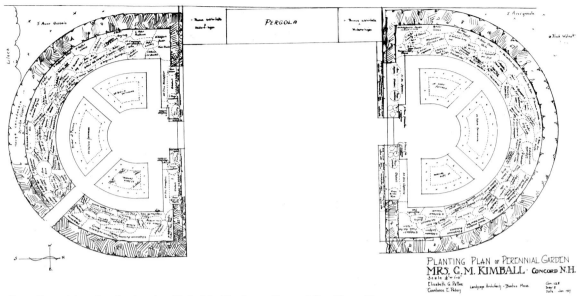

PERGOLA

PLANTING PLAN OF PERENNIAL GARDEN
MRS. G.M. KIMBALL · CONCORD N.H.

Above: Perennial garden planting plan, Kimball-Jenkins Estate, Concord, New Hampshire. (Kimball-Jenkins Estate Archives, Concord, NH)

Below: View of perennial garden, Kimball-Jenkins Estate, Concord, New Hampshire, ca. 1940s. (Kimball-Jenkins Estate Archives, Concord, NH)

Lowthorpe faculty members, including Pattee, transferred to the new program at RISD. Pattee was on the faculty at RISD from 1945 until her retirement in 1963. During her tenure at RISD, she served as department head from 1946 to 1952 and again from 1955 to 1959. By the time she retired in 1963, the program at RISD was no longer referred to as the Lowthorpe Department of Landscape Architecture. Throughout her career as an educator at RISD, Pattee continued to design residential properties throughout New England.

While on the RISD faculty, Pattee wrote numerous articles for professional publications, the content of which indicate an active interest and involvement in the International Federation of Landscape Architects (IFLA) and the American Society of Landscape Architects (ASLA). She attended numerous international conferences related to these professional associations. In November 1950, Pattee attended a seminar as a representative of the American Institute of Planners (AIP), the ASLA, and American Institute of Architects (AIA) in San Salvador, El Salvador. This seminar focused on housing and city planning issues in Central America. She coauthored a summary of this seminar entitled "Report on the Pan-American Regional Seminar on Housing and City Planning," prepared for the *Journal of the American Institute of Planners.* Pattee went on to attend both the 1954 and 1956 IFLA

World Congress. She reported on both for *Landscape Architecture* magazine. Her account of the 1956 IFLA Congress in Zurich commented on the public parks and open spaces, housing developments, and experiences that would be of interest to other professionals.

In her years at RISD, Pattee observed changes in the profession as well as in academics. During this time, the focus of landscape architecture was moving away from residential estate work and small commissions to large-scale urban and regional planning projects. Within her private practice, the majority of her landscape design work involved developing private grounds and gardens in New England. Generally, her work was practical and followed trends of the time, using plant materials to integrate architecture into the landscape.

Pattee was elected a Fellow of the American Society of Landscape Architects in 1961. She had been a member of the society since 1931, and her professional career spanned almost half a century. Pattee retired from professional practice in 1965 when she moved to a continual care elderly housing facility in Hightstown, New Jersey. She lived there until her death at age ninety-eight on February 27, 1991.

The Rhode Island School of Design Fleet Library, Special Collections, Providence, R.I., contains the archival collection of documents from the Lowthorpe School before and after the merger.

Pattee, Elizabeth Greenleaf. "Little Lessons in Landscape Design". *Horticulture,* March 15, 1939, 140.

Pattee, Elizabeth Greenleaf. "Planting the Herbaceous Border." *The House Beautiful,* October 1919, 245.

Pattee, Elizabeth Greenleaf. "The Rhode Island Shore." *Audubon Society of Rhode Island Bulletin* 17, nos. 3, 4 (June, October 1956). A discussion of large-scale planning issues associated with shoreline conservation and development. The planning and conservation issues emphasized in this article reflect the changing role of landscape.

Susanne Smith Meyer

PAUL, COURTLAND PRICE
(1927–2003)
LANDSCAPE ARCHITECT, DEVELOPER

Courtland Paul was on born March 11, 1927, in Pasadena, California, the city where he spent his childhood and began his career. Though he had no formal education in landscape architecture, he was responsible for helping to develop licensure in the state of California, and founded what was at the time, one of the nation's largest landscape architecture firms.

Upon his return from the U.S. Navy in 1946, Paul studied design at John Muir Jr. College, followed by ornamental horticulture at California Polytechnic State University's then southern campus in San Dimas. Leaving school prior to graduation to support his wife and children, he worked for Bamico Nursery in Pasadena, developing nascent landscape design skills through both design and installation of residential garden commissions.

W. Bennett Covert and Mike Engle were his first business partners in a 1951 landscape contracting business, Courtland Paul and Associates. By 1953, the company had grown to a staff of four designers and twenty landscape crew members. Paul shifted purely to design from design/building by 1954. Throughout the 1950s and early 1960s, Paul's office focused on residential

Courtland Paul. (Peridian Group, Inc.)

Illustrative site plan of Harbor Ridge, Newport Beach, California, 1976. (Peridian Group, Inc.)

design, winning awards such as "Landscaped Home of the Year" in 1958, from the American Institute of Landscape Architects.

When California was the first state to license landscape architects, Paul became one its first recipients, receiving license number 57. A passionate advocate of landscape architecture, Paul became a founding member of the American Institute of Landscape Architects in 1955. In 1959, he was president of the California Council of Landscape Architects, a group representing all licensed landscape architects in the state. In 1960, he was appointed by Governor Pat Brown to the California State Board of Landscape Architecture where he served as president in 1964. He served for eight years and developed the examination for state licensure.

The mid- to late 1960s were a notable time of evolution in Southern California housing developments. Master developers and landholders in the region included the Mission Viejo Company, Irvine Company, Newhall Land and Farming, and American Hawaiian. During this time, landholders began to work directly with landscape architects to plan and develop their holdings. In 1965, Paul's firm had evolved into Courtland Paul/Arthur Beggs and Associates with the partnership of Arthur G. Beggs. The firm added large, planned communities to the practice, designing the details in subdivisions to enact developers' visions. Significant to Courtland Paul's career was Orange County developer Donald Bren. When Bren left the Mission Viejo Company to establish his own building company, he hired Paul in 1968 for his first development of homes in Valencia, California, on a 50,000- to 60,000-acre land holding. It was the first master-planned residential community in north Los Angeles County. Gifted in both landscape design and attuned to market trends, Paul skillfully packaged the California lifestyle into his designs. Residential communities had strong entrance designs, providing identities to the new villages, and private landscapes meshed indoors and outdoors to reflect the temperate climate.

Renaming the firm Peridian Group, Paul and Beggs added more partners in the 1970s: Dennis Taylor, Rae Price, Shinji Nakagawa, and Jerry Pearson. Their new business name literally meant "about one's own." They described "peridian" as a "proper name coined to represent concern for the environment and environmental issues." Between 1976 and 1985, Peridian Group grew to one of the nation's largest landscape architecture and planning firms, with three offices in California (Irvine, San Diego, and Walnut Creek), as well as Fort Lauderdale, Florida, and Guadalajara, Mexico. Affiliated offices were located in Singapore and Tokyo. The firm specialized in such diverse areas as planning and landscape design, park and recreational facilities, commercial and industrial design, and residential community planning. Under Paul's guidance, Peridian was instrumental in major planning and design in the planned communities of Mission Viejo, Lake Forest, Irvine, Valencia, Westlake, El Dorado, Simi Valley, and Rancho Santa Margarita in California.

Paul's design at Harbor Ridge, Newport Beach, in 1976 was a key project that demonstrated his concern for the visual effects of designed hillside developments. It became one of his most important designs for its innovative concepts in land form grading techniques, which had a lasting effect on policy in Southern California. Harbor Ridge was a planned, Newport Beach community and the first Irvine Company village built in the hills. Historically when communities were developed in hills, housing pads were mass graded by machinery, completely changing the original aesthetics of the site. Paul's vision was to retain the identifying elements of the original landform—its ridgelines, knolls, and ravines. Beginning with intense visual analysis and assessment, grading was done to either preserve these integral elements or regrading was done so that the perception of the original landscape was maintained. House construction was prohibited on the ridges. Lots sloped in keeping with the site, and houses were only allowed to be built in predetermined, three-dimensional building envelopes. Adhering to strict design guidelines, non-removable specimen trees were planted to force homeowners to develop their sites in different ways while adding maturity to the new community. In an attempt to re-create the natural drainage systems, water was forced to flow into ravines that were interspersed with boulders and sycamores. The City of Los Angeles, upon seeing the success of Harbor Ridge, adopted Paul's grading concept for their hillside grading ordinances in 1981.

Throughout his career, Paul's guidebook was **Thomas Dolliver Church**'s *Gardens Are for People* in which design was driven by the client. In his public park designs, such as Irvine Regional Park (1976–1977), he was in the forefront of bringing the public into the facilitation and design process. His work was both large and small scale. The Hibbs Residence (Pasadena, 1978) was one of his most important residential designs. The clients were scuba divers and requested a swimming pool with underwater caves for them to practice their diving skills. Recreating a natural pool, the project meshed the clients' wishes with Paul's love of the mountains and outdoors into an innovative design.

In the 1980s, Paul was seminal in uniting the two professional landscape architecture groups, the American Institute of Landscape Architects (AILA) and the American Society of Landscape Architects (ASLA). In 1955, Paul had helped found the AILA, an association whose members did not fit the typical mold of the ASLA, and thus felt disenfranchised. Many AILA members had not received degrees in landscape architecture, but instead had experience and knowledge in the field. When the ASLA began to recognize the value of self-taught practitioners, Paul joined in 1968. He ultimately became a Fellow in 1982. Two professional groups of practitioners were both confusing to the public and clients, and hurtful to the advancement of the landscape architecture profession. Paul's role on the steering committee helped merge the two organizations, ending years of division.

Never forgetting his roots, nor believing his role in landscape architecture more important than those who constructed it, he worked closely with the National Association of Home Builders (NAHB) and the Building Industry of America (BIA). Among his many design awards, he received Gold Nugget Awards from the NAHB and Best Landscape Awards in 1976, 1978, and 1980. Three Grand Awards were received in 1975, 1980, 1982 from the BIA's Major Achievement in Merchandizing Award. In 1992, he received the prestigious Max Tipton Award for Marketing Excellence, the first landscape architect to win the award from the Sales and Marketing Council of the BIA.

Courtland Paul's forty-four years of practice helped influence the profession of landscape architecture in California. His career was devoted to professional practice, where he helped develop policy, but he did not publish his own writing. Instead, he allowed his work to speak for itself through photographs in the *Los Angeles Times Home Magazine, Sunset,* and *Landscape Architecture.*

Courtland Paul died January 28, 2003, in San Juan Capistrano, leaving his wife Nadine and adult children Pamela Burns, Kimberly Paul, Robyn Cueva, and Sanford Paul. A son, Scott Paul, predeceased Courtland Paul.

The Courtland Price Paul Archive, at Peridian International Inc., Newport Beach, Calif., includes images, drawings, and plans of Paul's work, as well as family photos.

French, Jere S. *The California Garden.* Washington, D.C.: The Landscape Architecture Foundation, 1993, 203. Excerpt contains a description of Paul's influence in the history of California landscape architecture.

Luna, Claire. "Courtland Paul, 75; Landscape Architect Helped Change Face of Southern California." *Los Angeles Times,* February 10, 2003, sec. B, 9. Biographical information regarding his early life and career.

Christine Edstrom O'Hara

PEARSE, RUBEE JEFFREY
(1887–1973)
LANDSCAPE ARCHITECT,
FAIRGROUND DESIGNER

Born in Geneva, Iowa, in 1887, Rubee Jeffrey Pearse, who was known as R. J., began and ended his career with fairground design. In between he made his mark in government work during and after the Great Depression. This farm-born landscape architect did not immediately find his calling. A graduate of Cornell College, in Mount Vernon, Iowa, Pearse taught both elementary and high school for five years. He then switched course at age twenty-eight and obtained a Master in Landscape Architecture from Harvard University. His first employment in his new vocation was with the extension program at Iowa State University in Ames. He designed model parks, school grounds, and farms, ostensibly for clientele too poor to afford professional services. The program aimed to provide services to one farm and one school per county.

While in Iowa, in 1919, Pearse founded the firm of Pearse, Robinson, and Sprague. Based in Des Moines, this multidisciplinary firm at one time also had offices in St. Louis and Chicago. The partnership planned and remodeled fairgrounds "in nearly every state east of the Rockies, north to Winnipeg and south to New Orleans." The group's work included four county fair grounds in North Dakota and the Champlain Valley Expo in Vermont. At the Arkansas State Fair grounds in Little Rock, the firm laid out the site and designed the buildings.

As a result of the firm's extensive portfolio, the City of Philadelphia hired Pearse to be Director of Works, from 1925 to 1926, for its Sesquicentennial Exposition, a gigantic 2,000-acre show with more than twenty foreign exhibitors. As chief of the drafting division, architect Louis

R. J. Pearse, ca. 1948. (Courtesy of Anne Willson and the Pearse family)

Kahn would have reported to Pearse. The Philadelphia experience was a prelude to the Iowa designer's breaking with both his firm and the Midwest.

In 1924, the amended partnership of Pearse-Robinson bid along with six of the nation's major planning and design firms (Charles Leavitt & Sons [**Charles Wellford**

Leavitt Jr.], Olmsted Brothers, John Nolen, Albert Davis Taylor, Earle Sumner Draper, Harland Bartholomew) for the contract to prepare a park and parkway plan for the City of Birmingham, Alabama. Although Pearse-Robinson lost to the Olmsted Brothers, the partners favorably impressed the Birmingham city officials. Pearse-Robinson won a contract to design one of the local parks in the city. The foundry city was booming. Samuel Parsons Jr. and Warren Henry Manning were both engaged in consulting projects; nevertheless, William Harry Kessler* was the only resident landscape architect. After the Sesquicentennial Fair, Pearse moved to Birmingham, entering the second and transitional phase of his career.

In 1931, Pearse designed tennis courts, a rose garden, and an open-air amphitheater for Avondale Park in an older residential area northeast of downtown. The Avondale project would be a prelude to one of the highlights of Pearse's extensive list of commissions. In 1938, he designed for the City of Raleigh, North Carolina, a combination amphitheater and municipal rose garden for the Works Progress Administration.

During the 1930s, Pearse provided landscape architecture services while employed by various government agencies. During the Depression, Pearse's responsibilities expanded proportionately with the enlarging role of government in the area of work relief. He began, at the county level, overseeing work done by the indigent. In 1933, Alabama was the first state to set up a Transient Bureau, authorized by the pioneering federal relief legislation of that same year. Pearse was responsible for its work program.

After operating at the state level, Pearse ascended in his next two jobs to regional responsibilities. From 1934 to 1936, he supervised park planning for the Tennessee Valley Authority (TVA). Pearse then moved on to Raleigh, where he was the regional landscape architect with the Resettlement Administration for two years.

According to historian Walter Creese, the TVA's two most accomplished parks were Big Ridge and Norris, both on Norris Lake in Tennessee. Pearse, working under Earle S. Draper, supervised six Civilian Conservation Corps camps with a total of twelve hundred men, six superintendents, and thirty-six foremen to build a dam,

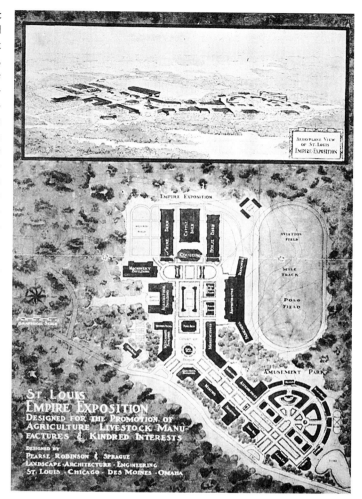

Pearse designed many exposition grounds; Empire Exposition plan, St. Louis, Missouri is an example of this type of work. (Courtesy of the Frances Loeb Library, Harvard School of Graduate Design)

two lodges, sixty-four cabins, a riding stable, and various piers and floats. Later recreational development by the TVA did not rise to the level of quality of these two founding parks.

The move to Raleigh to work with the Resettlement Administration expanded Pearse's territory. He developed community parks and forests in five southern states, including six still extant state parks. Particularly notable are two in North Carolina. Singletary Lake and Jones Lake State Parks encompasses two of the coastal area's unique freshwater lakes formed from former bays. Jones Lake also created a historical precedent. It was the first state park built specifically for African Americans.

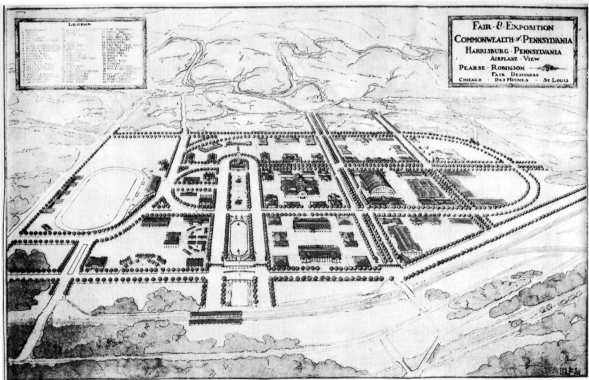

Above: Rustic cabins, ca. 1935, at Norris Dam State Park, Lakeville, Tennessee, 1985 view. (Norris Dam State Park archives)

Below: One of Pearse and Robinson's many fairground designs is the plan for the Fair and Exposition, Harrisburg, Pennsylvania, 1925. (Courtesy of Anne Willson and the Pearse family)

By 1937, the Resettlement Agency's work was winding down. Now permanently settled in Raleigh, in 1938, Pearse returned once more to private practice. He designed the grounds of textile mills and institutions, but continued to accept government commissions. Sometime during the 1930s, Pearse obtained a civil engineer's license, a logical step after designing numerous dams and lodges.

Following service during World War II with the Army Corps of Engineers, Pearse returned to Raleigh, and once again he immersed himself in fairground planning. He completed designs for Waco, Texas; Flint, Michigan; and Tallahassee, Florida. These are among almost thirty cities that owe all or part of their fairgrounds to this final phase of Pearse's career.

Pearse continued to work well into his sevenites. He died February 26, 1973, at age eighty-six, leaving a wife, one daughter, and four grandchildren.

Creese, Walter L. *TVA's Public Planning: The Vision, The Reality.* Knoxville: University of Tennessee Press, 1990. An examination of early recreational work at Lake Norris from the elevated vantage of planning history.

Munger, Guy. *Curtain Up! Raleigh Little Theatre's First Fifty Years.* Raleigh, N.C.: Raleigh Little Theatre, 1985. Pearse's part in the design of the associated park is documented. Linda Jewell, professor of landscape architecture at U.C. Berkeley, was inspired by this amphitheater to initiate her survey of the genre.

Pearse, Robinson, and Sprague. *Your Fair and Its Possibilities: A Few Thoughts for the Consideration of Fair Officials* (1920). This is the only known published work connected with Pearse.

Phoebe Cutler

PENDLETON, ISABELLA E.
(1891–1965)
LANDSCAPE ARCHITECT

Isabella E. Pendleton was born in Cincinnati, Ohio, in 1891. As a young woman, she showed an interest in gardening and landscape design, and her parents encouraged her. Pendleton was a founder of the Cincinnati Garden Club and became its president in 1915. Almost immediately, however, she relocated to the Boston area and enrolled in the Lowthorpe School of Landscape Architecture, Landscape Gardening, and Horticulture for Women in Groton, Massachusetts, graduating in 1917. Shortly afterward, Pendleton returned to Cincinnati, although no projects by her in that city have yet been identified. Around 1922, she moved again, this time to New York City, where her first office was initially subsidized by an uncle who also gave her a commission for his summer place on Long Island. (The identities of her uncle and first Long Island project remain elusive, although she eventually designed at least eight gardens on Long Island.) Pendleton seems never to have worked in the office of another landscape architect.

Pendleton was a member of the American Society of Landscape Architects (ASLA) and wrote a number of articles, but no books. Her projects were frequently published in garden periodicals and ASLA *Yearbooks.* In October 1920 her first article, "Striking Perennial Combinations," was published in *The Garden Magazine.* In 1924, she published a cottage-style garden, client and location unidentified, in the Architectural League of New York's *Yearbook and Catalogue* for that year. The following year, she implemented a Gertrude Jekyll design for Mr. and Mrs. Stanley Resor, former residents of Cincinnati, in Greenwich, Connecticut. Pendleton described her "main stamping grounds" as Cincinnati; Nassau County, on Long Island, New York; and Princeton, New Jersey. One Princeton client was a Miss Emma Martin for whom she designed a garden in two stages, the second one being an arboretum. Pendleton's preferred practice was to return to each client for yearly consultations, which she did with both the Resors and Miss Martin. She also lectured frequently.

Perhaps Pendleton's most striking project was a large iris garden for Z. G. Simmons in Greenwich, Connecticut, which was published in *Architectural Record* in August 1933. The iris garden was located on extensive acreage on a site with two ponds, as well as many stone outcroppings, which were used for picturesque effect. Except for the terraces immediately to the rear of the house, which were planted formally and included a flower garden, the irises and other plantings at the Simmons property were set in informal swirling beds that traversed the rear slopes. The bulk of the irises were tall bearded and Japanese varieties, which were set off by azaleas and white flowering dogwoods. The banks of the two ponds were planted with half a dozen moisture-loving irises. Dispersed among the low-growing irises were the vertical

Left: The flower garden and gazebo at The Braes, Glencoe, Long Island, New York, ca. 1926, is one of several of Pendleton's Long Island commissions. (Smithsonian Institution, Archives of American Gardens, Garden Club of America Collection)

Below: Boxwood Garden at The Braes, Glencoe, Long Island, New York, ca. 1930. (Nassau County Department of Parks, Recreation, and Museums—Long Island Studies Collection)

accents of trees, including cedars, hawthorns, flowering cherries, and individual specimens of oaks, elms, and ashes, as well as plantings of sumac and redbud. The various spaces within the garden were connected by numerous steps made of both masonry and turf. However naturalistic and casual its appearance, the Simmons garden would have been very labor-intensive. By 1954, the property had changed hands, and the iris garden was no longer maintained.

In 1938, Pendleton was commissioned by the Trenton, New Jersey, Garden Club to rehabilitate a colonial-era garden for Trent House, the early eighteenth-century home of William Trent, founder of the city. Her work there is best described as Colonial Revival rather than a "restoration." Although Pendleton conscientiously read old letters and other documents, it would have been impossible to bring the garden back to the era of the Trent-family ownership. The site had diminished in size from 800 acres to slightly less than 2 acres. Pendleton's plan included an herb garden, a small pear orchard, a boxwood circle with a groundcover of English ivy, and, to simulate the appearance of age, 300 yews planted so close together that they touched. The paths were brick. Among the deciduous trees were maples, beeches, lindens, horse chestnuts, and walnuts. When Pendleton designed the landscape at Trent House, it was in the midst of an industrial district, surrounded by factories. Pendleton created an oasis in the industrial area, which inspired her to urge that such gardens be planned for other factory districts. Trent House and its garden are owned by the city of Trenton and are listed in the National Register of Historic Places.

In the mid-1930s, Pendleton married Ezra Bowen, a retired professor of economics who was pursuing a new vocation as an artist. The couple kept a home in New York City and a cottage in Chilmark on Martha's Vineyard, where Pendleton developed a much-admired wildflower garden. The local daily, the *Vineyard Gazette,* reported frequently on the couple's nautical and horticultural activities. Generally using her maiden name, Pendleton designed gardens for her neighbors on the Vineyard, whose names are unrecorded. Ezra Bowen died in 1945, but Pendleton continued to summer on Martha's Vineyard until 1963.

Three years after her husband's death, Pendleton moved their Chilmark house to a site in Edgartown overlooking Vineyard Sound. Acting as her own architect, she remodeled the home. She also moved her Chilmark garden plantings with remarkably little plant loss but made significant changes, primarily to reduce maintenance. To the rear of the lot was a pitch pine grove, which was bordered with mass plantings of dwarf Japanese yews and cotoneaster. Also near the edge of the pine grove were a few small flowering trees, such as kousa dogwoods and hawthorns. Four small flowerbeds with perennials such as daylilies, delphiniums, and asters were located closer to the house.

Isabella Pendleton died in Princeton, New Jersey, on March 16, 1965, leaving a niece, Martha Hunt Nickerson of Lyme, Connecticut. No Pendleton archives have been located.

Arndt, Jessie Ash. "Gardens Don't Just Grow: Miss Pendleton Perfects Her Art." *Christian Science Monitor,* August 26, 1954, 10. A description of Pendleton's approach to garden making.

Pendleton, Isabella. "A House and Garden Built in Four Months: Moderate Garden Maintenance: A Major Consideration." *Landscape Architecture* 39, no. 3 (April 1949), 117–19.

Zaitzevsky, Cynthia. *Long Island Landscapes and the Women Who Designed Them.* New York: W. W. Norton & Company, 2004. Includes a brief biography of Pendleton and selected projects.

Cynthia Zaitzevsky

PESMAN, MICHIEL WALTER
(1887–1962)
LANDSCAPE ARCHITECT

Michiel Walter Pesman was born on May 28, 1887, in Thesinge, the Netherlands. In 1908, Pesman who was known as Walter immigrated to the United States and enrolled in Colorado Agricultural and Mechanics College (now Colorado State University) in Fort Collins, Colorado. He graduated in 1910 and moved to Denver, beginning a career in landscape architecture.

Little is known about Pesman's early career. In 1919, he formed DeBoer and Pesman Landscape Architects with Saco Rienk DeBoer. The partnership lasted for five productive years. Their commissions included both public and private work. The firm designed the grounds of many prestigious residences including the J. J. Hall home on Montview Boulevard and Forest Street; school grounds for Denver Public Schools, including Byers Middle School; civic landscapes for a number of Denver parks and parkways; and planning for many city plans, including the State and City Public Center in Cheyenne, Wyoming.

More important, the partnership yielded a design aesthetic that Pesman continued to refine throughout his career. From 1919 to 1924, Pesman's landscapes were formal design expressions in the tradition of English and European garden design where symmetrically arranged outdoor rooms complemented their buildings. Pesman articulated these spaces with thoughtful plantings, composed of a diverse array of species, frequently including an arboretum—a landscape feature that would become his signature. This style is exemplified at Skinner Middle School, located in northwest Denver and built in 1922, where formal landscape spaces transition in scale and complexity from building edge to street edge, wrapping the symmetrical Gothic-inspired building. Two arboreta, one an evergreen collection and the other composed of deciduous shade trees, contrast the axial symmetrical arrangement of the formal spaces.

Pesman's most significant work began soon after his partnership with DeBoer dissolved. Beginning in 1922 and lasting until 1932, the Denver Public Schools system enjoyed a major building period inspired by the City Beautiful Movement. With a $12 million bond, the Board of Education committed to civic architecture—defined by monumental buildings set amid beautiful landscapes—commissioning Denver's leading architects to design five high schools, ten middle schools, and twenty-four elementary schools. Pesman's contribution was twofold. He collaborated with Denver's elite architects, including Harry J. Manning and Burnham Hoyt, designing individual school grounds. He also served as landscape architect for the school system, independently designing

Country Club Gardens, Denver, Colorado. (Image courtesy of Tina Bishop)

Pesman combined a formal upper terrace at the primary building entry with a naturalistic lower lawn. His L-shaped rockery—a rustic stacked sandstone wall with crevices of native forbs—separated the two spaces and was the dominant landscape feature. A master of planting design, Pesman mixed exotics and native plant species to create distinct spaces providing shade, color, and fragrance. Pesman integrated his passion for educating others about the Colorado landscape with this project. He worked with the school community on a series of wood cuts illustrating the landscape, especially the rockery.

In 1940, construction began on Country Club Gardens, the largest private apartment project in Denver at that time. Walter Pesman was the landscape architect, working alongside the elite architecture firm of Fisher, Fisher & Hubbell, and prominent bankers and builders to create a model for modern apartment living for middle-class renters. Pesman's gardens are a series of private and public outdoor rooms that match the architecture in craft, material, and composition. While the buildings were sited symmetrically along a dominant north-south axis, Pesman's primary garden was composed along an east-west axis at the approximate center of the complex, creating the illusion that the buildings are subservient to the garden. Pesman's artful manipulation of plant material, topography, and building placement is evident. Topography and hedges defined landscape spaces, creating transitions from public open lawns to private gardens, which served as respites for the residents and play areas for the children. Pesman artfully employed the buildings as landscape features. Using the building edge as one side of an allée of trees, Pesman set evergreen trees as the other side to create a private walkway next to an open lawn. In keeping with his passion for the Colorado landscape, Pesman planted a rich

schools grounds as neighborhood centers with gardens, play areas, fields, and his signature arboreta.

Between 1926 and 1929, Pesman created his most memorable school landscape—Lake Middle School. Situated on a hillside on the shore of West Denver's Sloan's Lake and oriented to panoramic mountain views, Pesman masterfully integrated architect Burnham Hoyt's Tudor-inspired masterpiece with its commanding site. Employing an eclectic design vocabulary, variety of plant species, all carefully sited for composition, shade, color, and year-long interest. He was a landscape architect whose respect for and knowledge of the diverse and unique growing conditions of the Rocky Mountain region made him an originator of what would now be considered sustainable design.

Pesman's love of the Colorado landscape extended well beyond his design work, as did his desire to share his knowledge. He wrote extensively on the use of native plants and taught at Colorado State University and the University of Colorado. In 1928, he wrote about the importance of aesthetically improving the state's highways, presenting a paper entitled "A Landscape Architect's Views on Highway Planting." In 1942, he self-published *Meet the Natives; An Easy Way to Recognize Rocky Mountain Wildflowers, Trees, and Shrubs.* This easy-to-use field guide is a comprehensive resource on Colorado's climate and plant life. It is Pesman's treatise on the significance of Colorado's life zones and their symbiotic relationship to native plants. It has been so successful it is currently in its ninth edition, most recently reissued in 1992.

In 1959, Pesman presented a paper entitled "Little Known Ornamentals from the Land of the Rocky Mountains" at the 15th International Horticultural Congress in Nice, France, handing out packages of columbine seeds. In 1961, the year before his death, Pesman authored *Flora Mexicana,* a guide to recognizing Mexico's flora.

Throughout his life, Pesman was active in many civic affairs, including volunteering with the Colorado Forestry Association, and the Denver Society of Ornamental Horticulture, contributing regularly to their newsletter *Garden Hints.* In the early 1950s, Pesman was one of the influential city leaders who founded the Denver Botanic Gardens, beginning with a tree collection in Denver's City Park. When the Botanic Gardens moved to its permanent facility on the western edge of Cheesman Park in 1959, Pesman became a trustee.

Lake Middle School, Denver, Colorado. (Image courtesy of Tina Bishop)

Following a long illness, Pesman died at age seventy-five on November 15, 1962. At the time of his death, the Trustees of the Denver Botanic Gardens recognized his special contributions by the naming a popular mountain trail in his honor. The M. Walter Pesman trail is on Mount Goliath near Mount Evans.

The Denver Parks and Recreation Department Records 1861–2001, in the Western History Collection, Denver Public Library, Denver, Colo., includes numerous project drawings for the Park and Parkway system of Denver. The Denver Public Schools Archives contains project drawings for the Denver Public Schools and is not open to the public; special arrangements are needed to view documents. The Fisher Architectural Records Collection, in the Western History Collection, Denver Public Library, contains project drawings for the architectural firms of Fisher & Fisher and Fisher, Fisher & Hubbell, including those for Country Club Gardens for which M. Walter Pesman served as landscape architect.

Pesman, M. Walter. *Meet Flora Mexicana: An Easy Way to Recognize Some of the More Frequently Met Plants of Mexico as Seen from the Main Highways.* Globe, Ariz.: D. S. King, 1962. A guide to recognizing plants material of Mexico.

Pesman, M. Walter. *Meet the Natives: The Beginner's Field Guide to Rocky Mountain Wildflowers, Trees and Shrubs.* 10th ed. Denver: Denver Botanic Gardens and Roberts Rinehart Publishers, 2002.

Tina Bishop

PHILLIPS, WILLIAM LYMAN
(1885–1966)
LANDSCAPE ARCHITECT

William Lyman Phillips was born in West Somerville, Massachusetts, in 1885. Though he was raised in West Somerville, he took annual summer sojourns to East Boothbay, Maine. Phillips graduated from Somerville Latin High School in 1904 and entered Harvard College in the fall. Continuing at Harvard's newly established graduate program in landscape architecture in 1908, Phillips built a foundation of design principles that would inform fifty years of professional work in landscape architecture and planning.

Phillips's notebook from Professor **James Sturgis Pray**'s introductory course, Landscape Architecture I, cites **Charles Eliot**'s definition of the purpose of landscape architecture as the "art of arranging land and landscape for human use, convenience, and enjoyment." Phillips shared Eliot's view that landscape architects should be responsible for "the main lines" of the project, and Eliot's advocacy of unity as a dominant principle in which "the site, the scene, the landscape," and the buildings should be studied as one composition. Phillips supported Pray's belief that the goal of landscape architecture is a complex, but unified impression.

By 1911, Phillips was a member of the Boston Society of Landscape Architects and joined the firm of **Olmsted Brothers** as an assistant with responsibility for site work on the Boston Common, as well as for contracts and specifications. On leave in 1913, he traveled across Europe and subsequently was appointed landscape architect for the design and construction of the new town of Balboa, Panama, under the Isthmian Canal Commission, a position he held on site for the next sixteen months.

When Phillips returned to Cambridge in the winter of 1914, employment was scarce and for the next several years he worked across the United States until he joined the Quartermaster's Corps Construction Division, United States Army, at Camp Las Casas in San Juan, Puerto Rico. In 1919, he moved to Camp Bragg in North Carolina where he worked on layouts for army establishments. Over the next five years, Phillips successively practiced in Brookline, Massachusetts; spent a year based in Paris where he worked on American military cemeteries; and finally settled on the west coast of Florida where he planned a new town for the island of Boca Grande, to

William Lyman Phillips, Somerville Latin High School graduation photograph, ca. 1904. (Charles W. Tebeau Library of Florida History, Historical Museum of Southern Florida)

be developed by the American Agricultural Chemical Company. In 1925, when the company decided to abandon real estate development, Phillips moved to Lake Wales, Florida, where he renewed his association with Olmsted Brothers and began work on Mountain Lake Sanctuary with **Frederick Law Olmsted Jr.**, who had become the firm's senior partner.

Phillips's collaboration with the firm continued for the rest of the younger Olmsted's life and was the foundation for Phillips's long career in Florida. Later working as a designer for the National Park Service, Civilian Conservation Corps, and the Dade County Park and Recreation Department, Phillips created public landscapes that have defined the image of Florida. Matheson

Hammock, his first coastal park in Miami, also represents a prescient understanding of the vital role that the mangrove played in the composition of the park and in the ecology of the Florida shoreline. Phillips reported that while most viewed the mangrove swamp as hostile growth that must be removed, he realized that they were a disappearing type of forest that was unique and could play an important role in a total park effect. He noted that the mangrove swamps should be managed sympathetically and preserved as a significant cultural legacy.

Phillips's interest in the artistic potential of native materials engaged formal planning strategies within a tropical context. He used the principles of variety and contrast to heighten the experience of each landscape. At Matheson Hammock, he placed rusticated shelters made of native oolitic limestone at the edges of clipped lawns. Against a tropical hardwood hammock, he silhouetted an allée of Royal palms, each formal gesture carefully positioned to produce individual variety within a unified effect.

Fairchild Tropical Botanic Garden, in Coral Gables, named in honor of horticulturalist and plant explorer David Fairchild,* represents Phillips's longest association. He developed the original design and remained a consultant to the garden for more than two

Bok Mountain Lake Sanctuary Carillion Tower, ca. 1940. (Charles W. Tebeau Library of Florida History, Historical Museum of Southern Florida)

decades, establishing a model for the tropical botanic garden as a landscape of civic dimension. He described his intent in a report that was subsequently published in *Landscape Architecture* in January 1963. Phillips recalled his first decision to choose the principal families of plants to be exhibited. Once he determined the tropical basis of the collections, he chose to exhibit large shrubs and trees in families and turned to the site for organizational principles. He identified the upland of the garden as "the edge of an ancient marine terrace which appears as an abrupt cliff at other points along the Biscayne Bay shore," noting that the "escarpment was the boldest topographical feature and strongly influenced the plan-

ning." Phillips's determination to reveal the escarpment and to extend the major axes of two geometrically formal spaces—the Overlook and the Palm Glade—out over the lowland connected the upland to the lowland visually, thus unifying a series of botanic collections into composed, memorable scenes.

Unlike the broad axial views of French formal gardens, the vistas Phillips shaped for Fairchild were narrow. Phillips had discovered that "in Florida small landscape units and close views of vegetation are apt to be more attractive than wide views, and walks in the shade more agreeable than walks in the sun." He believed that the scenic effect was a product of organization and well-

Left: Palm Glade, Fairchild Tropical Botanic Garden, ca. 1945. (Courtesy of the Archive of Fairchild Tropical Botanic Garden)

Below: Phillips, working with the Civilian Conservation Corps, built roads and bridges at Greynolds Park, Miami, Florida, including the Lake Romeran oolitic limestone bridge and observation tower, pictured here ca. 1936. (Photo by Gleason Waite Romer; Romer Collection, Miami-Dade Public Library)

ity of Phillips's work throughout his life, Florida's isolation limited his profile in the national arena. He considered offers to return to Boston, but felt that since Florida had become his palette, he was reluctant to change his situation. His landscapes signified a sophisticated understanding of the authentic native landscape as both a frame and figure that could be accentuated by the exotic elements that had come to characterize Florida in popular culture. In recognition of his contribution to landscape architecture Phillips was awarded the Thomas Barbour Medal by Fairchild Tropical Garden in 1950, a medal previously awarded to Ernest F. Coe for his work on the establishment of Everglades National Park.

The range of Phillips's Miami work is extensive. He produced iconic scenes, such as the great allée of coconut palms at Crandon Park on Key Biscayne and more contemplative landscapes, such as the oolitic limestone gardens at the University of Miami and the greens of Woodlawn and Inman cemeteries. His landscapes include hundreds of private homes, businesses, and clubs, including the Indian Creek County Club and the Biscayne Bay Yacht Club, as well as public thoroughfares, including the Venetian and Rickenbacker Causeways. Across Florida his major works include a Riverfront Promenade for St. Augustine; Mountain Lake Sanctuary in Lake Wales; Highland Hammock Park in Sebring; McKee Jungle Gardens in Vero Beach; and at the southern tip of the peninsula, the Overseas Highway to the Keys. William Phillips passed away in 1966.

defined openings, both of which necessitated open space. In contrast to the axial geometry of the major vistas, Phillips juxtaposed the naturalistic edges of dense botanical plots. The entire plan, he wrote, "is essentially an articulated complex of openings."

After his work with Dade County concluded, Phillips maintained his association with Fairchild Tropical Garden as well as a private practice with numerous public, commercial, institutional, and residential clients. Although his immediate peers recognized the high qual-

Phillips's correspondence to clients and reports to his superintendents in the National Park Service can be found at the National Archives and Records Administration, the Historical Museum of Southern Florida Charlton W. Tebeau Research Center, the University of Miami Otto G. Richter Library, and the Harvard University Frances Loeb Library, Special Collections.

Ceo, Rocco, and Joanna Lombard. *The Historic Landscapes of Florida*. Miami: University of Miami School of Architecture and the Deering Foundation, 2001. In an essay on Phillips and studies of several of his landscapes, the author examines the design principles and impact of Phillips's work.

Jackson, Faith Reyher. *Pioneer of Tropical Landscape Architecture: William Lyman Phillips in Florida*. Gainesville: University Press of Florida, 1997. Mrs. Jackson, a journalist who was also a client of William Lyman Phillips, was authorized by Phillips's surviving daughter, Juliette Coyle, to write his biography. This book is the definitive work on Phillips's life and professional engagements.

Phillips, William Lyman. "Developing a Tropical Garden." *Landscape Architecture* 53, no. 2 (January 1963), 119–22. This article is based on Phillips's report on his intent for the design of Fairchild Tropical Botanic Garden.

Joanna Lombard

PILAT, IGNATZ ANTON
(1820–1870)
LANDSCAPE ARCHITECT, HORTICULTURALIST

Ignatz Anton Pilat was born in St. Agatha, Austria, on June 27, 1820. Although his parents wished for their son to enter the ministry, a love of gardening led Pilat to attend the University of Vienna where he studied horticulture while working for the university's botanical gardens. According to Pilat he "learned the art of gardening in the Gardens of the Earldom of Karrach in Aschach on the Danube." He later served as a gardener's assistant for Baron Charles von Hügel, one of Europe's premier horticulturalists, in the Heitzing Gardens near Vienna. The design for the estate grounds of Prince Klemens von Metternich, the Austrian foreign minister, at his home in the Rennweg in Vienna brought Pilat acclaim. On April 1, 1846, he was appointed assistant gardener in the Imperial Royal University Botanical Garden. Revolution broke out in Vienna in 1848. Metternich fled the country and Emperor Ferdinand I gave up his throne. With the loss of his patrons, Pilat and his brother, Carl Franz, immigrated to America, arriving in New York City and settling in Dalton, Georgia. Pilat landscaped Liberty Hall, the home of Alexander H. Stephens, the vice president of the Confederacy, in Augusta, Georgia. He also served as chief gardener on Thomas Metcalf's estate near Augusta.

Pilat held the post with Metcalf until 1852 when he returned to Vienna to serve as director of the botanical gardens. During this period he published in Vienna an elementary text on botany, and a small book on landscape gardening was published in Linz, Austria. He returned to the United States in 1856 and designed the garden of Miss Sarah Cumming of Augusta, Georgia, on The Sand Hills. Today, only the intricate pattern of the central flowerbed remains at what is now known as the Cumming-Langdon Place.

Pilat's work caught the attention of Andrew Haswell Green, chair of the Central Park Commission of New York, who appointed him chief landscape gardener of Central Park. Pilat and his colleague Charles Rawolle (1812–1867) wrote the report "Catalogue of Plants in August and September 1857 in the Ground of the Central Park," which identified 281 different plants that naturally occurred on the site. Egbert Viele, chief surveyor of the New York Park Department, praised Pilat, the "thorough botanist," for the "very valuable botanical reconnaissance of the exceedingly wild and unpromising area." In the 7th Annual Report of the Park Commission (December 31, 1863), Pilat included the "Catalogue of Trees, Shrubs and Herbaceous Plants on the Central Park . . . with the months of Flowering and Fruiting of such as have conspicuous blossoms or fruits." Pilat devoted the remaining thirteen years of his life to enhancing the plant collection in Central Park.

Samuel Parsons Jr. credited Pilat with the actual planting design for Central Park, stating that "the single specimens of trees [for Central Park] could only have been selected and arranged with the help of a plant expert who was also a landscape gardener, like Ignatz Pilat."

While serving as secretary of the Sanitary Commission during the Civil War, **Frederick Law Olmsted Sr.** spent a great deal of time away from New York City and assigned primary responsibility for the park to Pilat. In need of money, Pilat requested a promotion and was

Key individuals involved in the planning of Central Park standing on Willowdell Arch, 1862 (*from right to left*): Frederick Law Olmsted, Jacob Wrey Mould, Ignaz Anton Pilat, Calvert Vaux, George Waring, and Andrew Haswell Green; Victor Provost, photographer. (Charles Schwartz Ltd.)

creation of a pond, ornamental rock work, Bridge Number 25, the excavation of shaping land forms, the construction of through roads, and paths near the pool. Olmsted's respect for Pilat, however, clearly grew over time. When Olmsted and **Calvert Vaux** were reappointed to Central Park in 1865 they referred to Pilat as "brother artist," crediting him with having "freely rendered the design in our absence" and sending him a $500 bonus.

Critics lauded Pilat in the popular press. Numerous writers acknowledged his contributions to Central Park and enthusiastically credited him for his design expertise. Samuel Parsons Jr. acknowledged Pilat's plantings of the southern portion of the park as "one of the best landscapes in the Park." Parsons also credited Pilat with the planting design of the Ramble, a 38-acre wilderness garden in which Pilat and Olmsted highlighted not individual plants but mass plantings to create a naturalistic effect. The *Evening Post* said of the Ramble: "The Ramble is at present the very soul of the Park. So far as we have been able to learn, Ignatz A. Pilat is the gentlemen to whom the public is indebted for the fine effects in the arrangements of plants and the classification of colors which charm all visitors of taste to Central Park."

By 1873 with the park nearly complete, a survey indicated over 3,000 different plants were growing there. He brought to Central Park a formal education in design and horticulture, as well as a basic familiarity with American native plants.

In 1867, at the request of Olmsted and Vaux, Pilat submitted a list of trees found on the site of Prospect Park in Brooklyn, New York, and their condition. The next year he prepared detailed planting plans for the new park.

After his departure from Central Park, Calvert Vaux continued his private practice with Pilat who helped with "laying out several country places of small size." Pilat prepared a plan that was implemented from 1867 to 1870 for Mount Morris Square (now Marcus Garvey Park) in Harlem. His scheme remained largely intact until the 1930s.

made superintendent of a separate landscape gardening department in 1860. Despite Pilat's credentials and responsibilities, Olmsted's 1860 report on the park referred to him as "general foreman in charge of grubbing and nursery work."

In April 1862, Pilat wrote an unpublished report on the previous year's plantings to Andrew Haswell Green. Pilat was particularly concerned with the plantings of the northern portion of the park, starting this effort in November 1862. He reported to Olmsted regularly, describing in precise detail his planting plans and calling for creation of an arboretum and a flower garden. The arboretum was never realized. The flower garden was finally constructed in 1934. Central Park was constructed from the south to the north beginning at 59th Street. The entire northern portion, the greatest representation of Pilat's design philosophies, was completed by Pilat when Olmsted was not in New York. Construction included the

In 1870, New York City created its first Department of Public Parks with Ignatz Pilat as chief landscape architect. That year, Pilat and William Grant relandscaped Madison Square, a historically public open space that had existed since 1686 and which was formally opened as a public park in 1847. Pilat and Grant's design for Madison Square contained formal and pastoral elements, interspersing well-defined walkways with open lawns. He also transformed Washington Square Park that year with engineer Montgomery Alexander Kellogg. During his tenure he also prepared plans for the Battery, City Hall Park, Canal Street Park, Duane Street Park, and Beach Street Park. A simple diagram by Pilat for the Sixth Avenue Park, No. 1, at the intersection of Broadway and 6th Avenue, was also included in the first annual report of the New York Board of Park Commissioners in 1871. Pilat also prepared plans for Massachusetts Agricultural College and numerous private residences in the Northeast.

Ignatz Anton Pilat died of tuberculosis in New York City on September 17, 1870. In his obituary, the *New York Herald* said of Pilat's work, "He planned, superintended and directed the work on the [Central] Park from its commencement up to the time of his last illness, and to him more than to any other man is due the credit of the Park as it appears today." Pilat's nephew, Carl Franz, was appointed to the position of landscape architect of New York City Parks in 1913.

Graff, M. M. *The Men Who Made Central Park.* New York: Greensward Foundation, Inc., 1982. This makes a compelling case for the importance of Pilat's contribution to the design of the park.

Kirschner, Franziska. *Der Central Park in New York.* Worms, Germany: Werner, 2002. Provides an understanding of the contribution of Pilat and other German landscape designers, such as Wilhelm Fischer, to the design of Central Park. Also, the influence of German design thought on Frederick Law Olmsted.

Orange, Herbert J. "Frederick Law Olmsted: His Horticultural Philosophy and Practice." Master's thesis, University of Delaware, n.d. Offers the most comprehensive view of Pilat's relationship with Olmsted, as well as information gained from interviews with Pilat's grandsons, Oliver R. and William J. Pilat.

Kurt Culbertson

PITKIN, WILLIAM CHASE, JR.
(1884–1972)
LANDSCAPE ARCHITECT

William Chase Pitkin Jr. was born in Rochester, New York, in 1884 and he was raised there, where his family had lived for several generations and operated one of the many plant nurseries that gave Rochester acclaim as the Flower City in the nineteenth century. Rochester was one of the first cities after the Civil War to enact an ordinance requiring the planting of street trees, and flowering magnolias lined Oxford Street each spring. During his youth, Pitkin was exposed to the wonderful new parks and roadways being laid out by Frederick Law Olmsted Sr. between 1888 and 1900 and became accustomed to a cityscape that displayed a rich array of trees, shrubs, and flowers. He attended Cornell University from 1905 to 1907 where, in addition to horticulture, he likely studied landscape architecture under Bryant Fleming, whom Liberty Hyde Bailey chose to head the newly established Department of Landscape Art in the school's College of Agriculture. Also educated at Cornell, Fleming had worked with Warren Henry Manning before establishing his own practice designing Country Place–era estates, and appears to have strongly influenced Pitkin's specialization in residential design.

Pitkin returned to Rochester at a time when the city was expanding and many of the former nurseries and farms were being subdivided to form new residential neighborhoods. By 1909, Pitkin established a private practice with landscape architect Ralph A. Weinrichter. One of their earliest projects was the 1911 design of the grounds and garden at the Mrs. Minnie Matthews Nester Estate, in Geneva, New York, where they arranged a long, formal lawn with a series of low parterres connecting the house with a distant terrace overlooking Seneca Lake. Similarly working within a formal style, Pitkin designed the grounds of the Toledo Museum of Art from 1911 to 1912. At a time when formal landscapes were fashionable, Pitkin blended the naturalism of the Olmsted tradition with experimentation with formal Beaux-Arts and Renaissance-inspired conventions of early twentieth-century design. He frequently retained existing trees and substituted green hedges and shrubbery for the artificial balusters and parapets typically designed by architects of the period. Pitkin platted Home Acres (1910) and Highland Heights (1913), both Rochester subdivisions. He was greatly influenced by if not actually involved in the design and planting of the Browncroft neighborhood, which had deep setbacks and dense plantings of conifers and deciduous trees and shrubs.

In 1914, Pitkin partnered with Seward Hamilton Mott,* also of Rochester, who became his brother-in-law when he married Mott's sister. At that time, Pitkin was designing a housing subdivision in Flint for General Motors employees. Together they worked on many projects and in 1923 they incorporated and formed the firm of William Pitkin Jr. & Seward H. Mott—Landscape Architects. Mott the able civil engineer who described himself as a "land use engineer," complemented Pitkin's training in landscape architecture and strong horticultural knowledge, enabling the firm to take on large-scale projects that blended Olmsted-inspired principles with advances in Garden City planning.

In 1917, Pitkin designed the grounds of architect Ward Wellington Ward's home and studio in Syracuse, New York, and is believed to have worked with the architect on a number of homes in Syracuse and Rochester. Collaborating closely with architects throughout his career, Pitkin helped define the role of the professional landscape architect in twentieth-century residential design.

Pitkin's special talent lay in the design of domestic gardens and grounds ranging from estates to city lots. His highest priority in plant selection was the contribution the plant would make to structure and form. All his published designs featured carefully planted naturalistic borders of trees and shrubs surrounding the property's perimeter and dividing the interior space into smaller garden units. His small garden designs were typically rectilinear and featured enclosed flower gardens, sometimes sunken, with rectilinear perimeter walkways, open lawns, and garden views from the house. His designs emphasized continuous green foliage with seasonal displays of color, favoring the use of what he called "gardenesque shrubs" that, foremost, provided structural form

and, secondarily, supplied seasonal color when flowering. The firm's larger estate gardens were often a mix of naturalistic and formal designs. Pitkin took pride in his use of collected native plants, his ability to simulate natural plant communities, and designs that preserved mature trees already existing on site. For principles of small garden design he recommended **Fletcher Steele**'s 1926 book, *Design in the Little Garden.*

Most of Pitkin's known work dates from the 1920s when he was partnered with Mott and includes estates, subdivisions, parks, country clubs, and small garden designs. During this time, he wrote at least eight articles that appeared in a variety of periodicals, including *American Architect* and *National Real Estate Journal.* He also developed a personal reputation for campus design; his work included the grounds for Angell Hall (1924) at the University of Michigan, where he worked with architect Albert Kahn, and projects at the University of Rochester's River Campus (1934).

The firm gained a strong reputation for the design of fine estate grounds and residential subdivisions that attracted commissions across the Midwest and as far south as Florida. The combined talents enabled the firm to take on ambitious projects that required close attention to natural topography and streams, and to create idyllic, pastoral, and naturalistic environments.

Pitkin returned to Rochester in 1936 upon his father's death to assume the presidency of the family nursery and horticultural business, Chase Brothers Co., which had been founded by his mother's family about 1860. He sold the bulk of the business in 1940, but his son continued to operate the retail stores under the name Chase-Pitkin until they were sold in 1956. Pitkin served as the city's superintendent of parks from 1943 to 1950. He spent most of his later years in Asheville, North Carolina. Still practicing at the age of eighty, he contributed to master planning efforts for the College of Charleston in 1964. He died at Tryon, North Carolina, in 1972.

See also the individual entry on Seward Hamilton Mott and the joint entry on Pitkin & Mott. References follow the Pitkin & Mott entry.

Linda Flint McClelland and Charles T. Gleaves

PITKIN & MOTT

William Chase Pitkin Jr.* and Seward Hamilton Mott* formed a partnership in 1914 and incorporated as William Pitkin Jr. & Seward H. Mott— Landscape Architects in 1923. The firm quickly gained a strong reputation for the design of fine estate grounds and residential subdivisions that attracted commissions across the Midwest and as far south as Florida. In Cleveland after World War I, Pitkin and Mott worked for wealthy industrialists who were building fine homes along the shore of Lake Erie, out Fairmount Avenue, and in the fashionable new suburbs of Cleveland Heights and Shaker Heights. They continued to design spacious estates throughout western New York and the Midwest. *American Landscape Architecture,* the 1924 portfolio edited by **Philip Homer Elwood**, included examples of their work for William H. Murphy of Birmingham, Michigan; Truman H. Newberry of Grosse Point, Michigan; Herbert E. Crouch and George B. Montgomery of Buffalo, New York; and Mrs. E. K. Hays of Shaker Heights, Ohio. Their designs blended naturalistic design with a restrained formality and featured well-laid-out approaches and paths, formal sunken gardens, water features, and a wide variety of the garden types and planted features common to the larger Country Place–era estates. The combined talents enabled the firm to take on ambitious projects that required close attention to natural topography and streams, and to create idyllic, pastoral, and naturalistic environments, such as the mill pond at the Murphy Estate in Birmingham, Michigan, and the meadow stream at the Herbert Crouch Estate in Buffalo. In such water features, one perceives a Prairie-like feeling reminiscent of **Jens Jensen**'s work at Humboldt Park in Chicago and the Rubens Estate in Glencoe, Illinois.

The dynamism of the two partners was most emphatically expressed in the design of residential subdivisions, commonly called "allotments" by the real estate

Entrance to Lower Garden, Kingwood, estate of Charles Kelley King, Mansfield, Ohio, ca. 1940 view. (Kingwood Center)

community. Following their work for General Motors Corporation, the firm worked with the New York architectural firm of George B. Post & Sons on the influential plan for Eclipse Park (1916), in Beloit, Wisconsin, a residential community for the employees of Fairbanks, Morse and Company. At Eclipse Park, they introduced a broad sweeping diagonal to form an axial backbone from which lesser curvilinear roads symmetrically branched; the symmetry dissolved as the roads naturalistically bent away from the central axis and followed the natural contours of the site. The plan immediately attracted considerable attention to the possibilities of moderate priced housing for working-class Americans, receiving praise from *Architectural Record* as one of the nation's "most artistic and attractive" developments.

The most influential of the firm's early subdivisions was Upper Arlington in Columbus, Ohio, designed for developer King C. Thompson. The first plan for Upper Arlington was drawn by Pitkin in 1913 and was followed by a series of plats and improvements during the following decade for an area amounting to more than 1,000

Front Lawn of Toledo Museum of Art, ca. 1920, from P. H. Elwood, *American Landscape Architecture*, 1924.

acres. The firm's designs featured curvilinear roads following the natural contours of the land, deep setbacks, and abundant parks and open space. Other early projects by the firm included Old Beechwold, also in Columbus; Rosedale in Detroit; Wyomissing Hills near Reading, Pennsylvania; and several subdivisions in Shaker Village, Ohio.

As a result of their successes in Columbus and Shaker Village, the firm's commissions grew following World War I when economic prosperity brought renewed demand for suburban homes in upper-priced garden suburbs. Notable projects from this time include Forest Glen Estates in Youngstown, Ohio; Avondale in Jacksonville, Florida; and Rosedale Gardens in Detroit, which received recognition in *Architectural Record*. The most striking characteristic of their mature work was the abundance of evergreen and deciduous trees that filled the broad margins between street and sidewalk, and blended seamlessly with informal groupings of trees in spacious front yards.

Kingwood, the estate of Charles Kelley King in Mansfield, Ohio, now known as Kingwood Center, is currently a botanical garden open to the public. The formal garden designed by the firm in 1926 is intact and is being preserved as part of the center's long-term plans. Inspired by the English Arts and Crafts style of Gertrude Jekyll, Edward Lutyens, and Lawrence Weaver, the gar-

den reflects Pitkin and Mott's admiration for the craftsmanship, native stonework, and what they described in *The American Architect* as "the pictorial aspect of old English towns." The informal groupings of deciduous and evergreen trees surrounding the estate's perimeter and articulating the open lawns further reflect the firm's treatment of estate grounds.

The Great Depression brought an end to the sustained prosperity that fueled the firm's commissions through the 1920s. By the mid-1930s, the two designers had taken widely different paths, with Pitkin returning to Rochester to operate the family nursery and Mott locating to Washington, D.C., to promote neighborhood planning on a national scale.

Elwood, P. H., ed. *American Landscape Architecture*. New York: Architectural Book Publishing Company, 1924. Portfolio containing overall views, garden details, and one plan of the residential estates designed by Mott and Pitkin outside the industrial cities of the American Midwest. Includes residences of William H. Murphy and Truman H. Newberry near Detroit, George B. Montgomery and Herbert E. Crouch near Buffalo, and Mrs. E. K. Hays of Shaker Heights, Ohio.

Mott, Seward. "The Federal Housing Administration and Subdivision Planning," *Architectural Record* 19 (April 1936), 257–63; "The FHA Small Homes Program," *Landscape Architecture* 33, no. 1 (1942), 16; "Land Planning in the FHA: 1934–44," *Insured Mortgage Portfolio* 8, no. 4 (second quarter 1944), 12–14. Three articles explaining the

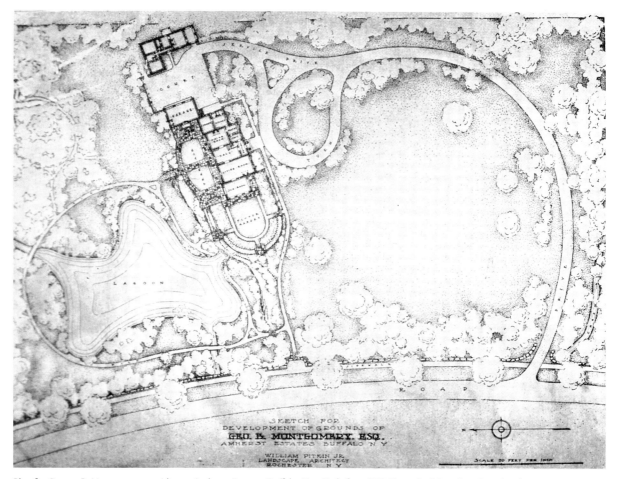

Plan for George B. Montgomery residence, Amherst Estates, Buffalo, New York, from P. H. Elwood edition, *American Landscape Architecture,* 1924.

philosophy, principles of subdivision design and neighborhood planning, and method for design review, which Mott, as head of the Land Planning Division, formulated for the Federal Housing Administration.

Pitkin, William, Jr. "The Relationship between the Architect and the Landscape Architect," *The American Architect* (March 17, 1920), 327–34 and 363–67; "The Problem of the Small City Lot," *Architecture* (March 1920), 86–92; and "How to Plan Allotments," *National Real Estate Journal* (Feb. 2, 1920), 16–20. A trilogy of articles with many examples examining the role of the landscape architect in residential design. Includes an index to the best practices, and business aspects, including collaboration with architects and community builders.

See also the individual entries on Seward Hamilton Mott and William Chase Pitkin Jr.

Research assistance for this entry was provided to Charles T. Gleaves by Rose Mary Hoge, librarian, Cleveland Public Library.

Linda Flint McClelland and Charles T. Gleaves

PITZMAN, JULIUS
(1837–1923)
SURVEYOR, PLANNER

Julius Pitzman was born in Halberstadt, Prussia, on January 11, 1837. He immigrated to the United States with his widowed mother and siblings, settling first in Waukesha, Wisconsin. At the age of seventeen, he went to St. Louis to work for his brother-in-law Charles E. Salomon, owner of a successful surveying and engineering firm. Salomon was elected St. Louis county engineer in 1858 and placed Pitzman in charge of the office. After supervising county work for less than two years, Pitzman established his own business, Pitzman's Company, Surveyors and Engineers.

When Salomon joined the Union army at the outbreak of the Civil War, officials made his young protégé the acting county engineer. Within three months, however, Pitzman too volunteered and was appointed first lieutenant of the Topographical Engineers. Serving under both William T. Sherman and Ulysses S. Grant, his surveying and mapmaking skills made him a highly regarded officer. During the Siege of Vicksburg, in June 1863, Pitzman was wounded in the hip while reconnoitering near enemy lines. He returned to St. Louis to recover and rejuvenate his business. Finding many inaccuracies in early maps of the area, Pitzman gained a reputation for precise and detailed survey work. He consulted for attorneys and served as an expert witness during boundary disputes and other property litigation.

In October 1863, he was elected county surveyor and settled into a lifelong occupation delineating, developing, and improving the city. He worked to mitigate the deleterious effects of the city's rapid growth, exhorting owners to improve their properties by grading, burying utilities, and planting trees. As rail service continued to expand into the growing city, Pitzman helped develop alternatives to street-level crossings near the depots. Over the next decade, Pitzman was responsible for surveying much of the area in and around St. Louis. His reputation as arbiter of the city's various boundaries and lot lines was secured with the publication of his St. Louis County maps in 1878 and 1886.

In 1867, Pitzman began work on a succession of private residential subdivisions, for which he was surveyor, investor, promoter, and occasionally resident. Called "private places," they would be his most notable con-

Julius Pitzman. (Courtesy of Kent and Mary Lou Salomon)

tribution to the shaping of St. Louis and to the field of urban design. These developments featured streets and open areas owned and maintained by the property owners rather than the municipality. Though originally unique to St. Louis, the concept of a privately administered urban enclave was a precursor to the homeowners' association common today.

Private places were a response by the increasingly prosperous middle and upper classes to the chaotic industrial growth of St. Louis and the slow development of that city's infrastructure. Located on the urban fringe, near enough to commute to the city center but sufficiently distant from the crowding and pollution, private places offered spacious, clean, and controlled environments. Deed restrictions stipulated the scale, massing, setback, building materials, and cost of construction, and regulated ongoing operation of the places. Taverns, shops, and other commercial functions were usually prohibited; only doctors and dentists could use their homes for business.

"Plan of Forest Park
Addition," lithograph,
1887. (Missouri
Historical Society)

Entrepreneurs, business executives, and other inves-
tors purchased and assembled tracts of land on the edge
of the city to develop these new residential enclaves.
Pitzman surveyed the sites, laid out the streets and lot
lines, and helped establish the regulations that would
govern the developments; he was also an occasional
investor, and trustee. Most private places featured a
combination of ornate masonry gateways, semicircular
entrances, parks, and parkways. Pitzman's designs separated the subdivisions not only from the larger city, but
from adjacent neighborhoods creating discrete communities of leafy quiet streets, substantial lots, and large
homes.

Some of the designs largely retained the urban grid
and rectilinear lots but restricted entry on the ends and
inserted landscaped parkways between the streets. This
was the case with Pitzman's first design (and the second
private place in the city), Benton Place, built in 1868 adjacent to Lafayette Park. In 1870, Pitzman improved upon
his first design with a development called Vandeventer
Place. Considered by many to be the most elegant and
successful private place design in St. Louis, it featured a
columned entrance gate and central parkway with water
fountains.

Other Pitzman-designed private places had curvilinear
street patterns similar to those introduced by the then-
popular picturesque rural cemeteries. An obviously in-
efficient division of land, Pitzman's arcing streets, seen
in Clifton Heights (1885) and Compton Heights (1889)
among others, suggested affluence and indulgence, further demarcating the developments as private property.

Upon his return from an 1874 trip to study European
parks and gardens, Pitzman placed his growing reputation behind efforts to establish a major park in the St.
Louis area. The county hired him to survey an undeveloped tract west of the city that totaled over 1,300 acres.
Pitzman was then instrumental in convincing the local
government to turn the site into Forest Park. When de-
tractors argued that the rugged site was ill-suited for use
as parkland, Pitzman asserted that its rough features
would remain in place and contribute to the design's
picturesque character. As chief engineer for the project, Pitzman played a substantial role in developing
Forest Park's plan, working alongside the main designer
Maximilian G. Kern. When the city and county governments were separated in 1876, Pitzman became city surveyor and engineer.

Forest Park's success stimulated the development

of new private places on nearby properties. In 1887, Pitzman platted (and Maximilian Kern landscaped) the Forest Park Addition, just north of the park and including Westmoreland and Portland Places. These linear places featured main entrance gates on either end. Just inside each gate, the entrance branched into streets divided by a central parkway. Pitzman's 1892 Washington Terrace, also north of the park, was a more modest design with an ornate entrance but no parkway.

In 1905, Pitzman laid out what would be the largest of his private place designs, the 70-acre Parkview. Straddling the line between the city of St. Louis and the newly incorporated University City, Parkview was meant to surpass all previous developments and become the most desirable subdivision in the area. As with other private places, Parkview set itself apart from the surrounding neighborhood with a gatehouse and deed restrictions. To further distinguish Parkview as an elite and separate enclave, Pitzman broke from the rectilinear street grid and established a pattern of six curved streets one set atop the next. Corner lots, where the curving streets and the linear street grid met, became park areas.

Pitzman was also active regionally, and to some extent nationally. He undertook several projects in East St. Louis and laid out the rectilinear plan for Granite City, Illinois, an industrial town founded in 1896 by an enamelware manufacturer. In addition, he designed City Park in Little Rock, Arkansas, and the 1884 West Side Park racetrack in Nashville, Tennessee (on property that is now part of Centennial Park).

Julius Pitzman died in 1923 at the age of eighty-seven. In all, he designed forty-seven private place residential developments in St. Louis. By the turn of the century, his firm had completed over half of all the surveys made in the St. Louis area. Pitzman's atlas and other maps still serve as reliable documentation of the city's growth, property ownership, and land use. In recent years his private places have been rediscovered and often rehabilitated. They are once again among the most desired residences in the city.

Hunter, Julius K. *Westmoreland and Portland Places: The History and Architecture of America's Premier Private Streets, 1888–1988.* Columbia: University of Missouri Press, 1988. Study of the history, design, and architecture of one of Pitzman's private places, with some biographical material.

Hyde, William. *Encyclopedia of the History of St. Louis.* Louisville, Ky.: The Southern History Company, 1899. Contains a detailed biography of Julius Pitzman with a special emphasis on his activities beyond the development of private places.

Loughlin, Caroline, and Catherine Anderson. *Forest Park.* Columbia: University of Missouri Press, 1986. A history of the largest park in St. Louis; as surveyor and then chief engineer, Julius Pitzman was instrumental in its creation.

Chad Randl

PRAGNELL, CECIL
(1881–1970)
LANDSCAPE ARCHITECT

Cecil Pragnell was born in Sherbourne Castle, England, on December 28, 1881. He became familiar with some of Europe's great landscapes at an early age. His father, who accompanied Charles Darwin on the historic voyage of the HMS *Beagle* that resulted in *The Origin of Species,* had worked in Queen Victoria's botanical gardens. Young Cecil learned the Latin names of the many plants in the royal gardens and traveled to Africa with his father to collect rare plant specimens. He was apprenticed to a Belgian orchid grower and spent fourteen months touring the royal gardens of Europe. Remarkably, he accomplished all this before the age of seventeen. Pragnell would complete his notable career decades later at the Glorieta Baptist Assembly in New Mexico, carrying out and embellishing the vision of Clarence Edmund "Bud" Hollied* for Glorieta Gardens.

From 1899 to 1902 Pragnell served in the Boer War in South Africa. By 1903, Pragnell had been pressed into the service of the British Crown to help prepare the presentation grounds in New Delhi for the coronation of Edward VII as emperor of India. He then ran a rubber plantation near Singapore and built a 40-acre water garden for the shah of Persia before leaving for North America in 1910. In Canada, he joined the gold rush to Alaska and the Yukon. In 1915, he arrived at the San Francisco World's Fair, where he managed the Philippine orchid and exotic plants exhibit.

Once Pragnell reached California, it took little time

Cecil Pragnell with his wife, New Mexico, 1957.
(LifeWay Glorieta Conference Center)

Garden path at the Glorieta Conference Center, New Mexico.
(Photo courtesy of Baker A. Morrow)

before his landscaping talents were recognized. He worked with Charles Gibbs Adams* on the grounds of the William Randolph Hearst estate at San Simeon, California, and with **Rose Ishbel Greely** at Los Poblanos Ranch of Albert G. and Ruth Hanna McCormick Simms in Albuquerque, New Mexico.

Pragnell fell in love with the bright blue skies and the endless open spaces of New Mexico. To earn a stable income, he became Bernalillo County (Agricultural) Agent in the 1950s, and served in that capacity for eight years. Pragnell managed the New Mexico Boys Ranch for several years in central New Mexico before moving to Glorieta, New Mexico, just east of Santa Fe, to take over landscape responsibilities for the grounds of the Glorieta Baptist Assembly from Hollied.

At the age of seventy-two, Pragnell undertook the implementation and expansion of his recently deceased friend's plans for the newly opened Glorieta Baptist Assembly. The Assembly grounds had been somewhat deforested during the railroad construction era beginning in the 1880s, so Pragnell had thousands of native trees moved from remote areas of the nearby mountains to improve the Assembly's property. He raised thousands of plants in Glorieta's greenhouses for his botanical creations that included a depiction of a Bible made of lobelias and gray flax, a globe of blue lobelias and yellow marigolds, and the World Mission Garden of hollyhocks. He grew and tested hundreds of varieties of plants for high-altitude gardening, including alyssum, begonia, balsam, calendula, celosia, columbine, clema-

tis, gaillardia, poppy, phlox, salvia, verbena, and yarrow, as well as numerous herbs. Pragnell's Glorieta Gardens, with acres of terraces and specialty plantings, became a late-life passion. He viewed the gardens as an "outdoor cathedral; above is the sky." He noted, "Its spires are the trees pointed upward to God. A foundation of rock is under this temple. The mountains are its only walls and the good earth is its floor." The grounds today exhibit the character of a somewhat rustic Italian villa garden, with wagon wheels at waterfalls along a central water axis. Stone terrace walls and paved pathways make for acres of breezy strolling grounds, quite rare in New Mexico. Though the thousands of flowers Pragnell cultivated and planted are no longer evident, the landscape still blazes with color, especially in fall, when the aspens turn a rich gold.

An extraordinary designer and landscape gardener, Pragnell left Glorieta in 1962 to live with his daughter in South Carolina. In a few singular works, he had helped to create a tradition of large-scale, European-influenced landscape design in a pocket of the Southwest that had scarcely seen anything of the sort in earlier centuries. He died in 1970 at the age of eighty-nine.

Danielson, Dale. "Glorieta, the Impossible Dream that Became Reality." *Impact Albuquerque Journal Magazine,* June 15, 1982. A brief history of the Glorieta Conference Center's development.
Danielson, Dale, and Betty Danielson. *Glorieta and Northern New Mexico Discovery Tours: The Impossible Dream That Became Reality. Volume 1: A History of Glorieta Baptist Conference Center.* Colorado Springs, Colo.: Great Western Press, 1985. Includes a chapter on

the development of Glorieta Gardens and a discussion of Cecil Pragnell's background and his contribution to the design of the grounds.

Morrow, Baker A. "Rio Grande Landscape Architecture." In *A Dictionary of Landscape Architecture*. Albuquerque: University of New Mexico

Press, 1987, 280–81. Cites Cecil Pragnell and Bud Hollied as influential figures in early twentieth-century Southwestern regional style.

Baker H. Morrow and Judy Kowalski

PRICE, THOMAS DREES
(1901–1989)
LANDSCAPE ARCHITECT

Thomas Drees Price was born in 1901 in Porto Alegre, Brazil, to a missionary family in the region of Rio Grande do Sul. At sixteen, his parents sent him to the United States, where he enrolled at Ohio State University. His initial goal, according to his sister, was to gain the knowledge of agriculture and farming needed to start a ranch in Brazil. His talents in art proved greater than his gifts for animal husbandry and by his second year, he changed to the course in landscape architecture, while working in his uncle's brass foundry. In 1923, Price moved to Cambridge, Massachusetts, and attended Harvard University to finish the coursework for his bachelor of science degree, which he completed in 1924. He then stayed on for his master of landscape architecture degree, which he earned in 1926.

Thomas Price was a modest man, a talented designer with the work ethic of his Welsh coalminer ancestors, according to his family. **James Sturgis Pray** encouraged him, and the academic system at Harvard rewarded his efforts. A classmate of Richard K. Webel* and **Thomas Dolliver Church**, Price won the intercollegiate design competitions of the day and the **Charles Eliot** traveling fellowship. After graduating, he worked for **Olmsted Brothers**, from 1926 to 1929, with a year off for the Eliot Fellowship. The firm's records indicate that he worked primarily on campuses and private residences. In 1929, the American Academy in Rome awarded him the Rome Prize in Landscape Architecture.

Price's background laid the groundwork for his travels and fellowship at the American Academy in Rome. He was able to use his fluency in Portuguese and Spanish to research in the libraries of Spain, and visited a standard itinerary of sites in Portugal and Spain. His work at the brass foundry fostered a continuing interest in metalwork, seen in his sketchbook, collected pieces, and publications in *Landscape Architecture*. He came to love urban life and would never return to a rural setting.

Thomas Drees Price at Horace's Villa, oil portrait by Donald Mattison (AAR painting fellow), ca. 1930. (Courtesy of John Gorsuch)

Price arrived in Rome in 1929 as the first Kate Lancaster Brewster Fellow in Landscape Architecture. With three landscape architects present (the others being Richard K. Webel and **Michael Rapuano**), they joined that year's annual collaborative project entitled "A Monument to Mechanical Progress," a highly contentious topic that brought the Fellows' interests in modern design into full conflict with the Academy Trustees' convictions about the value of classical inquiry. Price, never a diarist or correspondent, left no record of his position in these heated debates.

In 1929, the Italian authorities offered the foreign schools in Rome the chance to apprentice Fellows in the classics to Italian archaeologists at work on sites in the

Section of Horace's Villa, Licenza, Italy, by Price, 1930. (Courtesy of Henrique Price Grecchi)

area. The academy's archaeologists in that year had prior commitments, so Price conducted work with Guiseppe Lugli at Horace's Villa at Licenza in November and December 1930. Price participated in a second collaborative project, "A Small Museum for Classical Renaissance Sculpture on the Estate of a Wealthy Collector." The Fellows treated this project as a farce, but Price's team was close and visited him during the excavations in the spring of 1931. Price's essay, photographs, and drawings in the *Memoirs of the American Academy in Rome* form the only publication of the excavation. It is also the first time a landscape architect authored a paper in this scholarly publication, normally represented by classicists and humanists. Price also created measured drawings of the Villa Aldobrandini at Frascati and the House of Loreius Tiburtinus at Pompeii. His models and drawings of these projects were displayed at the Exhibition of Italian Gardens at the Palazzo Vecchio in Florence from 1931 to 1932. His productivity as a Fellow was widely praised and he was granted an additional year at the academy.

Returning to the United States in 1932, Price worked as a forester for the Civilian Conservation Corps in Massachusetts. Later that year **Gilmore David Clarke**, a new trustee of the American Academy, recruited him to the New York City Department of Parks and Recreation. Price's projects have yet to be inventoried, but his records and Parks publications indicate that he worked on the Central Park Zoo, Madison Square Park, Astoria Park, and various other smaller parks.

In 1934, Price worked on the design team for the Conservatory Gardens in Central Park. M. Betty Sprout, wife of Gilmore Clarke, designed the elegant planting scheme, which is the focus of the garden to many visi-

tors. Price was credited for the site design (including the terracing, architectural elements, and circulation) in later years by Richard Webel, Domenico Anese, and others. In a clearly collaborative context, the conceptual design may have been worked out by any combination of Sprout, Price, and Clarke. Price's ideas from his publications and sketchbook observations on ironwork of trellises and fencing, terracing, and well-head fountains are evident in the details of the project.

Price regarded the 1939 World's Fair as the apex of his design career. A member of the staff of the commission, Price developed Lucio Costa's conceptual sketch for the Brazil Pavilion's modern garden. Fluent in Portuguese and familiar with modernist ideas, he easily developed the design for Oscar Neimeyer's pavilion. Some scholars have suggested that the young Roberto Burle Marx was the designer, as he was working in Rio with Costa at the time, but Roberto Burle Marx scholars in Brazil credit Price, who is regarded as a Brazilian landscape architect. For Price, the project led to a promising design position in the firm of the fair's architects, Stephen Vorhees and Ralph Walker. With the onset of World War II, however, Price worked mainly in the Caribbean on military base designs with Walker, surviving the crash of a Pan Am flight in San Juan Bay in 1941.

In 1942, Price enlisted in the U.S. Army and served as a translator throughout the war. After he was decommissioned, the design world had changed. Price rejoined the office of Vorhees, Walker, Smith, Smith, and Haines in New York, but the position of landscape architect in the firm was greatly diminished, as it was for the profession, generally, during the period of the International Style. Price worked for the firm for the duration of his career

RESTORED · PLAN · OF
HORACE'S · SABINE · VILLA

Above: The Brazil Pavilion at the 1939 World's Fair, New York, New York. (American Academy in Rome Photographic Archive)

Left: Horace's Sabine Villa, a restored plan which appeared in Norman Thomas Newton's *Design on the Land.* (Courtesy of Charles A. Birnbaum)

Daniel Urban Kiley.* He lived, almost to the chapter, the twentieth-century landscape architecture of **Norman Thomas Newton**'s *Design on the Land:* His clean, simple designs show the attention to detail from his training at Harvard and the Olmsted office. His dedication to interdisciplinary teams reflects an American tradition of collaboration that was perhaps the best legacy of the American Academy in Rome in the early part of the century, seen also in the work of the New York City Department of Parks and Recreation and the World's Fair. His translation of classical lines and proportions to park design is akin to the work of Dan Kiley. Price, a bachelor, retired to live with his sister's family in Denver in 1978. He died of complications of Parkinson's disease in 1989.

Gleason, Kathryn. "Biographical Sketch of Thomas Drees Price." In Bernard Frischer, Jane Crawford, and Monica De Simone, *"The Villa of Horace" at Licenza, Final Report of the Excavations 1996–1999.* Oxford, U.K.: Archaeopress, 2006. Details on Price's work at the American Academy in Rome, full color publication of his drawings of Horace's Villa, and details on current location of his archives.

Price, Thomas Drees. "A Reconstruction of 'Horace's Sabine Villa.'" *Memoirs of the American Academy in Rome* 10 (1932), 135–42. Provides photographs, drawings and some detail on the excavations of the villa in 1931–1932, together with Price's views as a landscape architect on some of the construction problems at the site.

Price, Thomas Drees, "Some Mediterranean Wellheads." *Landscape Architecture* 23, no. 2 (January 1933), 97–109. One of three articles he published in the magazine, with earlier pieces in 1927 and 1929.

Kathryn L. Gleason

at a meager salary, yet he enjoyed the work and his colleagues in the New York design community and was active in the American Society of Landscape Architects and the Architectural League. Domenico Anese remembers him as a "designer's designer," a man who designed the bones of a project without a lot of self-promotion. Drawings from his projects with Ralph Walker remain in the uncataloged archives of the successor firm.

Thomas Drees Price's career offers a different view of landscape architecture's transition to modernism, now characterized by the lives of his classmates and the younger modernists, Garrett Eckbo,* James C. Rose, and

REHMANN, ELSA
(1886–1946)
LANDSCAPE ARCHITECT, AUTHOR

Elsa Rehmann was born in the Forest Hills section of Newark, New Jersey, in April 1886. Her father, an architect who emigrated from Germany, presided over the Newark Public Drawing School. Rehmann attended Wells College in Aurora, New York, from 1904 to 1906, intending to take up writing as a profession. She then transferred to Barnard College in New York City, where she received a bachelor of arts degree in 1908.

Following her graduation from Barnard, she studied at the Lowthorpe School of Landscape Architecture for Women in Groton, Massachusetts. The Lowthorpe School trained women to take an active and professional part in gardening, horticulture, and landscape architecture, emphasizing, in particular, design and construction. Rehmann remained at the school until 1911 and was probably among one of the first of eight to graduate from there.

In 1911, Rehmann began an apprenticeship, working in New York City for two landscape architects: Charles N. Lowrie, head of the Hudson County park system, and **Marian Cruger Coffin**, who specialized in estate gardens. During this apprenticeship, Rehmann produced her first book, *The Small Place: Its Landscape Architecture,* a selection of fifteen diverse landscape designs that represented her ideas of well-organized plans, published by the Knickerbocker Press in 1918. The idea for the book grew out of Rehman's "intensive study of the small place from the point of view of the landscape architect," and as such was one of the earliest publications to illustrate, and credit, a diversity of residential designs to the landscape architect who actually laid out the grounds. Landscape architects included in this residential survey of "complete and well organized plans" include Lowrie, Coffin, **Alling Stephen DeForest**, **Warren Henry Manning**, the **Olmsted Brothers**, **Arthur Asahel Shurcliff**, Elizabeth Leonard Strang,* and the firm of Pray, Hubbard and White (**James Sturgis Pray**, **Henry Vincent Hubbard**, and **Stanley Hart White**), among others. During this same time period, Rehmann also published many magazine articles in magazines such as *Garden Magazine, Country Life, House Beautiful,* and *Better Homes and Gardens.* The content of all these articles, in addition to her first two books, comprise the typical gardenesque theories of the period.

Elsa Rehman, ca. 1907. (Barnard College Archives)

In 1919, Rehmann established her own office, working out of her home. She planned gardens for clients in Essex County and in other parts of New Jersey, as well as in Pennsylvania, Delaware, New York, and parts of New England. These designs included the Saks Garden at Elberon, New Jersey, in 1921; the Watter Garden at Essex Fells, New Jersey, in 1923; the Dominick Garden at Rumson, New Jersey, in 1923; and the Hirshon Garden at New Rochelle, New York, in 1923. Rehmann produced a second book in 1926, *Garden-Making,* a discourse on garden theory, published by the Houghton Mifflin Company. This practical book is richly illustrated with photographs by her sister, Antoinette Perrett. In addition to including her own work, as with her earlier publication, the contributing landscape architect is always credited by name, and this book includes work by **Nathan Franklin Barrett**, **Beatrix Jones Farrand**, **James L. Greenleaf**, **Charles A. Platt**, **Ellen Biddle Shipman**, and the Olmsted Brothers.

During the 1920s, Rehmann became associated with Vassar College and entered into an association with Edith Roberts that would alter her landscape philosophy. Roberts, a botanist who was a pioneer in the new science

Vassar coeds planting in the Open Field Association, Dutchess County Botanical Garden, from The Ecology Society of America's *Ecology Journal*, ca. 1921.

of plant ecology, developed an outdoor botanical laboratory for experimental ecology. This site became known as the Dutchess County Botanical Garden. It was the first of its kind in the United States. Roberts and Rehmann established plants native to Dutchess County, New York, in their correct associations and demonstrated plants in artfully designed landscapes, and used the design and scientific data produced by this laboratory. In 1924, the Conservation Committee of the Garden Club of America published in their *Bulletin* a booklet by Roberts and Margaret F. Shaw on "The Ecology of Plants Native to Dutchess County, New York." This booklet in turn suggested the idea for a series of articles that later would appear in *House Beautiful*. Finally, in 1929, these articles were published as a book, *American Plants for American Gardens: Plant Ecology—The Study of Plants in Relation to their Environment,* by Roberts and Rehmann.

Although ideas about native plants had been generally supported by other gardeners and prominent American landscape architects, Rehmann and Roberts promoted a scientific view, stating that accurate environmental planting would guarantee a successful outcome and reduce the loss of plants, as well as create authenticity in the natural character, a view that addressed practicality, health, and accuracy. Rehmann's book included extensive listings of native plant associations. An advertisement promoted the value of these lists to the owner or developer of naturalistic plantings, noting that they were unavailable anywhere else. These lists included eleven types of associations, primarily for New England and the Mid-Atlantic states. The book developed ecological concepts in more detail than other books and promoted the use of plant associations for the entire property, including the siting and characteristics of the house as well. Not only did this book list native plants by association, but it also provided the patterns, or design compositions, in which they grew. Science was discussed as an art form.

Elsa Rehmann's book promoted the idea that art and nature could coexist. Her design theory springs from a desire for science, geographic diversity, and art to coexist. Although well received by the critics, the book never achieved any lasting visibility.

Rehmann apparently retired from her practice when she moved to Rockport, Massachusetts, in 1929, to live with her sister, Antoinette Perrett. During the 1930s, she participated in a series of lectures with Stephen F. Hamblin, sponsored by the Cambridge School's Boston alumnae group. She may have had some connections with the Rockport Summer School extension of the Cambridge School. She wrote poetry, some ecological in spirit, after she moved to Rockport; a volume called *First Poems* was published in 1933. Elsa Rehmann died on May 30, 1946, in Rockport. In 1996, *American Plants for American Gardens* was reprinted by the University of Georgia with an introduction by Dr. Darrel Morrison, wherein he remarked, "This volume has a message that is as solid today as it was the day it was published."

Rehmann, Elsa. *Garden-Making.* Boston/New York: Houghton Mifflin Co., 1926. This book includes, among others, her own garden designs in the gardenesque style. Discourse includes typical topics such as design, plant material, distribution, ornament, and fragrance. Reviews noted that this publication displays her enthusiastic and poetic style, her thoroughness and finish in her work, making it a readable, human, and yet scholarly book.

Rehmann, Elsa. *The Small Place.* New York: Knickerbocker Press, 1918. This work portrays residential designs by other notable landscape architects, and is accompanied by her personal design commentary.

Wurman, Dorothy. "Elsa Rehmann, Ecological Pioneer—A Patch of Ground." Proceedings of "A Century of Women" conference, Department of Landscape Architecture and Environmental Planning, University of California at Berkeley, California, November 2002. Paper discusses the content and significance of the book, *American Plants for American Gardens,* and presents some of Rehmann's life and the events surrounding the production.

Dorothy Wurman

REICH, ROBERT S.
(1913–   )

LANDSCAPE ARCHITECT, EDUCATOR

Robert S. Reich, often referred to as Doc, was born in New York City on March 22, 1913. Reich was the only child of Ulysses and Adele Reich. His mother was a school teacher in the New York public schools; his father grew up in Manhattan where his family ran a hotel, The Cambridge, which would eventually become the Astor, and later the Waldorf-Astoria, long after the family had lost the hotel to creditors.

Reich's colorful father Ulysses provided young Robert and his school friends with tickets to Broadway shows. Reich's early schooling in a New York City Montessori-like school gave him a sense of independence and love for learning that characterized him as a young boy. This independence of thought and voracious intellect would become defining traits of his personality as an adult.

Reich spent summers either on Long Island, or later at Rockville Center and Lynbrook. Reich was fascinated with trains at an early age and his lust for travel would lead to a belief that travel was one of the best teachers of the kind of observation necessary for one to become a successful designer.

When he was in the third grade, the Reich family moved to New Rochelle, seeking a smaller community in which to raise their son. As a cross-country runner, he was "great at coming in last," as he recounts, because he was "looking at and enjoying the landscape." Reich says that his team captain always encouraged him despite his poor performance, and that this example of leadership by encouragement and belief in the potential of "late bloomers" became important to him as a leader of groups in his service in the army and later as an educator.

An accidental occurrence during high school was responsible for Reich's exposure to landscape architecture. He won an essay contest and was invited to the home of the prize donor, where he was amazed by her garden of lovely plants. "I became greatly interested in her plantings, and the first thing I knew, through her interests, I decided to go to Cornell to study plants."

At Cornell University, Reich earned a bachelor of science degree in horticulture in 1934 and a doctorate in 1941, studying education. His Cornell experiences would shape his life's work; his commitment to the power of education led him to his career choice of educator, and

Dr. Robert S. Reich and friend, 2007. (Photo by Brian Goad, ASLA)

his strong foundation in plant sciences made him a persistent advocate for plants as the signature material of the profession.

Upon graduation, Reich was hired to teach courses in landscape architecture by the dean of the agriculture school at Louisiana State University (LSU). He arrived at the train station in Baton Rouge one night in 1941, and was in the classroom teaching the following morning. He has taught there nearly continuously since that morning, eventually founding an independent department of landscape architecture in 1946, moving it from the agriculture department to the College of Design, elevating its status to that of a School, and lobbying for a new building. Initially, Reich had only intended to stay in the South for a year, and planned to return to Cornell after that. However, a chance meeting with a young librarian, Helen Adams, altered his life plans permanently, and Cornell's loss was LSU's great fortune. Reich proposed to

Above: Grounds of St. Aloysius Catholic Church, Baton Rouge, Louisiana. (Photo by Brian Goad, ASLA)

Below: Repentance Park, Baton Rouge Riverside Centroplex. (Photo by Brian Goad, ASLA)

Reich endowed scholarships in his wife's name, and as their four children grew up, Reich poured more and more energy and attention into his university "family"—the students and the faculty in landscape architecture, and the congregation of the University Methodist Church. Reich was concerned for the welfare of students and faculty beyond the academic arena and sixty years after his arrival at LSU many alumni continued to correspond with "Doc" as extended family. For decades he has prepared a floral arrangement for the altar each Sunday morning, using the wildflowers and foliage of the native vegetation from rural roadsides. Reich officially retired from teaching in 1983, at the age of seventy, forced by a mandatory university retirement policy. He has taught part-time without compensation since then, serving as professor emeritus and continuing to influence classes of students who enroll in his seminars, travel on field trips with him, and attend ice cream socials in his home.

Reich's goal as educator and department head from the onset was to have landscape architecture recognized as a design profession, not as an extension of horticulture; and to make the services of the profession known to the residents and communities of the state. There was only one other landscape architect in Louisiana when Reich came to LSU, and few in the region at the time.

During the 1950s Reich became disillusioned with the pedagogical methods that he found being used at many schools of landscape architecture, and the reliance on the Beaux-Arts vocabulary that he saw in the profession, which he felt suppressed individuality. He believed that there should be a more creative approach and was considering leaving the profession when in 1950, he came across Garrett Eckbo's* just published *Landscape for Living*. The book struck a chord, and Reich requested a sabbatical to spend time in California

his sweetheart, but when called to the European theater to serve in World War II, he felt that it would be unfair to marry until after the war, not wanting her to risk becoming a young widow. They were wed shortly after Reich's return from the war, and Helen was Reich's partner in running LSU's landscape architecture program as well as his practice. Her untimely death in 1968 was a terrible blow to Reich as they had shared most aspects of their lives so closely, particularly their devotion to their faith.

in Eckbo's office. As a consequence of Reich's working so intensely with Eckbo he was not only exposed to innovative projects in the language of modernism as applied to residential design, but also to Eckbo's pioneering commitment to social justice and to environmental conservation.

After this work experience, Reich returned to LSU energized and determined. Reich explained that Eckbo had confirmed his belief in individual creativity: that one should never copy anyone else's work, that each person's life experience and interpretation of a landscape was a critical element in the design process. Reich refined the curriculum so that students were encouraged to take free electives, broadening their perspectives beyond the professional curriculum to include courses in the humanities and allied arts, and allowing students to pursue their personal interests beyond landscape architecture. He incorporated travel as a major component of the curriculum, with annual trips to the east and west coasts required before graduation. As recently as 2006, Reich escorted a class of students on a field trip to Texas to tour projects and visit offices of alumni. Enrichment trips abroad, to Europe, Asia, and Central and South America, were offered during the summers. Reich recognized that many of his students had never left the state of Louisiana, and that these opportunities to see "the world" would benefit them in immeasurable ways beyond their college years.

Reich's personal teaching included courses in design theory, site planning, plant materials, planting design, landscape history, and career planning. In teaching design, he used modernist ideas. His required Saturday morning field trips via bicycle to tour landscape projects served as a living laboratory, in which students experienced firsthand the work of their teacher and other faculty and professionals in the community. Reich would direct the group of students through these landscapes and residences, pointing out how he had created the "gasp" view from the front entrance straight through the interior spaces and out the back of the house to the landscape garden. Or he would point out the screening effect of the "baffle" of bamboo or parasol trees that separated one outdoor room from the next. This direct illustration of the theory carried from classroom to the built project stayed with students in a way that textbook teaching or slideshow illustrations did not.

In Reich's history courses, he included detailed units on the landscapes of the Orient long before there were published texts on the subject or general agreement on the significance of this material for the education of a designer practicing primarily in the Western world. Reich knew that he was preparing students for international practice, and he was particularly drawn to the tenets of Oriental design in his own practice and design aesthetic, as were the members of the California School. Not only was Reich one of the first landscape architects in the state of Louisiana to be trained and practice, but his progressiveness and contact with the larger concept of professional practice earned him the title of "father of landscape architecture in Louisiana."

Throughout Reich's career as an educator, he ran a professional practice with several different partners; today Reich and Associates is a partnership between Reich and his son Bill, a landscape architect. Over the years, the firm's work has included a wide range of project types including residential commissions, community master plans, state parks, and large municipal projects. Projects in which he has played a major role include the Baton Rouge Riverside Centroplex, Lake Claiborne State Park, St. Aloysius Catholic Church, University Methodist Church Complex, and Mountain Lake Sanctuary in Lake Wales, Florida. Many students have had the opportunity to gain professional experience by working in the office as interns while in school or after graduation.

Reich holds LSU's highest teaching honor, Alumni Professor, and in 1992 he was awarded the ASLA's highest honor, the ASLA Medal. In 2005, he was again honored by the ASLA with the Jot D. Carpenter Teaching Medal.

Reich's legacy as an educator has been his insistence that teaching should aim to "graduate educated, thinking people, not just landscape architect technologists." Reich recognized that the pace of change in the modern world made it impossible to expose a student in a limited number of years to all of the possible information and situations that would be needed or encountered in practice. His belief was in helping the individual realize his or her potential as a problem-solver, and helping the student gain the self-confidence to become a leader and a contributing member of the communities he or she would join. Reich strove for nearly three-quarters of a century to foster an educational environment that remained relevant to the particular social and cultural issues of the time.

Reich's remarkable zest for life is indeed contagious. He exercised daily in the university swimming pool, and rode his bicycle to work and home. Reich's uncanny ability to remain open to the thinking of the time has allowed him to continue to relate to students and faculty alike into his ninth decade of life, a quality that has meant that he continues to graciously participate in the growth and evolution of the school that he founded over sixty years ago.

Reich, Robert S. "Autobiographical Notes" (unpublished), 1999. Reich has systematically recorded the story of his life and his formation as a landscape architect, and there are plans for these to be published.

"A Voice from Landscape Architecture: The Life and Work of Dr. Robert S. Reich." Produced by Chad Danos, project of the Louisiana Chapter ASLA, Creative Media Solutions, 2000. Video interview with Reich, a good summary of design philosophy and approach to professional practice and education.

Nomination and announcement of award for ASLA Jot D. Carpenter Medal, March 2005. This tribute to Reich captures the qualities and accomplishments that distinguish his long, productive career.

Suzanne L. Turner

RIDDLE, THEODATE POPE
(1867–1946)
ARCHITECT

Born on February 2, 1867, in Salem, Ohio, Effie Brooks Pope was the only child of Alfred Atmore Pope, a Cleveland iron industrialist, and his wife, Ada Brooks. Like many privileged daughters of fashionable Gilded Age families, she attended exclusive girls' schools. At age nineteen, she changed her name to Theodate, in honor of her grandmother, Theodate Stackpole Pope. The same year she came east to Miss Porter's School in Farmington, Connecticut, to continue her education. The town had a profound impact on her. She fell in love with the rural landscape and the village's seventeenth- and eighteenth-century domestic architecture.

From 1898 to 1889, Pope, who later worked under her married name of Theodate Pope Riddle, took the Grand Tour of Europe with her parents and was introduced firsthand to a world of art, architecture, and landscape design. She especially loved England, and was drawn to the grand scale and beauty of the English countryside, as well as the Arts and Crafts aesthetic found in old English villages. While traveling in Europe, she decided to become an architect. Upon her return, she settled in Farmington. Here she undertook her first architectural project, the restoration of an eighteenth-century saltbox, which she dubbed The O'Rourkery. It became her romanticized vision of a colonial home.

Pope's second project was designing a traditional farmhouse as a retirement home for her parents. Her dream of owning a New England dairy farm coincided with her father's interest in returning to his New England roots. The property known as Hill-Stead, was completed in 1901. From the beginning, Hill-Stead had a sense of grandeur and permanence. Thirty-foot elm trees, hauled

Theodate Pope Riddle at Avon Old Farms School, Avon, Connecticut, ca. 1920. (Archives, Hill-Stead Museum, Farmington, CT)

Hill-Stead (Pope-Riddle House) from the entryway, 2002 view. (Archives, Hill-Stead Museum, Farmington, CT)

in by horse and wagon and planted close to the west facade of the house, provided scale and shade. A gracefully curving and gently rising drive, flanked by an allée of stately maples and stonewalls, created a dramatic sense of arrival.

As in the English Park movement, the natural characteristics of the land shaped Hill-Stead's features. After consulting with **Warren Henry Manning**, Pope located her buildings on the highest point of land to take advantage of sweeping vistas. From this vantage point, she created three distinct sight lines.

From the imposing west facade of the house (with its Mount Vernon–inspired veranda), the first sight line—a wide greensward, detailed with ha-ha and slate stone walkway—gently slopes down to the village of Farmington. It visually links Hill-Stead to the colonial-era homes of the village. Irregular massing of trees and shrubs reinforces the soft undulations of the landscape set against dramatic views of the distant Litchfield Hills.

A pond, located in a natural swale just north of the house, creates a second sight line, directing the eye to its reflective surface and through open pasture to farm buildings and an orchard beyond. In damming the Pope Brook, she created an aesthetic as well as a practical feature: spring run-off from the pastures drains into the pond. The pond also doubled as a water hazard for Alfred Pope's six-hole golf grounds and provided ice for domestic use. A large kitchen-and-cutting garden, located off the northeast side of the house, further defined the area. A theater, stable, and maintenance buildings were also present.

In contrast to this rather loose organization of the greater landscape, Pope created a third, intimate sight line to the south by locating her mother's formal flower garden in a natural depression near the house. Neoclassical in concept, the octagonal sunken garden was surrounded by massive, six-foot, stone walls and contained a summer house, pergola, and sundial. A small, boxed hedge bordered numerous flower beds filled with colorful, popular perennials.

Pope had this garden seeded over in the 1940s due to wartime shortages. In 1985, during an effort to rebuild a "period garden," a planting plan by **Beatrix Jones Farrand** was discovered and installed.

Just beyond the sunken garden is a wild garden, loosely planted with naturalizing indigenous vegetation and defined by gravel pathways. It provides a gentle transition from the domestic area to woodlands and a sheep meadow beyond.

Using native materials made popular in the Arts and

Crafts movement, Pope deftly made use of the rocky fields designing miles of new stone walls into the landscape.

In addition to Hill-Stead, Pope's built legacy is not extensive. She designed three schools, two country houses, the reconstruction and additions to the Theodore Roosevelt Birthplace in New York City, and countless ancillary buildings designed for workers and garden ornamentation.

Without formal training in architecture, Pope depended on her sketch pad and copious notes scribbled in her diary during her many trips abroad. What she did design was based on a principled set of moral values derived from the need to produce meaningful work. She eschewed the popular Beaux-Arts style, preferring the Arts and Crafts vernacular of contemporary English architects and the sensitive relationship between buildings and their environments.

In 1906, Pope drew up plans for Westover, a girl's school in Middlebury, Connecticut. Following her belief that institutional architecture can have a human scale, Pope minimized the imposing facade by adding steeply pitched roofs; projected east and west wings forward, and designed a cloistered quadrangle to convey a greater sense of community.

Shortly after, Pope was invited to design two country houses, Highfield in Middlebury, Connecticut, and the Dormer House in Locust Valley, Long Island. The design of both houses demonstrates her agility with the English vernacular idiom: steeply pitched roofs to create a low rambling type house, cozy, yet stately; multiple dormers piercing the roofs, decorative chimney pots, and a subtle selection of color and texture, visually fusing the house with its landscape setting.

In October 1913, Pope opened an architectural office in New York City. In 1916, she married John Wallace Riddle, a former Russian diplomat, and also became licensed as an architect in New York State. She began using the name Theodate Pope Riddle at that time. She was elected as a member of the American Institute of Architects in 1918. A year later she closed her New York office. Her most prestigious commission came in 1920, when she was invited to reconstruct and add a wing to the Theodore Roosevelt Birthplace in New York. Her reputation growing, her colleagues recommended her work to magazine editors and in 1926 the Architectural Club of New Haven appointed her as an honorary member.

Riddle's last significant commission was to found a boy's school as a memorial to her father. She would design the school and determine its educational program. She decided on the simplicity of an eighteenth-century English village to stimulate good citizenship in her students. The Pope School for Boys, later named Avon Old Farms, was to be a progressive school where students were required to work on the farm or in workshops as well as study academics for the development of the mind and body. Consequently Riddle purchased 3,000 acres on the west side of the Farmington River and clustered her school buildings on a bluff overlooking the river.

Construction began in 1921. She specifically chose a vernacular interpretation of English Cotswold architecture, well suited to traditional domestic farm and village architecture. The buildings utilized local materials, many quarried on site. Eschewing modern construction methods, she transported labor from England to construct the buildings by hand without measures or plumb lines.

Riddle created a sense of community by clustering the buildings in small groups around a central feature, the village green. Dormitories surround a quadrangle opening on central axis to the provost and dean's houses overlooking the green and distant farm fields, successfully combining the English college quadrangle and the English village vernacular.

Theodate Pope Riddle died on August 30, 1946, at her home in Farmington. Her will stipulated that Hill-Stead was to become a museum "for the benefit and enjoyment of the public," showcasing her architectural legacy and her father's renowned collection of French impressionist art.

Hewitt, Mark A. *The Architect and the American Country House 1890–1940.* New Haven, Conn.: Yale University Press, 1990. An overview of the breadth and aesthetic vitality of the era through the expert eye of a practicing architect.

Katz, Sandra L. *Dearest of Geniuses: A Life of Theodate Pope Riddle,* Windsor, Conn.: Tide-Mark Press, 2003. Biographical account of Riddle's personal life and experiences.

Smith, Sharon, *Theodate Pope Riddle: Her Life and Architecture.* Internet publication: www.valinet.com/˜smithash. An architectural survey of Riddle's work.

Margaret Carpenter

RIES, JANE SILVERSTEIN
(1909–2005)
LANDSCAPE ARCHITECT

Julia Jane Silverstein was born in Denver, Colorado, where she attended the city's public schools. She graduated from the Lowthorpe School of Landscape Architecture in 1932. She began her professional career in 1933 working with Denver landscape architect Irvin J. McCrary on planting plans for Colorado University. Two years later she opened her own office in Denver.

During World War II, Silverstein served in the U.S. Coast Guard as a property surveyor and port liaison officer, rising to the rank of lieutenant. She worked briefly after the war as a landscape architect in the New York City office of Skidmore, Owings & Merrill. In 1947 she returned to her Denver practice. She married Henry F. Ries in 1953. Known professionally as Julia Jane Silverstein until 1961, she then assumed her married name and established a brief professional partnership with Julia Andrews-Jones.

During her career, Ries concentrated on the design of gardens for both modest and fashionable homes, many of which were set on Denver's ubiquitous small lots. Her signature style was immediately recognizable as it differed from the established uniformity of the city's residential pattern of front lawn, foundation plantings, back lawn, and border garden. She designed a garden for an Art Moderne home, built in 1935 as a General Electric demonstration project, and gained wide and favorable notice. Her work reached a rich and versatile dignity in her middle years. And her services continued to be in great demand throughout the remainder of her career.

Ries walked into a space and saw potential. Her back gardens were private and livable, small spaces sequestered by hedges from the crowded urban scene. Elegant and usually formal, often intimate yet sculpted and articulated to seem grand, they were easy to maintain and not inordinately thirsty. For inspiration, she looked to the walled gardens of Beacon Hill in Boston, which enchanted her when she was at Lowthorpe. She later made her own contribution to the Beacon Hill ensemble with a garden design for a Pinckney Street residence, yet she was able to use the same themes and serve the same purposes in making modernist gardens.

As for the view from street and sidewalk, her sensibilities were captured in a charming collage made when she

Above: Jane Silverstein during her World War II tour of duty with the U.S. Coast Guard. (Jane Silverstein Ries Papers, 1934–1992, WH1785, Western History Collection, The Denver Public Library)

Below: Entrance garden of Art Moderne home (General Electric demonstration house), Denver, Colorado, planted 1936, shown here in 1977. (Photo by Don Etter © 1977)

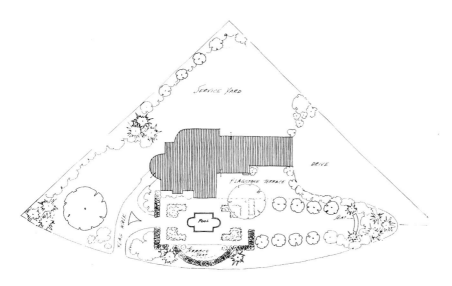

Landscape development plan for Touff residence Denver, Colorado, 1958. (Jane Silverstein Ries Papers, 1934–1992, WH1785, Western History Collection, The Denver Public Library)

was thirteen. A textured walk says welcome, sculpted trees dramatize a traditional house, and flowers in abundance evoke the spirit of joyful residents. Ries looked to these simple themes to guide her work, including her street-front plan for the 1935 Art Moderne house. Her 1958 design for a modernist garden in Denver's Hilltop neighborhood featured a shaded entry court punctuated by native plantings. And her own gateway garden was an experimental bramble, and was officially designated a Denver Landmark in 1992.

Though urban gardens were at the center of her practice, her commissions included federal housing projects, large estates, churches, courthouse grounds, and mortuary parking lots. And though her arcadian sensibilities were obvious, she adopted her own regional palette, incorporated local plant materials into her earliest gardens, and established a clear ethic for the development of suburban, prairie, and mountain sites. She could slip a home into the natural cover and topography without disturbing the existing land. Vistas and native vegetation thus became the garden, yet she would frame the home with comfortable viewing platforms and discreet specimen plantings.

Ries was the first woman in Denver to pursue a career in landscape architecture. Her office also served as headquarters for an array of other professional, civic, and social endeavors. She presided there as a role model and mentor for professional women, particularly in her profession; as a teacher to her dedicated assistants; and as a cheerleader, tireless volunteer, and sage. In her later years she became the doyenne of her regional colleagues. Her passion also extended to social causes not directly related to her profession, but which she saw at the ethical heart of awareness, understanding, and stewardship of the land.

Ries believed that every professional, indeed every citizen, had a responsibility to participate in civic debate. For over half a century, few land-use issues were addressed in Denver or Colorado without the benefit of her wisdom. She shared her knowledge of various topics, including the importance of prairie and mountain lands; the need for mass transit; the blight of poorly designed houses and rampant growth; the propagation of a shrub rose brought west by pioneers and a hardy boxwood now called "Julia Jane"; Dutch elm disease; the paucity of good planning; drought; and the replacement of street trees.

Ries was elected a Fellow of the American Society of Landscape Architects (ASLA) in 1965, and was the first president of the Rocky Mountain Chapter of the ASLA (now the Colorado Chapter). She was awarded the ASLA Medal in 2005. Ries was a consultant to mayors and governors and had the ear of the city's opinion makers. She nurtured collegial relationships among design professionals and, over her long career, her perspective, personality, and impact on the land were an inspiration to virtually every other Colorado landscape architect. She served on multiple boards, committees, and commissions, and she contributed her professional services when solutions were not otherwise available. After World War II, Ries was part of an informal yet influential group including horticulturist George W. Kelly and, in addition to Ries, landscape architects **Saco Rienk DeBoer**, Sam Leslie Huddleston, Irvin J. McCrary, and Michiel

Walter Pesman.* They led the way in promoting sustainable and satisfying landscapes for Colorado's semiarid, high altitude environment. Ries also became a key player in the maintenance of Denver as an exemplar of a green, tree-shaded, and flowered City Beautiful.

Ries was always as focused as she was indefatigable. Through ASLA and Colorado Chapter ASLA committees, she defined the importance of preserving historic landscapes. She helped spearhead early efforts to rehabilitate the grounds of Colorado's Executive Mansion. She volunteered as a consultant in the restoration of the Molly Brown House Museum garden and creation of the Ninth Street Historic Park. She developed early plans for the Larimer Square redevelopment. And she served on the Colorado Chapter ASLA publication committee for *Colorado: Visions of an American Landscape,* a 1991 book written by Kenneth Helphand and sponsored by the Landscape Architecture Foundation.

Ries became the institutional memory for the history of Denver's landscape and those who shaped it, particularly after S. R. DeBoer's death in 1974. She was responsible for a plethora of projects, including over 1,000 gardens, thus leaving her own direct mark on the landscape. Ultimately, an institution herself, she received numerous awards for her life's work, including induction into the Colorado Women's Hall of Fame and the AIA Denver Chapter's Community Service Award. In recognition of her pioneering sense of awareness and stewardship of land-use values in the Rocky Mountain region, the Colorado Chapter of the ASLA established the JSR Foundation in her honor. The foundation grants scholarships to students of landscape architecture, and offers a prestigious annual lecture program. Its first annual award was conferred on Ries.

Determined not to think about retirement, Ries joined Land Mark Design as a senior advisor in 1989, and encouraged that firm to carry on her legacy. Ries passed away in 2005.

Paper collage created by Julia Jane Silverstein (later Ries) at age thirteen. (Jane Silverstein Ries Papers, 1934–1992, WH1785, Western History Collection, The Denver Public Library)

The Jane Silverstein Ries Papers, 1934–1992 ("JSR Papers"). WH 1785, in the Western History Collection of the Denver Public Library, Colo., is an extensive collection of Ries's papers that includes plans, drawings, photographs, business files, and related memorabilia.

Etter, Don D. *Denver Going Modern: A Photographic Essay on the Imprint of the International Style on Denver Residential Architecture.* Denver: Graphic Impressions, Inc., 1977. Includes material relating to the garden designed by Ries for a 1935 Art Moderne demonstration house.

Ries, Jane Silverstein (as Julia Jane Silverstein). "Water in the Garden." *The Green Thumb* 16, no. 6 (1959), 198–201. Ries's writing was always direct and useful. This example appeared in this Denver Botanic Gardens periodical.

Shaw, Betty. "The Artistry of Landscape Design." *Colorado Homes & Lifestyles* 2, no. 1 (1982), 118–23. One of many news and feature articles about Ries. This piece includes several good illustrations.

Carolyn Etter and Don Etter

ROBINSON, FLORENCE BELL
(1885–1973)

EDUCATOR, HORTICULTURIST

Florence Bell Robinson was born on November 1, 1885, in Lapeer, Michigan, the only child of Dr. and Mrs. William Robinson. She graduated from Kalamazoo College in 1908 with a bachelor of philosophy, and obtained a second such degree from the University of Chicago by completing correspondence courses that same year. Her education was primarily in the sciences, and for the next eighteen years she taught such subjects as physics, chemistry, botany, biology, physiography, and drafting in high schools throughout Detroit. Robinson also studied for a degree in architecture at the University of Michigan from 1913 to 1915, and after the death of her parents in 1921, committed to a career change and completed her bachelor of science in architecture as well as a master's degree in landscape design at Michigan in 1924. She worked briefly as an architectural draftsman for J. W. Case in Detroit from 1918 to 1926, while also maintaining a small, private landscape design practice. Teaching landscape architecture would become the "right vocation," an ideal combination of her passion for teaching and her extensive knowledge of plants and design.

Robinson, at the age of forty-one, began her teaching career in the Department of Landscape Architecture at the University of Illinois as an associate faculty member in 1926. In 1929, she gained appointment as an assistant professor, decades before women were permitted entry to tenure track positions in professional design schools. She retired in 1951 with the rank of full professor, an achievement that no other woman teaching in landscape architecture was to accomplish until the 1970s.

Comments from alumni indicate that Miss Robinson, as students always addressed her, was the quintessential spinster schoolteacher. She was shy, reserved, and impersonal by comparison to her colleagues, but possessed a strong, personal resolve that enabled her to travel on her own or with a female companion to regions as remote as China, Japan, and Guatemala. She taught plant identification and planting design, assignments typical for women instructors during this time. Her courses were rigorous, often lasting hours longer than other studios, with an emphasis on mastering principles and rules of composition. Any work of landscape, according to Robinson, was to be a work of art "functionally con-

Professors Florence Bell Robinson, Walt Keith, and Otto Schaffer review student projects at the University of Illinois, March 1951. (Courtesy of the University of Illinois Department of Landscape Architecture Archives)

ceived, adequately presented, and beautifully clothed in harmonious masses of color and texture and form." Student reaction to her courses varied from dread to appreciation for the specificity and the contagious love of plants that she exhibited. Hideo Sasaki,* a former student, commented that Robinson "loved her work, and when a student expressed interest in plants, he could be showered with her generosity. Miss Robinson is one of those unappreciated teachers who have had greater influence than acknowledged. She was a pro through and through, and I admired her for it."

Since opportunities for private practice were limited in Champaign-Urbana, Robinson focused her activities

Right: "Approaches to planting around different styles of residential architecture," illustrations by Florence Bell Robinson for *Planting Design,* 1940. (Courtesy of the University of Illinois Archives)

Below: A 1938 card file of data on approximately 500 hardy woody plants in common use as ornamentals. (Photo by Charles A. Birnbaum)

House and dominant lines.

Columnar forms if used should be placed with regard for balance.

Planting and dominant lines.
"Upright and wing"—the country or farmhouse type.
Planting designed on the lines of the house as indicated in Problem XIV.

The modern version of the L and wing has a sturdiness of character that should be reflected in the trees used.

The design of this modern house in Tokyo shows a repeated rhythm of three horizontals. The same rhythm should be incorporated in the planting design. The plants used should have pronounced horizontal shadows to be in harmony with the building.

on academic pursuits. She used her understanding of art, architecture, science, and engineering coupled with an encyclopedic knowledge of plants to publish extensively in *Landscape Architecture, House and Garden, Country Life,* and other periodicals that also appealed to the general public. She was frequently invited to speak to garden clubs, cemetery associations, art leagues, and the local PBS radio station on such topics as choosing shrubs, use of hybridized plants, and garden design.

McGraw-Hill published Robinson's first major book, *Planting Design,* in 1941. It was one of the few available on the subject at the time and as such became the standard text in plant material courses throughout the United States and at universities in Australia, Russia, England, and the Philippines. It was essentially a textbook, containing exercises for students, including some examples of poorly designed buildings whose shortcomings were to be overcome by corrective planting. A noted strength of the text was the attention devoted to texture and its varied possibilities in design; few previous publications paid more than cursory attention to this attribute of plants. The text was also considered ahead of its time in its strong emphasis on ecological factors in planting design, and this may be a result of the influence of her close colleague at the University of Illinois, **Stanley Hart White.**

As early as 1932, Robinson's card index system of plants was made commercially available as *Deciduous Trees, Deciduous Shrubs and Conifers* later to be published in summary form as a book entitled *Tabular Keys for the Identification of the Woody Plants* (1941). The card index was a favorite of students that many graduates found useful in their professional careers; it was reissued periodically by Garrard Press of Champaign until only recently. Her final book, *Palette of Plants* (1950), was a romantic and poetic list of plant "personalities," which includes a chapter on plantings for cemeteries that placed Robinson in great demand as a speaker on the topic.

Robinson spent her summers traveling throughout the western United States, Europe, China, and Japan. In 1929, she joined a tour of China led by Professor **Philip Homer Elwood** of Iowa State College, during which she developed a deep passion and knowledge of Chinese garden design that eventually led to her translation of a French author's article entitled "The Imperial Palaces of Peking." In 1931, she led her own tour through China and Japan, a record of which includes a collection of 800 hand-tinted class lantern slides that have been digitally preserved in the landscape architecture archives at the University of Illinois. Researchers familiar with the collection indicate that many of the slides are the only depictions known to remain of places that were subsequently destroyed by earthquake or military action.

Throughout her career, Robinson was active in local business and women's clubs, the American Planning and Civic Association, and the National Conference of State Parks. In 1945, she achieved a listing in *Who's Who in Chicago and Illinois,* and in 1950, *Who's Who Among American Women.* She received a special citation as a distinguished alumnus from Kalamazoo College in January 1951.

Upon retirement at age sixty-five, Robinson moved from Urbana to St. Petersburg, Florida, and later to North Carolina. Although she was highly regarded by her colleagues, the record indicates only perfunctory contact with the department, and only for the first few years after her departure. Twenty-two years after she left campus, Robinson died in Hendersonville, North Carolina, on August 13, 1973, leaving the legacy of her writings.

Robinson, Florence Bell. *Palette of Plants.* Champaign, Ill.: Garrard Press, 1950. A sequel to *Planting Design* with emphasis on plant characteristics and appropriate use.

Robinson, Florence Bell. *Planting Design.* Champaign, Ill.: Garrard Press, 1940. A course text describing plants and their use in design.

Robinson, Florence Bell. *Tabular Keys for the Identification of the Woody Plants.* Champaign, Ill.: Garrard Press, 1941. A reference guide to 500 woody plants of the northern states and Canada.

This entry was written using the research notes of the late Natalie Alpert.

Gary Kesler and Natalie Alpert

ROCHE, ELEANOR LOUISE
(1892–1975)
LANDSCAPE ARCHITECT

Eleanor Louise Roche was born on January 21, 1892, in East Orange, New Jersey, into a large French family with longstanding gardening interests. At the family home, Eleanor's mother had a flower and vegetable garden, a lily bed, orchards, and a grape arbor. After graduation from East Orange High School, Roche studied at the Lowthorpe School of Landscape Architecture, Landscape Gardening, and Horticulture for Women in Groton, Massachusetts, graduating in 1917, the same year as Louise Payson and Isabella E. Pendleton.*

Roche and her classmate Payson worked together in the New York City office of **Ellen Biddle Shipman**, although it is unclear what projects Roche may have worked on. In 1926, Roche opened her own practice in New York City at 15 East 40th Street, the same year she was elected to membership in the American Society of Landscape Architects (ASLA). Like Shipman, Roche specialized in residential work, particularly gardens for small and moderate-size homes. Maud Sargent, however, recalled that Roche also worked for the New York City Parks Department in the 1920s. While Roche hired some staff, she worked primarily on her own, focusing on smaller projects. Her work was well represented in the ASLA yearbooks between 1931 and 1934 and in the yearbooks of the New York Chapter of the ASLA between 1930 and 1933.

By 1931, she moved her office to 295 Madison Avenue, sharing quarters with Mabel Parsons (daughter of **Samuel Parsons Jr.**) of the New York City Parks Department who had shared the 40th Street office. Roche moved again in 1934, to 424 Madison Avenue, by which time she was working in Grosse Pointe, Michigan, on a regular basis. In addition to maintaining a professional design practice, Roche was a frequent contributor to popular and professional journals, such as *Landscape Architecture.* She was also recognized for her work as a teacher, lecturer, and tour organizer. She organized a tour to Africa for the ASLA and one to Mediterranean gardens, and also traveled to Spain with Virginia Prince (another Lowthorpe graduate and employee in Shipman's office) to view gardens and landscapes. Like many of her classmates, Roche was committed to the Lowthorpe School, where she lectured and was an active member of the school's alumnae group. With Louise Payson, she organized a tour for Lowthorpe in 1933 of gardens designed by Ellen Biddle Shipman. In 1935, she was asked to serve as a professional advisor for a garden tour to benefit the Anne Browne Alumnae Free Kindergarten and Nursery School in New York City. With Helen Swift Jones,* **Nellie B. Allen**, and H. Stuart Orloff, she donated her services as a professional consultant to garden tour participants.

Roche designed a number of flower gardens, including one that she transformed from a vegetable garden for Jackson A. Dykman in Glen Cove on Long Island, begun in 1929. The Dykman garden and a project in Pelham Manor were published in the 1931 New York Chapter ASLA yearbook. Three more projects were published in 1932, including a flower garden with an arched entrance for Mrs. G. Peats and a rock garden for Mrs. Henry Hobbs, both in New Canaan, Connecticut, and a garden for Mrs. Maxine Furland in Princeton, New Jersey. Images of a garden she designed for Ralph W. Gwinn in Bronxville, New York, seem to best exemplify Roche's style. Its flower beds, stairs, and pergolas are similar to those in the work of Roche's mentor, Ellen Shipman. Roche's work was usually a combination of formal flower gardens and naturalistic open spaces with trees and lawn. Around 1933, Roche designed a pleasant courtyard garden for St. Luke's Hospital in New York City. The court was paved and surrounded with richly planted flower borders and raised beds. One side of the garden was covered with lattice over which grew vines, while a small table with chairs and a stone bench invited visitors to rest amid the greenery in an otherwise dense urban landscape.

Around 1935, Roche moved to Grosse Pointe, Michigan, where she worked with local clients and continued to lead tours and give lectures. She served as secretary and treasurer for the Detroit chapter of the ASLA and was a member of the Detroit Planning Committee. Little is known about her design work, but her obituary states that she designed numerous landscapes in Detroit and Grosse Pointe, including a rose garden at Christ Episcopal Church in Grosse Pointe. The Virginia Brush Ford Memorial Rose Garden, constructed in 1966 to honor the memory of a local woman, is still extant, with some modifications in planting. Roche also designed the trial garden at the Grosse Pointe War Memorial (formerly the Russell A. Alger residence, designed by **Charles A. Platt**, with a garden by Shipman) that is extant. Roche's only other known project is the Howard Smith garden in Grosse Pointe, initially designed by Shipman in 1928, and rehabilitated by Roche in the 1950s.

Eleanor Roche died at the Georgian East Nursing Home in Macomb County, Michigan, on July 30, 1975.

Above: Garden of the estate of Mrs. Maxine Furland, Princeton, New Jersey, from ASLA *Illustrations of Works of Members,* 1933.

Below: Garden of Mrs. Genevieve Peats, New Canaan, Connecticut, from *Gardens and Gardening,* 1933.

"Gardens in Bronxville, NY & Glen Cove, L.I." *Architecture,* June 1927, 321, 323.

"Miss Eleanor L. Roche." Obituary. *Grosse Pointe News,* August 7, 1975.

Prince, Virginia, and Eleanor Roche. "El Labertino: A Spanish Garden in the Neo-Classic Style." *Landscape Architecture* 24, no. 1 (October 1933), 5–15. An example of Eleanor Roche's writing where she describes a garden in Horta, Spain, which she and Virginia Prince visited on one of their European tours.

Cynthia Zaitzevsky, Thaïsa Way, and Judith B. Tankard

ROOT, RALPH RODNEY
(1884–1964)
LANDSCAPE ARCHITECT, AUTHOR

Ralph Rodney Root was born and raised in Jamestown, New York. He studied landscape architecture at Cornell University. According to Cornell archival records, from 1906 to 1910 he studied design under both department founder **Bryant Fleming** and **George Elberton Burnap**. Root was granted a scholarship to attend the landscape architecture program at Harvard in 1910, in the era when **Henry Vincent Hubbard** was an instructor. Root graduated from the Harvard program with a Master's in Landscape Architecture in 1912 and promptly was hired by the University of Illinois at Urbana.

As head of the landscape architecture program at Illinois from 1912 to 1918, Root taught formal principles of design. Notable students during this period included Annette Hoyt Flanders* and Charles Dudley Wagstaff. In 1914, Root along with Ohio State faculty member Charles Fabens Kelley, wrote *Design in Landscape Gardening,* a textbook intended to succinctly espouse the most definite principles of design as applied to landscape gardening. The preface to the book quotes Humphrey Repton, and draws on ties to a classic tradition, preceding that of **Andrew Jackson Downing** and **Frederick Law Olmsted Sr.** This book anticipated by three years the better-known *An Introduction to the Study of Landscape Design,* by Harvard's Henry Vincent Hubbard and Theodora Kimball (Hubbard).*

By 1916, Root relocated to the Chicago area to design, teach in the summer, observe, and begin to explain some of the new formal garden developments in the suburbs. In 1916, Root offered a summer program at Lake Forest College, under the sponsorship of the Garden Club of Illinois. Among the participants from around the country was Illinois landscape architecture student Annette Hoyt Flanders. Also in 1916, Root played a key role in documenting North Shore estates in *Lake Forest: Art and History Edition,* a booklet published by the American Communities Company that same year. Simultaneously, planning was underway for the Garden Club of America (GCA) to visit Chicago's North Shore. While Root was preparing for a second year of the Lake Forest summer school, his work attracted the attention of both his future horticulturalist partner Noble P. Hollister and Illinois urban planning professor **Charles Mulford Robinson**.

R. R. Root, 1916. (Department of Landscape Architecture Archives, University of Illinois)

Root was sketching estate plans for the anticipated GCA visit when the United States entered World War I, in April 1917. During wartime, Root's work at the University of Illinois ended. He proposed a four-year landscape program at Lake Forest, which was not approved.

However, from 1916 to 1917 in Lake Forest, Root embarked on a Chicago-area design career most notable for its collaborations with the firm of Beaux-Arts-trained architects David Adler and Robert Work. In early 1917, Root & Hollister worked with the Adler firm on the garden of the Charles B. Pike Italian villa. About this same time Root & Hollister designed gardens for A. Watson Armour's Elawa Farm, another Adler and Work project nearby. In the early 1920s, Root & Hollister contributed to Adler's design for the dramatic William McCormick Blair lakefront estate north of Lake Bluff. Around 1920, Root's firm also designed expansive estate gardens for

Robert R. McCormick estate plan, Wheaton, Illinois. (Lake Forest College Library Special Collections)

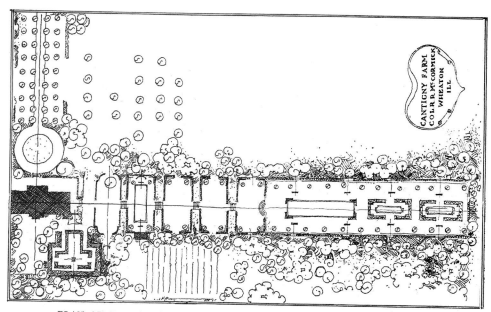

PLAN OF ESTATE OF COLONEL R. R. McCORMICK, WHEATON, ILLINOIS
Root & Hollister, Landscape Architects

two cousins who were partners in the *Chicago Tribune:* one for Joseph Medill Patterson, just west of Lake Forest; and the other for Robert R. McCormick, near Wheaton, just west of Chicago. These various schemes involved dramatic framed vistas, constructed walls and stairs, preserved woodland areas, abundant hedge-bounded flower beds, and stone borders. At the McCormick estate, Cantigny, the vista east toward the city led down from a hilltop mansion by a series of terraces to a reflecting pool, while a perpendicular southern vista was framed by two rows of trees. Another dramatic long view is within Lake Forest's Knollwood Club estate community, laid out in the mid-1920s by Edward Bennett with a Provencal-styled house designed in 1929 by Robert Work and his new partner Russell Walcott.

Root also designed a number of gardens beyond Chicago's North Shore, including several in and around Madison, Wisconsin, and elsewhere in the Midwest. Many of these commissions are employed as examples in three of the ten *Landscape Garden Series* pamphlets, published in 1921, and in his 1941 book, *Contourscaping.* Unlike Root's earlier 1914 publication, *Design in Landscape Gardening,* this publication was pitched to the general reader. In his 1941 textbook, *Contourscaping,* Root advanced ideas from his 1914 book, suggesting that for a

design to be successful from different, dynamic points, it must be conceived with a series of successful elevations. The many black and white plates with their geometric forms, in three and two dimensions, give *Contourscaping* a distinctly art moderne character. Thus, the book is both grounded in Beaux-Arts concepts and also looking forward to the modernist designs that dominated the postwar era. In 1942, Root authored *Camouflage with Planting,* a seventy-nine-page booklet that outlined strategies for protective planting for defense using trees, shrubs, vines and grass based on leaf color.

With the end of World War I, the Garden Club of America came to Chicago's North Shore in the summer of 1919. The visit was guided by Root's book of twenty-four garden sketch plans, still a major source of documentation. These and some later designs, such as Root's Patterson and R. R. McCormick estates, were featured in his January 1924 *Architectural Record* article entitled "Country Places Types of the Middle West," which showcased several formal landscape plans. The GCA visit and the 1924 article both led to increased awareness of this suburban Chicago formal-garden phenomenon.

In 1925, a revived Lake Forest summer school was held in conjunction with the University of Illinois, this time led by the new head of the landscape program, **Stanley**

Robert R. McCormick estate landscape. (Lake Forest College Library Special Collections)

Book cover, *Camouflage With Planting,* by Ralph Rodney Root. (Courtesy of Charles A. Birnbaum)

Hart White. By 1926, this had become the Foundation for Architecture and Landscape Architecture, a summer program for the leading graduates of the respective professions. It operated through 1931. Root raised the visibility of the Lake Forest initiative, but he played no role in the revived postwar program. Root continued to design and write in the Midwest through the 1940s. A notable later project was Ten Chimneys, the Genesee Depot, Wisconsin (near Milwaukee), estate of Alfred Lunt and Lynn Fontanne, a famous stage couple from the late 1920s to the 1950s. From 1939 to 1948 Root & Hollister, with offices in Chicago, designed formal, kitchen, and cutting gardens; an entry court; stone garden walls and walks; and an orchard. Through that period they collaborated with Charles Dornbusch, a Chicago architect and an instructor/colleague of Ludwig Mies van der Rohe at the Illinois Institute of Technology (IIT). Dornbusch was recalled as a friend of Lunt's by Ambrose M. Richardson, then an IIT student.

Root died May 29, 1964, at a time when the understanding and appreciation of the Beaux-Arts tradition in general and of formal gardens in particular largely was in eclipse. Through his surviving dramatic designs, writings, and work by students and other proponents, Root's contribution to the character of the Midwestern landscape has endured.

The Landscape Program Files in the Archives of the Lake Forest College Library, Lake Forest Ill., include Root's records and descriptions of the 1916 to 1917 summer program; the Lake Forest Garden Club Archives, in the Lake Forest College Library Special Collections, contain Root's 1919 GCA visit book of plans and other materials.

Ramsey, Leonidas, compiler. *Landscape Garden Series*. Davenport, Iowa: Garden Press, 1921. Ten pamphlets, of which Root authored three: the first (introductory and historical), the seventh (design), and the ninth (country estates).

Root, Ralph R. *Contourscaping*. Chicago: Ralph Fletcher Seymour, 1941. Root's three-dimensional approach to design theory drew on classic theory and looked forward to new, abstract, and asymmetrical forms.

Root, Ralph R., and Charles Fabens Kelley. *Design in Landscape Gardening*. New York: Century, 1914. One of the earliest textbooks in the field, emphasizing classic theory.

Arthur H. Miller

ROYSTON, ROBERT
(1918–2008)

LANDSCAPE ARCHITECT, EDUCATOR

Robert Norman Royston was born on April 25, 1918, in San Francisco. He grew up on a farm in the Santa Clara Valley of California, and at an early age displayed an interest in design. As a high school student he demonstrated a talent for drawing, dramatic performance, and athletics. One teacher advised him to be either an attorney or a ballet dancer. He pursued instead his interest in design and the natural environment. Upon graduation in 1936, he enrolled in the program in landscape design in the College of Agriculture at the University of California, Berkeley. Royston's mentor, Hollyngsworth Leland Vaughan,* allowed him to experiment on his own with the new design perspectives emerging in the work of **Thomas Dolliver Church** and the more avant-garde explorations of Daniel Urban Kiley,* Garrett Eckbo,* and **James C. Rose**. His university work also included courses in studio art, engineering, and architecture, an experience that convinced him of the value and necessity of interdisciplinary design collaboration, which he practiced throughout his long career. Royston's interest in painting, which he continued to pursue in order to explore aesthetic principles applicable to his design work, can be traced to the studio art classes that were a part of his early education.

While working his way through college, Royston was employed part-time in the office of Thomas Church and upon graduation in 1940 he became a full-time employee. At the time, Church was expanding his practice, which had been centered primarily on residential gardens, to include the design of larger-scale, planned, residential communities. Young Royston was given major responsibilities on such San Francisco projects as Valencia Gardens Housing Project, Potrero Hill Housing, and Parkmerced Apartments, along with James Rose. He was also an early member of Telesis, an informal interdisciplinary group of designers and planners concerned with environmental problems of the San Francisco Bay area. Here he met several of the architects he would later collaborate with on various projects as well as his future professional partner, Garrett Eckbo.

With the outbreak of World War II, Royston volunteered for the U.S. Navy. He served as a junior officer in the Pacific theater, logging some 150,000 miles at sea. In

Robert Royston, ca. 1950. (Royston, Hanamoto, Alley & Abey)

his spare time aboard ship, Royston experimented with design ideas, building models of residential gardens and creating jewelry out of scrap materials. He credited these efforts with developing many of the ideas on space and form he would utilize in his professional practice after the war. In 1945, Royston returned to the Bay Area and accepted Garrett Eckbo's invitation to form a partnership with him and landscape architect Edward Williams. The new firm, Eckbo, Royston, and Williams, eventually established offices in San Francisco and Los Angeles. Eckbo ran the Los Angeles office and Royston the one in San Francisco. The two offices worked mostly independently of each other, concentrating on projects in their regions.

In 1947, Royston accepted a teaching position at the University of California at Berkeley, while continuing his

Mitchell Park, Palo Alto, California, 1956.
(Royston, Hanamoto, Alley & Abey)

in 1948. Royston's specific design vocabulary of layered, non-axial spaces and bold asymmetrical arcs and polygons suggests such influences as analytical cubism, biomorphism, and the rectilinear geometry of Piet Mondrian's paintings. The approach to architectural space of Mies van der Rohe and Le Corbusier are also clearly visible. Royston regarded space as the primary medium of design and insisted on the absolute necessity of integrating design form with human use. For example, in a typical Royston park design, a wading pool for young children may be laid out as a visually engaging biomorphic form but at the same time is scaled to the distance a parent's voice can reach. The depth of the pool would also reflect function over pure form in that it would be shallowest in the middle where the child is farthest from parental aid. In Royston's design vocabulary there is no art for art's sake. Design form is always directly related to use and the psychological effect of space on its participants. For him, landscape architecture "practices the fine art of relating the structure of culture to the nature of landscape, to the end that people can use it, enjoy it, and preserve it."

professional practice. His students included both architects and landscape architects. He credited his interaction with students and faculty as a decisive influence on his professional work. His teaching career at Berkeley ended in 1951 when he resigned after refusing to sign a loyalty oath. Soon after leaving Berkeley, he accepted a part-time position at Stanford University and later at North Carolina State University. Over the course of his career, Royston taught and lectured at over twenty-five colleges and universities in the United States.

Royston's early professional work was concentrated in northern California and at first consisted mostly of residential site planning and garden design. This was a period of astronomical growth fueled by the postwar economic boom and an acute shortage of housing. From 1940 to 1950, the population of California increased by 42 percent, the largest increase of any state. Most of this growth occurred as low-density, suburban development, where Royston did much of his work. His practice soon expanded to include parks, plazas, and planned residential communities. Royston collaborated on numerous residential projects with many notable Bay Area architects, including Joseph Allen Stein, John Funk, Joseph Esherick, Campbell and Wong, and Robert Marquis. His site plans emphasized the integration of indoor and outdoor space with elegant, functional garden rooms for outdoor living. Important early residential designs by Royston include the Naify Garden in 1947, the Chinn Garden (date unknown), three gardens for the Appert family from 1947–1955, and twin gardens created for his own home and for his neighbor, Joseph Allen Stein, both

In dealing with more complex projects such as planned residential communities, Royston developed early in his practice his concept of the "landscape matrix," which he defined as "the linking of open space as a continuous system throughout the community establishing a strong framework whereby communities are controlled and given form." An early application of the landscape matrix was the plan for a 258-acre cooperative housing project, Ladera (1946), near Palo Alto. Royston's design featured a linear park that tied together the residential clusters and separated automobile and pedestrian circulation. The plan was built, but not according to Royston's specifications.

Royston's innovative park work also began during the 1950s. His first major commission in 1950 was for the Standard Oil Rod and Gun Club located at the Standard Oil Refinery near Point Richmond, California. It was a private recreation facility for workers at the refinery. Royston's carefully zoned design provided a gymnasium,

Plan of Mitchell Park, Palo Alto, California. (Royston, Hanamoto, Alley & Abey)

swimming pools, imaginatively designed custom play equipment, family picnic areas, and several multi-use areas in a series of skillfully layered spaces on the site of a former skeet range and fishing pier. The biomorphic forms he employed were reminiscent of his residential design work. Much of the actual construction was done by the refinery workers. The facility was an immediate success and attracted the attention of Bay Area planners representing several municipalities.

Royston soon was given important park and playground commissions, many of which gained attention in the national media. Among his more important works were Krusi Park in Alameda (1954); Pixie Place in Marin County (1954); Bowden (1960), Mitchell (1956), and

Rinconada (1965) parks all in Palo Alto; and, later, Santa Clara's Central Park (1960) and Mountain View's Cuesta Park (1974). Royston rejected the notion of parks as primarily outdoor gymnasiums catering to a narrow range of age groups. He envisioned parks as "public gardens" serving a wide spectrum of users, including families, very young children, and the elderly. Many of his parks contain elements that are more commonly used in residential design, such as pergolas and enclosed patio-like areas that create a sense of familiarity and intimacy. All play equipment, seating, and lighting were custom designed and were unique to each park. During the 1950s Royston also designed urban plazas, such as San Francisco's Portsmouth Square and St. Mary's Square.

Chinn Garden, San Francisco, California, 1949. (Royston, Hanamoto, Alley & Abey)

In 1958, Royston amicably left the firm of Eckbo, Royston, and Williams and formed a new professional office with Asa Hanamoto and David Mayes. The firm developed into Royston Hanamoto Alley & Abey and is still in existence. For fifty years, the office, now located in Mill Valley, California, has been engaged in a wide range of commissions in the United States, Venezuela, Chile, Mexico, Canada, Singapore, and Malaysia and has earned over seventy design awards for projects ranging from residential gardens to the design of new towns. Two of its most significant designs, which embody an effective application of Royston's landscape matrix con-cept, are Sun River, Oregon, a 5,500-acre residential community (1969), and North Bonneville, Washington, a new town (1974). Other notable projects include master plans for the Lawrence Livermore National Laboratory (1969), Los Alamos National Laboratory (1980), the Stanford University Linear Accelerator (1961), and Parque Recuerdo Cemetery, Santiago, Chile (1981), as well as various site plans for facilities at the University of California Berkeley (1977), Stanford University (1964), and the University of California at Santa Cruz (1967).

Robert Royston was the recipient of many profession-al awards, including Fellow of the American Society of

Landscape Architects (1975); the American Institute of Architects Medal (1978); the Bradford Williams Award (1978); the Award of Honor in Landscape Architecture of the City of San Francisco Art Commission (1980); Northern California Chapter of ASLA Award for Outstanding Contributions to the Stature of the Profession (1981); Honorary Fellow of the Australian Institute of Landscape Architects (1986); and the American Society of Landscape Architects Medal, the highest award of that professional organization. Royston, while officially retired, remained active as a consultant to his firm and to clients engaged in the restoration of his parks.

Robert Royston passed away at his home in Mill Valley, California, on September 19, 2008.

Robert Royston's design drawings are located in the Environmental Design Archives at the University of California, Berkeley.

Rainey, Reuben M., and JC Miller. *Modern Public Gardens: Robert Royston and the Suburban Park.* San Francisco: William Stout Publishers, 2006. This 128-page monograph celebrates Royston's own aesthetic as a native Californian.

Royston, Robert N. "Getting the Feel for a New Town Site and Its Design." *Landscape Architecture* 66, no. 5 (Spring 1976), 432–43.

Royston, Robert N. "Robert Royston's Thoughts on Landscape Architecture." *Landscape Australia* 8, no. 2 (Winter 1986), 152–64.

The authors wish to thank Robert Royston, who provided source material for this entry.

Reuben M. Rainey and JC Miller

SASAKI, HIDEO
(1919–2000)
LANDSCAPE ARCHITECT, EDUCATOR

Hideo Sasaki was born in Reedley, California, in the San Joaquin Valley on November 25, 1919. A farmer's son, bright, well-rounded, athletic, he graduated from Reedley Junior College in 1939. At the University of California at Los Angeles (UCLA), he studied business administration, with a minor in art; but after hearing about the field of city planning, Sasaki transferred to the University of California at Berkeley, where planning was taught in the landscape architecture department.

With the outbreak of war, Sasaki's studies in California abruptly ended. After a brief time in an internment camp for Japanese Americans, Sasaki worked in the sugar beet fields of Colorado and, later, in a photographer's darkroom in Chicago. At the University of Illinois in Urbana, he studied under **Stanley Hart White** and Karl B. Lohmann, both of whom had masters in landscape architecture degrees from Harvard. In 1946, Sasaki received a bachelor of fine arts in landscape architecture, with highest honors, from the University of Illinois. In 1948, from Harvard, he received a master of landscape architecture degree.

In those early postwar years at Harvard's Graduate School of Design (GSD), while Walter Gropius was dean, Sasaki came into contact with Bauhaus ideals of teamwork and mingled freely with architects and engineers. After graduation, Sasaki worked in the New York and Chicago offices of Skidmore, Owings & Merrill (SOM), and taught at the University of Illinois and at Harvard.

Ken DeMay (*seated left*), Stuart Dawson (*standing*), and Hideo Sasaki (*seated right*), ca. 1965. (Sasaki Associates, Inc.)

With the planner Reginald Isaacs and students at the University of Illinois, Sasaki also did research on housing and urban renewal in and around Chicago.

By the end of 1953, Sasaki was teaching at Harvard and practicing in Watertown, Massachusetts. At the GSD, both the new dean, Josep Lluís Sert, and the new planning department chairman, Reginald Isaacs, shared

Left: John Deere & Company World Headquarters, Moline, Illinois, 1959. (Sasaki Associates, Inc.)

Below: Sea Pines Plantation, Hilton Head, South Carolina, 1964. (Sasaki Associates, Inc.)

P. Dober, John W. Frey, Paul Gardescu, Don H. Olson, Donald K. Sakuma, and Lawrence W. Walquist Jr. Projects requiring diverse skills and talents included Sea Pines Plantation on Hilton Head Island, South Carolina, from 1958 for the developer Charles Fraser; Upjohn Corporation World Headquarters in Kalamazoo, Michigan, with SOM from 1957 to 1961; Deere & Company World Headquarters with architects Eero Saarinen and Associates from 1963; and projects in New England and beyond with the architects Pietro Belluschi, J. L. Sert, I. M. Pei, Paul Rudolph, and Edward L. Barnes—leading figures in the modern movement.

It was a unique moment in time, a "coalescing of different forces and ideas," Sasaki recalled. There was pent-up demand for revitalization and new construction after World War II. The environmental movement was gaining strength. New tools, such as aerial photo interpretation, computer graphics, and computer modeling, were being developed. A focus on research and regional planning opened up new opportunities for collaboration. As Dean Sert noted at Harvard's first annual urban design conference in April 1956, the era of individual, isolated work was over. It was a new era of synthesis.

Sasaki's commitment to collaboration. Before long, the lines between professions and departments became blurred. What mattered was the problem at hand and the diversity of professionals assembled to solve it.

As head of a large planning and design firm that, by the early 1970s, included several practicing architects and engineers, and as chairman of Harvard's department of landscape architecture from 1958 to 1968, Sasaki utilized a wide range of talents, regularly giving credit to others. Stamped on the cover of a 1959 report on Boston's Government Center—one of his firm's collaborative projects, with Kevin Lynch and others—is the firm's title block, which credits Hideo Sasaki, Peter E. Walker, Marvin I. Adelman, Stuart O. Dawson, Richard

For landscape architects this was a sea change. The individual who practiced or taught (or did both) in relative isolation, with a great deal of autonomy and control over the final product, became fairly rare. More common was the member of a team, who practiced or taught with less autonomy but perhaps more influence. It was a shift from lone generalist to team player. At Harvard's Department of Landscape Architecture, when Sasaki was chairman, this shift was evident in the emphasis on team

Greenacre Park, New York, New York, 1971.
(Sasaki Associates, Inc.)

teaching and group projects. The sequence of studies was divided into eight-week quarters, taught by a small core faculty and many guests, including specialists from other schools and colleagues from Sasaki's practice. The department's limited funds induced Sasaki to keep a flow of expertise moving from his office to the school and back again. Those who taught without pay would find stimulation, new ideas, perhaps other rewards as well. It was a remarkable symbiosis, recalled Professor Charles W. Harris, Sasaki's successor at Harvard.

Beyond introducing new kinds of knowledge, novel methods of teaching, and sophisticated new tools, in a two-phased sequence that Harris considered "almost revolutionary," Sasaki also contributed to teaching and practice by demonstrating clear, analytical thinking about a problem. Former students and colleagues recall the penetrating and intellectually satisfying manner in which Sasaki would arrive at a synthesis or conclude a jury. And yet his office's built work, subject to his review as chief design critic, was not overly cerebral. It was understated, uncluttered, seemingly natural, elegantly crafted. If the artist's hand was not evident in the landscape, still one could sense that the artist's eye and mind had been engaged there.

Such was Sasaki's legacy, an increasingly comprehensive approach to planning and design, such that many skills and talents—artistic, intellectual, technical—were given free range while none alone was dominant. Within his firm, two ideals are still upheld: *collaboration* among people from different fields; and *integration* of land, buildings, and the larger environment. Another of Sasaki's ideals was the *oasis*—a designed landscape where the human spirit could be refreshed, especially in the city—at Greenacre Park, in New York, for instance; at Constitution Plaza, in Hartford; within housing developments in Chicago and New York; and at the Christopher Columbus Park, in Boston. "As the world becomes more crowded and resources limited," he wrote in 1989, "we must treasure the oases we find and create new ones, no matter how small, with love and care."

Sasaki's legacy is widespread, traceable in landscapes and schools around the country and abroad. It can also be seen in the people at Sasaki Associates, including his successors as head of the firm—Paul Gardescu, James Sukeforth, Kenneth Bassett, and Dennis Pieprz and over 2,000 employees, past and present. Sasaki's office went through several configurations and spin-offs, including Sasaki, Walker and Associates; Sasaki, Dawson, DeMay Associates; and The SWA Group. The office's planned and built work garnered numerous awards. Sasaki personally served on the design review boards of the University of Colorado in Boulder, from 1961 to 1994; and of Arizona State University in Tempe, from 1982 to 1989. He served on the U.S. Commission of Fine Arts in Washington, D.C., from 1961 to 1971. He was often a juror for competitions, including those for the Vietnam Veterans Memorial in 1981 and the Astronauts' Memorial in 1988.

A Fellow of the American Society of Landscape Architects, Sasaki received the ASLA Medal in 1971 and the Allied Professions Medal of the American Institute of Architects in 1973. He was awarded honorary doctorates from the University of Illinois, the University of Colorado, and Ohio State University. In the spring of 2000, the Harvard Design School awarded him the Centennial Medal in honor of his extraordinary achievement in landscape architecture. He died on August 30, 2000. After his passing, many tributes were sent to Sasaki's widow and two daughters, and to Sasaki Associates. A former student wrote, "In addition to being a towering giant in his profession, he was always gentle as a human being."

Sasaki, Hideo "Thoughts on Education in Landscape Architecture: Some Comments on Today's Methodologies and Purpose." *Landscape Architecture* (July 1950), 158–60. Sasaki wrote very little for publication. His thoughts on ecological factors in planning and design appeared in *Forsite*, a student publication of the Department of City Planning and Landscape Architecture, University of Illinois, in 1951 and 1953.

Simo, Melanie. *The Offices of Hideo Sasaki, A Corporate History.* Berkeley, Calif.: Spacemaker Press, 2001. Traces the history of Sasaki's professional practice from 1953 to 1980, when he retired from the multidisciplinary, national firm of Sasaki Associates.

Considers several offices that developed from that firm, most notably Sasaki Walker and Associates, Sasaki, Dawson, DeMay Associates, and the SWA Group.

Walker, Peter, and Melanie Simo. *Invisible Gardens: The Search for Modernism in the American Landscape.* Cambridge, Mass.: MIT Press, 1994. Places the work of Sasaki, in teaching and in practice, within the context of his peers, including Ian L. McHarg,* Lawrence Halprin,* Daniel Urban Kiley,* Garrett Eckbo,* Roberto Burle Marx, Isamu Noguchi, Richard Haag,* and Stanley Hart White.

Melanie Simo

SCHERMERHORN, RICHARD, JR.
(1877–1962)
LANDSCAPE ARCHITECT, CIVIL ENGINEER

Richard Schermerhorn Jr. was born on October 17, 1877, in Brooklyn, New York. From age ten until 1894, Schermerhorn studied science at the Brooklyn Polytechnic Institute. He went on to Rensselaer Polytechnic Institute where he studied engineering from September of 1894 until the end of his sophomore year in 1897. The following year, Schermerhorn was employed by the Department of City Works in Brooklyn. In the fall of 1900, after assisting in his father's civil engineering practice, Schermerhorn embarked upon the study and practice of landscape architecture.

Commissioned by Andrew Carnegie in 1901 to design a terrace and garden for a residence on Fifth Avenue in New York City, Schermerhorn created a striking plan for what is today known as the Arthur Ross Terrace and Garden at the Cooper-Hewitt, National Design Museum. Bounded by a wide sidewalk, the largely unchanged rectangular garden features a distinctive rockery at one end, with trees and shrubbery bordering an expansive lawn.

Schermerhorn began his formal study of landscape architecture first working in the office of Boston architect **Guy Lowell**. From 1903 until 1905, he served in the office of New York landscape engineer, **Charles Wellford Leavitt Jr.** During this period, Schermerhorn completed work on private estates in Scarborough, New York, and Sea Bright, New Jersey. Schermerhorn continued to hone his craft, working for a brief time under landscape architect **Nathan Franklin Barrett**.

Just five years after the professional organization's founding, Schermerhorn joined the American Society of Landscape Architects (ASLA) in 1904. A year later, he opened an office in New York City, practicing both land-

Richard Schermerhorn Jr., ca. 1914. (Courtesy of the collection of William G. Crawford Jr.)

scape architecture and civil engineering. He devised formal plans based on classical styles for a number of properties, including those of William C. Whitney, William M. Sperry, and the City of New York. By 1912, Schermerhorn had also completed designs for C. K. G. Billings's estate stables in New York City; Arthur von Briesen's estate Gernda on Staten Island; Clarence Bonynge's North Bennington, Vermont, property; and Franklin Farrel Jr.'s property in New Haven, Connecticut.

Schermerhorn displayed a particular interest in Colonial Revival landscape architecture, beginning in 1908 with a submission to *House and Garden* for a collection of Long Island country estates. For the next thirty-eight years, Schermerhorn published a steady stream of thoughtful articles on landscape architecture, architecture, and gardening. Schermerhorn often argued that the profession of landscape architecture should transcend

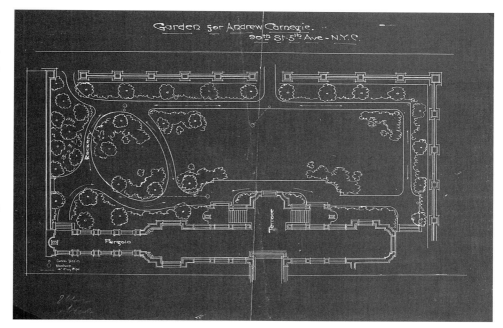

Right: Schermerhorn's plan for the Andrew Carnegie garden, 1901. (Collection of the New-York Historical Society, Architect & Engineer File, PR003-216-040-001, negative number 76056D)

Below: Arthur Ross Terrace and Garden, Cooper-Hewitt, National Design Museum, New York, New York, 2005. (Photo courtesy of William M. Singer, AIA)

the mere making of estate plans to tackle the modern challenges of state parks, transportation, and urban planning. In 1912, Schermerhorn presented an important paper on city planning before the Brooklyn Engineers' Club summarizing the planning efforts of several cities. "Distinguishing the City Practical from the City Beautiful," Schermerhorn argued that "if the City Practical is first realized there is no doubt that the City Beautiful will follow as a matter of course."

In 1915, one year after his election as a Fellow of the ASLA, Schermerhorn won the top prize in a competition conducted by the New York Department of Parks for the first plan in the development of Telewana, now Jacob Riis Park, in Queens. As a U.S. Army engineer during World War I, Schermerhorn helped to devise a plan for Camp Jackson in Columbia, South Carolina. From 1916 to 1924, Schermerhorn served as secretary of the New York chapter of the ASLA. While serving as president from 1924 to 1927, he opposed several uncontrolled efforts to develop Central Park. One plan called for a $15 million art and music center, and Schermerhorn successfully argued that the plan would destroy one of the park's natural vistas. Doubting the efficacy of gathering a number of different arts groups in one location, he believed that only structures ancillary to the park itself should be allowed and that a single encroachment would inevitably lead to others. Later Schermerhorn spearheaded a citywide protest against the use of the park for a $1 million war memorial, criticizing the proposal as inconsistent with both city and park planning.

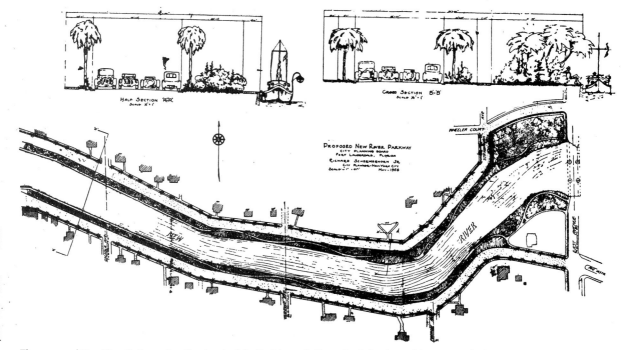

The proposed New River Parkway plan, Fort Lauderdale, Florida, 1926. (From the Collections of the Fort Lauderdale Historical Society. All rights reserved. Not to be reproduced without permission)

During the late 1920s, Schermerhorn's practice continued to grow. In 1926, Schermerhorn created a comprehensive zoning and street plan for Fort Lauderdale, Florida. The plan anticipated the city's rapid development and addressed growing concerns over traffic, zoning, and a lack of parks. He also completed city and regional plans for municipalities on Long Island, New York, including a 1933 zoning and master plan for Huntington; a 1927 zoning plan for North Hempstead; master and rezoning plans for Lawrence Village; and a master plan for Great Neck District. Schermerhorn's work in New Jersey included a master plan for Newark and a plan for Princeton. Schermerhorn designed parks at both the state and local levels, including Allegheny and Taconic state parks in New York, municipal parks throughout New York State, and a rural park surrounding a waterworks plant near Spartanburg, South Carolina, in 1927.

From 1928 to 1931, Schermerhorn served as an ASLA trustee. In 1929, he became chairman of the Landscape Architects Committee for the restoration of Colonial Williamsburg in Virginia. The distinguished group, which included ASLA founder **Warren Henry Manning**, Markley Stevenson, **Rose Ishbel Greely**, and **Fletcher Steele**, recommended studies on details such as the grasses, hitching rails, and rings, as well as the street lighting that existed during the colonial period. The committee also suggested reserving large open spaces as a rural backdrop for historic Williamsburg. Assisting in the commemoration of the 200th anniversary of George Washington's birth, the ASLA spearheaded the publication of *Colonial Gardens: The Landscape Architecture of George Washington's Time*. Published by the United States George Washington Bicentennial Commission in 1932, this work included Schermerhorn's essay on historic New York and New Jersey homes and gardens and landscape plans made as early as 1660.

From 1935 to 1939, Schermerhorn lectured on landscape architecture at Columbia University despite his never having graduated from college. In 1938, while serving as secretary of the Association for the Preservation of Lindenwald, Martin Van Buren's homestead at

Kinderhook, New York, Schermerhorn worked for the Hudson River Conservation Society as a consulting landscape architect for eight communities along the river.

Schermerhorn served during World War II as a landscape architect and planner for the U.S. Army at Fort Hamilton in New York, and as a consultant for the Federal Public Housing Authority on housing projects in Bound Brook, New Jersey. By the end of his career, Schermerhorn had planned over one hundred private country estates in New York, New Jersey, and elsewhere. He prepared plans for cemeteries in New York, New Jersey, and Pennsylvania, ranging in size from 20 to 250 acres. A life member of the American Society of Civil Engineers and a member of the American Institute of Planners, Schermerhorn also designed plans for colleges and universities in New York, including Albany College, Union College, and his alma mater, Rensselaer Polytechnic Institute.

Schermerhorn died on September 28, 1962, at the age of eighty-four, a resident of Montclair, New Jersey. Recognizing his fight to preserve Central Park in 1924, Schermerhorn's *New York Times* obituary noted that the landscape architect had long been "a strong advocate of the principle that land should be acquired early for park use and once acquired should be kept free of special installations."

American Society of Landscape Architects. *Colonial Gardens: The Landscape Architecture of George Washington's Time.* Washington, D.C.: United States George Washington Bicentennial Commission, 1932. Early collection of essays on the documentation and treatment of historic landscapes along with photographs, illustrations, and plans. Includes essays by Bradford Williams, **Arthur Asahel Shurcliff**, **Robert Wheelwright**, Richard Schermerhorn Jr., and Fletcher Steele, and a bibliography by region of early source materials on landscape architecture.

Schermerhorn, Richard, Jr. "A Few References to Illustrated Articles on American Estates." *Landscape Architecture* 2, no. 2 (1912), 89–92. A bibliography of illustrated articles on American estates and gardens by region and state published in American magazines between 1899 and 1911.

Schermerhorn, Richard, Jr. "Less Familiar Gardens: a Few References to Articles." *Landscape Architecture* 2, no. 3 (1912), 141–42. A bibliography of articles on gardens from around the world published in American magazines and journals between 1869 and 1909.

William G. Crawford Jr.

SCHUBARTH, NILES BIERRAGAARD
(1818–1889)
LANDSCAPE GARDENER, CEMETERY DESIGNER

Born in Drobak, Norway (a small town south of Oslo), on May 24, 1818, Niles Bierragaard Schubarth, named for his Danish maternal grandfather, was the paternal grandson of a German immigrant who had settled in nearby Kongsberg. His father died when he was ten, and through the patronage of a prosperous villager and his wife, Schubarth found work at fourteen in a local store and counting house.

The Romantic writings of James Fenimore Cooper aroused in Schubarth a strong desire to experience the United States firsthand, and he immigrated at the age of twenty-two to western New York, the setting for much of that author's early writing. His Norwegian patron then characterized him as possessing "a high mind and a good heart." He found work in 1840 with a Rochester civil engineering firm engaged in the first expansion of the Erie Canal. Although untutored, Schubarth demonstrated a special aptitude for drawing and was placed in charge of delineating surveys and plans for the canal. When financial difficulties shut down canal construction in 1842, Schubarth, described as "an ingenious and accomplished draftsman, and as a useful member in any office or company of engineers," moved to Providence, Rhode Island, then in need of civil engineers. He remained in Providence for the rest of his life.

Schubarth's first professional activity in Providence was in collaboration with Stephen Atwater (1816–1855) in the office of the bustling, rapidly growing, and culturally ambitious city's only established engineering firm. Active by the 1820s under Benoni Lockwood (1777–1852) and continued by his son Moses B. Lockwood (1815–1872), the firm had devolved by 1844 to Samuel B. Cushing (1811–1873). The relationship between Cushing and Atwater & Schubarth remains unknown; they occupied the same quarters in 1844, but by 1845 the new firm had moved to separate quarters.

The new firm burst onto Providence's landscape scene. Within two years after its appearance, Atwater

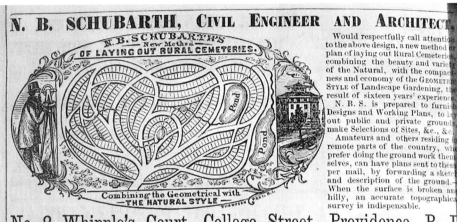

Schubarth's advertisement from the City Directory of Providence, Rhode Island, ca. 1840.

& Schubarth had garnered all three of the 1840s open-space landscape-design commissions in Providence: two public commissions in 1845, the Cove Basin and the new section of North Burial Ground, and, the following year, the original section of the privately subscribed Swan Point Cemetery. In addition to these landscaped open spaces, the firm became heavily involved in surveying and platting undeveloped land into house lots for the rapidly expanding Providence metropolitan area. William E. Haines joined the firm between mid-1848 and early 1849; the collaboration was known briefly as Atwater, Schubarth & Haines before Atwater's departure by April of 1849. By 1854, Schubarth and Haines too had gone their separate ways, both practicing independently in Providence.

Schubarth's professional activity included designing Romantic publicly accessible open space, pragmatic division of undeveloped land into house lots, designing buildings, and real-estate speculation. The North Burial Ground and Swan Point commissions led to similar undulating, curvilinear cemeteries at River Bend in Westerly, Rhode Island, and Oak Grove in Pawtucket, Rhode Island, both in 1852; Elm Grove in Mystic, Connecticut, in 1853; and Juniper Hill in Bristol, Rhode Island, in 1859. He may also have designed Mount Hope Cemetery (1850) in North Attleborough, Massachusetts. His advertisement in the 1860 *Providence Directory,* proclaiming "N.B. Schubarth's New Method OF LAYING OUT RURAL CEMETERIES, combining the Geometrical with THE NATURAL STYLE," seems oddly hollow today, for no new cemetery commissions followed. Indeed, beginning

in 1859, when Butler Hospital for the Insane, abutting Swan Point to the south, obtained the services of **Horace William Shaler Cleveland** to design a therapeutic setting for its patients' recovery, Schubarth was passed over for major public-works landscaping in the metropolitan area. He was, however, a founding member in 1883 of Providence's important, if not always influential, Public Park Association, an early exponent of sensible and attractive land-use planning. His stock in trade was surveying and platting house lots, which began in the mid-1840s and continued into the mid-1880s in Providence and the adjacent cities of Cranston and Warwick. Schubarth's architectural commissions include the Arnold Block (1854) in Providence, the Oriental Mill in Providence (1860) and the Willamantic Linen Thread Mill in Connecticut (1864), the Jefferson Street Baptist Church (1867), and several houses, including two for himself (1873 and 1874). He began to speculate in real estate in 1851 and by the mid-1850s was playing the multiple roles of surveyor, designer, and investor in several of the areas he platted.

Schubarth's career and position in American landscape design perhaps begs more questions than it answers. Cooper's lure to the vanishing frontier of the United States suggests a strong Romantic impulse, visible in his early cemetery designs. His decision to move to Providence to fill a need for civil engineers shows his practical side, even more fully revealed in his house-lot platting, where maximum return on investment (for others as well as for himself) drove the design. His venture into architecture, self-ratified in his own advertising by 1867, in some ways combines a Romantic willingness

Swan Point Cemetery, Providence, Rhode Island, 2002 view. (Photo by Charles A. Birnbaum)

for new challenges with practical need. His apparent lack of professional training did not hinder his brief, intense, early involvement in public aesthetic-driven designs but ultimately must have inhibited his involvement with larger-scale projects in the late nineteenth century. Constantly buying and selling real estate as well as moving his own office and household, he ultimately seems to have achieved the restlessness more characteristic of his adopted country than his native land.

Schubarth died at his home (the ninth he occupied during his forty-six years in Providence) on July 31, 1889. His remains were laid to rest on a knoll just inside the original entrance to Swan Point Cemetery, which he had designed more than forty years earlier.

Jordy, William H., and Christopher P. Monkhouse. "Atwater, Stephen." *Buildings on Paper: Rhode Island Architectural Drawings, 1825–1945.* Providence, R.I.: Brown University Press, 1982, 207–8. Catalog produced for the exhibition of architectural drawings includes an entry for Schubarth's Swan Point Cemetery.

Public Park Association of Providence. "Niles Bierragaard Schubarth." Parks of Providence and Other Cities. Providence, R.I.: Public Park Association of Providence, 1896, 111–14. The eleventh of a series of pamphlets published by the Association, advocated for increased public urban open spaces and to elevate the level of public discourse.

William McKenzie Woodward

SCOTT, GERALDINE KNIGHT
(1904–1989)
LANDSCAPE ARCHITECT

Geraldine Knight Scott was born in Wallace, Idaho, in 1904. Her parents died while she was young, and she was raised by relatives in Idaho and the San Francisco Bay area. According to an autobiographical article, she decided to become a landscape architect during her senior year at San Francisco's Girls High School. She en-rolled in the University of California at Berkeley, College of Agriculture in 1922, and received her degree in landscape architecture in 1926. Feeling that the curriculum was too focused on science, she extended her education with courses in art and architecture at Cornell University from 1926 to 1928, an experience she found wonderful

Above: Geraldine Knight Scott, date unknown. (Geraldine Knight Scott Collection [2000-3], Environmental Design Archives, University of California, Berkeley)

Right: San Francisco Funeral Service and Mortuary (Daphne Funeral Home, now demolished), San Francisco, California, ca. 1953. (Geraldine Knight Scott Collection [2000-3], Environmental Design Archives, University of California, Berkeley)

and stimulating. Following graduation from Cornell, she began her professional career in the offices of A. E. Hanson* in Southern California. During the next two years, she worked on various residential estates and gardens, including the Harold Lloyd estate in Beverly Hills.

A strong advocate of the role of travel for increasing one's self-knowledge and appreciation of different cultures and regionalism, Geraldine Knight spent twenty-two months in Europe beginning in 1930. She surveyed historic Italian villas through the Academia Della Arts in Rome and explored the famous gardens of France and Spain. She also attended the Sorbonne in Paris, where she pursued her interest in housing, studying projects in Germany and Austria. Upon her return to California, there were few employment opportunities because of the Great Depression, so she studied painting with Japanese artist Chiura Obata at the University of California at Berkeley. They remained lifelong friends and traveled to Japan together in 1954. (During World War II, she assisted his son Gyo, later of the architectural firm Hellmuth, Obata + Kassabaum, with admission to Washington University in St. Louis so the younger Obata would not be placed in an internment camp.) In 1933, she joined the office of Helen Van Pelt in Marin County. They were

partners for three years, and then worked independently in a shared office for three more.

In 1939, Geraldine Knight married Mellier Scott, a Los Angeles journalist who would later become a well-known writer interested in city and regional planning issues. With their shared interest in housing and planning, they traveled throughout Europe visiting housing projects and attended the 18th Congress of the International Federation for Housing and Town Planning in Stockholm in July of 1939. They were forced to end their travels when war broke out in September of that year.

They returned to Los Angeles where Geraldine Knight Scott worked as the director of the Citizens Housing Council and later became the first female member of the Los Angeles Regional Planning Commission, working on recreational planning and war housing. In Los Angeles, they were also actively involved with Telesis, a group interested in the social implications of architecture and landscape design, whose members included Gregory Ain, Robert Royston,* and **James C. Rose**. In 1941, the Scotts moved to Berkeley where they participated in the San Francisco Housing and Planning Commission and the San Francisco Telesis group, which included Garrett Eckbo,* Jack Kent, and Vernon DeMars. Combined with her inherent interest in housing, the involvement with Telesis persuaded Scott to continue working in the public sector.

Scott began working with landscape architect Katherine Imlay in 1947, and the following year opened her private practice in Berkeley, which she operated until 1968. She excelled in site planning, integrating the project with the land, and applying a collaborative vision of an artist and scientist. Scott focused her efforts on housing, schools, private gardens and professional office parks. Her projects varied widely and included the design and installation of the living plant exhibit in the Pacific House at the Golden Gate International Exposition in 1939; the Daphne Funeral Home in San Francisco in 1953; and the Menlo Park Professional Zone in 1950. In a 1949 article about the Scott & Imlay designed garden for the E. J. Nell residence in Atherton, California, Scott was quoted as saying, "A garden is a creation in space and time and must be planned as an ever-changing composition in which human beings at any moment can become the central figures." Her particular talent was the visual combination of plants, which, in conjunction with her knowledge of California flora, led to Daniel Urban Kiley's* invitation for Scott to join the design team as the horticultural consultant for his 1963 design for the garden of the Oakland Museum. Scott was involved from the beginning with this project that combined Kevin Roche's three-part museum and Kiley's design for an urban park created with roof-top gardens. She, with her colleague Mai Arbegast, worked to preserve, protect, and restore the museum's landscape for the next twenty-five years.

Scott also lectured and taught landscape architecture at the University of California, Berkeley, from 1952 to 1968. She developed a course in planting design, a subject about which she felt strongly. Scott felt that this subject was being de-emphasized in favor of broad analysis concerns—both in universities and professional

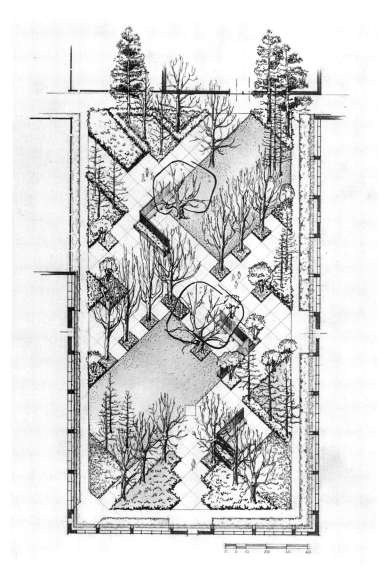

An example of Scott's designs is this site development axonometric drawing for the Food Machinery & Chemical Corporation, San Jose, California. (Geraldine Knight Scott Collection [2000-3], Environmental Design Archives, University of California, Berkeley)

practices. Scott espoused an approach that was both dynamic and multidisciplinary, involving many of the allied arts such as painting, sculpture, and dance as a way of getting the students to see and feel space before articulating it with design materials. She was asked by the landscape department in 1962 to assume management of the university's Blake Estate in Kensington, which resulted in her long-range unrealized plan completed 1964. Her publications included a 1957 article on highway aesthetics and a 1963 article on the Unitarian Church of Berkeley, both in *Landscape Architecture.*

In addition to her private practice and teaching engagements, Scott actively participated in professional organizations and public activities. She was elected a Fellow of the American Society of Landscape Architects, was a founding member of the California Horticultural Society in 1935, and was awarded a distinguished membership to the Sigma Lambda Alpha Honor Society in 1981. She also served as a member of the Berkeley Art Commission for many years. Scott established the Traveling Fellowship Program for landscape architecture students at UC Berkeley and the Endowment for Research into the History of Landscape Architecture, which included support for maintaining and preserving the Environmental Design Archives at the University of California, Berkeley. Scott died in Berkeley, California, on August 2, 1989.

The Geraldine Knight Scott Collection resides at the Environmental Design Archives, University of California, Berkeley. The collection documents projects and professional activities from 1914 to 1988. In addition, it includes travel journals, sketchbooks, scrapbooks from several tours of Europe; oral histories and interviews given by Scott; course materials and examples of her students' work; and project records including drawings, files, and photographs.

"Geraldine Knight Scott: A Woman in Landscape Architecture in California, 1926–1989." Berkeley, Calif.: Regional Oral History Office, 1990. An interview with Geraldine Knight Scott about her life, philosophy, education, professional development, practice, and teaching career.

Laurie, Michael. *75 Years of Landscape Architecture at Berkeley. Part II: Recent Years.* Berkeley: Department of Landscape Architecture, University of California, Berkeley, 1988. Appendix 1. Includes an appendix that consists of short biographies of significant members of the department.

Waverly B. Lowell

SEAVEY, FRANCES COPLEY
(1851–1920)
AUTHOR

Frances Copley was born in Illinois in 1851. She married Thomas Benton Seavey in St. Louis in 1876. Little is known about her early life or academic background. She wrote for *Garden and Forest,* a journal published in New York City under the auspices of **Charles Sprague Sargent**, from 1893 to 1897, sometimes using the name Fannie Copley Seavey. When it ceased publication, she began writing for *Park and Cemetery* and *Landscape Gardening,* published in Chicago.

An indication of her activities and ideas can be gleaned from her extensive writings, especially Victor F. Lawson's Current Topics Club, serialized in the *Chicago Record Herald* and *Los Angeles Times* (1901); "Railroad Gardening" in **Liberty Hyde Bailey**'s *Cyclopedia of American Horticulture* (1903); and "Trees on Small Home Grounds" in the *Chautauquan* (1905).

She supported the idea of women in the business arena, writing about the topic in the Current Topics Club. In the horticulture column, she listed landscape architects working across the country, stressing the importance of the profession. "In these days no man under-

takes to build house, factory mill, schoolhouse, church, store, railway station, city hall or post office without plans and specifications from a competent landscape architect, and still more fundamental advice of the landscape gardener is recognized as at least equally essential to the best results."

In "Railroad Gardening," she advocated the use of hardy trees and skillfully arranged shrubs, which she deemed interesting all year round, while scorning ornamental gardening for station parks. She prepared landscape plans for companies such as the Michigan Central Railroad. She favored planting hardy vines, shrubs, and trees—not decorative flower beds—so a part of the display preserves its "beautiful effects" during the winter, and cited station grounds at Niles and Ypsilanti in Michigan as examples of successful planting.

She started the article "Trees on Small Home Grounds" with a grand statement: "People who are deprived of intimate, friendly relations with trees are doubly unfortunate. They not only miss some of life's pleasantest occupations, associations, and memories, but they never

Open-air reading room, photo by Frances Seavey, from the *Chautauquan,* June 1905.

made the real acquaintance of trees, the noblest and most human of earth's ornaments." Two of her photos accompanied the text.

Seavey's monthly column, "Improvement Associations," for *Park and Cemetery* appeared from 1901 through 1904. She showed a clear understanding of international issues, writing that the Metropolitan Public Gardens Association of London, England, deserved to be called the most important improvement association in the world. Seavey wrote about a broad range of topics in her column, including women as landscape gardeners, trees and tree planting, and improving school grounds.

In "Possibilities of Small Home Gardens," she wrote, "Finally, make your home a picture, but let it harmonize with and enhance the pictures on either side of it; let your planting blend with that on adjoining properties; make yours one of a long gallery of pleasant homes."

As a resident of Chicago, she contributed to the *Chi-*

cago Tribune, writing about European and Japanese gardens and residential landscape architecture and penning letters to the editor.

Her writings ended about 1905, but she and her husband continued to live at 7554 South Shore Drive in Chicago for a number of years. She died in Los Angeles in 1920, and was buried in Brighton, Illinois, where she grew up.

Seavey, Frances Copley. "Railroad Gardening." In L. H. Bailey, *Cyclopedia of American Horticulture.* New York: Macmillan Co., 1903, 1489–95.

Seavey, Frances Copley. "Trees on Small Home Grounds." *Chautauquan* 41, no. 4 (June 1905).

Seavey, Frances Copley. "Women in Horticulture." *Los Angeles Times* and *Chicago Record Herald,* September 22, 1901. Part of a series on women in business that Seavey wrote for the newspapers' Current Topics Club.

John Gruber

SHAW, HENRY
(1800–1889)
AMATEUR BOTANIST, LANDSCAPE GARDENER

Henry Shaw was born in the industrial town of Sheffield, England, in 1800. At the age of eighteen, he left his birthplace, to sell manufactured goods from St. Louis throughout the Mississippi Valley and westward. Shaw purchased investment property and vast acreage and established businesses in St. Louis, achieving financial success in two decades. Shaw then turned over his business operations and took up more genteel pursuits, ultimately trading the life of a businessman for that of a landscape advocate. In 1840, he began nearly ten years of travel, visiting royal and botanical gardens in Europe, Asia Minor, and Russia. He was familiar with two important models for the new public park movement: J. C. Loudon's Derby Arboretum and Birkenhead Park outside Liverpool and, the Sheffield Botanic Garden (its curator of plants was Robert Marnock) and the Glasgow Botanical Garden.

According to his own admission, Shaw was particularly impressed by Chatsworth, the estate in Derbyshire, England, where, in 1851, he saw Joseph Paxton's arboretum, innovative glass conservatories, and the Duke of Devonshire's world-class collection of exotic specimens from South America and China. Shaw vowed to create a similar cultural enterprise in St. Louis, his adopted home.

Shaw located his botanical garden on his new country estate, Tower Grove, then 3.5 miles southwest of the city on the Prairie des Noyers. When construction of his Italianate villa was finished in 1849, he began ordering thousands of plants and arranging the grounds using J.C. Loudon's "three grand divisions" of garden, arboretum, and fruticetum, revealing his preference for contemporary sources rather than historical ones. Plants were ordered from sources including Robert Buist and Thomas Meehan (Philadelphia), Ellwanger & Barry (**George Ellwanger** and **Patrick Barry**, Rochester, New York), and nurseries in Germany, Holland, Scotland, and Russia. Details of his plans were sent to William Jackson Hooker, the director of the Royal Botanical Garden at Kew, and Shaw enlisted the Harvard botanist Asa Gray to guide him in establishing a research facility for scientists. St. Louis physician and botanist George Engelmann, foremost authority on American cacti, was Shaw's primary adviser for over thirty years. Still referred to today by lo-

Henry Shaw, watercolor portrait by Emile Herziger, 1859. (Missouri Botanical Garden Archives)

cals as Shaw's Garden, the Missouri Botanical Garden was ornamented with an observatory, a sunken parterre, and an "herbaceous ground" of scientifically arranged plants. Since its opening in 1859, the garden has had millions of visitors and it remains one of the finest botanical institutions in the world.

In 1868, Shaw began work on Tower Grove Park, a stretch of approximately 280 acres adjacent to the garden's southern end. Although Shaw understood picturesque vision and theory as defined by William Gilpin and Uvedale Price he chose to unite "utility, variety and beauty" using the gardenesque method rather than a more naturalistic aesthetic. He ornamented the landscape with vine-clad trellises, sculpture, and urns planted with exotic specimens. Eclectic and colorful pavilions and summerhouses, which are still extant, suggested a miniature grand tour and palm houses were constructed to overwinter the collection of exotic plants. Separate circulation routes were provided for visitors on foot, horseback, and carriage. Many of the park's trees were labeled in keeping with its educational mission. The December 1870 inventory lists 17,119 trees, shrubs, and vines ready for planting and suggests the size of the park's vast collection, which boasted greater diversity than any urban park in the country today. Shaw recorded the evolution of his ideas in his ten-page "Plan of the Park and Reasons for its Adoption," which outlines use, education, and matters of taste. Since the early 1990s, Tower Grove Park has been a leading example of how historic preservation and sensitivity to the historic designed landscape address the common goal of protecting place and context.

Henry Shaw contributed to the progress of nineteenth-century St. Louis, Missouri, in the areas of education, science, and politics until his death in 1889. He helped to found the Missouri Historical Society and the Mercantile Library, was the founder of the School of Botany at Washington University, and was a constant friend to local churches, hospitals, and charitable institutions. Shaw understood the capacity of botany to teach and reform and he chose to use this increasingly popular branch of science, against the broader context of landscape gardening, as a means of educating the public and improving its general well-being. According to Shaw, the combination of art and science found in "garden botany" would benefit all classes of society, be conducive to health and happiness, and aid in refinement through the cultivation of taste. Due largely to Shaw's vision and planning his botanical garden and public park, which he donated to the citizens of St. Louis, remain vital cultural institutions today and provide almost 360 acres of green space to the city.

Above: Half of stereoscopic view of the conservatory, Missouri Botanical Garden, St. Louis, Missouri, ca. 1880. (Missouri Botanical Garden Archives, GPN-0046)

Below: Tower Grove Park, St. Louis, Missouri, 2002 view. (Photo by Charles A. Birnbaum)

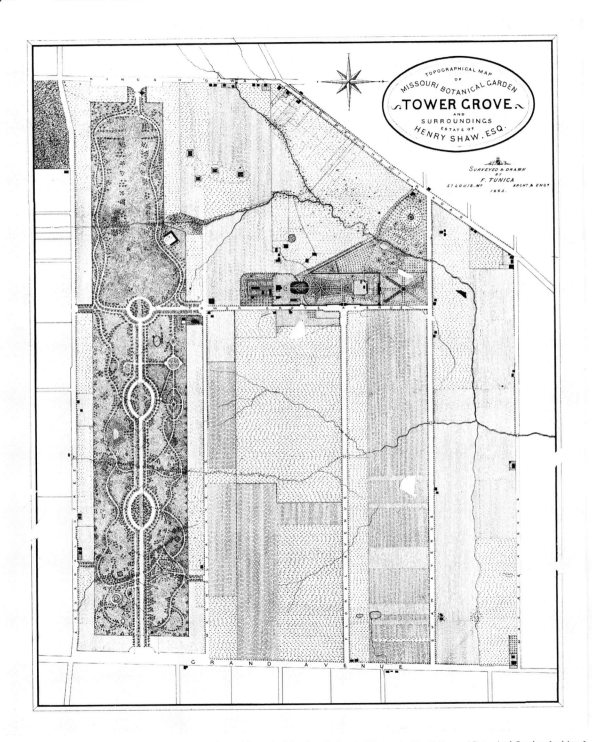

Plan of Shaw's property drawn by Francis Tunic, Missouri Botanical Garden, St. Louis, Missouri, 1865. (Missouri Botanical Garden Archives)

Figuratively, Shaw was a man of two centuries and his garden and park are evidence of his complex nature. He embodied characteristics that define the eighteenth century and public interests that defined the nineteenth: he was a gentleman and connoisseur, well read and well traveled. Grand tours of England and Europe provided him the opportunity to collect art, experience culture, and refine his appreciation of aesthetics. As a landscape gardener he was an "amateur" in the eighteenth-century sense: he was self-taught on a subject he loved; his skill and knowledge were gained by observation, experience, and by studying the hundreds of books in his personal library. These traits were balanced by thoroughly nineteenth century ones: his interest in innovation and improvement, and in the needs of the middle class. He recognized the power of education and the enjoyment of nature to reform society. In his lifetime he saw gardening change from a gentleman's avocation to the responsibility of hands-on gardeners and professionals trained in the increasingly specialized field.

Late in life Shaw wrote *The Rose* (1879), and a history of wine entitled *The Vine and Civilization* (1884). He never married and referred to his plants as his children. He died on August 25, 1889, in St. Louis.

Faherty, William Barnaby. *Henry Shaw: His Life and Legacies.* Columbia: University of Missouri Press, 1987. Biography of Henry Shaw and the city of St. Louis.

Grove, Carol. *Henry Shaw's Victorian Landscapes: The Missouri Botanical Garden and Tower Grove Park.* Amherst: University of Massachusetts Press in association with the Library of American Landscape History, Amherst, 2005. An assessment of Shaw's garden and park, including discussion of garden botany, aesthetics, the gardenesque method, and landscapes as vehicles of social reform.

MacAdam, David H. *Tower Grove Park and the City of St. Louis.* St. Louis, Mo.: R. P. Studley and Co., 1883. A contemporary account of the park based on Shaw's ten-page "Plan of the Park and Reasons for Its Adoption."

Carol Grove

SHELLHORN, RUTH PATRICIA
(1909–2006)
LANDSCAPE ARCHITECT

Ruth Patricia Shellhorn was born in Los Angeles, California, on September 21, 1909. Her parents, Dr. Arthur L. Shellhorn, a dentist, and Lodema Gould Shellhorn, encouraged their daughter at an early age to identify a profession that would make use of her mathematical skills and artistic abilities. A self-described tomboy who loved tree climbing and camping trips with her father, Shellhorn sought career advice from her neighbor, the already well-known landscape designer Florence Yoch. Attracted to a career that would provide regular contact with the out-of-doors, Shellhorn decided to become a landscape architect when she was fifteen years old.

In 1927, Shellhorn left South Pasadena to attend the School of Landscape Architecture at Oregon State College, now the University of Oregon. There, she received acclaim for her many significant achievements. She was the first woman to win the Alpha Zeta Scholarship Cup for the highest marks in the School of Agriculture. In addition, she won the Clara Waldo Prize for Most Outstanding Freshman Woman, was named

Ruth Shellhorn, 1955. (Department of Special Collections, Charles E. Young Research Library, UCLA)

Bullock's Wilshire exterior courtyard, 1953. (Photo by Douglas Simmonds; Department of Special Collections, Charles E. Young Research Library, UCLA)

sought professional opportunities. Exhibiting her typical gumption, she partnered with a local architect and interior designer to offer a full array of design services for eight residences in Whittier, California. Shellhorn earned $15 for her first landscape design.

Despite dim economic prospects, Shellhorn completed a number of commissions for private gardens, located throughout Southern California, before World War II broke out. During this time she worked briefly with **Ralph Dalton Cornell** and Florence Yoch, both of whom exerted a strong influence on her approach to design. As her practice grew, she gained the attention of wealthier clients and her body of work grew to include estates in Bel Air and Pacific Palisades.

On November 21, 1940, she married Harry A. Kueser. Shellhorn credits her prolific career to the special business partnership she and her husband created after he retired from banking in 1945 to join her firm. He took care of the financial aspects of the business, worked with her in the field surveying smaller properties, and helped supervise job installations. Shellhorn devoted herself to the creative work. Childless, they were constant companions until his death in 1991.

With private landscape commissions still scarce during the onset of

Phi Kappa Phi in her junior year, and earned a national prize in a Beaux-Arts competition.

Seeking to expand her design repertoire, Shellhorn transferred to Cornell University's College of Architecture. She distinguished herself with honors, capturing the Charles Goodwin Sands Memorial Medal for Most Outstanding Design in a collaborative senior project. She also served as president of Psi Chapter Kappa Kappa Gamma and was named national architect for her sorority for five years. Unable to afford a final year away at college, Shellhorn left Cornell in 1933, four units short of her degree.

Shellhorn returned to Southern California in the midst of the Great Depression and lived at home while she

World War II, Shellhorn began a two-year project working on the Shoreline Development Study for the Greater Los Angeles Citizens Committee, a private group of civic-minded businessmen. The study established restrictions on oil drilling in Santa Monica Bay and became a precedent for the goals of the later-enacted California Coastal Act. It also provided an advocacy framework for the use of public funding for recreation and parkland acquisition, and paved the way for the installation of Los Angeles's first sewage treatment plant. In a time and place where a woman's presence was unusual, Shellhorn perceived no gender discrimination.

Through professional connections made while working on the Shoreline Study, Shellhorn received a recom-

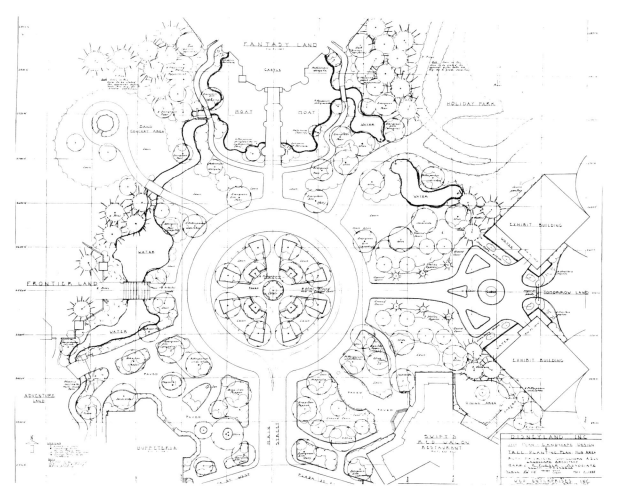

Disneyland, Plaza Hub landscape design plan, 1955. (Department of Special Collections, Charles E. Young Research Library, UCLA)

mendation to design the landscape plan for Bullock's department store in Pasadena, California, in 1945. Cooperating with the architect Welton Becket, a succession of Bullock's department stores followed, including Bullock's Wilshire, Bullock's Palm Springs, Bullock's Lakewood, a remodel of Bullock's Westwood, and the Fashion Squares in Santa Ana, Sherman Oaks, Del Amo, and La Habra.

The Bullock's projects were modernist landscape designs, evoking a sun-soaked, leisurely lifestyle, and came to epitomize the Southern California look. Company executives, anxious to lure post–World War II, middle-class disposable income to the stores, allowed Shellhorn to work directly with site planners and architects from the outset of each project. She recognized that the shopping experience began the moment a customer pulled into the parking lot, and she designed those areas with a generous number of trees and exuberant color. Especially on the Fashion Square projects, where different architects designed each of the stores, Shellhorn's goal was to create a harmonious transition between buildings with various styles, sizes, and shapes. She composed beautiful, courtyard-like settings, designed to attract customers who were, or wished to be, well-educated, traveled, and cultured. In these park-like settings, Shellhorn's designs redefined shopping as a relaxing and pleasant pastime.

Shellhorn was retained as landscape architect for the Bullock's/Fashion Squares from 1945 to 1978. During that time, she visited each of the sites several times a year to take notes and write voluminous recommendations for maintenance procedures.

Shellhorn exhibited a flair for site planning on another significant commission, Disneyland. Originally hired by Walt Disney just three months before opening day in July 1955, Shellhorn's task was to act as part-time liaison between Disney Studios and Jack and Bill Evans, who were responsible for plantings at the park. But with separate art directors in charge of each of the five Lands, and construction of many of the rides and attractions throughout the park already underway, there was still no final site plan for the park. Shellhorn ultimately turned her full-time attention to designing a comprehensive pedestrian circulation system for the entire park. She also created plans for the Entrance, Main Street, and Plaza Hub, successfully evoking the small-town America envisioned by Walt Disney. In addition, she oversaw design of many of the planted areas throughout the park and assisted with major tree placement and, in some cases, the outline of water courses.

In 1956, Shellhorn was appointed the Supervising and Executive Landscape Architect for the newly opened University of California at Riverside. The appointment included responsibility for site design and new landscaping as well as the design of roads, walks, lighting, and utilities on the campus. She held the post for eight years, completing a campus-wide master landscape plan and detailed plans for more than a dozen building areas. She also held other executive and consulting landscape architectural positions for Marlborough School for Girls in Los Angeles from 1968 to 1993, El Camino College in Torrence from 1970 to 1978, and Harvard School in North Hollywood from 1974 to 1990.

Shellhorn continued to design hundreds of private gardens and commercial projects throughout her fifty-seven-year career. Her residential client list included well-known motion picture stars Spencer Tracy, Gene Autry, and Barbara Stanwyck; R. Stanton Avery, founding president of Avery International; Edward Carter, president of Carter, Hawley, Hale; Norman and Dorothy Chandler, publisher of the *Los Angeles Times;* and, Ben Goetz, MGM Superintendent of Producers. Her numerous commercial projects included the Western Home Office for Prudential Insurance Company, the John Tracy Clinic, the Santa Monica Civic Auditorium, Vroman's Book Depository in Pasadena, and the Segerstrom Center in Santa Ana.

Shellhorn received numerous honors for her designs including eight Los Angeles Beautiful Awards, several National Industrial Landscape Awards by the American Association of Nurserymen, civic beautification awards, and chamber of commerce awards. For her leadership and dedication to her field of practice she was listed in *Who's Who in America* from 1978 on, named a Fellow of the American Society of Landscape Architects in 1971, and honored as Horticulturist of the Year by the Southern California Horticultural Institute in 1986. As a role model for professional women, she was named Woman of the Year by the *Los Angeles Times* and the South Pasadena, San Marino Business and Professional Women's Club in 1955.

Shellhorn retired in 1990. In June 2005, Cornell University recognized Shellhorn's earned units and granted her bachelor of landscape architecture and bachelor of architecture degrees. She died November 3, 2006, in California.

Shellhorn's papers and drawings are housed at the Charles E. Young Research Library's Department of Special Collections at the University of California in Los Angeles. The collection includes all of her original drawings, client files, photographs, and correspondence. Plans are underway to digitize the collection.

McElvey, Carl, with associates Ruth Patricia Shellhorn and Henry Klumb. "Shoreline Development Study, Playa del Rey to Palos Verdes." Greater Los Angeles Citizens Committee, Inc., April, 1944. A macro site-analysis and master plan for recreational development of 12 miles of shoreline property.

Shellhorn, Ruth. "Disneyland: Dream Built in One Year Through Teamwork of Many Artists." *Landscape Architecture,* April 1956, 125–36. Summarizes the fast-forward design and construction of the "happiest place on earth."

"A Study of Ruth Patricia Shellhorn: Award-Winning Landscape Architect." *Landscape Design and Construction* 13, no. 4 (October 1967). Discusses the design philosophy and development of the Bullock's department stores and Bullock's Fashion Squares.

Kelly Comras and Carolyn Doepke Bennett

PLATE 32 (*left*): Charles Blair Macdonald. "Punchbowl," hole 16, National Golf Links of America, Southampton, New York. (© Bob Labbance)

PLATE 33 (*below*): Emanuel Tillman Mische. Laurelhurst Park, Portland, Oregon. (Photo by Charles A. Birnbaum)

PLATE 34 (*left*): Kinsaku Nakane. Tenshin-en, the Garden of the Heart of Heaven, Museum of Fine Arts, Boston, Massachusetts. (Courtesy of Shiro Nakane)

PLATE 35 (*below*): Hallam Leonard Movius. Colt Road subdivision plan, Pittsfield, Massachusetts, 1927, illustrates Movius's residential planning work. (Courtesy of Geoffrey Movius)

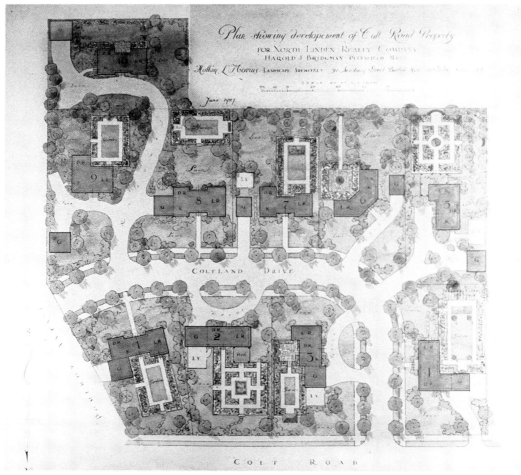

PLATE 36 (*left*): Theodore Osmundson. Kaiser Center Roof Garden, Oakland, California, photo by Ted Osmundson. (Courtesy of Lorraine Osmundson)

PLATE 37 (*below*): Cornelia Hahn Oberlander. Robson Square (Provincial Government Center and Courthouse Complex), Vancouver, British Columbia, Canada. (Photo by Milton Hicks)

PLATE 38 (*above*): John L. Paolano. Fellows Riverside Gardens, Mill Creek MetroParks, Youngstown, Ohio. (Courtesy of Mary Paolano Hoerner)

PLATE 39 (*below*): Courtland Price Paul. Harbor Ridge, Newport Beach, California. (Peridian Group, Inc.)

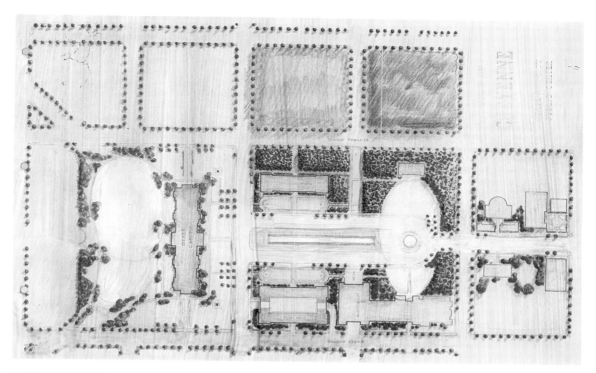

PLATE 40 (*above*): Michiel Walter Pesman. Plan of State and City Public Center, Cheyenne, Wyoming. (Denver Public Library Western History Collection, DeBoer, Z-2119)

PLATE 41 (*below*): William Lyman Phillips. Fairchild Tropical Botanic Garden, Coral Gables, Florida. (Photo by Charles A. Birnbaum)

PLATE 42 (*left*): Julius Pitzman. Entrance gates to Washington Terrace, a private residential street in St. Louis, Missouri. (Photo by Kevin Pasnik)

PLATE 43 (*below*): Thomas Drees Price. The Conservatory Gardens, Central Park, New York, New York. (Photo by Charles A. Birnbaum)

PLATE 44 (*above, left*): Cecil Pragnell. Prayer Garden, Glorieta Conference Center, Glorieta, New Mexico. (Photo by Baker A. Morrow, courtesy of Morrow Reardon Wilkinson Miller Ltd.)

PLATE 45 (*above, right*): Robert Royston. Central Park, Santa Clara, California. (Royston, Hanamoto, Alley & Abey)

PLATE 46 (*left*): Hideo Sasaki. Christopher Columbus Park, Boston, Massachusetts. (Sasaki Associates, Inc.)

PLATE 47 (*below*): Geraldine Knight Scott. Roof garden, Oakland Museum, Oakland, California. (Courtesy Jane Amidon)

PLATE 48 (*right*): Henry Shaw. Tower Grove Park, St. Louis, Missouri. (Photo by Charles A. Birnbaum)

PLATE 49 (*below, right*): Ruth Patricia Shellhorn. Shellhorn with Walt Disney, Disneyland, Anaheim, California, 1955, photo by Harry Kueser. (Department of Special Collections, Charles E. Young Research Library, UCLA)

PLATE 50 (*opposite*): Lawrence Vinnedge Sheridan. An example of Sheridan's planning work is seen in the Master plan, City of Columbus, Indiana, 1951. (Courtesy of the City of Columbus)

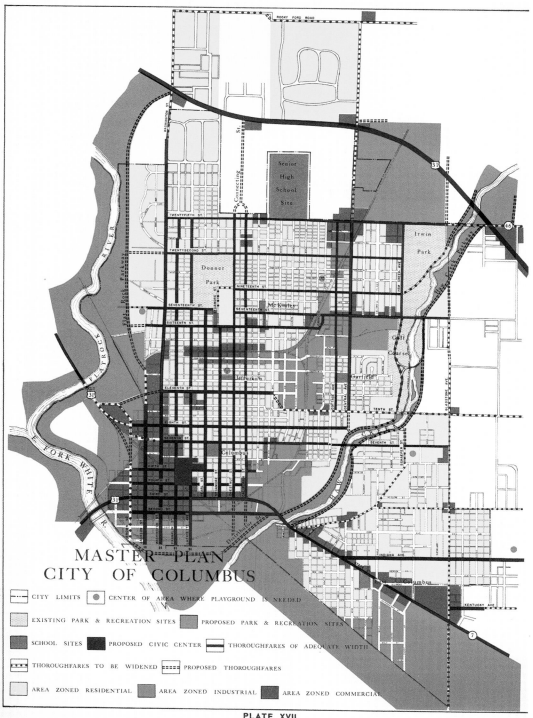

MASTER PLAN
CITY OF COLUMBUS

- - - CITY LIMITS   ⬤ CENTER OF AREA WHERE PLAYGROUND IS NEEDED

EXISTING PARK & RECREATION SITES   PROPOSED PARK & RECREATION SITES

SCHOOL SITES   PROPOSED CIVIC CENTER   THOROUGHFARES OF ADEQUATE WIDTH

THOROUGHFARES TO BE WIDENED   PROPOSED THOROUGHFARES

AREA ZONED RESIDENTIAL   AREA ZONED INDUSTRIAL   AREA ZONED COMMERCIAL

PLATE XVII

PLATE 51 (*above*): John Ormsbee Simonds. Pelican Bay, Dade County, Florida. (Environmental Planning & Design, LLC)

PLATE 52 (*opposite, top*): John Ormsbee Simonds. Mellon Square, Pittsburgh, Pennsylvania, 1956. (Environmental Planning & Design, LLC)

PLATE 53 (*opposite, bottom*): Wayne E. Stiles. Marshfield Fairways, Marshfield, Massachusetts. (Photo by Kevin R. Mendik)

PLATE 54 (*left*): Diego Suarez. Vizcaya, Miami, Florida. (Photo by Charles A. Birnbaum)

PLATE 55 (*below*): Rudolph Ulrich. The Arizona Garden at Stanford University (1891-1893), 2004 view, photo by Javier Chagoya, Naval Postgraduate School. (Courtesy of Christy L. Smith)

PLATE 56 (*opposite, top*): Hollyngsworth Leland Vaughan and Adele Wharton Vaughan. "Proposed Development for Mrs. H. B. Martin Residence, San Jose, California," 1937. (H. Leland and Adele W. Vaughn Collection [1999-18], Environmental Design Archives, University of California, Berkeley)

PLATE 57 (*opposite, bottom*): Richard K. Webel. French parterre garden, Hillwood Estate Museum and Garden, Washington, D.C. (Courtesy of Hillwood Estate, Museum and Gardens; bequest of Marjorie Merriweather Post, 1973; photo by G. Chesman)

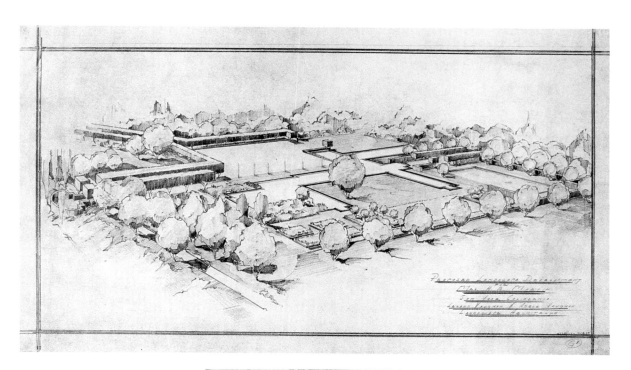

Proposed Landscape Development
for Mrs. H. B. Clark
San Jose California
Bruce Porter & Mrs. Vaughan
Landscape Architects

PLATE 58 (*left*): Perry Hunt Wheeler. White House Garden, Washington, D.C. (Smithsonian Institution, Archives of American Gardens, Maida Babson Adams American Garden Collection)

PLATE 59 (*below*): William S. Wiedorn. Rose garden, New Orleans City Park, New Orleans, Louisiana. (Photo by Charles A. Birnbaum)

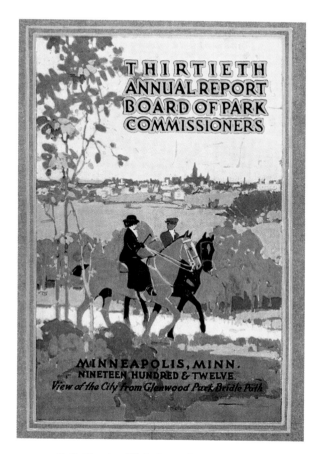

PLATE 60 (*left*): Theodore Wirth. Cover of park commissioners report, Minneapolis, Minnesota, 1913. (Minneapolis Park and Recreation Board)

PLATE 61 (*right*): Robert Lewis Zion. IBM World Headquarters atrium, New York, New York. (Zion Breen & Richardson Associates)

PLATE 62: Robert Zion. Waterfront park, Cincinnati, Ohio. (Photo by Charles A. Birnbaum)

SHEPHERD, HARRY WHITCOMB
(1890–1961)

LANDSCAPE ARCHITECT, EDUCATOR

Harry Whitcomb Shepherd was born September 8, 1890, in North Attleboro, Massachusetts, to Charles Pitman Shepherd and Alice Elizabeth Williamson Shepherd. He later moved with his family to Monrovia, California. As a youth, Shepherd was athletic and interested in the outdoors, attributes that suited his career choice of landscape architecture. He began his studies in agriculture at the University of California, Berkeley. In 1913, he transferred to the newly established Division of Landscape Gardening and Floriculture. He was the division's first graduate in 1914. As an undergraduate, Shepherd was a member of Alpha Zeta, Theta Xi, the Big C Society, and he was an outfielder for the varsity baseball teams of 1913 and 1914.

Completing his bachelor of science degree, Shepherd moved to Los Angeles, where he served as the assistant director of the Los Angeles Beautification Committee from 1914 to 1915. At this time, he also began his private landscape architecture practice in Monrovia, California. He married Elsinore Steinman in Klamath Falls, Oregon, on August 12, 1916. Concurrent with his early design work, Shepherd taught classes in landscape engineering and ornamental horticulture at the Manual Arts High School in Los Angeles, where he also coached baseball and basketball teams, through 1918. Leaving California in 1918, Shepherd served in World War I as a member of the 143rd Field Artillery of the American Expeditionary Forces in France.

Returning to California after the war, Shepherd opened his landscape engineering office in Lodi, California, where he also directed the vocational horticulture program at Lodi Union High School. In 1922, Shepherd began his long tenure with the University of California, first as an instructor of landscape design at the Davis campus through 1925. While at Davis, Shepherd was also in charge of landscape development for the Agriculture College grounds. He also served as an acting extension specialist in landscape engineering for many California counties, planning more than 200 projects that included farmsteads, county parks, and fairgrounds. In 1925, Shepherd was transferred to the Berkeley campus, where he was appointed assistant professor of landscape design. Bringing nearly a decade of experience back to his

Harry Whitcomb Shepherd, from a larger, undated group photo. (Harry Whitcomb Shepherd Collection [1998-11], Environmental Design Archives, University of California, Berkeley)

alma mater, Shepherd worked with Professors John W. Gregg* and Hollyngsworth Leland Vaughan* to develop Berkeley's landscape design program, which in 1959 became a recognized department and major within the College of Environmental Design.

During his long tenure at Berkeley, Shepherd taught plant materials, planting design, and landscape construction. His students best remember him for his encyclopedic knowledge of plants and his ability to recognize and identify them. In 1932, and again in 1948, Shepherd took sabbatical leaves during which he traveled extensively through Europe, Australia, New Zealand, and Tasmania, and studied parks and recreation, gardens, and native plants. Native Australian plants particularly interested Shepherd because of their adaptability to the California climate. Shepherd also taught classes for the University Extension Division, including a 1942 class on plant camouflage, in cooperation with the Office of Civilian Defense. Additionally, Shepherd was active in the campus landscape development plans, one important contribution being his advocacy for a campus tree planting committee.

In addition to his teaching career and work for the university, Shepherd maintained an active professional life. His early design practice consisted primarily of residential gardens, schools, and other institutional projects,

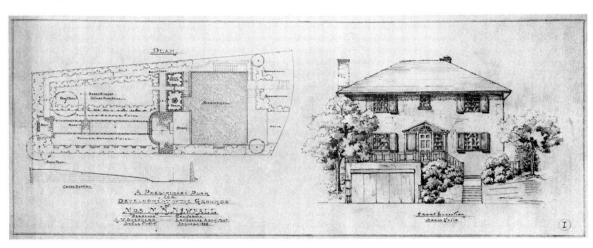

Above: Plan for the Alameda–Contra Costa Counties Court, Golden Gate International Exposition, Treasure Island, San Francisco, California, 1938. (Harry Whitcomb Shepherd Collection [1998-11], Environmental Design Archives, University of California, Berkeley)

Below: "A Preliminary Plan for Development of the Grounds of Mrs. M. H. Newhall," Berkeley, California, 1929. (Harry Whitcomb Shepherd Collection [1998-11], Environmental Design Archives, University of California, Berkeley)

Alameda–Contra Costa Counties Court, Golden Gate International Exposition, Treasure Island, San Francisco, California, 1938. (Harry Whitcomb Shepherd Collection [1998-11], Environmental Design Archives, University of California, Berkeley)

and consultations for public parks and highways. A few of his more significant private projects in California include the estates of Thomas Telfer (Berkeley, 1928) and Ernest J. Sweetland (Piedmont, 1929 to 1934), and the residential gardens of Edwin Ross (Piedmont, 1928), Albert Denton (Berkeley, 1928), V. S. Andrus (Alameda, 1928), and Mrs. M. N. Newhall (Berkeley, 1929). Institutional projects in California designed by Shepherd include the Juvenile Detention Home (Martinez, 1926), Davis Joint Union High School (1927 to 1929), Marysville Union High School (1927 to 1929), and the Veteran's Hospital (Livermore, 1928). From 1925 to 1929 he served as a landscape consultant and assistant for **Frederick Law Olmsted Jr.** at the **Olmsted Brothers**, and also as the landscape architect in charge of the California State Park Survey, a pioneering documentation initiative that resulted in the acquisition and protection of many of the state's park and recreation sites. He was the consulting landscape architect for the California State Park Commission from 1929 through 1930.

In the mid-1930s, Shepherd served as a chairman on the City of Berkeley's Regional Park Committee and worked on the Codornices Rose Garden, Aquatic Park, John Hinkel Amphitheater, the city tree planting plan, and the development of Live Oak Park. He was also a member of the city's Park and Recreation Commission, and in 1934, he was the acting consulting landscape engineer for the California State Highway Division. Shepherd designed and supervised the landscape development of the Alameda–Contra Costa Counties Court at the Golden Gate International Exposition from 1938 to 1939. During World War II, Shepherd was a chief observer in the Aircraft Warning Service, Fourth Fighter Command at Berkeley Post #1, and an issuance officer at the navy's V–12 Book Depository, University of California. For his volunteer service to the country during the war, Shepherd was honored with a "Wings" award for one hundred hours of service as Assistant Chief Ground Observer.

In 1931, Shepherd was elected a member of the American Society of Landscape Architects (ASLA); he was the North Pacific Chapter's president from 1941 to 1942 and, most significantly, led the society's committee on state registration of landscape architects. When the legislation finally passed in 1953, Shepherd was honored for his leadership and efforts with the first professional landscape architect license in the state. He was elected a Fellow of the ASLA in 1955. Shepherd was also a member of the California Association of Landscape Architects, the American Civic and Planning Association, the American Forestry Association, the Save-the-Redwoods League, and numerous other professional organizations. He was also an honorary member of the Northern California Golf Course Superintendents Association and was a board member of the State of California's Board of Landscape Architects. Shepherd presented his research and interest in plant materials and landscape design in a number of journal articles, lectures, papers, and brochures. He also contributed to the major reference works for the fields of landscape architecture and garden design and wrote numerous reports for the government and other agencies.

Shepherd retired in 1956, but maintained an appointment as emeritus professor. Harry Whitcomb Shepherd passed away January 3, 1961, at the age of seventy in Berkeley.

The Harry Whitcomb Shepherd Collection and Office Files are housed at the Environmental Design Archives, University of California, Berkeley; a finding aid and index are available online at www.ced.berkeley.edu/cedarchives.

Laurie, Michael. *75 Years of Landscape Architecture at Berkeley. Part I: The First 50 Years.* Berkeley: Department of Landscape Architecture, University of California, Berkeley, 1988. Laurie's study includes many notes on Shepherd's teaching and professional career.

Litton, R. B., Jr., M. K. Arbegast, and H. M. Butterfield. "Harry Whitcomb Shepherd, 1890–1961, Professor of Landscape Architecture, Emeritus [obituary]." *In Memoriam.* The University of California, 1962, 85–88.

Carrie Leah McDade

SHERIDAN, LAWRENCE VINNEDGE
(1887–1972)
LANDSCAPE ARCHITECT, CITY PLANNER, ENGINEER, EDUCATOR

Lawrence V. Sheridan, known as Sherry, was born in Frankfort, Indiana, on July 8, 1887, to Harry C. and Margaret Vinnedge Sheridan. He had one younger sister, Marjorie Ellen. He received a bachelor of science in civil engineering in 1909 and a professional civil engineering degree in 1912 from Purdue University.

His first position after graduation was with Central Station Engineering, a company with offices in Chicago and Crawfordsville, Indiana. He remained with that firm until April 1910, when he accepted a position in the engineering department of the T. Street L. and W. Railroad, and continued in that capacity until April 1911.

From 1911 through 1914, he was associated with the Park Board of Indianapolis working alongside **George Edward Kessler**, landscape architect for the City of Indianapolis. His responsibilities at the time included serving as the engineering inspector for the construction of the Capitol Street Bridge and later as chief inspector of construction. In July 1914, he accepted a position with the Bureau of Municipal Research, where he studied municipal playground systems and assisted with government surveys in various Midwest cities. In September 1916, he gave up his position to pursue coursework at the Harvard University School of Landscape Architecture until May 1917, when as part of the World War I mobilization, he was sent to Camp Pike, Arkansas, as a city planner of the division cantonment there.

During World War I, in January 1918, he entered 3rd Officers' Training School at Camp Sherman, Ohio, and was commissioned second lieutenant. For several months he served with an anti-aircraft battery near Verdun, France. He was discharged at Camp Devens, Massachusetts, on January 28, 1919. After his discharge, he went to Dallas, Texas, where he became the assistant to George Kessler, who was the consulting engineer of

Lawrence Sheridan, class picture from Purdue University yearbook, 1909. (Courtesy of Purdue University Libraries, Archives and Special Collections)

the Dallas Property Owners' Association. This group was promoting the development of part of the business district of Dallas.

Around that time, he married Grace Elizabeth Emmel of Chillicothe, Ohio. The couple had four sons including his second son Roderick Kessler Sheridan, whom he named after George Kessler. His other children were Roger Williams Sheridan, Harry C. Sheridan II, and Phillip Sheridan.

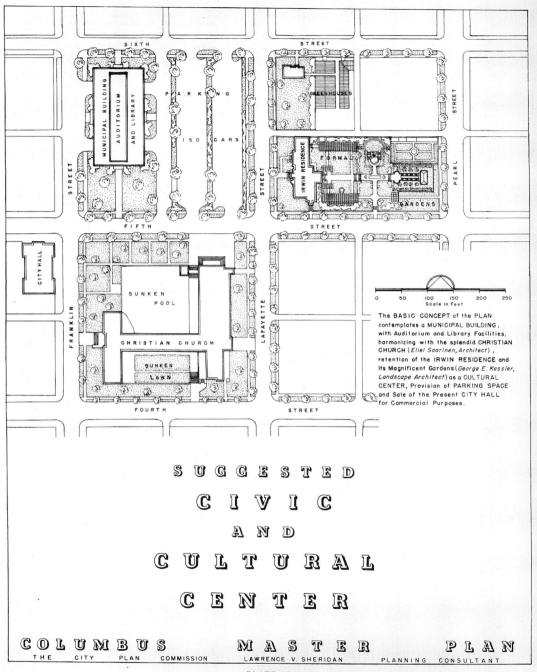

Columbus Civic and Cultural Center plan, plate XIX of the Columbus Master Plan, Lawrence Sheridan Planning Consultant, Columbus, Indiana, 1951. (Courtesy of the City of Columbus)

In December 1921, Sheridan returned to Indianapolis to serve as the executive secretary of the City Plan Commission. During his tenure, the commission wrote and passed the city's first zoning ordinance, and other city planning measures were under his direction. He resigned in May 1923 in order to give more attention to his private work. The city retained him as a consultant in order not to lose his valuable services. As a consultant to the Park Board, Sheridan completed a comprehensive plan of park development for Indianapolis and Marion County, in 1928 building upon the previous work of his friend and mentor, George Kessler. Sheridan was proactive in planning and promoting the development and extension of Kessler's park and boulevard plan for Indianapolis. Sheridan's work included Kessler Boulevard and the extension of the Kessler-designed Fall Creek Parkway north and east to Fort Harrison. The Indianapolis Park and Boulevard system, as designed by Kessler and expanded by Sheridan, included over 3,400 acres, and was listed in the National Register of Historic Places in March 2003. Lawrence Sheridan gained a pervasive reputation for the excellence of his work in landscape architecture and city planning, resulting in consulting work for other Indiana city planning commissions, including Richmond, Muncie, Anderson, Fort Wayne, and Terre Haute.

Sheridan's work included more than parks. It was during the 1920s that Sheridan designed an estate for Fredrick M. Ayres, the son of an Indianapolis department store founder. The estate, known as Walden, was built on fashionable Sunset Lane in the Crow's Nest district of Indianapolis. Sheridan's approach to the estate plan at Walden was to minimize disturbance of the existing site and preserve the natural character of the property on a ridge along the White River. He described his design approach for the 18 acres in the June 1931 issue of *American Landscape Architect:* "The planning of every feature was done with the idea of merging its outlines with its surroundings and denying emphasis to any one particular element." Sheridan's ability to integrate his landscape designs with existing site conditions, along with his desire and ability to work closely with the architect, produced dramatic results. The Walden estate was destroyed by fire, but the landscape still stands as a testament to the ability of Sheridan as a designer. Sheridan designed the golf course for Brendonwood, a subdivision planned by Kessler, in 1923. Later, in 1929, Sheridan built a house called Roundtoft, a Tudor Revival English cottage designed by architect Willard Osler, in Brendonwood.

During the 1930s, Sheridan with landscape architect Eunice Fenelon consulted for the Crown Hill Cemetery Association in Indianapolis. He also worked as the landscape architect for Lockefield Garden Apartments, a significant public housing project in Indianapolis now listed on the National Register of Historic Places. For this design Sheridan worked on the sensitive placement of the buildings to maximize sunlight in each of the apartment units. He planned the focal point of the development as a central court with a grove of red oaks.

From 1937 through 1941, Sheridan was principal of his company, Lawrence V. Sheridan and Son. In 1937, President Franklin Delano Roosevelt asked Sheridan to serve as the regional counselor for the National Resources Planning Board. In this position, Sheridan administered a seven-state planning group attempting to map state resources through a county by county survey. In 1939, the American Society of Landscape Architects inducted him as a Fellow, in recognition of his outstanding work in the fields of landscape architecture and city planning.

He returned to active military duty on October 1, 1941, during World War II, at Fort Harrison in Lawrence, Indiana, as a lieutenant colonel, Quartermaster Corps, assigned to Office of the Quartermaster General, Repairs and Utilities Branch, Washington D.C., and Deputy Service Command Engineer, Ninth Service Command at Fort Douglas, Utah. During this time he completed the development of site plans for Fort Eustis, Virginia; Billings General Hospital; Fort Benjamin Harrison, Indiana; Camp Chaffee, Arkansas; and Camp Atterbury, Indiana. He was released from active duty on February 10, 1946, and retired as a colonel in the Army Reserve on July 8, 1947.

After the war, Sheridan focused his attention on city planning in Indianapolis and elsewhere while serving as president of Metropolitan Planners, Inc., a company formed by the merger of Lawrence V. Sheridan and Son and Kenneth L. Schellie and Associates in 1953. In 1957, the American Institute of Planners awarded him their distinguished service award, honoring his work in over one hundred communities. Sheridan also contributed to the landscape architecture profession by serving as an instructor in the Landscape Architecture Department at Purdue University in the 1960s.

Sheridan's community involvement was extensive. He was a member of the Third Church of Christ, Scientist, Sigma Phi Epsilon Fraternity, and the Purdue Alumni Association, and was a commander of the John Holiday Post No. 186 of the American Legion. Sheridan was a

Map No. 6

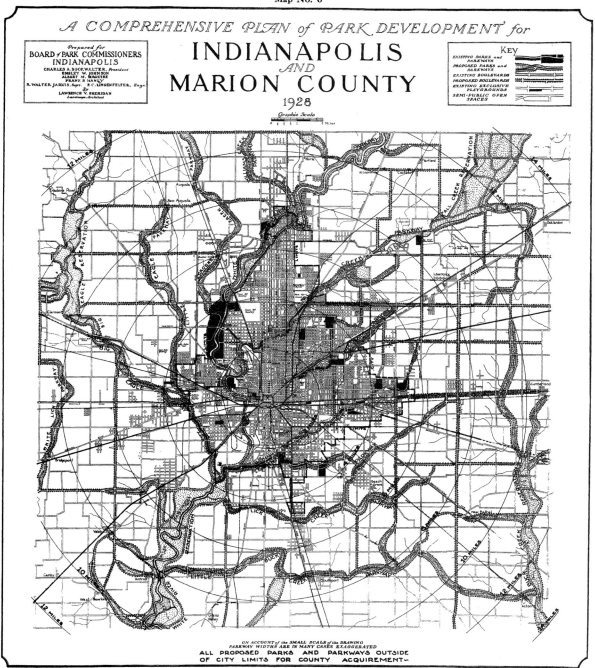

"A Comprehensive Plan of Park Development for Indianapolis and Marion County," 1928. (Courtesy of the City of Indianapolis)

member of the Freemasons. He also held memberships in the American Society of Civil Engineering, the American City Planning Institute, and the Service Club. In addition to being a Fellow of the American Society of Landscape Architects and the American Society of Engineers, Sheridan was a charter member of the American Society of Planning Officials and served as a past president of the American Institute of Planners.

Lawrence Sheridan was well known in Indianapolis as "one of the City's substantial and representative citizens and one who accomplished much for the public good." He retired from active partnership in 1957, but continued to serve as a planning counselor until he passed away in Indianapolis on January 26, 1972.

The History of Marion County, College of Architecture and Planning Archives, Ball State University, Muncie, Indiana, 827–828, contain several documents about Sheridan and his work.

Hinds, Lawrence H. *Memorial Resolution.* College of Architecture and Planning Drawing and Documents Archive, Ball State University, Muncie, Indiana, 1972, 1–2. Provides an overview of Sheridan's life and work.
Sheridan, Lawrence V. "Preserving the Native Charm of a Hoosier Setting." *American Landscape Architect* 4 (June 1931), 10–15. Sheridan's design for the Frederic Ayres estate.

The author wishes to thank Storrow Kinsella Associates for their support.

David A. Roth

SIMONDS, JOHN ORMSBEE
(1913–2005)
LANDSCAPE ARCHITECT, AUTHOR

John Simonds was born in Jamestown, North Dakota, in 1913. He was the second of five children born to Guy Wallace and Margueritte Simonds. His father, a Presbyterian minister, moved the family to rural Michigan when Simonds was young. Influenced by his father's love of the outdoor life, he developed a sense of adventure, and curiosity, which lead him to value the natural world all his life.

Simonds studied landscape architecture at Michigan State University. He graduated in 1935, and continued his education at Harvard, earning a master's degree in landscape architecture in 1938. He was a student during a pivotal time in which Garrett Eckbo,* **James C. Rose**, and Daniel Urban Kiley* led the "Harvard Revolution," a student revolt against the traditional teachings of the Beaux-Arts style. The arrival of Walter Gropius, former head of the Bauhaus in Europe, at Harvard in 1937 had a profound effect on the future of architecture and landscape architecture in the United States. Gropius promoted modernist ideas, which were reflected in Simonds's work.

In 1939, he moved to Pittsburgh, Pennsylvania, and began a landscape architecture practice with his brother Philip Simonds. Over the years, their firm Simonds and Simonds grew from a small residential practice to a suc-

John O. Simonds. (Photo courtesy of Lynn Johnson)

cessful multidisciplinary landscape architecture and planning firm with offices in Pittsburgh, Washington, D.C., and Miami Lakes, Florida. Reflecting the firm's success and growth, Lester Albertson Collins* joined Simonds and Simonds and the firm became Collins, Simonds and Simonds, from 1952 to 1970. Again renamed in 1970, the firm, Environmental Planning and Design (EPD), continues today.

John Simonds married Pittsburgh native Marjorie Todd in 1943. Marjorie was his lifelong friend and com-

Mellon Square plan, Pittsburgh, Pennsylvania. (Environmental Planning & Design, LLC)

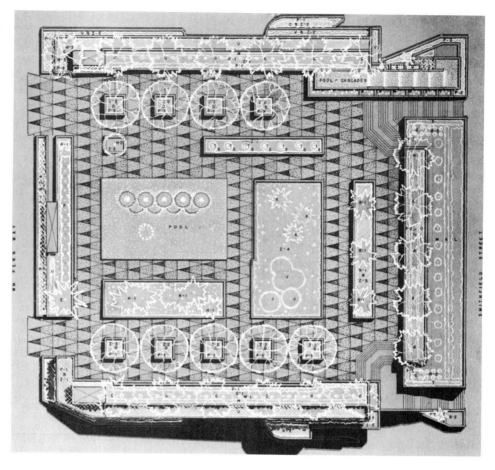

panion. She was a valued editor of his textbooks, several of which are dedicated to her. Simonds loved to travel; he and Marjorie made many trips together. He believed that travel was vital to growth and to the understanding of design. As a young man he traveled around the world twice, in 1933 and 1939. His trips to Europe, the Orient, and Latin America contributed to his evolving design ideas all his life. Learning from his years of traveling, he concluded that a good designer should design experiences rather than places.

Simonds and Simonds received many important public commissions after World War II, which reshaped Pittsburgh's downtown and suburbs. Two significant projects were Mellon Square and The Equitable Life Insurance Plaza. Mellon Square, built in 1951, was the first modernist garden plaza built over a parking garage, and the second park built over a garage in the United States. Reminiscent of the grand plazas of European

cities, Simonds intended Mellon Square to be an oasis, a civic monument, and a gathering space. Its well-conceived design has provided Pittsburgh with a downtown civic space, which has remained popular and active for more than fifty years.

In 1955, Collins, Simonds and Simonds designed The Equitable Plaza, part of The Gateway Center Development, designed by Clarke & Rapuano (**Gilmore David Clarke** and **Michael Rapuano**), at Pittsburgh's Golden Triangle. This modernist design included irregular-shaped planting beds, animated fountains, and a tricolor paving pattern. This group of buildings and plaza remains Pittsburgh's premiere example of International Style planning.

Another innovative project in the 1950s was Simonds's work on the Pittsburgh Aviary-Conservatory, which was designated by the U.S. Congress, in 1992, as the National Aviary in Pittsburgh. Simonds designed the grounds and interior exhibit space for a new kind of aviary and

Allegheny Commons, Pittsburgh, Pennsylvania, 2001 view. (Photo by Charles A. Birnbaum)

plant conservatory, which showcased tropical birds and plants in spaces that replicated the birds' native habitat. Simonds and his firm designed the rockwork, streams, pools, paving, fountains, and furnishings to complement the lush tropical environment.

He was instrumental in the 1966 rehabilitation of Allegheny Commons, the oldest park in Pittsburgh. Originally designed in 1867 by William H. Grant, of Mitchell Grant & Co, New York City, it was redesigned in the late 1930s by Ralph E. Griswold. Simonds's plan showed respect for the history of the site, sensitivity to the work of others, and consideration for contemporary needs.

In the 1960s, Simonds developed a master plan for a proposed botanic garden for the Chicago Horticultural Society. The proposed botanic garden site was an abandoned farm and polluted borrow pit in Glencoe, Illinois. Inspired by the Garden of Perfect Brightness, outside Beijing, Simonds created a series of gardens by shaping and mounding the farmland, and by creating lagoons and islands in the borrow pit. Unlike conventional research gardens, Simonds's plan offered a range of garden spaces and views reminiscent of a pleasure garden. It combined public education, narrated tram rides, and demonstration garden exhibits. The success of this master plan began a series of commissions for EPD, which shaped the designs of future botanic gardens around the country.

In the 1970s large-scale planning became the focus of much of Simonds's work. The communities of Miami Lakes, Saga Bay, Indian Trace, and Pelican Bay in Florida were among scores of planned developments, which were designed by EPD in the 1970s and 1980s. These new town plans followed planning concepts developed over years of community-based work. They drew from the design tradition of towns such as Radburn, New Jersey, designed in 1928 by **Henry Wright**, Clarence Stein, and **Marjorie Sewell Cautley**, and the emergence of environmental and systems design, made popular by Ian L. McHarg's* book, *Design with Nature.* These new towns succeeded because of a strong economic foundation, and a flexible master plan that met the needs of the individual as well as the community. They were designed to blend with the environment, by preserving the sites' unique natural systems. They offered cluster housing of various sizes, utilized a hierarchy of different types of transportation routes, and created a myriad of recreational opportunities.

In addition to his private practice, Simonds consulted for the federal government, including the Department of Housing and Urban Development, the Department of Transportation, The National Park Service, and the Corps of Engineers. He also served on the Board of Urban Advisors, Federal Highway Administration (1966–1968), the President's Task Force on Resources and the Environment (1968–1970), and was a member on the Design Advisory Panel, Operation Breakthrough, U.S. Department of Housing and Urban Development (1970–1974).

Complementing his professional practice, Simonds's career included a mixture of academic writing, teaching, and publishing. He taught courses in planning in the Architecture Department at Carnegie Mellon University from 1955 to 1968.

Among the lasting contributions to the profession of landscape architecture are his many textbooks. He had a unique ability to express the primary concepts of the land planning process, and his books are richly illustrated with case studies. His textbook *Landscape Architecture: A Manual of Site Planning and Design,* first published in 1961 (reprinted 1983 and 1998), is considered a classic. He also authored *Landscape Architecture: The Shaping of Man's Natural Environment, Earthscape: A Manual of Environmental Planning,* and *Garden Cities 21: Creating a Livable Urban Environment.* He was the editor of the seminal 1968 Federal Highway publication, *Freeway in the City: Principals of Planning Design,* by the Urban Advisors to the Federal Highway Administration, which included contributions from landscape architects Michael Rapuano and Lawrence Halprin.*

Simonds was made a Fellow of the American Society of Landscape Architects (ASLA) in 1965. He actively worked to promote the profession, serving as the president of the ASLA from 1963 to 1965. He was the recipient of numerous awards and honors including the ASLA Medal in 1973, and the ASLA President's Centennial Medal in 1999.

Still active in retirement, Simonds was consulted during the 1980s on the rehabilitation of Mellon Square. He died in Pittsburgh, Pennsylvania, on May 26, 2005.

The extensive John Ormsbee Simonds Collection, at the George A. Smathers Library, University of Florida, Gainsville, includes drawings, project files and plans, correspondence, and speeches.

Simonds, John Ormsbee. *Earthscape: A Manual of Environmental Planning*. New York: McGraw-Hill, 1978. Environmental and regional planning concepts.
Simonds, John Ormsbee. *Garden Cities 21: Creating a Liveable Urban Environment*. New York: McGraw Hill, 1994. Simonds looks at an organic approach to designing cities.
Simonds, John Ormsbee. *Landscape Architecture: A Manual of Site Planning and Design*. New York: McGraw-Hill, 1961 (revised and reprinted in collaboration with Barry Starke, 2006). Insight into the principles of landscape architecture and design.

Nancy Slade

SMITH, ALICE ORME
(1889–1980)
LANDSCAPE ARCHITECT

Alice Orme Smith was born on February 26, 1889, in the town of Normal, Illinois. From 1907 to 1911, she attended Smith College, a private liberal arts college for women in Northampton, Massachusetts, from which she earned her bachelor of arts degree. After finishing her undergraduate studies, Smith trained as a nurse at the New York Presbyterian Hospital where she worked until 1917. For the next two years, she served in France at a military base hospital during the height of World War I. Consequently, the French government awarded Smith the French Croix de Guerre for her service in a field hospital on the front lines.

After returning from France, Smith returned to her native Illinois to attend the Armour Institute's College of Architecture in Chicago, from which she received a master's degree in 1922. In 1926, Smith earned a master's degree in landscape architecture from the Cambridge School of Architecture and Landscape Architecture, which was officially awarded to her in 1935 after the Cambridge School merged with Smith College to create a master's degree program in landscape architecture.

From 1920 to 1923, while studying at the Armour Institute, Smith worked for architect Earl Reed and landscape architect Ralph Rodney Root* in Chicago. After graduating from the Cambridge School, she moved to New York City, where Harold Hill Blossom* employed her in his firm from 1925 to 1926. From 1926 to 1930, Smith worked with the preeminent landscape gardner

Alice Orme Smith, 1919. (Illinois State University Archives, Milner Library)

Beatrix Jones Farrand on plans for Dumbarton Oaks in Washington, D.C., and the walled Chinese garden at John D. Rockefeller's estate in Mount Desert, Maine. Following in her mentor's footsteps, Smith opened her own landscape design office in New York City in 1932.

During her lifetime, Smith traveled throughout the United States, as well as in the British Isles, France, Italy, and Japan. From 1930 to 1932, she worked in Peking, China, producing measured drawings of Chinese gardens for the Swedish architect Oswald Siren. Smith's travels facilitated her exceptionally thorough understanding of the broadest aspects of the practice of landscape architecture, including site evaluation, location of structures, grading and manipulation of ground forms, drainage, aesthetic appreciation, ecology, environment, and conservation, as well as all phases of landscape construction.

Smith's educational experiences, as well as her world travels, provided a firm base upon which to build a long and successful career. The majority of Smith's commissions were in the northeastern United States, where she operated offices in New York City and Fairfield, Connecticut. Examples of her work include the estates of Richard Rodgers (famed composer of the duo Rodgers and Hammerstein), Mrs. Marshall Field, Edwin Blair, and Senator William Benton in Connecticut, as well as the home of Marjorie Merriweather Post in the Adirondacks. In addition to designing many residences, her works include the grounds of the American Shakespeare Theater in Stratford, Connecticut (now the Stratford Festival Theater), as well as the landscape for the Bridgeport Museum of Art, Science, and Industry (now The Discovery Museum) in Bridgeport, Connecticut. Other work included land subdivisions of various sizes—from 12 acres in Green Farms, Connecticut, to 5,000 acres in Christian County, Illinois.

Throughout her career, Alice Orme Smith received many awards and accolades for her accomplishments. She won a *New York Times* award for her designs of the Main Vista and the "Garden of Religion" at the 1939 World's Fair in New York, which also brought her widespread publicity. She received a gold medal from the New York Horticultural Society at the 1947 Flower Show, and a year later, Smith won the Bulkley Medal from the Garden Club of America at the Brookside Gardens Exhibit. In 1969, the Massachusetts Horticulture Society awarded her a gold medal for her ground designs of the Ames Family Estate in North Easton, Massachusetts.

In 1973, Alice Orme Smith won the Smith College Medal for professional accomplishment, an award given to alumnae "who in the judgment of the Trustees of the College exemplify in their lives and service to their community or to the College, the true purpose of liberal arts education." During the ceremony, college president Thomas Corwin Mendenhall noted that Smith, along with the other three award recipients, had all done their part "in bringing men and nature into harmony in their landscape," and also cited their ability to "open up vistas rather than enclose spaces." A year later, in 1974, the prominent and highly accomplished landscape architect Helen Swift Jones* endorsed Alice Orme Smith's election to the American Society of Landscape Architects' Council of Fellows. Smith graciously accepted the honor with good humor and praise for her contemporaries, such as **Marian Cruger Coffin**, Florence Bell Robinson,* Sylvia Crowe, Brenda Colvin, and Beatrix Farrand, whom she called "the greatest woman landscape architect of them all." In her closing remarks to the American Society of Landscape Architects, Smith avowed, "I think it is a humble heart we all need in the face of environmental problems," proving her prescience for current issues in the ever-changing discipline.

In addition to landscape work, she also invested in real estate, remodeling old houses or designing buildings and gardens on exceptional parcels of land, selling the properties upon completion. In her personal life, Smith never married, but adopted two sons of her brother and sister-in-law, who were killed in an auto accident.

On April 4, 1980, Alice Orme Smith died at the age of ninety-one at her home in Fairfield, Connecticut. The American Society of Landscape Architects acknowledged that "Alice Orme Smith, in her long life, demonstrated how well a woman of taste, talent, and training can succeed as a landscape architect." Unfortunately, a fire in her Fairfield, Connecticut, home destroyed the majority of her drawings, records, and photographs as well as a large slide collection.

"Alice Orme Smith dies; landscape architect, 91." The Bridgeport (Connecticut) *Telegram,* April 7, 1980. Obituary outlining Smith's life and work.

Connecticut Chapter, American Society of Landscape Architects. Alice Orme Smith, Nomination to Fellowship, A.S.L.A. January 23, 1974. Files including nomination materials and Smith's acceptance speech text.

Zadik, Madelaine. "Designed Landscape Moves." *Botanic Garden News,* Fall 2005, 14. Summary of exhibit at Smith College that prominently featured Smith's work.

Emma Young

STEVENS, RALPH T.
(1882–1958)
LANDSCAPE ARCHITECT, HORTICULTURIST, EDUCATOR, WRITER

Ralph Tallant Stevens was the first child of the pioneering California nurseryman R. Kinton Stevens (1849–1896) and his wife, Lucy Tallant Stevens. Born at Tanglewood, the family property in Montecito, California, on December 15, 1882, Ralph was exposed at an early age to horticultural techniques and a vast array of exotic, sub-tropical vegetation—his father's specialty.

Stevens was just entering his teens when his father died suddenly of a heart attack. His mother took in borders to finance the education of her three children. Stevens graduated with a B.S. degree in landscape architecture from Michigan State College (now Michigan State University) around 1905. He was employed for two years in the office of **Ossian Cole Simonds** in Chicago, then returned to California to work for a nursery in Niles and as a landscape architect for the Southern California Acclimatizing Association (SCAA) in Santa Barbara, owned at that time by Dr. Francesco Franceschi* and Peter Riedel. One of the original faculty members in the Landscape Gardening Department of the University of California in Berkeley, Stevens was an assistant professor from 1913 to 1917. During this period he collaborated with department founder John W. Gregg* on a number of projects including entries in **Liberty Hyde Bailey**'s *Standard Cyclopedia of Horticulture.* Through John McLaren,* superintendent of Golden Gate Park, Stevens made contributions to the park and to San Francisco's 1915 Pan Pacific Exposition.

Stevens returned to Santa Barbara in 1917 and practiced landscape architecture for the next forty years. He was superintendent of the Parks Department from 1919 to 1921, then continued as an unpaid parks commissioner and consultant for the rest of his career, exerting a strong influence on park development. In the 1920s he taught landscape architecture at the Santa Barbara School of the Arts and married Ann Klein. Their marriage lasted until her death in 1957 but produced no children.

Because his papers are scattered, it is difficult to reconstruct his work, but his name seems to turn up frequently in California projects: at the Peabody estate in 1908 (when he was designing for the SCAA); working with the Carnegie Institution in an effort to establish a botanical garden in Santa Barbara (according to a 1924 letter from

Ralph T. Stevens, ca. 1910. (Courtesy of Gledhill Library, Santa Barbara Historical Museum)

the **Olmsted Brothers**); and he contributed to the 1949–1950 master plan for the University of California at Santa Barbara.

Many important Stevens commissions in the 1920s had gardens that (like the associated buildings) adapted formal Mediterranean ideas in the California context. The richness of Stevens's plant palette distinguishes these designs from routine exercises, including his use of palms and giant bird of paradise, *Strelitzia nicolai,* as foundation plantings to create interesting patterns against the building facades. An early commission

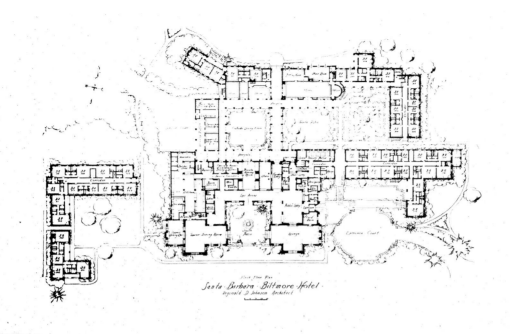

Santa Barbara Biltmore Hotel
Reginald D Johnson Architect

from 1921, the Walter E. Hodges residence by architect Windsor Soule, is situated on a city lot. In the walled, terraced, axial rear garden Stevens employed forced perspective tricks to increase the sense of space.

Designed by George Washington Smith and his client, George Steedman, Casa del Herrero in Montecito is an excellent example of the Spanish Colonial Revival architectural style. Although key site issues were resolved by **Francis Townsend Underhill** and **Lockwood de Forest III**, Stevens was the principal landscape architect for the gardens, which superbly demonstrate the new American synthesis of Anglo and Islamic design concepts.

Stevens's important commercial commissions include the Santa Barbara Biltmore Hotel in Montecito (Reginald D. Johnson, architect, 1926–1927), where tightly clipped box hedges contrast with lush palms; the Santa Barbara County Courthouse (William Moser & Company, architects, 1929); and the Royal Hawaiian Hotel (Warren and Wetmore, architects, 1927), where Stevens was recommended by McLaren for his ability to mass tropical plants. Still an icon of the tourist landscape, it is an early example of the commoditization of the native Hawaiian culture. Stevens retained palm trees believed to date to the royal grove of Chief Kakuhihewa in the Coconut Grove garden.

During the Great Depression, Stevens spearheaded the development of Franceschi Park, the former residence and commercial nursery of Dr. Franceschi, by involving the Works Progress Administration (WPA). The WPA plan for the park incorporates elements of his design.

Ganna Walska was the visionary who gradually transformed the Gavit estate (developed from Tanglewood) into Lotusland, but it was Stevens who gave form to many of her ideas. In the Blue Garden (installed sometime between 1944 and 1955), blue Atlas cedar (*Cedrus atlantica* "Glauca") and Mexican blue palm (*Brahea armata*) tower above *Agave franzosinii,* kleinia (*Senecio mandraliscae*) and blue fescue (*Festuca ovina* var. *glauca*) to create an unprecedented environment with cool blue shades. Stevens is also credited with the design of the Sycamore Canyon Road entry drive, the Swimming Pool and Beach (1947), the Rooster Grotto in the Bromeliad Garden (1940s), the Theatre Garden (1948), and the Horticultural Clock and Topiary Garden (1955–1957)—all extant, but altered to various degrees since Lotusland became a public, botanic garden.

In 1949, Stevens created the Succulent Garden for the Tremaine house, in Montecito, designed by Richard Neutra. Plants were massed for aesthetic effect, not as horticultural specimens. Stevens's free-form design had swirling colors only found elsewhere in the work of Brazil's Roberto Burle Marx. The Succulent Garden

Opposite: Plan of the Santa Barbara Biltmore Hotel, Montecito, California, from *The Architect and Engineer,* April 1929. (Courtesy of the collection of Susan Chamberlin)

Right: Garden of the Walter E. Hodges residence, Santa Barbara, California, from *California Southland* magazine, September 1922. (Courtesy of the collection of Susan Chamberlin)

Below: East facade and Coconut Grove, Royal Hawaiian Hotel, Honolulu, Hawaii, ca. 1927. (Courtesy of Gledhill Library, Santa Barbara Historical Museum)

was included in Elizabeth Kassler's seminal 1964 book, *Modern Gardens and the Landscape.* This and other publications established the garden as a landmark of mid-century modernism.

Stevens began his career in the era of the picturesque landscape garden, completed numerous important commissions in the formal, Mediterranean and Spanish Colonial Revival styles popular during the American Country Place era, and made a lasting contribution to the modernist canon. His best work expressed his flair for horticulture. Stevens Park in Santa Barbara was named in his honor a year before he died. Stevens knew that "the beauty of informal planting lies in the plants themselves." He passed away in 1958.

Stevens's papers are not collected in a single archive; Ganna Walska Lotusland Foundation, the Santa Barbara Botanic Garden, and the Santa Barbara Historical Society hold materials, but most of his drawings are apparently lost.

Chamberlin, Susan. "Tremaine Garden: A Mid-Century Modern Classic." *Pacific Horticulture* 62 (October 2001), 32–37. An examination of Stevens's career and bibliography with David C. Streatfield's important work.

Padilla, Victoria. *Southern California Gardens: An Illustrated History.* Berkeley and Los Angeles: University of California Press, 1961. An essential early reference and the first garden history book to feature Stevens.

Stevens, R. T. "Ornamental Shrubs and Their Landscape Value." *The Architect* 10 (1915), 254–56. An in-depth analysis of the role of plant material in various styles; complements the "Planting" lists Stevens coauthored for *Bailey's Standard Cyclopedia of Gardening.*

Susan Chamberlin

STILES, WAYNE E.
(1884–1953)
GOLF COURSE ARCHITECT

Born in 1884 in Boston, the son of John and Ada Stiles, Wayne E. Stiles spent his formative years as a draftsman and office boy for the landscape architect Franklin Brett beginning when he was eighteen. Stiles stayed with the Boston firm of Brett and Hall (**George Duffield Hall**) until 1914, ending up as a junior partner. He was primarily involved in city planning and land subdivisions in Canada and essentially learned the trade of landscape architecture without formal schooling, which was common at that time in the United States.

During his time at Brett and Hall, he was an avid golfer, peaking at a three handicap from 1909 through 1911 at his home course, the Brae Burn Country Club, in Newton, Massachusetts. He played numerous competitive matches, both individual and team efforts during the years 1905 through 1911, and competed both with and against some of the top professional and amateur golfers of the day, including Francis Ouimet, Alex Ross, and Walter Travis. Stiles won several club invitational tournaments as early as 1905, qualified for the Massachusetts Amateur Championship, and won a series of medals, among them for runner-up in the Club Championship of 1910 and for winning the 1910 MGA Team Championship, representing Brae Burn.

Among the projects he worked on prior to his golf-related work was the 1912 layout for the buildings, roads, and grounds for the Prentiss Estate, now known as Mount Hope Farm, in Williamstown, Massachusetts. He spent additional time in Williamstown during the late 1920s, designing what is widely considered his signature golf course, the Taconic Golf Club, operated by Williams College. In 1915, he formed his own landscape design firm on Newbury Street and became a Junior Member of the American Society of Landscape Architects, becoming a Fellow of the society in 1921. He also served a term as the president of the Boston Society of Landscape Architects.

Wayne Stiles (*highlighted, back row, second from left*), with the 1911 Massachusetts Golf Association (MGA) Team at Brae Burn Country Club, Newton, Massachusetts.

By 1916, he became involved in golf course design largely due to the tremendous proliferation of golf course construction in the United States at that time. Many golf courses during this period were designed for private estates and often involved a subcontract from a landscape architecture firm, among them the **Olmsted Brothers**. The earliest golf course design for which Stiles is credited came in 1916 when he completed a nine-hole course at the Nashua Country Club, in New Hampshire. He is not credited with any further golf projects until 1921. It is possible that his avoidance of golf-related work was coincidental with the United State Golf Association's 1916 ruling to remove the amateur status of golf course architects who received fees, which was reversed in 1921.

In 1916, there were fewer than 1,000 courses, but by the onset of the Great Depression, there were well over 5,500, with Stiles being involved in designs from Maine to Florida and as far west as Missouri. In 1924, he established the firm of Stiles and Van Kleek, with offices in Boston, New York, and St. Petersburg, Florida. The firm continued to be involved in non-golf projects, although Stiles's work was primarily golf related whereas Van Kleek focused more on landscape design. Stiles is credited with designing the City of Oldsmar, Florida, and spent considerable time in residence on the project in 1924, having originally flown the sight in an airplane. Golf professional Walter Hagen acted as a consultant to the firm, and associates of Stiles and Van Kleek included **Thomas Dolliver Church** and Butler Stevens Sturtevant,* both of whom later established themselves as nationally known landscape architects.

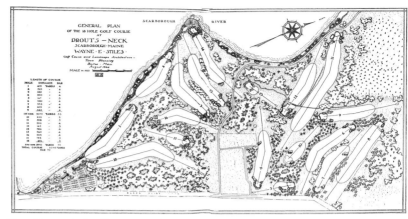

Plan of Prouts Neck golf course, Scarborough, Maine, from *The Story of Prouts Neck* by Rupert Sargent Holland (Prouts Neck, Maine: The Prouts Neck Association, 1924).

Stiles worked on many subdivisions and private estates, including the Massachusetts commissions for the L. K. Liggett estate in Chestnut Hill, and the Fiske Warren estate in Wellesley, which was subcontracted from the Olmsted Brothers. In addition, Stiles worked at the Ross subdivision in Pittsburgh; the C. C. Calder estate in Bronxville, New York, and the Edward S. Harkness estate, known as Eolia, now the Harkness Memorial State Park in Connecticut.

During the Great Depression when relatively few golf course projects were completed, Stiles managed to win contracts for several notable courses, including the Putterham Meadows, in Brookline, Massachusetts, where he beat out several competitors, including Albert Warren Tillinghast.* He also designed a private estate course in 1936 on Martha's Vineyard, today known as Mink Meadows. His work during this time also included the first municipal course in Maine known as the Riverside Municipal Golf Course (North) in Portland, which opened in 1935. Riverside was funded by the Works Progress Administration, for whom Albert Warren Tillinghast* also worked. Stiles also worked for a year during the 1930s supervising Civilian Conservation Corps projects for the National Park Service in New Hampshire.

Stiles remained involved in the reconstruction of many courses that deteriorated during the Great Depression and World War II. Much of the postwar reconstruction work was with William Mitchell, who subsequently redesigned several of Stiles's courses. The latest designs for which he is credited include Pontoosuc Lake, Massachusetts, in 1939, and Gulph Mills, Pennsylvania,

in 1941. In 1943, he was asked to design a course on Block Island, Rhode Island, which was not built but became Nathan Mott Park. He did, however, provide considerable information to the proponents as to how to remove stone walls and other features.

In 1944, Stiles built a cottage in Kennebunk, Maine, and utilized granite from an abandoned railroad bridge to form a retaining wall. His wife was from Kennebunk and they often spent time in Maine, especially considering the number of courses Stiles designed along the mid- and southern Maine coast.

Stiles left a significant number of golf courses throughout New England, where much of what is considered his best work remains. He worked as far west as Albuquerque, Omaha, and most notably, St. Louis, where he designed two eighteen-hole courses for the Norwood Hills Country Club.

Stiles had a distinctive style, and he was known for spending considerable time at those projects where he was hired. He would spend weeks walking the grounds when laying out a course. He took on fewer projects than many golf course architects and developed highly detailed drawings that formed the basis for plans and specifications. For most courses, he developed individual blueprints for each of the holes, often with substantial margin notes on each hole, enabling his foremen to implement his concepts accurately.

His background in landscape architecture enabled him to understand the importance of blending a golf course into the natural terrain. When he designed greenside bunker complexes and associated mounds, they had a natural look to them. He focused on selecting the best green sites first, then routing the course to link them. He was known for utilizing naturally elevated areas for greens, often fitting them into a hill. Many century-old deciduous trees guard these greens today, showing his cognizance of how they would look, and affect play, at maturity. Mounds were also placed around the putting surfaces, which distinguished him from his Massachusetts contemporary, Donald Ross, who usually made the putting surface the zenith of the green complex. Stiles is also known for matching green and fairway slopes, so the golfer often finds the approach shot resting on a side hill lie that slopes the same way as the green, creating the need for a precise shot. He employed the use of both saddle and reverse saddle greens. Many of his greenside approaches feature a narrow and sloping neck between bunkers guarding an elevated green. His greenside bunkers were often hidden and deep, only visible to the golfer upon finding his or her shot in the sand. Although much of this type of bunkering has surrendered to modern alterations, a few great examples

still exist, and several of his layouts are in close to original condition or have been restored.

In *Landscape Architecture* in 1953, the ASLA noted the passing of one of its more dynamic members. Stiles passed away on February 8, 1953, leaving a legacy of approximately seventy original designs. He is buried in the Evergreen Cemetery in Portland, Maine.

Cornish, Geoffrey S., and Ronald E. Whitten. *Architects of Golf: A Survey of Golf Course Design from Its Beginnings to the Present, with an Encyclopedic Listing of Golf Architects and Their Courses.* New York: Harper Information, 1993. Includes a comprehensive listing of Stiles's designs and revisions.

Cornwell, David. "The Stiles Style." *Commonwealth Golf Magazine* (2000), 58–65. Includes biographical information as well as Stiles's golf architecture commissions in the Commonwealth of Massachusetts.

Healey, James F. *Norwood Hills Country Club: A Family Tradition, 1922–2003.* St. Louis, Mo.: Norwood Hills Country Club, 2003. Comprehensive discussion of Stiles's work in St. Louis, along with reference to his complete Planting Plan for both courses.

Kevin R. Mendik

STRANG, ELIZABETH LEONARD
(1886–1948)
LANDSCAPE ARCHITECT

Elizabeth Leonard was born into a middle-class farm family in upstate New York in 1886. Leonard entered Cornell University in 1905 with the intention of studying art, but later transferred to the Rural Art Department from which she graduated in 1910. During her final year at Cornell, Leonard wrote an article entitled "Landscape Architecture from the Point of View of an Undergraduate," which represented the first such description drafted by a student of landscape architecture. Writing in a clear, concise style filled with personal observations, Leonard exhibited her gift for prose, which became her major contribution to the profession in over twenty years of active practice. With her droll sense of humor, Leonard noted that "nearly everyone whom I consulted in regard to taking landscape work advised me not to do it—or at least they did not encourage me. Now that I have nearly completed the course I am convinced that they knew a good thing and wanted to keep it for themselves." Following a lengthy description of the great amount of time and work involved in preparation for the profes-

sion, she closed rather bluntly, saying, "If you have any idea of entering upon a pleasant occupation which will take you out among the flowers, I say—Don't!"

Completing her studies, Leonard began a busy period of apprenticeship in some of the best-known landscape architecture firms of the day. After working in the New York office of **Ferruccio Vitale** for a few months, she took a position with the firm of Hinchman & Pilat, also in New York City. (Carl Franz Pilat, one of the two partners, was the nephew of Ignatz Anton Pilat.*) Writing of her experiences some years later, Leonard observed that, "I stayed with the second firm until Christmas, when I had an opportunity to enter the office of Miss Lorrie A. Dunnington in London, which I did. I returned in March 1911, and entered the office of **John Nolen**, City Planner, in Cambridge, Mass."

While Leonard later acknowledged that her jobs at Vitale and at Hinchman & Pilat were primarily to create planting plans, her experience with John Nolen proved very different. Nolen's career as a city planner was just be-

Above: Elizabeth Leonard (Strang), from the 1910 *Cornellian.* (Carl A. Kroch Library, Cornell University)

Left: The garden at the Hollis, Hingham, Massachusetts residence, from *House Beautiful,* 1930, is an example of Strang's work.

ginning, and during the two years with his firm Leonard discharged "responsibilities in field and office work of a general planning nature" and demonstrated "a considerable command of useful information with regard to engineering features." Leonard, like many women designers, valued her own skills in planting design, but she also realized that women hired primarily for those skills often found their professional opportunities limited. While working for Nolen, Leonard also offered her drafting services to practitioners in the Boston area, including **Warren Henry Manning**, **Samuel Pike Negus**, and **Stephen Child**. The relationship with Child proved particularly fortunate. As a member of the board of directors of the Lowthorpe School in Groton, Massachusetts, he encouraged Leonard to accept a part-time teaching position. She later wrote, "The teaching which seemed to me at first a side issue has developed very much." In 1913, Child nominated Leonard for membership in the American Society of Landscape Architects, writing that she "had not only shown a thorough grasp of the subject and a knowledge of how to teach it, but had inspired

the interest and confidence of the young women whom she had taught." Another beneficiary of Leonard's drafting skills was then little-known garden designer **Ellen Biddle Shipman**, who, from her home in Cornish, New Hampshire, was taking on a growing clientele. Leonard was the first of many young women who Shipman hired.

In 1915, Elizabeth Leonard married the writer Robert Strang, whom she had met aboard ship while returning from England in 1911, and she began using his last name professionally. With the outbreak of World War I, the family, which now included two young sons, moved to Leominster, Massachusetts, where Elizabeth Strang continued to practice, but also began writing on landscape architecture topics. Unlike the majority of women who wrote about gardens and design and acquired much of their information from personal experiences or apprenticeships, Strang's study at a major university, travel to Europe, teaching experience, and professional work placed her in a unique position. Her work and study were presented in her writings, which she illustrated with plans and images of the rather modest projects for which she became known. Collectively, they revealed another side of the profession of landscape architecture that at the time was perceived primarily as a province of the wealthy. Over four dozen articles authored by Strang appeared in popular periodicals from 1918 to 1930.

While many of Strang's articles discussed the maintenance and daily care of gardens, the majority focused on good design principles and an understanding of the design process. Accompanied with photographs and drawings of her own projects, these articles offered a wealth of information to the average homeowner. Strang also encouraged young women to become landscape architects and discussed this in her writings. Just as she was reaching the pinnacle of her career in the late 1920s, illness and accompanying depression forced Strang to be institutionalized. She remained incapacitated until she died in 1948. Upon her death, a former instructor at Lowthorpe

remembered Strang's legacy, saying, "Elizabeth Leonard Strang did much—especially through her writing and photographs—to awaken public consciousness in this country to the meaning of landscape design and the realization of it in home surroundings."

Krall, Daniel W. "The Landscape Architect as Advocate: The Writings of Elizabeth Leonard Strang." *Journal of the New England Garden History Society* 11 (Fall 2003), 12–21. Reviews many of Strang's articles and lists known projects.

Leonard, Elizabeth. "Landscape Architecture from the Point of View of an Undergraduate." *The Cornell Countryman,* December 1909. Discusses the challenges faced by the landscape architecture undergraduate.

Strang, Elizabeth Leonard. "Women in Landscape Architecture." *Farm and Garden,* March 1925. On the opportunities for young women in landscape architecture.

Daniel Krall

STURTEVANT, BUTLER STEVENS
(1899–1971)
LANDSCAPE ARCHITECT

Butler Stevens Sturtevant was born on September 1, 1899, in Delevan, Wisconsin, to James Brown and Ada Belle Sturtevant. In 1918 he enrolled in the undergraduate horticulture program at the University of California, Southern Branch (now UCLA). He graduated in 1921. Concurrent with his studies, he gained practical construction experience working with several landscape architects in Southern California including **Florence Yoch,** Charles Gibbs Adams,* A. E. Hanson,* and the firm of Cook, Hall and Cornell (**George Duffield Hall** and **Ralph Dalton Cornell**). In 1921, he sharpened his knowledge of plant materials and gained nursery experience working with Theodore Payne, the well-known specialist in California native plants.

In 1922 he enrolled in the Harvard University Graduate School of Landscape Architecture and City Planning. He completed all work but his thesis, and did not earn his graduate degree. His classmates included **Thomas Dolliver Church** and Charles W. Eliot II.* Immediately following Harvard, Sturtevant worked for a series of offices. Initially, he returned to the firm of Cook Hall & Cornell in Los Angeles, from 1924 to 1925, where he served as an office draftsman. This was followed by brief stints from 1925 to 1926 at Stiles & Van Kleek, in their

Butler Sturtevant, from *Architect and Engineer,* March 1936.

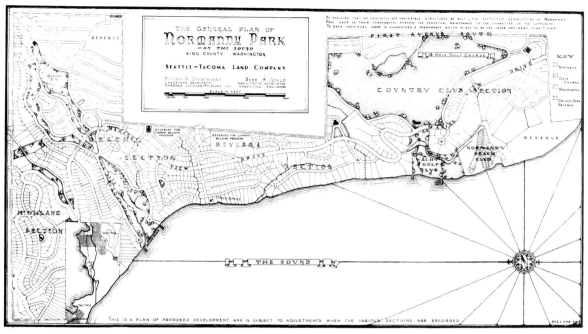

Plan of Normandy Park, Washington, 1927. (University of Washington Libraries, Special Collections, UW13573)

St. Petersburg, Florida, office; office manager and head designer for **Fletcher Steele** in Boston, from 1926 to 1927; and as a designer with Gardner, Gardner & Fischer in Los Angeles, from 1927 to 1928. In 1928, he opened his own office in Seattle, Washington, to participate with architects Charles Herbert Bebb & Carl Freylinghausen Gould in the design of the Normandy Park Subdivision Master Plan (1928–1929).

For the next decade Sturtevant's practice flourished. A recommendation from Carl Gould led to Sturtevant's design for the New Rose Garden at Butchart Gardens, in Victoria, British Columbia (1928–1933); and a courtyard garden at the Children's Orthopedic Hospital in Seattle (1930–1931), which is no longer extant. Gould, who was the key figure in the creation of the 1915 Regents Plan that forever shaped the University of Washington campus, also recommended Sturtevant for the campus landscape architect position, which he held from 1931 to 1939. Using Work Progress Administration (WPA) funds, Sturtevant directed nearly 900 laborers to rework portions of the campus master plan and landscape around new construction projects including the planting of Anderson Hall (1931–1932), the construction of a new 2.5-acre Medicinal Herb Garden (1934–1936), the recon-

struction of Rainier Vista (1935–1937), the renovation of Drumheller Fountain (1935–1936), and the planting of cedar trees on Stevens Way in 1938.

Beginning in 1931, Sturtevant served as the campus landscape architect for Principia College, a small Christian Science school in Elsah, Illinois, where he was responsible for both the planning and landscape architecture. The road system laid out by Sturtevant was largely in place when the land was purchased from the previous owner, wealthy St. Louisan Lucy V. Semple Ames. Notchcliff, the original Ames mansion, had burned in 1911, and in November 1930 the Principia Corporation purchased the spectacular bluff land along the Mississippi River.

Bernard Maybeck and his successor, Henry Gutterson, were the principal architects at Principia. The Sturtevant relationship with Maybeck was tumultuous and the client had to beg Maybeck to continue working with Sturtevant, acknowledging that Sturtevant was "tactless and impulsive and has not always remembered that we began with the definite understanding that the architect was to have general supervision of the landscape plans," but noting that Sturtevant was enthusiastic and "unquestionably in love with his work here." Maybeck completed his portion

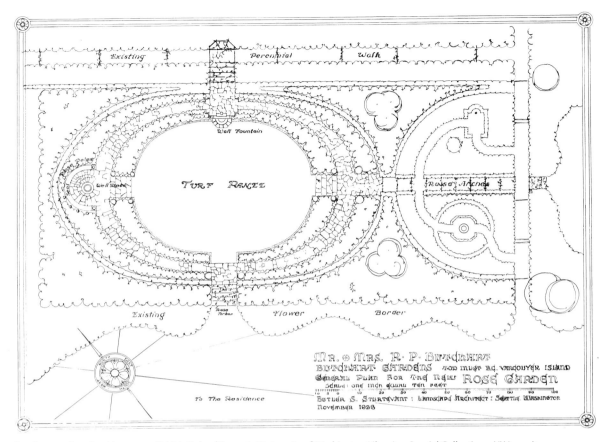

Butchart garden plan, Vancouver, British Columbia, 1928. (University of Washington Libraries, Special Collections, UW13574)

of the commission, leaving Sturtevant to work on various campus projects until 1969.

Sturtevant's work at the Frederick Remington Green Garden in The Highlands (1931–1933) and the William O. McKay Roof Garden in Seattle (1931–1932) established his reputation as a residential landscape designer. His 1936–1937 design for the Ambrose Patterson Garden in Seattle was shown as Seattle's first modern garden, at the San Francisco Museum of Art's exhibition "Contemporary Landscape Architecture and Its Sources." He collaborated with J. Lister Holmes on the Arnold Dessau house in The Highlands (1937–1939), to "bring the outdoors inside." Across the road, another project, the Paul Piggott residence (formerly Norcliffe; 1943–1945) included a cliffside pool, which was unique in the Northwest. Sturtevant, while working around the country, maintained an office in Elsah, Illinois. From 1931 to 1940, he kept a desk in Thomas Church's San Francisco office. When in the Bay Area, Sturtevant was involved in the design of a series of small gardens for the 1939 Golden Gate Exposition on Treasure Island.

In 1941, Sturtevant served as the first president of the San Francisco Chapter of the American Society of Landscape Architects. Later that year he joined the U.S. Army Air Corps, where he served as a major in the Army Air Force and chief of their Airport Unit. During this time he formed a partnership with Edwin Grohs. This partnership allowed Sturtevant to work on wartime housing projects such as Yesler Terrance and Holly Park in Seattle. He also contributed to Westpark, Eastpark, and Bremerton Gardens, all in Bremerton, while he was laying out military airfields throughout the southern United States.

At the end of the war, Sturtevant opened a San Francisco office under succeeding names: Western Engineers (1945-1946) and Sturtevant & French (1946-1947). The work during this time emphasized airport design, but only

Rendering of the development of Rainier Vista, University of Washington Campus, Seattle, Washington, from *Architect and Engineer,* July 1937.

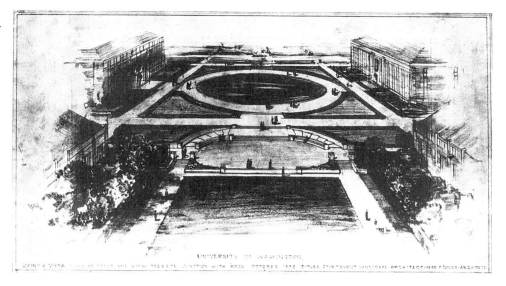

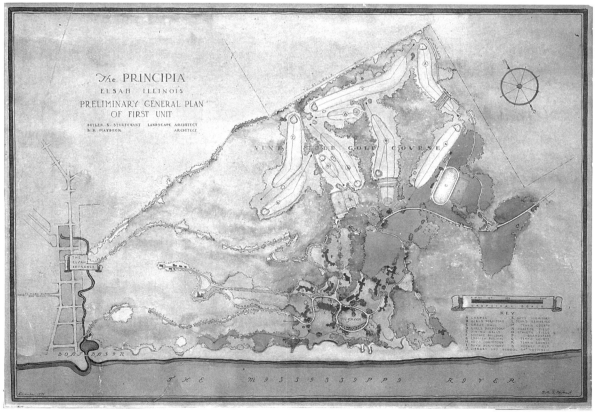

Plan of Principia College, Elsah, Illinois. (Papers of Mary Kimball Morgan, The Principia, Archives Department)

the Portland Airport in Portland, Oregon, (1945–1948) can be confirmed. He also began to do larger land planning work, executing master plans for the Pope Estate in Burlingame, California (1946–1947), and the Village of Hana, on the Island of Maui, Hawaii, (1947–1949).

In 1954, Sturtevant moved back to his native Midwest, settling in St. Louis to work on the design of the Principia School campus (1948–1969) for grades K–12. He also executed the American University Campus Master Plan, in Beirut, Lebanon (1961–1962); worked for John Brown University, in Siloam Springs, Arkansas (1962–1963); and the Mason Woods Development, in St. Louis, Missouri (1966–1969). He fell ill with colon cancer and died at the Christian Science Sanatorium in San Francisco on April 11, 1971.

The Special Collections Division at the University of Washington, Seattle, includes two drawings of Butchart Gardens' Rose Garden and two sketches of the University of Washington Rainier Vista. In addition the holdings at Principia College include correspondence, plans, and sketches.

"Garden for Mrs. Frederick Remington Greene, Seattle, Wash." *Country Life,* January 1936, 31–33. Plan and photos of the Greene Garden overlooking Puget Sound.

Sturtevant, Butler. "Houses for Defense: Westpark, Bremerton, WA." *Architectural Forum,* December 1941, 410–16. Site plan and images of a military housing development west of Seattle.

Sturtevant, Butler. "Small English Stone Bridges." *Landscape Architecture,* October 1933, 16–23. Article and photos on small bridges in England.

Duane A. Dietz

SUAREZ, DIEGO
(1888–1974)
GARDEN DESIGNER

Diego Suarez was born on May 25, 1888, to Roberto Suarez, a diplomat and historian, and Maria Costa Suarez, the great-granddaughter of General Francisco de Miranda, an entrepreneur who organized two expeditionary attacks on Spanish holdings in Venezuela. Suarez spent his early years in Bogotá, Colombia. After his father's death, the family moved to Italy in 1906.

In 1912, industrialist James Deering began the acquisition of 180 acres in northern Coconut Grove, Florida, that would ultimately become Villa Vizcaya. The estate contained a farm, railroad stop, and pleasure grounds that not only included the 10 acres of gardens closest to the house, but also 17 acres of gardens throughout the native mangrove and hammock along a series of winding canals and lagoons. Diego Suarez was, by his own account, the chief designer for this significant American landscape.

Deering's closest advisor, Paul Chalfin, later referred to Suarez as a draftsman in his office that Chalfin organized to design and plan the estate. However, recent scholarship credits Chalfin as the leading strategic planner of the estate with a vast scope of responsibilities that ranged from land acquisition to the monogramming of the linens. Chalfin appears to have been an intense and informed owner's advocate who made crucial design decisions in coordination with the architect, F. Burall Hoffman Jr. Suarez established the principle strategy and design of the garden, while Chalfin made the on-site decisions and directed implementation.

A more definitive understanding of design authorship of garden elements still remains elusive. A review of the surviving correspondence between Deering and Chalfin revealed few specific references to Suarez on the garden's design while a 1958 interview with Suarez offers a thorough and credible account of his inspirations and intentions for the garden. Those statements were bolstered by interviews with F. Burall Hoffman Jr., as well as references to Suarez's ideas that appear in some of the Chalfin letters.

Suarez described his preliminary engineering education in Bogotá until the family relocated to Italy, where he graduated from the Florence Architectural School in 1912. Suarez first encountered James Deering, a vice president of The International Harvester Company (the result of the merger of the Deering and McCormick companies) and Paul Chalfin, an artist and recipient of the Rome Prize, and former curator of the Boston Museum of Fine Arts, at the home of Arthur Acton, near Florence, Italy. A friend and mentor to Suarez, Acton hosted the group at La Pietra, his renowned villa and garden. Upon Acton's

Right: Diego Suarez at Vizcaya, ca. 1925. (Vizcaya Museum & Gardens, Miami, Florida)

Below: Vizcaya casino in 1926. (Photo by William Fishbaugh; Florida State Archive)

suggestion, Suarez spent several days showing Mr. Deering and Mr. Chalfin the gardens in and around Florence. Suarez included two of his own projects, the Villa Schifanoia for Lewis Einstein and the Villa Loeser for Charles Loeser. In recalling these events forty years later, Suarez expressed his concern that Acton "be known to future generations as mainly responsible, together with the great French landscape architect, Achille Duchêne, for the revival of the great art of classical design." Certainly the publication of **Charles A. Platt**'s *Italian Gardens* in 1894 and the 1903 edition of Edith Wharton's *Italian Villas and Their Gardens,* illustrated with Maxfield Parrish's luxuriant watercolors, generated an enthusiastic audience among patrons. John Singer Sargent, longtime friend of James and Charles Deering, would later portray Vizcaya with the same animating spirit in a series of watercolors he produced during a sojourn there in the winter of 1917.

Just as World War I opened, Suarez, having set sail to the United States en route to Colombia, found himself stranded in New York, where he accidentally met Chalfin. Shortly thereafter, Suarez began work on the gardens of Vizcaya, where Deering and Chalfin hoped to create a villa and garden in the great Italian tradition. Suarez was shocked by his first encounter with the actual site, where he discovered that the primary view of the gardens from the villa was obliterated by the brilliance of the tropical sun that reflected blindingly off the surface of the lake. Suarez immediately set to reworking the project. His "new conception consisted principally in the idea of going down from the house terrace to the garden level, and of going up again to a higher level; and in the building of a high mound, crowned by a curtain of high trees between the gardens and the lake." Now he faced the unwanted side effect of obscuring the water entirely, a dilemma that led Suarez to what he believed was his

"most original idea in relation to the Vizcaya gardens"— the planning of the gardens and mound in a V-shape, flanking the mound by two grass avenues. The design, inspired by Villa Gamberaia, just outside of Florence at Settignano, included a balustrade and a statue in the middle at the end of each vista, so that one could have a glimpse of the lake from the house.

Supporting the high mound, "heroic figures guard access to deep grottoes on either side of the cascade, and these shadowed openings are reflected directly upon the water at the extreme end of the great pool." Along the central axis that extends from the center of the southern facade of the house, are "the waters of a great pool ornamented with pyramids." Here, stone vases surround an island lawn, connected by two bridges with the adjacent

View from grounds to the casino at Vizcaya, 2005. (Photo by Bill Sumner; Vizcaya Museum & Gardens, Miami, Florida)

gardens, and at one end, a Roman cascade, flanked by steps, ascends to the higher end of the terrace. Suarez is credited with executing the working drawings for the elaborate boxwood parterres in the main garden, inspired principally by the gardens of the palace of Caserta near Naples. Eventually, the boxwood was replaced by a native jasmine, which provided similar structure and the requisite hardiness.

Atop the mound, Suarez placed the casino, which offered refuge from the tropical day. With allusions to the Farnese casino at Caprarola, the tripartite organization of two rooms flanking a central, open pavilion, positioned at the head of the water stair, which Suarez based on his survey of the cascade and stair of the Roman Villa Corsini, offers a significant platform from which to view the estate. Originally, the lower lawn also led southeast to a bridge lined with palms, which in turn defined a path into the woods where a network of diminutive canals and waterways threaded through small islands housing tennis courts, a boathouse, and the Casbah, a Sicilian-inspired pavilion and fish garden.

Like Villa Lante's original forest, the tropical hammock surrounded Vizcaya, punctuated with theatrical openings to reveal carefully planned views of the villa, gardens, and bay front. In 1917, William Patterson, writing in *Town & Country*, noted the dramatic "progress along the allée, with its low voiced waterways hidden

under the Ilex trees . . . full of the pleasantest surprises. And the climax of the unexpected is in the house itself, which has been carefully screened by the planting and which is finally reached through the iron grilles and open arcades of the first loggia."

On the bay side, a terrace along the water faces the stone barge, which, with its lattice teahouse and garden, framed the vista of Biscayne Bay. Suarez identified his source as the famous barge at the Villa Borromeo at Isola Bella on Lake Maggiore in northern Italy. His model of the Vizcaya barge was submitted to the distinguished sculptor Stirling Calder, and the result is what Suarez referred to as the proudest architectural creation of his life.

Suarez subsequently parted company with Chalfin and never saw him after 1921. Noting that American taste had shifted from the classical design of gardens to the naturalistic school, Suarez described his interest to be the "architectural design in gardens." Since he believed himself to be almost completely ignorant in the field of agriculture and botany, Suarez determined that he would focus on architecture. References to Suarez begin appearing in society columns as he attended various events, including the 1926 Beaux-Arts Ball in New York. His marriage in 1937 to divorcée Evelyn Marshall Field further enhanced Suarez's social profile.

An interesting figure in her own right, Evelyn Marshall

was a passenger on the *Carpathia* on April 15, 1912, and witnessed the predawn rescue of *Titanic* survivors. While married to Marshall Field III, she worked with architect David Adler and landscape architects **Umberto Innocenti** and Richard K. Webel* in designing Easton, the celebrated Field estate in Syosset, Long Island. After her marriage to Suarez, she consulted interior designer Eleanor Brown of McMillen, Inc., to redesign their River House apartment. In addition to documentation of Easton, the firm Gottscho-Schleisner photographed the couple's Brookville residence in 1957.

Suarez turned to writing and diplomacy, acting as press attaché and minister counselor under Eduardo Zuleta Angel at the Colombian Embassy in Washington, D.C., until 1952. Vizcaya remains his significant contribution to landscape design in the United States. In 1972, Suarez and Hoffman returned to Vizcaya for a final tour of the project they both considered "one of the finest examples of garden planning in the great Italian tradition ever built in America." Diego Suarez passed away two years later at his home, at 435 East 52nd Street, New York, on September 15, 1974.

Vizcaya maintains its own archives. Historic images and materials relating to Vizcaya are also available at the University of Miami, Otto G. Richter Library, Archive and Special Collections.

Ceo, Rocco, and Joanna Lombard. *The Historic Landscapes of Florida.* Miami: University of Miami School of Architecture and the Deering Foundation, 2001. In essays on the Deering landscapes, the author discusses the design principles evident at Vizcaya.

Harwood, Kathryn Chapman. *The Lives of Vizcaya: Annals of a Great House.* Miami: Banyan Books, 1985. Harwood includes a chapter on Diego Suarez in a full history of the estate.

Maher, James T. *The Twilight of Splendor: Chronicles of the Age of American Palaces.* Boston: Little Brown & Company, 1975. Maher's focus is Vizcaya and material from two interviews with Diego Suarez.

Joanna Lombard

THIENE, PAUL G.

(1880–1971)

LANDSCAPE ARCHITECT

Paul George Thiene was born in 1880 in Germany, where he was educated. He received a Landscape Technical degree and served an apprenticeship there before immigrating to the United States in 1903. He was employed as a nurseryman around 1910 by the **Olmsted Brothers** when their office was hired to plan and landscape the Panama-California Exposition. This World's Fair was scheduled to open in 1915 in Balboa Park in San Diego, California. Both the Olmsted Brothers and their West Coast associate, **James Frederick Dawson,** had already completed a great deal of preliminary work on the Exposition when fundamental disagreements with architect Bertram G. Goodhue arose. In 1911, the Olmsted firm quit. Thiene assumed head gardener and landscape designer tasks and helped make the Exposition a sensation. Its Spanish Colonial Revival–style buildings in a formal garden setting became the most important influence on architecture and landscape architecture in Southern California, decisively shifting the aesthetic toward the climate-appropriate Mediterranean styles. Thiene's association with the Exposition and contacts he made, including Lloyd Wright, the son of Frank Lloyd Wright, launched his career as a landscape architect.

Paul G. Thiene, ca. 1910. (From *The California Garden* by Jere Stuart French, used by permission)

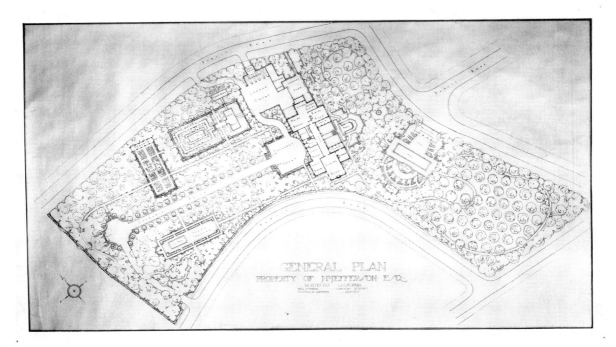

"General Plan, Property of J. P. Jefferson, Esq., [Mira Flores], Montecito, California, Paul G. Thiene, Landscape Architect, Reginald D. Johnson, Architect." (Paul Thiene Collection, [1962-1], Environmental Design Archives, University of California, Berkeley)

Thiene's specialty was horticulture. One of his earliest jobs was a planting consultation in 1914 for the A. H. Sweet garden in San Diego, by Frank Mead and Richard Requa, architects. Lloyd Wright became Thiene's partner around this time, and the two had a landscape architecture office in Los Angeles. Thiene later practiced in Pasadena. His most notable early garden was the 1918 J. P. Jefferson estate, Mira Flores, in Montecito near Santa Barbara, one of the first and most acclaimed estates in the new Mediterranean style.

The Jefferson house was a remodel by the Los Angeles architect Reginald D. Johnson. The site was organized in a symmetrical, axial manner in relation to the main building. Cross axes led to rose, cutting, and formal gardens hidden in the hedges. The main axis extended through the house to the fabulous views from the rear terraces. An allée of clipped black acacia trees (*Acacia melanoxylon*) was a feature at the Exposition. There is also an allée of clipped black acacias at Mira Flores. Combined with lighter green *Pittosporum undulatum* hedges, this simple, architectonic composition in tones of evergreen foliage was based on Thiene's favorite style, the Italian

Renaissance. The entrance court is an early example of the use of subtropicals for foundation planting. Florence Yoch added an exquisite "Don Quixote" courtyard to Mira Flores in 1932.

The Jefferson estate was the first of several collaborations between Thiene and Johnson. Its site plan is typical of the era in general. Formal gardens extend the architecture of the house, which is hidden within an informal, wooded setting. Thiene's office structure was also typical. He relied on talented designers, such as Wright and A. E. Kuehl, to complement his own skills.

Thiene worked with Johnson on the lushly planted Edward Lowe estate, El Eliseo in Montecito (1920). They also are associated with the Neptune Fountain formal garden area behind the house designed by Johnson at the E. Palmer Gavit estate, Cuesta Linda, also in Montecito (1920; formerly Tanglewood, later Lotusland). Other collaborations include the Max Fleischmann estate, Edgewood in Summerland (1920), and the J. L. Severance estate in Pasadena (1922), which was much admired for its lushly planted, brook-like water feature.

The sophisticated site plan by Wright for the Benjamin

Loggia and swimming pool,
La Collina, Benjamin R. Meyer
estate, Beverly Hills, California,
1923. (Paul Thiene Collection,
[1962-1], Environmental Design
Archives, University
of California, Berkeley)

R. Meyer estate, La Collina, in Beverly Hills (Gordon B. Kaufmann, architect, 1922), featured a winding drive through an orchard to the hilltop house. Thiene created a unique California interpretation of European traditions with a swimming pool serving as a reflecting pool and an edging of drought-tolerant plants substituting for English-style perennial borders. This pool garden was hidden below the house. Also with Kaufmann, Thiene completed the Isadore Eisner estate in Los Angeles (1925); the Milton E. Getz estate in Beverly Hills (1927), where palm trees played the role usually filled by Italian cypresses; the Benjamin R. Meyer Hope Ranch house in Santa Barbara (1930); and the enormous Edward L. Doheny Jr. estate, Greystone, in Beverly Hills, real-

ized from 1925 to 1929. There a long entry drive curved through an arboretum-like collection of trees to a hilltop of extensive formal gardens surrounding the fifty-five-room mansion. Included within the 400 acres were tennis courts, stables and riding trails, a huge swimming pool, an artificial waterfall, lakes and fountains, and that essential California element, a barbecue.

Widely published and included in Frank Albert Waugh's book *Formal Design in Landscape Architecture,* Thiene had a national reputation by the end of the 1920s. He was a significant figure in the American Country Place era. He made a substantial contribution to the emergence of the regionally appropriate California interpretation of Mediterranean-style gardens, which would dominate in

Cascades, Milton E. Getz estate, Beverly Hills, California, ca. 1925. (Paul Thiene Collection, [1962-1], Environmental Design Archives, University of California, Berkeley)

the 1920s and in subsequent revivals. Thiene specialized in horticulture and relied on his associates for much of the design work. His office was noted for its water features including: the still, rectangular lily pool at the Jefferson estate; the artificial streams and ponds at the Meyer and Severance estates; the formal, Italian-style cascades at the Getz estate; and the artificial waterfall at the Doheny estate. A member of the American Society of Landscape Architects since 1926, Thiene was elected a Fellow of the society before he retired in 1951. He died twenty years later in 1971.

Thiene's papers are in the University of California, Berkeley, Environmental Design Archives.

French, Jere Stuart. *The California Garden: And the Landscape Architects Who Shaped It.* Washington, D.C.: The Landscape Architecture Foundation, 1993. This survey highlights numerous important individuals including Thiene.

Gebhard, David. "The Design of the Landscape in the Work of Reginald D. Johnson, Gordon B. Kaufmann, and Roland E. Coate." *Johnson, Kaufmann, Coate: Partners in the California Style,* ed. Jay Belloli et al. Santa Barbara, Calif.: Capa Press, 1992, 56–69. The definitive examination of Thiene's early work and the California context for his style.

Lucas, James J. "Paul G. Thiene: A Biographical Research Paper." Unpublished manuscript, 1962. Interviews with Thiene were the basis for this illustrated student project housed in the Environmental Design Library at the University of California, Berkeley.

Susan Chamberlin

TIBBITTS, ARMAND RHODES
(1891–1987)
LANDSCAPE ARCHITECT

Armand Rhodes Tibbitts was born in Hingham, Wisconsin, to Ulysses J. and Elizabeth Rhodes Tibbitts on August 30, 1891. The family later moved to Waukesha, Wisconsin, where Tibbitts attended Carroll Academy. He continued his education at Cornell University and earned a bachelor of science degree in 1915. Tibbitts

spent the following summer working as a draftsman for Jens Jensen in Chicago, Illinois. During this time, Tibbitts traveled to Fair Lane, Henry Ford's private estate in Dearborn, Michigan, and observed firsthand the naturalistic approach Jensen took in designing the property. These experiences with Jensen and his work introduced

Greenhouse plan and section, Riegel estate, Fairfield, Connecticut. (Courtesy of Historic New England)

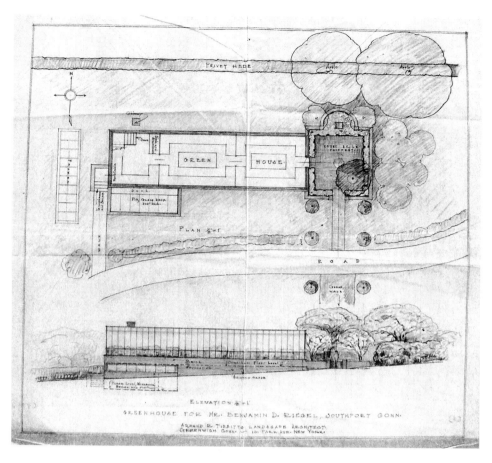

Tibbitts to the concept of integrating local natural resources, especially stone, into landscape design. Tibbitts never fully adopted Jensen's naturalistic style, but he did frequently use stone walkways, walls, and benches, as well as native plantings, in his designs.

In 1916, Tibbitts returned to Cornell and completed his master's degree in landscape design. He spent the following year as a draftsman for the landscape architecture firm Townsend and Fleming (**Bryant Fleming**) in Buffalo, New York, before taking a position with Vitale, Brinckerhoff, and Geiffert in New York City (**Ferruccio Vitale** and **Alfred Geiffert Jr.**). While working in New York, Tibbitts met and married Emma G. Smith, with whom he had two children, Armand Jr. and Phyllis Anne. By 1921, Tibbitts had moved to Greenwich, Connecticut, and started his own practice.

Shortly after opening his firm, Tibbitts began work on the Benjamin DeWitt Riegel and Leila Edmonston Riegel

estate in Fairfield, Connecticut. The New York businessman commissioned Tibbitts and architect Henry C. Pelton to create a grand estate on farmland that he had purchased. Riegel Point, as the 20-acre property came to be known, included a summer house surrounded by a rock garden, walkways lined with apple trees, and mature elm trees transplanted to shade the main house.

In 1922, while finishing his work on the Riegel estate, Tibbitts undertook the most extensive project of his career. In association with developer Arthur Waterman, Tibbitts designed a planned community of upper-class homes in Connecticut called Millbrook. Tibbitts sited and landscaped the development's houses, golf course, clubhouse, roads, and pathways. By the time the well-publicized project was complete, Tibbitts's reputation was firmly established in Greenwich.

In 1927, during the first of several three-month-long garden study trips, Tibbitts focused his attentions on

Benjamin DeWitt Riegel and Leila Edmonston Riegel estate, Fairfield, Connecticut, from ASLA *Illustrations of Works of Members,* 1932.

a formal English garden, a 100-foot pergola, lily pond, and a collection of specimen trees.

Tibbitts also completed the plan for Mrs. Eugene Atwood's estate on Long Island Sound. The estate sits on a narrow tract of land bounded on one side by the town of Stonington and on the other by the steep banks of Long Island Sound. Tibbitts incorporated the rocky banks by installing a series of terraces on the southeastern end of the property. The uppermost terrace features the property's two houses, which Tibbitts connected by a long, stone walkway flanked by plantings. The remaining terraces are connected by a series of stone and gravel walkways and include an expansive lawn sparsely planted with elm trees; a rose garden; twin garden houses; and a swimming pool. The swimming pool occupies the largest terrace and is highlighted by decorative stone and ironwork. Throughout the property, Tibbitts installed decorative features made from wrought iron and local stone, including garden benches, a wellhead, and entry gates. He integrated both native plantings and more traditional plants, such as boxwoods, in order to create a formal yet contemporary design.

Tibbitts's other projects included the Connecticut estates of Florence De Bevoise in Greens Farms and George Platt Brett in Fairfield, as well as plans for Hobart and William Smith Colleges in Geneva, New York. He completed master plans for Greenwich Point, commonly known as Todd's Point, and a planting plan for Bruce Park, both in Greenwich. Tibbitts was also responsible for designing the Jackson and Perkins rose gardens at nearly thirty International Flower Shows in New York, Chicago, Boston, and Washington, D.C. His awards include the Horticultural Society of New York Trophy for his show design in 1959 and the Director's Trophy for the hybridized roses in 1961.

Tibbitts became a member of the American Society of Landscape Architects in 1925 and a Fellow in 1933. He

the romantic gardens of Italy and the formal gardens of England. His experience likely influenced his estate designs, as he often chose to combine several types of gardens in one plan. In 1932, Tibbitts designed the landscape for Clarence Wooley's Sunridge Farm estate on Quaker Ridge in western Greenwich. Along with flowerbeds and gardens, Tibbitts installed vineyards, tobacco fields, and vegetable gardens for use by residents of the estate. He integrated diverse garden types for the estate of New York attorney Charles Frueauff as well. Frueauff's estate on Mead's Point included vegetable and fruit gardens, and a vast lawn that was located between the house and Long Island Sound. Other features included

served as a Trustee for the organization's Connecticut Chapter during the early 1950s. Tibbitts was also a member of the Architecture League of New York from 1928 to 1932.

During the mid-1930s, Tibbitts was employed by the federal government's Resettlement Administration, the predecessor to the Farm Securities Administration, to work on the development of Greenhills, Ohio. The planned community outside of Cincinnati was developed as one of three government subsidized greenbelt communities completed during the Depression era. In 1944, Tibbitts joined the war effort, spending a year working with the U.S. Army Air Corps Camouflage Division, disguising defense factories along the eastern seaboard with special paint finishes and landscaping.

After the war, Tibbitts returned to private practice and continued to produce landscape plans for properties throughout southeastern Connecticut. He also continued traveling, spending three months in Greece in 1955 and four months in Asia and the South Pacific in 1967.

In 1968, Tibbitts returned to Riegel Point. The Riegels' daughter Katherine Riegel Emory, who inherited the property, and her husband, German H. H. Emory, commissioned Tibbitts to renovate the landscape. It was one of his last projects before retiring from his formal practice later that year. He continued to oversee the gardens at his own home in Southbury, Connecticut, including his rose hybridization garden.

Throughout his life, Tibbitts had been active in community activities, including serving on the Planning Commission and Zoning Board of Appeals in Greenwich. Upon retiring, he continued with many of these endeavors. He also continued traveling, painting, and playing golf. Armand Tibbitts died on January 24, 1987.

The Armand Tibbitts Papers, Department of Manuscripts and University Archives, Cornell University Library, accession number 4899, contain over one hundred of Tibbitts's drawings for several clients, including Hobart and William Smith Colleges. The Society for the Preservation of New England Antiquities holds a significant collection of drawings and photographs chronicling the history of the Riegel estate.

Anner, Rosemarie T. "Digging in the Past." *Greenwich,* May 1994. A general discussion of several of Tibbitts's projects including a discussion of his work on Millbrook.
Tibbitts, Armand R. "A Terrace Garden by the Sea." *The American Landscape Architect,* n.d. Tibbitts provides details regarding his work on Mrs. Eugene Atwood's estate.

Melanie Macchio

TILLINGHAST, ALBERT WARREN
(1874–1942)
GOLF COURSE DESIGNER

Albert Warren Tillinghast was born in Philadelphia in 1874. An only child of prosperous parents, he was known as A. W., and also as "Tillie the Terror" during much of his youth in the 1880s, running with a group of wealthy and hard-drinking playboys called the Kelly Street Gang that operated out of the Philadelphia Cricket Club, whose golf course Tillinghast would later design. He bragged about never having graduated from any school he attended, and there were several. However, when he turned twenty, he abruptly left the gang, immersed himself in relatively refined social circles, and married Lillian Quigley; they had two daughters, Marion and Elsie. For the next several years, he lived the life of a wealthy connoisseur, collecting art and furniture and writing self-published novels. Tillinghast was an avid sportsman, indulging in billiards, bridge, polo, cricket, and golf. In 1896, his interest in golf was peaked when he visited St. Andrews in Scotland and was fortunate to take lessons from renowned player Old Tom Morris, returning each year through 1901 to play and visit with the game's grand old man. Back in the United States, he competed at the highest levels in golf, playing in the U.S. Amateur Championship several times between 1905 and 1915. He lost his amateur standing in 1915, having been classified as a professional due to his income from golf architecture and writing, and he consequently stopped playing competitive golf. He is credited with coining the term "birdie" to describe holing out in one stroke under par.

Despite his lack of formal training in golf course design or landscape architecture, he laid out his first course in 1909, at the request of Charles Worthington on land at the Worthington family's farm at Shawnee-on-Delaware,

Above: Albert Tillinghast (*right*) consulting with construction foreman. (The Tillinghast Association)

Below: Baltusrol clubhouse, Springfield, New Jersey. (The Tillinghast Association)

Pennsylvania. For perhaps the first time in his life, he was working for pay. He immediately found that he not only enjoyed the work, but sensed, quite correctly, that he had a natural affinity for golf course design. He formed his own design and construction firm that was quite successful, making A.W. Tillinghast a millionaire within twenty years. His aristocratic image was further cemented during his most successful years as a golf designer. During much of that time he lived in Harrington Park, New Jersey. Tillie, as he was known, had an office in midtown Manhattan, commuting in a chauffeur-driven Rolls Royce. He was not the type to spend his time scrutinizing working drawings and detailed plans; instead, he preferred to bushwhack through the undeveloped site, laying out the course with an innate sense of the best locations for the greens and other features. He always dressed in his three-piece suit and was not hard to spot in the field, sitting in the shade propped up by his walking stick, drinking from his flask, and shouting directions to the workers. He claimed he invented the clipboard to assist in his fieldwork.

He worked throughout the United States and is credited with approximately seventy original designs. His courses range from Marble Island Golf & Yacht Club in Chittenden County, Vermont, to Brook Hollow in Texas and included such outstanding designs as Winged Foot's East and West courses in Mamaroneck, New York; Baltusrol's Upper and Lower courses in Springfield, New Jersey; Bethpage Black State Park in Farmingdale, New York; and the San Francisco Golf Club. He was highly cognizant of the need to include the entire site in his planning. He often spent considerable time working (or arguing) with club committees to determine the proper sites for

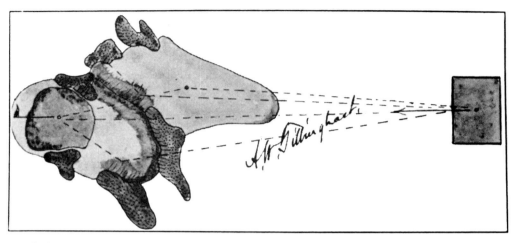

A Reef hole drawing by Tillinghast. (The Tillinghast Association)

clubhouses. Many clubs wanted their clubhouses on the highest point of land, but Tillinghast recognized that this often resulted in a starting hole teeing off a high elevation and a blind or arduous uphill trek to the home green. He often worked with notable landscape architects, including **Albert Davis Taylor** and **Charles Wellford Leavitt Jr.** His work with Leavitt on the 400-acre Philadelphia Cricket Club site involved selecting the clubhouse location prior to designing the thirty-six holes. Tillie and Leavitt agreed that the clubhouse should be located on a lower level that allowed for entrance roads along the ridges, providing the first view of the clubhouse in a valley setting. He stressed that while scenic values were important, golfing values were of greater importance. During the 1920s, most of his designs were on inland locations, usually containing specimen trees, which club members were quite fond of. He would often site a putting green adjacent to such trees, but not so close as to adversely affect play. Americans were also fond of water on their golf courses, and in designing holes, Tillinghast made use of existing watercourses whenever possible. Relocating streams was a simple matter in those days, and often had a dramatic effect on play. Clumps of shrubs and trees were commonly planted along teeing grounds to prevent shots from ending up on adjacent or parallel holes, a design element still common today.

He also designed what he called "Lilliput Links," which were usually nine-hole layouts on private estates, such as the Rainey Estate in Huntington, New York, where he worked in collaboration with well-known landscape architects. His golf architecture business thrived until the Great Depression, when a series of ill-advised investments (into such things as a Broadway show) left Tillinghast nearly a pauper. During the 1930s, he worked for the Professional Golf Association of America (of which he was a founding member), touring members' courses throughout the country and recommending changes. He also worked for the Works Progress Administration, where he designed the classic Bethpage Black State Park course, including the Blue and Red courses there, among others. He retained his trademark mannerisms, using his hickory walking stick to point and shout out tree and bunker locations to workers. During that time, many clubs were struggling to survive and were either not keen, or unable to implement, his suggestions. After a few years, he largely abandoned golf course design and, thinking that Hollywood was the last place the Depression would hit, moved to Beverly Hills to open an antique shop, using primarily his and his family's furniture and art collections for inventory. After a few years, when that business failed along with his health, he moved in with his daughter Marion in Toledo, Ohio. He wrote often for *The American Golfer* and *Golf Illustrated* and served as the latter's editor briefly before World War II. He died in Toledo on May 19, 1942, largely forgotten by the golfing world.

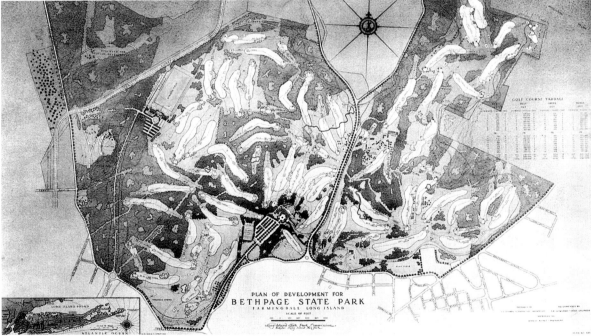

Above: San Francisco Golf and Country Club, hole 7, ca. 1922. (The Tillinghast Association)

Below: Bethpage State Park development plan. (The Tillinghast Association)

Tillinghast, Albert W. *The Course Beautiful: A Collection of Original Articles and Photographs on Golf Course Design,* ed. Richard C. Wolffe Jr., Robert S. Trebus, and Stuart F. Wolffe. Lynchburg, Va.: Progress Printing, 1995. A collection of numerous articles written by Tillinghast, some originally published in the Professional Golfer of America. Assembled by the founders of the Tillinghast Association.

Tillinghast, Albert W. *Gleanings From the Wayside: My Recollections as a Golf Architect,* ed. Richard C. Wolffe Jr., Robert S. Trebus, and Stuart F. Wolffe. Rockville, Md.: Smith Lithographic Corporation, 2001. Final volume of the series with additional articles by Tillinghast

and photographs. Assembled by the founders of the Tillinghast Association.

Tillinghast, Albert W. *Reminiscences of the Links, A Treasury of Essays and Vintage Photographs on Scottish Design and Early American Golf,* ed. Richard C. Wolffe Jr., Robert S. Trebus and Stuart F. Wolffe. Rockville, Md.: Smith Lithograph Corporation, 1998. Second volume includes early essays by Tillinghast along with many historical photographs. Assembled by the founders of the Tillinghast Association.

Kevin R. Mendik

ULRICH, RUDOLPH
(1840–1906)

LANDSCAPE GARDENER, LANDSCAPE ARCHITECT, HORTICULTURIST

Rudolph Ulrich was born in Weimar, Thuringia, Germany, and educated at the Royal Gardener's Institute at Potsdam and at Van Houtte's School of Horticulture in Gendbrugge-lez-Gand, Belgium. Henry Probasco, a wealthy merchant from Cincinnati, Ohio, induced Ulrich to come to America in 1868 and take charge of Probasco's private grounds in the suburb of Clifton Heights. Ulrich married Karlina Linck Hartman at Indianapolis in 1872 and their first two children were born in Ohio. Between 1875 and 1876, Ulrich moved his family to California, where two more children were born.

Ulrich spent the next several years designing and installing gardens on the large summer estates of the San Francisco Peninsula. His use of formal design, combined with an opulent palette of plant material, provided the European-style landscape preferred by newly wealthy clients such as D. O. Mills, James C. Flood, and Leland Stanford. Design features that Ulrich employed typically included arboreta, artificial lakes, hedge mazes, large conservatories, elaborate mosaiculture designs, and botanical specimens set in large expanses of lawn in the gardenesque style.

In 1879, Ulrich sought new commissions through two German-owned florist shops in San Francisco. The following year he added his design skills to the services offered by a third German florist and seedsman, Hugo Leopold, but new opportunities soon led to the dissolution of this partnership.

Having completed the monumental task of building an intercontinental railroad, the owners of the Southern Pacific found that they lacked sufficient paying custom-

Rudolph Ulrich, from D. H. Burnham's World's Columbian Exposition senior management staff group portrait, ca. 1893. (D. H. Burnham, Ryerson and Burnham Archives, The Art Institute of Chicago. Reproduction © The Art Institute of Chicago)

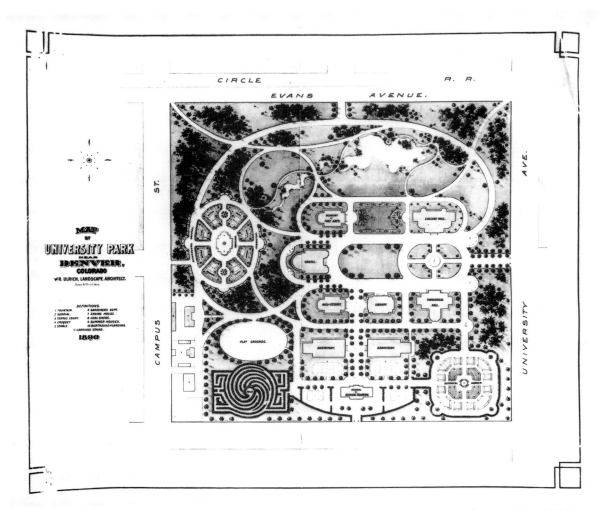

Plan for University Park, Denver, Colorado, 1890. (Courtesy of the National Park Service, Frederick Law Olmsted National Historic Site)

ers. To remedy this situation, they chose Monterey as the site for the Hotel del Monte, the first western destination resort. Wealthy Easterners and Europeans were induced to visit by the prospect of a balmy climate and the magnificent grounds of this seaside resort. Hotel advertising heavily emphasized the year-round beauty of the gardens, and in 1881, Ulrich was hired to make this promise a reality. He landscaped the 126 acres that surrounded the hotel, bringing in plants from all over the world to create the necessary four seasons of garden interest. **Stephen Child** wrote in his 1927 publication, *Landscape Architecture, A Series of Letters,* that the hotel

grounds were "perhaps unexcelled in America." He believed this was due in part to Ulrich's long tenure at Del Monte, which ensured "the continuity of purpose in the consummation of well-studied plans."

The crown jewel of the Hotel del Monte property was the Arizona Garden, a design concept unique to Ulrich. A series of symmetrical beds were lushly stocked with a large assortment of cacti, succulents, and semitropical plants that Ulrich collected from the Sonoran Desert and points south, using the railroads to transport plants. (Southern Pacific owner Leland Stanford's Palo Alto Stock Farm also boasted one of these gardens.) Every hotel room had a view of the grounds. Ulrich surrounded the buildings with formal designs of mosaiculture and ribbon bedding. The axial East Garden was laid out in line with the hotel lobby, and continued down in a series of terraces to the large ornamental lake Ulrich created from the existing marsh. Formal landscaping gradually gave way to the native forest of Coast live oaks and Monterey pines, enhanced with a collection of exotic trees "from every country in the world." A hedge maze of Monterey cypress was topped with topiary chess pieces. Themed walks (Ivy Walk, Cypress Row, Sylvan Walk, and Lover's Lane) encouraged guests to explore the grounds. Two formal rose gardens were augmented with climbing roses trained up trees and trellises throughout the grounds.

During his employment by the railroad tycoons, Ulrich also designed the grounds of at least three other California resort hotels, at Pasadena, San Rafael, and Redondo Beach. His plan for Pasadena's Hotel Raymond included the adjacent residential tract. He was hired to design Mission Park Plaza in Santa Cruz, and to improve the appearance of St. James Park in San Jose. Ulrich also was awarded numerous private commissions from wealthy hotel guests and influential local residents. These ranged in scale from the 40-acre Edenvale estate at San Jose to the block-long grounds of Bishop Henry Warren's summer cottage at Santa Cruz. This latter connection soon brought Ulrich a larger commission and provided the transition to a new phase of his career.

In 1890, Bishop Warren recommended that Ulrich be hired to create landscape plans for the new Denver University grounds and its flanking residential neighborhood, the whole to be called University Park. The campus plan continued Ulrich's utilization of both formal and informal landscaping, including a hedge maze, formal parterres, and a lake encircled by shrubbery and curvilinear paths. The larger plan for the neighborhood included four smaller formal parks, a formula for "parking the streets and avenues" with trees, and the landscaping of the grounds of the Warrens' newly built mansion. A surviving photograph of the campus plan shows the first known instance of Ulrich adopting the title "landscape architect." While Ulrich initially expected the Denver job to be another long-term installation, justifying his resignation from the Del Monte, the changing economic climate resulted in the majority of this plan never being executed. Instead of moving to Colorado, Ulrich received and accepted an invitation to work under **Frederick Law Olmsted Sr.** as Superintendent of Grounds for the World's Columbian Exposition of 1893 in Chicago.

Leaving his family behind in Berkeley, Ulrich spent the next three years in Chicago, bringing Olmsted's plans to fruition. When Olmsted later spoke before the American Institute of Architects, he said of Ulrich, "We had seen the results of rapid work carried out under difficulties by him and formed a good opinion of his ability to meet emergencies." The Exposition's Director of Works, Daniel Burnham, was also impressed by Ulrich's abilities, and soon asked him to assume additional duties as Superintendent of the Miscellaneous Department, a division that handled jobs not readily assignable to any other departmental category. A year later, he was asked to take on the work of Superintendent of Roads as well. During the construction phase of this Exposition, Ulrich was supervising up to 500 men at any given time. These additional responsibilities were a source of friction with Olmsted, who wanted Ulrich's entire attention given to the landscape.

At the close of the Exposition, Ulrich was hired as General Superintendent of Parks for the city of Brooklyn, New York. The job was enormous, entailing the renovation of all the old park properties, and overseeing the construction of several new ones, but it was routine work for a man of Ulrich's experience. While land acquisitions doubled the total of park properties during this time, the firm of Olmsted, Olmsted & Eliot, hired as Advisory Landscape Architects, controlled all design work for the new parks as well as the old. At Prospect Park, laid out by Olmsted and **Calvert Vaux** in 1866, Ulrich made many improvements, but designed only a new rosery in the former Children's Playground (which displeased Olmsted) and an arboretum in front of the Institute of Arts & Sciences. After two years, Ulrich resigned his position at Brooklyn and eventually accepted an offer to landscape the Trans-Mississippi & International Exposition at Omaha, Nebraska. Ulrich's two designs at Prospect Park were completed by his successor, landscape architect J. A. Pettigrew, who added his own touches to the work.

In the fall of 1901, a Buffalo newspaper reported that Ulrich had received commissions in Paris, Canada, Indiana, Illinois, and Ohio. In 1902, he completed plans for landscaping Indiana State University at Bloomington and designed Maplewood Cemetery at Anderson, Indiana. In 1904, Ulrich was rehired by M. Theodore Kearney of Fresno, California, to give the finishing gloss to the grounds of his 240-acre estate, Chateau Fresno Park, first laid out by Ulrich in 1889. He spent some portion of the next three years making further additions to the grounds, including a hedge maze and what he described as "the finest and most expensive rose garden in California, if not in the United States." Unfortunately Kearney died in May 1906, and all work on the estate came to a halt. Ulrich died at San Diego the same year, on October 7. His body was shipped back to the family in Brooklyn, New York.

Cain, Julie. "Landscaping the Gilded Age: Rudolph Ulrich at Monterey's Hotel del Monte, 1880–1890." *Noticias del Puerto de Monterey, Journal of the Monterey History and Art Association* 33, no. 3 (Fall 2004), 2–57.

Cain, Julie, and Marlea Graham. "Rudolph Ulrich on the San Francisco Peninsula." *Eden, Journal of the California Garden & Landscape History Society* 6, no. 3 (Fall 2003), 1–8.

Graham, Marlea. "The Rose Garden at Chateau Fresno." *Eden, Journal of the California Garden & Landscape History Society* 8, no. 1 (Spring 2005), 6–10.

Julie Cain and Marlea Graham

VAUGHAN, HOLLYNGSWORTH LELAND
(1905–1974)
LANDSCAPE ARCHITECT, EDUCATOR

VAUGHAN, ADELE WHARTON
(1916–1955)
LANDSCAPE ARCHITECT

Hollyngsworth Leland Vaughan was born in 1905 in Alliance, Ohio. His parents, both teachers, instilled in him an open attitude to learning, which later guided his own teaching career. He completed three years of study at Mount Union College in his hometown, and then went on to complete his bachelor's degree in landscape architecture at Ohio State University in 1929. At the university, Vaughan studied with **Thomas Dolliver Church**, who taught there from 1927 to 1929. Following his graduation, Vaughan continued his studies as a Fellow at the Lake Forest Foundation in Lake Forest, Illinois, and further enhanced his education through extensive travel in Europe. From his travels in Italy, France, and Spain, Vaughan developed an early affinity for the similar northern California climate and landscape, just as his mentor, Thomas Church, a Sheldon Traveling Fellow in 1927, recognized and studied. Following his studies, Vaughan eventually settled in California in the early 1930s. Both his home in Point Richmond and his vacation retreat on the Mendocino Coast embodied the special feelings Vaughan felt for the region and were open to his students, colleagues, and friends.

As an educator and university professor, as well as a civic activist and professional landscape architect, Punk Vaughan, as he was referred to by his friends and colleagues, was generous, patient, and self-assured. Rather than impressing his own ideas upon his students, he encouraged innovation and individualistic courses of

H. Leland Vaughan, undated photograph. (H. Leland and Adele W. Vaughn Collection [1999-18], Environmental Design Archives, University of California, Berkeley)

academic and professional development. One of his students, Michael Laurie, remembers him as "a young maverick, an inspiring teacher, who encouraged his students to keep an open mind and to form their own opinions." A number of promising landscape architecture students passed through the University of California, Berkeley, program during Vaughan's long career, including Garrett Eckbo* (B.S., 1935), Robert Royston* (B.S., 1940), Kathryn

An example of the Vaughans' residential design work is this rendered garden plan for the residence of Mr. and Mrs. J. O. Turner, Berkeley, California, 1939. (H. Leland and Adele W. Vaughn Collection [1999-18], Environmental Design Archives, University of California, Berkeley)

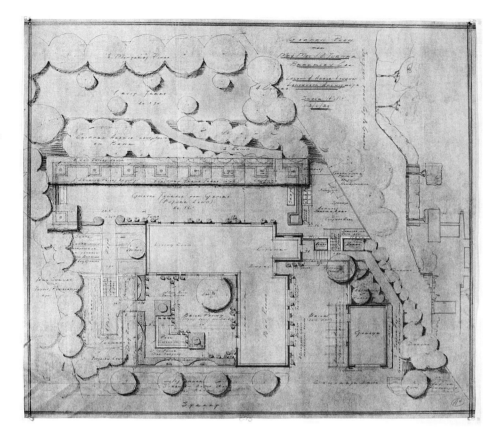

Imlay (B.S., 1946), Asa Hanamoto (B.S., 1950), Robert Tetlow (M.S., 1951), and Mai Arbegast (M.S., 1953).

A landscape architecture professor at the University of California, Berkeley, from 1930 to 1969, including emeritus status, Vaughan was particularly instrumental in guiding the department's critical years of growth from 1947 to 1962, serving as departmental chairman. During these years he increased faculty size and introduced the first visiting lecturers to the department. He also helped establish the Department of City and Regional Planning in the late 1940s and the comprehensive College of Environmental Design in 1959. Prior to his retirement in 1969, Vaughan served several years as assistant dean of the College of Environmental Design. Professor Vaughan was also responsible for securing **Beatrix Jones Farrand**'s papers and her Reef Point Collection for the university, as well as a large endowment that continues to support student scholarships and research in the field today.

Concurrent with his teaching, Vaughan practiced in the private sector, initially with F. H. Mick in Oakland, from 1930 to 1931, and then with Thomas Church's office from 1931 to 1945. Some of the landscape projects that he was associated with in California include Park Merced in San Francisco with Church in 1942; the Federal War Housing program, and the Richmond Civic Center in 1949; as well as the University of California at Berkeley campus projects: Fernwald Dormitories in 1948, and the Alumni House with Lawrence Halprin,* in 1954. Many of his residential projects were collaborations with his wife, Adele Wharton, who received her bachelor of science degree in landscape architecture from the University of California at Berkeley, in 1937, and her master of science from the same department in 1938. Adele's student work, specimens of which are held by the Environmental Design Archives at the university, reveal a strong resemblance to the many drawings and plans designed by the Vaughan team, therefore suggesting that Adele ran the private practice while her husband concentrated on his academic responsibilities.

H. Leland Vaughan was an active member of the

California Association of Landscape Architects and the American Society of Landscape Architects. He was elected a Fellow to the latter in 1954. In other professional-related service, Vaughan was chairman of the education committee of the International Federation of Landscape Architects, a member of the American Planning and Civic Association, a member of the National Shade Tree Conference, a member of the American Association of University Professors, an advisor for the California Spring Garden Show, a trustee for the Nature Conservancy, a board member of the Saratoga Horticulture Foundation, a member of the California State Outdoor Recreation Planning committee, and a member of the Bohemian Club. For this last organization, Vaughan helped redesign its wooded retreat, the Bohemian Grove, in Monte Rio, California. In addition to his professional activities, Vaughan took an active role in civic activities contributing an innovative and liberal perspective; he was a member of the City Planning Commission and the Parks and Recreation Commission of Richmond.

Adele Wharton Vaughn died in 1955, and H. Leland Vaughn died in 1974.

The H. Leland Vaughan and Adele W. Vaughan Collection [1999–18], in the Environmental Design Archives, University of California, Berkeley (with a finding aid and project index available online at www.ced .berkeley.edu/cedarchives/), spans the years 1931–1955 and contains records relating to the couple's professional partnership as landscape architects. Included are project files, drawings, and photographs. Projects by Thomas Church and in collaboration with Church are also included. The collection is divided into two series: Professional Papers and Project Records. The College of Environmental Design also houses a collection of student work, at the Environmental Design Archives, and includes some student work by Adele Wharton (March 1938), wife of H. Leland Vaughan.

Biographical Record compiled by R. B. Litton for the American Society of Landscape Architects, 1977. A copy is housed at the Environmental Design Archives, University of California, Berkeley.
Laurie, Michael. *75 Years of Landscape Architecture at Berkeley. Part I: The First 50 Years.* Berkeley: Department of Landscape Architecture, University of California, 1988. A history of the landscape architecture program at the University of California, Laurie's study includes many notes on Vaughan's teaching and professional career.
Violich, Francis, Michael M. Laurie, and R. Burton Little Jr. "Hollysworth Leland Vaughan, 1905–1974, Professor of Landscape Architecture, Emeritus [obituary]" *In Memoriam.* The University of California, 1976, 125–127.

Carrie Leah McDade

VICK, JAMES
(1818–1882)
SEEDSMAN, HORTICULTURIST, NURSERY OWNER, PUBLISHER, WRITER

James Vick was born in Chichester, near Portsmouth, in the south of England on November 23, 1818. In 1833, at the age of fifteen, he and his family immigrated to America. Arriving in New York City, Vick was soon hired as a typesetter at the *Knickerbocker Magazine,* a small journal that celebrated the rural nature of the New York countryside, thus beginning his twenty-year career in the publishing industry. After three years working with Horace Greeley, Vick left New York City for Rochester, New York, where he promoted liberal social causes in his work for newspapers and magazines, including the *Democrat and Chronicle, Workingman's Advocate,* and Frederick Douglass's *The North Star.*

In 1842, Vick married Mary Elizabeth Seelye. Mary, a quiet and deeply religious woman, was very influential in many aspects of Vick's life. When he turned to retail seed enterprises in the late 1850s, his pious nature was strongly reflected in his work. Vick's ability to convey a righteous overtone to the marketing of his flower seeds appealed to the middle-class suburban homeowner during an era when formalized religion was at its height. It was also through his association with the Seelye family that Vick increased his interest in and knowledge of horticulture: Mary's brother Charles W. Seelye had established Rochester Central Nurseries in 1844. Seelye, an accomplished garden artist, would go on to serve as an occasional editor for Vick's periodical, *Vick's Illustrated Monthly Magazine.*

Late in 1852, Vick bought *The Horticulturist,* a journal that had previously been edited by **Andrew Jackson Downing,** the famous aesthete and landscape gardener, whose untimely death in 1852 left the editorial position vacant. Vick hired **Patrick Barry,** a prominent local horticulturist, to assume the role of horticultural editor at

James Vick, from *Vick's Illustrated Monthly Magazine,* January 1878.

the magazine and Alexander J. Davis, the well-known architect, as architectural editor. This was Vick's first real experience with a publication in the field of ornamental design. *The Horticulturist*'s consumer base was comprised of middle-class suburban homeowners—the target of Vick's business endeavors. But only two years later, under pressure from the rising cost of publication, Vick sold *The Horticulturist* to Robert Pearsall Smith of Philadelphia. In 1856, Vick published the *Rural Annual and Horticultural Directory.* This too was unsuccessful and he sold it after one year.

Vick began experimenting with seed propagation during the late 1840s at his home on Union Street in Rochester. His first excursion into seed propagation was a small affair, growing the plants in his backyard and packaging the seeds in his attic. He purchased some of his seeds from France in 1848 and in 1856 first advertised French vegetable and flower seeds in the *Genesee Farmer.* Unlike many seed companies, which were paid only upon the receipt of the seeds ordered, Vick organized his business so that only "envelopes containing money" would receive the ordered seeds. This policy transferred

the risk associated with the failure of the seeds to germinate to the customer, and insured that he did not lose money to nonpayment.

By 1862, his business of growing flowers, both annuals and perennials for seed, was consuming so much of his time that he quit his position as horticultural editor at the *Rural New Yorker* and began his seed business in earnest. That year he began publication of his seed catalog, *Vick's Illustrated Catalogue and Floral Guide,* issued twice annually. Although the earliest catalogs were merely price lists, they soon developed into much more extensive publications, self-proclaimed manuals for the novice gardener. The plants, annuals, perennials, and ornamental grasses were divided into categories, based on their potential use in the landscape. With the publication of his catalog, almost all of his business was conducted by mail order, as opposed to local distributors. In 1866, Vick sent out over 20,000 packages of seeds to more than 16,000 customers. By this point he was both importing seeds from Germany, France, and England and growing seeds himself. The seeds averaged about five to twenty-five cents per package. Though novelties, flowers recently introduced or rare often sold for four to five times the normal price.

In 1866, Vick purchased the Union Tavern and established 35 acres of flowerbeds along East Avenue, then just outside the Rochester city limits. Here he built his family house and lived with his wife Mary, their eight children, Vick's mother and father, and assorted nephews who apprenticed with Vick in the seed business. Although the property was not designed for show, the mere numbers of plants created a spectacle that the Vick firm used to its advantage in advertising.

After only a few years, the area around Vick's business had grown up remarkably with upper-middle-class homes, and finding that the 35 acres were not large enough to support his industry Vick was forced to establish another farm further from the city core, in Greece, 5 miles north of Rochester near the Lake Ontario shore. By 1870, about 140,000 catalogs were printed, with arrangements made for printing nearly 200,000 during 1871. In 1875, he introduced garden related items into his catalogs, including iron hedge-hog boot scrapers, lawn mowers, vases, and plant stands.

Around 1869, Vick purchased a four-story building on Mill Street in Rochester and set up his seed warehouse. A few years later—finding this building too small—he built a warehouse on State Street. At the height of the business, he employed more than 100 people. The building was

Vick home and flower fields in Rochester, New York, from *Vick's Illustrated Catalogue and Floral Guide* for 1877.

five stories, including the basement, and filled the entire block, containing everything from the printing press to the seeds themselves. The exterior of the structure was typical of the time period, an Italianate brick commercial building with an arcade of fluted Corinthian columns and plate glass windows on the first story. Vick organized and oversaw all aspects of his enterprise, from the importation of bulbs and seeds to the publication of his journals and catalogs. By doing these things, he was able to decrease the cost of shipment and ensure the quality of his product—at least according to the advertising copy.

The building's cool basement was ideally suited for the storage of bulbs, coarse seeds, and tubers; additionally, it was used for packing heavy shipments. The first floor, known as "Floral Hall," was dedicated to retail sales. The second floor was dedicated to packing and shipping. The third was devoted to publishing the German editions of Vick's catalogs (entitled *Vick's Blumen Furhrer*). The printing and bindery operations were located on the fourth floor. Here artists and typesetters created the catalogs and the chromolithograph plates that were offered as subscription bonuses and as retail items. The invention of the chromolithographs aided Vick immensely in his advertising. Lithographs, printed from ink applied to the surface of a smooth chemically treated stone, proved to be much cheaper to produce than earlier steel engravings or woodcuts. Vick quickly took advantage of the new technology, publishing a chromolithograph in his 1864 catalog, one of the earliest uses of such technology in the publication of a seed catalog.

In 1878, with his seed business well established, Vick started his monthly periodical, *Vick's Illustrated Monthly Magazine.* The aim of the journal unlike that of earlier widely published American periodicals was to increase the general practice of ornamental flower gardening; increasing a love of flowers would sell more seeds. *Vick's Illustrated Monthly,* at $1.25 per annum, was inexpensive. In contrast *The Horticulturalist,* Vick's first publication venture, sold for twice as much twenty years earlier. Vick was determined to reach as broad a readership as possible, comprised of people who could afford to purchase his seeds.

Vick's Illustrated Monthly Magazine combined the formats of two of the most widely read horticultural periodicals in America at the time, Downing's *The Horticulturist* and Thomas Meehan's *Gardener's Monthly.* In every month's introductory article, Vick adopted the genteel voice of Downing in his self-proclaimed moral quest to achieve the Beautiful. Vick mimicked the practical organization of *Gardener's Monthly* by dividing the text of *Vick's Illustrated Monthly* into subheadings that allowed for quick reference and was easily used by the amateur gardener; later journals such as *American Gardener* followed this format. Each issue of *Vick's* began with a colored plate of one of the flowers for sale, engraved and painted expressly for the monthly. His audience, consisting mainly of women, would write in to share gardening experiences and design ideas from New York to Oregon.

James Vick died of pneumonia at the age of sixty-four on May 16, 1882. However, gardeners from across the country continued to address their correspondence to Vick at *Vick's Illustrated Monthly Magazine* until 1909 when the journal was discontinued. The Vick seed com-

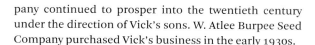

pany continued to prosper into the twentieth century under the direction of Vick's sons. W. Atlee Burpee Seed Company purchased Vick's business in the early 1930s.

Hanna, Jennifer. "Cultivating the Amateur Gardener: James Vick, Seedsman and Editor." *Journal of the New England Garden History Society,* Fall 2001. An article summarizing the life and work of James Vick, providing detailed woodcut illustrations of the mid-ninetenth-century technological processes used in the publication of his periodical and his seed business.
Vick's Illustrated Catalogue and Floral Guide. Published bi-annually 1862 to 1873; published quarterly until 1887. The catalog grew quickly from a simple price list of available seed to a self-proclaimed manual for the novice gardener, including extensive, opinionated descriptions of plants organized by their potential use in the landscape.
Vick's Illustrated Monthly. James Vick and James Vick's Sons, Rochester, New York, 1878–1909. Published and edited by James Vick Sr. until his death in 1882, the magazine was created to teach the public about the art of flowers and the joy of gardening and thus increase the number of seed packets sold. The magazine was one of the first and largest journals to be devoted solely to ornamental gardening.

Jennifer Hanna Reive

WEBEL, RICHARD K.
(1900–2000)
LANDSCAPE ARCHITECT

Richard Webel, born in Frankenthal, Germany, in 1900, but raised from his first year in Washington, D.C., studied the fine arts in his youth and continued to do so as a Harvard College undergraduate. Upon the recommendation of a career adviser, he continued on to Harvard's School of Landscape Architecture, matriculating as part of the class of 1926. There, his outstanding drawing abilities, keen eye, and confident demeanor propelled him to the top of his class.

Webel studied at Harvard during a period of strenuous but ultimately pointless debate over fidelity to two "opposing" manners of organizing landscapes. One was rooted in French and Italian references and generally symmetrical or axial organization in plan; the other tended to suppress fixed geometries by arranging vegetation irregularly according to naturalistic principles, deriving from compositions more familiar from well-known British precedents. Webel's school projects favored symmetry, but he also converged these tendencies—and generally proved the folly of seeing them as distinct. In his thesis work, he examined published theories of pictorialism and empathy in art and speculated on their application to axial organization and sequence in landscape design.

Upon graduation, he received Harvard's Sheldon Traveling Fellowship and the Rome Prize in Landscape Architecture. His travels to gardens and his production of carefully measured drawings of villas while living at the American Academy in Rome legitimized the authority of

Richard Webel (*highlighted, fifth from front*) at the ASLA Conference dinner, 1936. (Courtesy of Charles A. Birnbaum)

the traditions explored in his thesis. Moreover, his precisely executed watercolor plans of Italian Renaissance and Baroque gardens show ample evidence that these precedents incorporated overlapping and varied design languages and never depended on a singular design rhetoric. Webel adhered to this convergence in his professional work for decades to come.

Forecourt of Evelyn Marshall Field residence, Syosset, New York, 1936. (Samuel Gottscho, photographer; Library of Congress, Prints and Photographs division, Gottscho-Schleisner Collection [LC-G612-27378])

During the summers between academic years, Webel worked as an intern in the office of **Warren Henry Manning** in Boston and in the office of **Bremer Whidden Pond**. Upon return from the three-year fellowship in Rome, he began an apprenticeship at the prominent New York firm, Vitale & Geiffert. Here he became chief designer for many of the firm's projects, working with **Ferruccio Vitale** and **Alfred Geiffert Jr.** on public and private commissions. From Vitale, Webel learned much about professional practice and the value of cultivating successful client relationships—socially and professionally. Geiffert's influence came more directly in the discipline of analytical topographic studies and the testing of alternative approaches to evolving plans for each site. Webel also met **Umberto Innocenti** at Vitale & Geiffert; Innocenti was responsible for implementing the firm's estate projects and developed great expertise in horticulture and construction. When Vitale's work load became significantly reduced in 1930 due to the failing economy, Webel and Innocenti secured several commissions and started their own firm in the Long Island studio of the sculptor John Whitney Hay.

Innocenti & Webel became widely known for a series of gardens for private clients during the 1930s. This work was well documented for promotional reasons and the carefully staged photographs demonstrate a consistent

and practiced design language. Built from the belief that a shifting pictorial view is the primary device of landscape experience, the projects were shaped by large formal gestures, always conceived in plan, often axial in organization. Other common characteristics include long single or multiple rows of trees; clear and simple shapes—arcs or hemicycles or compartment squares or rectangles, sometimes with chamfered corners; and typically shaped with symmetrical terraces, balustrades, and stairs borrowed from Baroque gardens, at times distorted to fit irregularly shaped sites or architectural conditions. Departures from symmetry were rare. Many of the works included references to European garden iconography in features such as brick piers and ornamental gates, water jets or quiet fonts, urns, bronze birds, and other objects that punctuated and amplified the traditional flavor.

These gardens, exemplified by the commissions for wealthy Long Island clients such as Robert Winthrop, Howard Phipps, and Mrs. Evelyn Marshall Field, achieved an Old World, aristocratic feel almost immediately upon completion. Though they were smaller and simpler than the colossal estate projects of the previous generation of landscape architects such as the **Olmsted Brothers**, **Samuel Parsons Jr.**, and Vitale, they achieved for their clients a kind of decorum of space and maturity of landscape character that suited their family legacies, if more modestly than that of their forebears. This first decade of the partnership's finely executed works drew most assiduously on the combination of Webel's skill at adapting traditional formal devices and Innocenti's deep knowledge of planting, soils, and landscape construction. It was an attitude they would carry beyond the estate garden into the challenging new commissions of the post-Depression and post–World War II periods.

Janet Darling, a young landscape architect who joined the office in the 1940s, married Richard Webel and worked in the practice in Long Island for many years. (Janet Darling Webel later opened her own practice in New York City, where she worked independently on commissions for public housing projects, schools, and residences. She died in 1966.)

During the late 1940s and 1950s, Webel pursued new project types including the design of small prototype gardens associated with mass-produced contemporary housing. He also took on commissions for corporate headquarters, newly developed suburban college campuses, airports, cemeteries, retirement communities, resort hotels, and public spaces. Projects from this period include two pavilions for the 1939 World's Fair in New York; the American Cemetery in Ardennes, Belgium; Doubleday headquarters in Garden City, Long Island; the new campus of Furman University (completed with architects Perry, Shaw and Hepburn, Kehoe and Dean) in Greenville, South Carolina; headquarters for the Reader's Digest Association in Pleasantville, New York; the Greenbrier Hotel in White Sulphur Springs, West Virginia; the corporate headquarters of Milliken & Company (with SOM as architects), in Spartanburg, South Caroina; Keeneland Raceway in Lexington, Kentucky; the Greenville-Spartanburg Airport (with SOM) in Greer, South Carolina; Damrosch Park in New York's Lincoln Center; studies for the Mall and associated spaces for the U.S. Commission of Fine Arts in the nation's capital; and

Villa Dona Dalle Rose near Padua, Italy, measured drawing, watercolor on paper, by Richard K. Webel, 1928. (Courtesy of Gary Hilderbrand)

the planning and design of dozens of homes in the retirement communities of Hobe Sound and Jupiter Island in Florida.

Innocenti & Webel received recognition throughout the long period of their partnership, which lasted until Innocenti died in 1968. Webel published two small guidebooks of European Gardens under the imprint of the Garden Club of America, his American Academy fellowship sponsor, in 1930. Several of the firm's designs for estates and homes appeared in published garden compilations by Joseph Howland and James Marston

Fitch. During the 1950s, Webel participated in competitions and expositions of newer house types in land subdivisions and new corporate projects in publications including *Architectural Record, House and Garden, House Beautiful, Horticulture, American Nurseryman,* and *Landscape Architecture.* He was profiled in *Town and Country* in 1980, and the work of his firm continued to be published in *Garden Design* throughout the 1980s. In 1997, an exhibition of Webel's Rome watercolors, along with vintage and contemporary photographs and plans of the firm's work, was mounted at Harvard and at the American Academy in Rome's New York gallery space.

Webel's career demonstrated a deliberate consistency of spatial approach—a reliably simple formal repertoire that he believed worked at every scale of experience. A believer in loyalty and professional service, his client relationships sometimes lasted for three or four decades. Another consistent trait, also simple but more profoundly enduring, is evidenced in the projects themselves: Webel's dedication to structuring and ordering space with trees, in large numbers and single species, carefully matched and beautifully spaced. The spatial beauty that was realized in many of the projects is abundantly evident, and seems sustainable by any measure, now fifty or more years later.

Webel had an exceptionally long career as principal of Innocenti & Webel, working with institutions, corporations, landowners, and homeowners, finally retiring in his mid-nineties. He died in 2000, four months past his one-hundredth birthday. His firm continues to practice as Innocenti & Webel.

Because the firm still practices in Locust Valley, Long Island, Innocenti & Webel retains the record of their work. However, many original drawings, photographs, typescripts, and ephemera related to key projects up to the 1960s are housed in the Special Collections of the Frances Loeb Library, Harvard University Graduate School of Design. Photographs of Innocenti gardens by Samuel Gottscho, from 1931 through the mid-1950s, may also be viewed in the collections of the Avery Library, Columbia University.

Architecture and Design. "This issue devoted to the work of Umberto Innocenti and Richard K. Webel, Landscape Architects." New York: Architectural Catalog, 1937. A volume, in the format of a firm portfolio or monograph, reproduces outstanding photographs by Samuel Gottscho of the firm's projects.

Fitch, James Marston, and F. F. Rockwell. *Treasury of American Gardens.* New York: Harper Brothers, 1956, 40–41, 57–59, 65–67, 71, 150–152. Features several projects by the firm, including the residences of both Webel and Innocenti, among a broad survey of traditional and contemporary American gardens.

Hilderbrand, Gary R. *Making a Landscape of Continuity: The Practice of Innocenti & Webel.* Cambridge, Mass.: Harvard Graduate School of Design and Princeton Architectural Press, 1997. A monograph to the 1997 exhibition on the firm; includes essays on its practices, a catalog of major projects, chronology, complete list of commissions, and bibliography.

Gary R. Hilderbrand

WEST, JAMES ROY
(1880–1941)
LANDSCAPE ARCHITECT

James Roy West was born in 1880. West's family had moved from Montreal, Canada, eight years before his birth, to a large frame house in the neighborhood of Lakeside, now Hubbard Woods in Winnetka, Illinois. He would live in this same house for his entire life. His father owned the largest personal library in town, and required his children to learn Latin, Greek, French, Spanish, and German. West grew up with neighbors such as future architects Marion Mahony and her cousin Dwight Perkins, and nationally influential figures including Harold Ickes and Henry Demarest Lloyd.

After going to a local elementary school, West attended the Chicago Manual Training School. Founded by the Chicago Commercial Club in 1882, with a board of trustees that included such notable Chicagoans as Marshall Field, George Pullman, Martin Ryerson, and Charles L. Hutchinson, the school's focus was on literature, science, and drawing for industrial purposes. It offered architectural drawing during the senior year. West's fellow students included architect Joseph Lyman Silsbee, and David Lloyd and Henry Demarest Lloyd Jr.

Graduating in 1898, he began an internship with **Ossian Cole Simonds**, serving as an apprentice on Graceland Cemetery in Chicago, learning landscape design on the job. He would spend his entire career with Simonds's firm, becoming a partner in 1925. The company name then became Simonds and West, Landscape Designers. A congenial man who was known for mentoring new

McPherson Holt garden, Lake Forest, Illinois, circa 1930. (Smithsonian Institution, Archives of American Gardens, Garden Club of America Collection)

staff members, West handled many of the company's major projects, but because projects were signed with only the firm's name, there is often no clear distinction between Simonds's and West's work.

West assumed the company's daily management in the 1920s, continuing the naturalistic design principles and planting traditions of Simonds who, because of failing health, had begun to spend his winters in Florida. Pragmatically, West was willing to change with the times, and although he had long believed that "wild portions" of the garden should go right up to the walls of a house, West and junior partner Erle O. Blair began to create terraces and formal outdoor spaces for clients in the mid-1920s.

West was a principal for scores of projects that included the more than 4,000-acre Sinnissippi estate of Frank and Florence Pullman Lowden; the Belle Meade Farm subdivision in Nashville, Tennessee; many country clubs including the Indian Hill Club in his home town of Winnetka; and the Mount Auburn Cemetery in Summit, Illinois. In 1930, his project list included a wooded ravine for *Janesville Gazette* owner H. H. Bliss in Wisconsin; a sanatorium in Muskegon, Michigan; and St. Mary's Church in Freeport, Illinois. He also designed estates for Arthur Marks in Palm Beach, Florida; Bar Harbor, Maine; and Westchester County, New York. He had numerous residential commissions along Chicago's North Shore, including several in Hubbard Woods, the Kuppenheimer estate in central Winnetka, the McPherson Holt Arts and Crafts cottage and the Whipple house, by architect Russell Walcott, in Lake Forest, as well as civic work for Lake Forest High School and Public Library.

West continued to be influenced by Simonds through-

out his career. West moved mature trees with heavy tops for clients, a trademark planting effect of the Simonds's firm. West continued to educate himself, frequenting a variety of cultural venues. After attending **Fletcher Steele**'s talk "The Modern Tendencies in Garden Design" at the Fortnightly Club in February of 1930, West reminisced about his early assignments from Simonds, for which he wore overalls and carried a hoe on a streetcar in downtown Chicago to go to such upscale sites as the Newberry Library and Bryan Lathrop's mansion, which became the Fortnightly Club.

Another major project for West and Blair in 1930 was the development of the Skokie Road from Chicago to Glencoe. Initially employed to provide planting advice for a narrow margin along the roadside, the firm also consulted with the developers regarding the nature of the entire highway, and adapted the native forest preserves along the Skokie River at the northern portion into picturesque scenery. Within a few years, the Civilian Conservation Corps would channel this marshy river into lagoons, which, thanks to West's early planning, are still visible from the road today.

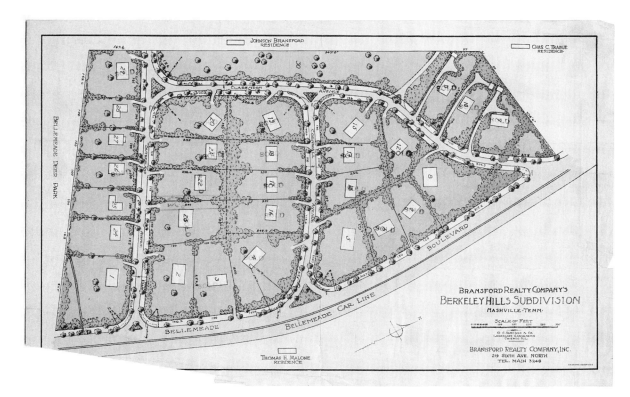

Above: One of many Simonds and West subdivision plans is the plan of Berkeley Hills, Waddey Subdivision, Nashville, Tennessee, 1920. (Courtesy of the Tennessee State Library and Archives)

Below: Belle Meade Farm subdivision, Nashville, Tennessee, 2006 view. (Photo by Charles A. Birnbaum, courtesy of The Cultural Landscape Foundation)

West held a lifelong interest in the natural environment, native plants, and in Chicago culture. He was a founding member of the Prairie Club with **Jens Jensen,** Dwight Perkins, and Simonds's daughter Gertrude, and served as an early officer. He was also a director of the Playground Association, a Winnetka Park District commissioner, and was a member of the Chicago Regional Planning Association and Friends of Our Native Landscape. The American Society of Landscape Architects made West a Fellow in 1939; he also belonged to the American Forestry Association, American Iris Society, American Rose Society, Chicago Academy of Sciences, Field Museum, the Cliff Dwellers, Art Institute of Chicago, and the Norge Club. A bachelor who lived with his siblings and nieces and nephews, West took a brotherly interest in fostering an appreciation of nature in young people through many of these organizations.

West's letters show his gentle sense of

Water fowl sanctuary, Brookwood Farm, Mentor, Ohio, by Simonds, West and Blair, from ASLA *Illustrations of Work of Members*, 1934.

humor, in which he described one client's property as being "such an uneven piece that nobody . . . had the temerity to build on it and it escaped the expansion of the city which has grown about it." Referring to his own blood pressure, West described it as "too high for even this fast jazz age." And his account of the Cliff Dwellers annual meeting noted that the event included "much singing and real old time comradeship . . . helped along . . . by a beautiful silver bowl. . . . Its contents had a kick in it."

Also apparent is the enduring regard between West and "Mr. Simonds," as West always addressed him, who sent West fresh apples from his orchard in Michigan every fall and oranges from Florida in the winter. West had a special cold cellar built onto to his house to properly store the fruit, and used his own heavily wooded property to try out new plants and ideas for his clients. For Roy West, his pleasure in nature and people provided a base for creating a career and personal life that flowed together naturally, and influenced the conservation of native Midwest landscapes that citizens still enjoy. West died at his home in Hubbard Woods on November 25, 1941.

Harnsberger, Caroline Thomas. *Winnetka: The Biography of A Village.* Evanston, Ill.: Schori Press, 1977, 157–58. References to West's contributions to the Winnetka landscape.

"J. Roy West: A Biographical Minute." *Landscape Architecture* 32, no. 3 (April 1942), 120–21. A short summary of West's career accomplishments.

Obituary. *Winnetka Talk,* November 27, 1941, p. 67.

Barbara Geiger

WEST, MYRON HOWARD
(1880–1960)
LANDSCAPE ARCHITECT, ENGINEER, PLANNER

Myron Howard West was born on December 19, 1880, in Belchertown, Massachusetts. His parents were Marietta Cady and Howard Chauncey West. Myron Howard West graduated from Belchertown High School in 1899. He went on to earn degrees from Massachusetts Agricultural College (now the University of Massachusetts at Amherst) in 1903 and Boston University in 1904. He had degrees in both landscape architecture and engineering and took some of the first courses offered in city planning.

West was trained in the discipline of landscape architecture by Professor **Frank Albert Waugh**, who in 1902 established the Landscape Department at the Massachusetts Agricultural College in Amherst. This was only the second such formal landscape gardening program in the nation. Waugh taught that certain design principles—the entrance, points of interest, and the finale—were essential in park design. As a student of Waugh, West incorporated these concepts into his work throughout his prolific career. West was also a musician and, like his mentor, Frank Waugh, who was known for his love of music, used music to inspire landscape design.

Aerial postcard view of City Park Lake, Baton Rouge, Louisiana, before development, 1929.

West began his professional career as the chief engineer on Keney Park, the Olmsted, Olmsted & Eliot–designed landscape (**Frederick Law Olmstead Sr.**, **John Charles Olmstead**, and **Charles Eliot**) in Hartford, Connecticut. In October of 1905, West married his high school sweetheart, Rachel Curtis of Belchertown. That same year, West moved to Chicago where the city planner, Daniel H. Burnham, was drawing up his Chicago plan, now known as the Burnham Plan. When Burnham learned that West had formal education in city planning, he called upon him for service. West became the general superintendent and secretary of the Lincoln Park System in Chicago, serving during the years 1906 to 1912.

When West arrived in Chicago in 1905, much of Chicago's renowned lakefront was under water. A breakwater extended east and south from Oak Street, and the area within was used as a city dump. The eventual development of this area into parklands and handsome business property was largely through the efforts of West, who planned extensively for Chicago's twentieth-century growth. West became general superintendent of the Lincoln Park system. He was in charge of building the

northern extension of 270 acres along the shore of Lake Michigan. He also planned and supervised the installation of the playground system, the paving and rejuvenation of Lincoln Park proper, and the erection of many buildings, including the zoo.

Myron West's theory was to plan for growth. West was an early proponent of zoning and in one of his many lectures on the subject he said, "Many city planners plan only for a city as it is. They don't take into account the fact that a city soon grows." The idea of planning for growth became a religion for West. He gave one of the first lectures on the subject of zoning in the United States.

West was among the first city planners to take advantage of an Illinois law passed in 1923 that governed regional city planning. Under this law, he prepared comprehensive city plans for Decatur and Springfield that went beyond the city limits and planned for future growth. West believed that city planning was unworthy of the name unless it provided for the future of the city in question and therefore qualified more accurately as regional planning.

West founded the American Park Builders, Inc., a professional corporation for the practice of city planning and landscape architecture that operated from 1912 until 1932. He continued to work extensively in Chicago, but his professional endeavors were not limited to that city. The business was devoted to the designing of comprehensive city plans, subdivisions, country clubs, golf courses, city park systems, and cemeteries throughout the United States and Canada. West noted in a 1926 company publication that he had developed city plans and large landscape projects worth millions of dollars throughout the entire country, including such cities as Auburn, Maine; Lincoln, Nebraska; Poughkeepsie, New York; St. Augustine Florida; Beloit, Wisconsin; Mobile, Alabama; and Springfield, Illinois.

City Park Golf Course, Baton Rouge, Louisiana, 2005 view. (Photo by Charles A. Birnbaum)

Many of the company's golf courses were designed by Tom Bendelow,* a noted golf course architect. Medina and Olympia Fields, renowned golf courses in Illinois, were among these projects. City Park in Baton Rouge, Louisiana, was established in 1928 as a project of West/Bendelow and the American Park Builders, Inc. It includes a nine-hole golf course that is now listed in the National Register of Historic Places. A list of over 200 parks and golf courses by American Park Builders, Inc, can be documented.

Golf courses were of particular interest to West as American's interest in the sport exploded and its popularity in the 1910s and 1920s was instantaneous. Through American Park Builders, Inc., West developed a comprehensive operation for a community to organize and establish a stand-alone park or one that would include a golf club, golf course, and club house. He had an exceptional staff of professionally trained architects, designers, and engineers who were all specialists in their fields. He marketed his company's organizational, landscape, and golf-course design expertise to cities and municipalities throughout the nation. In advocating for a golf course for one community, West wrote, "Golf tunes the muscles, makes the mind keener, develops the highest in sportsmanship, engenders a delightful social contact and brings about the fullest appreciation of the beautiful out-of-doors; it builds up broken arches, reduces obesity, cures indigestion, retards senility and is good for the soul."

Unfortunately, by 1937, the Depression took its toll on the building and expansion of America's private and municipal parks. West was forced to close his company. He retired to his home in Wilmette, Illinois, on the shores of Lake Michigan but maintained a limited, prestigious consulting practice with cities and corporations. He was always anxious to demonstrate that landscape architecture consisted of more than "fixing grounds and setting out flower beds." He died in Wilmette of heart disease in 1960, just one day shy of his fifty-fifth wedding anniversary. He is buried in Mount Hope Cemetery in Belchertown, Massachusetts. At the time of his death, he was survived by his widow, Rachel, one son, Myron Howard West Jr., and two grandchildren.

Bruce, Marjorie. "Wilmette's Myron West Lifted Chicago Shore Out of Water: Landscape Architect Recalls Activities at Turn of Century." *Wilmette Life,* September 6, 1951. Focuses on a fifty-year recollection of Myron West's career.

Waugh, Frank A. *Landscape Gardening: Treatise on the General Principles Governing Outdoor Art.* New York: Orange Judd Co., 1902. Waugh's retrospective of a personal philosophy on outdoor gardening as an art form.

West, Myron Howard. *The Story of the American Park Builders.* Chicago: American Park Builders Inc., 1926. A lengthy text-based promotional booklet used by the American Park Builders, Inc, to describe its turnkey municipal-park design services. An addendum includes an extended list of golf courses designed by Tom Bendelow.

Lillie Petit Gallagher

WHEELER, PERRY HUNT
(1913–1989)
LANDSCAPE ARCHITECT

Perry Hunt Wheeler was born on October 5, 1913. He lived with his parents, Sarah H. and John L. Wheeler; a sister, Pauline; and a brother, John L. Jr., on a small farm in Cordele, Georgia, a flourishing railroad town.

Wheeler pursued his education at Emory University, transferring to the University of Georgia to attain a bachelor of fine arts degree in 1937. Here, he met Helen Hawkins Clarke.* After receiving a landscape architecture degree at Harvard Graduate School in 1938, Wheeler entered a partnership with Clarke in Atlanta. One of their landscape plans shows a paved tile terrace near a client's house and a children's play yard on the upper terrace. Walls, plantings, and terraced land separated each utilitarian space.

World War II interrupted Wheeler and Clarke's partnership as Wheeler moved to Washington, D.C., to serve under the Office of Civilian Defense and the Office of Strategic Services Camouflage Division. In correspondence to Clarke, Wheeler mentioned visiting landscape architect and Washington, D.C., native **Rose Ishbel Greely**'s gardens in 1942.

A 1944 letter to Clarke placed Wheeler in Georgetown, in Washington, D.C. Following the war, Georgetown flourished with new upper-middle to upper-class homeowners, and it was during this time that Wheeler began to make his mark. Wheeler wrote the Easton family, "I feel that your garden would mean a lot to me in the future. There are very few jobs where a LA has such a good rear elevation to begin with." His success resulted in an *American Home* article titled "Three-level, Three-Purpose Garden" that was published in 1951. Wheeler's design included simple plantings of evergreens, flowering trees, and ground covers. Areas for storage, entertaining, relaxing, and play featured in many of his future designs. Since many owners lived elsewhere during the summer, low maintenance—at least on the homeowner's part—was crucial. The gardens also needed to shine during the winter months when nothing bloomed.

Despite his successes, in 1950, Wheeler questioned whether he could make a living as a landscape architect in Washington, D.C. His reticence and quiet modesty belied the fact that he was establishing an enviable clientele. Gossip columns reported on his parties

Perry Wheeler. (Smithsonian Institution, Archive of American Gardens, Perry Wheeler Collection)

with Hollywood stars and the top echelon of the political circuit. Publications such as *House and Garden* and *American Home* featured many of Wheeler's new Washington gardens. For example, in *House and Garden* in 1953, Wheeler provided advice for shady backyards in "Why Not Brighten Your Own Backyard?" Later that year in the same magazine he guided postwar newlyweds in the article "Bride's First Garden."

A job at a Georgetown shop, Garden House, afforded Wheeler the opportunity to socialize with homeowners and suggest tasteful designs and items for their gardens.

The McGuire garden (Washington, D.C., 1959) is an example of Perry Wheeler's residential work. (Smithsonian Institution, Archive of American Gardens, Perry Wheeler Collection)

Nancy Gray Pyne, a former employee of Garden House, knew Wheeler well. She later employed him in 1958 to modernize her newly acquired garden, originally designed by Rose Greely, by replacing curved brick lines with straight Belgian block. Pyne recalled that Wheeler was "wonderful, always thinking ahead of you. He always kept things simple."

Wheeler's clientele grew from word of mouth in Washington's social circles and through sharing office space with Greely and, later, architect Gertrude Sawyer. In 1959, Mrs. Rachel "Bunny" Mellon hired Wheeler to consult on her gardens. This led to Wheeler's contributions to the White House Rose Garden. In 1973, Mrs. Mellon recalled, "Both he [Whitey Williams] and I were aided by the knowledge and loyalty of Perry Wheeler. . . .His never-ending quiet presence and experience had a great deal to do with the perfection of this garden."

Churches and organizations called on Wheeler to redesign spaces in Washington and elsewhere. Specifically, in Washington, the National Cathedral, Hillwood Estate Museum and Garden, and Christ Church Georgetown contracted his services. The Garden Club of America hired Wheeler to plan for their gazebo project at the National Arboretum in 1963. Wheeler intended the building to appear "as a surprise as one first sees it from a distance through the trees." The plant palette included collections of cotoneasters and other plants including styrax, clethra, azaleas, masses of Rhododendrons, and Kingsville box for accents. Wheeler cherished his relationship with Henry Hohman of Kingsville Nursery, which was known for its exclusive client list.

Despite being one of the most popular landscape architects in Washington, he kept clients' privacy with charming modesty. Wheeler told a friend, Gordon Riggle, to keep his mouth shut and eyes open. Riggle remembers Wheeler using little hedges and not liking flash or a lot of summer-blooming flowers. He was hands-on, although he never picked up a tool, but knew all the men working for him. Wheeler's garden-side manner won him the respect of fellow professionals. In 1963, the University of

Georgia's Department of Landscape Architecture honored him with an Award of Merit.

Wheeler continued to be much sought after for the next several decades and his work and new responsibilities continued to flourish. The Trustees for Harvard University appointed Wheeler to the Garden Advisory Committee at Dumbarton Oaks where he served from 1964 to 1974. This Harvard-appointed committee began in 1956 with **Alden Hopkins** and **Michael Rapuano** among its first advisers. Wheeler's tenure coincided with Rapuano, **Ralph E. Griswold**, Mrs. Paul Mellon and others. With the John F. Kennedy Memorial at Arlington Cemetery, Wheeler worked again with Mrs. Mellon, acting as her authorized representative.

By 1968, Washington, D.C., had suffered in the aftermath of the assassination of Martin Luther King Jr. and the race riots that followed. The departure of long-term residents to the suburbs may have contributed to Wheeler's decision to move to Middleburg, Virginia. Taking on new clients was not a priority; however, he continued to travel, lecture to the Garden Club of America, and consult with former clients. In October 1977, Wheeler received a citation from the American Horticulture Society "for outstanding contributions to Horticulture landscaping . . . to expand the influence and improve the effectiveness of American horticulture nationwide."

Wheeler received his license to practice landscape architecture in Virginia in 1981, and enjoyed semi-retirement at his property, Budfield. Wheeler's health declined with the diagnosis of cancer. On August 17, 1989, Wheeler died at Loudon County Hospital and was buried at Sunnyside Cemetery in Cordele, Georgia.

The Perry Wheeler Collection is housed at the Archives of American Gardens, Smithsonian Institution. The collection contains letters, plans, magazine articles, and correspondence with clients and businesses. The collection also includes travel slides and slides and snapshots of family and gardens.

Wheeler, Perry. "Three-level, Three-Purpose Garden." *American Home,* August 1951, 36–37. Features the Easton property and describes the three garden areas to accommodate the owners' lifestyle. Includes photographs and drawings.

Wheeler, Perry H. "The Bride's First Garden: A Five Year Plan." *House and Garden,* May 1953, 138–43. Wheeler outlines the process of building the landscape for a modern suburban home. Plant lists and drawings are included.

Beth Page

WHYTE, WILLIAM HOLLINGSWORTH, JR.
(1917–1999)
AUTHOR, JOURNALIST, URBAN THEORIST

William Hollingsworth Whyte Jr., known as "Holly" by his friends and family, was born October 1, 1917, in West Chester, Pennsylvania, in the Brandywine Valley, about 25 miles west of Philadelphia. He often said that he was educated at St. Andrew's School (in Middletown, Delaware), Princeton University, and in the United States Marines. As an intelligence officer in the First Marine Division, he landed on Guadalcanal as part of the initial invasion on August 7, 1942, and fought with his unit for four and one-half months until, sick and exhausted, his unit was relieved by the U.S. Army.

Discharged from the Marines as a captain in 1945, Whyte was hired by *Fortune* magazine in 1946. As noted in Joseph Nocera's foreword to the 1956 publication *The Organization Man,* Whyte joined "writers and editors who were genuinely interested in the subject of big corporations and business in general, and most of them loved writing about it. But more than that there was a feeling of enormous intellectual ferment at the magazine, a sense that they were creating a new kind of business journalism. . . . Eventually Fortune took as its mission the goal of exploring not just corporate life but American life and the way the two intertwined. And the person most responsible for turning *Fortune* in this new and exciting direction was William H. Whyte."

His best-selling book, *The Organization Man,* made Whyte internationally famous and was translated into a dozen languages. The book grew out of a series of *Fortune* articles that traced the long-range shift that American organizational life was bringing to Americans' personal values. Whyte pointed out how pervasive the organization had become in the lives of millions of Americans.

"The fault is not in organization, it is in our worship of it." He said, "there must always be a conflict between the individual and society and it is the price of being an individual that he must face these conflicts."

The importance of open space and ways to make it available and useful constantly fascinated Whyte. While on leave from *Fortune,* he wrote a paper for the Urban Land Institute, "Securing Open Space for Urban America: Conservation Easements." He condensed his findings in a *Life* magazine article, "A Plan to Save Vanishing U.S. Countryside," later reprinted in *Readers Digest,* and in his book *The Last Landscape.* Whyte argued that open space itself was a public good justifying condemnation, but that conservation easements were a more practical and effective way of saving much-needed open space.

He left *Fortune* in 1958 and spent the rest of his life observing, studying, lecturing, and writing. He believed passionately that the quality of life was enhanced by public spaces and the street life of cities. He called streets "the river of life of the city, the place where we come together, the pathway to the center."

The American Conservation Association in 1964 published Whyte's influential study, *Cluster Development,* with a foreword by Laurence Rockefeller. Here Whyte was concerned with the unbridled development in the suburbs where "Cape Cods, ranches, and Hansel and Gretels" were gobbling up land at a prodigious rate. In response to this dilemma, Whyte posed the question, "Why couldn't we bring the density principle to the suburbs?" The study, backed by the American Conservation Association, proposed such a concept that resulted in grouping houses closely together and using the pro-

William "Holly" Whyte in Paley Park, New York, New York, ca. 1988. (Courtesy of Alexandra Whyte)

tected and preserved land to create common greens and squares.

In 1968, Whyte published *The Last Landscape,* a major work on the future of open space in the United States. He attacked the then-current planning orthodoxy of decentralized city growth resulting in low-density sprawl and advocated increased density in the center city. He went on to discuss many techniques, including scenic easements, cluster development, play areas, small spaces, roadsides, and townscape, and concluded with the case for crowding.

Whyte served as a consultant to the New York City Department of City Planning and wrote the first volume of the *Plan for New York City,* published in 1969. The "thrust of the Plan was unusually challenging: it was concerned with the major issues of the growth and workability of the city and its government rather than with specific land-use projections and the kind of futuristic projects typical of such plans. There was also a strong

emphasis on urban design and the use of incentive zoning to provide parks and plazas." The plan contained a ringing endorsement of concentration of economic activity in the core of the city.

In 1971, Whyte established the Street Life Project. Assisted by young students and able observers, using time lapse photography, movie cameras, and many interviews, Whyte used direct observation to understand and describe human behavior in the urban environment. Over a sixteen-year period, Whyte studied and recorded how people behaved on New York City's streets and in its public spaces. This work informed and confirmed his judgments about density and disproved much of the conventional wisdom about urban spaces. The result of the project was a preliminary booklet published in 1980 by the Conservation Foundation, *The Social Life of Small Urban Spaces,* and a companion 55-minute film, which was shown on public television as part of the *Nova* science series titled *Public Spaces/Human Places.* The final report on the project, *City: Rediscovering the Center,* was published by Doubleday in 1989. It included analysis and recommendations for the design and management of public spaces. Every chapter is illustrated with specific examples from New York City and many other cities.

While involved in the Street Life Project, Whyte visited Tokyo under the auspices of the Japan Society in New York and the International House Tokyo and compared the pedestrian environments of the two cities. In 1977, he published a report, *New York and Tokyo: A Study in Crowding.*

Perhaps the most dramatic example of the principles Whyte developed is New York's Bryant Park, 9 acres in the heart of the city. Bryant Park had been redesigned in 1930 by Clarke & Rapuano (**Gilmore David Clarke** and **Michael Rapuano**) through a competition based on the theory that it was to be a refuge from the city. The implementation of this theory in fact isolated Bryant Park, and for the next fifty years it was a disaster. The park was frequented by drug addicts and the downtrodden, and as a result was forsaken by the general public. The park was rehabilitated by Bob Hanna and Laurie Olin following Whyte's ideas, and today it is one of the most successful and heavily used parks in the city, filled at noon with office workers from the surrounding buildings, and often the scene of events in the evening. Seating is on movable chairs, the plant materials are magnificent, a diverse population meets to socialize, eat lunch, read, play chess, sit, and enjoy the scene—and the public treats it like a gem.

Whyte traveled the globe, invited by people fascinated with his ideas. He received many awards and honors. He was active in the Municipal Art Society in New York City, was a trustee of the Conservation Foundation, and was a visiting Distinguished Professor for a year at Hunter College. After he left *Fortune* he was never again willing to work for a large organization or developer because he wanted to maintain his independence and objectivity. He passed away on January 12, 1999.

LaFarge, Albert, ed. *The Essential William H. Whyte.* Bronx, N.Y.: Fordham University Press, 2000. Written by Whyte's former editor, an overview and celebration of Whyte's career. Includes earlier essays by Whyte.

Whyte, William H., Jr. *The Last Landscape.* Garden City, N.Y.: Doubleday and Company, 1968. Reprinted 2002 by University of Pennsylvania Press. A strategy and a legal toolbox for protecting open space in metropolitan America.

Whyte, William H., Jr. *The Organization of Man.* Garden City, N.Y.: Doubleday Anchor, 1956. Reprint. Philadelphia: University of Pennsylvania Press, 2002. An important evaluation of living in postwar America.

Donald Elliott

WIEDORN, WILLIAM S.
(1896–1990)
LANDSCAPE ARCHITECT, CITY PLANNER

Born in Baltimore, Maryland, on May 2, 1896, William S. Wiedorn attended Cornell University, receiving his bachelor of science in 1919 and his master of landscape architecture in 1921. After graduation he married, accepted a teaching position in landscape architecture at Kansas State College, served in the U.S. Army as a second lieutenant, and became an associate with John Watson in St. Petersburg, Florida, from 1924 to 1927. He also worked briefly in the **Olmsted Brothers** office in Brookline, Massachusetts. In 1927, he moved to Cleveland, Ohio, and became the chief designer at the landscape architecture firm of Pitkin & Mott.* Seeking a new direction in 1932, Wiedorn returned to Florida and opened a private practice as a landscape architect and city planner in St. Petersburg and worked on the Committee for Beautification in Tampa.

Wiedorn's practice included golf course design, and in 1932, at the height of the Works Progress Administration (WPA), Wiedorn was called on for a brief consultation in the design of the golf course at City Park in New Orleans. Wiedorn then moved from St. Petersburg to New Orleans and he immediately became instrumental in the landscape design of some of the city's most significant institutions. After his golf course design, he continued in other elements of the design and construction of City Park from 1935 to 1960, collaborating with New Orleans architects Richard Koch and Samuel Wilson Jr. in modifying the master plan of Bennett, Parsons and Frost of Chicago. As he later recalled, he came to New Orleans for two weeks but stayed for a lifetime. Wiedorn's work

William Wiedorn, 1959. (Courtesy of Kathy Wiedorn)

focused primarily on utilitarian and government-sponsored projects. Wiedorn's career spanned three states: Florida, Ohio, and Louisiana. He maintained these connections throughout his career and continued to accept projects that took him away from New Orleans for short periods of time.

Wiedorn resumed teaching when in 1934 he accepted an offer to lead a landscape gardening course at the New

New Orleans City Park Rose Garden plan. (Architectural Archive, Special Collection, Tulane University Libraries)

Orleans Art School, located in a building in City Park. His subjects included the art of design and landscape design, plant materials, and construction. His teaching style emphasized fieldwork, as the study of nature was as important to Wiedorn as book knowledge. In Wiedorn's opinion, City Park's burgeoning botanical gardens and arboretum positioned it in the forefront for the study of landscape gardening in the lower South. Although Wiedorn lived only 75 miles from Louisiana State University in Baton Rouge, he never became involved with its program in landscape architecture.

In 1936, Wiedorn began a project in City Park that was more intimate in scale than some of his other WPA projects: the City Park Botanical Garden (today known as the New Orleans Botanical Gardens). This public botanical garden—one of the few remaining in America from the Art Deco period—united art and nature through a series of garden rooms arranged along a central axis.

This project, which remains relatively intact and is the project for which Wiedorn is today largely remembered, was an interdisciplinary collaboration among Wiedorn, Koch, and Mexican-American artist Enrique Alferez, all of whom were strong-willed designers. Deprived of city and state funds over time, the garden deteriorated until a revitalization initiative began in the late 1980s. Wiedorn, professionally inactive by that time, was briefly involved in early discussions.

In addition to work in City Park, Wiedorn's landscape design projects in New Orleans included work at Tulane University, Dillard University, Audubon Park riverfront, residential subdivisions and public housing developments, swimming pools, golf courses, and residential landscape designs. He continued to collaborate on projects with architect Koch, and in 1941, they completed the design for St. Anthony's Garden at the rear of the St. Louis Cathedral in the city's historic Vieux Carre. Wiedorn con-

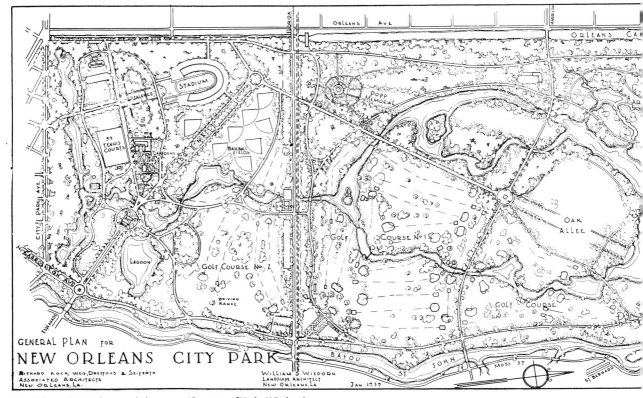

New Orleans City Park general plan, 1939. (Courtesy of Kathy Wiedorn)

tinued his working relationship with City Park throughout his lifetime. His latest involvement was a golf course revision in 1978.

Wiedorn published little, and there is little written about him. He voiced his opinion advocating the standardization of plant nomenclature in a letter that appeared in the July 1947 issue of *Landscape Architecture,* and several years later he wrote an article on the landscape use of camellias for the 1949 publication of *The American Camellia Yearbook.*

Prior to his death on October 15, 1990, Wiedorn bequeathed his professional library and selected plans and other documents to the Southeastern Architecture Archive at Tulane University. With his wife Marguerite, William Wiedorn is buried in the Chalmette National Cemetery, southeast of New Orleans.

The William S. Wiedorn Office Records are housed at the Southeastern Architectural Archive Collection 21, Tulane University, New Orleans, La. Included are project drawings, correspondence, several books, and his photograph.

New Orleans *Times Picayune* article, October 4, 1934. Highlights a gardening course offered at City Park and taught by Wiedorn.

Reeves, Sally K. Evans, William D. Reeves, Ellis P. Laborde, and James S. Janssen. *Historic City Park New Orleans.* New Orleans, La.: Friends of City Park, 1982. This publication, though flawed with factual errors, contains extensive information about the beginning of City Park in New Orleans, including Wiedorn's contributions.

Wiedorn, William S. "Landscape Use of Camellias." *American Camellia Yearbook,* ed. R. J. Wilmot. Gainesville, Fla.: American Camellia Society, 1949, 78–81. An essay by Wiedorn on the use of camellias in the residential garden; a plan is included.

Barry Fitzpatrick

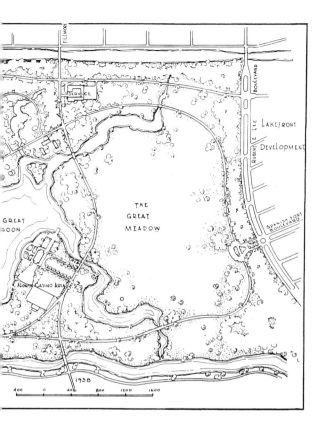

WILLISTON, DAVID AUGUSTUS
(1868–1962)

LANDSCAPE ARCHITECT, HORTICULTURIST, EDUCATOR

David A. Williston, the first professionally trained black landscape architect in United States and the first to establish his own professional office, was born on a rural farm outside of Fayetteville, North Carolina. He was the second child in a large family of twelve siblings. His parents, Frank and Henrietta Williston, soon moved to town where the middle-class, educated family became respected pillars of the community. Williston's older brother, Edward Davis, became a physician and head of Pediatrics at the Black Freedman's Hospital in Washington, D.C., adjacent to Howard University. Edward supported his younger brother's educational undertakings, including two years at the Howard University Normal School from which David earned a diploma in 1895. David then enrolled in the School of Agriculture at Cornell University

where he studied under the horticulturist **Liberty Hyde Bailey**. Although there was no formal school of landscape architecture at Cornell, Williston, along with other future landscape practitioners such as **Frank Albert Waugh**, **Bryant Fleming**, and Carl Pilat, was enrolled in a group of courses recommended by Bailey. Graduating in 1898 with a B.S. in agriculture, Williston was one of the first African Americans to receive a degree from Cornell. A few years later Williston completed an additional degree in municipal engineering from the International Correspondence School in Scranton, Pennsylvania.

Following his graduation from Cornell, Williston returned to his home state where he was employed as a professor of agriculture at the State College of North Carolina in Greensboro. Williston vacated this position

David A. Williston. (D. A. Williston Papers/Moorland-Spingarn Research Center, Howard University)

in 1900 and by 1901 was listed as an instructor at the Lincoln Institute in Lincoln, Missouri. Remaining there for just one year, Williston was identified as an instructor of chemistry, biology, and agriculture. In 1902, Booker T. Washington, president of Tuskegee Institute, where a Department of Mechanical Industries for instruction in architecture had just been initiated, recruited Williston to serve as horticulturist and landscape architect under the title of horticulture curator. At the Alabama school, Williston joined black architect Robert R. Taylor and together the two men planned much of the physical layout of the Tuskegee campus. Prior to his arrival, Williston had also been responsible for the landscaping of the private residence of Booker T. Washington.

In 1907, Williston left Tuskegee for an appointment at Fisk University in Nashville, Tennessee, where he was named Professor of Agriculture and Horticulture. Williston may have been enticed by the expanded offering of courses that the university had undertaken the previous year with new courses in industrial education,

pure sciences, as well as floriculture, architectural drawing, and agricultural chemistry. Recognized at this time as one of the top black schools in the country, Fisk offered Williston what he considered advancement in his teaching career. Additionally, he realized the opportunity for interaction with privileged blacks and wealthy white donors associated with the Tennessee school might provide further professional opportunities. Returning to Tuskegee two years later, Williston remained in the position of adjunct professor there from 1909 to 1929. During his tenure he was also given the official title of "Landscape Architect and Superintendent."

With the onset of the Great Depression in late 1929, a major decrease in student enrollments and loss of donors forced many black colleges and universities to cut programs and eliminate faculty positions. Leaving Tuskegee, Williston taught for one year at Tennessee State University before relocating to Washington, D.C., where he spent the remainder of his life as an active professional. Williston had opened a small office in the city in the late 1920s while teaching, but it was only with the deteriorating economic conditions that his private work became his full-time vocation.

Listing his profession as "Landscape Architect and Site Planner," some of Williston's earliest consultations appear to have been with the government-sponsored Public Works Administration and particularly in association with the Tennessee Valley Authority. However, by far the largest part of Williston's practice was his site planning and campus development for dozens of historically black institutions. In addition to those previously listed, Williston worked at differing levels with Clark University in Atlanta, on Alcorn State University near Lorman, Mississippi, Lane College in Jackson, Tennessee, and Philander Smith College in Little Rock. Other projects emanating from Williston's office included Langston Terrace Housing Project and Parkside Dwellings Project in Washington, D.C.; Roberts Airfield in the Republic of Liberia; 99th Pursuit Squadron Airfield in Chehaw, Alabama; Centennial City Planning Project in Monrovia, Liberia; and Veterans Administration Hospital in Tuskegee, Alabama. One of his major projects was the expansion of the Howard University campus, which he undertook with Cornell-trained, African American architect Albert Cassell in the 1930s. The campus plan and many of the buildings one sees today are the result of their collaboration.

While Williston was a member of several professional societies, he never became a member of the American

Society of Landscape Architects. As Dreck Wilson and Kirk Muckle noted, however, "In private practice and in public service, Williston's contribution to the profession was made in full measure. . . . This is his legacy for enthusiastic and talented young, black horticulturists, architects, and landscape architects." David Williston died on July 28, 1962, following a lengthy illness.

The David A. Williston Collection, in the Moorland-Spingarn Research Center, Howard University, Washington, D.C., contains an extensive, though incomplete, collection of Williston's project drawings.

Muckle, Kirk, and Dreck Wilson. "David Augustus Williston: Pioneering Black Professional." *Landscape Architecture,* January 1982. A good overview of Williston's life and professional work.
Wilson, Dreck S., ed. *African-American Architects: A Biographical Dictionary, 1865–1945.* Ontario, Canada: Routledge, Taylor & Francis Group, 2004. Entry by Douglas A. Williams from his unpublished master's thesis on David A. Williston, Cornell University, 2002.

Douglas A. Williams and Daniel Krall

WIRTH, CONRAD LOUIS
(1899–1993)
ADMINISTRATOR

Conrad Louis Wirth was born in 1899. At the time of his birth, his father, Theodore Wirth,* was the superintendent of the Hartford, Connecticut, park system, and Conrad was born in the superintendent's residence in Elizabeth Park. The family moved in 1906 when the elder Wirth took the position of superintendent of Minneapolis parks, and the family lived in the superintendent's residence in Lyndale Park.

As an adolescent, Wirth attended military school in Wisconsin. He went on to study landscape architecture with his father's choice of teachers, **Frank Albert Waugh**, who established a landscape degree program at the Massachusetts Agricultural College (later the University of Massachusetts, Amherst) in 1903. Wirth graduated with a bachelor of science in landscape architecture in 1923 and moved to San Francisco, where he went to work for nurseryman Donald McLaren, the son of John McLaren,* the Scottish designer of Golden Gate Park who was another close friend of his father. After two years of this apprenticeship, Wirth moved to New Orleans and started his own landscape architecture firm with a partner. The new business did well at first, mainly in the design of subdivisions. However, the development boom soon turned to bust on the Gulf Coast and elsewhere, and by 1927 Wirth was out of business.

Conrad Wirth (*seated on left*) reviews Mission 66 plans for Yosemite National Park with the park's superintendent and staff in 1956. (National Park Service Photo Archive)

At that point, he again relied on his father's connections and moved to Washington, D.C., where **Frederick Law Olmsted Jr.** secured a job for him with the National Capital Park and Planning Commission in 1928. In 1931, Park Service director Horace M. Albright offered him a transfer to the National Park Service (NPS), where Wirth became assistant director in charge of the Branch of Lands, or essentially chief land planner, in 1931.

YOUR MISSION 66 AND THE NATIONAL PARKS

A PASSPORT TO ADVENTURE

Presented by: PHILLIPS 66 PHILLIPS PETROLEUM COMPANY

A Mission 66 brochure, highlighting the influence of automotive tourism on the planning of the project. (National Park Service History Collection, Harpers Ferry, WV, Photo Archive)

additions to the park system for the previous two years. He now became the principal liaison to dozens of state governments, many of which had virtually no state parks, but which were rapidly acquiring land in order to take advantage of the federal government's offer to develop them with CCC labor and funds. Wirth oversaw and reviewed all planning, design, and construction undertaken by the NPS-CCC state park program. By 1941, more than 560 state, county, and municipal parks had been created or redeveloped by Wirth's program, in partnership with 140 state and local park agencies.

In 1936, the NPS consolidated its CCC programs, bringing together Wirth's state park program and the national park CCC camps, now all under Wirth. That year Congress passed the Park, Parkway, and Recreational-Area Study Act, which expanded the role of Wirth's national recreational planning. The act also authorized a national plan for the recreational use of public lands in every state, in cooperation with state agencies, using CCC funds and labor. The Land Planning Committee of the National Resources Board gave the NPS responsibility to produce that agency's national recreation plan, *Recreational Use of Land in the United States,* which it published in 1938. Wirth's prewar recreational planning activities culminated in 1941, when he published *A Study of the Park and Recreation Problem of the United States,* a report that summarized and analyzed recreational land-use data collected over the previous eight years.

American entry into World War II put an end to the CCC and other New Deal programs. Following the end of the war, Congress kept national park appropriations low, but at the same time, visitors inundated state and national parks. In 1955, there were 56 million visits to the national park system compared to 17 million in 1940. In the developed areas of many parks, people found traffic jams, long lines outside bathrooms, overflowing parking lots, and no available accommodations or campgrounds. Superintendents could not adequately protect

Known as Connie by many of his colleagues, Wirth remained in the NPS's Washington Office for the next thirty-three years, running the agency from 1951 until 1964, the longest tenure of any director before or since. His first decade in Washington shaped many of his future attitudes. A transformation of the NPS began in the spring of 1933, when Franklin Delano Roosevelt mobilized the Civilian Conservation Corps (CCC). In his position as chief land planner, Wirth investigated possible

their parks, much less staff their museums and interpretive programs. Many park concessionaires struggled unsuccessfully to reopen aging and inadequate hotels and restaurants.

These were the challenges facing Wirth when he became NPS director near the end of 1951. After three years, however, the situation changed with the inauguration of President Dwight D. Eisenhower and the end of the Korean War. As armed forces demobilized and recession threatened, Eisenhower looked favorably on public works spending that would stimulate the economy. Wirth decided the time was right, and after eight months of intensive planning he and his staff had outlined the scope of Mission 66, a ten-year program to improve, modernize, and expand the national park system in time for the fiftieth anniversary of the NPS in 1966.

Mission 66 responded to a generally perceived crisis that resulted from a period of low funding combined with heavy use of the park system. It proved to be an effective strategy for capturing Congress's interest. By 1966 the lawmakers had spent about $1 billion on land acquisition, new staff and training, general operations, and all types of construction activity in national parks. The NPS constructed or reconstructed thousands of miles of roads and hundreds of miles of trails. Hundreds of park residences, administration buildings, comfort stations, and other buildings for public use and park administration were built. Mission 66 expanded and professionalized NPS staff and established new training centers. Above all, Mission 66 funded more than 100 visitor centers, a new building type invented by the agency's planners and architects, which was at the heart of revised park master planning goals.

Mission 66 forged a new identity for the park system, represented by a new idiom of modernist park architecture that made full use of steel, concrete, prefabricated elements, unusual fenestration, climate control, and other aspects of contemporary architecture. The new park architecture also expressed contemporary planning ideas. The arrowhead NPS agency logo was introduced in 1951 and subsequently was featured prominently on buildings, publications, and redesigned uniforms. In the end Mission 66 accomplished much of what Wirth intended: the reinvention of the NPS to meet the needs of postwar American society.

Mission 66 was greeted at first with enthusiasm by Congress, government officials, and by many preservationists. The program was also criticized, however, for emphasizing construction as a one-dimensional solution to the complex social and environmental problems park managers were facing. Critics also complained that Mission 66 abandoned the Rustic style of park architecture and landscape design. If Mission 66 began in an atmosphere of intense optimism, the program soon led the NPS into bitter controversy as the postwar environmental movement began to take shape and exert its strength. Mission 66 hastened the advent of environmentalism by creating concern that the NPS was overdeveloping parks while failing to take other steps to preserve wilderness. Wirth stepped down as NPS director at the beginning of 1964, two years before his program was to have been completed. The creation of the Bureau of Outdoor Recreation in 1962 and the passage of the Wilderness Act of 1964 signaled the advent of what Secretary of the Interior Stewart L. Udall described as New Conservation. Many park acquisitions and expansions completed over the next decade, however, had their roots in Mission 66 proposals.

Wirth remained active in conservation affairs after his retirement, and he published many articles and speeches in his lifetime. In 1962, he was elected president of the American Institute of Park Executives and played an important role in the organization and growth of that organization. He was a trustee of the National Geographic Society and a consultant to Laurance S. Rockefeller's American Conservation Association. He received many awards, including the Department of the Interior's Distinguished Service Award, the American Forestry Association's Conservation Award, and several honorary doctorates. The American Scenic and Historic Preservation Society awarded him its Pugsley Gold Medal twice. In 1972 the American Society of Landscape Architects gave him its highest honor, the ASLA Medal. In 1980, Wirth published an important memoir, *Parks, Politics, and the People,* in which he describes his professional activities in detail. Conrad Wirth died in 1993 and was buried in his family's plot at Lakewood Memorial Cemetery in Minneapolis.

Wirth, Conrad L. "The Landscape Architect in National Park Work." *Landscape Architecture Magazine* 46, no. 1 (1955).

Wirth, Conrad L. "Parks and Their Uses." In *American Planning and Civic Annual.* Washington, D.C.: American Planning and Civic Association, 1935.

Wirth, Conrad L. *Parks, Politics, and the People.* Norman: University of Oklahoma Press, 1980.

Ethan Carr

WIRTH, THEODORE
(1863–1949)
PARK SUPERINTENDENT, HORTICULTURALIST

Born in 1863, Theodore Wirth exhibited an interest in horticulture from an early age, playing in the greenhouses and gardens of a florist near his home in Winterthur, Switzerland. Wirth graduated from high school in 1878 and spent three years as an apprentice gardener with the Stahel Brothers, one of the country's largest horticultural businesses. After returning to Winterthur for an engineering course, he moved to London in 1883 and was employed as a gardener and floral designer. Two years later, he was in Paris working for a commercial florist and at the Jardin des Plantes. Back in Switzerland in 1887, he spent the winter in the employ of the city gardener of Zurich.

While in Zurich, Wirth studied English in anticipation of moving to the United States. He arrived in New York in April 1888, and worked briefly as a private gardener and rose grower in New Jersey. He was hired by New York City's Department of Parks later in 1888, initially serving on greenhouse, planting, and forestry crews and studying landscape gardening in his off hours. His knowledge and skills attracted the attention of Central Park superintendent **Samuel Parsons Jr.** When political changes foiled Wirth's ambitions within the department, Parsons helped him secure work in New York and New England. During this time Wirth worked at the Niagara Reservation, perhaps on the recommendation of Parson's supervisor, **Calvert Vaux**. Vaux collaborated with **Frederick Law Olmsted Sr.** on the 1887 plan for the reservation, and was also the landscape architect for the New York Department of Public parks from 1888 to 1895.

Around this time, Wirth was introduced to the French-American horticulturalist Felix H. Mense. Wirth began courting Mense's daughter, Leonie Alexandrine, and the couple married in 1895. Two of their three sons followed in their father's footsteps: Conrad Louis Wirth,* who headed the National Park Service, and Walter Wirth, who directed city and state parks around the United States.

Wirth became superintendent of parks in Hartford, Connecticut, in 1896, initially implementing plans prepared by Frederick Law Olmsted Sr., **John Charles Olmsted** and **Charles Eliot** and their successor firm, the **Olmsted Brothers**. Wirth's first independent design was a master plan for Elizabeth Park, prepared in 1900. Three

Theodore Wirth, 1935. (Minneapolis Park and Recreation Board)

years later, he introduced the country's first public rose garden there. Wirth believed that public rose gardens should not only be great floral displays but should also be educational, assisting visitors to select rose varieties for their personal use. While in Hartford Wirth also designed Rocky Ridge and Hyland parks.

The concern for public benefit was a hallmark of Wirth's approach to the Minneapolis park system, which he oversaw for three decades. His work in Hartford had attracted the attention of the Minneapolis Park Board, which invited him to become superintendent in 1905. Wirth was intrigued by the fledging system, which offered an array of natural amenities, but he was inclined to stay in Hartford. After months of persuasion and the promise of a new house built to his specifications within a park, Wirth moved west to assume his new position in January 1906.

The city's park system had a strong foundation. **Horace William Shaler Cleveland** had proposed a network of parks and parkways for Minneapolis and St. Paul in the 1870s, and Cleveland was hired to implement that plan in Minneapolis after a board of park commissioners was formed by a city referendum in 1883. The vote was authorized by the state legislature after the city council refused to expand the nascent community's 6-acre park "system."

When Wirth arrived in Minneapolis, the system's potential remained far from realized. He began an aggressive campaign to develop the fifty-seven properties on approximately 1,800 acres already owned by the board and to acquire additional parkland. Wirth shaped the system

Lake of the Isles, Minneapolis Park and Recreation Board Park, Minneapolis, Minnesota. (Minneapolis Park and Recreation Board)

both physically and philosophically, serving as chief landscape architect as well as superintendent. The lower level of his house held a drafting room where designers sketched plans under his watchful eye. Most of the plans ultimately bore his name. By the time he reached the mandatory retirement age of seventy-two in 1935, the system's 144 properties covered 5,241 acres and were valued at over $18 million. The nation's second public rose garden (now part of the Lyndale Park Gardens), only a short distance from his house, had opened in 1907. Marshes were dredged and filled to complete a chain of lakes, the crown jewels in the Grand Rounds park and parkway system encircling the city. The dramatic urban gorge of the Mississippi River was protected and enhanced. Acquisitions placed a park within six blocks of every residence in the city.

This reflected his commitment to providing parks for rich and poor, young and old. One of his first accomplishments when he arrived in Minneapolis was removing the "Keep Off the Grass" signs on park lawns. In the winter, he encouraged children to use snowy hills for sledding. Parks appeared in neighborhoods occupied by immigrants and minorities, areas often ignored by nineteenth-century park planners.

Wirth also advocated for a system of regional parks around Minneapolis, extending up the valleys of the Mississippi and Minnesota Rivers and along their tributaries. He realized the exceptional scenic value of these rural lands and knew they would eventually be threatened by development. He continued to lobby for the plan after becoming superintendent emeritus. Hennepin County ultimately established this system in 1957.

Wirth promoted his approach and philosophy on the national as well as the local level, being an important influence during a formative period for park administration. He was a charter member of the New England Association of Park Superintendents, established in 1898. It became the American Association of Park Superintendents in 1904, the American Institute of Park Executives in 1921, and, upon merging with three other organizations, the National Recreation and Park Association in 1965. Wirth served as president of the American Association of Park Superintendents and treasurer, director, and three terms as president of the American Institute of Park Executives. Upon Wirth's death, Robert E. Everly, then president of the American Institute of Park Executives, reflected: "Every profession, or professional organization, which has weathered the pioneer stage and become a national institution, has numbered among its membership one or two outstanding leaders to whom it practically owes its existence. . . . Wirth was such a leader in the American Institute of Park Executives." Wirth was also involved

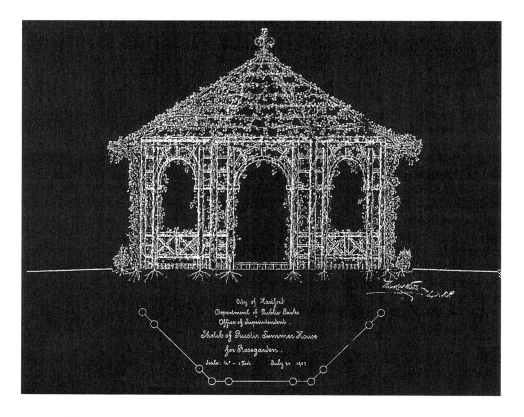

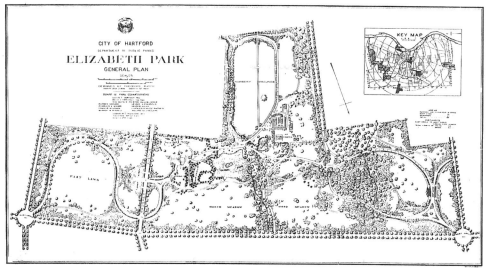

Above: Design of public rose garden summer house elevation, Department of Public Parks, Hartford, Connecticut, 1903. (Courtesy of Charles A. Birnbaum)

Below: Plan of Elizabeth Park, Hartford, Connecticut. (Courtesy of Charles A. Birnbaum)

with the Playground Association of America, founded in 1906 with President Theodore Roosevelt as its honorary president, and headed the Society of American Florists and Ornamental Horticulturists and the Minnesota State Florists Association.

Despite his interest in the common man, Wirth was not one of them. He never learned to drive, requiring the park board to provide him with a chauffeur. Nor was he a timid man: his longtime secretary remarked on his "genial, forceful, and colorful personality." His assistant, Charles Doell, who succeeded him as superintendent, described Wirth as "stern, steady, courageous, and unflinchingly devoted to the task before him, sometimes impetuous, impatient, and short-tempered," but added that "he loved sociability, jovial conversation, friends, fun, and a good time."

Wirth died in La Jolla, California, his retirement home, in January 1949, only a few months after being feted at the golden anniversary of the American Institute of Park Executives in Boston. He was eighty-five. Some 200 people attended his funeral at Lakewood Cemetery in Minneapolis. His grave overlooks the superintendent's residence, where he did so much to shape the city's park system and the nation's park philosophy. The house was listed in the National Register of Historic Places in 2002 for its association with Wirth.

The collections of the Minnesota Historical Society include thousands of photographs of Minneapolis parks. Many can be viewed with the online Visual Resources Database. In addition, the history collection of the Minneapolis Public Library contains some excellent photographs of the city's parks, many of which are in an online database.

"Theodore Wirth, A Great Park Builder and Administrator and a Great Man" and "Tributes to Theodore Wirth: Life of Veteran Park Executive Commented on by His Associates." *Parks and Recreation* 32 (March 1949), 132–44. Memorials to Wirth upon his death by associates and friends from around the country, including **Frederick Law Olmsted Jr.**, Robert Everly, Francis Gross, and his long-time secretary, Emily Merkert.

Wirth, Theodore. *Minneapolis Park System, 1883–1944.* Minneapolis: Board of Park Commissioners, 1945. Reprint, Minneapolis: Minneapolis Parks Legacy Society, 2006. An engaging, copiously illustrated book, by far the best history of this nationally significant park system.

Wirth, Theodore. "Value of Rose Culture in Public Parks." *Park and Cemetery* 17 (March 1907), 2–7. The philosophical and technical aspects of public rose gardens, using Elizabeth Park in Hartford, Connecticut, as an illustrated example.

Charlene K. Roise

WODELL, HELEN PAGE
(1891–1973)
LANDSCAPE AND GARDEN DESIGNER, AUTHOR

Helen Page was born in Summit, New Jersey, in 1891. She attended The Masters School in Dobbs Ferry, New York (class of 1908). In 1914, she married Ruthven Adriance Wodell, whose families were among the first European settlers of the lands along the Hudson River near Millbrook, New York. Around 1924, she began creating gardens for friends and neighbors in Short Hills, New Jersey, who had noted her own attractive plantings. Quickly realizing that she had a gift for design but lacked business skills, she asked her younger sister, Lois Page Cottrell,* to help her. In 1931, the sisters officially formed the firm of Wodell and Cottrell,* Landscape and Garden Consultants, focusing primarily on designs for private residences.

In addition to her design work, Helen Page Wodell was a prolific writer of articles on garden design, flower arranging, and a wide variety of subjects in the decorative arts. Her charming volume for children, *Beginning to Garden,* provides practical information on planting and design, as well as addressing social aspects of the subject, such as starting a garden club for young people. Wodell herself was a popular speaker on garden design, flower show staging, and flower arranging at garden club and other civic association meetings.

In 1948, Helen Page Wodell brought her daughter, Lois Wodell Poinier, into the firm, and effectively retired the following year, although she continued some consulting work through the 1960s in and around Summit, New Jersey, where she had moved with her second husband, Ernest K. Halbach. Helen Page Wodell died on August 5, 1973.

See also the individual entry on Lois Page Cottrell and the joint entry on Wodell and Cottrell. References follow the Wodell and Cottrell entry.

Rebecca Warren Davidson

WODELL AND COTTRELL

The sisters Helen Page Wodell* and Lois Page Cottrell* established their practice by designing gardens for their families and friends. Commissions for private residences comprise the majority of their work, although during World War II they were asked to design plantings at Fort Dix in New Jersey, and at Halloran General Hospital in Staten Island, New York. Notable designs in Short Hills include those for William K. Wallbridge, Bancroft Gherardi, Dean Emery, Waldron Ward, Ralph Rumery, and Frederick B. Ryan. They also designed a garden for the Ryans in East Hampton, New York. In Summit, New Jersey, Wodell and Cottrell created gardens for Ernest K. Halbach, Waldron Ward, and what is now the Reeves-Reed Arboretum. They also designed gardens in Connecticut, New York, and Pennsylvania.

These residential designs contain both formal and informal elements, with axial connections between the house and a series of garden rooms created with hedges, fencing, or stone walls. Luxuriant plantings of traditional cottage garden favorites such as iris, phlox, and roses fill the geometrically shaped beds. Wodell and Cottrell's designs usually included a pool or fountain, and often a central birdbath or sundial. These features are typical of early twentieth-century American Colonial gardens, which were based on earlier models, but adapted to meet a contemporary function. Wodell and Cottrell had a particular interest in practical garden architecture, and their extant plans include numerous playhouses, tool sheds, gazebos, and housing for domestic animals. Helen Wodell's suggestions on this topic appeared in her article "Garden Houses Old and New," published in *House Beautiful* in September 1933.

Helen Page Wodell garden, Short Hills, New Jersey, 1936. (Image courtesy of the Millburn–Short Hills Historical Society)

Wodell and Cottrell always referred to their business as "Landscape and Garden Consultants." In an interview she gave in later life, Lois Cottrell said that because neither she nor her sister had received any formal training in the field, they did not feel it was appropriate to call themselves landscape architects. At the same time, neither felt such a designation was necessary. Instead, they credited their early experiences working in their family's

Pool for Mrs. Bancroft Gherardi, Short Hills, New Jersey, 1934. (Image courtesy of the Millburn–Short Hills Historical Society)

large gardens, which gave them knowledge of plant requirements as well as an understanding of good design, with the success of their firm.

Wodell and Cottrell retired from active practice in 1949–1950. Helen's daughter, Lois Wodell Poinier, who had begun working with her mother and aunt in 1948, took on the firm name, and subsequently designed numerous gardens in New Jersey until her retirement in 1983. Lois Poinier's daughter, Helen Page Sanders, is also a landscape architect who practices in Palo Alto, California, making this a rare and perhaps unique example of a garden-design firm founded by women and continued for three generations.

The archives of Wodell and Cottrell, including drawings, slides, photographs, and written documentation, are housed at the Millburn–Short Hills (New Jersey) Historical Society and at the Smithsonian Archives of American Gardens in Washington, D.C. A portion of the Smithsonian collection, including images, is available online at www .siris.si.edu/.

Filzen, Patricia Louise. "Garden Designs for the Western Great Lakes Region: Annette Hoyt Flanders and Early Twentieth Century Women Landscape Architects." Master's thesis, University of Wisconsin–Madison, 1988. The work of Annette Hoyt Flanders* is the primary focus of this thesis, but the author also interviewed other women practitioners in the Midwest, including Lois Page Cottrell.

Wodell, Helen Page. *Beginning to Garden.* The Work and Play series. Illustrated by Jack Rosé. New York: Macmillan, 1928. A book written for young people, emphasizing the social and cultural benefits of gardening as well as practical information on planning, planting, harvesting, and garden-related crafts.

Wodell, Helen Page. "Garden Houses Old and New." *House Beautiful* 74 (September 1933), 81–84. One of the structures discussed is the Chinese "Let-go-pagoda" and how it can be adapted to contemporary gardens. Wodell's many other articles appeared frequently in *Charm, House & Garden, House Beautiful, Real Gardening, The Spur,* and *Woman's Home Companion* during the 1920s, 1930s, and 1940s.

See also the individual entries on Lois Page Cottrell and Helen Page Wodell

Rebecca Warren Davidson

ZACH, LEON HENRY
(1895–1966)
LANDSCAPE ARCHITECT

Born in Jamaica Plain, Massachusetts, on January 23, 1895, Leon Henry Zach grew up in a multilingual, cultured household. His father, Max W. Zach, an Austrian émigré, was the principal viola of the Boston Symphony Orchestra and part-time conductor of the Boston Pops. In 1907, the elder Zach was appointed the principal conductor of the St. Louis Symphony Orchestra, a post he held until his death in 1921.

Graduating from Roxbury Latin School, Leon Zach attended Harvard College during the tumultuous years of 1914–1918, taking courses in preparation for graduate work in landscape architecture. Although his Harvard A.B. degree is registered as 1918, Zach had entered the military in January of that year and was stationed in France as of April. With his diverse language skills, he was assigned as a second lieutenant to intelligence duty at a prisoner-of-war enclosure in Richelieu, which he described as a "nice nine-months stay in the châteaux country which . . . gave opportunity to [study] local examples of landscape work." He was discharged in September 1919 and promptly entered Harvard School of Landscape Architecture, graduating in 1922. He wrote a thesis on the various methods used by cities across the country to promote city planning and educate their populace as to its benefits. Additionally, after spending the summer of 1921 traveling in Europe, Zach had an article on visiting the various Italian villas published in *Landscape Architecture.*

Upon graduation, Zach was immediately employed by **Olmsted Brothers**, and set to work producing plans of all types for parks, estates, subdivisions, and schools. He spent part of 1923–1924 in Bermuda, supervising construction for the Mid Ocean Club grounds; developed entrance sketches for the Middlesex School in Concord, Massachusetts; and made various studies for the Cleveland Museum of Art. Over the next twenty years, he worked closely with **Frederick Law Olmsted Jr.** on projects for socially prominent clients such as George Widener in Chestnut Hill, Pennsylvania, Mrs. Oliver Iselin in Providence, Rhode Island, and Edward and Mary Curtis Bok in Mountain Lake, Florida, Wyncote, Pennsylvania, and in Rockport and Camden, Maine. After she was widowed, Mrs. Bok sponsored numerous projects in

Leon Henry Zach, ca. 1950. (Courtesy of the National Park Service, Frederick Law Olmsted National Historic Site)

the Maine communities, several of which involved residential designs for musicians, which Zach, with his own musical affiliations, appropriately supervised. Over the decades, Mrs. Bok's landscape endeavors in these communities shaped much of the streetscape and public spaces. In particular, for the notable Camden, Maine, amphitheater, designed by **Fletcher Steele**, he coordinated her interests in this project with other Camden/Rockport public planning endeavors for which she paid for Olmsted's design work.

Zach was also engaged in numerous projects in the New York area, planning several of the individual properties for the Chocomount development on Fisher's Island. In 1924, he began planning a playground for Riverside

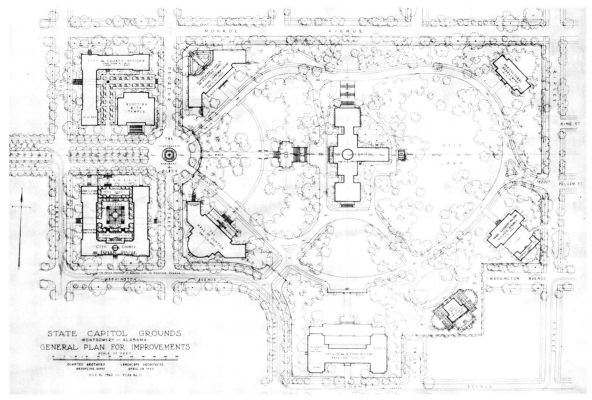

"State Capitol Grounds General Plan for Improvements," Montgomery, Alabama, April 28, 1930. (Courtesy of the National Park Service, Frederick Law Olmsted National Historic Site)

Church, a project funded by John D. Rockefeller Jr. As Rockefeller projects increased in number in the Olmsted office, Zach's responsibilities for this client's work grew, as he became Olmsted Jr.'s main onsite contact for the Fort Tryon, Cloisters, and Claremont Park (all in New York) constructions from 1929 to 1936. At the same time he was preparing studies for several drives in Acadia National Park, another Rockefeller public park donation. Zach continued to design elements for other Rockefeller properties into the late 1930s, mainly in Pocantico Hills, New York.

From the correspondence, plans, and other records of the Olmsted Brothers, some of Zach's individual works are slowly being identified. His design sketches reveal his artistic hand, but his real strength was in planning and administration. Thus, he was well suited to the complex coordination of extensive design and engineering tasks and multiple work crews involved in the concurrent Rockefeller projects. Likewise, working with Olmsted

Brothers partner **James Frederick Dawson**, Zach supervised numerous simultaneous projects throughout Alabama during the late 1920s and 1930s for parks, educational institutions, and the state capitol at Montgomery. While it is difficult to point to any specific element as being his design, his extraordinary management skills are reflected in the quality of the final product.

In 1924, Zach married Gertrude Robinson, whom he described as having "similar wanderlust . . . [agreeing] to take a trip at least every three years." Over the next decade they traveled to Europe for pleasure and for the jury of the Prix de Rome at the American Academy (1933); to Venezuela for work on the Caracas Country Club (1928); to Bermuda for the Biological Research Station (1930); and to Vancouver, British Columbia, for the 4,000-acre development of Capilano for the British Pacific Properties (1930–1934), with pleasure trips to Havana, the Panama Canal, and across the country from the California coast to the Grand Canyon to New Orleans (1934).

Left: Sketch by Pertzoff of the state capitol, Montgomery, Alabama, n.d. (Courtesy of the National Park Service, Frederick Law Olmsted National Historic Site)

Below: One of Zach's campus designs is the "General Plan for Troy State Teachers College," Troy, Alabama, April 1930. (Courtesy of the National Park Service, Frederick Law Olmsted National Historic Site)

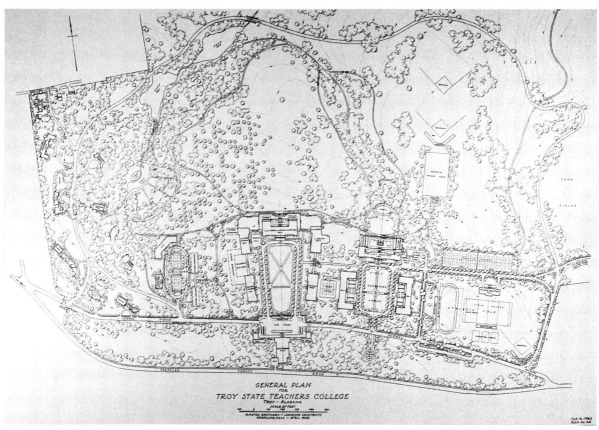

Zach became a partner of the Olmsted firm in 1938, but as he noted in his Harvard *25th Anniversary Report* (1943), this was "no help to the pocketbook." Therefore, in 1941 he went to Washington, D.C., "for a few months" to set up the functions for the Site Planning Unit in the Construction Division of the Quartermaster General's Office. Finding the planning problems for military cantonments, internment camps, hospitals, and the like, of great interest, he never returned to Olmsted Brothers. Instead, he spent the rest of his career traveling around the world, planning military bases of all sizes, for which he was awarded the Commendation for Exceptional Civilian Service by the War Department in 1944. As a result of his efforts, comprehensive master planning was instituted for military installations, instead of the formerly haphazard approach. Zach was active at both the local and national levels of the American Society of Landscape Architects, serving at different times as president of both the nationwide organization and the local chapter. He became a Fellow in 1943. Additionally, he represented the U.S. Army on the National Capital Planning Commission (1953–1956); was active with alumni affairs for the Harvard Graduate School of Design; served on the Advisory Committee of Dumbarton Oaks; was a vice president of the International Federation of Landscape Architects (1962–1964); and was an honorary member of the American Institute of Architects (1956). Having no children, he had time to pursue these activities and his avocations of music and painting.

Zach wanted the landscape profession to be respected as a distinct discipline and desired educational training for landscape architects that was responsive to new needs. Consequently, he wrote numerous articles on these topics, for *Landscape Architecture* and other such journals. In addition to book reviews and obituary tributes for colleagues, he explored issues of collaboration among the related professions; the developing opportunities of government service for landscape architects; and the need to strengthen educational programs to include fine arts as well as the study of land forms. He was an early supporter of preservation efforts and of interpreting sites of interest in American history and culture for the public benefit.

In 1965, at age seventy, Zach retired as chief of the Planning Branch, Engineering Division of the U.S. Army. He died in Washington, D.C., on July 11, 1966.

Zach, Leon. "The Value of Landscape Treatment in Cemeteries." Paper read by Zach at the Annual Meeting of the American Association of Cemetery Superintendents, September 12, 1935. Zach recommended that training for cemetery design and management be tempered with an aesthetic point of view about land arrangements to balance the man-made and the natural, suggesting restrictions concerning size and shape of ornaments. He sought decoration from varied yet dignified plantings to give pleasure over long periods, while also recognizing maintenance implications. The design must imply function (a cemetery was not to appear as a public park), but he considered the best-selling point for one's last resting place was to have a total visual effect of serene and picturesque tranquility.

Zach, Leon H. "The Education of the Landscape Architect. American Aims and Achievements in Historical Perspective." *Landscape Architecture* 39 (October 1948), 27–32. Zach sets forth his credo for landscape architects, what they should study and why. He sees the landscape profession as "a social art" that "requires in its practitioners a knowledge of the ideals and the living requirements of many sorts of man. . . ."

Zach, Leon H. "Landscape Beauty and Use: Some Examples from Claremont Park." *Landscape Architecture* 26 (January 1936), 57–67. Analysis of the site constraints and design considerations that influenced the Olmsted plans for this important small park situated between Riverside Church and the International House, across the street from Grant's Tomb. Zach emphasizes the intent to coordinate the park with its important surroundings in a "good landscape composition," while providing "the greatest value per dollar . . . the interlocking relations of esthetic values and economic values."

Arleyn A. Levee

ZION, ROBERT LEWIS
(1921–2000)
LANDSCAPE ARCHITECT

Robert Lewis Zion was born March 3, 1921, in Lawrence, on Long Island, New York, one of two children. He attended a private boarding school, and Hamilton College. He was attending Harvard College when he was drafted into the U.S. Army during World War II. He was assigned to Washington, D.C., as a translator of Chinese, and later reassigned to Europe during the Battle of the Bulge.

Zion first entertained the notion of becoming a landscape architect when, during the Battle of the Bulge, he was alone in a foxhole and heard movement, so he opened fire on the supposed enemy. The next morning he discovered, to his delight, he had survived the night, but later realized he had eliminated an entire hedgerow. He decided to become a landscape architect to restore the landscape he had destroyed.

Zion returned to the United States to finish Harvard College under the G.I. Bill. He received the following degrees from Harvard University: bachelor of arts (cum laude), Industrial Administrator in 1943, master of business administration in 1946, and master of landscape architecture in 1951. During his time at Harvard, he was strongly influenced by Lester Albertson Collins,* Walter Gropius, Joseph Hudnut, and especially **Norman Thomas Newton**, his friend and mentor. Upon graduation from the School of Design, he was awarded the Charles Eliot Traveling Fellowship. Returning from a year of travel and study in Europe and North Africa, Zion entered private practice in New York City.

From the beginning, Zion's work was deft and mature. The garden he designed for his parents in 1956 was featured in *House and Garden* that year. Zion joined the firm of I. M. Pei, Architect, and completed numerous projects. He formed a partnership with Harold Breen, a classmate at Harvard, in 1957. Their office remained in New York City.

In 1962, he wrote an article, "Some Impractical Ideas for the Improvement of Cities," for the *Journal of the American Institute of Architects.* Zion proposed a series of urban plans for New York City, including the need to build parklets, zoolets, and recognize the waterfront of New York. Many of his proposals were eventually realized. During the Wagner and Lindsay administrations,

Robert Zion and friends, ca. 1982. (Zion Breen & Richardson Associates)

he served on the City's Arts Commission. He was also vice president of the Architectural League of New York. In 1963, Zion designed the first prototype for the "vest-pocket" park for an exhibition organized by the League along with the Park Association of New York, titled *New Parks for New York.*

Zion was later commissioned by William S. Paley, Chairman of CBS, to create the first "vest-pocket" park in memory of his father. Paley Park, located on 53rd Street just east of Fifth Avenue, was a small space (50 feet by 100 feet) with an unlimited budget. Zion's vision was a simple "outdoor room": the floor was granite block; the walls covered with vines of English ivy, creating a "vertical lawn," the ceiling—a dense canopy of leaves pro-

Sculpture Garden, Museum of Modern Art, New York, New York. (Courtesy of Charles A. Birnbaum)

vided by locust trees planted 12 feet to 15 feet apart; the furniture did not include traditional park benches, but rather, light and portable single chairs and tables. The park, with its 20-foot high water wall, recirculating 3,500 gallons of water every minute, drowns out the harsh city sounds, and provides an oasis for people to meet and gather. William H. Whyte* photographed and studied the use of Paley Park with time-lapse photography, and found that it was the most actively used park, per square foot, in the City of New York. The 1967 success of Paley Park forced New York officials to reconsider such spaces, which had long been deemed too small to be properly used or maintained. As a result, for the next thirty years, small parks and plazas became part of the city plan.

In the late 1960s, Zion purchased and restored Bilyeu Farm, in Cream Ridge, New Jersey, reestablishing the building's eighteenth-century character. Later, he purchased an adjoining farm and began raising animals. He also started a tree nursery, nurturing seedlings while, as he liked to point out, his urban friends were going to cocktail parties.

At first, the farm was a weekend retreat for Zion, who continued to work in New York City. As his weekends

began to stretch from two to three days, then to four, he realized he needed to move his business into the country. He purchased a condemned mill in Imlaystown, New Jersey, and began restoring the 1695 structure for his office. In 1973, Zion and Breen Associates, Inc., relocated to Imlaystown, where Zion often made his three-mile commute to the office on horseback.

From the early 1960s, the firm was retained as a consultant to the Museum of Modern Art, working with Philip Johnson for the additions to the Museum Garden in 1965; with Cesar Pelli, Architect, for the Museum Tower addition; and directing the renovation of the garden in 1989 for the museum's fiftieth anniversary celebration. The Museum Garden, which consists of weeping European beech, birch, and London plantrees; unpolished, gray marble pavement; and reflecting pools and fountains, is a sculptural element in itself.

From 1967 to 1982, Zion's firm served as landscape architects to Yale University, designing a garden for the president's residence. The firm also served as consultants to Princeton University from 1976 to 1983, and completed numerous master plans for universities throughout the country.

Paley Park (former site of the Stork Club), midtown Manhattan, New York, New York. (Zion, Breen & Richardson Associates)

The 1970s also brought several significant commissions including the site analysis of a 2,000-acre site in Concord, North Carolina, which became the Philip Morris Manufacturing Plant. The firm also completed the Philip Morris Corporate Offices in Richmond, Virginia; the development of a master plan design for Liberty State Park in New Jersey, and the Cincinnati Riverfront Park. The original design commission for the City of Cincinnati, contained four or five small parcels of land designated by the city for park use. Zion convinced a Citizens Riverfront Commission that the public deserved a far better development of the waterfront. Zion made a Recreational Master Plan Proposal for the waterfront accompanied by a "concept-of-use" report. The result was a phased implementation of the master plan with a green park located above and behind the riverside concrete, serpentine embankment to encourage river views, which rises approximately 25 feet from the Ohio River. The embankment serves as a series of stadium steps from which crowds watch river traffic, water-borne boat shows, and civic events.

Several equally important commissions were completed in the 1980s, including the new landscape design for Liberty Island for the 1986 Statue of Liberty Centennial ceremonies, which provided an overlay to Newton's earlier plan. The plan involved the redesign and repaving of the main malls leading to the Statue of Liberty flanked by plantings of mature Littleleaf Lindens, and many other elements throughout the island. Architect Edward Larrabee Barnes designed the IBM World Headquarters corporate plaza in New York City, and Zion and his firm created the planting design for the large, ground-level atrium with eleven bamboo groves rising from diamond-shaped cut-outs in the plaza pavement. The planting was intended to create a contrast to the hardness of the surrounding architecture and to allow intimate seating areas for the public.

Zion was quick-witted and an eloquent writer. He was tireless in his pursuit of innovative ideas to improve cities and the environment. His great interest in trees resulted in his book *Trees for Architecture and Landscape,* first published in 1968.

Zion designed the environment to function as needed, and then attempted to provide as much delight as possible. Zion's simple and elegant designs remain timeless, and are still considered innovative and fresh. Sustainability is one of the most important aspects of landscape design, and many of Robert Zion's landscapes have endured for decades. Throughout his life, he remained committed to humanizing and beautifying the urban landscape by maintaining high standards and impeccable design instincts. Later in life, he became an eccentric country gentleman, enjoying the things that made him happy: his work, a donkey, a pony, seven dogs, four horses, thirteen barn cats and more than one hundred deer, living on his 200-acre tree nursery. "Solitude," he declared "is the greatest luxury."

During his almost fifty-year career, he completed projects in Israel, France, and Japan. Zion worked with some of the country's most distinguished architects, including Philip Johnson, Edward Larrabee Barnes, I. M. Pei, Robert A. M. Stern, Eero Saarinen, Kohn Pedersen Fox, Beyer Blinder Belle, Skidmore Owings & Merrill, and Paul Rudolph. Under Zion's direction, his firm completed over 1,000 projects, before his death in an automobile accident in April 2000, at the age of seventy-nine.

Robert Zion: A Profile in Landscape Architecture, Process: Architecture, No. 94. Tokyo, Japan: Process Architecture Co., Ltd., 1991. Essays and articles by Zion. Introductory essay by Susan Tamulevich. A Japanese monograph of the life of Robert Zion and the work of the firm.

Zion, Robert L. "Some Impractical Ideas for the Improvement of Cities." *Journal of the American Institute of Architects* 37, no. 2 (February 1962), 25–29. Zion's vision for gateways, recognizing waterfronts as recreational spaces.

Zion, Robert L. *Trees for Architecture and Landscape.* 2nd ed. New York: Van Nostrand Reinhold, 1995. First published in 1968. A pictorial resource and guide on tree design characteristics, and a reference on all aspects of using trees in architecture and landscapes.

Donald Richardson

Sites Accessible to the Public

Following is a selected list of landscapes open to the public (or by appointment) for those practitioners whose landscapes survive. Addresses of small and discrete sites have been included, and, where possible, streets, directions, phone numbers, and Web sites have been provided.

Note: Many sites listed here are credited to more than one practitioner, a reflection of various layers of design. Conversely, although some are credited to an individual practitioner, often more than one designer was involved.

ADAMS, CHARLES GIBBS
Hearst Castle, San Simeon, near Paso Robles, California, (800) 444-7275, www.hearstcastle.org
The Succulent Garden, W. K. Kellogg Arabian Horse Ranch (now the campus of the California State Polytechnic University), Pomona, California

AUST, FRANZ
Circulation system and rockwork at the northeast quadrant (corner at Pleasant and Bushnell Streets) of the Beloit College campus, Beloit, Wisconsin
Glenwood Children's Park, Madison, Wisconsin
The Nakoma neighborhood, Madison, Wisconsin (with Ossian Cole Simonds and Hare & Hare)

BALTIMORE, GARNET DOUGLASS
Forest Park Cemetery, Pinewoods Avenue, Brunswick, New York, Brunswick Historical Society, (518) 279-4024
Prospect Park, Pawling Avenue, Troy, New York, (518) 270-4401

BAYER, HERBERT
Anderson Park, Aspen Institute for Humanistic Studies, 1000 North Third Street, Aspen, Colorado, (970) 925-7010
ARCO Plaza, 555 South Flower Street, Los Angeles, California
Grass Mound, Aspen Institute for Humanistic Studies, 1000 North Third Street, Aspen, Colorado, (970) 925-7010
Marble Garden, Aspen Institute for Humanistic Studies, 1000

North Third Street, Aspen, Colorado, (970) 925-7010
Mill Creek Canyon Earthworks Park, 742 E. Titus Street, Kent, Washington

BAYLIS, DOUGLAS
Monterey Freeway, California
San Bruno Mountain and Housing Preserve, California
San Francisco Bay Area Rapid Transit, Glen Park Station, California
San Francisco's Civic Center Plaza, California
Washington Square, San Francisco, California

BENDELOW, TOM
City Park Golf Course (public), 1442 City Park Avenue, Baton Rouge, Louisiana, (225) 387-9523
City Park Golf Course (public), 2500 York Street, Denver, Colorado, (303) 295-4420
Helfrich Hills Golf Course (public), 1550 Mesker Park Drive, Evansville, Indiana, (812) 435-6075
Medinah Country Club (private), 6N001 Medinah Road, Medinah, Illinois, (630) 773-1700, www.medinahcc.org
Van Cortlandt Park Golf Course (public), Bailey Avenue and Van Cortlandt Park South, Bronx, New York, (718) 543-4595

BOERNER, ALFRED L.
Charles A. Wustum Museum of Fine Arts, 2519 Northwestern Avenue, Racine, Wisconsin, (262) 636-9177, www.ramart.org

Milwaukee County Parks, including Brown Deer Park, Estabrook Park, Greenfield Park, McGovern Park, and Sheridan Park

Milwaukee County Parkways, including Menomonee River Parkway and Oak Creek Parkway

Whitnall Park Arboretum and Boerner Botanical Gardens, 9400 Boerner Drive, Hales Corners, Wisconsin, (414) 525-5600, www.boernerbotanicalgardens.org

BOGART, JOHN

Branch Brook Park, Southern Division at Clifton Avenue, Newark, New Jersey, www.newark1.com/branchbrook/

Echota, Niagara Falls, New York, southern section of city, west of intersection of Buffalo Avenue and Hyde Park Boulevard

Grounds of the Tennessee State Capitol, Nashville, Tennessee

Washington Park, entrance at New Scotland Avenue, Albany, New York, www.shingtonparkconservancy.com

BRINLEY, JOHN ROWLETT

Henry Villard Estate Burial Plot at Sleepy Hollow Cemetery, 540 North Broadway, Tarrytown, New York, (914) 631-0081, www.sleepyhollowcemetery.org

Morristown Park and Stone Fountain, Park Place, Morristown, New Jersey

New York Botanical Garden, Peggy Rockefeller Rose Garden, 200th Street and Southern Boulevard, Bronx, New York, (718) 817-8700, www.nybg.org

Rye Town Park, Forrest Avenue, between Rye Beach and Dearborn Avenue, Rye, New York

BROOKS, JOHN A.

Fair Lane, 4901 Evergreen Road, Dearborn, Michgan, (313) 593-5590, www.henryfordestate.org

CALVERT, FRANCIS

East Lake Forest street plan of 1857, Lake Forest, Illinois; see especially the lawns of 570 and 660 North Sheridan Road and 644, 747, 888, 920, and 965 East Deerpath and the ravine-scape on the southeast corner of Deerpath (500 block) and Washington Road

CAPARN, HAROLD AP RHYS

The Bronx Zoo, Fordham Road and the Bronx River Parkway, Bronx, New York, (718) 367-1010, www.bronxzoo.com

Brooklyn Botanic Garden, 1000 Washington Avenue, Brooklyn, New York, (718) 623-7200, www.bbg.org

Grant Park, Park Avenue, and Columbus Park, Park Hill Avenue, Yonkers, New York

Lebanon Valley College, 101 N. College Avenue, Annville, Pennsylvania, www.lvc.edu

Mountain Branch, National Home for Volunteer Disabled Soldiers, Johnson City, Tennessee, (423) 979-2888, www.jcedb.org/history

CHRISTY, ELIZABETH (LIZ)

Bergen Block Association Garden, Bergen Street between Nostrand and New York Avenues, Brooklyn, New York

Cherry Park, Bryant Avenue between E. 174th Street and Cross Bronx Expressway, The Bronx, New York

Liz Christy's Bowery-Houston Garden, northeast corner of the Bowery and Houston Street, Manhattan, New York, www.lizchristygarden.org

Our Lady of the Presentation Garden, Rockaway Avenue and Bergen Street, Brownsville, Brooklyn, New York

Wyckoff-Bond Garden, northwest corner of Wyckoff and Bond Streets, Brooklyn, New York

COLLINS, LESTER ALBERTSON

Enid Haupt Garden, Smithsonian, 10th Street and Independence Avenue SW, Washington, D.C.

Hirshhorn Sculpture Garden, Smithsonian, Seventh Street SW and Independence Avenue, Washington, D.C., hirshhorn.si.edu

Innisfree Garden, Millbrook, New York, (845) 677-8000, www.innisfreegarden.org

Miami Lakes, Florida

CRET, PAUL PHILIPPE

National Naval Medical Center, 8901 Rockville Pike, Bethesda, Maryland, www.bethesda.med.navy.mil

Rittenhouse Square, Walnut and 19th Streets, Philadelphia, Pennsylvania

University of Texas, Austin, Texas, www.utexas.edu

CULYER, COLONEL JOHN YAPP

Eastern and Ocean Parkways, Brooklyn, New York

Eastside Park, Paterson, NJ

Prospect Park, Brooklyn, New York, www.prospectpark.org/

CURTIS, JOSEPH HENRY

Asticou Terraces, Northeast Harbor, Maine

DAHL, HILBERT EINAR

Albany Rural Cemetery, 48 Cemetery Avenue, Menands, New York, (518) 463-7017, www.albanyruralcemetery.org

Baha'i Temple, 100 Linden Avenue, Wilmette, Illinois, (847) 853-2300, www.bahai.us/bahai-temple

Croton Aqueduct and Water Works: Old Croton Aquaduct State Historic Park, Bronx to Cortlandt, New York; 15 Walnut Street, Dobbs Ferry, New York, (914) 963-5259

Erie Canalway National Heritage Corridor–Visitor's Center at Peebles Island State Park, Delaware Avenue, off of Ontario Street, Cohoes, New York, (518) 237-7000

Green-Wood Cemetery, 500 25th Street, Brooklyn, New York, (718) 768-7300, www.green-wood.com

Old Erie Canal State Park, RD 2, Andrus Road, Kirkville, New York, (315) 687-7821

DE FOREST, ELIZABETH KELLAM

Alice Keck Park Memorial Gardens, intersection of Santa Barbara and Arrellaga Streets, Santa Barbara, California

Laguna Cottages for Seniors (formerly known as Santa Barbara Senior Center), 803 Laguna Street, Santa Barbara, California, (805) 965-1179

Lamont Garden at Mount Vernon, 3200 Mount Vernon Memorial Highway, Mount Vernon, Virginia, (703) 780-2000

DORMON, CAROLINE CORONEOS

Briarwood, The Caroline Dormon Nature Preserve, 216 Caroline Dormon Road, Saline, Louisiana, (318) 576-3379, www.cp-tel.net/dormon

Chicot State Park and Louisiana State Arboretum, 4213 Chicot Park Road, Ville Platte, Louisiana, (337) 363-6289, www.stateparks.com/chicot.html

Hodges Gardens, Park and Wilderness Area, P.O. Box 340, Florien, Louisiana, (318) 586-3523, www.crt.state.la.us/parks/ihodges.aspx

Longue Vue Gardens, 7 Bamboo Road, New Orleans, Louisiana, (504) 488-5488, www.longuevue.com

DOUGLASS, DAVID BATES

Albany Rural Cemetery, 48 Cemetery Avenue, Menands, New York, (518) 463-7017, www.albanyruralcemetery.org

Croton Aqueduct and Water Works, Old Croton Aqueduct State Historic Park, Bronx to Cortlandt, New York, 15 Walnut Street, Dobbs Ferry, New York, (914) 963-5259

Erie Canalway National Heritage Corridor, Visitor's Center at Peebles Island State Park, Deleare Avenue, off of Ontario Street, Cohoes, New York, (518) 237-7000

Green-Wood Cemetery, 500 25th Street, Brooklyn, New York, (718) 768-7300, www.green-wood.com

Old Erie Canal State Park, RD 2, Andrus Road, Kirkville, New York, (315) 687-7821

ECKBO, GARRETT

Ambassador College, Pasadena, California

Fulton Street Mall, Fresno, California

Mar Vista Housing, Los Angeles, California

Tucson Downtown Community Center, Tucson, Arizona

Union Square Bank, Downtown Los Angeles, California

EGAN, WILLIAM CONSTANTINE

Two signature trees—a Gingko and a Katsuratree—along the 2200 block of Egandale Road, Highland Park, Illinois

ENGELHARDT, HEINRICH ADOLPH

Belleville Cemetery, 631-B Dundas Street West, 3.7 miles south of Highway 401, exit 538, near Belleville, Ontario, (613) 962-8468, www.bellevillecemetery.com

Mount Pleasant Cemetery, between Yonge Street and Mount Pleasant Road, north of St. Clair Avenue, Toronto, Ontario, (416) 485-9129, www.mountpleasantgroupofcemeteries.ca/our_cemeteries/mount_pleasant_cemetery.asp

FAIRCHILD, DAVID

Cherry Trees, Tidal Basin, Washington, D.C., (202) 426-6841

The Kampong, 4013 S. Douglas Road, Coconut Grove, Florida, (305) 442-7169

FLANDERS, ANNETTE HOYT

Lawrence C. Phipps Memorial Conference Center at the University of Denver, 3400 Belcaro Drive, Denver, Colorado, (303) 777-4441, www.du.edu/phipps

Morven Farm Gardens, Charlottesville, Virginia, www.uvafoundation.com/morvenfarms

FRANCESCHI, DR. FRANCESCO

Franceschi Park, Franceschi Road off Mission Ridge Road, Santa Barbara, California, (805) 564-5418, www.santabarbara.com/Activities/parks/franceschi/

FRIEDBERG, M. PAUL

Battery Park City, North Cove, New York City, New York

Peavey Plaza and Loring Greenway, Nicollet Mall, Minneapolis, Minnesota

Pershing Park, Pennsylvania Avenue, Washington, D.C.

67th Street Playground, Central Park, New York City, New York

Yerba Buena Gardens Playground, San Francisco, California

FURLONG, ETHELBERT ELY

Clayton E. Freeman property, Hawthorne Avenue, Glen Ridge, New Jersey

Freeman Gardens, Glen Ridge, New Jersey

GRÉBER, JACQUES-HENRI-AUGUSTE

Casa De Serralves, Porto, Portugal

Ottawa Park System, Ottawa, Canada

Philadelphia Museum of Art, 2600 Benjamin Franklin Parkway, Philadelphia, Pennsylvania, (215) 763-8100, www.philamuseum.org/visit

Rodin Museum Grounds, 22nd Street and the Benjamin Franklin Parkway, Philadelphia, Pennsylvania, (215) 568-6026, www.rodinmuseum.org

Villa Reale di Marlia, Tuscany, Italy

GREGG, JOHN W.

Campus, University of California, Berkeley, California, www.berkeley.edu

Campus, University of California, Los Angeles, California, www.ucla.edu

Campus, University of California, Riverside, California, www.ucr.edu

John Hinkel Park, 41 Somerset Avenue between Southampton Avenue and San Diego Road, Berkeley, California, www.ci.berkeley.ca.us/parks

GUNN, RALPH ELLIS

Centennial House, 411 Upper Broadway, Corpus Christi, Texas, (361) 882-8691, www.ccahs.com

Key West Tropical Forest & Botanical Garden, 5210 College Road, Key West, Florida, (305) 296-1504, www .keywestbotanicalgarden.org

Liendo Plantation, www.tsha.utexas.edu/handbook/online/ articles/view/LL/ccl1.html

Rienzi, 1406 Kirby Drive, Houston, Texas, (713) 639-7800

Rosedown Plantation, 2501 LA Highway 10, St. Francisville, Louisiana, (225) 635-3332, www.crt.state.la.us/crt/parks/ rosedown/rosedown.htm

HAAG, RICHARD

Bloedel Reserve, Bainbridge Island, Puget Sound, Washington, http://www.bloedelreserve.org/

Jordan Park, Everett, Washington

Victor Steinbrueck Park, 1984 Western Avenue, Seattle, Washington

Washington Gas Works Park, North Northlake Way and Wallingford Street, Seattle, Washington

Western Washington State University: Ridgeway Dorms, Red Square, Admin. Building, Fairhaven College, Humanities and Science Complex, Bellingham, WA

HALL, ALFRED V. *SEE* **HARRIES, HALL & KRUSE**

HALPRIN, LAWRENCE

Auditorium Forecourt, Pettigrove Plaza, Lovejoy Plaza, Transit Mall, Portland, Oregon

Downtown Pedestrian Mall, between 2nd Street NW and 4th Street NE, Charlottesville, Virginia

Franklin Delano Roosevelt Memorial, Tidal Basin, Washington, D.C., www.nps.gov/fdrm

Freeway Park, Seattle, Washington

The Sea Ranch community, Gualala, Sonoma County, California

HANSON, A. E.

Doheny Memorial Library and Alumni Lawn, University of Southern California, Los Angeles, California

Getty House (former Lockhart Garden; now official residence of the Mayor of Los Angeles), 605 S. Irving, Los Angeles, California, (323) 930-6430

Palos Verdes Peninsula, the original entrance to Rolling Hills, Los Angeles County, California

HARRIES, HALL & KRUSE

Amsterdam Square Park and Fountain, 525 Avenue Road at St. Clair Avenue, Toronto, Ontario, www.toronto.ca/legdocs/ bylaws/2003/law0437.pdf

Kapuskasing, Ontario, town center north of Kapuskasing River, www.kapuskasing.ca/portal/en/kapuskasing/ourtown

Parker/Chappell House, Mississauga Garden Park, 1447

Burnhamthorpe Road West, Mississauga, Ontario, www .mississaugagardenpark.com

HAVEY, RUTH MILDRED

Dumbarton Oaks Garden, R Street and 32nd Street NW, Washington, D.C., (202) 339-6401, www.doaks.org

HEGEMANN, WERNER

Original neighborhood, Kohler, Wisconsin

Washington Highlands, Wauwatosa, Wisconsin

Wyomissing Park, Reading, Pennsylvania

HERTRICH, WILLIAM

Huntington Botanical Gardens, 1151 Oxford Road, San Marino, California, (626) 405-2100, www.huntington.org

Lacey Park, between Virginia and St. Albans Roads, and North of Monterey Road, San Marino, California

HOLLIED, CLARENCE EDMUND "BUD"

Glorieta Gardens, Glorieta Baptist Conference Center, Glorieta, New Mexico, (800) 797-4222

Roosevelt Park, Coal and Spruce SE, Albuquerque, New Mexico

HOLZBOG, WALTER CHARLES

Bradley Sculpture Gardens, Rose Garden, 2145 W. Brown Deer Road, River Hills, Wisconsin, (414) 224-3850

Community United Methodist Church, 14700 Watertown Plank Road, Elm Grove, Wisconsin, (262) 782-4060

Pattison State Park, 6294 S. State Road 25, Superior, Wisconsin, (715) 399-3111

St. Matthew's Lutheran Church, 1615 Wauwatosa Avenue, Wauwatosa, Wisconsin, (414) 774-0441

HOTCHKISS, ALMERIN

Bellefontaine Cemetery, 4947 W. Florissant Avenue, St. Louis, Missouri

Chippiannock Cemetery, 12th Street and 31st Avenue, Rock Island, Illinois, www.chippiannock.com

Green-Wood Cemetery, 500 25th Street, Brooklyn, New York, (718) 768-7300, www.green-wood.com

Lake Forest, Illinois, roughly 30 miles north of Chicago

HOWLAND, BENJAMIN CREGAN, JR.

Assateague Island National Seashore, Virginia and Maryland, www.nps.gov/asis/index.htm

Baltimore-Washington Parkway, 29-mile scenic parkway, also known as I-295, from Washington, D.C., to Baltimore, Maryland, www.nps.gov/bawa/

Cape Cod National Seashore, along the Atlantic coast of Massachusetts, www.nps.gov/caco/

George Washington Memorial Parkway, Memorial Bridge to Great Falls, Virginia, www.nps.gov/gwmp/

Point Reyes National Seashore, Point Reyes, California, 30 miles north of San Francisco on Highway 1, www.nps.gov/ pore/

HUBBARD, LOUISE STONE

Old Mill Farm, Albert Lasker estate (400 acres subdivided), between Everett and Old Mill Roads, east of I-94, Lake Forest, Illinois (especially Estate Lane and its associated plantings and spaces)

IREYS, ALICE RECKNAGEL

Alice Recknagel Ireys Fragrance Garden for the Blind, Brooklyn Botanic Garden, 1000 Washington Avenue, Brooklyn, New York, (718) 623-7200, www.bbg.org/exp/stroll/fragrance.html

Clark Botanic Garden (designed entire facility), 193 I. U. Willets Road, Albertson, New York, (516) 484-8600, http://www.clarkbotanic.org/

Davis Square Park Capitol and Summer Streets, Charleston, West Virginia

Garden of the Mount Vernon Hotel Museum, 421 East 61st Street, New York, New York, (212) 838-6878, http://www.mvhm.org/

Red Hook Housing Project Tree Plantings, between W. 9th and Creamer Streets, Dwight and Clinton Streets, Brooklyn, New York

JOHNSON, CAROL R.

John F. Kennedy Memorial Park, Memorial Drive and JFK Street, Cambridge, Massachusetts

Lechmere Canal Park, CambridgeSide Place, East Cambridge, Massachusetts

Mystic River Reservation, Mystic Valley Parkway, Somerville, Massachusetts

Old Harbor Park, 24 Oyster Bay Road, Boston, Massachusetts

Rollins College, 1000 Holt Avenue, Winter Park, Florida

JOHNSON, MARSHALL LISTON

The Clearing, 12171 Garrett Bay Road, Ellison Bay, Wisconsin, (920) 854-4088, www.theclearing.org

Columbus Park, 500 S. Central Avenue, Chicago, Illinois

Cook Memorial Rose Garden, 400 block Milwaukee Avenue, Libertyville, Illinois

Greenfield Village, The Henry Ford, 20900 Oakwood Boulevard, Dearborn, Michigan, (313) 982-6100, www.hfmgv.org/village/index.aspx

Villa Turicum subdivision, south of East Westleigh Road and east of Sheridan Road, Lake Forest, Illinois (especially South Circle Lane)

KELLAWAY, HERBERT J.

Faxon Park, Quincy Avenue, Quincy, Massachusetts

Hammond Pond Parkway, connects Beacon Street to Route 9 through Hammond Pond Reservation, Brookline, Massachusetts

Hastings Park, corner of Massachusetts Avenue and Worthen Road, Lexington, Massachusetts

Merrymount Park, intersection of Merrymount (Route 3A) and Furnace Brook Parkways, Quincy, Massachusetts

Mill Pond stepped dam; Waterfield Road and Main Street bridges; Wedge Pond (town center), Leonard Pond (Washington Street), and Davidson Park (Cross Street), Winchester, Massachusetts

Newton Center Playground, near Center Street and Commonwealth Avenue, Newton, Massachusetts

KESSLER, WILLIAM HARRY

The Country Club of Birmingham (private), 3325 Country Club Road, Birmingham, Alabama

Mountain Brook Club (private), 19 Beechwood Road, Birmingham, Alabama, (205) 871-3769

Mountain Brook Estates and Redmont Park neighborhoods, Birmingham, Alabama

Mountain Brook Village, Birmingham, Alabama

Old Mill house, Mountain Brook Estates, Birmingham, Alabama (view from road)

Tutwiler estate, Mountain Brook Estates, Birmingham, Alabama (view from road)

KILEY, DANIEL URBAN

Air Force Academy, Exit 156B on Interstate 25, 14 miles north of Colorado Springs, Colorado, (719) 333-2025, www.usafa.af.mil/

Art Institute of Chicago, 111 South Michigan Avenue, Chicago, Illinois, (312) 443-3600, www.artic.edu/

Fountain Place, 1445 Ross Avenue, Dallas, Texas

Jefferson National Expansion, St. Louis, Missouri, (314) 655-1700, www.nps.gov/jeff/

Oakland Museum, 1000 Oak Street, Oakland, California, (510) 238-2200, www.museumca.org/

KRUSE, ARTHUR M. *SEE* HARRIES, HALL & KRUSE

LAWRENCE, ELIZABETH

The Elizabeth Lawrence House and Garden (open by appointment), 348 Ridgewood Avenue (between Selwyn Avenue and Westfield Road), Charlotte, North Carolina, tours@elizabethlawrence.org

Elizabeth Lawrence Perennial Border at the J. C. Raulston Arboretum, North Carolina State University, 4415 Beryl Road, off Hillsborough Street, Raleigh, North Carolina, (919) 515-3132, www.ncsu.edu/jcraulstonarboretum

The Herb Garden at the Country Doctor's Museum, 4165 Vance Street, Bailey, North Carolina, (252) 235-4165, www.countrydoctormuseum.org

Historic Hope Plantation, off NC Highway 308, Windsor, North Carolina, (252) 794-3140, www.hopeplantation.org

LAWSON, EDWARD GODFREY

No known surviving gardens; however, Italian baroque gardens he measured include:

Villa Borghese, Borghese gardens, Rome, a short walk form Porta via Veneto

Villa Gamberaia, Settignano, northeast of Florence, reachable by bus and a country road walk

Villa Torlonia (now in ruins), Frascati, site of the terminus of the bus line from Rome

LEE, CLERMONT "MONTY" HUGER

Juliette Gordon Low Birthplace, 10 East Oglethorpe, Savannah, Georgia

Owen-Thomas House, 124 Abercorn Street, Savannah, Georgia

Warren, Washington, Green, and Troup Squares, Savannah, Georgia

LIPP, FRANZ

Cantigny Park, Wheaton, Illinois

Chicago Botanic Garden, Education Building, West Court, Glencoe, Illinois, www.chicagobotanic.org

Henri-Chapelle American Cemetery and Memorial, Liege, Belgium

LONDON, RUTH

Bayou Bend Collection and Gardens, 1 Westcott Street, Houston, Texas, (713)639-7750, www.mfah.org/bayoubend

Houston Museum of Fine Arts, South Garden, at Main Street and Montrose Boulevard, Houston, Texas, www.mfah.org

MACDONALD, CHARLES BLAIR

Annapolis Golf Club (public), 2836 Carrolton Road, Annapolis, Maryland, (410) 263-2771, www.annapolisroads.net/

Chicago Golf Club (private), 25W253 Warrenville Road, Wheaton, Illinois, (630) 665-2988, www.golflink.com/golf-courses/course.asp?course=318945

The Course at Yale (private), 200 Conrad Drive, New Haven, Connecticut, (203) 392-2376, yalegolfcourse.com

National Golf Links of America (private), Sabonet Inlet Road, Southampton, New York, (631) 283-3559, www.golfclubatlas.com/ngla2.html

St. Louis Country Club (private), 400 Barnes Road, St. Louis, Missouri, (314) 994-0017, www.golfclubatlas.com/stlouis2.html

MARVIN, ROBERT E.

Finlay Park, 930 Laurel Street, Columbia, South Carolina, (803) 733-8331, www.columbiasouthcarolina.com/parks-city.html

Glencairn Garden, Charlotte Avenue and Crest Street, Rock Hill, South Carolina, (803) 329-5620, /rockhillrocks.com/facilities.asp#regional

Governor's Mansion, 800 Richland Street, Columbia, South Carolina (Monday to Friday, 9:00 AM to 4:00 PM), (803) 737-1710, www.scgovernorsmansion.org

Harbortown at Sea Pines plantation, Hilton Head Island, South Carolina

Sibley Center and Cecil B. Day Butterfly House, Callaway Gardens, Pine Mountain, Georgia, (706) 663-2281, www.callawaygardens.com

MCHARG, IAN L.

Cemetery for British Soldiers Killed in Action in Greece, Athens, Greece

Central Waterfront, Toronto, Canada

Edith Macy Conference Center, Girl Scouts of America, 550 Chappaqua Road, Briarcliff Manor, New York

Gateway National Recreational Area, 210 New York Avenue, Staten Island, New York, www.nps.gov/gate/

Township of Medford, 17 North Main Street, Medford, New Jersey

The Woodlands, Texas

MCLAREN, JOHN

Dunsmuir House, 2960 Peralta Oaks Court, Oakland, California, (510) 615-5555, www.dunsmuir.org/contact.htm

Golden Gate Park, Fell and Stanyan Streets, San Francisco, California, (415) 666-7106

Graceada Park, Sycamore Street, Modesto, California, www.historicmodesto.com/graceadapark.html

Palace of Fine Arts, Baker Street at Beach Street, San Francisco, California (the structure at the rear is now the Exploratorium), (415) 666-7106, www.nps.gov/archive/prsf/places/palace.htm

MISCHE, EMANUEL TILLMAN

Boulevard Drive, Henry Vila Park, and Tenney Park, Madison, Wisconsin

Elk Rock garden at Bishop's Close, 11800 SW Military Lane, Portland, Oregon, (503) 636-5613, www.diocese-oregon.org/theclose/

Laurelhurst, Peninsula Park, and Mt. Tabor Park, Portland, Oregon, www.portlandonline.com/parks/index.cfm?c=39473

Lloyd Frank Estate (Lewis & Clark College), 615 SW Palatine Hill Road, Portland, Oregon, www.lclark.edu/dept/pres/history.html

MOTT, SEWARD HAMILTON. *SEE* PITKIN AND MOTT

MOVIUS, HALLAM LEONARD

Since most of the projects designed by Hallam Movius were private residential grounds, there is little opportunity to review what remains of these plans. The public work, whether institutional or for public housing, retains little of the original Movius planning.

NAKANE, KINSAKU

Carter Center, 441 Freedom Parkway, Atlanta, Georgia, www.cartercenter.org

Tenshin-en, The Museum of Fine Arts, 465 Huntington Avenue, Boston, Massachusetts, www.mfa.org

NICHOLSON, SIR FRANCIS

City of Annapolis, Maryland, www.visit-annapolis.org

City of Williamsburg, Virginia, www.colonialwilliamsburg.com

OBERLANDER, CORNELIA HAHN

C. K. Choi Building–Institute of Asian Research, University of British Columbia, greater Vancouver, Canada

Museum of Anthropology, University of British Columbia, Vancouver, Canada, www.moa.ubc.ca

Northwest Territories Legislative Assembly Building, Yellowknife, Northwest Territories, Canada

Robson Square, Vancouver, Canada

Vancouver Public Library green roof garden, Vancouver, Canada (for viewing only; not accessible)

OGLETHORPE, JAMES EDWARD

City of Augusta, Georgia, www.augustaga.org/index.cfm

City of Savannah, Georgia, www.savannah-visit.com/

Fort Frederica, Georgia, www.nps.gov/fofr/, Fort Frederica National Monument, 6515 Frederica Road, St. Simons Island, Georgia, (912) 638-3639

Town of Darien, Georgia, www.mcintoshcounty.com/index.html

Town of New Ebenezer, Georgia

OSMUNDSON, THEODORE

J. F. Kennedy Park, Cutting Boulevard between 39th and 41st Streets, Richmond, California

Kaiser Center Rooftop, Kaiser Center, 300 Lakeside Drive, Oakland, California

Keller Beach Park, Western Drive and Garrard Boulevard, Richmond, California

Recreation–Swimming Pool Complex, Hutchison Drive, University of California at Davis, Davis, California, www.ucdavis.edu/index.html

Standard Oil Plaza, Standard Oil Company of California, 555 Market Street, San Francisco, California

OWENS, HUBERT BOND

Founders Memorial Garden, corner of Lumpkin and Bocock Streets, University of Georgia, Athens, Georgia, (706) 542-4776, www.sed.uga.edu/facilities/founders.htm

PALMER, MILTON MEADE

Bull Run Regional Park, 7700 Bull Run Drive, Centreville, Virginia, (703) 631-0550, www.nvrpa.org/parks/bullrun

Capitol Street Development and Darden Garden, Capitol Street adjacent to State Capitol Grounds, Virginia State Capitol, Richmond, Virginia

Carter's Grove Country Road, Colonial Williamsburg, Virginia, www.colonialwilliamsburg.org

The Garth at Washington National Cathedral, Massachusetts and Wisconsin Avenues, Washington, D.C., www.cathedral.org

Lyndon B. Johnson Memorial Grove, Washington, D.C., George Washington Memorial Parkway, www.nps.gov/lyba/

PAOLANO, JOHN L.

Fellows Riverside Gardens, Mill Creek MetroParks, 123 McKinley Avenue, Youngstown, Ohio, (330) 740-7116, www.millcreekmetroparks.com/riversidegarden.htm

Lake Anna Park, 565 West Park Avenue, Barberton, Ohio, (330) 848-6739

PARK, WILLIE, JR.

Battle Creek Country Club (private), 318 Country Club Drive, Battle Creek, Michigan, (269) 962-6121

Huntercombe Golf Club (visitors accommodated, contact the club), Nuffield, Henley-on-Thames, Oxfordshire, England, O1491-641207, http://www.huntercombegolfclub.co.uk/

Maidstone Club (private), Old Beach Lane, East Hampton, New York, (631) 324-5530

Olympia Fields Country Club (private), 2800 Country Club Drive, Olympia Fields, Illinois, (708) 748-0495

Sunningdale Golf Club (public, visitors are welcome on Mondays, Tuesdays, Wednesdays and Thursdays only) Ridgemount Road, Sunningdale, Berkshire, England, 01344-621681, http://golftravel.about.com/od/unitedkingdomireland/qt/sunningdale.htm

PARKER, CARL RUST

Blaine Memorial Park, intersection of Blaine Avenue and Green Street, Augusta, Maine

Capitol Park and Driving Grounds, intersection of State and Capitol Streets, Augusta, Maine

George Washington Masonic Memorial, 101 Callahan Drive, Alexandria, Virginia, www.gwmemorial.org

Governor's Mansion/James G. Blaine House, intersection of State and Capitol Streets, Augusta, Maine, www.blainehouse.org

Village Green, intersection of Main and South Streets, Yarmouth, Maine

PATTEE, ELIZABETH GREENLEAF

Kimball-Jenkins Estate, 266 North Main Street, Concord, New Hampshire, (603) 225-3932, www.kimballjenkins.com

PAUL, COURTLAND PRICE

Irvine Regional Park, 1 Irvine Park Road, Orange, California, (714) 633-8072, www.ocparks.com/irvinepark

Rancho Madera Park (Wood Ranch), 556 Lake Park, Simi Valley, California

Rancho Simi Park, 1692 Sycamore Drive, Simi Valley, California

Rancho Tapo Community Park, 3700 East Avenida Simi, Simi Valley, California

Tri-City Park, 2301 North Kraemer Boulevard, Placentia, California

PEARSE, RUBEE JEFFREY

Arkansas State Fairgrounds, 2401 West Roosevelt Road, Little Rock, Arkansas, www.arkansasstatefair.com

Cedars of Lebanon State Park, 328 Cedar Forest Road, Lebanon, Tennessee, (615) 443-2769, www.state.tn.us/environment/parks/Cedars

Dutchess County Fairgrounds, Route 9, Rhinebeck, New York, www.dutchessfair.com

North Florida Fair, intersection of Monroe Street and Paul Russell Road, Tallahassee, Florida, (850) 671-8400, www.northfloridafair.com/

Singletary Lake State Park, 6707 NC 53 Highway, East Kelly, North Carolina, (910) 669-2928, www.ncparks.gov/Visit/parks/sila/main.php

PENDLETON, ISABELLA E.

William Trent House Museum, 15 Market Street, Trenton, New Jersey, (609) 989-3027, www.williamtrenthouse.org

PESMAN, MICHIEL WALTER

Country Club Gardens, 1-23 Downing Street, 2-22 South Ogden Street, and 1010-1140 West Ellsworth Street, Denver, Colorado

Lake Middle School, 1820 Lowell Boulevard, Denver, Colorado (check-in required), (720) 424-0260

Skinner Middle School, 3435 West 40th Avenue, Denver, Colorado (check-in required), (720) 424-1420

PHILLIPS, WILLIAM LYMAN

Fairchild Tropical Botanic Garden, 10901 Old Cutler Road, Coral Gables, Florida, (305) 667-1651, www.fairchildgarden.org

Greynolds Park, 17530 West Dixie Highway, North Miami, Florida, (305) 949-1741

Matheson Hammock, 9610 Old Cutler Road, Coral Gables, Florida, (305) 665-5475

McKee Jungle Gardens (now McKee Botanical Garden), 350 U.S. Highway 1, Vero Beach, Florida, (561) 794-0601, www.mckeegarden.org

Mountain Lake Sanctuary (now Bok Tower Gardens), 1151 Tower Boulevard, Lake Wales, Florida, (863) 676-1408

PILAT, IGNATZ ANTON

Central Park, New York, New York, www.centralparknyc.org

Madison Square, New York, New York, www.madison-squarepark.org

Marcus Garvey Park (formerly Mount Morris Square), New York, New York, partnershipsforparks.org/brochures/marcus_garvey.html

Prospect Park, Brooklyn, New York, www.prospectpark.org

PITKIN & MOTT

Angell Hall, University of Michigan, State Street between Huron and South University, Central Campus, Ann Arbor, Michigan, www.umich.edu

Applewood, 1400 East Kearsley Street, Flint, Michigan (open on a limited basis), (810) 233-3031

Avondale Historic District, bounded by Roosevelt Boulevard, Belvedere Avenue, Seminole Road, St. Johns River, and Talbot Avenue, Jacksonville, Florida, vicinity, www.riverside-avondale.com

Forest Glen Estates Historic District, bounded by Homestead Drive, Glenwood Avenue, Alburn Drive, and Market Street, Youngstown, Ohio

Kingwood Center, 900 Park Avenue West, Mansfield, Ohio, (419) 522-0211, www.kingwoodcenter.org

Old Beechwold Historic District, bounded by W. Jeffrey Place, N. High, River Park Drive, and Olentangy Boulevard, Columbus, Ohio

Shaker Village Historic District, bounded by Fairmount Boulevard, Greene Street, Warrensville Center Road, Lytle Road, Scottsdale Boulevard, and Lindholm Road, Shaker Heights, Ohio

Toledo Museum of Art, Old West End Historic District, 2445 Monroe Street at Scottwood Avenue, Toledo, Ohio, (419) 255-8000, www.toledomuseum.org

Upper Arlington Historic District, bounded by Lane Avenue, Andover Road, Fifth Avenue, and Riverside Drive, Columbus, Ohio, www.ua-ohio.net/aboutua/history/

PITZMAN, JULIUS

Benton Place, north of Lafayette Park, St. Louis, Missouri

Compton Heights, Longfellow and Hawthorne Boulevards, St. Louis, Missouri

Fullerton's Westminster Place, northeast corner of Forest Park, St. Louis, Missouri

Parkview, northwest corner of Forest Park, St. Louis, Missouri

Portland and Westmoreland Places, northeast corner of Forest Park, St. Louis, Missouri

PRAGNELL, CECIL

Glorieta Gardens, Glorieta Baptist Conference Center, Glorieta, New Mexico, (505) 757-6161

Los Poblanos Ranch, 4803 Rio Grande Boulevard NW, Albuquerque, New Mexico, (505) 344-9297

PRICE, THOMAS DREES

The Conservatory Garden, Central Park, New York, New York, www.centralparknyc.org

Horace's Villa at Licenza, northeast of Rome, Italy, near Tivoli

REICH, ROBERT S.

Baton Rouge Centroplex Repentance Park, 275 River Road South, Baton Rouge, Louisiana

St. Aloysius Catholic Church, 2025 Stuart Avenue, Baton Rouge, Louisiana

St. Timothy United Methodist Church, Mandeville, Louisiana

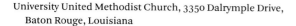

University United Methodist Church, 3350 Dalrymple Drive, Baton Rouge, Louisiana

RIDDLE, THEODATE POPE

Avon Old Farms School, 500 Old Farms Road, Avon, Connecticut, (860) 404-4100, www.avonoldfarms.com

Hill-Stead Museum, 35 Mountain Road, Farmington, Connecticut, (860) 677-4787, www.hillstead.org

Westover School, 1237 Whittemore Road, Middlebury, Connecticut, (203) 758-2423, www.westoverschool.org

RIES, JANE SILVERSTEIN

Herb and Scripture Gardens for Denver Botanic Gardens, 1005 York Street, Denver, Colorado, (720) 865-3500, www.botanicgardens.org

Ninth Street Historic Park on the Auraria Higher Education Campus, Denver, Colorado, www.ahec.edu/

Rehabilitated gardens of Colorado's Executive Mansion, 400 E. 8th Avenue, Denver, Colorado.

The restored Molly Brown House gardens, 1340 Pennsylvania Street, Denver, Colorado, (303) 832-4092, mollybrown.org/househistory.asp

Urban Renewal development of Larimer Square, 1400 block, Larimer Street, Denver, Colorado

ROOT, RALPH RODNEY

Cantigny Park, 1 South 151 Winfield Road, Wheaton, Illinois, (630) 668-5161, www.rrmtf.org/cantigny

Elawa Farm, 900 North Waukegan Road, Lake Forest, Illinois, (847) 234-0713, www.elawafarm.org

Ten Chimneys, Box 225 (S43 W31575 Depot Road), Genesee Depot, Wisconsin, (262) 958-4161, www.tenchimneys.org

ROYSTON, ROBERT

Central Park, 909 Kiely Boulevard, Santa Clara, California

Cuesta Park, 615 Cuesta Drive, Mountain View, California

Mitchell Park and Bowden Park, Palo Alto, California

Santa Clara Civic Center Park, Lincoln and El Camino Real, Santa Clara, California.

St. Mary's Square, 651 Kearny St, San Francisco, California.

SASAKI, HIDEO

Christian Science Center, 175 Huntington Avenue, Boston, Massachusetts, (617) 450-2000

Constitution Plaza, Hartford, Connecticut, (860) 524-4965

Greenacre Park, 217 East 51st Street, between Second and Third Avenues, New York, New York, (212) 838-0528

Newburyport, Massachusetts, (978) 462-6680, www.newburyportchamber.org

University of Colorado at Boulder, Colorado, (303) 492-7097, www.colorado.edu

SCHERMERHORN, RICHARD, JR.

Arthur Ross Terrace and Garden, Cooper-Hewitt, National Design Museum, 2 East 91st Street, New York, New York, (212) 849-8400, cooperhewitt.org

Cemetery of the Holy Rood, 111 Old Country Road, Westbury, Long Island, New York, (515) 334-7990

SCHUBARTH, NILES BIERRAGAARD

Elm Grove Cemetery, Greenmanville Avenue, Mystic, Connecticut, (860) 536-7834

Juniper Hill Cemetery, Sherry Avenue, Bristol, Rhode Island

North Burial Ground, 5 Branch Avenue, Providence, Rhode Island, (401) 331-0177

River Bend Cemetery, 117 Beach Street, Westerly, Rhode Island, (401) 596-2724

Swan Point Cemetery, 585 Blackstone Boulevard, Providence, Rhode Island, (401) 272-1314, swanpointcemetery.com

SCOTT, GERALDINE KNIGHT

Arts Court, Unit number 1 Santa Clara County Governmental Center, 70 West Hedding Street, San Jose, California

Blake Garden Master Plan, 70 Rincon Road, Kensington, California, (510) 524-2449

James Lick High School, 57 N. White Road, San Jose, California, (408) 347-4400

Oakland Museum of California, roof garden, 1000 Oak Street, Oakland, California, (510) 238-2200

SHAW, HENRY

Missouri Botanical Garden, 4344 Shaw Boulevard, St. Louis, Missouri, (314) 577-9400, www.mobot.org

Tower Grove Park, 4256 Magnolia Avenue, St. Louis, Missouri, (314) 771-2679, www.towergrovepark.org

SHELLHORN, RUTH PATRICIA

Disneyland Park, Disneyland Drive off Interstate Highway 5, Anaheim, California (entrance, Main Street, Plaza Hub, and pedestrian circulation), disneyland.disney.go.com

Macy's (formerly Bullock's Pasadena), south of the 210 Freeway at 401 South Lake Avenue, Pasadena, California

Macy's at Mainplace (formerly Bullock's Fashion Square, Santa Ana), 2800 N. Main Street, Santa Ana, California (Shellhorn's perimeter landscape design is still intact)

Marlborough School for Girls, 250 S. Rossmore Avenue, Los Angeles, California (perimeter and some courtyards are still intact), www.marlboroughschool.org

University of California at Riverside, University Avenue off the 60 Freeway, east of the 91 Freeway, www.ucr.edu

SHEPHERD, HARRY WHITCOMB

Aquatic Park, 80 Bolivar Drive, Berkeley, California

Codornices Rose Garden, Berkeley, California

John Hinkel Park Amphitheater, 41 Somerset Avenue, Berkeley, California

Live Oak Park, 1201 Shattuck Avenue, Berkeley, California, www.ci.berkeley.ca.us/parks

SHERIDAN, LAWRENCE VINNEDGE

The Indianapolis Park and Boulevard System, incorporating Fall Creek Parkway from 38th Street to Fort Benjamin Harrison, and Kessler Boulevard, Indianapolis, Indiana

Lockefield Gardens Apartments, 737 Lockefield Lane, Indianapolis, Indiana, (317) 631-2922

Master plan, incorporating the Levee Shopping Center, at the Wabash River, northeast of State Road 26 (State Street) and U.S. 231/State Road 43 (River Road), West Lafayette, Indiana

SIMONDS, JOHN ORMSBEE

Mellon Square, 6th Avenue at Smithfield Street, Pittsburgh, Pennsylvania, www.city.pittsburgh.pa.us/wt/html/mellon_square.html

Miami Lakes, Florida

The National Aviary, Allegheny Commons West, Pittsburgh, Pennsylvania, (412) 323-7235, www.aviary.org

Pelican Bay, Naples, Florida, www.pelicanbay.com

SMITH, ALICE ORME

Abby Aldrich Rockefeller Garden, Mount Desert Island, Maine (by appointment), (207) 276-3727

American Shakespeare Theater (now Stratford Festival Theater) grounds, 1850 Elm Street, Stratford, Connecticut, (203) 385-4001, www.stratfordfestival.com

Bridgeport Museum of Art, Science, and Industry (now The Discovery Museum) grounds, 4450 Park Avenue, Bridgeport, Connecticut, (203) 372-3521, www.discoverymuseum.org

STEVENS, RALPH T.

Casa del Herrero, 1387 East Valley Road, Montecito, California (by appointment), (805) 565-5653, www.casadelherrero.com

Fielding Graduate Institute (the former Hodges residence), 2112 Santa Barbara Street, Santa Barbara, California (by appointment), (805) 687-1099

Four Seasons Biltmore Hotel, 1260 Channel Drive, Montecito, California, (805) 969-2261

Ganna Walska Lotusland Foundation, Sycamore Canyon Road at Cold Spring Road, Montecito (Santa Barbara), California (by appointment), (805) 969-9990, www.lotusland.org

Sheraton Royal Hawaiian Hotel, 2259 Kalakaua Avenue, Honolulu, Hawaii, (808) 923-7311

STILES, WAYNE E.

Hooper Golf Club (semi-private), Prospect Hill Street, Walpole, New Hampshire, (603) 756-4020

Mink Meadows Golf Club (Martha's Vineyard Island) (semi-public), 320 Golf Club Road, Vineyard Haven, Massachusetts, (508) 693-0600, www.minkmeadowsgc.com

North Haven Island Golf Club (private), North Haven, Maine, (207) 867-4476

Rutland Country Club (private), 275 Grove Street, Rutland, Vermont, (802) 773-3254, www.rutlandcountryclub.com

The Taconic Golf Club (Williams College) (semi-private), Meacham Street, Williamstown, Massachusetts, (413) 458-3997, www.taconicgolf.com

STURTEVANT, BUTLER STEVENS

Medicinal Herb Garden, Anderson Hall, Rainier Vista, and Drumheller Fountain at University of Washington, Seattle, Washington

Normandy Park Subdivision Master Plan, Normandy Park, Washington

Principia College, Elsah, Illinois, www.prin.edu/college

Rose Garden, Butchart Gardens, Victoria, British Columbia, www.butchartgardens.com

SUAREZ, DIEGO

Vizcaya, 3251 South Miami Avenue, Miami, Florida, (305) 250-9133, www.vizcayamuseum.com

THIENE, PAUL G.

Ganna Walska Lotusland Foundation, Sycamore Canyon Road at Cold Spring Road, Montecito (Santa Barbara), California (by appointment; Thiene's Neptune Fountain garden was altered when the Gavit estate became Lotusland), (805) 969-9990

Greystone Park (former Doheny estate), 905 Loma Vista Drive, Beverly Hills, California, (310) 550-4654

Music Academy of the West (former J. P. Jefferson estate), 1070 Fairway Road, Santa Barbara (Montecito), California (by appointment), (805) 969-4726

TILLINGHAST, ALBERT WARREN

Bethpage State Park Golf Course (Black Course 1936, Blue Course 1935, Red Course 1935) (public), Bethpage, New York, (516) 249-0700

The Shawnee Inn and Golf Resort (public), Shawnee on Delaware, Pennsylvania, (570) 424-4000

ULRICH, RUDOLPH

Indiana University, 400 East 7th Street, Bloomington, Indiana, (812) 855-6494, www.indiana.edu

Kearney Park, 7160 West Kearney Boulevard, Fresno, California, (209) 441-0862

Naval Postgraduate School (formerly the Hotel del Monte number 3), Public Affairs Office, 1 University Circle–Code 004, Monterey, California, (831) 656-2023

Stanford University, the Arizona garden, near the Stanford Mausoleum (formerly the Palo Alto Stock Farm), Stanford, California, www.stanford.edu

VAUGHAN, HOLLYNGSWORTH LELAND
VAUGHAN, ADELE WHARTON

Alumni House, University of California, Berkeley, California, (510) 642-7026, www.berkeley.edu

Richmond Civic Center, Richmond, California

WEBEL, RICHARD K.

Elizabethan Gardens, 1411 Highway 64 and 24, Roanoke Island, North Carolina

Furman University, Greenville, South Carolina, www.furman.edu

Greenbrier Hotel, 300 West Main Street, White Sulphur Springs, West Virginia, www.greenbrier.com

Greenville-Spartanburg Airport, Greer, South Carolina

Keeneland Race Course, 4201 Versailles Road, Lexington, Kentucky, ww2.keeneland.com

Rector Park, Battery Park City, New York, www.bpcparks.org

WEST, JAMES ROY

Belle Meade Farm, subdivision around Belle Meade Country Club, Nashville, Tennessee

Lake Forest High School, 1285 N. McKinley Road, Lake Forest, Illinois, (847) 234-3600, www.lfhs.org

Maytag Park, 301 W. 11th Street S., Newton, Iowa

WEST, MYRON HOWARD

City Park, 1442 City Park Avenue, Baton Rouge, Louisiana

WHEELER, PERRY HUNT

Hillwood Museum and Gardens, Pet Cemetery, 4155 Linnean Avenue NW, Washington, D.C., (202) 686-5807, www .hillwoodmuseum.org/

National Arboretum Asian Garden (pagoda), 3501 New York Avenue NE, Washington, D.C., (202) 245-2726, www.usna .usda.gov/

Trinity Episcopal Church, 9114 John S. Mosby Highway, Upperville, Virginia, (540) 592-3343

Washington National Cathedral Bishop's Garden, Massachusetts and Wisconsin Avenues NW, Washington, D.C., (202) 537-6200, www.cathedral.org

White House Rose Garden, 1600 Pennsylvania Avenue NW, Washington, D.C., (202) 456-7041, www.whitehouse.gov

WIEDORN, WILLIAM S.

New Orleans Botanical Garden, City Park, New Orleans, Louisiana, www.neworleanscitypark.com

WIRTH, CONRAD LOUIS

Bastrop State Park, Bastrop County, Texas, www.tpwd.state .tx.us/spdest/findadest/parks/bastrop/

Cape Cod National Seashore, Massachusetts, www.nps.gov/ caco/

Grand Canyon National Park, Colorado, www.nps.gov/grca/

Pine Mountain State Park (FDR State Park), Harris County, Georgia, www.gastateparks.org/info/fdr/

Yosemite National Park, California, www.nps.gov/yose/

WIRTH, THEODORE

Elizabeth Park, 1555 Asylum Avenue, West Hartford, Connecticut, www.elizabethpark.org

Hyland/Rocky Ridge, Summit Terrace, Hartford, Connecticut, www.healthy.hartford.gov/OpenSpace/osParks.htm#Hyland

Lake of the Isles Park (Chain of Lakes Regional Park), 2500 Lake Isles Parkway, Minneapolis, Minnesota, (612) 230-6400, www.minneapolisparks.org/default. asp?PageID=4&parkid=258

Rose Garden (Lyndale Park Gardens), 1500 E. Lake Harriet Parkway, Minneapolis, Minnesota, (612) 230-6400, www .minneapolisparks.org/default.asp?PageID=4&parkid=347

Theodore Wirth Park, 1339 Theodore Wirth Parkway, Minneapolis, Minnesota, (612) 230-6400, www .minneapolisparks.org/default.asp?PageID=4&parkid=255

ZACH, LEON HENRY

Acadia National Park, Mount Desert, Maine

Alabama State Capitol, Montgomery, Alabama

Camden Village Green, Camden, Maine

Campuses of the University of Alabama at Tuscaloosa and Huntsville, and the University of North Alabama at Florence and Troy University, among others

Claremont and Fort Tryon parks, Upper West Side of New York City

ZION, ROBERT LEWIS

Cincinnati Riverfront Park, Cincinnati, Ohio, www.crpark.org

IBM World Headquarters Atrium (recently purchased by Minskoff Developers), southwest corner of Madison Avenue and 57th Street, New York

Liberty State Park, Jersey City, New Jersey, www .libertystatepark.com

Museum of Modern Art, 11 West 53rd Street, New York, New York, (212) 708-9400, www.moma.org

Paley Park, 5 East 53rd Street (between Fifth and Madison Avenues), New York, New York, (212) 355-4171 (park superintendent)

Contributors

ARNOLD R. ALANEN is a professor in the Department of Landscape Architecture at the University of Wisconsin–Madison.

LAURIE MUENCH ALBANO is a landscape architect with the Milwaukee County Parks.

NATALIE ALPERT served as instructor and assistant department head from 1971 to 1991 in the Department of Landscape Architecture at the University of Illinois, where she taught courses in history and planting design.

STEVEN BARONTI is an attorney who lives in Pound Ridge, New York, with his wife and two children, and is writing a book on the life and works of Julian Francis Detmer.

AMANDA GRAHAM BARTON is a landscape architect in private practice in Charleston, South Carolina.

SYDNEY BAUMGARTNER is a landscape architect in Santa Barbara, California, and was the protégé of Elizabeth Kellam de Forest, assisting her in her later years with projects at Mount Vernon and in Santa Barbara/Montecito.

VIRGINIA LOPEZ BEGG is a landscape historian who has written widely about the role of women in shaping the American landscape, in particular through American garden literature.

STUART BENDELOW is the grandson of golf course designer Tom Bendelow.

CAROLYN DOEPKE BENNETT is a writer, lecturer, landscape preservation advocate, and consultant based in Los Angeles, California.

CHARLES A. BIRNBAUM, FASLA, FAAR, is the founder and president of The Cultural Landscape Foundation.

TINA BISHOP is a landscape architect and partner with Mundus Bishop Design Inc.

JOHN BRYAN is professor emeritus of Art and Architectural History at the University of South Carolina.

JULIE CAIN is a landscape historian and operations manager of the Engineering Library at Stanford University, Stanford, California.

MARGARET CARPENTER lives in central Vermont. She is a researcher and lecturer on historic preservation and works as the project manager for the restoration of the gardens and landscape of the Justin Morrill Homestead, a National Historic Landmark, in Strafford, Vermont.

ETHAN CARR, FASLA, is associate professor of landscape history at the University of Virginia.

SUZANNE CARTER MELDMAN is a landscape historian, urban planner, and preservationist.

STACI L. CATRON is director of the Cherokee Garden Library at the Atlanta History Center.

OLIVER CHAMBERLAIN taught, performed, and conducted music at university level, retiring as executive director of the Center for the Arts, University of Massachusetts–Lowell; he is the fifth generation of the Caparn-Chamberlain family with interests in horticulture, landscape design, and the arts.

SUSAN CHAMBERLIN is the author of *Hedges, Screens & Espaliers,* and is a licensed landscape architect.

DIANE BRANDLEY CLARKE is a volunteer garden researcher for the Archives of American Gardens at the Smithsonian Institution through her membership in the Rumson Garden Club, and is a member of the Garden Club of America.

KAREN COLE is associate director of the Gillespie Museum of Minerals at Stetson University in DeLand, Florida.

KELLY COMRAS is a landscape architect in private practice in Pacific Palisades, California. She is former staff landscape architect for the National Park Service in the Santa Monica Mountains National Recreation Area and a member of the California State Bar Association.

PLEASANCE K. CRAWFORD is a landscape historian in Toronto, Ontario, and an honorary member of the Canadian Society of Landscape Architects and the Ontario Association of Landscape Architects.

WILLIAM G. CRAWFORD JR. is an attorney in Fort Lauderdale, Florida, past president of the Fort Lauderdale Historical Society, and past chair of the Broward County Historical Commission.

KURT CULBERTSON, FASLA, is chairman of Design Workshop, in Aspen, Colorado.

ELIZABETH HOPE CUSHING is a practicing landscape historian who writes and lectures on landscape matters.

PHOEBE CUTLER writes and lectures about garden history. She is the author of *The Public Landscape of the New Deal,* and is currently researching the landscape heritage of Oakland, California.

REBECCA WARREN DAVIDSON is the author of a number of articles on pioneering American landscape architects. She is currently an independent architectural and landscape historian living in Ithaca, New York.

DUANE A. DIETZ, ASLA, is a landscape architect and historian on Vashon Island, Washington.

CED DOLDER is with the Historic Preservation Division of the Georgia Department of Natural Resources in Atlanta, Georgia.

LAKE DOUGLAS, ASLA, is a landscape architect and garden historian based in New Orleans, Louisiana. He is associate professor of landscape architecture and graduate coordinator at Louisiana State University, Baton Rouge.

MARC DUTTON is president of Marc Dutton Irrigation, in Waterford, Michigan, and the current president of John A. Brooks, Inc.

DONALD ELLIOTT is a lawyer in New York City. He was chairman of the New York City Planning Commission and worked closely with William H. Whyte Jr. when he wrote the first volume of the plan for New York City and remained a close friend the rest of his life.

CAROLYN ETTER and **DON ETTER**, historians, are former joint managers of Denver's Department of Parks and Recreation, and honorary members of the ASLA.

BARRY FITZPATRICK is a landscape architect and a graduate of Louisiana State University, Baton Rouge, Louisiana.

STEPHANIE S. FOELL is an architectural and landscape historian. She completed the National Register of Historic Places documentation for the Statue of Liberty National Monument and is the senior curator of *Fred J. Orr, Architect, Athens, Georgia.*

LILLIE PETIT GALLAGHER is a former college professor and education administrator who has a long personal interest in history, historic preservation, and heritage landscapes. She writes and publishes on the subject.

BARBARA GEIGER is an adjunct professor in the College of Architecture at the Illinois Institute of Technology and a landscape historian and consultant in the Chicago area.

KATHRYN L. GLEASON is director of undergraduate studies and associate professor of landscape architecture at Cornell University and co-principal investigator of the current American Academy in Rome excavations of Horace's Villa.

CHARLES T. GLEAVES is director of Kingwood Center in Mansfield, Ohio.

ISABELLE GOURNAY is an associate professor of architecture at the University of Maryland.

MARLEA GRAHAM is a landscape historian and editor of *Eden, Journal of the California Garden & Landscape History Society.*

CAROL GROVE teaches art history and landscape studies at the University of Missouri–Columbia. She is a historian of nineteenth-century and Midwestern landscapes, and works to promote historic preservation.

JOHN GRUBER, a writer and photographer, is founder of the Center for Railroad Photography & Art, Madison, Wisconsin.

KEN GUZOWSKI is a senior planner with the Planning & Development Department, Eugene, Oregon, where he oversees the city's Historic Preservation Program.

GARY R. HILDERBRAND, FASLA, FAAR, is a principal of Reed Hilderbrand Landscape Architects and is adjunct professor of landscape architecture at the Harvard Design School.

MARY PAOLANO HOERNER is John L. Paolano's niece. She is working on a survey of Ohio historic designed landscapes.

HEIDI HOHMANN is an assistant professor of landscape architecture at Iowa State University.

DOROTHÉE IMBERT is an associate professor in landscape architecture at the Harvard Design School.

CHRISTINE JOCHEM is head of the North Jersey History Center at the Morristown and Morris Township Library, Morristown, New Jersey.

BRIAN KATEN, ASLA, is chairman of the Landscape Architecture Program and associate professor, School of Architecture and Design at Virginia Tech and a former landscape adviser to Dumbarton Oaks.

GARY KESLER, FASLA, is associate dean for undergraduate studies and outreach at the College of Art and Architecture, Pennsylvania State University. He is a recipient of a Distinguished Educator award from the Council of Educators in Landscape Architecture and the President's Medal from the American Society of Landscape Architects.

JOY KESTENBAUM is director of the Adam and Sophie Gimbel Design Library at the New School, in New York, and has served as historian for numerous preservation projects and historic structures and landscape reports.

JULIE KHUEN is a landscape designer in Winchester, Massachusetts.

JUDY KOWALSKI, MLA, RLA, is a landscape architect and researcher and the primary author of "Santa Fe Plaza: A Cultural Landscape Report" (2006).

DANIEL KRALL, FASLA, is director of graduate studies and an associate professor in the Department of Landscape Architecture at Cornell University.

DEBBIE LANG is an activist in Miami, Florida, with an interest in research on landscape architecture.

ARLEYN A. LEVEE, from Belmont, Massachusetts, is a landscape historian and preservation consultant specializing in the work of the Olmsted firm.

DONNA TUNKEL LILBORN earned a master of landscape architecture degree, writing a thesis on Alice Ireys. This followed twenty years as a soil scientist, horticulturist, and garden designer.

DONALD LOGGINS, a former associate of Liz Christy, is the senior member of the Liz Christy Garden.

JOANNA LOMBARD is a professor at the University of Miami School of Architecture, and she practices architecture with Denis Hector. She has recently completed work on a garden originally designed in 1945 by William Lyman Phillips.

WAVERLY B. LOWELL is the curator of the Environmental Design Archives in the College of Environmental Design at the University of California, Berkeley, and editor of *Architectural Records in the San Francisco Bay Area: A Guide to Research.*

MELANIE MACCHIO is an architectural historian at The Cultural Landscape Foundation, Washington, D.C.

CATHERINE MAGGIO splits her time between her lighting design business and project management of large-scale, civic urban design projects in Seattle, Washington.

BRICE MARYMAN, ASLA, is a Seattle-based practicing landscape architect whose professional interests include historic preservation, ecological design, and urban studies.

THERESA MATTOR is a landscape architect, historian, and lecturer in Hollis, Maine.

KELLY MCCAUGHEY DENT holds a Master in Landscape Architecture from Louisiana State University. She is a registered landscape architect living in Austin, Texas.

LINDA FLINT MCCLELLAND is a historian and cultural landscape specialist for the National Register and National Historic Landmarks Programs of the National Park Service in Washington, D.C.

CARRIE LEAH MCDADE is an independent researcher and formerly the assistant curator, Environmental Design Archives, University of California, Berkeley.

KAREN MCLAREN is president of McLaren Advertising in Rochester Hills, Michigan.

LAUREN G. MEIER, ASLA, is a landscape preservation specialist with Pressley Associates, Inc. in Cambridge, Massachusetts, and coauthor of the National Historic Landmark nomination for Green-Wood Cemetery.

KEVIN R. MENDIK is a water resource specialist for the Northeast Regional Office of the National Park Service.

JULIE MOIR MESSERVY, a former student of Kinsaku Nakane, is a designer, author, and lecturer who practices in Vermont.

ELIZABETH K. MEYER, FASLA, is on the faculty of the University of Virginia School of Architecture.

SUSANNE SMITH MEYER, ASLA, is a registered landscape architect in private practice in Concord, New Hampshire.

ARTHUR H. MILLER is archivist and librarian for Special Collections, Donnelley and Lee Library, Lake Forest College (Illinois) and a coauthor of *Classic Country Estates of Lake Forest.*

JC MILLER is a landscape architect and a director for the landscape architecture certificate program at the University of California Berkely Extension. He is coauthor of *Modern Public Gardens: Robert Royston and the Suburban Park.*

BAKER H. MORROW, FASLA, is the founder of the Master of Landscape Architecture program at the University of New Mexico and the author of *Best Plants for New Mexico Gardens and Landscapes* and *A Dictionary of Landscape Architecture.*

DONNA M. NEARY serves as executive director of the Kentucky Heritage Council and State Preservation Officer. Neary formerly served as president of Donna M. Neary, Inc., a historical consulting business in Louisville, Kentucky.

SUSAN S. NELSON is a landscape architect and worked in the office of Meade Palmer from 1974 to 1982.

CHRISTINE EDSTROM O'HARA is a landscape architect and historian who teaches at California Polytechnic State University, San Luis Obispo, and practices in Atascadero, California.

LAURIE D. OLIN, FASLA, FAAR, a student and sometime employee of Richard Haag, has taught landscape architecture and urban design at the University of Pennsylvania in Philadelphia since 1974, where he also cofounded Hanna/Olin (1976-1996), now Olin.

THERESE O'MALLEY, associate dean of the Center for Advanced Study in the Visual Arts at the National Gallery of Art, is an art historian specializing in the history of landscape architecture and garden design in the colonial period and early nineteenth century.

BETH PAGE lives in Pennsylvania and writes on landscape history.

ELIZA PENNYPACKER is a professor of landscape architecture at Penn State. She co-curated the 1990 exhibition *Abstracting the Landscape: The Artistry of Landscape Architect A. E. Bye.*

DOUG PULAK is a historic preservation specialist for the federal government with a background in preservation policy and urban planning.

SUSAN M. RADEMACHER succeeded Grady Clay as editor of *Landscape Architecture* in 1984; was founding executive director and president of the Louisville Olmsted Parks Conservancy; and is now Parks Curator for the Pittsburgh Parks Conservancy.

REUBEN M. RAINEY is the William Stone Weedon Professor Emeritus in the Department of Architecture and Landscape Architecture at the University of Virginia.

CHAD RANDL is an architectural historian and author of the 2004 book *A-frame.*

JENNIFER HANNA REIVE, landscape architect and historic preservation planner, is executive director of Greenwood Gardens, a historic public garden in Short Hills, New Jersey.

MARION L. RENNEKER, MLA, has worked for Oehme van Sweden & Associates in Washington, D.C., and for Nimrod Long & Associates in Birmingham, Alabama. The author grew up in the former residence of William H. Kessler.

DONALD RICHARDSON, FASLA, is principal of Zion Breed & Richardson Associates, and was a friend and business associate of Robert Zion for forty years. The firm continues to practice at the Mill in Imlaystown.

GARY O. ROBINETTE, FASLA, is a professor of landscape architecture at the University of Texas at Arlington.

SETH RODEWALD-BATES is a landscape architect in Baton Rouge, Louisiana.

ANNEMARIE VAN ROESSEL is archivist in the Drawings and Archives Department of Avery Architectural and Fine Arts Library, Columbia University.

CHARLENE K. ROISE is an architectural and landscape historian with the consulting firm Hess, Roise and Company in Minneapolis, Minnesota.

DAVID A. ROTH, a registered landscape architect and preservation consultant, is the manager of the Sustainable

Solutions Group for Hannum Wagle and Cline Engineering in Indianapolis.

R. TERRY SCHNADELBACH, FAAR, is professor of landscape architecture at the University of Florida, Gainesville, and its Paris Research Center, Paris, France

RENÉ D. SHOEMAKER is director, librarian, and archivist at the Owens Library in the School of Environmental Design at the University of Georgia, Athens.

MELANIE SIMO is the author of *Forest and Garden: Traces of Wildness in a Modernizing Land* (2003) and other books on landscape architecture and planning.

NANCY SLADE, ASLA, is a landscape architect practicing in Washington, D.C.

FREDERICK STEINER, FASLA, FAAR, is dean of the School of Architecture at the University of Texas at Austin.

DAVID STREATFIELD is professor emeritus of Landscape Architecture at the University of Washington, Seattle.

TIM TAMBURRINO is an architectural historian living in Baltimore, Maryland.

JUDITH B. TANKARD has taught at the Landscape Institute, Harvard University, for twenty years and is the author of six books on landscape history. She is also a preservation consultant and a frequent lecturer.

MARIA M. THOMPSON is a historian living and working in suburban Philadelphia who has written and lectured on several members of the Furness family.

WILLIAM H. TISHLER, FASLA, is professor emeritus of Landscape Architecture at the University of Wisconsin–Madison.

SUZANNE L. TURNER, FASLA, is a Louisiana State University professor emerita of landscape architecture.

MARY ALICE VAN SICKLE is the marketing director at Carol R. Johnson Associates, Inc., and has been with the firm since 1981.

NOEL D. VERNON, ASLA, is a professor of Landscape Architecture at California State Polytechnic University–Pomona. Her areas of expertise are cultural landscape history and preservation.

DIANA S. WAITE is president and founder of Mount Ida Press in Albany, New York, and editor of the *APT Bulletin: The Journal of Preservation Technology*.

PETER WALKER is a landscape architect and founder of Peter Walker & Partners, Berkeley, California.

THAÏSA WAY is an assistant professor of landscape architecture at the University of Washington and the author of *Unbounded Practice: Women and Landscape Architecture in the Early Twentieth Century*.

DOUGLAS A. WILLIAMS is a Ph.D. candidate, Department of Landscape Architecture, University of Illinois, Champaign-Urbana.

EMILY HERRING WILSON is the author of *No One Gardens Alone: A Life of Elizabeth Lawrence* and editor of *Two Gardeners/ Katharine S. White & Elizabeth Lawrence: A Friendship in Letters*.

WILLIAM MCKENZIE WOODWARD, architectural historian at the Rhode Island Historical Preservation and Heritage Commission, is the author of *Historic Landscapes of Rhode Island*.

DOROTHY WURMAN is an architect and a landscape architect engaged in professional and academic practice.

EMMA YOUNG is an architectural historian living in Adams County, Pennsylvania.

CYNTHIA ZAITZEVSKY is a historian of architecture and landscape architecture.

Index